Fourth Edition

D0879346

The Encyclopedia of Journal Entries

Available from AIPB

Continuing Professional Education Home-Study Courses
Mastering Inventory I
Mastering Financial Statement Analysis
Mastering Correction of Accounting Errors
Mastering Payroll I
Mastering Payroll II
Mastering the C Corporation Tax Return (Form 1120)
Mastering the S Corporation Tax Return (Form 1120S)
Mastering the Partnership Tax Return (Form 1065S)
Mastering the Form 1040, Schedule C (sole proprietorship)
Mastering Adjusting Entries
Mastering Depreciation
Mastering Collections: Business to Business
Mastering Internal Controls and Fraud Prevention

Employee Training Home-Study Courses
Mastering Double-Entry Bookkeeping

Periodicals
The General Ledger newsletter

To order or obtain information call 1-800-622-0121. FAX: 1-800-541-0066

Fourth Edition

The
Encyclopedia of
Journal Entries

Edited by
Gordon S. May, MBA, Ph.D., CPA

AIPB

ABOUT THE EDITOR

Gordon S. May, MBA, Ph.D., CPA is emeritus faculty of the University of Georgia's J.M. Tull School of Accounting in the Terry College of Business. Dr. May has had practical experience at every level of accounting, from write-up and auditing work to in-house consulting. He has worked at firms of every kind, from national (Touche Ross and Price Waterhouse) to regional (Stoy, Malone and Company, Washington, D.C.) to the small, local firm (Dogan & Roby, Valpariso, Indiana). Dr. May is co-author of *Accounting Principles* (Random House) and co-editor or the accompanying *Solutions Manual*, *Working Papers*, *Instructors' Resource Manual* and *Test Bank*. He has published widely in leading professional and business publications including *The Journal of Accountancy*, *The CPA Journal*, and *National Public Accountant*.

INTRODUCTION

The Encyclopedia of Journal Entries is designed to help you find the right journal entry for transactions, postings, adjustments, or corrections quickly and easily. Whether you work in industry, the service sector, or public accounting, the *Encyclopedia* can save you time. It also provides you with clear, concise explanations of the information you need to calculate the debit and credit amounts.

The *Encyclopedia* is up to date and in conformity with all Generally Accepted Accounting Principles in effect as of January 1, 2004.

It is our belief that there are few individuals who could have taken the concept of an encyclopedia of journal entries and made it a reality. It was our extraordinary good fortune to be introduced to Dr. Gordon S. May by Dr. Stephen E. Loeb. Dr. May brought to this volume the rare combination of traits required to realize it: a superior knowledge and grasp of accounting, the intellectual capacity to organize and execute a project of this scope, and the unrelenting attention to detail at every level needed for a reference that is, in fact, a practical compilation of thousands of details.

The Publishers

ACKNOWLEDGMENTS

I would like to extend my thanks to the contributors to and reviewers of the Encyclopedia, who include experts in financial, managerial, and not-for-profit accounting from all over the country.

Some of the experts who helped were both contributors and reviewers and their names are mentioned twice.

Contributors

Ajay Adhikari, Ph.D.	The American University
Robert M. Bracken, DBA, CPA	University of South Alabama
Gadis J. Dillon, Ph.D., CPA	Oakland University
Karen A. Fortin, Ph.D., CPA	University of Baltimore (Retired)
Rita H. Grant, MBA, CPA	Grand Valley State University
David J. Harr, Ph.D., CPA	George Mason University
Pamela Z. Jackson, Ph.D., CPA	Augusta State
Susan A. Lynn, DBA, CPA	University of Baltimore
J. Lowell Mooney, Ph.D, CPA	Georgia Southern University
Robert H. Sanborn, Ph.D.	University of Richmond
Douglas K. Schneider, Ph.D.	East Carolina University
Jalal Soroosh, Ph.D., CMA	Loyola College in Maryland

Reviewers

Ajay Adhikari, Ph.D.	The American University
Cynthia E. Bird, Ph.D., CPA	California State University - San Bernardino
Wayne G. Bremser, Ph.D., CPA	Villanova University
Janet D. Daniels, DBA, CPA	Boston University
David F. Fetyko, Ph.D., CPA	Kent State University
Mary L. Fischer, Ph.D.	University of Texas at Tyler
Karen A. Fortin, Ph.D., CPA	University of Baltimore (Retired)
Charles H. Gibson, DBA, CPA	University of Toledo (Retired)
Teresa P. Gordon, Ph.D., CPA	University of Idaho
Martin L. Gosman, Ph.D., CPA	Quinnipiac College
David P. Kirch, Ph.D., CPA	Ohio University
Susan A. Lynn, DBA, CPA	University of Baltimore
Stanley Martens, Ph.D., CPA	DePaul University
Richard W. Metcalf, DBA, CPA	University of Arizona (Deceased)
Philip E. Meyer, DBA, CPA	Boston University
Mary D. Myers, Ph.D., CPA	Shippensburg University
Laurie W. Pant, DBA, CMA	Suffolk University
Philip M.J. Reckers, Ph.D.	Arizona State University
Ann J. Rich, Ph.D., CPA	Quinnipiac College
Robert A. Semenza, BBA, CPA	Quinnipiac College
Kathleen Simione, BA, CPA	Quinnipiac College
Jalal Soroosh, Ph.D., CMA	Loyola College in Maryland
Barbara R. Stewart, Ph.D., CPA	Towson State University
Martin E. Taylor, Ph.D., CPA	University of Texas - Arlington
Deborah H. Turner, Ph.D., CPA	Georgia Institute of Technology
Herbert N. Watkins, Ph.D., CPA	Alabama State

Special thanks to those who helped in developing the concept of the Encyclopedia to make it a reality. They are Stephen Loeb, CPA, Ph.D., Lita Schloss, Thomas Gilgut, Jr., and Adrienne Seiffert. Thanks to Joanne Brodsky who patiently did the proofreading.

Gordon S. May

TABLE OF CONTENTS

HOW TO USE THE ENCYCLOPEDIA

■ Index of Journal Entries
Use the extensive topical Index beginning on page 705 to find the entry or group of entries you need.

■ Account Classification Index
Use the Account Classification Index, beginning on page 697, to see what kind of account you are dealing with — asset, liability, revenue, expense, etc. For example:

Direct Labor Efficiency Variance [G or O]   This is a Gain or Loss account

Purchase Discounts [CA]   This is a Contra Asset account

■ General Table of Contents
Use the general Table of Contents on page vii to find the area of accounting or tax you are interested in. For example, Section 2000 is Receivables, Section 12000 is Income Tax, and Section 23000 is Not-for-Profit Organization journal entries.

■ Table of Contents for Each Section
Each section begins with a Table of Contents that offers a second way, in addition to the index, to find the journal entry you need. It lists all subjects for the section in the order in which they appear. To illustrate, here is a portion of the Table of Contents for Section 4, Inventories:

GEN4000. "GEN" means that you are in one of the general accounting sections. "4000" is the prefix for all entries in Section 4, which is Inventories.

Each journal entry has its own i.d. number on the left and is also described by one or more headings above. When you find the entry that you want, apply the headings as follows:

- Apply only headings with i.d. numbers that have the same starting digits. For example, do not apply headings that begin 4000.2 to entries that begin 4000.1.

- Apply all headings with *shorter* i.d. numbers.

- Apply *no* headings with longer i.d. numbers.

For example, take the entry Cash Purchase. Reading up the ladder, you see that this entry is specifically for Purchase of Merchandise for Resale (shorter i.d. number) under the Periodic System (shorter i.d. number) for Merchandising Inventories (shorter i.d. number).

How Entries Are Defined on Each Page of the *Encyclopedia*

Each page of entries in the *encyclopedia* uses the same system as the table of contents described on the previous page.

All the headings you need for your entry are supplied at the top of each page in boldface type.

- Apply only those headings at the top of the page with i.d. numbers that have the same starting digits as that entry you want.

  For example, do not apply headings that begin 4000.1.4. to entries that begin 4000.1.3.

- Apply all headings with *shorter* i.d. numbers.

- Do *not* apply headings with longer i.d. numbers.

Sample page explained

❶ GEN indicates a general accounting section, the prefix 4000 indicates that this is the section on inventories and .1.2.1.2.2 is the i.d. number of the first entry on the page.

❷ The decimal .1.2.3 is the i.d. number of the last entry on the page.

❸ These are the headings from previous pages that apply to the entries on this page (because the heading i.d. numbers begin with the same digits as the entry i.d. numbers and are shorter than the entry i.d. numbers).

Thus, the entry on this page for Purchase of Merchandise for Resale is used only under the Perpetual Inventory System (shorter i.d. number) for Merchandising Inventories (shorter i.d. number).

Applying the descriptive headings for each entry is important because many entries appear several times in a handbook and involve different accounts in each instance.

For example, in the Inventories section the entry for Cash Purchase appears in Merchandising Inventories under both the perpetual and periodic systems and appears twice more in Manufacturing Inventories under both the perpetual and periodic systems with different accounts used in each instance.

(continued on page viii)

Important: Make sure all appropriate subheads apply to your entry.

4000.1	**Merchandising Inventories**	
4000.1.2	**Perpetual Inventory System**	
4000.1.2.1	**Purchase of Merchandise for Resale**	❸
4000.1.2.1.2	**Purchase on Credit (on Account)**	

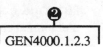

SAMPLE
PAGE

4000.1.2.1.2.2   **Purchase Recorded Net of Anticipated Cash Discount**

> *Inventory   xxxx
>   Accounts Payable   xxxx
> *To record purchase of merchandise*

*Inventory is debited for the invoice amount net of any cash discount that may be taken for prompt payment. For example, a $1,000 purchase subject to a 2% cash discount if paid within 10 days will be recorded at $980 even though $1,000 will be paid if the account is not paid within 10 days.

4000.1.2.2   **Payment of Freight-In (Transportation-In)**

Freight-In (Transportation-In) is the cost of freight necessary to acquire goods purchased on an F.O.B. (free on board) shipping point basis, i.e., when the supplier does not bear the cost of freight. Freight-In (Transportation-In) must be recorded in a separate account from Freight-Out (Transportation-Out), which is a selling expense.

> *Inventory   xxxx
>   Cash   xxxx
> *To record payment of freight-in*

*Transportation-In may be debited (instead of Inventory) if the amount is immaterial, or if it is not feasible to allocate these costs to Inventory.

4000.1.2.3   **Return of Merchandise to or Price Adjustment by Supplier**

> *Accounts Payable   xxxx
>   *Inventory   xxxx
> *To record purchase return or allowance*

*The amount recorded will be the gross invoice amount of the return or the amount of the allowance (price reduction because of product damage, etc.) if the purchase was originally recorded at the gross amount (*see GEN4000.1.2.1.2.1*). If the purchase was originally recorded net of the cash discount, the amount of this entry will be the net invoice amount of the return or allowance (*see GEN4000.1.2.1.2.2*).

Journal Entry Format

All journal entries are given in standard form, such as the following:

Accounts Payable	xxxx	
Purchase Discounts Lost	xxxx	
Cash		xxxx
To record payment of accounts payable		

1. <u>Alternative account titles and wording</u>: Alternative account titles and wording are shown in two ways. First, they may be shown in parentheses with the account. Here are two examples:

Factory Overhead (Manufacturing Overhead)	xxxx	
Raw Materials Inventory		xxxx
To record indirect materials used		

Cash	xxxx	
Common (Preferred) Stock		xxxx
To record issuance of stock		

When it is too cumbersome to show alternative account titles or wording with the account, they are provided in a note to the entry, such as the following:

Cash	xxxx	
*Additional Paid-In Capital - Common (Preferred) Stock		xxxx
Common (Preferred) Stock		xxxx
To record issuance of stock		

    *Common alternative account titles include:
        Contributed Capital In Excess Of Stated Value - Common (Preferred) Stock
        Paid-In Capital In Excess Of Stated Value - Common (Preferred) Stock

2. <u>Descriptions in Brackets</u>: brackets indicate *types* of accounts (e.g., assets, payables, or receivables):

[Various Assets]	xxxx	
Donated Capital		xxxx
To record donation of capital		

Depreciation Expense	xxxx	
Accumulated Depreciation - [Various Assets]		xxxx
To record depreciation		

When you begin to look up entries, you will find the *Encyclopedia* simple to use.

If you have a special way of recording a transaction or use entries that are not generally known, we would like to hear about it. Please write to us at:

Encyclopedia
AIPB, 6001 Montrose Road, Suite 207, Rockville, MD 20852

TABLE OF CONTENTS

GEN1000   ACCOUNTING CYCLE

1000.1   **Definition of the Accounting Cycle**

The accounting cycle is the process by which accountants analyze, record, and report an entity's measurable economic business transactions for a specific period of time. The accounting cycle is a series of steps that are repeated on a cyclical basis (i.e., each accounting period). Generally, the complete cycle occurs over a 12-month period, which may be the calendar year or any 12-month fiscal year (e.g., July 1 through June 30)

1000.2   **Phases of the Accounting Cycle**

The accounting cycle occurs in three distinct phases. The first phase consists of work performed at the beginning of the accounting period. The second phase consists of work performed during the accounting period. The third phase consists of work performed at the end of the accounting period.

1. Work performed at the beginning of the accounting period includes:

    - Reviewing the balances of all general ledger accounts or reviewing the post-closing trial balance at the end of the last accounting period to be sure the accounts are ready to begin the new accounting period. *See GEN1000.2.1.1.*
    - Recording reversing entries in the general journal and posting to the general ledger accounts if the policy of the firm is to record reversing entries. The use of reversing entries is optional. *See GEN1000.2.1.2.*

2. Work performed during the accounting period includes:

    - Collecting transaction data from business documents. *See GEN1000.2.2.1.*
    - Analyzing transactions and making appropriate journal entries. *See GEN1000.2.2.2.*
    - Posting journal entries to general ledger accounts. *See GEN1000.2.2.3.*

3. Work performed at the end of the period includes:

    - Preparing a trial balance to prove the equality of debits and credits in the general ledger accounts. *See GEN1000.2.3.1.*
    - Recording adjusting entries in the general journal and posting to the general ledger accounts. *See GEN1000.2.3.2.*

Important: Make sure all appropriate subheads apply to your entries (see page v for instructions)

1000.2   **Phases of the Accounting Cycle**

- Preparing an adjusted trial balance to prove the equality of debits and credits in the general ledger accounts. *See GEN1000.2.3.3.*
- Preparing financial statements including *(see GEN1000.2.3.4):*
  - a. Income Statement
  - b. Balance Sheet
  - c. Statement of Owner's Equity (for a sole proprietorship) or Statement of Retained Earnings (for a corporation)
  - d. Statement of Cash Flows
- Recording closing entries in the general journal and posting to the general ledger accounts. *See GEN1000.2.3.5.*
- Preparing a post-closing trial balance to prove the equality of debits and credits in the general ledger accounts. *See GEN1000.2.3.6.*

1000.2.1   **Work Performed at the Beginning of the Accounting Cycle**

1000.2.1.1   **Reviewing Account Balances in the General Ledger at the Beginning of the Accounting Period**

Newly Formed Company - All balances in general ledger accounts will be zero.

Established Company -
  (a) Asset, liability, and owner's equity accounts will have balances carried over from the prior year.
  (b) Revenue, expense, dividend, and drawings (withdrawals) accounts will have zero balances.

1000.2.1.2   **Recording and Posting Reversing Entries (Optional)**

Recording and posting reversing entries are not required steps in the accounting cycle. However, reversing entries may be desirable to save time or to simplify record-keeping in the new accounting period.

Reversing entries reverse certain adjusting entries made at the end of the previous accounting period. When the recording of revenue and expense transactions of the new period would be affected by adjusting entries of the past period, reversing

Important: Make sure all appropriate subheads apply to your entries (see page v for instructions)

1000.2   **Phases of the Accounting Cycle**
1000.2.1   **Work Performed at the Beginning of the Accounting Cycle**
1000.2.1.2   **Recording and Posting Reversing Entries (Optional)**

---

entries eliminate the need to consider any balances in asset or liability accounts created by the prior period's adjusting entries.

For example, assume that the prior accounting period ended on Monday, 12/31/x1. Also assume that the company makes a weekly cash payroll every Friday. The adjusting entry made on 12/31/x1 would accrue one day (Monday) of wage expense for 20x1 that had not been paid and would establish a liability account, Wages Payable, for that amount. The following entry must be made:

Wages Expense	xxxx	
Wages Payable		xxxx
To accrue wages expense		

Now, assume that the standard journal entry to record the cash payroll consists of a debit to Wages Expense and a credit to Cash. On the first Friday of the new year (20x2) when the cash payroll is recorded, to avoid recording the wage expense for Monday (12/31/x1) again, the following entry must be made:

*Wages Payable	xxxx	
**Wages Expense	xxxx	
Cash		xxxx
To record weekly cash payroll		

*Wages Payable must be debited to remove the amount of the credit made in the adjusting entry at the end of the prior period.

**Wages Expense must be debited for the amount of wages expense incurred in 20x2, i.e., for Tuesday through Friday only.

The preceding entry can be avoided if a reversing entry is made at the beginning of the new year (20x2). In the example, the reversing entry would reverse the previous adjusting entry by debiting what was credited in the entry and crediting what was debited. The following entry must be made:

Wages Payable	xxxx	
Wages Expense		xxxx
To reverse the adjusting entry made to accrue wages		
expense at 12/31/x1		

Important: Make sure all appropriate subheads apply to your entries (see page v for instructions)

1000.2   **Phases of the Accounting Cycle**
1000.2.1   **Work Performed at the Beginning of the Accounting Cycle**
1000.2.1.2   **Recording and Posting Reversing Entries (Optional)**

This reversing entry will cause a credit to be recorded in the Wages Expense account for the amount of the 12/31/x1 wages (for Monday) which was accrued and expensed in the prior period. On Friday, the standard cash payroll entry can now be made, i.e., Wages Expense can be debited for the entire amount of the wages paid for the five-day week. This would cause a debit in the Wage Expense account for a full five-day week, which is partially offset by the credit created by the reversing entry. The effect is a net debit in the Wage Expense account for the expense pertaining to the four days of the new period, i.e., the appropriate amount of expense for the new accounting period.

1000.2.2   **Work Performed During the Accounting Cycle**

1000.2.2.1   **Collection of Transaction Data from Business Documents**

Transaction data must be collected from business documents, e.g., sales slips and purchase invoices (which may be computerized records) to be used as a basis for making journal entries.

1000.2.2.2   **Analyzing Transactions and Making Appropriate Journal Entries**

1000.2.2.2.1   **Normal Asset Transactions**

1000.2.2.2.1.1   **Investment by Owner(s) (Sole Proprietorship or Partnership)**

    *[Various Assets]   xxxx
      [J. Doe], Capital   xxxx
    To record investment by owner

*Assets that may be debited include (but are not limited to) Cash, Inventory, Supplies, Prepaid Expenses, and Equipment.

Important: Make sure all appropriate subheads apply to your entry (see page v for instructions)

1000.2   **Phases of the Accounting Cycle**
1000.2.2   **Work Performed During the Accounting Cycle**
1000.2.2.2   **Analyzing Transactions and Making Appropriate Journal Entries**
1000.2.2.2.1   **Normal Asset Transactions**

1000.2.2.2.1.2   **Investment by Owner(s) (Corporation)**

*[Various Assets]	xxxx
Common (Preferred) Stock	xxxx
Additional Paid-In Capital	xxxx
To record investment by stockholder	

*Assets that may be debited include (but are not limited to) Cash, Inventory, Supplies, Prepaid Expenses, and Equipment.

1000.2.2.2.1.3   **Asset Purchases**

*[Various Assets]	xxxx
Accounts Payable (Cash, [Various Liabilities])	xxxx
To record purchase of assets	

*Assets that may be debited include (but are not limited to) Cash, Inventory, Supplies, Prepaid Expenses, and Equipment.

1000.2.2.2.1.4   **Assets Acquired by Sales Transactions**

Accounts Receivable (Cash, [Various Assets])	xxxx
Sales	xxxx
To record sales	

1000.2.2.2.1.5   **Assets Acquired by Collection of Accounts Receivable**

Cash (Notes Receivable)	xxxx
Accounts Receivable	xxxx
To record collection of accounts receivable	

1000.2.2.2.1.6   **Sale of Assets**

The recording of the sale of assets can be quite complicated. The entries below do not deal with many of the complications. For complete coverage of the sale of assets, *see GEN5000.3.1.*

Important: Make sure all appropriate subheads apply to your entry (see page v for instructions)

1000.2	**Phases of the Accounting Cycle**
1000.2.2	**Work Performed During the Accounting Cycle**
1000.2.2.2	**Analyzing Transactions and Making Appropriate Journal Entries**
1000.2.2.2.1	**Normal Asset Transactions**
1000.2.2.2.1.6	**Sale of Assets**

1000.2.2.2.1.6.1   **Sale of Assets with Realization of Gain**

Cash	xxxx	
Accumulated Depreciation - [Various Assets]	xxxx	
Gain On Sale Of Assets		xxxx
[Various Assets]		xxxx
To record sale of assets and realization of gain		

1000.2.2.2.1.6.2   **Sale of Assets with Realization of Loss**

Cash	xxxx	
Accumulated Depreciation - [Various Assets]	xxxx	
Loss On Sale Of Assets	xxxx	
[Various Assets]		xxxx
To record sale of assets and realization of loss		

1000.2.2.2.2   **Normal Liability Transactions**

1000.2.2.2.2.1   **Purchases of Inventory on Credit**

*Inventory (Purchases)	xxxx	
Accounts Payable (Notes Payable)		xxxx
To record purchase of inventory		

*Purchases would be debited if the periodic system of inventory is used. *See GEN4000.1.1.1.2.* Inventory would be debited if the perpetual system of inventory is used. *See GEN4000.1.2.1.2.*

1000.2.2.2.2.2   **Purchases of Assets Other than Inventory on Credit**

*[Various Assets]	xxxx	
Accounts Payable (Notes Payable, Mortgage Payable)		xxxx
To record purchase of assets		

*Assets that may be debited include (but are not limited to) Supplies, Prepaid Expenses, Land, Buildings, and Equipment.

Important: Make sure all appropriate subheads apply to your entry (see page v for instructions)

1000.2	**Phases of the Accounting Cycle**
1000.2.2	**Work Performed During the Accounting Cycle**
1000.2.2.2	**Analyzing Transactions and Making Appropriate Journal Entries**
1000.2.2.2.2	**Normal Liability Transactions**

1000.2.2.2.2.3 **Borrowing Money**

Cash   xxxx
    Notes Payable (Bonds Payable)   xxxx
*To record borrowing cash by issuing notes or bonds
payable*

1000.2.2.2.2.4 **Payment of Liability**

  *[Various Liabilities]   xxxx
    Cash   xxxx
To record payment of liability

*Liabilities may include (but are not limited to) Accounts Payable, Notes Payable, Mortgage Payable, Bonds Payable, Interest Payable, and Salaries Payable.

1000.2.2.2.3 **Owner's Equity Transactions**

Owner's equity transactions are transactions relating to an owner's claim to the assets of the business. In a proprietorship or in a partnership, these transactions are split into separate accounts — one (or more in the case of a partnership) for owner(s') capital and one (or more in the case of a partnership) for owners' drawings (withdrawals). In a corporation, the owners' equity accounts are comprised of a variety of contributed (or paid-in) capital accounts (e.g., Common Stock, Preferred Stock, and Additional Paid-In Capital), and Retained Earnings.

1000.2.2.2.3.1 **Investment by Stockholders**

  *[Various Assets]   xxxx
    Common (Preferred) Stock   xxxx
    Additional Paid-In Capital   xxxx
To record investment by stockholders

*Assets that may be debited include (but are not limited to) Cash, Inventory, Supplies, Prepaid Expenses, and Equipment.

Important: Make sure all appropriate subheads apply to your entry (see page v for instructions)

1000.2	**Phases of the Accounting Cycle**
1000.2.2	**Work Performed During the Accounting Cycle**
1000.2.2.2	**Analyzing Transactions and Making Appropriate Journal Entries**
1000.2.2.2.3	**Owner's Equity Transactions**

1000.2.2.2.3.2   **Investment by Sole Proprietor or Partner**

> *[Various Assets]   xxxx
> [J. Doe], Capital   xxxx
> *To record investment by owner*

*Assets that may be debited include (but are not limited to) Cash, Inventory, Supplies, Prepaid Expenses, and Equipment.

1000.2.2.2.3.3   **Withdrawal by a Sole Proprietor or Partner**

> *[J. Smith], Withdrawals   xxxx
> Cash [Various Assets]   xxxx
> *To record an owner's withdrawal*

*An alternative account title would be [J. Smith], Drawings.

1000.2.2.2.3.4   **Dividends Declared and Paid to Stockholders**

> *Dividends (Retained Earnings)   xxxx
> **Dividends Payable   xxxx
> *To record declaration of dividends*

*If Dividends is debited, this account is later closed to Retained Earnings.

**Dividends Payable is credited if the dividend is to be paid in cash. If a noncash asset is to be distributed, the credit should be made to Property Dividend Payable. If notes payable (debt) is to be distributed, the credit should be made to Scrip Dividend Payable. *See GEN9000.12* for a complete discussion of dividends.

> *Dividends Payable   xxxx
> *Cash   xxxx
> *To record payment of cash dividends*

*This entry is made for the payment of a cash dividend. If another type of dividend is to be paid, a different entry will be made. *See GEN9000.12* for a complete discussion of dividends.

Important: Make sure all appropriate subheads apply to your entry (see page v for instructions)

1000.2   **Phases of the Accounting Cycle**
1000.2.2   **Work Performed During the Accounting Cycle**
1000.2.2.2   **Analyzing Transactions and Making Appropriate Journal Entries**

1000.2.2.2.4   **Revenue Transactions**

1000.2.2.2.4.1   **Revenue from Services Provided**

   Accounts Receivable (Cash)   xxxx
    *Service Revenue   xxxx
   To record service revenue

  *Fees Earned is a common alternative account title.

1000.2.2.2.4.2   **Revenue from Sale of Merchandise**

   Accounts Receivable (Cash)   xxxx
    *Sales   xxxx
   To record sale of merchandise

  *Sales Revenue is a common alternative account title.

1000.2.2.2.4.3   **Revenue from Interest Earned**

   Cash (Interest Receivable)   xxxx
    *Interest Revenue   xxxx
   To record interest revenue

  *Interest Income is a common alternative account title.

1000.2.2.2.4.4   **Revenue from Rent Earned**

   Cash (Unearned Rent)   xxxx
    *Rent Revenue   xxxx
   To record rent revenue

  *Rent Income is a common alternative account title.

Important: Make sure all appropriate subheads apply to your entry (see page v for instructions)

1000.2   **Phases of the Accounting Cycle**
1000.2.2   **Work Performed During the Accounting Cycle**
1000.2.2.2   **Analyzing Transactions and Making Appropriate Journal Entries**

1000.2.2.2.5   **Expense Transactions**

1000.2.2.2.5.1   **Expense Incurred (Cash Paid or Liability Incurred)**

     *[Various Expenses]   xxxx
       **Cash [Various Liabilities]   xxxx
    To record incurrence of expense

*Various expenses, e.g., Advertising Expense, Wages Expense, Rent Expense, Taxes Expense, and Utility Expense, may be debited.

**Instead of Cash, various liabilities such as Accounts Payable, Wages Payable, and Taxes Payable, may be credited.

1000.2.2.2.5.2   **Expense Incurred (Use of an Asset Other than Cash)**

The consumption of an asset will usually result in an expense. The following three entries are common examples:

    Supplies Expense   xxxx
      *Supplies   xxxx
    To record supplies used

*Supplies On Hand is a common alternative account title.

    Insurance Expense   xxxx
      Prepaid Insurance   xxxx
    To record insurance expense

    Depreciation Expense   xxxx
      Accumulated Depreciation - [Various Assets]   xxxx
    To record depreciation expense

1000.2.2.3   **Post Journal Entries to General Ledger Accounts**

Periodically, amounts must be transferred (posted) from the journal(s) to the general ledger accounts.

Important: Make sure all appropriate subheads apply to your entry (see page v for instructions)

1000.2   **Phases of the Accounting Cycle**

1000.2.3   **Work Performed at the End of the Accounting Cycle**

1000.2.3.1   **Preparation of a Trial Balance**

A trial balance contains a listing of all accounts in the general ledger with their balances. It is prepared with debit balances in one column and credit balances in another. The columns are totaled to prove the equality of debits and credits. A trial balance is used only to prove this equality; it cannot detect omitted transactions, nor does it test the correctness of accounting entries.

1000.2.3.2   **Recording Adjusting Entries**

Adjusting entries update the general ledger account balances so that they properly and more accurately reflect the revenues earned, the expenses incurred, the assets owned, the liabilities owed, and the owners' equity in the business. Adjustments are necessary because some transactions have effects that cover more than one accounting period. There are six types of adjustments that result from one of two categories: *deferrals*, and *accruals*.

1000.2.3.2.1   **Deferrals**

Deferrals occur when cash is paid or received in the current period but the related expense or revenue is not recognized until a future period. When a deferral occurs, it is necessary to make an adjusting entry to record the expense or revenue at a later date.

1000.2.3.2.1.1   **Prepaid Expenses**

Prepaid expenses represent the cost of future benefits that have been paid in advance and that must be allocated to expense over the accounting periods in which the benefits are received.

1000.2.3.2.1.1.1 **Prepaid Expenses Initially Recorded as an Asset**

Examples of original entries include:

Important: Make sure all appropriate subheads apply to your entry (see page v for instructions)

1000.2	**Phases of the Accounting Cycle**
1000.2.3	**Work Performed at the End of the Accounting Cycle**
1000.2.3.2	**Recording Adjusting Entries**
1000.2.3.2.1	**Deferrals**
1000.2.3.2.1.1	**Prepaid Expenses**
1000.2.3.2.1.1.1	**Prepaid Expenses Initially Recorded as an Asset**

Prepaid Insurance   xxxx
    Cash   xxxx
*To record payment of an insurance premium covering
several periods*

*Supplies   xxxx
    Cash   xxxx
To record purchase of supplies

*Supplies On Hand is an alternative account title.

Examples of adjusting entries include:

Insurance Expense   xxxx
    Prepaid Insurance   xxxx
To record insurance expense

Supplies Expense   xxxx
    *Supplies   xxxx
To record amount of supplies used

*Supplies On Hand is an alternative account title.

1000.2.3.2.1.1.2   Prepaid Expenses Initially Recorded as an Expense

Examples of original entries include:

Insurance Expense   xxxx
    Cash   xxxx
*To record payment of an insurance premium covering
several periods*

Supplies Expense   xxxx
    Cash   xxxx
To record purchase of supplies

Important: Make sure all appropriate subheads apply to your entry (see page v for instructions)

1000.2	**Phases of the Accounting Cycle**
1000.2.3	**Work Performed at the End of the Accounting Cycle**
1000.2.3.2	**Recording Adjusting Entries**
1000.2.3.2.1	**Deferrals**
1000.2.3.2.1.1	**Prepaid Expenses**
1000.2.3.2.1.1.2	**Prepaid Expenses Initially Recorded as an Expense**

Examples of adjusting entries include:

Prepaid Insurance	xxxx	
Insurance Expense		xxxx
To record prepaid insurance		

*Supplies	xxxx	
Supplies Expense		xxxx
To record supplies on hand		

*Supplies On Hand is an alternative account title.

1000.2.3.2.1.2   **Depreciation**

Depreciation results from the most common deferral (the allocation of the cost of a tangible asset over its useful life). The adjusting entry is in the form of:

Depreciation Expense	xxxx	
*Accumulated Depreciation - [Various Assets]		xxxx
To record depreciation		

*Allowance For Depreciation - [Various Assets] is an alternative account title

1000.2.3.2.1.3   **Unearned Revenue**

Unearned revenue represents cash amounts that have been received before merchandise has been delivered or before services have been rendered. Because these amounts have not yet been earned, they are usually (but not always) initially recorded in liability accounts. Unearned revenue adjustments transfer revenue earned during the current period from liability account(s) to revenue account(s) or vice versa, depending on how the amounts were originally recorded.

1000.2.3.2.1.3.1   **Unearned Revenue Originally Recorded as a Liability**

Examples of original entries include:

Important: Make sure all appropriate subheads apply to your entry (see page v for instructions)

1000.2	**Phases of the Accounting Cycle**
1000.2.3	**Work Performed at the End of the Accounting Cycle**
1000.2.3.2	**Recording Adjusting Entries**
1000.2.3.2.1	**Deferrals**
1000.2.3.2.1.3	**Unearned Revenue**
1000.2.3.2.1.3.1	**Unearned Revenue Originally Recorded as a Liability**

Cash   xxxx

    Unearned Rent   xxxx

To record advance collection of rent

Cash   xxxx

    Unearned Subscription Revenue   xxxx

To record advance collection of subscription revenue

Examples of adjusting entries include:

Unearned Rent   xxxx

    Rent Revenue   xxxx

To record amount of unearned rent revenue earned during the period

Unearned Subscription Revenue   xxxx

    Subscription Revenue   xxxx

To record amount of unearned subscription revenue earned during the period

1000.2.3.2.1.3.2   **Unearned Revenue Originally Recorded as a Revenue**

Examples of original entries include:

Cash   xxxx

    Rent Revenue   xxxx

To record advance collection of rent

Cash   xxxx

    Subscription Revenue   xxxx

To record advance collection of subscription revenue

Examples of adjusting entries include:

Rent Revenue   xxxx

    Unearned Rent Revenue   xxxx

To record unearned rent revenue previously recorded as earned

Important: Make sure all appropriate subheads apply to your entry (see page v for instructions)

1000.2   **Phases of the Accounting Cycle**
1000.2.3   **Work Performed at the End of the Accounting Cycle**
1000.2.3.2   **Recording Adjusting Entries**
1000.2.3.2.1   **Deferrals**
1000.2.3.2.1.3   **Unearned Revenue**
1000.2.3.2.1.3.2   **Unearned Revenue Originally Recorded as a Revenue**

Subscription Revenue	xxxx	
Unearned Subscription Revenue		xxxx

*To record unearned subscription revenue previously
recorded as earned*

1000.2.3.2.2   Accruals

Accruals occur when expense or revenue is recognized before cash is paid or received. At the end of an accounting period, it is necessary to make an adjusting entry to record certain expenses and revenues before the cash flow occurs to properly reflect revenue and expense for the period.

1000.2.3.2.2.1   Accrued Revenues

Accrued revenues are revenues that have been earned during the current accounting period but have not been received in cash or recorded in the accounts. The adjustment consists of recording the amount of revenue earned during the period and establishing an appropriate receivable account for the amount to be collected.

Examples of adjusting entries include:

Rent Receivable	xxxx	
*Rent Revenue		xxxx

To record accrued rent revenue

*Rent Income is an alternative account title.

Interest Receivable	xxxx	
*Interest Revenue		xxxx

To record accrued interest revenue

*Interest Income is an alternative account title.

1000.2.3.2.2.2   Accrued Expenses

Accrued expenses are expenses that have been incurred during the current accounting period but have not been paid in cash or recorded in the accounts. The adjustment

Important: Make sure all appropriate subheads apply to your entry (see page v for instructions)

1000.2	**Phases of the Accounting Cycle**
1000.2.3	**Work Performed at the End of the Accounting Cycle**
1000.2.3.2	**Recording Adjusting Entries**
1000.2.3.2.2	**Accruals**
1000.2.3.2.2.2	**Accrued Expenses**

---

consists of recording the amount of expense incurred during the period and establishing an appropriate liability for the amount to be paid.

Examples of adjusting entries include:

Wages Expense	xxxx	
Wages Payable		xxxx
To record accrued wages expense		
Interest Expense	xxxx	
Interest Payable		xxxx
To record accrued interest expense		
*Bad Debt Expense	xxxx	
**Allowance For Doubtful Accounts		xxxx
To accrue bad debt expense		

*Uncollectible Accounts Expense is an alternative account title.

**Allowance For Uncollectible Accounts is an alternative account title.

1000.2.3.3

Preparation of an Adjusted Trial Balance

An adjusted trial balance contains a listing of all accounts in the general ledger with their balances after adjusting entries have been made and posted. It is prepared with debit balances in one column and credit balances in another. The columns are totaled to prove the equality of debits and credits. A trial balance is used only to prove this equality; it cannot detect omitted transactions or adjusting entries, nor does it test the correctness of accounting entries.

1000.2.3.4

Preparation of Financial Statements

At this point, financial statements, including Balance Sheet, Income Statement, Statement of Cash Flows, and Statement of Owner's Equity or Statement of Retained Earnings, are prepared.

Important: Make sure all appropriate subheads apply to your entry (see page v for instructions)

1000.2   **Phases of the Accounting Cycle**
1000.2.3   **Work Performed at the End of the Accounting Cycle**

1000.2.3.5   **Recording and Posting Closing Entries**

Closing entries are made to transfer all expense, revenue, gain, loss, and dividend (or withdrawal if a sole proprietorship or partnership) account balances to Retained Earnings (or owner capital accounts if a sole proprietorship or partnership). This leaves zero balances in these accounts, so that they are ready for the new accounting period.

1000.2.3.5.1   **Closing Revenue and Gain Accounts to Income Summary**

To close revenue and gain accounts, each revenue or gain account is debited for the amount of its credit balance, and Income Summary is credited for the total of all the debits, e.g.:

Sales	xxxx	
Interest Revenue	xxxx	
[Various Revenues]	xxxx	
[Various Gains]	xxxx	
*(Merchandise Inventory)	xxxx	
*(Purchases Returns And Allowances)	xxxx	
*(Purchases Discounts)	xxxx	
Income Summary		xxxx
To close all revenue accounts		

*If a firm accounts for merchandise inventory using the periodic method, it may treat its year-end inventory adjustment as part of the closing process. In that case, purchases related accounts are closed along with revenue accounts and Merchandise Inventory is debited for its ending balance. *See GEN4000.1.1.7* for a discussion of alternative year-end procedures for merchandise inventory under the periodic method.

1000.2.3.5.2   **Closing Expense and Loss Accounts to Income Summary**

To close expense and loss accounts, credit each expense and loss account for its debit balance and debit Income Summary for the total credits, e.g.:

Important: Make sure all appropriate subheads apply to your entry (see page v for instructions)

1000.2	**Phases of the Accounting Cycle**
1000.2.3	**Work Performed at the End of the Accounting Cycle**
1000.2.3.5	**Recording and Posting Closing Entries**
1000.2.3.5.2	**Closing Expense and Loss Accounts to Income Summary**

Income Summary	xxxx	
Sales Discounts		xxxx
Sales Returns And Allowances		xxxx
*Cost Of Goods Sold		xxxx
*(Purchases)		xxxx
*(Merchandise Inventory)		xxxx
Rent Expense		xxxx
Wages Expense		xxxx
Depreciation Expense		xxxx
Supplies Expense		xxxx
[Various Expenses]		xxxx
[Various Losses]		xxxx

To close all expense accounts

*If a firm accounts for merchandise inventory using the periodic method, it may treat its year-end inventory adjustment as part of the closing process. In that case, Purchases will be closed along with expense accounts, Merchandise Inventory is credited for its beginning balance and Cost Of Goods Sold is not used. *See GEN4000.1.1.7* for a discussion of alternative year-end procedures for merchandise inventory under the periodic method.

1000.2.3.5.3   **Closing Income Summary to Retained Earnings or Owner Capital Accounts**

After closing all revenues, expenses, gains, and losses to Income Summary, Income Summary will have either a credit balance (indicating net income) or a debit balance (indicating net loss). This balance must then be closed to Retained Earnings (for a corporation) or to owner capital accounts (if a sole proprietorship or a partnership). Thus, if Income Summary has a credit balance, debit Income Summary for the amount of this credit balance and credit Retained Earnings (or owner capital accounts). If Income Summary has a debit balance, credit Income Summary for theamount of this debit balance and debit Retained Earnings (or owner capital accounts). If Income Summary has a credit balance, the proper entry is one of the following:

For a corporation:

Income Summary	xxxx	
Retained Earnings		xxxx

To close Income Summary to Retained Earnings

Important: Make sure all appropriate subheads apply to your entry (see page v for instructions)

1000.2   **Phases of the Accounting Cycle**
1000.2.3   **Work Performed at the End of the Accounting Cycle**
1000.2.3.5   **Recording and Posting Closing Entries**

For a sole proprietorship:

Income Summary	xxxx	
[J. Smith], Capital		xxxx
To close Income Summary to owner capital		

For a partnership:

Income Summary	xxxx	
[Partner A], Capital		xxxx
[Partner B], Capital		xxxx
To close Income Summary to partner capital		

1000.2.3.5.4   **Closing a Dividends or Drawings (Withdrawals) Account**

If the firm is a corporation, it may have a Dividends account with a debit balance, indicating that dividends have been declared that have been paid or will be paid to stockholders. If the firm is a sole proprietorship or partnership, it will have one or more Withdrawals (Drawings) accounts (one for each owner) containing debit balances. Dividends must be closed to Retained Earnings. Withdrawals accounts must be closed to the respective owner capital account. The proper entry is one of the following:

For a corporation:

Retained Earnings	xxxx	
Dividends		xxxx
To close Dividends to Retained Earnings		

For a sole proprietorship:

[J. Smith], Capital	xxxx	
[J. Smith], Withdrawals		xxxx
To close the owner withdrawal account to owner capital		

Important: Make sure all appropriate subheads apply to your entries (see page v for instructions)

1000.2	**Phases of the Accounting Cycle**
1000.2.3	**Work Performed at the End of the Accounting Cycle**
1000.2.3.5	**Recording and Posting Closing Entries**
1000.2.3.5.4	**Closing a Dividends or Drawings (Withdrawals) Account**

For a partnership:

[Partner A], Capital	xxxx	
[Partner B], Capital	xxxx	
[Partner A], Withdrawals		xxxx
[Partner B], Withdrawals		xxxx

To close owner withdrawals accounts to owner capital accounts

1000.2.3.6   **Preparation of a Post-Closing Trial Balance**

A post-closing trial balance contains a listing of all accounts in the general ledger with their balances after closing entries have been made and posted. It is prepared with debit balances in one column and credit balances in another. The columns are totaled to prove the equality of debits and credits. A trial balance is used only to prove this equality; it cannot detect omitted transactions or adjusting entries, nor does it test the correctness of accounting entries.

TABLE OF CONTENTS

GEN2000   CASH

2000.1	**Cash in Banks**

2000.1.1	**Disbursements of Cash**

2000.1.1.1   **Advances**

Advances To Employees [Various Advances]	xxxx	
Cash		xxxx
To record advances made		

2000.1.1.2   **Accounts Payable or Vouchers Payable**

See GEN7000.1 for a more complete treatment of Accounts Payable including purchases discounts, returns, and allowances.

Accounts Payable (Vouchers Payable) - [Creditor A]	xxxx	
Cash		xxxx
To record payment of accounts payable		

2000.1.1.3   **Assets**

The purchase of assets often involves other accounts. For complete coverage, see the section covering transactions involving the particular asset.

[Various Assets]	xxxx	
Cash		xxxx
To record purchase of assets		

2000.1.1.4   **Deposits**

Deposits On Utilities [Various Deposits]	xxxx	
Cash		xxxx
To record deposits made		

CASH

Important: Make sure all appropriate subheads apply to your entry (see page v for instructions)

2000.1   **Cash in Banks**
2000.1.1   **Disbursements of Cash**

2000.1.1.5   ### Dividends Payable

Dividends Payable - Common (Preferred)	xxxx	
Cash		xxxx
To record payment of dividends payable		

2000.1.1.6   ### Drawings by a Partner or Sole Proprietor

Drawings (Withdrawals) - [Partner A]	xxxx	
Cash		xxxx
To record drawings by a partner (or sole proprietor)		

2000.1.1.7   ### Expense—No Liability Previously Recorded

[Various Expenses]	xxxx	
Cash		xxxx
To record payment of an expense for which a liability has not been previously recorded		

2000.1.1.8   ### Investments

The purchase of investments often involves other accounts. See GEN10000 for complete coverage.

Investments - [Investment A]	xxxx	
Cash		xxxx
To record purchase of investments		

2000.1.1.9   ### Liabilities

[Various Liabilities]	xxxx	
Cash		xxxx
To record payment of liabilities		

Important: Make sure all appropriate subheads apply to your entry (see page v for instructions)

2000.1   **Cash in Banks**
2000.1.1   **Disbursements of Cash**

2000.1.1.10   **Notes Payable**

See GEN7000.2 for a more complete treatment of Notes Payable, including interest and discount or premium amortization.

Notes Payable - [Creditor A]	xxxx	
Cash		xxxx

To record payment of a note payable

2000.1.1.11   **Treasury Stock**

See GEN9000.8 for a more complete treatment of Treasury Stock purchases.

Treasury Stock - Common (Preferred)	xxxx	
Cash		xxxx

To record purchase of treasury stock

2000.1.2   **Receipts of Cash**

2000.1.2.1   **Accounts Receivable**

See GEN3000.1 for a more complete treatment of collection of Accounts Receivable, including discounts and allowances.

Cash	xxxx	
Accounts Receivable - [Customer A]		xxxx

To record collection of an account receivable

2000.1.2.2   **Dividends Receivable**

Cash	xxxx	
Dividends Receivable		xxxx

To record receipt of dividends for which a receivable has been previously recorded

CASH

Important: Make sure all appropriate subheads apply to your entry (see page v for instructions)

2000.1　　　　　　**Cash in Banks**
2000.1.2　　　　　　　**Receipts of Cash**

2000.1.2.3　　　　**Dividend Revenue (Dividend Income)**

　　　　　　　　　　Cash　　　　　　　　　　　　　　　　　　xxxx
　　　　　　　　　　　　*Dividend Revenue　　　　　　　　　　　　xxxx
　　　　　　　　　　*To record receipt of dividends for which a receivable has
　　　　　　　　　　not been previously recorded*

　　　　　　　　*Dividend Income is an alternate account title.

2000.1.2.4　　　　**Interest Receivable**

　　　　　　　　　　Cash　　　　　　　　　　　　　　　　　　xxxx
　　　　　　　　　　　　Interest Receivable　　　　　　　　　　　xxxx
　　　　　　　　　　*To record receipt of interest for which Interest Receivable
　　　　　　　　　　has been previously recorded*

2000.1.2.5　　　　**Interest Revenue (Interest Income)**

　　　　　　　　　　Cash　　　　　　　　　　　　　　　　　　xxxx
　　　　　　　　　　　　*Interest Revenue　　　　　　　　　　　　xxxx
　　　　　　　　　　*To record receipt of interest for which Interest Receivable
　　　　　　　　　　has not been previously recorded*

　　　　　　　　*Interest Income is an alternate account title.

2000.1.2.6　　　　**Investment by Partner or Sole Proprietor**

　　　　　　　　　　Cash　　　　　　　　　　　　　　　　　　xxxx
　　　　　　　　　　　　[Partner A], Capital　　　　　　　　　　　xxxx
　　　　　　　　　　To record investment by a partner (or sole proprietor)

2000.1.2.7　　　　**Notes Receivable**

　　　　　　　　See GEN3000.2 for a more complete treatment of Notes Receivable, including
　　　　　　　　interest.

Important: Make sure all appropriate subheads apply to your entry (see page v for instructions)

2000.1	**Cash in Banks**
2000.1.2	**Receipts of Cash**
2000.1.2.7	**Notes Receivable**

Cash   xxxx
       Notes Receivable - [Debtor A]   xxxx
To record collection of a note receivable

2000.1.2.8   **Revenue (Income)**

Cash   xxxx
       [Various Revenue (Various Income)]   xxx
*To record receipt of revenue for which a receivable has
not been previously recorded*

2000.1.2.9   **Sales**

Cash   xxxx
       Sales   xxxx
To record cash sales

2000.1.2.10   **Stock**

*See GEN9000.1 for a more complete treatment of stock issuance, including
premiums and discounts.*

Cash   xxxx
       Stock - Common (Preferred)   xxxx
To record receipt of cash from issuance of stock

2000.1.3   **Transfer of Cash Between Bank Accounts**

Cash - [Bank Account A]   xxxx
       Cash - [Bank Account B]   xxxx
*To record transfer of cash from Bank Account B to Bank
Account A*

Important: Make sure all appropriate subheads apply to your entry (see page v for instructions)

2000.1 **Cash in Banks**

2000.1.4 **Reconciliation of Bank Account—Adjustments and Corrections**

2000.1.4.1 **Accounts Payable or Vouchers Payable**

2000.1.4.1.1 **Check Recorded for Too Much**

Cash	xxxx	
Accounts Payable (Vouchers Payable) - [Creditor A]		xxxx

To correct an error caused by recording a check for an amount greater than it was written for

2000.1.4.1.2 **Check Recorded for Too Little**

Accounts Payable (Vouchers Payable) - [Creditor A]	xxxx	
Cash		xxxx

To correct an error caused by recording a check for an amount less than it was written for

2000.1.4.2 **Accounts Receivable**

2000.1.4.2.1 **Check Recorded for Too Much**

Accounts Receivable - [Customer A]	xxxx	
Cash		xxxx

To correct an error caused by recording a customer's check for an amount greater than it was written for

2000.1.4.2.2 **Check Recorded for Too Little**

Cash	xxxx	
Accounts Receivable - [Customer A]		xxxx

To correct an error caused by recording a customer's check for an amount less than it was written for

---

Important: Make sure all appropriate subheads apply to your entry (see page v for instructions)

2000.1   **Cash in Banks**
2000.1.4   **Reconciliation of Bank Account—Adjustments and Corrections**
2000.1.4.2   **Accounts Receivable**

2000.1.4.2.3   **Return of Customer's Check for Lack of Funds**

Accounts Receivable - [Customer A]	xxxx	
Cash		xxxx

To record return of customer's check by bank for lack of funds

2000.1.4.3   **Banking Expense**

*Banking Expense	xxxx	
Cash		xxxx

To record a bank charge other than interest that has not been previously recorded

*A common alternative account title is Bank Service Charges.

2000.1.4.4   **Expenses**

2000.1.4.4.1   **Check Recorded for Too Much**

Cash	xxxx	
[Various Expenses]		xxxx

To correct an error caused by recording a check for an amount greater than it was written for

2000.1.4.4.2   **Check Recorded for Too Little**

[Various Expenses]	xxxx	
Cash		xxxx

To correct an error caused by recording a check for an amount less than it was written for

Important: Make sure all appropriate subheads apply to your entry (see page v for instructions)

2000.1   **Cash in Banks**
2000.1.4   **Reconciliation of Bank Account—Adjustments and Corrections**

2000.1.4.5   **Interest Expense**

> Interest Expense   xxxx
>   Cash   xxxx
> *To record interest expense that the bank deducted from*
> *your account*

2000.1.4.6   **Interest Revenue (Interest Income)**

> Cash   xxxx
>   *Interest Revenue   xxxx
> *To record interest revenue paid or collected by the bank*
> *on your behalf that has not been previously recorded*

*Interest Income is a common alternative account title.

2000.1.4.7   **Notes Payable**

2000.1.4.7.1   **Check Recorded for Too Much**

> Cash   xxxx
>   Notes Payable - [Creditor A]   xxxx
> *To correct an error caused by recording a check for an*
> *amount greater than it was written for*

2000.1.4.7.2   **Check Recorded for Too Little**

> Notes Payable - [Creditor A]   xxxx
>   Cash   xxxx
> *To correct an error caused by recording a check for an*
> *amount less than it was written for*

Important: Make sure all appropriate subheads apply to your entry (see page v for instructions)

2000.1   **Cash in Banks**
2000.1.4   **Reconciliation of Bank Account—Adjustments and Corrections**

2000.1.4.8   **Notes Receivable**

2000.1.4.8.1   **Check Recorded for Too Much**

Notes Receivable - [Customer A]   xxxx
    Cash   xxxx
To correct an error caused by recording a customer's
check for an amount greater than it was written for

2000.1.4.8.2   **Check Recorded for Too Little**

Cash   xxxx
    Notes Receivable - [Customer A]   xxxx
To correct an error caused by recording a customer's
check for an amount less than it was written for

2000.1.4.8.3   **Collection of Customer's Note by Bank**

See GEN2000.1.4.6 if interest was also collected by the bank.

Cash   xxxx
    Notes Receivable - [Customer A]   xxxx
To record collection of a customer's note by the bank on
your behalf that has not been previously recorded

2000.1.4.8.4   **Return of Customer's Check for Lack of Funds**

Notes Receivable - [Customer A]   xxxx
    Cash   xxxx
To record return of customer's check by bank for lack
of funds

CASH

Important: Make sure all appropriate subheads apply to your entry (see page v for instructions)

2000.1   **Cash in Banks**
2000.1.4   **Reconciliation of Bank Account - Adjustments and Corrections**

2000.1.4.9   **Sales**

2000.1.4.9.1   **Cash Sales Recorded for Too Much**

Sales	xxxx	
Cash		xxxx

To correct an error caused by recording cash sales for an amount that is too large

2000.1.4.9.2   **Cash Sales Recorded for Too Little**

Cash	xxxx	
Sales		xxxx

To correct an error caused by recording cash sales for an amount that is too small

2000.1.4.10   **Various Accounts**

2000.1.4.10.1   **Increase in Cash Account**

Cash	xxxx	
[Various Accounts]		xxxx

To increase Cash as necessary as a result of a bank reconciliation

2000.1.4.10.2   **Decrease in Cash Account**

[Various Accounts]	xxxx	
Cash		xxxx

To decrease Cash as necessary as a result of a bank reconciliation.

Important: Make sure all appropriate subheads apply to your entry (see page v for instructions)

2000.2	**Petty Cash**

2000.2.1	**Imprest Petty Cash System**

2000.2.1.1 Establishment of Petty Cash Fund

*Petty Cash	xxxx	
Cash		xxxx

To record establishment of an imprest petty cash fund

*Petty Cash is never debited or credited again unless the size of the account is permanently changed.

2000.2.1.2 Disbursements from Petty Cash Fund

No entry required. *See GEN2000.2.1.3 for replenishment of fund.*

2000.2.1.3 Replenishment of Petty Cash Fund

[Various Expenses]	xxxx	
*Cash Over And Short	xxxx	
*Cash Over And Short		xxxx
Cash		xxxx

*To record replenishment of the petty cash fund to the
originally established amount and to record expenses*

*Cash Over And Short is debited if there is a shortage of Cash in the fund, or credited if there is an overage of Cash in the fund. It is treated as a miscellaneous expense account if it has a debit balance, or a miscellaneous revenue account if it has a credit balance.

2000.2.1.4 Increasing the Size of the Petty Cash Fund Permanently

Petty Cash	xxxx	
Cash		xxxx

To permanently increase the size of the petty cash fund

Important: Make sure all appropriate subheads apply to your entry (see page v for instructions)

2000.2   **Petty Cash**
2000.2.1   **Imprest Petty Cash System**

2000.2.1.5   **Decreasing the Size of the Petty Cash Fund Permanently**

         Cash   xxxx
             Petty Cash   xxxx
         To permanently decrease the size of the petty cash fund

2000.2.2   **Non-imprest Petty Cash System**

2000.2.2.1   **Establishment of Petty Cash Fund**

         Petty Cash   xxxx
             Cash   xxxx
         To record the establishment of a petty cash fund

2000.2.2.2   **Disbursements from Petty Cash Fund**

         [Various Expenses]   xxxx
             Petty Cash   xxxx
         To record disbursements from petty cash fund

2000.2.2.3   **Replenishment of Petty Cash Fund**

         Petty Cash   xxxx
             Cash   xxxx
         To record replenishment of petty cash fund

TABLE OF CONTENTS

GEN3000   ACCOUNTS AND NOTES RECEIVABLE

3000.1   **Accounts Receivable**

3000.1.2   **Credit Sales and Collection**

3000.1.2.1   **Gross Method**

Under the gross method, Accounts Receivable is initially debited for the gross amount of the receivable, which includes the amount of any cash discount that may be taken by the customer. Thus, a $100 receivable subject to a 2% discount would be recorded at $100 even though only $98 may be collected if the discount is taken.

3000.1.2.1.1   **Sales**

*Accounts Receivable - [Customer A]	xxxx
Sales	xxxx
To record sales on credit	

*Accounts Receivable is debited for the gross amount of the sale. This reflects the assumption that a sales discount will not be taken.

3000.1.2.1.2   **Cash Collection within Discount Period**

3000.1.2.1.2.1 **Allowance for Sales Discounts (Allowance for Cash Discounts or Allowance for Unearned Discounts) Is Not Used**

Cash	xxxx
*Sales Discounts	xxxx
Accounts Receivable - [Customer A]	xxxx
To record collection of accounts receivable	

*Cash Discounts is an alternative account title.

Important: Make sure all appropriate subheads apply to your entry (see page v for instructions)

3000.1	**Accounts Receivable**
3000.1.2	**Credit Sales and Collection**
3000.1.2.1	**Gross Method**
3000.1.2.1.2	**Cash Collection within Discount Period**

3000.1.2.1.2.2 **Allowance for Sales Discounts (Allowance for Cash Discounts, Allowance for Unearned Discounts, or Allowance for Finance Charges) Is Used**

*Sales Discounts	xxxx	
**Allowance For Sales Discounts		xxxx

To periodically establish Allowance For Sales Discounts as a percentage of accounts receivable

*Cash Discounts is an alternative account title.

**Common alternative account titles include:
-Allowance For Cash Discounts
-Allowance For Unearned Discounts
-Allowance For Finance Charges

Cash	xxxx	
*Allowance For Sales Discounts		xxxx
Accounts Receivable - [Customer A]		xxxx

To record collection of accounts receivable

*Common alternative account titles include:
-Allowance For Cash Discounts
-Allowance For Unearned Discounts
-Allowance For Finance Charges

3000.1.2.1.3 **Cash Collection after Discount Period**

Cash	xxxx	
Accounts Receivable - [Customer A]		xxxx

To record collection of accounts receivable

3000.1.2.2 **Net Method**

Under the net method, Accounts Receivable is initially debited for the net amount of the receivable, which excludes the amount of any cash discount that may be taken by the customer. Thus, a $100 receivable subject to a 2% discount would be recorded at $98 even though $100 may be collected if the discount is not taken.

Important: Make sure all appropriate subheads apply to your entry (see page v for instructions)

3000.1	**Accounts Receivable**
3000.1.2	**Credit Sales and Collection**
33000.1.2.2	**Net Method**

3000.1.2.2.1 **Sales**

*Accounts Receivable - [Customer A]	xxxx	
Sales		xxxx
To record a sale on credit		

*Accounts Receivable is debited for the net amount of the sale, which reflects the assumption that a sales discount will be taken.

3000.1.2.2.2 **Cash Collection within Discount Period**

Cash	xxxx	
Accounts Receivable - [Customer A]		xxxx
To record collection of accounts receivable		

3000.1.2.2.3 **Cash Collection after Discount Period**

3000.1.2.2.3.1 **Adjusting Entries Are Not Made to Record Sales Discounts Forfeited (Cash Discounts Forfeited) when the Discount Period Passes**

Cash	xxxx	
*Sales Discounts Forfeited		xxxx
Accounts Receivable - [Customer A]		xxxx
To record collection of accounts receivable		

*Cash Discounts Forfeited is an alternative account title.

Important: Make sure all appropriate subheads apply to your entry (see page v for instructions)

3000.1   **Accounts Receivable**
3000.1.2   **Credit Sales and Collection**
3000.1.2.2   **Net Method**
3000.1.2.2.3   **Cash Collection after Discount Period**

3000.1.2.2.3.2   **Adjusting Entries Are Made to Record Sales Discounts Forfeited (Cash Discounts Forfeited) when the Discount Period Passes**

3000.1.2.2.3.2.1   **Adjusting Entry**

Accounts Receivable - [Customer A]   xxxx
     *Sales Discounts Forfeited   xxxx
To record sales discounts forfeited on uncollected accounts receivable

*Cash Discounts Forfeited is an alternative account title.

3000.1.2.2.3.2.2   **Collection**

Cash   xxxx
     Accounts Receivable - [Customer A]   xxxx
To record collection of accounts receivable

3000.1.3   **Uncollectible Accounts (Bad Debts or Doubtful Accounts)**

If notes receivable are involved instead of accounts receivable, substitute Notes Receivable for Accounts Receivable in all entries.

3000.1.3.1   **Percentage of Sales Approach**

3000.1.3.1.2   **Recording Bad Debt Expense**

*Bad Debt Expense   xxxx
     **Allowance For Doubtful Accounts   xxxx
To record bad debt expense

*Bad Debt Expense is debited for an amount equal to a percentage of sales or net sales for the period.

Important: Make sure all appropriate subheads apply to your entry (see page v for instructions)

3000.1	**Accounts Receivable**
3000.1.3	**Uncollectible Accounts (Bad Debts or Doubtful Accounts)**
3000.1.3.1	**Percentage of Sales Approach**
3000.1.3.1.2	**Recording Bad Debt Expense**

**Common alternative account titles include:
-Allowance For Uncollectible Accounts
-Allowance For Bad Debts

3000.1.3.1.3   **Write-Off of Customer's Account**

*Allowance For Doubtful Accounts	xxxx	
Accounts Receivable - [Customer A]		xxxx
To write off customer's account		

*Common alternative account titles include:
-Allowance For Uncollectible Accounts
-Allowance For Bad Debts

3000.1.3.1.4   **Collection (Recovery) of Previously Written-Off Account**

Accounts Receivable - [Customer A]	xxxx	
*Allowance For Doubtful Accounts		xxxx
To record recovery of previously written-off account		

*Common alternative account titles include:
-Allowance For Uncollectible Accounts
-Allowance For Bad Debts

Cash	xxxx	
Accounts Receivable - [Customer A]		xxxx
To record collection of accounts receivable		

3000.1.3.2   **Percentage of Receivables Approach**

3000.1.3.2.1   **Adjustment of Allowance for Doubtful Accounts (Allowance for Uncollectible Accounts or Allowance for Bad Debts)**

Bad Debt Expense	xxxx	
*Allowance For Doubtful Accounts		xxxx
To record Allowance for Doubtful Accounts		

Important: Make sure all appropriate subheads apply to your entry (see page v for instructions)

3000.1	**Accounts Receivable**
3000.1.3	**Uncollectible Accounts (Bad Debts or Doubtful Accounts)**
3000.1.3.2	**Percentage of Receivables Approach**
3000.1.3.2.1	**Adjustment of Allowance for Doubtful Accounts (Allowance for Uncollectible Accounts or Allowance for Bad Debts)**

---

*The desired balance in Allowance For Doubtful Accounts is calculated as a percentage of receivables, and this entry is then made to increase the account balance to the desired amount. If the balance needs to be decreased, Allowance For Doubtful Accounts would be debited and Bad Debt Expense would be credited.

Common alternative account titles include:
- Allowance For Uncollectible Accounts
- Allowance For Bad Debts

3000.1.3.2.2   **Write-Off of Customer's Account**

*Allowance For Doubtful Accounts	xxxx	
Accounts Receivable - [Customer A]		xxxx
To write-off customer's account		

*Common alternative account titles include:
- Allowance For Uncollectible Accounts
- Allowance For Bad Debts

3000.1.3.2.3   **Collection (Recovery) of Previously Written-Off Account**

Accounts Receivable - [Customer A]	xxxx	
*Allowance For Doubtful Accounts		xxxx
To reinstate previously written-off account		

*Common alternative account titles include:
- Allowance For Uncollectible Accounts
- Allowance For Bad Debts

Cash	xxxx	
Accounts Receivable - [Customer A]		xxxx
To record collection of accounts receivable		

3000.1.3.3   **Direct Write-Off Approach**

This is not a generally accepted method and should be used only when uncollectible accounts are not material or for tax purposes.

ACCOUNTS AND NOTES RECEIVABLE

Important: Make sure all appropriate subheads apply to your entry (see page v for instructions)

3000.1   **Accounts Receivable**
3000.1.3   **Uncollectible Accounts (Bad Debts or Doubtful Accounts)**
3000.1.3.3   **Direct Write-Off Approach**

3000.1.3.3.1   **Write-Off of Uncollectible Account**

Bad Debt Expense   xxxx
  Accounts Receivable - [Customer A]   xxxx
To write-off customer's account

3000.1.3.3.2   **Collection (Recovery) of Previously Written-Off Account**

Accounts Receivable - [Customer A]   xxxx
  *Uncollectible Amounts Recovered   xxxx
To record recovery of previously written-off account

*This is a revenue account. A common alternative account title is Bad Debts Recovered. Sometimes Bad Debt Expense is credited (reduced) instead of a revenue account.

Cash   xxxx
  Accounts Receivable - [Customer A]   xxxx
To record collection of accounts receivable

3000.1.4   **Sales Returns and Allowances**

3000.1.4.1   **Allowance for Sales Returns and Allowances Is *Not* Used**

3000.1.4.1.1   **Sales Returns Received or Allowances Granted**

Sales Returns And Allowances   xxxx
  Accounts Receivable - [Customer A]   xxxx
To record a sales return or price adjustment

Important: Make sure all appropriate subheads apply to your entry (see page v for instructions)

3000.1   **Accounts Receivable**
3000.1.4   **Sales Returns and Allowances**

3000.1.4.2   **Allowance for Sales Returns and Allowances Is Used**

3000.1.4.2.1   **Establishment of Allowance for Sales Returns and Allowances**

> Sales Returns And Allowances   xxxx
>   Allowance For Sales Returns And Allowances   xxxx
> *To establish Allowance For Sales Returns And Allowances*

3000.1.4.2.2   **Sales Returns Received or Allowances Granted**

> Allowance For Sales Returns And Allowances   xxxx
>   Accounts Receivable - [Customer A]   xxxx
> *To record a sales return or price adjustment*

3000.1.5   **Collection Expense**

Past due accounts may be sent to a collection agent, or other means may be used to collect these accounts which result in additional collection expense.

3000.1.5.1   **Allowance for Collection Expense Is *Not* Used**

> Collection Expense   xxxx
>   Cash   xxxx
> *To record payment of collection expense*

3000.1.5.2   **If Allowance for Collection Expense Is Used**

3000.1.5.2.1   **Establishment of Allowance for Collection Expense**

> Collection Expense   xxxx
>   Allowance For Collection Expense   xxxx
> *To establish Allowance For Collection Expense*

Important: Make sure all appropriate subheads apply to your entry (see page v for instructions)

3000.1	**Accounts Receivable**	
3000.1.5	**Collection Expense**	
3000.1.5.2	**If Allowance for Collection Expense Is Used**	

3000.1.5.2.2 Payment of Collection Expense

Allowance For Collection Expense	xxxx	
Cash		xxxx
To record payment of collection expense		

3000.1.6 Assignment of Accounts Receivable (Accounts Receivable as Security for Loan)

In this type of assignment, accounts receivable are assigned as security for a note payable.

3000.1.6.1 Initial Assignment of Specific Accounts Receivable

Cash	xxxx	
Finance Charge Expense	xxxx	
Notes Payable		xxxx
To record issuance of note payable and receipt of proceeds		

*Accounts Receivable Assigned	xxxx	
*Accounts Receivable		xxxx
To record assignment of specific accounts receivable as security for the note payable		

*The debit to Accounts Receivable Assigned and the credit to Accounts Receivable are for the same amount. Rather than making this entry, the amount of accounts receivable assigned is sometimes only indicated in the notes to the financial statements.

3000.1.6.2 Sales Returns and Allowances Involving Accounts Receivable Assigned

*Sales Returns And Allowances	xxxx	
Accounts Receivable Assigned		xxxx
To record sales return or price adjustment		

*Instead of debiting Sales Returns And Allowances, Allowances For Sales Returns And Allowances may be debited. *See GEN3000.1.3.*

Important: Make sure all appropriate subheads apply to your entry (see page v for instructions)

3000.1   **Accounts Receivable**
3000.1.6   **Assignment of Accounts Receivable (Accounts Receivable as Security for Loan)**

3000.1.6.3   ### Collection of Assigned Accounts Receivable by Assignor (Borrower)

Cash	xxxx	
Sales Discounts (Cash Discounts)	xxxx	
Accounts Receivable Assigned		xxxx

To record collection of assigned accounts receivable

3000.1.6.4   ### Remittance to Assignee (Lender)

Notes Payable	xxxx	
Interest Expense	xxxx	
Cash		xxxx

To record remittance to assignee (lender)

3000.1.6.5   ### Write-Off of Uncollectible Accounts Receivable Assigned

Allowance For Doubtful Accounts	xxxx	
Accounts Receivable Assigned		xxxx

To write off uncollectible assigned accounts receivable

3000.1.7   ### Sale (Transfer) of Accounts Receivable

Accounts receivable may be sold with or without recourse. If the sale is *without* recourse and a particular account is never collected, the seller of the account has no liability to the purchaser. This type of sale is called *factoring*. If the sale is *with* recourse, the seller does have a liability to the purchaser if an account is not collected. In the latter case, the seller may account for the transaction as if (a) it were a borrowing instead of a sale or as if (b) it were a factoring type sale, i.e., as if there were no recourse.

3000.1.7.1   ### Sale without Recourse (Factoring)

Cash	xxxx	
Due From Factor	xxxx	
Loss On Sale Of Receivable	xxxx	
Accounts Receivable - [Various Customer Accounts]		xxxx

To record sale of accounts receivable without recourse

Important: Make sure all appropriate subheads apply to your entry (see page v for instructions)

3000.1   **Accounts Receivable**
3000.1.7   **Sale (Transfer) of Accounts Receivable**

3000.1.7.2   **Sale with Recourse**

3000.1.7.2.1   **Treated as Borrowing**

Cash	xxxx
Due From Factor	xxxx
*Discount On Transferred Accounts Receivable	xxxx
**Liability On Transferred Accounts Receivable	xxxx

To record sale of accounts receivable with recourse

*An alternative account title is Discount On Accounts Receivable Sold.

**An alternative account title is Liability On Accounts Receivable Sold.

3000.1.7.2.2   **Treated as Sale (Factoring)**

Cash	xxxx
Due From Factor	xxxx
*Loss On Transfer Of Accounts Receivable	xxxx
Accounts Receivable - [Various Customer Accounts]	xxxx

To record sale of accounts receivable with recourse

3000.1.8   **Installment Accounts Receivable**

See GEN11000.2.

3000.2   **Notes Receivable**

3000.2.1   **Receipt of Notes Receivable**

3000.2.1.1   **Receipt for Cash**

3000.2.1.1.1   **Note Carries Realistic Interest Rate**

ACCOUNTS AND NOTES RECEIVABLE

Important: Make sure all appropriate subheads apply to your entry (see page v for instructions)

3000.2	**Notes Receivable**
3000.2.1	**Receipt of Notes Receivable**
3000.2.1.1	**Receipt for Cash**
3000.2.1.1.1	**Note Carries Realistic Interest Rate**

3000.2.1.1.1.1   **Receipt of Note**

Notes Receivable - [Customer A]	xxxx	
Cash		xxxx
To record receipt of a note receivable for cash		

3000.2.1.1.1.2   **Accrual of Interest at End of Accounting Period**

Interest Receivable	xxxx	
*Interest Revenue		xxxx
To accrue interest revenue		

*Interest Income is an alternative account title.

3000.2.1.1.1.3   **Receipt of Interest Periodically if Reversing Entries Are *Not* Made**

Cash	xxxx	
Interest Receivable		xxxx
*Interest Revenue		xxxx
To record receipt of interest		

*This account is credited interest received that has not been previously accrued.
Interest Income is an alternative account title.

3000.2.1.1.1.4   **Receipt of Interest Periodically if Reversing Entries Are Made**

Cash	xxxx	
*Interest Revenue		xxxx
To record receipt of interest		

*Interest Income is an alternative account title.

3000.2.1.1.2   **Noninterest-Bearing Note or Note Carrying Unrealistically Low Interest Rate**

ACCOUNTS AND NOTES RECEIVABLE

Important: Make sure all appropriate subheads apply to your entry (see page v for instructions)

3000.2　　　　　　**Notes Receivable**
3000.2.1　　　　　　　　**Receipt of Notes Receivable**
3000.2.1.1　　　　　　　　　**Receipt for Cash**
3000.2.1.1.2　　　　　　　　　　**Noninterest-Bearing Note or Note Carrying Unrealistically Low Interest Rate**

3000.2.1.1.2.1　　　**Receipt of Note**

Notes Receivable	xxxx	
Discount On Notes Receivable		xxxx
Cash		xxxx

To record receipt of notes receivable for cash

3000.2.1.1.2.2　　　**Accrual of Interest at End of Accounting Period**

*Interest Receivable	xxxx	
Discount On Notes Receivable	xxxx	
**Interest Revenue		xxxx

To accrue interest revenue

*This account is not used if the note is noninterest bearing.

**Interest Income is an alternative account title.

3000.2.1.1.2.3　　　**Receipt of Interest Periodically if Reversing Entries Are *Not* Made**

The following entry is not made if the note is noninterest bearing. It is made only if the note carries an unrealistically low interest rate.

Cash	xxxx	
*Discount On Notes Receivable	xxxx	
Interest Receivable		xxxx
*Interest Revenue		xxxx

To record receipt of interest

*These accounts are debited or credited as shown for interest received that has not been previously accrued. Interest Revenue may also be called Interest Income.

3000.2.1.1.2.4　　　**Receipt of Interest Periodically if Reversing Entries Are Made**

The following entry is not made if the note is noninterest bearing. It is made only if the note carries an unrealistically low interest rate.

ACCOUNTS AND NOTES RECEIVABLE

Important: Make sure all appropriate subheads apply to your entry (see page v for instructions)

3000.2	**Notes Receivable**	
3000.2.1	**Receipt of Notes Receivable**	
3000.2.1.1	**Receipt for Cash**	
3000.2.1.1.2	**Accrual of Interest at End of Accounting Period**	
3000.2.1.1.2.4	**Receipt of Interest Periodically if Reversing Entries Are Made**	

Cash	xxxx	
Discount On Notes Receivable	xxxx	
Interest Revenue		xxxx
To record receipt of interest		

3000.2.1.2   Receipt to Replace Accounts Receivable

Notes Receivable - [Customer A]	xxxx	
*Discount On Notes Receivable		xxxx
Accounts Receivable - [Customer A]		xxxx
To record receipt of a note receivable		

*This account is used only if the note is noninterest bearing or does not carry a realistic interest rate, in which case the credit here is for the difference between the face value of the note and its present value when discounted at a realistic interest rate. The present value amount should also equal the amount of the credit to Accounts Receivable.

3000.2.1.2.1   Accrual of Interest

3000.2.1.2.1.1   Discount on Notes Receivable Is *Not* Involved

See GEN3000.2.1.1.1.2.

3000.2.1.2.1.2   Discount on Notes Receivable Is Involved

See GEN3000.2.1.1.2.

3000.2.1.2.2   Receipt of Interest

3000.2.1.2.2.1   Discount on Notes Receivable Is *Not* Involved

See GEN3000.2.1.1.1.3 and GEN3000.2.1.1.1.4.

Important: Make sure all appropriate subheads apply to your entry (see page v for instructions)

3000.2	**Notes Receivable**
3000.2.1	**Receipt of Notes Receivable**
3000.2.1.2	**Receipt to Replace Accounts Receivable**
3000.2.1.2.2	**Receipt of Interest**

3000.2.1.2.2.2   **Discount on Notes Receivable Is Involved**

See GEN3000.2.1.1.2.3 and GEN3000.2.1.1.2.4.

3000.2.1.3   **Receipt for Sales**

Notes Receivable - [Customer A]	xxxx	
*Discount On Notes Receivable		xxxx
Sales		xxxx

To record receipt of a note receivable for sales

*This account is used only if the note is noninterest bearing or does not carry a realistic interest rate.

3000.2.1.3.1   **Accrual of Interest**

3000.2.1.3.1.1   **Discount on Notes Receivable Is *Not* Involved**

See GEN3000.2.1.1.1.2.

3000.2.1.3.1.2   **Discount on Notes Receivable Is Involved**

See GEN3000.2.1.1.2.2.

3000.2.1.3.2   **Receipt of Interest**

3000.2.1.3.2.1   **Discount on Notes Receivable Is *Not* Involved**

See GEN3000.2.1.1.1.3 and GEN3000.2.1.1.1.4.

3000.2.1.3.2.2   **Discount on Notes Receivable Is Involved**

See GEN3000.2.1.1.2.3 and GEN3000.2.1.1.2.4.

Important: Make sure all appropriate subheads apply to your entry (see page v for instructions)

3000.2   **Notes Receivable**
3000.2.1   **Receipt of Notes Receivable**

3000.2.1.4   **Receipt for Cash and Prepaid Rights**

Examples of prepaid rights include the right to receive a product (e.g., prepaid purchases) or service (e.g., prepaid rent or prepaid consulting services).

Notes Receivable	xxxx	
[Various Prepaid Rights]	xxxx	
*Discount On Notes Receivable		xxxx
Cash		xxxx

To record receipt of a note receivable

*This account is used only if the note is noninterest bearing or does not carry a realistic interest rate, in which case the credit here is for the difference between the face value of the note and its present value when discounted at a realistic interest rate.

3000.2.1.4.1   **Accrual of Interest**

3000.2.1.4.1.1   **Discount on Notes Receivable Is *Not* Involved**

See GEN3000.2.1.1.1.2.

3000.2.1.4.1.2   **Discount on Notes Receivable Is Involved**

See GEN3000.2.1.1.2.2.

3000.2.1.4.2   **Receipt of Interest**

3000.2.1.4.2.1   **Discount on Notes Receivable Is *Not* Involved**

See GEN3000.2.1.1.1.3 and GEN3000.2.1.1.1.4.

3000.2.1.4.2.2   **Discount on Notes Receivable Is Involved**

See GEN3000.2.1.1.2.3 and GEN3000.2.1.1.2.4.

Important: Make sure all appropriate subheads apply to your entry (see page v for instructions)

3000.2   **Notes Receivable**
3000.2.1   **Receipt of Notes Receivable**

3000.2.1.5   **Receipt for Property or Goods**

Notes Receivable	xxxx	
*Accumulated Depreciation - [Various Assets]	xxxx	
**Discount On Notes Receivable		xxxx
[Various Assets]		xxxx
***Gain On Sale Of [Various Assets]		xxxx

To record receipt of a note receivable

*This account is used only if the asset sold is a depreciable asset.

**This account is used only if the note is noninterest bearing or does not carry a realistic interest rate.

***If a loss occurred, Loss On Sale Of [Various Assets] would be debited instead.

3000.2.1.5.1   **Accrual of Interest**

3000.2.1.5.1.1   **Discount on Notes Receivable Is *Not* Involved**

See GEN3000.2.1.1.1.2.

3000.2.1.5.1.2   **Discount on Notes Receivable Is Involved**

See GEN3000.2.1.1.2.

3000.2.1.5.2   **Receipt of Interest**

3000.2.1.5.2.1   **Discount on Notes Receivable Is *Not* Involved**

See GEN3000.2.1.1.1.3 and GEN3000.2.1.1.1.4.

3000.2.1.5.2.2   **Discount on Notes Receivable Is Involved**

See GEN3000.2.1.1.2.3 and GEN3000.2.1.1.2.4.

Important: Make sure all appropriate subheads apply to your entry (see page v for instructions)

3000.2   **Notes Receivable**
3000.2.1   **Receipt of Notes Receivable**

3000.2.1.6   **Receipt for Services**

Notes Receivable	xxxx
*Discount On Notes Receivable	xxxx
Revenue From Services [Various]	xxxx

To record receipt of a note receivable

*This account is used only if the note is noninterest bearing or does not carry a realistic interest rate.

3000.2.1.6.1   **Accrual of Interest**

3000.2.1.6.1.1   **Discount on Notes Receivable Is *Not* Involved**

See GEN3000.2.1.1.1.2.

3000.2.1.6.1.2   **Discount on Notes Receivable Is Involved**

See GEN3000.2.1.1.2.2.

3000.2.1.6.2   **Receipt of Interest**

3000.2.1.6.2.1   **Discount on Notes Receivable Is *Not* Involved**

See GEN3000.2.1.1.1.3 and GEN3000.2.1.1.1.4.

3000.2.1.6.2.2   **Discount on Notes Receivable Is Involved**

See GEN3000.2.1.1.2.3 and GEN3000.2.1.1.2.4.

3000.2.2   **Uncollectible Notes Receivable (Bad Debts or Doubtful Accounts)**

See GEN3000.1.3.

Important: Make sure all appropriate subheads apply to your entry (see page v for instructions)

3000.2   **Notes Receivable**

3000.2.3   **Collection**

Cash	xxxx	
*Discount On Notes Receivable	xxxx	
Notes Receivable		xxxx
**Interest Receivable		xxxx
***Interest Revenue		xxxx

To record collection of a note receivable

*Discount On Notes Receivable will be involved only if (a) the note was originally issued at a discount, and (b) interest is collected that has not been previously accrued or if interest has been accrued, reversing entries have been made.

**Interest Receivable will be involved only if interest is collected that has been previously accrued and reversing entries have not been made.

***Interest Revenue will be involved only if interest is collected that has not been previously accrued or if interest has been accrued, reversing entries have been made. Interest Income is an alternative account title.

3000.2.4   **Discounting Notes Receivable at the Bank**

3000.2.4.1   **Recorded as a Sale of Notes Receivable with Recourse**

3000.2.4.1.1   **Recording Discount**

Cash	xxxx	
Loss On Sale Of Notes Receivable	xxxx	
*Notes Receivable Discounted		xxxx
Interest Receivable		xxxx

To record discounting of notes receivable

*Instead of crediting Notes Receivable Discounted (the preferred method), Notes Receivable may be credited, and the amount of discounted notes receivable disclosed in the notes to the financial statements.

ACCOUNTS AND NOTES RECEIVABLE

Important: Make sure all appropriate subheads apply to your entry (see page v for instructions)

3000.2	**Notes Receivable**
3000.2.4	**Discounting Notes Receivable at the Bank**
3000.2.4.1	**Recorded as a Sale of Notes Receivable with Recourse**

3000.2.4.1.2 **Payment of Note Receivable by Maker at Maturity**

No entry is necessary.

3000.2.4.1.3 **Maker Defaults**

*Notes Receivable Past Due	xxxx	
Cash		xxxx
To record defaulted discounted notes receivable		

*Accounts Receivable is sometimes debited instead of this account. This account would be debited for an amount that includes any interest paid to the bank as a result of the default.

3000.2.4.2 **Recorded as a Borrowing with Recourse**

3000.2.4.2.1 **Recording Discount**

Cash	xxxx	
Interest Expense	xxxx	
Interest Receivable		xxxx
Liability On Notes Receivable Discounted		xxxx
To record discounting of notes receivable		

3000.2.4.2.2 **Payment of Note Receivable by Maker at Maturity**

Liability On Notes Receivable Discounted	xxxx	
Notes Receivable		xxxx
To record payment of notes receivable		

Important: Make sure all appropriate subheads apply to your entry (see page v for instructions)

3000.2   **Notes Receivable**
3000.2.4   **Discounting Notes Receivable at the Bank**
3000.2.4.2   **Recorded as a Borrowing with Recourse**

3000.2.4.2.3   **Maker Defaults**

> *Notes Receivable Past Due (Accounts Receivable)   xxxx
> Liability On Notes Receivable Discounted   xxxx
>   Notes Receivable   xxxx
>   Cash   xxxx
> *To record defaulted discounted notes receivable*

*The amount should include any interest paid to the bank as a result of the default.

3000.3   **Impairment of a Loan Receivable**

A loan receivable is a contractual right to receive money on demand, or on fixed or determinable dates, that is recognized as an asset. Examples include but are not limited to accounts receivable (with terms exceeding one year) and notes receivable. A loan receivable is impaired when, based on current information and events, it is probable that a creditor will be unable to collect all principal and interest due.

The amount of the impairment is measured as the difference between the carrying (book) value of the loan receivable (including accrued interest, net deferred loan fees or costs, and unamortized premium or discount) and either (a) the present value of its expected future cash flows discounted at the loan's effective interest, (b) the loan's observable market price, or (c) the fair value of any collateral involved. *If foreclosure is probable, the impairment is measured using the fair value of the collateral.*

3000.3.1   **Recognition of Impairment of a Loan Receivable**

> *Loss Due To Impairment Of A Loan Receivable   xxxx
>   [Various Loans Receivable or Valuation Allowance]   xxxx
>   Accrued Interest Receivable   xxxx
> *To record a loss due to impairment of a loan receivable*

*The loss amount is the carrying (book) value of the loan receivable (including accrued interest, net deferred loan fees or costs, and unamortized premium or discount) less the measure of the impaired loan receivable. *See GEN3000.3.*

For recognition of a loss due to restructuring a loan, *see GEN20000.1.1.2.*

TABLE OF CONTENTS

GEN4000   INVENTORIES

INVENTORIES

4000.1	**Merchandising Inventories**

4000.1.1	**Periodic Inventory System**

Under the periodic system, all purchases, purchase returns and allowances, and purchase discounts are initially recorded in accounts other than Inventory. Cost of goods sold is not recorded as sales are made but instead is calculated at the end of the period by adding net purchases and costs of freight-in to beginning inventory and subtracting ending inventory.

4000.1.1.1	**Purchase of Merchandise for Resale**

4000.1.1.1.1	**Cash Purchase**

Purchases	xxxx	
Cash		xxxx
To record purchase of merchandise		

4000.1.1.1.2	**Purchase on Credit (on Account)**

4000.1.1.1.2.1	**Purchase Recorded at Invoice (Gross) Amount**

*Purchases	xxxx	
Accounts Payable		xxxx
To record purchase of merchandise		

*Purchases are recorded at the full invoice amount before any cash discount that may be taken for prompt payment. For example, a $1,000 purchase subject to a 2% cash discount if paid within 10 days will be recorded at $1,000 even though only $980 will be paid if payment is made promptly.

Important: Make sure all appropriate subheads apply to your entry (see page v for instructions)

4000.1   **Merchandising Inventories**
4000.1.1   **Periodic Inventory System**
4000.1.1.1   **Purchase of Merchandise for Resale**
4000.1.1.1.2   **Purchase on Credit (on Account)**

4000.1.1.1.2.2   **Purchase Recorded Net of Anticipated Cash Discount**

    *Purchases   xxxx
        Accounts Payable   xxxx
    To record purchase of merchandise

*Purchases are recorded net of any cash discount that may be taken for prompt payment (regardless of whether or not the discount is eventually taken). For example, a $1,000 purchase subject to a 2% cash discount if paid within 10 days will be recorded at $980.

4000.1.1.2   **Payment of Freight-In (Transportation-In)**

Freight-In (Transportation-In) is the cost of freight necessary to acquire goods purchased on an F.O.B. (free on board) shipping point basis, i.e., when the supplier does not bear the cost of freight. Freight-In (Transportation-In) must be recorded in a separate account from Freight-Out (Transportation-Out), which is a selling expense.

    Freight-In (Transportation-In)   xxxx
        Cash (Accounts Payable)   xxxx
    To record payment of freight-in

4000.1.1.3   **Return of Merchandise to or Price Adjustment (Allowance) by Supplier**

    *Accounts Payable   xxxx
        Purchase Returns And Allowances   xxxx
    To record purchase return or allowance

*The amount recorded will be the gross invoice amount of the return or allowance if the purchase was originally recorded at the gross amount *(see GEN4000.1.1.1.2.1)*. If the purchase was originally recorded net of the cash discount, the amount of this entry will be the net invoice amount of the return or allowance *(see GEN4000.1.1.1.2.2)*. Allowances may be granted for a variety of reasons including minor defects in the merchandise sold or damage incurred during shipping.

Important: Make sure all appropriate subheads apply to your entry (see page v for instructions)

4000.1   **Merchandising Inventories**
4000.1.1   **Periodic Inventory System**

4000.1.1.4   **Payment for Merchandise Purchased on Credit (on Account)**

4000.1.1.4.1   **Payment Made Within Discount Period**

4000.1.1.4.1.1   **Payment Made Within Discount Period When Purchase Was Initially Recorded at Invoice (Gross) Amount**

Accounts Payable	xxxx	
*Purchase Discounts		xxxx
Cash		xxxx

To record payment of accounts payable

*Purchase Discounts is credited for the amount of the cash discount taken.

4000.1.1.4.1.2   **Payment Made Within Discount Period When Purchase Was Initially Recorded Net of Anticipated Cash Discount**

Accounts Payable	xxxx	
Cash		xxxx

To record payment of accounts payable

4000.1.1.4.2   **Payment Made After Discount Period Ends**

4000.1.1.4.2.1   **Payment Made After Discount Period Ends and Purchase Was Initially Recorded at Invoice (Gross) Amount**

Accounts Payable	xxxx	
Cash		xxxx

To record payment of accounts payable

Important: Make sure all appropriate subheads apply to your entry (see page v for instructions)

4000.1   **Merchandising Inventories**
4000.1.1   **Periodic Inventory System**
4000.1.1.4   **Payment for Merchandise Purchased on Credit (on Account)**
4000.1.1.4.2   **Payment Made After Discount Period Ends**

4000.1.1.4.2.2   **Payment Made After Discount Period Ends and Purchase Was Initially Recorded Net of Anticipated Cash Discount**

Accounts Payable	xxxx	
*Purchase Discounts Lost	xxxx	
Cash		xxxx

To record payment of accounts payable

*Purchase Discounts Lost is an expense account representing finance charges for delayed payment.

4000.1.1.5   **Sale of Merchandise**

The reduction in inventory is not recorded under the periodic system of inventory at the time a sale is made.

Accounts Receivable (Cash)	xxxx	
Sales		xxxx

To record sales

4000.1.1.6   **Return of Merchandise by Customer**

The effect on Inventory is not recorded under the periodic system of inventory when a sales return is made.

Sales Returns And Allowances	xxxx	
Accounts Receivable		xxxx

To record sales returns

4000.1.1.7   **End of Period Inventory Adjustment**

4000.1.1.7.1   **Adjusting Entry Method**

Under the adjusting entry method, Inventory is debited or credited to adjust its balance to match the amount of inventory on hand established by physical count; the

Important: Make sure all appropriate subheads apply to your entry (see page v for instructions)

4000.1	**Merchandising Inventories**
4000.1.1	**Periodic Inventory System**
4000.1.1.7	**End of Period Inventory Adjustment**
4000.1.1.7.1	**Adjusting Entry Method**

balances in Purchases, Purchase Returns And Allowances, Purchase Discounts, and Freight-In (Transportation-In) are eliminated (closed); and Cost Of Goods Sold is debited to balance the entry. Subsequently, Cost Of Goods Sold is closed similar to any other expense account.

4000.1.1.7.1.1   **Adjusting Inventory and Recording Cost of Goods Sold**

*Inventory	xxxx	
**Purchase Returns And Allowances	xxxx	
**Purchase Discounts	xxxx	
***Cost Of Goods Sold	xxxx	
****Freight-In (Transportation-In)		xxxx
****Purchases		xxxx

To record inventory adjustment and cost of goods sold

*Inventory is debited for the excess of the amount determined by physical count over the existing balance in the account. If the amount determined by physical count is less than the existing balance in the account, Inventory is credited for this excess instead of debited. An alternative method is to debit Inventory for the amount of the ending balance and to credit Inventory for the amount of the beginning balance.

**Purchase Returns And Allowances and Purchase Discounts are debited sufficiently to eliminate their existing credit balances. If purchases are recorded net of anticipated cash discounts, there will be no Purchase Discounts account.

***Cost Of Goods Sold is debited for the amount necessary to balance the entry.

****Freight-In (Transportation-In) and Purchases are credited sufficiently to eliminate their existing debit balances.

4000.1.1.7.1.2   **Closing Cost of Goods Sold**

*Income Summary	xxxx	
Cost Of Goods Sold		xxxx

To close Cost Of Goods Sold

*A common alternative account title is Expense And Revenue Summary.

Important: Make sure all appropriate subheads apply to your entry (see page v for instructions)

4000.1   **Merchandising Inventories**
4000.1.1   **Periodic Inventory System**
4000.1.1.7   **End of Period Inventory Adjustment**

4000.1.1.7.2   **Closing Entry Method**

Under the closing entry method, Inventory is debited or credited to adjust its balance to match the amount of inventory on hand established by physical count; the balances in Purchases, Purchase Returns And Allowances, Purchase Discounts, and Freight-In (Transportation-In) are eliminated (closed); and Income Summary (Expense And Revenue Summary) is debited to balance the entry. A Cost Of Goods Sold account is not used.

*Inventory	xxxx	
**Purchase Returns And Allowances	xxxx	
**Purchase Discounts	xxxx	
***Income Summary (Expense And Revenue Summary)	xxxx	
****Freight-In (Transportation-In)		xxxx
****Purchases		xxxx

To close purchases-related accounts and adjust inventory

*Inventory is debited for the excess of the amount determined by physical count over the existing balance in the account. If the amount determined by physical count is less than the existing balance in the account, Inventory is credited for this excess instead of debited. An alternative method is to debit Inventory for the amount of the ending balance and to credit Inventory for the amount of the beginning balance.

**Purchase Returns And Allowances and Purchase Discounts are debited sufficiently to eliminate their existing credit balances. If purchases are recorded net of anticipated cash discounts, there will be no Purchase Discounts account.

***Income Summary (Expense And Revenue Summary) is debited for whatever amount is necessary to balance the entry.

****Freight-In (Transportation-In) and Purchases are credited sufficiently to eliminate their existing debit balances.

4000.1.1.8   **Application of Lower-of-Cost-or-Market**

If market value falls below cost, Inventory must be reduced. This must be done so that Inventory is reported within a range of values. The upper limit of this range (the ceiling) is the net realizable value of the inventory (selling price less normal costs of

---

Important: Make sure all appropriate subheads apply to your entry (see page v for instructions)

4000.1   **Merchandising Inventories**
4000.1.1   **Periodic Inventory System**
4000.1.1.8   **Application of Lower-of-Cost-or-Market**

---

disposal). The lower limit of the range (the floor) is the net realizable value of the inventory less a normal profit margin. If replacement cost of the inventory falls within the range, market value equals replacement cost. If replacement cost is not within the range, the amount within the range (ceiling or floor) closest to replacement cost is established as market value.

4000.1.1.8.1   **Reduction of Inventory to Market**

4000.1.1.8.1.1   **Direct Method**

Under the direct method, the entries to establish ending inventory under either the adjusting entry method *(GEN4000.1.1.7.1)* or the closing entry method *(GEN4000.1.1.7.2)* are made. But in either case, Inventory is debited or credited for an amount sufficient to value the ending inventory at the lower market value.

4000.1.1.8.1.2   **Indirect Method**

Under the indirect method, the entries to establish ending inventory under either the adjusting entry method *(GEN4000.1.1.7.1)* or the closing entry method *(GEN4000.1.1.7.2)* are made. Subsequently, a separate entry is made to write down Inventory to market using an allowance account.

> *Loss Due To Write Down Of Inventory To Market   xxxx
>   *Allowance To Reduce Inventory To Market   xxxx
> *To write down inventory to market*

*Allowance To Reduce Inventory To Market is shown as a contra account to Inventory (i.e., deducted from Inventory) in the balance sheet. It is adjusted at year end to reflect whatever balance is necessary to value Inventory at the lower of cost or market. If the amount of the allowance must be increased (i.e., if the allowance account must be credited), Loss Due To Write Down Of Inventory To Market is debited as shown here. If the amount of the allowance must be decreased (i.e., if the allowance account must be debited), Gain On Recovery Of Market Value Of Inventory is credited instead of debiting the loss account. However, the allowance account can never have a debit balance because the inventory can never be written up above original cost.

Important: Make sure all appropriate subheads apply to your entry (see page v for instructions)

4000.1   **Merchandising Inventories**

4000.1.2   **Perpetual Inventory System**

Under the perpetual inventory system all purchases, purchase returns and allowances, and purchase discounts, are recorded directly in Inventory. Cost of goods sold is recorded as sales are made. As a result, Inventory contains a continuous running balance (perpetual balance) representing the amount of inventory on hand. An adjustment to Inventory may be needed at the end of the period if there is a discrepancy between the balance in Inventory and the physical inventory count (normal inventory overage or shortage), or if there has been a theft loss or casualty loss, e.g., from a fire.

4000.1.2.1   **Purchase of Merchandise for Resale**

4000.1.2.1.1   **Cash Purchase**

      Inventory   xxxx
          Cash   xxxx
      To record purchase of merchandise

4000.1.2.1.2   **Purchase on Credit (on Account)**

4000.1.2.1.2.1   **Purchase Recorded at Invoice (Gross) Amount**

      *Inventory   xxxx
          Accounts Payable   xxxx
      To record purchase of merchandise

*Inventory is debited for the full invoice amount before any cash discount that may be taken for prompt payment. For example, a $1,000 purchase subject to a 2% cash discount if paid within 10 days will be recorded at $1,000 even though only $980 will be paid if payment is made promptly.

Important: Make sure all appropriate subheads apply to your entry (see page v for instructions)

4000.1	**Merchandising Inventories**
4000.1.2	**Perpetual Inventory System**
4000.1.2.1	**Purchase of Merchandise for Resale**
4000.1.2.1.2	**Purchase on Credit (on Account)**

4000.1.2.1.2.2   **Purchase Recorded Net of Anticipated Cash Discount**

*Inventory	xxxx	
Accounts Payable		xxxx
To record purchase of merchandise		

*Inventory is debited for the invoice amount net of any cash discount that may be taken for prompt payment. For example, a $1,000 purchase subject to a 2% cash discount if paid within 10 days will be recorded at $980 even though $1,000 will be paid if the account is not paid within 10 days.

4000.1.2.2   **Payment of Freight-In (Transportation-In)**

Freight-In (Transportation-In) is the cost of freight necessary to acquire goods purchased on an F.O.B. (free on board) shipping point basis, i.e., when the supplier does not bear the cost of freight. Freight-In (Transportation-In) must be recorded in a separate account from Freight-Out (Transportation-Out), which is a selling expense.

*Inventory	xxxx	
Cash		xxxx
To record payment of freight-in		

*Transportation-In may be debited (instead of Inventory) if the amount is immaterial, or if it is not feasible to allocate these costs to Inventory.

4000.1.2.3   **Return of Merchandise to or Price Adjustment by Supplier**

*Accounts Payable	xxxx	
*Inventory		xxxx
To record purchase return or allowance		

*The amount recorded will be the gross invoice amount of the return or the amount of the allowance (price reduction because of product damage, etc.) if the purchase was originally recorded at the gross amount *(see GEN4000.1.2.1.2.1)*. If the purchase was originally recorded net of the cash discount, the amount of this entry will be the net invoice amount of the return or allowance *(see GEN4000.1.2.1.2.2)*.

Important: Make sure all appropriate subheads apply to your entry (see page v for instructions)

4000.1   **Merchandising Inventories**
4000.1.2   **Perpetual Inventory System**

4000.1.2.4   **Payment for Merchandise Purchased on Credit (on Account)**

4000.1.2.4.1   **Payment Made Within Discount Period**

4000.1.2.4.1.1   **Payment Made Within Discount Period When Purchase Was Initially Recorded at Invoice (Gross) Amount**

Accounts Payable	xxxx	
*Inventory		xxxx
Cash		xxxx

To record payment of accounts payable

*Inventory is credited for the amount of the cash discount taken, i.e., the amount by which the price was reduced for early payment.

4000.1.2.4.1.2   **Payment Made Within Discount Period When Purchase Was Initially Recorded Net of Anticipated Cash Discount**

Accounts Payable	xxxx	
Cash		xxxx

To record payment of accounts payable

4000.1.2.4.2   **Payment Made After Discount Period Ends**

4000.1.2.4.2.1   **Payment Made After Discount Period Ends and Purchase Was Initially Recorded at Invoice (Gross) Amount**

Accounts Payable	xxxx	
Cash		xxxx

To record payment of accounts payable

Important: Make sure all appropriate subheads apply to your entry (see page v for instructions)

4000.1	**Merchandising Inventories**
4000.1.2	**Perpetual Inventory System**
4000.1.2.4	**Payment for Merchandise Purchased on Credit (on Account)**
4000.1.2.4.2	**Payment Made After Discount Period Ends**

4000.1.2.4.2.2   **Payment Made After Discount Period Ends and Purchase Was Initially Recorded Net of Anticipated Cash Discount**

Accounts Payable	xxxx	
*Purchase Discounts Lost	xxxx	
Cash		xxxx

To record payment of accounts payable

*Purchase Discounts Lost is an expense account representing finance charges for delayed payment.

4000.1.2.5   **Sale of Merchandise**

The reduction in inventory is recorded under the perpetual system of inventory when a sale is made.

Accounts Receivable	xxxx	
Sales		xxxx

To record sales

Cost Of Goods Sold	xxxx	
Inventory		xxxx

To record cost of goods sold

4000.1.2.6   **Return of Merchandise by Customer or Price Adjustment (Allowance) Granted**

The effect on inventory is recorded under the perpetual system of inventory when a sales return is made.

4000.1.2.6.1   **Return of Merchandise by Customer**

Sales Return And Allowances	xxxx	
Accounts Receivable		xxxx

To record sales returns
          (see next page)

INVENTORIES

Important: Make sure all appropriate subheads apply to your entry (see page v for instructions)

4000.1	**Merchandising Inventories**	
4000.1.2	**Perpetual Inventory System**	
4000.1.2.6	**Return of Merchandise by Customer or Price Adjustment (Allowance) Granted**	
4000.1.2.6.1	**Return of Merchandise by Customer**	

Inventory   xxxx
    Cost Of Goods Sold   xxxx
To adjust cost of goods sold and inventory for sales returns

4000.1.2.6.2   Price Adjustment (Allowance) Granted

Sales Return And Allowances   xxxx
    Accounts Receivable   xxxx
To record sales returns

4000.1.2.7   End of Period Inventory Adjustment

An adjustment to Inventory may be needed at the end of the period if there is a discrepancy between the balance in the inventory account and the physical inventory count (normal inventory overage or shortage), or if there has been a theft loss or casualty loss, e.g., from a fire.

4000.1.2.7.1   Normal Inventory Overage or Shortage

*Inventory Over Or Short   xxxx
    Inventory   xxxx
To record inventory shortage

*If a physical count of the inventory shows there is less inventory on hand than indicated by the balance in Inventory, Inventory Over Or Short is debited and Inventory is credited as shown here. If the physical count shows there is more inventory on hand than indicated by the balance in Inventory, Inventory is debited and Inventory Over Or Short is credited. A debit balance in Inventory Over Or Short indicates a loss from a shortage, and a credit balance indicates a gain from an overage. As long as the amount of shortage or overage is not material, some companies debit the amount of shortage or credit the amount of overage to Cost Of Goods Sold instead of using a separate "over or short" account.

INVENTORIES

Important: Make sure all appropriate subheads apply to your entry (see page v for instructions)

4000.1   **Merchandising Inventories**
4000.1.2   **Perpetual Inventory System**
4000.1.2.7   **End of Period Inventory Adjustment**

4000.1.2.7.2   **Adjustment of Inventory for Casualty or Theft Loss**

> Fire Loss (Theft Loss, [Various Casualty Loss])   xxxx
>   Inventory   xxxx
> *To record inventory loss*

4000.1.2.8   **Reduction of Inventory to Market**

4000.1.2.8.1   **Direct Method**

Under the direct method, Inventory is credited directly to write down the inventory to market.

> *Loss Due To Write Down Of Inventory To Market   xxxx
>   Inventory   xxxx
> *To write down inventory to market*

*If the amount of the loss is not material, Cost Of Goods Sold may be debited instead of this loss account.

4000.1.2.8.2   **Indirect Method**

Under the indirect method, an allowance account is credited instead of Inventory. The allowance account is a contra account to (i.e., deducted from) Inventory in the balance sheet.

> Loss Due To Write Down Of Inventory To Market   xxxx
>   *Allowance To Reduce Inventory To Market   xxxx
> *To write down inventory to market*

*Allowance To Reduce Inventory To Market is shown as a contra account to (i.e., deducted from) Inventory in the balance sheet. It is adjusted at year end to reflect whatever balance is necessary to value Inventory. If the amount of the allowance must be increased (i.e., if the allowance account must be credited) Loss Due To Write Down Of Inventory To Market is debited as shown here. If the amount

Important: Make sure all appropriate subheads apply to your entry (see page v for instructions)

4000.1   **Merchandising Inventories**
4000.1.2   **Perpetual Inventory System**
4000.1.2.8   **Reduction of Inventory to Market**
4000.1.2.8.2   **Indirect Method**

---

of the allowance must be decreased (i.e., if the allowance account must be debited) Gain On Recovery Of Market Value Of Inventory is credited instead of debiting the loss account. However, the allowance account can never have a debit balance because the inventory can never be written up above original cost.

4000.2   **Manufacturing Inventories**

4000.2.1   **Raw Materials**

4000.2.1.1   **Periodic Inventory System**

Under the periodic inventory system, all purchases, purchase returns and allowances, and purchase discounts are recorded initially in accounts other than Raw Materials Inventory. Raw Materials Inventory is not reduced as raw materials are requisitioned (used) but instead is calculated at the end of the period by adding net purchases and freight-in (transportation-in) to beginning raw materials inventory and subtracting ending raw materials inventory. If the periodic system is used for Raw Materials Inventory, it is also used for Work-In-Process and Finished Goods Inventories.

4000.2.1.1.1   **Purchase of Raw Materials**

4000.2.1.1.1.1   **Purchase Recorded at Invoice (Gross) Amount**

              *Purchases   xxxx
                    Accounts Payable   xxxx
                 To record purchase of raw materials

*Purchases are recorded at the full invoice amount before any cash discount that may be taken for prompt payment. For example, a $1,000 purchase subject to a 2% cash discount if paid within 10 days will be recorded at $1,000 even though only $980 will be paid if payment is made promptly.

Important: Make sure all appropriate subheads apply to your entry (see page v for instructions)

4000.2   **Manufacturing Inventories**
4000.2.1   **Raw Materials**
4000.2.1.1   **Periodic Inventory System**
4000.2.1.1.1   **Purchase of Raw Materials**

4000.2.1.1.1.2   **Purchase Recorded Net of Anticipated Cash Discount**

>   *Purchases   xxxx
>   Accounts Payable   xxxx
>   *To record purchase of raw materials*

*Purchases are recorded net of any cash discount that may be taken for prompt payment (regardless of whether or not the discount is eventually taken). For example, a $1,000 purchase subject to a 2% cash discount if paid within 10 days will be recorded at $980.

4000.2.1.1.2   **Payment of Freight-In (Transportation-In)**

Freight-In (Transportation-In) is the cost of freight necessary to acquire goods purchased on an F.O.B. (free on board) shipping point basis, i.e., when the supplier does not bear the cost of freight. Freight-In (Transportation-In) must be recorded in a separate account from Freight-Out (Transportation-Out), which is a selling expense.

>   Freight-In (Transportation-In)   xxxx
>   Cash (Accounts Payable)   xxxx
>   *To record payment of freight-in*

4000.2.1.1.3   **Return of Merchandise to or Price Adjustment by Supplier**

>   *Accounts Payable   xxxx
>   Purchase Returns And Allowances   xxxx
>   *To record purchase return or allowance*

*The amount recorded will be the gross invoice amount of the return or allowance if the purchase was originally recorded at the gross amount *(see GEN4000.2.1.1.1.1)*. If the purchase was originally recorded net of the cash discount, the amount of this entry will be the amount of the allowance(s) or the net invoice amount of the return or allowance *(see GEN4000.2.1.1.1.2)*.

Important: Make sure all appropriate subheads apply to your entry (see page v for instructions)

4000.2   **Manufacturing Inventories**
4000.2.1   **Raw Materials**
4000.2.1.1   **Periodic Inventory System**

4000.2.1.1.4   **Payment for Raw Materials**

4000.2.1.1.4.1   **Payment Made Within Discount Period**

4000.2.1.1.4.1.1   **Payment Made Within Discount Period When Purchase Was Initially Recorded at Invoice (Gross) Amount**

Accounts Payable	xxxx	
*Purchase Discounts		xxxx
Cash		xxxx

To record payment of accounts payable

*Purchase Discounts is credited for the amount of the cash discount taken. This account will eventually be closed to Manufacturing Summary, thereby reducing cost of goods manufactured *(see GEN4000.2.1.1.5).*

4000.2.1.1.4.1.2   **Payment Made Within Discount Period When Purchase Was Initially Recorded Net of Anticipated Cash Discount**

Accounts Payable	xxxx	
Cash		xxxx

To record payment of accounts payable

4000.2.1.1.4.2   **Payment Made After Discount Period Ends**

4000.2.1.1.4.2.1   **Payment Made After Discount Period Ends and Purchase Was Initially Recorded at Invoice (Gross) Amount**

Accounts Payable	xxxx	
Cash		xxxx

To record payment of accounts payable

Important: Make sure all appropriate subheads apply to your entry (see page v for instructions)

4000.2	**Manufacturing Inventories**
4000.2.1	**Raw Materials**
4000.2.1.1	**Periodic Inventory System**
4000.2.1.1.4	**Payment for Raw Materials**
4000.2.1.1.4.2	**Payment Made After Discount Period Ends**

4000.2.1.1.4.2.2   **Payment Made After Discount Period Ends and Purchase Was Initially Recorded Net of Anticipated Cash Discount**

Accounts Payable	xxxx	
*Purchase Discounts Lost	xxxx	
Cash		xxxx
To record payment of accounts payable		

*Purchase Discounts Lost is an expense account representing finance charges for delayed payment.

4000.2.1.1.5   **End-of-Period Raw Materials Inventory Adjustment**

*Raw Materials Inventory	xxxx	
**Purchase Discounts	xxxx	
**Purchase Returns And Allowances	xxxx	
***Manufacturing Summary	xxxx	
**Freight-In (Transportation-In)		xxxx
**Purchases		xxxx
*Raw Materials Inventory		xxxx
To adjust Raw Materials Inventory		

*Raw Materials Inventory is debited for the amount of the ending balance (established by physical count) and credited for the amount of the beginning-of-period balance. Alternatively, Raw Materials Inventory may just be debited for any increase or credited for any decrease. (This method does not distinguish between direct and indirect materials. If it is important to distinguish between them, they may be kept in two different inventory accounts each handled in this manner.)

**Purchase Discounts, Purchase Returns And Allowances, Freight-In (Transportation-In), and Purchases are all closed, i.e., they are debited or credited to remove any existing balance.

***Manufacturing Summary is debited for whatever amount is necessary to balance the entry. When combined with entries to adjust Work-In-Process Inventory, Finished Goods Inventory, Direct Labor, and Factory Overhead (Manufacturing Overhead), this entry will produce a balance in Manufacturing Summary equal to the cost of goods manufactured during the period.

Important: Make sure all appropriate subheads apply to your entry (see page v for instructions)

4000.2   **Manufacturing Inventories**
4000.2.1   **Raw Materials**

4000.2.1.2   **Perpetual Inventory System**

Under the perpetual inventory system, all purchases, purchase returns and allowances, purchase discounts, and freight-in (transportation-in) are recorded directly in Raw Materials Inventory. As materials are requisitioned (used) Raw Materials Inventory is reduced. As a result, Raw Materials Inventory contains a continuous running balance (perpetual balance) representing the amount of inventory on hand. At the end of the accounting period, the physical count of raw materials is compared with the balance in the inventory account which is adjusted if necessary to account for overages or shortages. If the perpetual system is used for raw materials inven-tory, it is also used for work-in-process and finished goods inventories.

4000.2.1.2.1   **Purchase of Raw Materials**

4000.2.1.2.1.1   **Purchase Recorded at Invoice (Gross) Amount**

*Raw Materials Inventory	xxxx	
Accounts Payable		xxxx
To record purchase of raw materials		

*Raw Materials Inventory is debited for the full invoice amount before any cash discount that may be taken for prompt payment. For example, a $1,000 purchase subject to a 2% cash discount if paid within 10 days will be recorded at $1,000 even though only $980 will be paid if payment is made promptly.

4000.2.1.2.1.2   **Purchase Recorded Net of Anticipated Cash Discount**

*Raw Materials Inventory	xxxx	
Accounts Payable		xxxx
To record purchase of raw materials		

*Raw Materials Inventory is debited for the invoice amount net of any cash discount that may be taken for prompt payment. For example, a $1,000 purchase subject to a 2% cash discount if paid within 10 days will be recorded at $980 regardless of when actual payment occurs.

INVENTORIES

Important: Make sure all appropriate subheads apply to your entry (see page v for instructions)

4000.2   **Manufacturing Inventories**
4000.2.1   **Raw Materials**
4000.2.1.2   **Perpetual Inventory System**

4000.2.1.2.2   **Payment of Freight-In (Transportation-In)**

Freight-In (Transportation-In) is the cost of freight necessary to acquire goods purchased on an F.O.B. (free on board) shipping point basis, i.e., when the supplier does not bear the cost of freight. Freight-In (Transportation-In) must be recorded in a separate account from Freight-Out (Transportation-Out), which is a selling expense.

    *Raw Materials Inventory   xxxx
         Cash   xxxx
       To record payment of freight-in

*Freight-In (Transportation-In) may be debited (instead of Raw Materials Inventory) if the amount is immaterial, or if it is not feasible to allocate these costs to inventory.

4000.2.1.2.3   **Return of Raw Materials to or Price Adjustment by Supplier**

    *Accounts Payable   xxxx
         *Raw Materials Inventory   xxxx
       To record purchase return or allowance

*The amount recorded will be the gross invoice amount of the return or allowance if the purchase was originally recorded at the gross amount *(see GEN4000.2.1.2.1.1)*. If the purchase was originally recorded net of the cash discount, the amount of this entry will be the amount of allowance or the net invoice amount of the return *(see GEN4000.2.1.2.1.2)*.

4000.2.1.2.4   **Payment for Raw Materials**

4000.2.1.2.4.1   **Payment Made Within Discount Period**

Important: Make sure all appropriate subheads apply to your entry (see page v for instructions)

4000.2   **Manufacturing Inventories**
4000.2.1   **Raw Materials**
4000.2.1.2   **Perpetual Inventory System**
4000.2.1.2.4   **Payment for Raw Materials**
4000.2.1.2.4.1   **Payment Made Within Discount Period**

4000.2.1.2.4.1.1   **Payment Made Within Discount Period When Purchase Was Initially Recorded at Invoice (Gross) Amount**

Accounts Payable	xxxx	
*Raw Materials Inventory		xxxx
Cash		xxxx

To record payment of accounts payable

*Raw Materials Inventory is credited for the amount of the cash discount taken.

4000.2.1.2.4.1.2   **Payment Made Within Discount Period When Purchase Was Initially Recorded Net of Anticipated Cash Discount**

Accounts Payable	xxxx	
Cash		xxxx

To record payment of accounts payable

4000.2.1.2.4.2   **Payment Made After Discount Period Ends**

4000.2.1.2.4.2.1   **Payment Made After Discount Period Ends and Purchase Was Initially Recorded at Invoice (Gross) Amount**

Accounts Payable	xxxx	
Cash		xxxx

To record payment of accounts payable

4000.2.1.2.4.2.2   **Payment Made After Discount Period Ends and Purchase Was Initially Recorded Net of Anticipated Cash Discount**

Accounts Payable	xxxx	
*Purchase Discounts Lost	xxxx	
Cash		xxxx

To record payment of accounts payable

*Purchase Discounts Lost is an expense account representing finance charges for delayed payment.

Important: Make sure all appropriate subheads apply to your entry (see page v for instructions)

4000.2   **Manufacturing Inventories**
4000.2.1   **Raw Materials**
4000.2.1.2   **Perpetual Inventory System**

4000.2.1.2.5   **Requisition (Use) of Raw Materials**

A reduction in Raw Materials Inventory is recorded under the perpetual system of inventory when material is requisitioned (used).

4000.2.1.2.5.1   **Direct Materials Used**

Direct materials are materials that become a physical part of the product.

Work-In-Process Inventory	xxxx	
Raw Materials Inventory		xxxx
To record direct materials used		

4000.2.1.2.5.2   **Indirect Materials Used**

Indirect materials are materials that do not become a physical part of the product, e.g., sandpaper or buffing compounds.

*Factory Overhead (Manufacturing Overhead)	xxxx	
Raw Materials Inventory		xxxx
To record indirect materials used		

*See GEN16000.1.3 for a discussion of the use of this account.

4000.2.1.2.6   **End-of-Period Raw Materials Inventory Adjustments**

An adjustment to Raw Materials Inventory may be needed at the end of the period if there is a discrepancy between the balance in the inventory account and the physical inventory count (normal inventory overage or shortage) or if there has been a theft loss or casualty loss, e.g., from a fire.

4000.2.1.2.6.1   **Normal Inventory Overage or Shortage**

*Raw Materials Inventory Over Or Short	xxxx	
Raw Materials Inventory		xxxx
To record inventory shortage		

Important: Make sure all appropriate subheads apply to your entry (see page v for instructions)

4000.2	**Manufacturing Inventories**
4000.2.1	**Raw Materials**
4000.2.1.2	**Perpetual Inventory System**
4000.2.1.2.6	**End-of-Period Raw Materials Inventory Adjustments**
4000.2.1.2.6.1	**Normal Inventory Overage or Shortage**

---

*If a physical count of the Raw Materials Inventory shows there is less inventory on hand than indicated by the balance in the Raw Materials Inventory account, Raw Materials Inventory Over Or Short is debited and Raw Materials Inventory is credited as shown here. If the physical count shows there is more inventory on hand than indicated by the balance in the inventory account, Raw Materials Inventory is debited and Raw Materials Inventory Over Or Short is credited. A debit balance in Raw Materials Inventory Over Or Short indicates a loss from a shortage, and a credit balance indicates a gain from an overage. As long as the amount of shortage or overage is not material, some companies debit the amount of shortage or credit the amount of overage to Manufacturing Summary instead of using a separate "over or short" account.

4000.2.1.2.6.2   **Adjustment of Raw Materials Inventory for Casualty or Theft Loss**

          *Fire Loss (Theft Loss, [Various Casualty Loss])   xxxx
                Raw Materials Inventory   xxxx
          To record inventory loss

*See GEN5000.3.3.3 for subsequent treatment of this account when proceeds from insurance are received.

4000.2.2   **Work-In-Process Inventory**

4000.2.2.1   **Periodic Inventory System**

4000.2.2.1.1   **Transfer of Raw Materials, Direct Labor, and Factory Overhead (Manufacturing Overhead) to Work-In-Process Inventory**

No entries are necessary under the periodic system.

4000.2.2.1.2   **Transfer of Work-In-Process Inventory to Finished Goods Inventory**

No entries are necessary under the periodic system.

Important: Make sure all appropriate subheads apply to your entry (see page v for instructions)

4000.2   **Manufacturing Inventories**
4000.2.2   **Work-In-Process Inventory**
4000.2.2.1   **Periodic Inventory System**

4000.2.2.1.3   **End-of-Period Work-In-Process Inventory Adjustment**

*Work-In-Process Inventory	xxxx	
**Manufacturing Summary	xxxx	
*Work-In-Process Inventory		xxxx

To adjust balance of Work-In-Process Inventory

*Work-In-Process Inventory is debited for the amount of its ending balance and credited for the amount of its beginning balance. Alternatively, if its balance has increased, it may just be debited for the amount of increase, or if its balance has decreased, it may just be credited for the amount of the decrease.

**Manufacturing Summary is debited or credited to balance the entry. A debit to this account represents the amount of decrease in Work-In-Process Inventory and a credit represents the amount of increase in Work-In-Process Inventory.

4000.2.2.2   **Perpetual System**

4000.2.2.2.1   **Transfer of Raw Materials, Direct Labor, and Factory Overhead (Manufacturing Overhead) to Work-In-Process Inventory**

Work-In-Process Inventory	xxxx	
Raw Materials Inventory		xxxx
Direct Labor		xxxx
Factory Overhead (Manufacturing Overhead)		xxxx

To record transfer of manufacturing costs to Work-In-Process Inventory

4000.2.2.2.2   **Transfer of Work-In-Process Inventory to Finished Goods Inventory**

Finished Goods Inventory	xxxx	
*Inventory Over Or Short	xxxx	
Work-In-Process Inventory		xxxx

To record transfer of Work-In-Process Inventory to Finished Goods Inventory

Important: Make sure all appropriate subheads apply to your entry (see page v for instructions)

4000.2   **Manufacturing Inventories**
4000.2.2   **Work-In-Process Inventory**
4000.2.2.2   **Perpetual System**
4000.2.2.2.2   **Transfer of Work-In-Process Inventory to Finished Goods Inventory**

If there is less work-in-process inventory on hand at the time of the transfer than there should be, Inventory Over Or Short is debited for the amount of the shortage (see GEN4000.1.2.7.1 for further discussion of the use of this account).

4000.2.3   **Finished Goods Inventory**

4000.2.3.1   **Periodic Inventory System**

4000.2.3.1.1   **Transfer of Work-In-Process Inventory to Finished Goods Inventory**

No entries are necessary under the periodic system.

4000.2.3.1.2   **Transfer of Finished Goods Inventory to Cost of Goods Sold**

No entries are necessary under the periodic system.

4000.2.3.1.3   **End-of-Period Finished Goods Inventory Adjustment**

*Finished Goods Inventory	xxxx	
***Income Summary (Expense And Revenue Summary)	xxxx	
**Manufacturing Summary		xxxx
*Finished Goods Inventory		xxxx
To adjust balance in Finished Goods Inventory		

*Finished Goods Inventory is debited for the amount of its ending balance and credited for the amount of its beginning balance. Alternatively, if its balance has increased, it may just be debited for the amount of increase, or if its balance has decreased, it may just be credited for the amount of the decrease.

**Manufacturing Summary is credited sufficiently to close out its debit balance.

***Income Summary (Expense And Revenue Summary) is debited for whatever amount is necessary to balance the entry. The amount of the debit will equal the cost of goods sold.

Important: Make sure all appropriate subheads apply to your entry (see page v for instructions)

4000.2   **Manufacturing Inventories**
4000.2.3   **Finished Goods Inventory**

4000.2.3.2   **Perpetual Inventory System**

4000.2.3.2.1   **Transfer of Work-In-Process Inventory to Finished Goods Inventory**

Finished Goods Inventory	xxxx	
*Inventory Over Or Short	xxxx	
Work-In-Process Inventory		xxxx

To record transfer to Finished Goods Inventory

*If there is less work-in-process inventory on hand at the time of the transfer than there should be, Inventory Over Or Short is debited for the amount of the shortage (*see GEN4000.1.2.7.1* for further discussion of the use of this account).

4000.2.3.2.2   **Sale of Finished Goods**

Accounts Receivable	xxxx	
Sales		xxxx

To record sales

Cost Of Goods Sold	xxxx	
Finished Goods Inventory		xxxx

To record cost of goods sold

4000.3   **Changes in Valuation Method**

4000.3.1   **Change or Adjustment from First-In-First-Out (FIFO) or Weighted Average to Last-In-First-Out (LIFO)**

4000.3.1.1   **Permanent Change from First-In-First-Out (FIFO) or Weighted Average to Last-In-First-Out (LIFO)**

Usually, the LIFO method is adopted assuming the current beginning inventory valuation is the beginning LIFO inventory. Thus, no entry is required. An entry is required only if the inventory has been previously written down under the appli-

INVENTORIES

Important: Make sure all appropriate subheads apply to your entry (see page v for instructions)

4000.3   **Changes in Valuation Method**
4000.3.1   **Change or Adjustment from First-In-First-Out (FIFO) or Weighted Average to Last-In-First-Out (LIFO)**
4000.3.1.1   **Permanent Change from First-In-First-Out (FIFO) or Weighted Average to Last-In-First-Out (LIFO)**

---

cation of lower-of-cost-or-market. In this case, the inventory must be restated to cost using the entry below.

    *Inventory (Allowance To Reduce Inventory To Market)   xxxx
        Adjustment To Record Inventory At Cost   xxxx
    To restate inventory

*If a balance exists in Allowance To Reduce Inventory To Market as a result of entries such as those presented at *GEN4000.1.1.8.1.2*, it should be debited instead of Inventory.

4000.3.1.2   **Temporary Adjustment from First-In-First-Out (FIFO) or Weighted Average to Last-In-First-Out (LIFO)**

If a firm uses LIFO for tax and external reporting purposes but maintains another inventory costing system (e.g., FIFO or weighted average) for internal reporting purposes, inventory value may be adjusted at the end of the period to LIFO using Allowance To Reduce Inventory To LIFO as a contra account (i.e., deducted from Inventory in the balance sheet). At the end of each period, this account is adjusted up or down to reflect the difference between the value of inventory under the method used for internal reporting purposes (e.g., FIFO or weighted average) and its LIFO value as follows:

    Cost Of Goods Sold   xxxx
        *Allowance To Reduce Inventory To LIFO   xxxx
    To increase the allowance to adjust inventory to LIFO

                  or

    *Allowance To Reduce Inventory To LIFO   xxxx
        Cost Of Goods Sold   xxx
    To reduce the allowance to adjust inventory to LIFO

*Allowance To Reduce Inventory To LIFO is a contra account deducted from Inventory in the balance sheet. Assuming rising prices, it will never have a debit balance because LIFO will always result in the lowest inventory value.

Important: Make sure all appropriate subheads apply to your entry (see page v for instructions)

4000.3   **Changes in Valuation Method**

4000.3.2   ## Change from Last-In-First-Out (LIFO) to First-In-First-Out (FIFO) or Weighted Average

A change from LIFO to FIFO is treated as a retroactive accounting change. For a complete discussion of retroactive accounting changes, *see GEN15000.1.1*. All of the financial statements included in the comparative statements issued for the year of change should be reported on a retroactive restated basis. Income tax effects should also be considered *(see GEN15000.1.1)*.

> Inventory   xxxx
>   Retained Earnings (Prior Period Adjustment)   xxxx
> *To record change from LIFO to FIFO*

4000.3.3   ## Change in Valuation Method Other Than from LIFO or to LIFO

A change in valuation method other than from LIFO or to LIFO is treated as a cumulative-effect ("catch-up") accounting change. For a complete discussion of cumulative-effect accounting changes *see GEN15000.1.3*.

A catch-up adjustment is required as of the beginning of the year in which the change is made. Assuming the value of inventory under the new method is greater than under the old method, the following entry must be made:

> Inventory   xxxx
>   Cumulative Effect Of Change In Accounting
>   Principle   xxxx
> *To record change in inventory valuation method*

If the value of inventory under the new method is less than under the old method, this entry would be reversed, i.e., Inventory would be credited and Cumulative Effect Of Change In Accounting Principle would be debited. Income tax effects should also be considered *(see GEN15000.1.3.)*.

4000.3.4   ## Temporary Reduction in LIFO Inventory in Interim Period Financial Statements

When inventory quantities have decreased and the LIFO valuation method is used, applying LIFO to interim periods and totaling the results of interim periods will give

Important: Make sure all appropriate subheads apply to your entry (see page v for instructions)

4000.3   **Changes in Valuation Method**
4000.3.4   **Temporary Reduction in LIFO Inventory in Interim Period Financial Statements**

---

different results than if LIFO is applied only once at the end of the fiscal year. Therefore, if LIFO inventory is reduced during an interim period, the following entry is usually made:

Cost Of Goods Sold	xxxx	
*Excess Of Replacement Cost Of LIFO Inventory Temporarily Liquidated		xxxx
To record temporary reduction of LIFO inventory		

*This account is reported as a current liability and is reported only in interim financial statements.

When additional inventory is purchased, Excess Of Replacement Cost Of LIFO Inventory Temporarily Liquidated is eliminated as follows:

Inventory (Purchases)	xxxx	
Excess Of Replacement Cost Of LIFO Inventory Temporarily Liquidated	xxxx	
Accounts Payable (Cash)		xxxx
To record purchase of inventory and replenishment of a temporary reduction of LIFO inventory		

4000.4   **Correction of Errors in Inventory**

4000.4.1   **Ending Inventory Overstated**

This may result from an error in the physical count.

4000.4.1.1   **Error Corrected Before the Books Are Closed for the Period in Which the Error Was Made**

*Cost Of Goods Sold (Income Summary)	xxxx	
Inventory		xxxx
To correct error in inventory		

*If the periodic method is used, Cost Of Goods Sold (Income Summary) is debited as indicated. If the perpetual method is used, Inventory Over Or Short is debited instead.

INVENTORIES

Important: Make sure all appropriate subheads apply to your entry (see page v for instructions)

4000.4   **Correction of Errors in Inventory**
4000.4.1   **Ending Inventory Overstated**

4000.4.1.2   **Error Corrected After the Books Are Closed for the Period in Which the Error Was Made**

Prior Period Adjustment (Retained Earnings)	xxxx	
Inventory		xxxx
To correct error in inventory		

4000.4.2   **Ending Inventory Understated**

4000.4.2.1   **Purchases Properly Recorded**

4000.4.2.1.1   **Error Corrected Before the Books Are Closed for the Period in Which the Error Was Made**

Inventory	xxxx	
Cost Of Goods Sold (Income Summary)		xxxx
To correct error in inventory		

4000.4.2.1.2   **Error Corrected After the Books Are Closed for the Period in Which the Error Was Made**

Inventory	xxxx	
Prior Period Adjustment (Retained Earnings)		xxxx
To correct error in inventory		

4000.4.2.2   **Purchases Not Recorded**

4000.4.2.2.1   **Error Corrected Before the Books Are Closed for the Period in Which the Error Was Made**

*Purchases (Inventory)	xxxx	
Accounts Payable		xxxx
To record purchase		

Important: Make sure all appropriate subheads apply to your entry (see page v for instructions)

4000.4   **Correction of Errors in Inventory**
4000.4.2   **Ending Inventory Understated**
4000.4.2.2   **Purchases Not Recorded**
4000.4.2.2.1   **Error Corrected Before the Books Are Closed for the Period in Which the Error Was Made**

---

*Purchases is debited if the periodic inventory method is used. If the perpetual inventory method is used, Inventory is debited.

4000.4.2.2.2   **Error Corrected After the Books Are Closed for the Period in Which the Error Was Made**

Retained Earnings (Prior Period Adjustment)	xxxx	
*Purchases (Inventory)		xxxx
To correct error		

*This credit assumes the purchase was eventually recorded in the period following the period in which the error was made and before this entry is made. Purchases is credited if the periodic inventory method is used. If the perpetual inventory method is used, Inventory is credited. If the purchase was not recorded before this entry is made, this credit should be to Accounts Payable.

4000.5   **Purchase Commitments**

4000.5.1   **Contracted for and Executed Within the Same Fiscal Year**

4000.5.1.1   **When Contract Is Signed**

No entry is required.

4000.5.1.2   **When Contract Is Executed (Delivery Is Taken)**

4000.5.1.2.1   **Market Price Is Greater than or Equal to the Contract Price**

*Inventory (Purchases)	xxxx	
*Accounts Payable (Cash)		xxxx
To record execution of purchase commitment		

*Inventory (Purchases) is debited and Accounts Payable credited for the contract price.

Important: Make sure all appropriate subheads apply to your entry (see page v for instructions)

4000.5	**Purchase Commitments**
4000.5.1	**Contracted for and Executed Within the Same Fiscal Year**
4000.5.1.2	**When Contract Is Executed (Delivery Is Taken)**

4000.5.1.2.2   **Market Price Is Below the Contract Price**

*Inventory (Purchases)	xxxx	
**Loss On Purchase Commitment	xxxx	
***Accounts Payable (Cash)		xxxx

To record execution of purchase commitment

*Inventory (Purchases) is debited for the current fair market value of the inventory acquired.

**Loss On Purchase Commitment is debited for the excess of the contract price over the fair value of the inventory acquired.

***Accounts Payable (Cash) is credited for the contract price of the inventory acquired.

4000.5.2   **Purchase Contract Extends Beyond the End of the Buyer's Fiscal Year**

4000.5.2.1   **Year-End Market Price Is Below Contract Price and the Price Decline Is a Reasonable Estimate of the Probable Loss at the Time of Actual Purchase**

*Estimated Loss On Purchase Commitment	xxxx	
*Estimated Liability For Purchase Commitment		xxxx

To record estimated loss on purchase commitment

*The debit and credit to these accounts are made in the amount of the excess of the contract price over the year-end market price for the amount of goods the firm is still obligated to take delivery of under the contract. If the estimated liability account already has a balance in it from a previous entry of this nature relating to the same contract, the debit and credit to these accounts are made for whatever amount is necessary to increase the balance in the estimated liability account to reflect the excess contract price. Accounting principles are not clear concerning whether the estimated liability account may be reduced if the excess contract price has been reduced because of a decline in market price so that there is a balance in the estimated liability account that is too large.

Important: Make sure all appropriate subheads apply to your entry (see page v for instructions)

4000.5   **Purchase Commitments**
4000.5.2   **Purchase Contract Extends Beyond the End of the Buyer's Fiscal Year**

4000.5.2.2   **Purchase Commitment Is Executed (Delivery of Goods Is Taken)— Market Price Is Equal to or Greater than the Market Price at the Last Time the Estimated Liability Account Was Adjusted to Reflect End-of-Year Market Prices**

*Inventory (Purchases)	xxxx	
**Estimated Liability For Purchase Commitment	xxxx	
***Accounts Payable (Cash)		xxxx

To record execution of purchase commitment

*Inventory (Purchases) is debited for whatever amount is necessary to balance this entry.

**The estimated liability account is debited to reduce its balance by the amount of liability previously recorded for the quantity of goods for which delivery is now taken. For example, assume the last time the estimated liability account was adjusted at year end, the balance in the estimated liability account was $100,000 after the adjustment and 80,000 units were yet to be received. If delivery is now taken on 20,000 units, the estimated liability account will be debited for $25,000 ($100,000 X 20/80).

***Accounts Payable (Cash) is credited for the amount owed or paid under the contract for the goods delivered.

4000.5.2.3   **Purchase Commitment Is Executed (Delivery of Goods Is Taken)— Market Price Is Less than the Market Price at the Last Time the Estimated Liability Account Was Adjusted to Reflect End-of-Year Market Prices**

*Inventory (Purchases)	xxxx	
**Estimated Liability For Purchase Commitment	xxxx	
***Loss On Purchase Commitment	xxxx	
****Accounts Payable (Cash)		xxxx

To record execution of purchase commitment

*Inventory (Purchases) is debited for the current market price.

**The estimated liability account is debited to reduce its balance by the amount of liability previously recorded for the quantity of goods for which delivery is now

Important: Make sure all appropriate subheads apply to your entry (see page v for instructions)

4000.5	**Purchase Commitments**
4000.5.2	**Purchase Contract Extends beyond the End of the Buyer's Fiscal Year**
4000.5.2.3	**Purchase Commitment Is Executed (Delivery of Goods Is Taken)— Market Price Is Less than the Market Price at the Last Time the Estimated Liability Account Was Adjusted to Reflect End-of-Year Market Prices**

taken. For example, assume the last time the estimated liability account was adjusted at year end, the balance in the estimated liability account was $100,000 after the adjustment and 80,000 units were yet to be received. If delivery is now taken on 20,000 units, the estimated liability account will be debited for $25,000 ($100,000 X 20/80).

***Loss On Purchase Commitment is debited for whatever amount is necessary to balance the entry.

****Accounts Payable (Cash) is credited for the amount owed or paid under the contract for the goods delivered.

4000.6	**Consignments of Inventory**

Under a consignment, a consignor ships goods to a consignee who holds the goods for resale with no obligation to the consignor (other than to take reasonable care of the goods) until the goods are sold. Thus, goods held on consignment by a consignee are the property of the consignor (not of the consignee).

4000.6.1	**Accounting for Consigned Inventory by Consignee**

No entries are made by a consignee to account for consigned inventory. *See GEN4000.6* for an explanation. For other entries made by a consignee *see GEN11000.4.2.*

4000.6.2	**Accounting for Consigned Inventory by Consignor**

4000.6.2.1	**Shipment of Inventory on Consignment to Consignee**

Inventory On Consignment	xxxx	
Inventory		xxxx
To record shipment to consignee		
Inventory On Consignment	xxxx	
Accounts Payable (Cash)		xxxx
To record shipping costs		

Important: Make sure all appropriate subheads apply to your entry (see page v for instructions)

4000.6   **Consignments of Inventory**
4000.6.2   **Accounting for Consigned Inventory by Consignor**

4000.6.2.2   **Sales and Remittance by Consignee**

Sales are recorded by a consignor upon receipt of a periodic report by the consignee concerning the quantity of sales. Such a report is usually accompanied by remittance by the consignee for the sales price of the inventory sold less the consignee's commission and less any expenses (e.g., for advertising) for which the consignor has previously agreed to reimburse the consignee.

Cash	xxxx	
Commission Expense	xxxx	
*[Various Expenses]	xxxx	
Consignment Sales		xxxx
To record consignment sales		

*Expenses of various kinds (e.g., advertising) may be debited for amounts withheld by the consignee to reimburse it for expenses according to provisions of the consignment contract.

Cost Of Consignment Sales	xxxx	
Inventory On Consignment		xxxx
To record cost of consignment sales		

TABLE OF CONTENTS

PROPERTY, PLANT, AND EQUIPMENT

5000.1

Acquisition of Plant Assets

Plant assets include land, buildings, machinery, and various types of equipment including trucks and automobiles used in primary revenue-producing activities. Plant assets are recorded at the cash or cash equivalent price of obtaining the assets. The cost of a plant asset also includes any expenditure required to get the asset in place and ready for use (e.g., sales commissions, sales taxes, freight, installation, and testing). Finally, when a group of plant assets is acquired for a single lump sum (e.g., when an entire factory is purchased for one lump sum price), the lump sum must be allocated among the various assets based on their fair market values.

5000.1.1

Plant Assets Acquired for Cash and/or Liabilities

5000.1.1.1

Land

5000.1.1.1.1

Land Acquired for Cash

*Land		xxxx
Cash		xxxx
To record acquisition of land		

*Land cost includes the purchase price plus all purchase-related costs such as:
- commissions
- closing costs such as
  - attorney fees
  - title search fees
  - insurance
  - recording fees
- property taxes paid at acquisition
- cost of preparing land for use (*see GEN5000.1.1.1.3*).

If the land is acquired as part of a lump sum purchase (i.e., more than just land is acquired in the same transaction), *see GEN5000.1.2*. Land acquired for speculation or investment purposes rather than for primary revenue-producing activities should be recorded in a separate land account and classified as Other Assets rather than Property, Plant, and Equipment.

Important: Make sure all appropriate subheads apply to your entry (see page v for instructions)

5000.1   **Acquisition of Plant Assets**
5000.1.1   **Plant Assets Acquired for Cash and/or Liabilities**
5000.1.1.1   **Land**

5000.1.1.1.2   ## Land Acquired for Liabilities (or Liabilities and Cash)

For a more complete coverage of plant assets acquired with debt *see GEN5000.1.4.*

*Land		xxxx
Property Tax Payable		xxxx
[Various Liabilities]		xxxx
Mortgage Payable		xxxx
Notes Payable		xxxx
Cash		xxxx

To record acquisition of land

*Land is debited for the cash paid plus all liabilities assumed. Land acquired for speculation or investment purposes rather than for primary revenue-producing activities should be recorded in a separate land account and classified as Other Assets rather than Property, Plant, and Equipment.

5000.1.1.1.3   ## Costs Incurred in Preparing Land for Intended Use

*Land	xxxx
Cash (Accounts Payable, [Various Liabilities	
Or Expenses])	xxxx

To record costs incurred to prepare land for intended use

*Land cost includes all expenditures required to prepare the land for its intended purpose such as:
      -appraisal costs at acquisition
      -clearing and filling costs
      -grading costs
      -improvements with indefinite lives such as
            landscaping
            special assessments for road construction, street lighting, and sewage
            and drainage.
If land is purchased as a site for new construction, all costs incurred up to the excavation for the new structures, including removal of existing structures, are debited to Land.

Important: Make sure all appropriate subheads apply to your entry (see page v for instructions)

5000.1	**Acquisition of Plant Assets**
5000.1.1	**Plant Assets Acquired for Cash and/or Liabilities**
5000.1.1.1	**Land**

5000.1.1.1.4

Amounts Received from Salvage or Timber During Preparation of Land for Its Intended Use

Cash		xxxx
*Land		xxxx

To record amounts received from salvage or cleared timber during preparation of land for intended use

*Amounts received as salvage for existing structures or for unneeded timber cleared from the land are assumed to reduce the land's cost and therefore are credited to Land.

5000.1.1.1.5

Land Improvements

Some expenditures related to land have finite lives. Expenditures for items such as:
- parking lots
- outdoor fixtures (e.g., picnic tables)
- fencing

are not charged to Land. These kinds of items are debited to Land Improvements and depreciated over their useful lives.

Land Improvements		xxxx
Cash		xxxx

To record cost of land improvements

5000.1.1.2

Buildings

5000.1.1.2.1

Buildings Acquired for Cash

*Buildings		xxxx
Cash		xxxx

To record acquisition of buildings

Important: Make sure all appropriate subheads apply to your entry (see page v for instructions)

5000.1	**Acquisition of Plant Assets**
5000.1.1	**Plant Assets Acquired for Cash and/or Liabilities**
5000.1.1.2	**Buildings**
5000.1.1.2.1	**Buildings Acquired for Cash**

---

*The cost of a building includes the purchase price and all other purchase-related costs such as:
        -realtor commissions
        -closing costs.
If the building is acquired as part of a lump sum purchase such as when an entire factory is purchased at one time for a lump sum price, *see GEN5000.1.2.*

5000.1.1.2.2   ## Buildings Acquired for Liabilities (or Liabilities and Cash)

For a more complete coverage of plant assets acquired with debt *see GEN5000.1.4.*

*Buildings		xxxx
[Various Liabilities]		xxxx
Mortgage Payable		xxxx
Notes Payable		xxxx
Cash		xxxx
To record acquisition of buildings		

*Buildings is debited for the cash paid plus all liabilities assumed by the purchaser.

5000.1.1.2.3   ## Costs Incurred in Preparing Buildings for Intended Use

*Buildings		xxxx
Cash (Accounts Payable)		xxxx
To record costs incurred to prepare buildings for intended use		

*The cost of a building includes all expenditures required to prepare it for its intended use. For example, costs incurred to repair or remodel a building are also charged to Buildings.

5000.1.1.2.4   ## Amounts Received from Salvage During Preparation of Buildings for Intended Use

Cash		xxxx
*Buildings		xxxx
To record amounts received from salvage		

Important: Make sure all appropriate subheads apply to your entry (see page v for instructions)

5000.1	**Acquisition of Plant Assets**
5000.1.1	**Plant Assets Acquired for Cash and/or Liabilities**
5000.1.1.2	**Buildings**
5000.1.1.2.4	**Amounts Received from Salvage During Preparation of Buildings for Intended Use**

---

*Amounts received as salvage of materials removed during remodeling, e.g., for the sale of used lumber or bricks, are assumed to reduce the cost of remodeling. The amount received is therefore credited to Buildings.

5000.1.1.3   **Equipment**

Common alternative account titles for equipment include:
- Machinery
- Office Equipment
- Office Furnishings
- Furniture And Fixtures
- Delivery Equipment
- Factory Equipment
- Autos And Trucks
- Vehicles.

5000.1.1.3.1   **Equipment Acquired for Cash**

*Equipment	xxxx	
Cash		xxxx

To record acquisition of equipment for cash

*The cost of equipment includes the purchase price plus all purchase-related costs such as:
- sales or use taxes
- handling charges
- freight and insurance during transit.

If the equipment is acquired as part of a lump sum purchase, such as when a factory is purchased for one lump sum price, *see GEN5000.1.2.*

5000.1.1.3.2   **Equipment Acquired for Liabilities (or Liabilities and Cash)**

For a more complete coverage of plant assets acquired with debt *see GEN5000.1.4.*

Important: Make sure all appropriate subheads apply to your entry (see page v for instructions)

5000.1	**Acquisition of Plant Assets**
5000.1.1	**Plant Assets Acquired for Cash and/or Liabilities**
5000.1.1.3	**Equipment**
5000.1.1.3.2	**Equipment Acquired for Liabilities (or Liabilities and Cash)**

---

*Equipment	xxxx	
[Various Liabilities]		xxxx
Accounts Payable		xxxx
Cash		xxxx

To record acquisition of equipment

*Equipment is debited for the cash paid plus all liabilities assumed by the purchaser.

5000.1.1.3.3 **Equipment Acquisition Subject to Cash Discounts on Related Accounts Payable**

5000.1.1.3.3.1 **Equipment and Accounts Payable Recorded Net of Cash Discount at Time of Acquisition (Recorded at Cash Equivalent)**

5000.1.1.3.3.1.1 **Cash Discount Is Taken**

Accounts Payable	xxxx	
Cash		xxxx

To record payment of Accounts Payable

5000.1.1.3.3.1.2 **Cash Discount Is Not Taken**

Accounts Payable	xxxx	
*Loss Due To Discounts Forfeited	xxxx	
Cash		xxxx

To record payment of Accounts Payable

*Because accounting principles require that a plant asset be recorded at the cash or cash equivalent price of acquisition, a loss should be recognized when available cash discounts are not taken.

5000.1.1.3.3.2 **Equipment and Accounts Payable Recorded Including (Gross of) Cash Discount at Time of Acquisition**

Important: Make sure all appropriate subheads apply to your entry (see page v for instructions)

5000.1	**Acquisition of Plant Assets**
5000.1.1	**Plant Assets Acquired for Cash and/or Liabilities**
5000.1.1.3	**Equipment**
5000.1.1.3.3	**Equipment Acquisition Subject to Cash Discounts on Related Accounts Payable**
5000.1.1.3.3.2	**Equipment and Accounts Payable Recorded Including (Gross of) Cash Discount at Time of Acquisition**

5000.1.1.3.3.2.1 **Cash Discount Is Taken**

Accounts Payable	xxxx	
*Equipment		xxxx
Cash		xxxx

To record payment of Accounts Payable

*Because accounting principles require that a plant asset be recorded at the cash or cash equivalent price of acquisition, the amount of the cash discount taken is credited to Equipment.

5000.1.1.3.3.2.2 **Cash Discount Is Not Taken**

Accounts Payable	xxxx	
Cash		xxxx

To record payment of Accounts Payable

Loss Due To Discounts Forfeited	xxxx	
*Equipment		xxxx

To reduce Equipment by amount of discount forfeited

*Because accounting principles require that a plant asset be recorded at the cash or cash equivalent price of acquisition, the amount of the cash discount not taken must be removed from Equipment.

5000.1.1.3.4 **Expenditures Incurred in Preparing Equipment for Its Intended Use**

*Equipment	xxxx	
Cash (Accounts Payable)		xxxx

To record costs incurred to prepare equipment for intended use

*The cost of equipment includes all expenditures required to prepare it for its intended purpose. For example,
-costs of special wiring
-assembly and installation costs
-equipment testing costs
are also charged to Equipment.

Important: Make sure all appropriate subheads apply to your entry (see page v for instructions)

5000.1   **Acquisition of Plant Assets**

5000.1.2   **Plant Assets Acquired in a Lump Sum Purchase**

If, for example, an entire factory is purchased for one lump sum price, the lump sum purchase price is allocated to the individual plant assets based on fair market values of the individual assets. The percentage of the lump sum (purchase price or cost) to be allocated to a particular plant asset is found by dividing that asset's fair market value by the sum of all the acquired asset's fair market values.

Land	xxxx	
Buildings	xxxx	
Equipment	xxxx	
Cash (Notes Payable, Mortgage Payable)		xxxx

To record acquisition of plant assets

5000.1.3   **Plant Assets Acquired by Self-Construction**

5000.1.3.1   **Buildings Self-Constructed**

The cost of buildings includes all costs from excavation to completion. Costs associated with preparing the land for the construction of the building are debited to Land if the land was purchased with the intent to construct the building (*see GEN5000.1.1.1*). In addition to material, labor, and overhead costs, the costs of related items such as

-architect and other building-related consulting fees
-building permits
-interest during construction (*see GEN5000.1.3.3*)
-taxes during construction should be debited to Building (*see GEN5000.1.1.2.*).

Buildings	xxxx	
*Direct Materials		xxxx
*Direct Labor		xxxx
*Factory Overhead		xxxx
*[Various Accounts]		xxxx
Cash (Accounts Payable)		xxxx

To record costs of self-constructed building

Important: Make sure all appropriate subheads apply to your entry (see page v for instructions)

5000.1   **Acquisition of Plant Assets**
5000.1.3   **Plant Assets Acquired by Self-Construction**
5000.1.3.1   **Buildings Self-Constructed**

---

*This journal entry assumes that the costs of production (direct materials, direct labor, factory overhead, and other costs) are initially accumulated in (debited to) temporary accounts. The above entry then transfers the balances from these accounts to Buildings. Some firms debit a single temporary account such as Construction In Progress (or Construction In Process) instead of these accounts. In that case, Construction In Progress would be credited instead of these accounts in the above entry. Finally, some firms initially debit Buildings directly to record the costs of production, thereby bypassing the use of these accounts altogether.

5000.1.3.2   **Machinery and Other Self-Constructed Plant Assets**

*Machinery [Various Plant Assets]	xxxx	
**Direct Materials		xxxx
**Direct Labor		xxxx
**Factory Overhead		xxxx
Cash		xxxx

To record costs of self-constructed plant asset

*A plant asset should not be recorded for more than its fair market value. Thus, if a similar plant asset is available from an outside supplier for less than the cost of self-construction, the plant asset is recorded at the lower fair market value. The difference is debited to Loss On Self-Construction Of Plant Assets. *See GEN5000.1.3.3* for treatment of interest capitalized during construction.

**This journal entry assumes that the costs of production (direct materials, direct labor, factory overhead, and other costs) are initially accumulated in (debited to) temporary accounts. The above entry then transfers the balances from these accounts to Buildings. Some firms debit a single temporary account such as Construction In Progress (or Construction In Process) instead of these accounts. In that case, Construction In Progress would be credited instead of these accounts in the above entry. Finally, some firms initially debit Buildings directly to record the costs of production, thereby bypassing the use of these accounts altogether. Some firms charge the plant asset account with only the variable overhead cost if construction of the plant asset does not reduce normal production.

Important: Make sure all appropriate subheads apply to your entry (see page v for instructions)

5000.1   **Acquisition of Plant Assets**
5000.1.3   **Plant Assets Acquired by Self-Construction**

5000.1.3.3   **Interest During Construction**

5000.1.3.3.1   **Interest Not Capitalized**

    Interest Expense   xxxx
        Cash (Interest Payable, Prepaid Interest)   xxxx
    To record interest expense incurred during construction

5000.1.3.3.2   **Interest Capitalized**

Only interest associated with plant assets that are self-constructed for the firm's own use or associated with assets constructed for others on a project or contract basis is eligible for capitalization. Interest associated with the purchase of land may be capitalized if the land is acquired with the intent to develop it further (e.g., to construct a building on the land). Interest may not be capitalized on items such as
    -inventory
    -assets already in use or ready for use
    -assets not being used in the normal course of business (e.g., land held for
     speculation).

    *Buildings [Various Plant Assets]   xxxx
    **Interest Expense   xxxx
        Cash (Interest Payable, Prepaid Interest)   xxxx
    To capitalize interest incurred during construction

*This debit to the plant asset account is for interest expense capitalized during the current period. Interest may not be capitalized until the following three conditions are met:

    1. construction expenditures have been made

    2. activities necessary to prepare the asset for its intended use are under way

    3. interest cost is being incurred.

The amount of interest to be capitalized (i.e., debited to the plant asset account) is the lesser of the amount of actual interest incurred (on all debt) during the construction period and the amount of interest that might have been avoided had no expenditures for the asset been made.

Important: Make sure all appropriate subheads apply to your entry (see page v for instructions)

5000.1	**Acquisition of Plant Assets**
5000.1.3	**Plant Assets Acquired by Self-Construction**
5000.1.3.3	**Interest During Construction**
5000.1.3.3.2	**Interest Capitalized**

Avoidable interest is found by multiplying the appropriate interest rate by the weighted-average amount of construction expenditures. The weighted-average amount of construction expenditures is found by multiplying each construction expenditure by the amount of time (fraction of year; for example, 9/12 if the expenditure was made on April 1) that interest could have been incurred on that expenditure. The individual weighted amounts are then added to determine the total weighted-average amount of construction expenditures for the entire year.

The following interest rates should be used to determine the amount of avoidable interest: (a) if the total weighted-average amount of construction expenditures is equal to or less than the amount actually borrowed to finance the asset's construction, use the actual interest rate incurred on the specific borrowings; (b) otherwise, use the actual interest rate incurred on the specific borrowings for the portion of the total weighted-average amount of construction expenses equal to the amount actually borrowed, and the weighted-average interest rate incurred on all other outstanding debt during the period for the remaining portion of the total weighted-average amount of construction expenditures.

The weighted-average interest rate is found by dividing the total amount of interest incurred on all other outstanding debt during the period by the total amount of related principal on that debt.

**The amount debited to Interest Expense is the difference between the amount of interest capitalized (the debit to the plant asset account) and the amount of interest actually incurred (the credit to Cash, Interest Payable, or Prepaid Interest).

5000.1.3.3.3

Interest Revenue Earned on Funds Borrowed to Finance Asset Construction

Cash	xxxx	
*Interest Income (Interest Revenue)		xxxx
To record interest income		

*Borrowed funds not presently needed for construction are often invested in short-term securities. Interest earned on these funds does not offset the interest expense incurred on the borrowed funds.

Important: Make sure all appropriate subheads apply to your entry (see page v for instructions)

5000.1 **Acquisition of Plant Assets**

5000.1.4 **Plant Assets Acquired with Debt (Deferred Payment Contracts)**

*Buildings [Various Plant Assets]	xxxx	
**Discount On Notes (Bonds) Payable	xxxx	
Notes Payable (Bonds Payable)		xxxx
To record plant assets acquired with debt		

*Plant assets acquired under a deferred payment contract (e.g., by issuing long-term notes, bonds, mortgages, or equipment obligations) will require future cash flows that exceed the purchase price of the asset. This is because the future cash payments will cover not only the cost of the asset but will also incorporate an interest element. If known, the cash price of the asset is debited to the asset account. If the cash price is not known, then the asset should be recorded at the present value of the notes or bonds issued. The present value of the notes or bonds is determined by discounting the payments required by the purchase contract to the present using the interest rate stated in the contract. If no interest rate is specified, then a rate should be imputed that closely approximates the interest rate that would have been paid if the purchaser had borrowed the funds and paid cash for the asset.

**The discount represents the difference between the cash price or present value of the plant asset acquired and the face value or principal amount of the debt issued. The discount is amortized (written off) to interest expense over the term of the debt. *See GEN8000* for accounting for long-term liabilities such as notes payable and bonds payable.

5000.1.5 **Plant Assets Acquired with Issuance of Stock**

Plant assets acquired by issuing stock should be recorded at the fair market value of the stock issued. If the stock is not actively traded and a fair market value cannot be established, the fair market value of the asset acquired should be used. If fair market values cannot be determined for either the stock or the asset, then management usually establishes the asset's value.

Important: Make sure all appropriate subheads apply to your entry (see page v for instructions)

5000.1   **Acquisition of Plant Assets**
5000.1.5   **Plant Assets Acquired with Issuance of Stock**

5000.1.5.1   **Fair Market Value of Stock Issued or Asset Received Is Greater than the Par or Stated Value of Stock Issued**

[Various Plant Assets]	xxxx	
*Common (Preferred) Stock		xxxx
**Additional Paid-In Capital		xxxx

To record acquisition of plant asset with issuance of stock

*The stock account is credited for the par or stated value of the shares issued. If no-par stock is issued, the stock account is credited for the same amount as the debit to the plant asset account (i.e., the fair market value of the stock issued or the asset received), and no additional paid-in capital is recorded. For more complete coverage of issuance of stock for plant assets *see GEN9000.1.6.*

**Alternative account titles include Premium On Common (Preferred) Stock and Paid-In Capital In Excess Of Par. For more complete coverage of issuance of stock for plant assets see *GEN9000.1.6.*

5000.1.6   **Plant Assets Acquired by Donation**

*[Various Plant Assets]	xxxx	
Donated Capital		xxxx
Cash (Accounts Payable, [Various Liabilities,		
Various Expenses])		xxxx

To record plant assets acquired by donation

*The plant asset account is debited for the fair market value of the asset received plus any expenses associated with the transfer (e.g., closing costs to effect the transfer of ownership).

5000.2   **Costs Subsequent to Acquisition of Plant Assets**

In general, costs incurred after acquisition are added to the plant asset accounts if these expenditures provide future service potential. If such expenditures benefit only the current period, they are expensed in the period incurred. As a matter of expediency, many firms follow a policy of expensing small amounts regardless of the impact of the expenditure.

Important: Make sure all appropriate subheads apply to your entry (see page v for instructions)

5000.2   **Costs Subsequent to Acquisition of Plant Assets**

5000.2.1   **Repairs and Maintenance**

Repairs may be ordinary or major. Ordinary repairs are periodic (i.e., regularly scheduled) expenditures that keep plant assets in normal working condition such as:
> -oil changes
> -tune-ups
> -scheduled maintenance, e.g.,
>> cleaning, oiling, and adjusting machinery,
>> paint jobs,
>> periodic safety inspections.

These are usually expensed as incurred.

Major repairs (e.g., a new roof) should be accounted for as replacements (*see GEN5000.2.2*) or improvements (*see GEN5000.2.3*), or additions (*see GEN5000.2.4*).

5000.2.1.1   **Expensing Repairs and Maintenance Costs**

*Repairs And Maintenance Expense	xxxx	
Cash		xxxx
To record repairs and maintenance expense		

*Common alternative account titles include Repairs Expense and Maintenance Expense.

5000.2.1.2   **Use of Allowance Method to Record Repairs and Maintenance Costs**

The allowance method is particularly useful when monthly or quarterly financial statements are prepared. For example, an entry might be made quarterly to allocate the year's expected repair expense equally to each quarter even though most of the expense is incurred during the plant's annual two-week shut-down during the summer.

5000.2.1.2.1   **Recording Repairs and Maintenance Expense**

Repairs And Maintenance Expense	xxxx	
Allowance For Repairs And Maintenance		xxxx
To record repairs and maintenance expense		

Important: Make sure all appropriate subheads apply to your entry (see page v for instructions)

5000.2   **Costs Subsequent to Acquisition of Plant Assets**
5000.2.1   **Repairs and Maintenance**
5000.2.1.2   **Use of Allowance Method to Record Repairs and Maintenance Costs**

5000.2.1.2.2   **Recording Actual Repairs and Maintenance Expenditures**

> Allowance For Repairs And Maintenance   xxxx
>   Cash   xxxx
> *To record repairs and maintenance expenditures*

5000.2.2   **Replacements**

A replacement occurs when an asset or a portion of an asset is replaced with an-other asset (e.g., a manual conveyor belt for another manual conveyor belt). If the replacement involves the substitution of a better asset for the existing asset (e.g., an automated conveyor belt for a manual belt), or if the cost and accumulated depreciation amounts for the replaced asset cannot be practically determined and written off, the expenditure should be accounted for as an improvement or betterment (*see GEN5000.2.3*).

> Trucks [Various New Plant Assets]   xxxx
> Accumulated Depreciation - [Various Plant Assets]   xxxx
> *Loss On Retirement Of Plant Assets   xxxx
>   Trucks [Various Plant Assets Being Replaced]   xxxx
>   **Cash   xxxx
> *To record new plant asset acquired as replacement for*
> *old plant asset*

*If the book value (cost - accumulated depreciation) of the existing plant asset is different from its actual salvage value (the fair market value received for it), a gain (actual salvage value exceeds book value) or loss (actual salvage value is less than book value) is recognized. Loss On Retirement Of Plant Assets would be debited to record a loss. Gain On Retirement Of Plant Assets would be credited to record a gain.

**Cash is credited for the cash paid for the replacement less the cash received as salvage value for the existing asset. If the salvage value is not immediately available in cash, a receivable such as Proceeds Due From Plant Asset Retirement or Salvage Value Of Retired Plant Asset may be debited for the expected salvage value in the above entry.

Important: Make sure all appropriate subheads apply to your entry (see page v for instructions)

5000.2   **Costs Subsequent to Acquisition of Plant Assets**

5000.2.3   **Improvements (or Betterments)**

An improvement or betterment extends the useful life of the asset and/or increases its quality or quantity of output.

5000.2.3.1   **Useful Life Is Not Extended, but Quality or Quantity of Output Is Increased**

[Various Old Plant Assets]	xxxx	
Cash		xxxx
To record improvement or betterment		

The asset's new book value is determined, and that amount (less salvage value) is depreciated over the plant asset's remaining useful life.

5000.2.3.2   **Useful Life Is Extended, but Quality or Quantity of Output Is Not Increased**

Accumulated Depreciation - [Various Old Plant Assets]	xxxx	
Cash		xxxx
To record improvement or betterment		

The asset's new book value is determined and that amount (less salvage value) is depreciated over the plant asset's remaining useful life.

5000.2.4   **Additions**

Additions are often confused with improvements. The distinction is that an addition results in the creation of a new plant asset, whereas an improvement does not. Examples of additions include a new wing added to a building or a new assembly line added to a manufacturing plant.

*Buildings [Various New Plant Assets]	xxxx	
Cash		xxxx
To record addition		

Important: Make sure all appropriate subheads apply to your entry (see page v for instructions)

5000.2   **Costs Subsequent to Acquisition of Plant Assets**
5000.2.4   **Additions**

---

*The new plant asset's cost (less salvage) is depreciated over its useful life, not over the life of the related old asset.

5000.2.5   Rearrangements (or Reinstallations)

5000.2.5.1   Cost and Accumulated Depreciation Amounts for Previous Arrangement or Installation Are Known

*[Various Plant Assets]	xxxx	
Accumulated Depreciation - [Various Plant Assets]	xxxx	
*[Various Plant Assets]		xxxx
Cash [Various Accounts]		xxxx
To record rearrangement cost		

*The rearrangement is accounted for as a replacement. The book value of the old rearrangement or installation is removed (e.g., Machinery is credited) and replaced with the new cost (e.g., Machinery is debited). *See GEN5000.2.2.* The new plant asset is depreciated over its expected useful life.

5000.2.5.2   Cost and Accumulated Depreciation Amounts for Previous Arrangement or Installation Are Not Known

*[Various Plant Assets]	xxxx	
Cash [Various Assets]		xxxx
To record rearrangement cost		

*The rearrangement is accounted for as an addition. The new plant asset is depreciated over its useful life and not that of the related old asset. *See GEN5000.2.4.*

5000.2.6   Relocations

No definitive guidelines exist for accounting for relocation costs. Some firms capitalize relocation costs and amortize them over some future time period, while other firms expense such costs in the period incurred.

Important: Make sure all appropriate subheads apply to your entry (see page v for instructions)

5000.2   **Costs Subsequent to Acquisition of Plant Assets**
5000.2.6   **Relocations**

5000.2.6.1   **Capitalizing Relocation Costs**

Relocation Costs	xxxx	
Cash [Various Accounts]		xxxx

To capitalize relocation costs

5000.2.6.1.1   **Amortization of Relocation Costs**

Amortization Expense - Relocation Costs	xxxx	
Relocation Costs		xxxx

To record amortization of relocation costs

5000.2.6.2   **Expensing Relocation Costs**

Relocation Expense	xxxx	
Cash [Various Accounts]		xxxx

To expense relocation costs

5000.3   **Disposition of Plant Assets**

The first entry that must be made when a plant asset is disposed of is to record depreciation up to the date of disposal. This brings the book value current so that any gain or loss on disposal can be properly computed.

5000.3.1   **Sale of Plant Assets**

5000.3.1.1   **Updating Book Value of Plant Asset**

Depreciation Expense - [Various Plant Assets]	xxxx	
Accumulated Depreciation - [Various Plant Assets]		xxxx

To record depreciation up to the date of disposition

Important: Make sure all appropriate subheads apply to your entry (see page v for instructions)

5000.3   **Disposition of Plant Assets**
5000.3.1   **Sale of Plant Assets**

5000.3.1.2   **Recording Sale of Plant Assets**

5000.3.1.2.1   **Proceeds from Sale of Plant Assets Are Equal to Book Value**

Cash	xxxx	
Accumulated Depreciation - [Various Plant Assets]	xxxx	
[Various Plant Assets]		xxxx

To record sale of plant assets

5000.3.1.2.2   **Proceeds from Sale of Plant Assets Exceed Book Value**

Cash	xxxx	
Accumulated Depreciation - [Various Plant Assets]	xxxx	
[Various Plant Assets]		xxxx
*Gain On Sale Of Plant Assets		xxxx

To record sale of plant asset

*The excess of the proceeds over the asset's current book value is recorded as a gain. Such gains are not considered extraordinary.

5000.3.1.2.3   **Proceeds from Sale of Plant Assets Are Less than Book Value**

Cash	xxxx	
Accumulated Depreciation - [Various Plant Assets]	xxxx	
*Loss On Sale Of Plant Assets	xxxx	
[Various Plant Assets]		xxxx

To record sale of plant asset

*The excess of the asset's current book value over the proceeds is recorded as a loss. Such losses are not considered extraordinary.

5000.3.2   **Exchange (Trade) of Plant Assets**

The cost of the asset acquired in a nonmonetary exchange (trade), e.g., one truck for another truck is assumed to equal the fair market value of the asset given up.

Important: Make sure all appropriate subheads apply to your entry (see page v for instructions)

5000.3   **Disposition of Plant Assets**
5000.3.2   **Exchange (Trade) of Plant Assets**

However, if the fair market value of the asset given up cannot be determined, the fair market value of the asset received should be used.

5000.3.2.1   **Updating Book Value of Plant Asset**

Depreciation Expense - [Various Plant Assets]	xxxx	
Accumulated Depreciation - [Various Plant Assets]		xxxx

To record depreciation up to the date of disposition

5000.3.2.2   **Exchange (Trade) of Dissimilar Plant Assets**

Similarity or dissimilarity is determined based on *function served*. Thus, a mechanical bookkeeping machine and a computer may be similar assets if they are both used for accounting purposes, or they may be dissimilar assets if the computer is used for other than accounting functions. A small truck and a tractor-trailer may be similar assets if both are used for delivery purposes, but they are considered dissimilar if one is used for long-distance hauling and the other for local nondelivery purposes.

5000.3.2.2.1   **Fair Market Value of Asset Given Up Exceeds Its Book Value**

*[Various Plant Assets Acquired]	xxxx	
Accumulated Depreciation - [Various Plant Assets]	xxxx	
[Various Plant Assets Given Up]		xxxx
**Gain On Disposal Of Plant Assets		xxxx
Cash		xxxx

To record exchange of dissimilar plant assets

*The cost of the plant asset acquired equals the fair market value of the asset given up plus any cash paid.

**The gain represents the excess of the fair market value of the asset given up over its book value.

Important: Make sure all appropriate subheads apply to your entry (see page v for instructions)

5000.3   **Disposition of Plant Assets**
5000.3.2   **Exchange (Trade) of Plant Assets**
5000.3.2.2   **Exchange (Trade) of Dissimilar Plant Assets**

5000.3.2.2.2   **Fair Market Value of Asset Given Up Is Less than Its Book Value**

*[Various Plant Assets Acquired]	xxxx
**Loss On Disposal Of Plant Assets	xxxx
Accumulated Depreciation - [Various Plant Assets]	xxxx
[Various Plant Assets Given Up]	xxxx
Cash	xxxx

To record exchange of dissimilar plant assets

*The cost of the plant asset acquired equals the fair market value of the asset given up plus any cash paid.

**The loss represents the excess of the book value of the asset given up over its fair market value.

5000.3.2.3   **Exchange (Trade) of Similar Plant Assets (Like-Kind Exchanges)**

Similarity or dissimilarity is determined based on function served. Thus, a mechanical bookkeeping machine and a computer may be similar assets if they are both used for accounting purposes, or they may be dissimilar assets if the computer is used for other than accounting functions. A small truck and a tractor-trailer may be similar assets if both are used for delivery purposes, but they are considered dissimilar if one is used for long-distance hauling and the other for local nondelivery purposes.

5000.3.2.3.1   **Fair Market Value of Asset Given Up Is Less than Its Book Value**

*[Various Plant Assets Acquired]	xxxx
**Loss On Disposal Of Plant Assets	xxxx
Accumulated Depreciation - [Various Plant Assets]	xxxx
[Various Plant Assets Given Up]	xxxx
Cash	xxxx

To record exchange of similar plant assets

*The cost of the plant asset acquired equals the fair market value of the asset given up plus any cash paid.

Important: Make sure all appropriate subheads apply to your entry (see page v for instructions)

5000.3   **Disposition of Plant Assets**
5000.3.2   **Exchange (Trade) of Plant Assets**
5000.3.2.3   **Exchange (Trade) of Similar Plant Assets (Like-Kind Exchanges)**
5000.3.2.3.1   **Fair Market Value of Asset Given Up Is Less than Its Book Value**

**The loss equals the excess of the book value of the asset given up over its fair market value.

5000.3.2.3.2

Fair Market Value of Asset Given Up Exceeds Its Book Value, and No Cash Is Received

The resulting gain (the excess of the fair market value of the asset given up over its book value) is not recorded and instead reduces the cost of the acquired asset.

*[Various Plant Assets Acquired]	xxxx	
Accumulated Depreciation - [Various Plant Assets]	xxxx	
[Various Plant Assets Given Up]		xxxx
Cash		xxxx
To record exchange of similar plant assets		

*The cost of the plant asset acquired equals its fair market value less the unrecorded gain or, equivalently, the book value of the asset given up plus the cash paid.

5000.3.2.3.3

Fair Market Value of Asset Given Up Exceeds Its Book Value, and Cash Is Received

The total gain represents the excess of the fair market value of the asset given up over its book value. However, only a portion of the total gain may be recognized as explained in the note below.

Cash	xxxx	
*[Various Plant Assets Acquired]	xxxx	
Accumulated Depreciation - [Various Plant Assets]		xxxx
[Various Plant Assets Given Up]		xxxx
**Gain On Disposal Of Plant Assets		xxxx
To record exchange of similar plant assets		

*The cost of the plant asset acquired equals its fair market value less the portion of the gain deferred or, equivalently, the total book value of the asset given up less the portion of the book value presumed exchanged.

Important: Make sure all appropriate subheads apply to your entry (see page v for instructions)

5000.3	**Disposition of Plant Assets**
5000.3.2	**Exchange (Trade) of Plant Assets**
5000.3.2.3	**Exchange (Trade) of Similar Plant Assets (Like-Kind Exchanges)**
5000.3.2.3.3	**Fair Market Value of Asset Given Up Exceeds Its Book Value, and Cash Is Received**

**The amount of gain recognized is determined by multiplying the total gain by a fraction. The numerator of the fraction is the amount of cash received, and the denominator of the fraction is the sum of the cash received plus the fair market value of the new asset acquired. For example, if the total gain is $1,000, cash of $4,000 is received, and the fair market value of the new asset is $20,000, only $200 of the gain is recognized [$1,000 X ($4,000/$20,000)].

5000.3.3   ## Involuntary Conversion (Casualty Loss) of Plant Assets

Plant assets are sometimes unintentionally lost as a result of an act of nature (e.g., earthquake, fire, flood, etc.) or of the government (e.g., condemnation). These dispositions are known as involuntary conversions. If such events are both unusual and nonrecurring, any gains and losses from the event are reported on the income statement as extraordinary.

5000.3.3.1   ## Updating Book Value of Plant Asset

Depreciation Expense - [Various Plant Assets]	xxxx	
Accumulated Depreciation - [Various Plant Assets]		xxxx
To record depreciation up to the date of disposition		

5000.3.3.2   ## Recording the Loss

Fire ([Various Casualty]) Loss	xxxx	
Accumulated Depreciation - [Various Plant Assets]	xxxx	
[Various Plant Assets]		xxxx
To record casualty loss		

5000.3.3.3   ## Receipt of Insurance Proceeds (Reimbursement from Insurance Company)

Cash	xxxx	
*Fire ([Various Casualty]) Loss		xxxx
To record receipt of insurance proceeds		

Important: Make sure all appropriate subheads apply to your entry (see page v for instructions)

5000.3	**Disposition of Plant Assets**
5000.3.3	**Involuntary Conversion (Casualty Loss) of Plant Assets**
5000.3.3.3	**Receipt of Insurance Proceeds (Reimbursement from Insurance Company)**

---

*If the cash is received in a different period than the loss was recorded, this account will have been closed and this credit must be made to a gain account. It is not unusual for the amount of insurance proceeds to exceed the amount of loss recorded, in which case a gain must be recorded for the difference.

5000.3.4   **Scrapping (or Abandoning) of Plant Assets**

5000.3.4.1   **Updating Book Value of Plant Asset**

Depreciation Expense - [Various Plant Assets]	xxxx	
Accumulated Depreciation - [Various Plant Assets]		xxxx
To record depreciation up to the date of disposition		

5000.3.4.2   **Recording Scrapping (or Abandoning) of Plant Assets**

Accumulated Depreciation - [Various Plant Assets]	xxxx	
*Loss On Sale Of Plant Assets	xxxx	
[Various Plant Assets]		xxxx
To record abandonment of plant assets		

*The loss recognized is equal to the asset's current book value and is not considered extraordinary.

5000.3.5   **Donation (Contribution) of Plant Assets**

*Donation (Contribution) Expense	xxxx	
Accumulated Depreciation - [Various Plant Assets]	xxxx	
**Loss On Disposal Of Plant Assets	xxxx	
[Various Plant Assets]		xxxx
To record donation of plant assets		

*Donation (Contribution) Expense is debited for the fair market value of the donated asset.

**The difference between the asset's fair market value and its current book value is recorded as a gain or loss. Such gains and losses are not considered extraordinary.

Important: Make sure all appropriate subheads apply to your entry (see page v for instructions)

5000.4   **Depreciation of Plant Assets**

5000.4.1   **Depreciation Methods**

Because plant assets, with the exception of land, have limited lives, their cost is allocated to the periods during which they help to generate revenue. This process is called *depreciation*. Regardless of the depreciation method used, a plant asset cannot be depreciated below its expected salvage, or residual, value. A plant asset's cost (less salvage value) is depreciated over its expected service life, which may be less than its actual physical life. Salvage value may be zero.

5000.4.1.1   **Straight-line Depreciation Method**

The straight-line method is used to depreciate a plant asset uniformly over its service life. The assumption behind charging a constant amount to depreciation each period is that the quality and quantity of the benefits of the asset and the expense of repairs and maintenance are constant over the asset's service life. *See GEN5000.4.2* for partial period depreciation and *GEN5000.4.3* for revision of depreciation rates.

> *Depreciation Expense - [Various Plant Assets]   xxxx
>   Accumulated Depreciation - [Various Plant Assets]   xxxx
>   *To record depreciation*

*Current period depreciation expense (D) is determined by dividing the basis for depreciation [cost (C) less salvage value (SV)] by the number of months or years (N) of expected service life:

$$D = (C - SV)/N$$

5000.4.1.2   **Units-of-Production Depreciation Method**

The units-of-production method is used to depreciate plant assets whose service lives are more affected by use than by the mere passage of time. Because the amount of depreciation is tied to asset use, this method usually results in a depreciation charge that varies from year to year.

Important: Make sure all appropriate subheads apply to your entry (see page v for instructions)

5000.4	**Depreciation of Plant Assets**	
5000.4.1	**Depreciation Methods**	
5000.4.1.2	**Units-of-Production Depreciation Method**	

---

*Depreciation Expense - [Various Plant Assets]   xxxx
        Accumulated Depreciation - [Various Plant Assets]   xxxx
    To record depreciation*

*Current period depreciation expense (D) is determined by multiplying the number of units produced during the current period (CU) by a predetermined deprecia- tion rate per unit (R). The predetermined rate is found by dividing the basis for depreciation [cost (C) less salvage value (SV)] by the total number of units the asset is estimated to produce during its useful life (TU). Thus,

$$R \; 5 \; (C - SV)/TU$$
$$\text{and}$$
$$D = R \; X \; CU$$

For example, if a truck with a cost of $25,000 and a salvage value of $5,000 is estimated to be driven a total of 150,000 miles during its life and it is driven 20,000 miles in one period, the predetermined depreciation rate is $0.13 per mile [$25,000 - $5,000)/150,000] and current depreciation is $2,600 ($0.13 X 20,000).

5000.4.1.3

Sum-of-the-Years'-Digits (SYD) Depreciation Method

The sum-of-the-years'-digits (SYD) method and the declining balance method are referred to as accelerated depreciation methods in that they result in higher depreciation in earlier years and lower depreciation charges in later years (i.e., these methods result in a declining depreciation charge). Accelerated depreciation methods are used for plant assets that are expected to be more productive (efficient) in earlier years than in later years and whose repair and maintenance costs are expected to increase significantly over time.

*Depreciation Expense - [Various Plant Assets]   xxxx
        Accumulated Depreciation - [Various Plant Assets]   xxxx
    To record depreciation*

*Current period depreciation expense (D) is determined by multiplying the basis for depreciation [cost (C) less salvage value (SV)] by a fraction whose numerator is the number of years of remaining life (RL) at the beginning of the year, and whose denominator is the sum-of-the-years'-digits (SYD) for the total useful life. Thus,

$$D = (C - SV) \; X \; (RL/SYD)$$

Important: Make sure all appropriate subheads apply to your entry (see page v for instructions)

5000.4   **Depreciation of Plant Assets**
5000.4.1   **Depreciation Methods**
5000.4.1.3   **Sum-of-the-Years'-Digits (SYD) Depreciation Method**

The SYD for an asset having a three-year useful life is 6 (1 + 2 + 3), while the SYD for a five-year useful life is 15 (1 + 2 + 3 + 4 + 5). (The following formula may be used to determine the SYD for any period: $N(N + 1)/2$ where N = number of years of useful life.) Thus, the fraction applied to calculate depreciation for the second year of life of an asset with a total useful life of 5 years is 4/15.

For example, an asset with a cost of $35,000, a salvage value of $2,000, and a life of 5 years would be depreciated $11,000 the first year [($35,000 -$2,000)/(5/15)] and $8,800 the second year [($35,000 - $2,000)/(4/15)]. *See GEN5000.4.2* for partial period depreciation and *GEN5000.4.3* for revision of depreciation rates.

5000.4.1.4   **Declining Balance Depreciation (Double Declining Balance Depreciation)(150% Declining Balance Depreciation)**

Declining balance and sum-of-the-years'-digits depreciation methods are referred to as accelerated depreciation methods in that they result in higher depreciation in earlier years and lower depreciation charges in later years. These methods are used for plant assets that are expected to be more productive (efficient) in earlier years than in later years and whose repair and maintenance costs are expected to increase significantly over time.

> *Depreciation Expense - [Various Plant Assets]   xxxx
>   Accumulated Depreciation - [Various Plant Assets]   xxxx
>   *To record depreciation*

*Current period depreciation expense (D) is determined by multiplying the basis for depreciation [cost (C) less accumulated depreciation (AD) at the beginning of the period] by a fraction whose numerator is 2 (some companies use 1.5) and whose denominator is the total number of periods of useful life (N); e.g., for an asset with a 10-year useful life, this fraction would be 2/10. Thus,

$$D = (C - AD) \times (2/N)$$

For example, an asset with a cost of $20,000 and a useful life of 5 years would be depreciated $8,000 the first year [$20,000 X (2/5)], $4,800 the second year [($20,000 - $8,000) X (2/5)], and $2,880 the third year [($20,000 - $12,800) X (2/5)].

This method will usually result in the asset being fully depreciated before its estimated useful life is expired. Because of this, when the current period depreciation expense

Important: Make sure all appropriate subheads apply to your entry (see page v for instructions)

5000.4   **Depreciation of Plant Assets**
5000.4.1   **Depreciation Methods**
5000.4.1.4   **Declining Balance Depreciation (Double Declining Balance Depreciation)(150% Declining Balance Depreciation)**

---

calculated under this method would be less than that under the straight-line method, some companies switch to the straight-line method for the remaining useful life of the asset. Under the declining balance depreciation method, salvage value is never deducted from cost in the calculation of depreciation, and the asset is never depreciated below its salvage value or below zero. *See GEN5000.4.2* for partial period depreciation and *GEN5000.4.3* for revision of depreciation rates.

5000.4.1.5   **Inventory Depreciation Method**

The inventory method is used to depreciate small plant assets such as hand tools and is based on physical inventories taken at the beginning and end of the period.

       *Depreciation Expense - Tools ([Various Small
            Plant Assets])   xxxx
           **Tools ([Various Small Plant Assets])   xxxx
       To record depreciation

*Current period depreciation is determined as follows: Beginning of Period Inventory Value + Cost of Tools Acquired During the Period - End of Period Inventory Value.

**An accumulated depreciation account is not normally used with this depreciation method.

5000.4.1.6   **Retirement and Replacement Depreciation Methods**

The retirement and replacement depreciation methods are used to depreciate quantities of similar low value plant assets based on their retirement or replacement. These methods are used primarily, but not exclusively, by public utility firms.

5000.4.1.6.1   **Retirement Depreciation Method**

       *Depreciation Expense - Telephone Poles ([Various
            Plant Assets])   xxxx
           **Telephone Poles ([Various Plant Assets])   xxxx
       To record depreciation

Important: Make sure all appropriate subheads apply to your entry (see page v for instructions)

5000.4   **Depreciation of Plant Assets**
5000.4.1   **Depreciation Methods**
5000.4.1.6   **Retirement and Replacement Depreciation Methods**
5000.4.1.6.1   **Retirement Depreciation Method**

---

*Depreciation expense is recorded only when the plant asset is retired. At that time, the retired asset's cost (less salvage value) is charged to Depreciation Expense. This results in a first-in-first-out (FIFO) depreciation cost flow because it is the cost of the old (earlier acquired) asset that is charged to depreciation.

**Accumulated depreciation accounts are often not used with retirement and replacement depreciation methods.

5000.4.1.6.2   **Replacement Depreciation Method**

    *Depreciation Expense - Telephone Poles ([Various
       Plant Assets])   xxxx
      **Telephone Poles ([Various Plant Assets])   xxxx
   To record depreciation

*Depreciation expense is recorded only when the plant assets are purchased to replace existing assets. At that time, the cost of the asset that replaces the existing asset (less salvage value) is charged to Depreciation Expense. This results in a last-in-first-out (LIFO) depreciation cost flow because it is the cost of the new (newly acquired) asset that is charged to depreciation.

**Accumulated depreciation accounts are often not used with retirement and replacement depreciation methods.

5000.4.1.7   **Group and Composite Depreciation Methods**

Group and Composite depreciation methods are used to depreciate multiple asset accounts using a single depreciation rate. When the assets being depreciated are similar in nature, the method is referred to as a group method. When the assets are dissimilar in nature, the method is referred to as a composite method.

    *Depreciation Expense - [Various Plant Assets]   xxxx
      Accumulated Depreciation - [Various Plant Assets]   xxxx
   To record depreciation

*Under this method, the plant assets are depreciated by multiplying the total original cost of assets being depreciated by a rate determined by dividing the total individual asset annual depreciation (determined on a straight-line basis taking

Important: Make sure all appropriate subheads apply to your entry (see page v for instructions)

5000.4   **Depreciation of Plant Assets**
5000.4.1   **Depreciation Methods**
5000.4.1.7   **Group and Composite Depreciation Methods**

---

salvage value into account) by the total original cost of the assets being depreciated. A new rate must be determined in any subsequent period in which a new asset is acquired or an old asset is disposed of. The composite life is determined by dividing the total individual asset annual depreciation into the total depreciable cost (cost less salvage value) of all assets being depreciated.

5000.4.1.7.1

Disposing of Plant Assets Depreciated Using Group or Composite Depreciation Methods

No gains or losses are recognized upon disposal when the group or composite depreciation method is used.

*Cash	xxxx	
Accumulated Depreciation - [Various Plant Asset]	xxxx	
[Various Plant Assets]		xxxx
To record disposal of plant assets		

*Cash is debited for the amount received for salvage value.

5000.4.2

Partial Period Depreciation

When plant assets are not acquired on the first day of the accounting period, partial year depreciation must be computed. Many variations exist for computing depreciation in the year of acquisition and disposal. Common approaches are described below. Regardless of how depreciation is computed, many firms record depreciation only once a year.

5000.4.2.1

Depreciation Computed to Nearest Full Month

Under this approach, a full month of depreciation is taken if the asset is purchased during the first half of the month or disposed of during the last half of the month. No depreciation is taken for the month if the asset is purchased during the last half of the month or disposed of during the first half of the month.

For example, a plant asset acquired on February 7, 2003, and disposed of on September 10, 2004, would be depreciated 11 months during 2003 and 8 months during 2004 but not below zero or salvage value.

Important: Make sure all appropriate subheads apply to your entry (see page v for instructions)

5000.4   **Depreciation of Plant Assets**
5000.4.2   **Partial Period Depreciation**

5000.4.2.2

Depreciation Computed to Nearest Fraction of a Month

Partial month depreciation is possible under this approach. For example, the plant asset acquired on February 7, 2003, and disposed of on September 10, 2004, would be depreciated 10 3/4 months during 2003 and 8 1/3 months during 2004 but not below zero or salvage value.

5000.4.2.3

Depreciation Computed to Nearest Year

Under this approach, a full year of depreciation is taken if the asset is acquired during the first half of the year or disposed of during the second half of the year and no depreciation if the asset is acquired during the second half of the year or disposed of during the first half of the year.

For example, the plant asset acquired on February 7, 2003, and disposed of on September 10, 2004, would be depreciated for a full year in both 2003 and 2004 but not below zero or salvage value.

5000.4.2.4

Half Year of Depreciation Taken in Year of Acquisition and Half Year in Year of Disposal

The actual dates of acquisition and disposal are not important. For example, a plant asset acquired on February 7, 2003, and disposed of on September 10, 2008, would be depreciated one-half year in 2003, a full year in each year during 2004-2007, and one-half year in 2008 (but not below zero or salvage value).

5000.4.2.5

Full Year of Depreciation Taken in Year of Acquisition and None in Year of Disposal (Vice Versa)

The actual dates of acquisition and disposal are not important. For example, the plant asset acquired on February 7, 2003, and disposed of on September 10, 2004, would be depreciated for a full year in 2003 and not depreciated at all in 2004. Alternatively, no depreciation may be taken in 2003 while a full year is taken in 2004.

Important: Make sure all appropriate subheads apply to your entry (see page v for instructions)

5000.4   **Depreciation of Plant Assets**
5000.4.2   **Partial Period Depreciation**

5000.4.2.6   ## Partial Period Depreciation Illustrated

Assume that a plant asset acquired on March 12, 2003 has a three-year useful life and that depreciation is computed to the nearest full month. Thus, in 2003 it will be depreciated for only 10 months and in 2006 it will be depreciated for only 2 months, as follows:

Straight-Line Depreciation Method

>   2003 The asset will be depreciated for only 10 months (10/12 X Full Year Depreciation Amount)

>   2004: Full Year Depreciation Amount

>   2005: Full Year Depreciation Amount

>   2006: The asset will be depreciated for only 2 months (2/12 X Full Year Depreciation Amount)

Units-of-Production Depreciation Method (Not applicable)

Sum-of-the-Years'-Digits and Declining Balance Depreciation Methods

>   2003: The asset will be depreciated for only 10 months of its first year's life (10/12 X First Year Depreciation Amount)

>   2004: The asset will be depreciated for 12 months, the remaining 2 months of its first year life and 10 months of its second year life (2/12 X First Year Depreciation Amount and 10/12 X Second Year Depreciation Amount)

>   2005: The asset will be depreciated for 12 months, the remaining 2 months of its second year life and 10 months of its third year life (2/12 X Second Year Depreciation Amount and 10/12 X Third Year Depreciation Amount)

>   2006: The asset will be depreciated for only 2 months which are the last 2 months of its third year life (2/12 X Third Year Depreciation Amount)

Important: Make sure all appropriate subheads apply to your entry (see page v for instructions)

5000.4   Depreciation of Plant Assets

5000.4.3   ### Revision of Depreciation Rates

From time to time, it may be necessary to revise a plant asset's depreciation rate due to changes in its estimated useful life and/or salvage value. Revisions are handled on a current and prospective basis (i.e., no changes should be made to prior period results).

> *Depreciation Expense - [Various Plant Assets]   xxxx
>   Accumulated Depreciation - [Various Plant Assets]   xxxx
>   *To record depreciation*

*Current period depreciation is determined as follows: First, compute the asset's current book value. Treat the asset's current book value as its new depreciable basis. Depreciate this new basis (less salvage value) over the asset's remaining useful life as of the beginning of the current period using whatever depreciation method is being used for that asset.

5000.4.4   ### Income Tax Depreciation

Depreciation for tax purposes may be different from depreciation computed for financial reporting purposes. For example, for assets acquired prior to 1981, the IRS permits only the use of the straight-line, sum-of-the-years'-digits, and declining balance depreciation methods. For assets acquired between 1981 and 1986, the IRS requires the use of either straight-line depreciation or the IRS-created Accelerated Cost Recovery System (ACRS). For assets acquired after 1986, the IRS requires the use of either straight-line depreciation or the Modified Accelerated Cost Recovery System (MACRS). ACRS and MACRS specify useful lives for different classes of assets (usually shorter than the assets' actual expected useful lives), zero salvage values, and accelerated depreciation patterns. These methods are generally not acceptable for financial accounting purposes and should not be used except to calculate income taxes. To account for timing differences caused by using ACRS or MACRS for tax purposes and some other method for financial accounting, *see GEN12000.2*.

5000.5   ### Impairment of Value of Plant Assets (Long-Lived Assets)

According to FASB Statement No. 121, *Accounting for the Impairment of Long-Lived Assets and for Long-Lived Assets to Be Disposed Of*, value impairment has occurred if an asset's current book value cannot be fully recovered over its useful life.

Important: Make sure all appropriate subheads apply to your entry (see page v for instructions)

5000.5　　　　　**Impairment of Value of Plant Assets (Long-Lived Assets)**

The following events or changes in circumstances may indicate that the recoverability of the carrying (book) value of an asset should be assessed:

- Significant reduction in the extent to which a plant asset is used.
- Significant change in the manner in which an asset is used
- Significant drop in the market value of an asset
- Significant change in law or environment that could affect the asset's value
- Forecast showing lack of long-term profitability associated with the use of the asset
- Excess cost over originally expected acquisition or construction cost

If events or changes in circumstances indicate the book value of an asset to be held and used may not be recoverable, expected future net cash flows from use and eventual disposition of the asset should be estimated. Future net cash flows are expected future cash inflows to be generated by the asset less expected future cash outflows necessary to obtain those inflows. For the purpose of determining future cash flows, it may be necessary to group assets whose cash flows can be identified and are for the most part independent of cash flows from other assets or groups of assets. If grouping is necessary it should be done only at the lowest level for which there are identifiable independent cash flows. If the future net cash flows (undiscounted and without interest charges) are less than the book value of the asset(s), an impairment loss is recognized.

For example, assume an asset has a book value of $500,000 ($700,000 cost less $200,000 accumulated depreciation). If the asset's undiscounted future net cash flow is $600,000 ($100,000 a year for six years), the asset is not impaired and no loss is recognized. If its undiscounted future net cash flow is $360,000 ($60,000 a year for six years), its value is impaired and a loss is recognized. Calculation of the amount of the loss depends on whether or not the fair market value of the asset is known.

If the assets' fair market value is known, the loss is the excess of the book value over the fair market value. If the fair market value is not known, it must be estimated using the present value of expected future cash inflows. The expected cash flow approach uses all expectations about possible cash flows instead of the single most-likely cash flow. For example, the following table shows by year the range and probability of possible cash inflows expected to result from the use and eventual disposition of an asset or a group of assets over their remaining useful lives of two years. The total present value of future cash inflow (sell in two years) is $42,895,000.

Important: Make sure all appropriate subheads apply to your entry (see page v for instructions)

5000.5   **Impairment of Value of Plant Assets (Long-Lived Assets)**

Year	Cash Flow Estimates (000's)	Probability Assessment	Expected Cash Flows (000's)	Risk-Free Discount Rate	Expected Present Value (000's)
1	$8,000	20%	$1,600		
	$10,000	55%	$5,500		
	$15,000	25%	$3,750		
		100%	$10,850	5.0%	$10,333
2	$7,000	20%	$1,400		
	$10,000	55%	$5,500		
	$15,000	25%	$3,750		
		100%	$10,650	5.0%	$9,660
Total	$15,000	20%	$3,000		
From	$20,000	55%	$11,000		
Use	$30,000	25%	$7,500		
Sale	$20,000	20%	$4,000		
of	$25,000	55%	$13,750		
Asset	$30,000	25%	$7,500		
		100%	$25,250	5.0%	$22,902
Total					$42,895

The Present value of future expected cash inflows ($42,895,000) is used to determine the assets' impairment loss.

If the plant (long-lived) assets acquired in a business combination that resulted in the recognition of goodwill are impaired and are subject to an impairment loss the carrying value of the identified goodwill should be eliminated before making any reduction in the carrying amounts of the impaired assets. *See GEN6000.1.1.3.*

5000.5.1   **Recording Impairment of Value**

Recording impairment of value differs slightly depending on whether the assets involved are to be held and used or disposed of.

Important: Make sure all appropriate subheads apply to your entry (see page v for instructions)

5000.5   **Impairment of Value of Plant Assets (Long-Lived Assets)**
5000.5.1   **Recording Impairment of Value**

5000.5.1.1   **Assets to Be Held and Used**

> *Loss Due To Impairment Of Value Of Assets   xxxx
>   Accumulated Depreciation - [Various Plant Assets]   xxxx
> *To record impairment of value of assets*

*The loss recognized equals the excess of the asset's current book value over its fair value, if known, or its discounted net future cash flows. Such losses are not considered extraordinary.

Once the loss is recorded, the resulting new book value becomes the asset's new cost. Therefore, future depreciation charges reflect the change in the carrying value of the asset due to impairment (see revision of depreciation rates in *GEN5000.4.3*).

For assets to be held and used, restoration of previously recognized impairment losses and carrying value due to increased future net cash flows or fair value is not allowed.

5000.5.1.2   **Assets to Be Disposed Of**

Assets to be disposed of by sale or abandonment *(see GEN5000.3.4)* are reported at the lower of carrying value or fair value less cost to sell and are not depreciated.

> *Loss Due To Impairment Of Value Of Assets   xxxx
>   Accumulated Depreciation - [Various Plant Assets]   xxxx
> *To record impairment of value of assets*

*The loss recognized is the excess of the asset's carrying (book) value over its fair market value adjusted for additional costs necessary to sell the asset.

If the fair value of the assets to be disposed of increases before disposal, recovery of impairment losses previously recognized can be recorded.

5000.5.2   **Recovery of Impairment Losses**

Recovery of impairment losses previously recognized for assets to be held and used cannot be recorded. Recovery of impairment losses previously recognized for assets to be disposed of are recorded as follows:

Important: Make sure all appropriate subheads apply to your entry (see page v for instructions)

5000.5   **Impairment of Value of Plant Assets (Long-Lived Assets)**
5000.5.2   **Recovery of Impairment Losses**

---

*Accumulated Depreciation - [Various Assets]	xxxx	
*Recovery of Impairment Losses		xxxx

To record recovery of impairment losses

*The amount of the recovery is the lower of the amount of the impairment loss originally recorded or the increase in the asset's fair value. After this entry is made, the carrying value of the asset(s) cannot be greater than it was immediately before the impairment loss was recognized.

5000.6   **Natural Resources**

Natural Resources include oil, gas, coal, ore, and timber. Depletion expense measures the amount of the natural resource used up during the current period.

5000.6.1   **Acquisition of Natural Resources**

Natural resources are assets that can be produced only by nature and are consumed by extraction or harvest such as:
-oil and gas deposits
-mineral deposits
-timber tracts.

5000.6.1.1   **Acquisition Costs of Known Resources**

Acquisition costs may include costs of property or property rights and lease or royalty payments.

[Various Natural Resources]	xxxx	
Cash ([Various Accounts])		xxxx

To record acquisition of natural resource

5000.6.1.2   **Acquisition Costs Where Resource Presence Is Uncertain**

Acquisition costs are costs of property, property rights and leases or royalties.

Important: Make sure all appropriate subheads apply to your entry (see page v for instructions)

5000.6   **Natural Resources**
5000.6.1   **Acquisition of Natural Resources**
5000.6.1.2   **Acquisition Costs Where Resource Presence Is Uncertain**

5000.6.1.2.1   **Property on Which the Natural Resource Is Located Is Owned**

    *Undeveloped Property   xxxx
      Cash ([Various Accounts])   xxxx
    To record acquisition of natural resource

    *If a natural resource is found, the costs are transferred to a natural resource account.
    If no resource is found, the costs (except salvage value) are written off as a loss.

5000.6.1.2.2   **Property on Which the Natural Resource Is Located Is Not Owned**

    *Undeveloped [Various Natural Resources]   xxxx
      Cash ([Various Accounts])   xxxx
    To record acquisition of natural resource

    *If a natural resource is found, the costs are transferred to a natural resource account.
    If no resource is found, the costs are written off as a loss.

5000.6.1.2.3   **Natural Resource Is Found After Prior Recognition of Acquisition with
Resource Presence Unknown**

    [Various Natural Resources]   xxxx
      Undeveloped [Various Natural Resources]   xxxx
    To record natural resource found

5000.6.1.2.4   **Natural Resource Not Found After Prior Recognition of Acquisition
with Resource Presence Unknown**

    Loss On Exploration   xxxx
      Undeveloped [Various Natural Resources]   xxxx
    To record loss on exploration

5000.6.2   **Exploration Costs Associated with Natural Resources**

Three acceptable treatments of exploration costs are (1) to expense all exploration
costs, (2) to capitalize (i.e., debit a natural resource asset account) exploration costs

Important: Make sure all appropriate subheads apply to your entry (see page v for instructions)

5000.6   **Natural Resources**
5000.6.2   **Exploration Costs Associated with Natural Resources**

---

related to successful projects, and expense exploration costs related to unsuccessful projects, and (3) to capitalize all exploration costs.

5000.6.2.1   **Expensing Exploration Costs**

Exploration Expense	xxxx	
Cash ([Various Accounts])		xxxx
To record exploration expense		

5000.6.2.2   **Capitalizing Exploration Costs**

[Various Natural Resources]	xxxx	
Cash ([Various Accounts])		xxxx
To capitalize exploration costs		

5000.6.3   **Development Costs**

Development costs include tangible equipment and intangible costs associated with finding and preparing natural resources for extraction. For example, such tangible equipment includes oil rigs, conveyor systems, and tree cutters, Intangible costs include the remaining costs associated with extracting the resource (i.e., the costs of using the tangible equipment).

5000.6.3.1   **Tangible Equipment Development Costs**

These are the costs of machinery, equipment, and buildings located at the site of the natural resource and used in extraction operations.

*[Various Equipment Accounts]	xxxx	
Cash ([Various Accounts])		xxxx
To record tangible equipment development costs		

*Tangible assets that can be moved are depreciated over their useful life. Tangible assets that cannot be moved should be depreciated over the shorter of their own useful lives or over the life of the natural resource. *See GEN5000.4.1* for depreciation methods.

Important: Make sure all appropriate subheads apply to your entry (see page v for instructions)

5000.6   **Natural Resources**
5000.6.3   **Development Costs**

5000.6.3.2   **Intangible Development Costs**

> [Various Natural Resources]   xxxx
>   Cash ([Various Accounts])   xxxx
> *To record development costs*

5000.6.4   **Depletion of Natural Resources**

5000.6.4.1   **Determining Depletion Rate**

Natural resources are depleted using an approach similar to units-of-production depreciation. The depletion rate is determined by dividing the total cost of the natural resource (including appropriate acquisition, exploration, and development costs) by the total estimated units extractable. *See GEN5000.6.1 to GEN5000.6.3.*

5000.6.4.2   **Recording Current Period Depletion**

> *Depletion Expense - [Various Natural Resources]   xxxx
>   **Accumulated Depletion - [Various Natural
>   Resources]   xxxx
> *To record depletion*

*Amount = Current Period Units Extracted X Depletion Rate. *See GEN5000.6.4.1.*

**The natural resource account, e.g., Oil Deposits, may be credited instead

5000.6.5   **Revision of Depletion Rate**

It may be necessary to revise the depletion rate for changes in management's estimate of a natural resource's recoverable reserves. Such revisions are handled on a current and prospective basis (i.e., no changes are made to prior period amounts).
The revised rate is undepleted cost divided by newly estimated recoverable reserves.

> Depletion Expense - [Various Natural Resources]   xxxx
>   Accumulated Depletion - [Various Natural
>   Resources]   xxxx
> *To record depletion*

Important: Make sure all appropriate subheads apply to your entry (see page v for instructions)

5000.6   **Natural Resources**

5000.6.6   **Impairment of Value of Natural Resources**

If the value of a natural resource has been impaired, a loss should be recognized.

*Loss Due To Impairment Of Natural Resource	xxxx	
Accumulated Depletion - [Various Natural Resources]		xxxx

To record loss due to impairment of natural resource

5000.6.7   **Impairment of Value of Tangible Equipment Associated with Natural Resources**

An impairment loss for these assets is recognized as shown at *GEN5000.5.1*.

5000.6.8   **Liquidating Dividends**

Liquidating dividends are sometimes paid to shareholders to return their capital investments when a corporation, whose single purpose is to extract natural resources from a specific property, decides to discontinue or reduce the scope of its operations.

*Retained Earnings	xxxx	
Additional Paid-In Capital - Common (Preferred) Stock	xxxx	
Cash		xxxx

To record declaration and payment of liquidating dividend

*Retained Earnings is debited for amounts up to its current balance.

**This debit is for the excess of cash paid over the debit to Retained Earnings..

TABLE OF CONTENTS

GEN6000   INTANGIBLE ASSETS

6000.1 | **Acquisition and Amortization of Intangible Assets**

Intangible assets include:
- goodwill
- patents
- copyrights
- trademarks and trade names
- franchises and licenses
- purchased computer software
- leasehold improvements
- organization costs.
- computer software development costs.

Intangible assets are recorded at cost. Cost includes the purchase price plus any expenditure required to get the asset in place ready for use, such as:
- legal fees
- filing fees.

If an intangible asset is acquired in exchange for a noncash asset or by issuing stock, the intangible asset is recorded at its fair market value or the fair market value of the consideration given, whichever is most readily determined. Finally, when a group of intangible assets is acquired in a single transaction (i.e., a lump sum purchase), the cost must be allocated among the various assets based on their fair market value or their relative sales value.

The illustrations below are for acquisition of intangible assets for cash or cash and liabilities. For acquisition for stock, *see GEN9000.1.6.*

6000.1.1 | **Goodwill**

Goodwill is recorded only when an entire business is purchased. Goodwill is the excess of the purchase price paid over the sum of the fair market values of the purchased entity's separately identifiable assets less liabilities assumed.

Important: Make sure all appropriate subheads apply to your entry (see page v for instructions)

6000.1   **Acquisition and Amortization of Intangible Assets**
6000.1.1   **Goodwill**

6000.1.1.1   **Acquisition of Goodwill**

6000.1.1.1.1   **Purchase Price Exceeds Total Fair Market Value of Separately Identifiable Assets Less Liabilities Assumed**

[Various Receivables]	xxxx	
[Various Inventories]	xxxx	
[Various Current and Noncurrent Assets]	xxxx	
*Goodwill	xxxx	
Cash		xxxx
[Various Liabilities]		xxxx

To record purchase of a business

*The assets and liabilities acquired in the purchase are recorded at their fair market value. The excess of the purchase price over the total fair market value of the acquired net assets (assets less liabilities) is debited to Goodwill.

6000.1.1.1.2   **Price Is Less than Total Fair Market Value of Separately Identifiable Assets Less Liabilities Assumed (Negative Goodwill)**

*[Various Receivables]	xxxx	
*[Various Inventories]	xxxx	
*[Various Other Current Assets]	xxxx	
**[Various Noncurrent Assets]	xxxx	
***Extraordinary Gain -- Excess Of Fair Market Value Over Cost Of Net Assets Acquired		xxxx
[Various Liabilities]		xxxx
Cash		xxxx

To record gains arising from negative goodwill

*These assets are recorded at their fair market value.

**These noncurrent assets are recorded at their fair market value less a proportionate share of the excess of the sum of the fair market values of the net assets acquired over the purchase price. See the next note (***).

***The assets and liabilities acquired in the purchase are recorded at their fair market value. In some cases, the sum of the amounts assigned to assets acquired and

Important: Make sure all appropriate subheads apply to your entry (see page v for instructions)

6000.1   **Acquisition and Amortization of Intangible Assets**
6000.1.1   **Goodwill**
6000.1.1.1   **Acquisition of Goodwill**
6000.1.1.1.2   **Price Is Less than Total Fair Market Value of Separately Identifiable Assets Less Liabilities Assumed (Negative Goodwill)**

---

liabilities assumed will exceed the cost of the acquired entity *(excess over cost* or *excess)*. That excess must be allocated as a pro rata reduction of the amounts that otherwise would have been assigned to all NONCURRENT assets acquired in the transaction except (a) financial assets other than investments accounted for by the equity method, (b) assets to be disposed of by sale, (c) deferred tax assets, and (d) prepaid assets relating to pension or other postretirement benefit plans.

If any excess remains after reducing to zero the amounts that otherwise would have been assigned to those assets, any remaining credit is then recognized as an extraordinary gain in the period in which the business combination is completed.

6000.1.1.2   **Impairment of Goodwill**

Goodwill and other intangible assets that have indefinite useful lives will not be amortized but rather will be tested at least annually for impairment. Impairment is the condition that exists when the carrying amount of goodwill exceeds its implied fair value.

Determination of goodwill consists of two steps. The first step compares the fair value of a reporting unit with its carrying amount, including goodwill, to identify potential impairment. If the fair value of a reporting unit exceeds its carrying amount, goodwill is considered not impaired, thus the second step is not necessary. If the carrying amount of a reporting unit exceeds its fair value, the second step must be performed to measure the amount of impairment loss, if any.

In the second step the implied fair value of the reporting unit goodwill is compared with the carrying amount of goodwill. If the carrying amount exceeds the implied fair value, an impairment loss must be recognized in an amount equal to that excess. After a goodwill impairment loss is recognized, the adjusted carrying amount of goodwill shall be its new accounting basis. Subsequent reversal of a previously recognized goodwill impairment loss is phohibited once the measurement of that loss is completed. A goodwill impairment loss, if any, is recognized as follows:

Loss Due to Impairment of Goodwill	xxxx	
Goodwill		xxxx
To record impairment loss		

Important: Make sure all appropriate subheads apply to your entry (see page v for instructions)

6000.1   **Acquisition and Amortization of Intangible Assets**

6000.1.2   **Patents**

A patent is granted by the U.S. government giving the patent holder the exclusive right to use, manufacture, and sell a product or process for 17 years.

6000.1.2.1   **Acquisition of Patents**

6000.1.2.1.1   **Acquisition of Patents for Cash**

*Patents	xxxx	
Cash		xxxx

To record purchase of patent

*The cost of a purchased patent includes the price paid plus other costs necessary for the purchase, such as legal fees. Costs of developing a patented product are research and development (R&D) costs and expensed when incurred. *See GEN6000.3*

6000.1.2.1.2   **Acquisition of Patents for Liabilities (or Liabilities and Cash)**

*Patents	xxxx	
Notes Payable		xxxx
[Various Liabilities]		xxxx
Cash		xxxx

To record purchase of patent

*Patents is debited for the cash paid plus all liabilities assumed.

6000.1.2.2   **Legal Fees and Other Costs Incurred to Defend or Protect a Patent**

6000.1.2.2.1   **Legal Fees and Other Costs Incurred if Patent Is Successfully Defended or Protected**

See GEN6000.1.2.2.2 if the patent is not successfully defended or protected.

INTANGIBLE ASSETS

Important: Make sure all appropriate subheads apply to your entry (see page v for instructions)

6000.1   **Acquisition and Amortization of Intangible Assets**
6000.1.2   **Patents**
6000.1.2.2   **Legal Fees and Other Costs Incurred to Defend or Protect a Patent**
6000.1.2.2.1   **Legal Fees and Other Costs Incurred if Patent is Successfully Defended or Protected**

---

*Patents	xxxx	
Cash		xxxx

To record costs of successfully defending or protecting a patent

*Patents is debited for all costs of successfully defending or protecting a patent. The new balance in Patents is amortized over the remaining useful life of the patent.

6000.1.2.2.2   **Legal Fees and Other Costs Incurred if Patent Is Unsuccessfully Defended or Protected**

See GEN6000.1.2.2.1 if the patent is successfully defended or protected.

*Loss From Unsuccessful Defense Of Patent	xxxx	
**Patents		xxxx
Cash		xxxx

To record costs of unsuccessful defense of patent and to write off the patent

*This loss account is debited for all costs incurred in the unsuccessful defense of the patent. The cost of the patent that was unsuccessfully defended or protected is also written off against this loss account if the patent is consequently considered generally indefensible.

**The cost of the patent that was unsuccessfully defended or protected is written off against the loss account if the patent is consequently considered generally indefensible.

6000.1.2.3   **Amortization and Impairment of Patents**

Patents are amortized over their useful lives to the reporting entity, or their legal lives (17 years) whichever is shorter as follows:

Amortization Expense - Patents	xxxx	
Patents		xxxx

To record amortization of patent

If a patent becomes worthless or its value is impaired, it should be written off or reduced to its remaining fair market value as follows:

Important: Make sure all appropriate subheads apply to your entry (see page v for instructions)

6000.1   **Acquisition and Amortization of Intangible Assets**
6000.1.2   **Patents**
6000.1.2.3   **Amortization and Impairment of Patents**

Loss Due to Impairment of Patents	xxxx	
Patents		xxxx
To record impairment loss		

6000.1.3   **Copyrights**

A copyright is granted by the U.S. government, giving the holder the exclusive right to reproduce and sell a:
　　　　　-book
　　　　　-musical composition
　　　　　-film
　　　　　-other work of art
for a period of 50 years beyond the death of the author or artist.

6000.1.3.1   **Acquisition of Copyrights**

6000.1.3.1.1   **Acquisition of Copyrights for Cash**

*Copyrights	xxxx	
Cash		xxxx
To record purchase of copyright		

*Copyrights should be debited for the cost of acquiring copyrights. However, research and development (R&D) costs of creating a copyright should be expensed as incurred. *See GEN6000.3* for a discussion of R&D.

6000.1.3.1.2   **Acquisition of Copyrights for Liabilities (or Liabilities and Cash)**

*Copyrights	xxxx	
Notes Payable		xxxx
[Various Liabilities]		xxxx
Cash		xxxx
To record purchase of copyright		

*Copyrights is debited for the amount of cash paid plus all liabilities assumed.

Important: Make sure all appropriate subheads apply to your entry (see page v for instructions)

6000.1   **Acquisition and Amortization of Intangible Assets**
6000.1.3   **Copyrights**

6000.1.3.2   **Legal Fees and Other Costs Incurred to Defend or Protect a Copyright**

6000.1.3.2.1   **Legal Fees and Other Costs Incurred if Copyright Is Successfully Defended or Protected**

See GEN6000.1.3.2.2 if the copyright is not successfully defended or protected.

*Copyrights	xxxx	
Cash		xxxx

To record costs of successfully defending or protecting a copyright

*Copyrights is debited for all costs of successfully defending or protecting a copyright. The new balance in Copyrights is amortized over the remaining useful life.

6000.1.3.2.2   **Legal Fees and Other Costs Incurred if Copyright Is Unsuccessfully Defended or Protected**

See GEN6000.1.3.2.1 if the copyright is successfully defended or protected.

*Loss From Unsuccessful Defense Of Copyright	xxxx	
**Copyrights		xxxx
Cash		xxxx

To record costs of unsuccessful defense of copyright and to write off the copyright

*This loss account is debited for all costs incurred in the unsuccessful defense of the copyright. The cost of the copyright that was unsuccessfully defended or protected is also written off against this loss account if the copyright is consequently considered generally indefensible.

**The cost of the copyright that was unsuccessfully defended or protected is written off against the loss account if the copyright is consequently considered generally indefensible.

INTANGIBLE ASSETS

Important: Make sure all appropriate subheads apply to your entry (see page v for instructions)

6000.1 **Acquisition and Amortization of Intangible Assets**
6000.1.3 **Copyrights**

6000.1.3.3 **Amortization and Impairment of Copyrights**

Copyrights are amortized over their legal lives (the life of the artist or author plus 50 years), or their useful lives whichever is shorter.

Amortization Expense - Copyrights	xxxx	
Copyrights		xxxx
To record copyright amortization		

If a copyright becomes worthless or its value is impaired, it should be written off or reduced to its remaining fair market value as follows:

Loss Due to Impairment of Copyright	xxxx	
Copyrights		xxxx
To record impairment loss		

6000.1.4 **Trademarks and Trade Names**

Trademarks and trade names include:
- designs
- brand names
- symbols
- and any other feature that permits the easy recognition of a product or service.

6000.1.4.1 **Acquisition of Trademarks and Trade Names**

6000.1.4.1.1 **Acquisition of Trademarks and Trade Names for Cash**

*Trademarks (Trade Names)	xxxx	
Cash		xxxx
To record purchase of trademark (or trade name)		

*The cost of a purchased trademark (or trade name) includes the purchase price plus any purchase-related costs such as:
- consulting fees
- legal fees
- registration fees.

INTANGIBLE ASSETS

Important: Make sure all appropriate subheads apply to your entry (see page v for instructions)

6000.1   **Acquisition and Amortization of Intangible Assets**
6000.1.4   **Trademarks and Trade Names**
6000.1.4.1   **Acquisition of Trademarks and Trade Names**
6000.1.4.1.1   **Acquisition of Trademarks and Trade Names for Cash**

The costs of successfully defending or protecting trademarks and trade names are also debited to Trademarks (or Trade Names). The costs related to developing a trademark (or trade name) should be expensed when incurred. *See GEN6000.3* for a discussion of R&D costs.

6000.1.4.1.2   **Acquisition of Trademarks and Trade Names for Liabilities (or Liabilities and Cash)**

*Trademarks (Trade Names)	xxxx	
Notes Payable		xxxx
[Various Liabilities]		xxxx
Cash		xxxx
To record purchase of trademarks (or trade names)		

*Trademarks (or Trade Names) is debited for the amount of cash paid plus all liabilities assumed.

6000.1.4.2   **Legal Fees and Other Costs Incurred to Defend or Protect a Trademark or Trade Name**

6000.1.4.2.1   **Legal Fees and Other Costs Incurred if a Trademark or Trade Name Is Successfully Defended or Protected**

See GEN6000.1.4.2.2 if the trademark or trade name is not successfully defended or protected.

*Trademarks (Trade Names)	xxxx	
Cash		xxxx
To record costs of successfully defending or protecting a trademark (or trade name)		

*Trademarks (or Trade Names) is debited for all costs of successfully defending or protecting a trademark (or trade name). The new balance in Trademarks (or Trade Names) is amortized over the remaining useful life of the trademark (or trade name).

Important: Make sure all appropriate subheads apply to your entry (see page v for instructions)

6000.1	**Acquisition and Amortization of Intangible Assets**
6000.1.4	**Trademarks and Trade Names**
6000.1.4.2	**Legal Fees and Other Costs Incurred to Defend or Protect a Trademark or Trade Name**

6000.1.4.2.2   **Legal Fees and Other Costs Incurred if a Trademark or Trade Name Is Unsuccessfully Defended or Protected**

See GEN6000.1.4.2.1 if the trademark or trade name is successfully defended or protected.

*Loss From Unsuccessful Defense Of Trademark (Trade Name)	xxxx	
**Trademarks (Trade Names)		xxxx
Cash		xxxx

To record costs of unsuccessful defense of trademark (or trade name) and to write off the trademark or (trade name)

*This loss account is debited for all costs incurred in the unsuccessful defense of the trademark (or trade name). The cost of the trademark (or trade name) that was unsuccessfully defended or protected is also written off against this loss account if the trademark (or trade name) is consequently considered generally indefensible.

**The cost of the trademark (or trade name) that was unsuccessfully defended or protected is written off against the loss account if the trademark (or trade name) is consequently considered indefensible.

6000.1.4.3   **Amortization and Impairment of Trademarks and Trade Names**

Trademarks and trade names registered with the U.S. Patent Office are protected for 20 years. Because registration can be renewed, trademarks and trade names can be protected indefinitely and are not amortized. If a trademark or trade name becomes worthless or its value impaired, it should be written off or reduced to its remaining fair market value as follows:

Loss Due to Impairment of Trademark (Trade Name)	xxxx	
*Trademark (Trade Name)		xxxx

To record impairment loss

6000.1.5   **Franchises and Licenses**

A franchise is a right to use property or to provide a product or service. Licenses include agreements with government units or agencies granting a firm the right to use

Important: Make sure all appropriate subheads apply to your entry (see page v for instructions)

6000.1   **Acquisition and Amortization of Intangible Assets**
6000.1.5   **Franchises and Licenses**

---

government property for business purposes. For example, an electric utility is permitted to install power lines over public property.

6000.1.5.1   **Acquisition of Franchises and Licenses**

6000.1.5.1.1   **Acquisition of Franchises or Licenses for Cash**

*Franchises (Licenses)	xxxx	
Cash		xxxx
To record purchase of franchise (or license)		

*The cost of a purchased franchise (or license) includes the purchase price (includ-ing any lump sum advance payments) plus all purchase-related costs such as legal fees. Subsequent annual payments required by the franchise agreement are not charged to Franchises but are expensed in the period incurred.

6000.1.5.1.2   **Acquisition of Franchises or Licenses for Liabilities (or Liabilities and Cash)**

*Franchises (Licenses)	xxxx	
Notes Payable		xxxx
[Various Liabilities]		xxxx
Cash		xxxx
To record purchase of franchise (or license)		

*Franchises (or Licenses) is debited for the cash paid plus all liabilities assumed.

6000.1.5.2   **Amortization and Impairment of Franchises and Licenses**

Franchises and licenses may be granted for a definite or an indefinite period. If they are granted for an indefinite period, they *are not* subject to annual amortization. If they are granted for a definite period, they should be amortized over the lesser of their useful lives or contractual lives as follows:

Amortization Expense - Franchises (Licenses)	xxxx	
*Franchises (Licenses)		xxxx
To record amortization		

INTANGIBLE ASSETS

Important: Make sure all appropriate subheads apply to your entry (see page v for instructions)

6000.1   **Acquisition and Amortization of Intangible Assets**
6000.1.5   **Franchises and Licenses**
6000.1.5.2   **Amortization and Impairment of Franchises and Licenses**

If a franchise or license agreement becomes worthless or its value is impaired, it should be written off or reduced to its remaining fair market value as follows:

Loss Due to Impairment of Franchise (License)	xxxx	
Franchise (License)		xxxx
To record impairment loss		

6000.1.6   **Purchased Computer Software**

Purchased computer software is an intangible asset rather than a tangible asset because what is purchased is a license to use the software in a limited and prescribed manner.

6000.1.6.1   **Acquisition of Purchased Computer Software**

6000.1.6.1.1   **Acquisition of Purchased Computer Software for Cash**

*Computer Software	xxxx	
Cash		xxxx
To record purchase of software		

*The cost of purchased software may be debited to Computer Software only if it has alternative future uses. Otherwise, the costs should be expensed.

6000.1.6.1.2   **Acquisition of Computer Software for Liabilities (or Liabilities and Cash)**

*Computer Software	xxxx	
Notes Payable		xxxx
[Various Liabilities]		xxxx
Cash		xxxx
To record purchase of software		

*The cost of purchased software may be debited to Computer Software only if it has alternative future uses. Otherwise, the costs should be expensed. If Computer Software is debited, it is debited for the amount of cash paid plus *all liabilities* assumed.

Important: Make sure all appropriate subheads apply to your entry (see page v for instructions)

6000.1   **Acquisition and Amortization of Intangible Assets**
6000.1.6   **Purchased Computer Software**

6000.1.6.2   ## Amortization of Purchased Computer Software

Purchased computer software is amortized over the lesser of its estimated economic life or 40 years.

Amortization Expense - Purchased Computer Software	xxxx	
Computer Software		xxxx
To record amortization of software		

6000.1.7   ## Leasehold Improvements

Leasehold improvements are the cost of construction, reconstruction, or improve-ment of facilities on leased property. Because the leased property is not owned, neither are the facilities located on the property. At the termination of the lease, title to the facilities reverts to the lessor. Because the constructed, reconstructed, or improved facilities on leased property are not owned, many accountants classify leasehold improvements as an intangible asset. However, other accountants classify leasehold improvements as tangible assets (i.e., Property, Plant, and Equipment). Either classification is acceptable.

6000.1.7.1   ## Acquisition of Leasehold Improvements

Leasehold Improvements	xxxx	
[Various Accounts]		xxxx
Cash		xxxx
To record leasehold improvements		

6000.1.7.2   ## Amortization of Leasehold Improvements

Amortization Expense - Leasehold Improvements	xxxx	
*Leasehold Improvements		xxxx
To record amortization of leasehold improvements		

*Usually Leasehold Improvements is credited directly when amortized. However, some firms credit Accumulated Amortization - Leasehold Improvements.

Important: Make sure all appropriate subheads apply to your entry (see page v for instructions)

6000.1   **Acquisition and Amortization of Intangible Assets**

6000.1.8   ## Organization Costs

Organization costs are costs of business formation including items such as:
- legal fees
- fees of printing and issuing stock or bonds
- incorporation fees paid to the state.

Operating losses incurred during the start-up phase of the business are not organization costs.

6000.1.8.1   ## Recording Organization Costs

Organization Costs	xxxx	
[Various Accounts]		xxxx
Cash		xxxx
To record organization costs		

6000.1.8.2   ## Amortization of Organization Costs

Organization costs should be amortized over a period not to exceed 40 years. Many firms use a 5-year period because the IRS requires that such costs be amortized over a period of at least 5 years.

Amortization Expense - Organization Costs	xxxx	
Organization Costs		xxxx
To record amortization of organization costs		

6000.1.9   ## Computer Software Development Costs

6000.1.9.1   ## Computer Software Developed for External Use

Costs associated with developing computer software for external use are expensed until technical feasibility has been established which occurs once a detailed program design or working model has been completed.

Important: Make sure all appropriate subheads apply to your entry (see page v for instructions)

6000.1   **Acquisition and Amortization of Intangible Assets**
6000.1.9   **Computer Software Development Costs**
6000.1.9.1   **Computer Software Developed for External Use**

6000.1.9.1.1   **External Use Software Development Costs Incurred Before Technical Feasibility Has Been Established**

Research and Development Expense	xxxx	
Cash		xxxx
To record research and development costs		

6000.1.9.1.2   **External Use Software Development Costs Incurred After Technical Feasibility Has Been Established**

Software Development Costs	xxxx	
[Various Accounts]		xxxx
Cash		xxxx
To record software development costs		

6000.1.9.1.3   **Amortization of Software Development Costs**

The amount of Software Development Costs to be amortized during a period is the greater of (a) the straight-line amount (the amount of Software Development Costs divided by the number of periods in the software's useful life) or (b) the amount found by multiplying the amount of Software Development Costs (SDC) by the ratio of current period revenues (CR) from the software divided by anticipated total revenues (ATR):

$$SDC \times (CR/ATR)$$

Because software is subject to rapid obsolescence, many firms use a short useful life (e.g., two to four years). If computer software becomes worthless or its net realizable value falls below cost, it should be immediately written off or written down (*see GEN6000.1.9.1.4*).

Amortization Expense - Software Development Costs	xxxx	
*Software Development Costs		xxxx
To record amortization of software development costs		

*Most companies credit Software Development Costs directly. However, Accumulated Amortization - Software Development Costs may be credited instead.

Important: Make sure all appropriate subheads apply to your entry (see page v for instructions)

6000.1   **Acquisition and Amortization of Intangible Assets**
6000.1.9   **Computer Software Development Costs**
6000.1.9.1   **Computer Software Developed for External Use**

6000.1.9.1.4   **Write-Down of Software Development Costs**

Software Development Costs must be reported on the balance sheet at the lower of
unamortized cost or net realizable value (expected revenues less costs of selling).
When net realizable value falls below cost, the Software Development Costs should
be written down to net realizable value. Once Software Development Costs has been
written down, it cannot be written back up even if the net realizable value increases.

Unrealized Loss On Valuation Of Computer Software		
Costs	xxxx	
Software Development Costs		xxxx

*To write down software development costs to net realizable
value*

6000.1.9.2   **Internal Use Software Development Costs**

Most firms expense costs to develop internal use software. However, there are no
official guidelines for this.

Software Development Expense	xxxx	
[Various Accounts]		xxxx
Cash		xxxx

To expense costs of software development

6000.2   **Intangible Assets Acquired in a Lump-Sum (Basket) Purchase**

*Patents	xxxx	
*Trademarks	xxxx	
*Copyrights	xxxx	
*[Various Intangible Assets]	xxxx	
Cash		xxxx
[Various Liabilities]		xxxx

To record purchase of intangible assets

*The lump sum purchase price is allocated to the individual intangible assets based on
fair market values or relative sales values. The percentage of the lump sum to be
allocated to a particular intangible asset is found by dividing that asset's fair market
value or sales value by the sum of all of the acquired assets' fair market or sales
values.

Important: Make sure all appropriate subheads apply to your entry (see page v for instructions)

6000.3

Research and Development Costs

Research and development (R&D) costs are not intangible assets. However, these costs are a necessary part of developing intangible assets. R&D costs should be expensed in the period incurred.

The Financial Accounting Standards Board's definition of R&D is as follows:

"Research is planned search or critical investigation aimed at discovery of new knowledge with the hope that such knowledge will be useful in developing a new product or service . . . or a new process or technique . . . or in bringing about a significant improvement to an existing product or process.

"Development is the translation of research findings or other knowledge into a plan or design for a new product or process or for a significant improvement to an existing product or process whether intended for sale or use. It includes the conceptual formulation, design, and testing of product alternatives, construction of prototypes, and operation of pilot plants. It does not include routine or periodic alterations to existing products, production lines, manufacturing processes, and other on-going operations even though those alterations may represent improvements and it does not include market research or market testing activities."

*Research and Development Expense	xxxx
Supplies	xxxx
Accounts Payable	xxxx
[Various Accounts]	xxxx
Cash	xxxx

To record costs of research and development

*R&D-related costs that should be expensed in the period incurred include the cost of:
   -salaries and wages
   -supplies
   -materials
   -equipment
   -depreciation
   -purchased intangibles
   -etc.
However, if items have alternative future uses, they should be debited to appropriate asset accounts and expensed as used. The costs of R&D-related services performed by others and an appropriate amount of indirect costs (i.e., overhead) are also expensed in the period incurred.

TABLE OF CONTENTS

GEN7000   CURRENT LIABILITIES

7000.1   **Accounts Payable (Trade Accounts Payable)**

Accounts payable are amounts owed for goods, supplies, or services purchased on account.

7000.1.1   **Recording Accounts Payable (Trade Accounts Payable)**

Inventory	xxxx	
Supplies	xxxx	
Delivery Expense	xxxx	
[Various Accounts]	xxxx	
Accounts Payable		xxxx

To record purchases on account

7000.1.2   **Payment of Accounts Payable (Trade Accounts Payable)**

Accounts Payable	xxxx	
Cash		xxxx

To record payment of accounts payable

7000.2   **Notes Payable**

Current notes payable include trade notes payable, short-term notes payable, and the currently maturing portion of long-term debt such as bonds and mortgages. Trade notes payable are promissory notes given to suppliers in lieu of or in settlement of accounts payable. Short-term notes payable are promissory notes issued to banks and finance companies usually to obtain a cash loan.

7000.2.1   **Recording Trade Notes Payable and Short-Term Notes Payable**

Important: Make sure all appropriate subheads apply to your entry (see page v for instructions)

7000.2   **Notes Payable**
7000.2.1   **Recording Trade Notes Payable and Short-Term Notes Payable**

7000.2.1.1   **Interest-Bearing Notes Payable**

*Cash	xxxx	
**Notes Payable		xxxx

To record issuance of notes payable

*In the case of an interest-bearing note payable, the cash received is equal to the face value of the note issued. Other accounts may be debited if the note payable is issued for assets other than cash. For example, if a trade note payable is issued to purchase equipment, Equipment would be debited.

**Notes Payable is credited for the face value (principal) amount of the note.

7000.2.1.2   **Noninterest-Bearing Notes Payable**

*Cash	xxxx	
**Discount On Notes Payable	xxxx	
***Notes Payable		xxxx

To record issuance of a noninterest-bearing note payable

*The amount of cash received (proceeds) is found by subtracting the discount amount (the cost of obtaining the loan) from the note's face value. The discount amount is found by using the interest formula: Principal X Rate X Time. *For example,* on a $1,000 note discounted at 8% for 6 months the discount would be $40 ($1,000 X .08 X 6/12). The proceeds would then be $960 ($1,000 - $40).

**When a noninterest-bearing note is issued, the bank or finance company discounts the note and remits the proceeds to the borrower. The discount balance (debited to Discount On Notes Payable) represents future interest expense. Discount On Notes Payable is deducted from Notes Payable on the balance sheet.

***Notes Payable is credited for the face value amount of the note payable, which in the case of a noninterest-bearing note payable is also equal to its maturity value.

Important: Make sure all appropriate subheads apply to your entry (see page v for instructions)

7000.2   **Notes Payable**

7000.2.2   **Currently Maturing Portion of Long-Term Debt**

No entry is used to record the currently maturing portion of long-term debt. The currently maturing portion is classified separately from the rest of the long-term debt in the balance sheet as a current liability unless:
- It is to be converted into stock; or
- It is to be refinanced on a long-term basis; or
- It is to be retired by assets accumulated for this purpose that properly have not been classified as current assets.

7000.2.3   **Recording Interest Expense on Trade Notes Payable and Short-Term Notes Payable**

7000.2.3.1   **Recording Interest Expense on an Interest-Bearing Note Payable**

> *Interest Expense   xxxx
>   Interest Payable   xxxx
> *To record interest expense*

*The amount of interest expense is found by using the interest formula: Principal X Rate X Time, where Time equals the number of periods since interest expense was last recorded. *For example,* interest on a $1,000 note payable at 6% for three months would be $15 ($1,000 X .06 X 3/12).

7000.2.3.2   **Recording Interest Expense on a Noninterest-Bearing Note Payable**

> *Interest Expense   xxxx
>   Discount On Notes Payable   xxxx
> *To record interest expense*

*Discount On Notes Payable is amortized to Interest Expense on the straight-line basis. *For example,* if the original amount of discount on a six-month note payable was $60 and this entry was made to record two months of interest, the amount of interest expense would be $20 ($60 X 2/6).

Important: Make sure all appropriate subheads apply to your entry (see page v for instructions)

7000.2   Notes Payable

7000.2.4   **Payment of Trade Notes Payable and Short-Term Notes Payable**

7000.2.4.1   **Payment of an Interest-Bearing Note Payable**

Notes Payable	xxxx	
*Interest Expense	xxxx	
**Cash		xxxx
To record payment of note payable		

*The amount of interest expense is found by using the interest formula: Principal X Rate X Time, where Time equals the number of periods since interest expense was last recorded. *For example*, interest on a $1,000 note payable at 6% for three months would be $15 ($1,000 X .06 X 3/12).

**The amount of cash to be paid, the maturity value of the note, is found by adding the total amount of interest to be paid at maturity (see the above note (*) pertaining to Interest Expense) to the face value (principal) of the note.

7000.3   **Dividends Payable**

Dividends payable are amounts owed to stockholders as a result of a cash dividend declaration by the corporation's board of directors. For dividends payable in additional shares of stock (stock dividends), *see GEN9000.12.4*. For dividends payable with assets other than cash (property dividends), *see GEN9000.12.2*. For dividends distributed in the form of debt (scrip dividends), *see GEN9000.12.3*.

7000.3.1   **Recording Dividends Payable**

Retained Earnings (Dividends Declared)	xxxx	
*Dividends Payable		xxxx
To record declaration of cash dividend		

*The dividend liability is found by multiplying the number of shares outstanding by the per share cash dividend declared by the board of directors. Dividends not yet declared by the board of directors are not liabilities.

Important: Make sure all appropriate subheads apply to your entry (see page v for instructions)

7000.3   **Dividends Payable**

7000.3.2   **Payment of Dividends Payable**

Dividends Payable   xxxx
    Cash   xxxx
To record payment of cash dividend

7000.4   **Returnable Cash Deposits**

Returnable cash deposits are amounts received from customers and employees as payment guarantees or to guarantee performance.

7000.4.1   **Recording Returnable Cash Deposits**

Cash   xxxx
    *Deposits Payable   xxxx
To record receipt of deposit

*Common alternative account titles include:
    -Customer Deposits Payable
    -Employee Deposits Payable
    -Dealer Deposits Payable.

7000.4.2   **Refunding Cash Deposits**

*Deposits Payable   xxxx
    Cash   xxxx
To record refund of deposit

*Common alternative account titles include:
    -Customer Deposits Payable
    -Employee Deposits Payable
    -Dealer Deposits Payable.

Important: Make sure all appropriate subheads apply to your entry (see page v for instructions)

7000.5   **Unearned Revenues**

Unearned revenues are liabilities resulting from collecting cash before earning the revenue. They are sometimes called deferred revenues, revenues collected in advance, or customer prepayments. Examples include:
- magazine subscriptions
- rent received in advance
- interest received in advance
- advance sale of tickets
- advance sale of tokens
- sale of gift certificates.

7000.5.1   **Recording Unearned Revenues**

Cash	xxxx	
Unearned [Various] Revenue		xxxx
To record receipt of unearned revenue		

7000.5.2   **Realizing Unearned Revenues**

Unearned [Various] Revenue	xxxx	
[Various] Revenue		xxxx
To record realization of revenue		

7000.6   **Sales Taxes**

7000.6.1   **Recording Sales Taxes**

7000.6.1.1   **Sales Tax Recorded Separately At the Time of Sale**

Accounts Receivable (Cash)	xxxx	
Sales		xxxx
*Sales Taxes Payable		xxxx
To record sales and sales taxes		

Important: Make sure all appropriate subheads apply to your entry (see page v for instructions)

7000.6   **Sales Taxes**
7000.6.1   **Recording Sales Taxes**
7000.6.1.1   **Sales Tax Recorded Separately At the Time of Sale**

---

*Sales Taxes Payable should be credited for the amount of sales taxes collected and owed to the government.

7000.6.1.2   Sales Tax Not Recorded Separately at the Time of Sale

Sales		xxxx
*Sales Taxes Payable		xxxx

To record sales taxes originally included in sales

*Businesses using this approach do not segregate the sales tax and the amount of the sale at the time of sale. To correctly reflect the actual amount of sale and the liability for sales taxes, Sales must be debited and Sales Taxes Payable must be credited for the amount of sales taxes due to the government.

The sales tax amount for the period is determined as follows: amount credited to Sales - (amount credited to Sales / (1 + sales tax rate)). *For example,* if Sales has been credited for $10,600 and the sales tax rate is 6% the amount is $600 ($10,600 - ($10,600 / 1.06)).

7000.6.2   Payment of Sales Taxes Payable

Sales Taxes Payable		xxxx
Cash		xxxx

To record payment of sales taxes payable

7000.7   Property Taxes

Property taxes are taxes levied by local governments on the real and personal property of citizens, including corporations. Property taxes should be accrued monthly during the fiscal period of the taxing authority.

7000.7.1   Recording Monthly Property Tax Expense

Important: Make sure all appropriate subheads apply to your entry (see page v for instructions)

7000.7   **Property Taxes**
7000.7.1   **Recording Monthly Property Tax Expense**

7000.7.1.1

Recording Monthly Property Tax Expense Prior to Making Any Property Tax Payments

*Property Tax Expense	xxxx
Property Tax Payable	xxxx

To record monthly property tax expense

*Property tax expense should be first accrued at the end of the month in which property taxes become a lien. The date at which taxes become a lien is determined by law, although it is usually the assessment date. The monthly expense (and payable) amount is found by dividing the property tax lien by 12 months.

7000.7.1.2

Recording Monthly Property Tax Expense After Making Property Tax Payments

Property Tax Expense	xxxx
*Prepaid Property Taxes	xxxx

*To record property tax expense and reduce the prepaid
asset balance*

*Prepaid Property Taxes is reduced monthly until its balance is zero. At that point, Property Tax Payable should again be credited. *See GEN7000.7.2* for creation of this account.

7000.7.2

Recording Payment of Property Tax Installment

*Property Tax Payable	xxxx
*Prepaid Property Tax	xxxx
**Cash	xxxx

To record payment of property tax installment

*If the cash paid is less than the balance in Property Tax Payable, Property Tax Payable is reduced by an amount equal to the cash paid. If the cash paid exceeds the balance in Property Tax Payable, then the entire payable balance is eliminated and Prepaid Property Tax is debited for the excess.

**The amount to be paid in each property tax installment is specified by the taxing authority.

Important: Make sure all appropriate subheads apply to your entry (see page v for instructions)

7000.8   **Income Taxes Payable**

This section does not deal with deferred taxes and some other tax topics. *See GEN12000* for additional topic coverage.

7000.8.1   **Recording Periodic Income Tax Expense**

Income Tax Expense	xxxx
*Income Tax Payable	xxxx
To record income tax expense	

*The amount payable is based on an estimate of the firm's total annual tax liability and may change from period to period. For deferred taxes and other tax topics, *see GEN12000*.

7000.8.2   **Making Periodic Income Tax Payments**

Income Tax Payable	xxxx
Cash	xxxx
To record payment of income tax	

7000.9   **Contingent Liabilities**

A contingent liability is an obligation that may occur in the future depending on the occurrence (or lack of occurrence) of some event or circumstance. To be recorded, a contingent liability must meet both of the following conditions:
-it is probable that a liability will be incurred; and
-the amount of the liability can be reasonably estimated.
Contingent liabilities include possible litigation-related obligations, possible losses due to expropriation of assets, and possible liabilities due to guarantees and warranties or outstanding premiums and coupons. Several examples are given in the following sections.

Important: Make sure all appropriate subheads apply to your entry (see page v for instructions)

7000.9   **Contingent Liabilities**

7000.9.1   **Litigation, Claims, and Assessments**

These are estimated obligations arising out of lawsuits in which the firm is a defendant.

7000.9.1.1   **Recording Contingent Liability for Litigation, Claims, and Assessments**

Estimated Loss From Pending Lawsuit	xxxx	
*Estimated Liability From Pending Lawsuit		xxxx
To record estimated lawsuit liability		

*The amount of the liability is determined by considering factors such as legal advice, the nature of the litigation, and experience.

7000.9.1.2   **Payment of Contingent Liability for Litigation, Claims, and Assessments**

*Estimated Liability From Pending Lawsuit	xxxx	
**Loss From Lawsuit	xxxx	
Cash		xxxx
To record payment of lawsuit loss		

*This account is debited for an amount sufficient to eliminate its balance as it pertains to the lawsuit involved.

**Loss From Lawsuit is debited for any excess of the cash paid over the amount of the previously estimated liability. If the estimated liability is in excess of the cash paid, this excess is credited to Gain From Overestimated Lawsuit Liability rather than debiting the loss account.

7000.9.2   **Expropriation of Assets**

Expropriation of assets refers to the seizure of company assets by a foreign government.

GEN7000.9.2.1   GEN7000.9.3

Important: Make sure all appropriate subheads apply to your entry (see page v for instructions)

7000.9   **Contingent Liabilities**
7000.9.2   **Expropriation of Assets**

7000.9.2.1   **Recording Probable Expropriation**

*Loss Due To Probable Expropriation Of Assets   xxxx
**Liability For Probable Expropriation Of Assets   xxxx
To record probable loss due to expropriation of assets

*A loss should be recognized when expropriation appears imminent and experience indicates that a loss will be incurred upon settlement.

**Allowance For Expropriation Of Assets may be credited instead of this liability account. The allowance account is a contra asset account; i.e., it is deducted from the asset account involved in the expropriation.

7000.9.2.2   **Recording Expropriation Settlement**

*Cash ([Various Assets])   xxxx
**Liability For Probable Expropriation Of Assets   xxxx
***Loss From Expropriation Of Assets   xxxx
****[Various Accounts]   xxxx
To record settlement of expropriation

*If any cash or other assets such as receivables are received in the settlement, appropriate asset accounts are debited.

**Liability For Probable Expropriation Of Assets is debited for an amount sufficient to eliminate its credit balance.

***Loss From Expropriation Of Assets is debited for any excess of the book value of the assets expropriated over the sum of the debits for assets received and the debit to the liability account.

****Whatever assets have been expropriated are written off.

7000.9.3   **Warranties and Guarantees**

Warranties and guarantees are obligations made by a seller to a buyer to repair or replace defective products.

Important: Make sure all appropriate subheads apply to your entry (see page v for instructions)

7000.9   **Contingent Liabilities**
7000.9.3   **Warranties and Guarantees**

7000.9.3.1   ### Warranty or Guarantee Costs that Cannot Be Reasonably Estimated

When warranty or guarantee costs cannot be reasonably estimated, when they are expected to be immaterial, or when the warranty period is very short, warranty costs are not estimated in advance but are charged to expense as incurred.

Warranty Expense (Guarantee Expense)	xxxx	
Materials (Parts)		xxxx
Wages Payable		xxxx
[Various Accounts]		xxxx
Cash		xxxx

To record actual warranty (or guarantee) costs

7000.9.3.2   ### Warranty or Guarantee Costs that Can Be Reasonably Estimated

70000.9.3.2.1   ### Recording Estimated Warranty or Guarantee Costs

*Warranty Expense (Guarantee Expense)	xxxx	
Estimated Liability Under Warranties		
(Guarantees)		xxxx

To record estimated warranty (or guarantee) costs

*The amount of Warranty Expense or Guarantee Expense to be recognized during the current period is that amount of expected warranty (or guarantee) costs related to the current period's sales.

7000.9.3.2.2   ### Recording Actual Warranty or Guarantee Costs

Estimated Liability Under Warranties (Guarantees)	xxxx	
Materials (Parts)		xxxx
Wages Payable		xxxx
[Various Accounts]		xxxx
Cash		xxxx

To record actual warranty (or guarantee) costs

Important: Make sure all appropriate subheads apply to your entry (see page v for instructions)

7000.9   **Contingent Liabilities**

7000.9.4   **Sales Warranties**

Sales warranties are separate contracts offered to customers to extend the manufacturer's original warranty. Such extended warranties are recorded separately from the related product.

7000.9.4.1   **Recording Warranty Sales**

Cash	xxxx	
*Unearned Warranty Revenue		xxxx
To record sale of extended warranty		

*Unearned Warranty Revenue is credited because the revenue must be deferred and recognized over the period of the warranty.

7000.9.4.2   **Recording Warranty Revenue**

Unearned Warranty Revenue	xxxx	
*Warranty Revenue		xxxx
To record warranty revenue on extended warranty sales		

*Warranty revenue is usually recognized on a straight-line basis over the life of the warranty contract.

7000.9.5   **Premiums and Coupons**

Premiums and coupons are plans used to promote sales of certain products. Under these plans, customers are offered premiums or prizes in exchange for:
- coupons
- product code labels
- wrappers
- box tops
- certificates.

The cost of premium and coupon plans should be charged to expense in the period of sales produced by the plans.

Important: Make sure all appropriate subheads apply to your entry (see page v for instructions)

7000.9   **Contingent Liabilities**
7000.9.5   **Premiums and Coupons**

7000.9.5.1

Recording Receipt of Premiums or Coupons During the Period Related Sales Were Made

*Premium Expense (Coupon Expense)	xxxx	
*Cash	xxxx	
Inventory ([Asset Being Awarded])		xxxx
To record premium (or coupon) expense		

*Premium plans often require customers to send cash along with the coupon. The amount of Premium Expense is the difference between the book value of the asset given to the customer and the cash received.

7000.9.5.2

Recording Premium Expense for Premiums or Coupons Outstanding at the End of the Period

Premium Expense (or Coupon Expense)	xxxx	
*Estimated Liability For Premiums		xxxx
To record estimated premium liability for outstanding premiums (coupons)		

*The liability for premiums or coupons outstanding that can be expected to result in expense is estimated at the end of the period and the balance in Estimated Liability For Premiums is adjusted to reflect that amount. If the balance in the liability account must be increased, an entry such as this is made for the amount of the increase. If the balance in the liability account must be reduced, Estimated Liability For Premiums is debited and Premium Expense is credited for the amount of the reduction.

7000.9.6

Losses Due to Lack of Insurance

Only contingent liabilities arising out of past events are recognized. Liabilities resulting from anticipated future events are not recognized.

Loss From Uninsured Accident ([Various Event])	xxxx	
Liability For Uninsured Accident ([Various Event])		xxxx
To record estimated liability due to uninsured event		

Important: Make sure all appropriate subheads apply to your entry (see page v for instructions)

7000.10

Employee-Related Liabilities

Employee-related liabilities include salaries and wages, payroll deductions, employer payroll taxes, postretirement benefits, compensated absences, and bonuses. *See GEN13000* for pension accounting entries.

7000.10.1

Payroll Liabilities

7000.10.1.1

Recording Salaries and Wages Liabilities (Payroll Liabilities)

Salaries And Wages Expense	xxxx	
*Federal Income Tax Withheld		xxxx
*State Income Tax Withheld		xxxx
**F.I.C.A. Tax Withheld		xxxx
***[Other Withholdings Payable]		xxxx
****Salaries And Wages Payable		xxxx

To record payroll

*Federal and state withholdings are found in the tax withholding tables provided by the federal and state governments.

**An alternative account title is Social Security Tax Withheld.

***Other withholdings may include amounts withheld for insurance premiums, savings plans, union dues, and uniforms.

****Salaries And Wages Payable is credited for the amount of net salaries and wages; i.e., gross salaries and wages minus all payroll deductions.

7000.10.1.2

Payment of Payroll Liabilities

Although the payment of payroll liabilities is illustrated below in one entry, the individual liabilities will usually be paid separately.

CURRENT LIABILITIES

Important: Make sure all appropriate subheads apply to your entry (see page v for instructions)

7000.10	**Employee-Related Liabilities**	
7000.10.1	**Payroll Liabilities**	
7000.10.1.2	**Payment of Payroll Liabilities**	

Federal Income Tax Withheld	xxxx	
State Income Tax Withheld	xxxx	
F.I.C.A. Tax Withheld	xxxx	
[Other Withholdings Payable]	xxxx	
Salaries And Wages Payable	xxxx	
Cash		xxxx

To record payment of payroll liabilities

7000.10.2   Employer Payroll Taxes

7000.10.2.1   Recording Employer Payroll Taxes

Payroll Tax Expense	xxxx	
*F.I.C.A. Tax Payable		xxxx
**Federal Unemployment Tax Payable		xxxx
State Unemployment Tax Payable		xxxx

To record employer payroll taxes

*The employer must match dollar for dollar the amounts contributed by employees.

**The federal government grants a credit to states that have an unemployment tax. The amount of the credit is the lesser of the state unemployment rate or a maximum rate contained in federal law.

7000.10.2.2   Payment of Employer Payroll Taxes

Although the payment of payroll tax is illustrated below in one entry, not all payroll tax liabilities will be paid at the same time.

F.I.C.A. Tax Payable	xxxx	
Federal Unemployment Tax Payable	xxxx	
State Unemployment Tax Payable	xxxx	
Cash		xxxx

To record payment of employer payroll tax

Important: Make sure all appropriate subheads apply to your entry (see page v for instructions)

7000.10   **Employee-Related Liabilities**

7000.10.3   ### Accrued Salaries and Wages at the End of the Accounting Period

Many firms do not accrue employee payroll deductions as separate liabilities because payroll taxes are not a liability until the payroll is actually paid.

Salaries And Wages Expense	xxxx	
Salaries And Wages Payable		xxxx
To record accrued salaries and wages		

7000.10.4   ### Postretirement Health Care and Life Insurance Benefits

Financial accounting standards require all companies to record as expense each year a portion of the expected cost of postretirement medical insurance and other benefits for every employee regardless of age or length of service.

Postretirement Medical (Life Insurance) Benefits Expense	xxxx	
Liability For Postretirement Medical (Life Insurance) Benefits		xxxx
To record postretirement medical (life insurance) benefits		

7000.10.5   ### Compensated Absences (Vacation Pay, Sick Pay, Etc.)

7000.10.5.1   ### Recording Liability for Compensated Absences

Liabilities for compensated absences are recorded in the period earned by the employee. The rate used to accrue the cost is usually the wage rate in effect when the employee earned the benefit.

Salaries And Wages Expense	xxxx	
Vacation Wages Payable		xxxx
Sick Pay Wages Payable		xxxx
[Various Other Compensated Absences]		xxxx
To record liabilities for compensated absences		

Important: Make sure all appropriate subheads apply to your entry (see page v for instructions)

7000.10   **Employee-Related Liabilities**
7000.10.5   **Compensated Absences (Vacation Pay, Sick Pay, Etc.)**

7000.10.5.2   **Payment of Compensated Absence Liability**

*Vacation (Sick Pay, etc.) Wages Payable	xxxx	
**Salaries And Wages Expense	xxxx	
Cash		xxxx

To record payment of compensated absence liability

*The debit to Vacation (Sick Pay, etc.) Wages Payable is calculated using the wage rate in effect when the employee earned the benefit; i.e., the same rate as used to calculate the initial credit to the account (*see GEN7000.10.5.1*).

**If the current wage rate is greater than the rate in effect when the benefit was earned by the employee, the credit to Cash will be in excess of the debit to Vacation (or Sick Pay, etc.) Wages Payable. This excess amount is debited to Salaries And Wages Expense. If the current wage rate has not increased since the liability was recorded, Salaries And Wages Expense will not appear in this entry.

7000.10.6   **Bonus Agreements**

Employees' Bonus Expense	xxxx	
Employees' Bonuses Payable		xxxx

To record employees' bonuses

TABLE OF CONTENTS

8000.1	**Bonds Payable**

8000.1.1	**Issuance of Bonds Payable**

8000.1.1.1	**Issuance at Par (Face, Stated, or Nominal) Value**

Bonds are issued at par (face, stated, or nominal) value when the current market rate of interest at issuance is equal to the interest rate printed on the bond (face, stated, coupon, or nominal rate).

8000.1.1.1.1	**Issuance at Par on Interest Payment Date**

```
Cash                                                    xxxx
    *Bonds Payable                                          xxxx
    To record issuance of bonds payable
```

*Bonds Payable will be credited for the par (face, stated, or nominal) value of the bonds. Because the bonds were issued on an interest payment date, this amount should also be the amount of the cash received. If bond issuance costs are involved *see GEN8000.1.1.4.*

8000.1.1.1.2	**Issuance at Par Between Interest Payment Dates**

Bonds normally pay half of the annual interest every six months. One of the interest payment dates is the maturity date of the bond; e.g., a bond that matures April 1, 2010, will pay interest on April 1 and October 1 each year. If bonds are issued between interest payment dates, interest calculated from the last interest payment date (even though no interest may have been paid then) is added to the price of the bond. Thus, if there are only two months until the next interest payment date when the bonds are sold, four (6 - 2 = 4) months of interest will be collected by the seller from the purchaser. Two months later the purchaser will receive six months interest, which will include interest for the two months' he or she held the bond plus a reimbursement for the four months' interest advanced to the seller.

Important: Make sure all appropriate subheads apply to your entry (see page v for instructions)

8000.1   **Bonds Payable**
8000.1.1   **Issuance of Bonds Payable**
8000.1.1.1   **Issuance at Par (Face, Stated, or Nominal) Value**
8000.1.1.1.2   **Issuance at Par Between Interest Payment Dates**

---

*Cash	xxxx
**Bonds Payable	xxxx
***Bond Interest Payable	xxxx
To record issuance of bonds payable	

*Cash will be debited for the total of the cash received. This will include the issuance price of the bond plus interest accrued from the last interest payment date until the date of issuance. If bond issuance costs are involved, *see GEN8000.1.1.4.*

**Bonds Payable will be credited for the par (face, stated, or nominal) value of the bonds.

***Common alternative account titles include:
- Interest Payable
- Bond Interest Expense
- Interest Expense.

Bond Interest Payable is credited for the amount of interest accrued since the last interest payment date. This amount is collected from the purchaser along with the purchase price of the bonds at the time the bonds are issued. See note in *GEN8000.1.1.1.2.*

8000.1.1.2   **Issuance at a Premium**

Bonds are issued at a premium (above par value) when the current market rate of interest at issuance is less than the interest rate printed on the bond (face, stated, coupon, or nominal rate).

8000.1.1.2.1   **Issuance at a Premium on an Interest Payment Date**

Cash	xxxx
*Bonds Payable	xxxx
**Premium On Bonds Payable	xxxx
To record issuance of bonds payable	

*Bonds Payable will be credited for the par (face, stated, or nominal) value of the bonds.

Important: Make sure all appropriate subheads apply to your entry (see page v for instructions)

8000.1	**Bonds Payable**
8000.1.1	**Issuance of Bonds Payable**
8000.1.1.2	**Issuance at a Premium**
8000.1.1.2.1	**Issuance at a Premium on an Interest Payment Date**

**Premium on Bonds Payable will be credited for the excess of the issuance price over the par (face, stated, or nominal) value of the bonds. If there are bond issuance costs, *see GEN8000.1.1.4.* For amortization of premium on bonds payable, *see GEN8000.1.2.1.2.*

8000.1.1.2.2   **Issuance at a Premium Between Interest Payment Dates**

Bonds normally pay half of the annual interest every six months. One of the interest payment dates is the maturity date of the bond; e.g., a bond that matures April 1, 2010, will pay interest on April 1 and October 1 each year. If bonds are issued between interest payment dates, interest calculated from the last interest payment date (even though no interest may have been paid then) is added to the price of the bond. Thus, if there are only two months until the next interest payment date when the bonds are sold, four (6 - 2 = 4) months of interest will be collected by the seller from the purchaser. Two months later the purchaser will receive six months' interest, which will include interest for the two months he or she held the bond plus a reimbursement for the four months' interest advanced to the seller.

*Cash	xxxx
**Bonds Payable	xxxx
***Premium On Bonds Payable	xxxx
****Bond Interest Payable	xxxx
To record issuance of bonds payable	

*Cash will be debited for the total of the cash received. This will include the issuance price of the bond plus interest accrued from the last interest payment date until the date of issuance. If bond issuance costs are involved, *see GEN8000.1.1.4.*

**Bonds Payable will be credited for the par (face, stated, or nominal) value of the bonds.

***Premium On Bonds Payable will be credited for the excess of the issuance price (disregarding accrued interest) over the par (face, stated, or nominal) value of the bonds. If bond issuance costs are involved, *see GEN8000.1.1.4.* For amortization of premium on bonds payable, *see GEN8000.1.2.1.2.*

Important: Make sure all appropriate subheads apply to your entry (see page v for instructions)

8000.1	**Bonds Payable**
8000.1.1	**Issuance of Bonds Payable**
8000.1.1.2	**Issuance at a Premium**
8000.1.1.2.2	**Issuance at a Premium Between Interest Payment Dates**

****Common alternative account titles include:
- Interest Payable
- Bond Interest Expense
- Interest Expense.

Bond Interest Payable is credited for the amount of interest accrued since the last interest payment date. This amount is collected from the purchaser along with the purchase price of the bonds at the time the bonds are issued.

8000.1.1.3	## Issuance at a Discount

Bonds are issued at a discount (below par value) when the current market rate of interest at issuance is more than the interest rate printed on the bond (face, stated, coupon, or nominal rate).

8000.1.1.3.1	## Issuance at a Discount on an Interest Payment Date

Cash	xxxx	
*Discount On Bonds Payable	xxxx	
**Bonds Payable		xxxx

To record issuance of bonds payable

*Discount On Bonds Payable will be debited for the excess of the par (face, stated, or nominal) value of the bonds over the issuance price, disregarding any bond interest costs. If there are bond issuance costs, see *GEN8000.1.1.4*. For amortization of discount on bonds payable, *see GEN8000.1.2.1.3*.

**Bonds Payable will be credited for the par (face, stated, or nominal) value of the bonds.

8000.1.1.3.2	## Issuance at a Discount Between Interest Payment Dates

Bonds normally pay half of the annual interest every six months. One of the interest payment dates is the maturity date of the bond; e.g., a bond that matures April 1, 2010, will pay interest on April 1 and October 1 each year. If bonds are issued between interest payment dates, interest calculated from the last interest payment date (even though no interest may have been paid then) is added to the price of the bond. Thus, if

Important: Make sure all appropriate subheads apply to your entry (see page v for instructions)

8000.1	**Bonds Payable**
8000.1.1	**Issuance of Bonds Payable**
8000.1.1.3	**Issuance at a Discount**
8000.1.1.3.2	**Issuance at a Discount Between Interest Payment Dates**

there are only two months until the next interest payment date when the bonds are sold, four (6 - 2 = 4) months of interest will be collected by the seller from the purchaser. Two months later the purchaser will receive six months' interest, which will include interest for the two months he or she held the bond plus a reimbursement for the four months' interest advanced to the seller.

*Cash	xxxx	
**Discount On Bonds Payable	xxxx	
***Bonds Payable		xxxx
****Bond Interest Payable		xxxx
To record issuance of bonds payable		

*Cash will be debited for the total of the cash received. This will include the issuance price of the bond plus interest accrued from the last interest payment date until the date of issuance. If there are bond issuance costs, *see GEN8000.1.1.4.*

**Discount On Bonds Payable will be debited for the excess of the par (face, stated, or nominal) value of the bonds over the issuance price, disregarding accrued interest or any bond issuance costs. If there are bond issuance costs, *see GEN8000.1.1.4.* For amortization of discount on bonds payable, see *GEN8000.1.2.1.3.*

***Bonds Payable will be credited for the par (face, stated, or nominal) value of the bonds.

****Common alternative account titles include:
- Interest Payable
- Bond Interest Expense
- Interest Expense.

Bond Interest Payable is credited for the amount of interest accrued since the last interest payment date. This amount is collected from the purchaser along with the purchase price of the bonds at the time the bonds are issued. See note in *GEN8000.1.1.3.2.*

8000.1.1.4	**Bond Issuance Costs**

Bond issuance costs may include underwriter costs, legal fees, and securities registration fees. Some of these costs may be incurred other than at the time of issuance. However, underwriter costs may include a fee payable at issuance that is deducted directly from the cash received by the issuer at issuance.

Important: Make sure all appropriate subheads apply to your entry (see page v for instructions)

8000.1	**Bonds Payable**
8000.1.1	**Issuance of Bonds Payable**
8000.1.1.4	**Bond Issuance Costs**

8000.1.1.4.1

Bond Issuance Costs that Reduce the Amount of Cash Received at Issuance

The entry shown below assumes there is no bond premium or discount. The point to be made is that the amount of any bond issuance costs deducted by the underwriter at the time of issuance of the bonds reduces the amount of cash received by the issuer. This would be no different if there were a premium or discount; the bond issuance costs would reduce the debit to Cash and would not alter the amount of premium or discount otherwise recorded. *See GEN8000.1.1.2* for treatment of a bond premium and *GEN8000.1.1.3* for treatment of a bond discount.

Cash	xxxx	
Unamortized Bond Issue Cost	xxxx	
Bonds Payable		xxxx
To record issuance of bonds at par with issuance cost		

8000.1.1.4.2

Bond Issuance Costs that Are Not Deducted from the Amount of Cash Received at Issuance

Unamortized Bond Issue Cost	xxxx	
Accounts Payable (Cash)		xxxx
To record bond issuance costs		

8000.1.1.4.3

Amortization of Bond Issuance Costs

Bond Issuance Costs are amortized to expense on a straight-line basis over the life of the bonds.

Amortization Of Bond Issuance Costs	xxxx	
Unamortized Bond Issue Costs		xxxx
To record amortization of bond issuance costs		

8000.1.2

Interest on Bonds Payable

8000.1.2.1

Payment of Interest

Important: Make sure all appropriate subheads apply to your entry (see page v for instructions)

8000.1	**Bonds Payable**
8000.1.2	**Interest on Bonds Payable**
8000.1.2.1	**Payment of Interest**

8000.1.2.1.1   **Bonds Originally Issued at Par**

*Bond Interest Expense	xxxx
**Bond Interest Payable	xxxx
Cash	xxxx
To record payment of bond interest	

*Bond Interest Expense is debited for whatever is necessary to balance the entry.

**Bond Interest Payable is debited for any bond interest payable previously recorded. This may have resulted from year-end (or monthly) interest expense accruals or because Bond Interest Payable was the account credited for accrued interest collected at the time the bonds were issued. *See GEN8000.1.1.1.2.*

8000.1.2.1.2   **Bonds Originally Issued at a Premium**

8000.1.2.1.2.1   **Premium Is Amortized at Interest Payment Dates as well as at Year End**

*Bond Interest Expense	xxxx
**Bond Interest Payable	xxxx
***Premium On Bonds Payable	xxxx
Cash	xxxx
To record payment of bond interest and amortization of premium	

*Bond Interest Expense is debited for whatever is necessary to balance the entry.

**Bond Interest Payable is debited for any bond interest payable previously re-corded; i.e., for the balance in Bond Interest Payable. *See GEN8000.1.1.2.2.*

***Premium On Bonds Payable is amortized (debited) over the life of the bonds. This may be done on interest payment dates and at year end (as assumed here) or only at year end. If it is amortized on interest payment dates, the debit to Bond Interest Expense is reduced by the amount of the amortization. Premium On Bonds Payable should be amortized using the effective interest method. However, the straight-line method is often used if the result is not materially different from that achieved by using the effective interest method.

Important: Make sure all appropriate subheads apply to your entry (see page v for instructions)

8000.1	**Bonds Payable**
8000.1.2	**Interest on Bonds Payable**
8000.1.2.1	**Payment of Interest**
8000.1.2.1.2	**Bonds Originally Issued at a Premium**

8000.1.2.1.2.2   ## Premium Is Not Amortized at Interest Payment Dates

*Bond Interest Expense	xxxx	
**Bond Interest Payable	xxxx	
Cash		xxxx
To record payment of bond interest		

*Bond Interest Expense is debited for whatever is necessary to balance the entry.

**Bond Interest Payable is debited for any bond interest payable previously re-corded; i.e., for the amount of its credit balance. *See GEN8000.1.1.2.2.*

8000.1.2.1.3   ## Bonds Originally Issued at a Discount

8000.1.2.1.3.1   ## Discount Is Amortized at Interest Payment Dates as well as at Year End

*Bond Interest Expense	xxxx	
**Bond Interest Payable	xxxx	
***Discount On Bonds Payable		xxxx
Cash		xxxx
To record payment of bond interest and amortization of discount		

*Bond Interest Expense is debited for whatever is necessary to balance the entry.

**Bond Interest Payable is debited for any bond interest payable previously re-corded; i.e., for the amount of its credit balance. *See GEN8000.1.1.3.2.*

***Discount On Bonds Payable is amortized (credited) over the life of the bonds. This may be done on interest payment dates and at year end (as assumed here) or only at year end. If it is amortized on interest payment dates, the debit to Bond Interest Expense is increased by the amount of the amortization. Discount On Bonds Payable should be amortized using the effective interest method. However, the straight-line method is often used if the result is not materially different from that achieved using the effective interest method.

LONG-TERM LIABILITIES

Important: Make sure all appropriate subheads apply to your entry (see page v for instructions)

8000.1	**Bonds Payable**
8000.1.2	**Interest on Bonds Payable**
8000.1.2.1	**Payment of Interest**
8000.1.2.1.3	**Bonds Originally Issued at a Discount**

8000.1.2.1.3.2   **Discount Is Not Amortized at Interest Payment Dates**

*Bond Interest Expense	XXXX	
**Bond Interest Payable	XXXX	
Cash		XXXX
To record payment of bond interest		

*Bond Interest Expense is debited for whatever is necessary to balance the entry.

**Bond Interest Payable is debited for any bond interest payable previously re-corded because of year-end interest expense accruals or because Bond Interest Payable was the account credited for accrued interest collected at the time the bonds were issued. *See GEN8000.1.1.3.2.*

8000.1.2.2   **Accrual of Interest on Bonds Payable**

Interest on bonds payable may be accrued monthly, quarterly, semi-annually, or annually, but it must be accrued at least annually. The period of the accrual runs from the date of the last payment or accrual. Because interest is stated at an annual rate, the amount of the accrual can be calculated by multiplying the stated rate (coupon or face rate) times the par value (face or stated value) times the period of accrual stated as a fraction of a year (e.g., one month is 1/12 of a year).

8000.1.2.2.1   **Bonds Originally Issued at Par**

Bond Interest Expense	XXXX	
*Bond Interest Payable		XXXX
To record accrued interest		

*For calculation of bond interest payable, see note in *GEN8000.1.2.2.*

8000.1.2.2.2   **Bonds Originally Issued at a Premium**

*Bond Interest Expense	XXXX	
**Premium On Bonds Payable	XXXX	
***Bond Interest Payable		XXXX
To record accrued interest and amortization of premium		

Important: Make sure all appropriate subheads apply to your entry (see page v for instructions)

8000.1	**Bonds Payable**
8000.1.2	**Interest on Bonds Payable**
8000.1.2.2	**Accrual of Interest on Bonds Payable**
8000.1.2.2.2	**Bonds Originally Issued at a Premium**

---

*Bond Interest Expense is debited for whatever is necessary to balance the entry.

**Premium On Bonds Payable is amortized (debited) over the life of the bonds. Premium On Bonds Payable should be amortized using the effective interest method. However, the straight-line method is often used if the result is not materially different from that achieved by using the effective interest method.

***For calculation of bond interest payable, see note in *GEN8000.1.2.2*.

8000.1.2.2.3 — Bonds Originally Issued at a Discount

*Bond Interest Expense	xxxx	
**Discount On Bonds Payable	xxxx	
***Bond Interest Payable		xxxx
To record accrued interest and amortization of discount		

*Bond Interest Expense is debited for whatever is necessary to balance the entry.

**Discount On Bonds Payable is amortized (credited) over the life of the bonds. Discount On Bonds Payable should be amortized using the effective interest method. However, the straight-line method is often used if the result is not materially different from that achieved by using the effective interest method.

***For calculation of bond interest payable, see note in *GEN8000.1.2.2*.

8000.1.3 — Redemption or Other Reduction of Bonds Payable

8000.1.3.1 — Redemption at Maturity

If unamortized bond issuance costs exist, *see GEN8000.1.3.2.4*.

Bonds Payable	xxxx	
Cash		xxxx
To record redemption of bonds		

Important: Make sure all appropriate subheads apply to your entry (see page v for instructions)

8000.1   **Bonds Payable**
8000.1.3   **Redemption of Other Reduction of Bonds Payable**

8000.1.3.2   **Reacquisition in the Market and Cancellation**

8000.1.3.2.1   **Bonds Originally Issued at Par**

If unamortized bond issuance costs exist, see GEN8000.1.3.2.4.

Bonds Payable	xxxx	
Cash		xxxx
*Gain On Reacquisition Of Bonds Payable		xxxx

To record reacquisition of bonds

*Gain On Reacquisition Of Bonds Payable is credited if the purchase price is less than the carrying value of the bonds reacquired. If the carrying value is less than the purchase price, Loss On Reacquisition Of Bonds Payable is debited for the difference instead of this gain account. On rare occasions, the purchase price may equal the carrying value of the bonds and there is no gain or loss recorded. Any gain or loss should be reported as an extraordinary item.

8000.1.3.2.2   **Bonds Originally Issued at a Premium**

If unamortized bond issuance costs exist, *see GEN8000.1.3.2.4.*

*Premium On Bonds Payable	xxxx	
Bond Interest Expense		xxxx

To amortize premium up to the date of reacquisition

*Amortization of Premium On Bonds Payable must be brought up to date. Thus, amortization must be recorded for the period since the last time it was amortized. See note in *GEN8000.1.2.1.2* concerning how the premium is amortized.

*Bonds Payable	xxxx	
*Premium On Bonds Payable	xxxx	
Cash		xxxx
**Gain On Reacquisition Of Bonds Payable		xxxx

To record reacquisition of bonds

Important: Make sure all appropriate subheads apply to your entry (see page v for instructions)

8000.1	**Bonds Payable**
8000.1.3	**Redemption or Other Reduction of Bonds Payable**
8000.1.3.2	**Reacquisition in the Market and Cancellation**
8000.1.3.2.2	**Bonds Originally Issued at a Premium**

---

*Bonds Payable and Premium On Bonds Payable will be debited for the portion of the balances in those accounts pertaining to the bonds reacquired. If the entire bond issue is reacquired, the entire balances in these accounts are eliminated.

**Gain On Reacquisition Of Bonds Payable is credited if the purchase price is less than the carrying value (the sum of the debits to Bonds Payable and Premium On Bonds Payable) of the bonds reacquired. If the carrying value is less than the purchase price, Loss On Reacquisition of Bonds Payable is debited for the difference instead of this gain account. On rare occasions, the purchase price may equal the carrying value of the bonds and there is no gain or loss recorded. Any gain or loss should be reported as an extraordinary item.

8000.1.3.2.3   **Bonds Originally Issued at a Discount**

If unamortized bond issuance costs exist, *see GEN8000.1.3.2.4.*

Bond Interest Expense	xxxx	
*Discount On Bonds Payable		xxxx
To amortize discount up to the date of reacquisition		

*Amortization of Discount On Bonds Payable must be brought up to date. Thus, amortization must be recorded for the period since the last time it was amortized. See note in *GEN8000.1.2.1.3* concerning how the discount is amortized.

*Bonds Payable	xxxx	
*Discount On Bonds Payable		xxxx
Cash		xxxx
**Gain On Reacquisition Of Bonds Payable		xxxx
To record reacquisition of bonds		

*Bonds Payable will be debited and Discount On Bonds Payable will be credited for the portion of the balances in those accounts pertaining to the bonds reacquired. If the entire bond issue is reacquired, this will result in the elimination of the entire balances of these accounts.

**Gain On Reacquisition Of Bonds Payable is credited if the purchase price is less than the carrying value (the debit to the Bonds Payable less the credit to Discount On Bonds Payable) of the bonds reacquired. If the carrying value is less than the purchase price, Loss On Reacquisition of Bonds Payable is debited for the difference instead of

Important: Make sure all appropriate subheads apply to your entry (see page v for instructions)

8000.1   **Bonds Payable**
8000.1.3   **Redemption or Other Reduction of Bonds Payable**
8000.1.3.2   **Reacquisition in the Market and Cancellation**
8000.1.3.2.3   **Bonds Originally Issued at a Discount**

---

this gain account. On rare occasions, the purchase price may equal the carrying value of the bonds and there is no gain or loss recorded. Any gain or loss should be reported as an extraordinary item.

8000.1.3.2.4   ## Unamortized Bond Issuance Cost at Reacquisition

Bond issuance costs are amortized to expense on a straight-line basis over the life of the bonds. At reacquisition the amortization of bond issuance costs must be brought up to date. The remaining unamortized balance must then be written off, resulting in either a reduction in the gain on redemption or an increase in the loss on redemption.

Amortization Of Bond Issuance Costs	xxxx	
Unamortized Bond Issue Costs		xxxx

To record amortization of bond issuance costs to the date of redemption

*Gain On Reacquisition Of Bonds Payable	xxxx	
Unamortized Bond Issue Costs		xxxx

To write off the remaining balance in Unamortized Bond Issue Costs

*If Gain On Reacquisition Of Bonds Payable was originally credited at reacquisition, it is reduced as shown in this entry. If Loss On Reacquisition Of Bonds Payable was originally debited at reacquisition, it is increased (debited) instead of the gain account. If the amount of unamortized bond issue costs to write off exceeds the amount of gain originally recorded at reacquisition, the gain account is debited with an amount sufficient to reduce its balance to zero, and the loss account is debited with an amount sufficient to balance this entry. Any gain or loss should be reported as an extraordinary item.

8000.1.3.3   ## Reacquisition in the Market Without Cancellation (Treasury Bonds)

8000.1.3.3.1   ## Bonds Originally Issued at Par

*Treasury Bonds Payable	xxxx	
Cash		xxxx
**Gain On Acquisition Of Treasury Bonds Payable		xxxx

To record acquisition of treasury bonds payable

Important: Make sure all appropriate subheads apply to your entry (see page v for instructions)

8000.1	**Bonds Payable**
8000.1.3	**Redemption or Other Reduction of Bonds Payable**
8000.1.3.3	**Reacquisition in the Market Without Cancellation (Treasury Bonds)**
8000.1.3.3.1	**Bonds Originally Issued at Par**

---

*Treasury Bonds Payable is debited for the par value (face, stated, or nominal value) of the bonds payable reacquired. This account is shown as a deduction from (contra account to) Bonds Payable on the balance sheet.

**Gain On Acquisition Of Treasury Bonds Payable is credited if the purchase price is less than the carrying value of the bonds reacquired. If the carrying value is less than the purchase price, Loss On Acquisition Of Treasury Bonds Payable is debited for the difference instead of this gain account. On rare occasions, the purchase price may equal the carrying value of the bonds and there is no gain or loss recorded. Any such gain or loss should be reported as an extraordinary item. If there are unamortized bond issuance costs, *see GEN8000.1.3.3.4.*

8000.1.3.3.2   **Bonds Originally Issued at a Premium**

*Premium On Bonds Payable	xxxx	
Bond Interest Expense		xxxx

To amortize premium up to the date of reacquisition

*Amortization of Premium On Bonds Payable must be brought up to date. Thus, amortization must be recorded for the period since the last time it was amortized. See note in *GEN8000.1.2.1.2* concerning how the premium is amortized.

*Treasury Bonds Payable	xxxx	
**Premium On Bonds Payable	xxxx	
Cash		xxxx
***Gain On Acquisition Of Treasury Bonds Payable		xxxx

To record acquisition of treasury bonds payable

*Treasury Bonds Payable is debited for the par value (face, stated, or nominal value) of the bonds payable reacquired. This account is shown as a deduction from (contra account to) Bonds Payable in the balance sheet.

**Premium On Bonds Payable will be debited for the portion of the balance in this account pertaining to the bonds reacquired. If the entire bond issue is reacquired, the entire balance in this account is eliminated.

***Gain On Acquisition Of Treasury Bonds Payable is credited if the purchase price is less than the carrying value (par value plus unamortized premium) of the bonds reacquired. If the carrying value is less than the purchase price, Loss On Acquisition

Important: Make sure all appropriate subheads apply to your entry (see page v for instructions)

8000.1	**Bonds Payable**
8000.1.3	**Redemption or Other Reduction of Bonds Payable**
8000.1.3.3	**Reacquisition in the Market Without Cancellation (Treasury Bonds)**
8000.1.3.3.2	**Bonds Originally Issued at a Premium**

Of Treasury Bonds Payable is debited for the difference instead of this gain account. On rare occasions, the purchase price may equal the carrying value of the bonds and there is no gain or loss recorded. Any gain or loss should be re-corded as an extraordinary item. If there are unamortized bond issuance costs, *see GEN8000.1.3.3.4.*

8000.1.3.3   **Bonds Originally Issued at a Discount**

Bond Interest Expense	xxxx	
*Discount On Bonds Payable		xxxx
To amortize discount up to the date of reacquisition		

*Amortization of Discount On Bonds Payable must be brought up to date. Thus, amortization must be recorded for the period since the last time it was amortized. See note in *GEN8000.1.2.1.3* concerning how the discount is amortized.

*Treasury Bonds Payable	xxxx	
**Discount On Bonds Payable		xxxx
Cash		xxxx
***Gain On Acquisition Of Treasury Bonds Payable		xxxx
To record reacquisition of bonds		

*Treasury Bonds Payable is debited for the par value (face, stated, or nominal value) of the bonds payable reacquired. This account is shown as a deduction from (contra account to) Bonds Payable in the balance sheet.

**Discount On Bonds Payable will be credited for the portion of the balance in this account pertaining to the bonds reacquired. If the entire bond issue is reacquired, the entire balance of this account is eliminated.

***Gain On Acquisition Of Treasury Bonds Payable is credited if the purchase price is less than the carrying value (par value less unamortized discount) of the bonds reacquired. If the carrying value is less than the purchase price, Loss On Acquisition Of Treasury Bonds Payable is debited for the difference instead of this gain account. On rare occasions, the purchase price may equal the carrying value of the bonds and there is no gain or loss recorded. Any gain or loss should be reported as an extraordinary item. If there are unamortized bond issuance costs, *see GEN8000.1.3.3.4.*

Important: Make sure all appropriate subheads apply to your entry (see page v for instructions)

8000.1   **Bonds Payable**
8000.1.3   **Redemption or Other Reduction of Bonds Payable**
8000.1.3.3   **Reacquisition in the Market Without Cancellation (Treasury Bonds)**

8000.1.3.3.4   **Unamortized Bond Issuance Cost at Acquisition of Treasury Bonds**

Bond issuance costs are amortized to expense on a straight-line basis over the life of the bonds. At acquisition of treasury bonds, the amortization of bond issuance costs must be brought up to date. The remaining unamortized balance must then be written off, resulting in either a reduction in the gain on redemption or an increase in the loss on redemption.

Amortization Of Bond Issuance Costs	xxxx	
Unamortized Bond Issue Costs		xxxx
To record amortization of bond issuance costs to the date of redemption		
*Gain On Acquisition Of Treasury Bonds Payable	xxxx	
Unamortized Bond Issue Costs		xxxx
To write off the remaining balance in Unamortized Bond Issue Costs		

*If Gain On Acquisition Of Treasury Bonds Payable was originally credited at acquisition, it is reduced as shown in this entry. If Loss On Acquisition Of Treasury Bonds Payable was originally debited at acquisition, it is increased (debited) instead of the gain account. If the amount of unamortized bond issue costs to write off exceeds the amount of gain originally recorded at acquisition, the gain account is debited with an amount sufficient to reduce its balance to zero, and the loss account is debited with an amount sufficient to balance this entry. Any gain or loss should be reported as an extraordinary item.

8000.1.3.4   **Extinguishment of Debt**

If debt is paid at its maturity date, the payment amount is usually the same as the carrying value, where no gain or loss is recognized *(see GEN8000.1.3.4.1)*. In some cases, however, a debt may be settled for an amount less than its carrying value under a troubled debt restructuring process *(see GEN8000.3.1)*.

Extinguishment of debt may take place through an in-substance defeasance. In-substance defeasance occures when cash and securities are placed in an irrevocable trust for the purpose of paying off the principle and interest of bonds as they mature.

Important: Make sure all appropriate subheads apply to your entry (see page v for instructions)

8000.1	**Bonds Payable**	
8000.1.3	**Redemption or Other Reduction of Bonds Payable**	
8000.1.3.4	**Extinguishment of Debt**	

8000.1.3.4.1

Extinguishment of Debt for its Carrying Value at its Maturity Date

*Bonds Payable	xxxx	
Cash		xxxx

To record extinguishment of debt at its maturity date

*Any remaining premium or discount is amortized as part of the interest expense (*see GEN8000.1.2.1.3* and *GEN8000.1.2.2.2*).

8000.1.3.4.2

Early Extinguishment of Debt

In some cases, a company may extinguish its debt or part of it before its maturity date. In these cases, the reacquisition price may be different from the carrying value of the debt at that time. The difference between the carrying value of the debt and its re-acquisition price will result in a gain or a loss to be recognized at the redemption date.

8000.1.3.4.2.1

Bonds Originally Issued at Par

Bonds Payable	xxxx	
Cash		xxxx
*Gain on Redemption of Bonds Payable		xxxx

To record early extinguishment of debt

*Gain On Redemption of Bonds Payable is credited if the reacquisition price is less that the carrying value of the bonds redeemed. If the carrying value is less than the reacquisition price, Loss on Redemption of Bonds Payable is debited for the difference, instead of this gain account.

8000.1.3.4.2.2

Bonds Originally Issued at a Premium

*Premium on Bonds Payable	xxxx	
Bond Interest Expense		xxxx

To amortize premium up to the date of redemption

*Amortization of Premium On Bonds Payable must be brought up to date. Thus, amortization must be recorded for the period since the last time it was amortized. See note in *GEN8000.1.2.1.2* concerning how the premium is amortized.

Important: Make sure all appropriate subheads apply to your entry (see page v for instructions)

8000.1	**Bonds Payable**
8000.1.3	**Redemption or Other Reduction of Bonds Payable**
8000.1.3.4	**Extinguishment of Debt**
8000.1.3.4.2	**Early Extinguishment of Debt**
8000.1.3.4.2.2	**Bonds Originally Issued at a Premium**

*Bonds Payable	xxxx	
*Premium On Bonds Payable	xxxx	
Cash [Various Securities]		xxxx
**Gain On Redemption Of Bonds Payable		xxxx

To record early extinguishment of debt

*Bonds Payable and Premium on bonds Payable will be debited for the portion of the balances in those accounts pertaining to the bonds redeemed. If the entire bond issue is redeemed, the entire balances in these accounts are eliminated.

**Gain On Redemption Of Bonds Payable is credited if the value of the cash and securities contributed to the trust are less than the carrying value (the sum of the debits to Bonds Payable and Premium On Bonds Payable) of the bonds redeemed. If the carrying value is less than the value of the cash and securities contributed, Loss On Redemption Of Bonds Payable is debited for the difference instead of this gain account. On rare occassions, the value of the cash and securities contributed may equal the carrying value of the bonds and there is no gain or loss recorded. If there are unamortized bond issuance costs, *see GEN8000.1.3.4.4.*

8000.1.3.4.2.3.   **Bonds Originally Issued at a Discount**

Bond Interest Expense	xxxx	
*Discount On Bonds Payable		xxxx

To amortize discount up to the date of redemption

*Amortization of Discount On Bonds Payable must be brought up to date. Thus, amortization must be recorded for the period since the last time it was amortized. See note in *GEN8000.1.2.1.3* concerning how the discount is amortized.

*Bonds Payable	xxxx	
*Discount On Bonds Payable		xxxx
Cash [Various Securities]		xxxx
**Gain On Redemption Of Bonds Payable		xxxx

To record early extinguishment of debt

*Bonds Payable and Discount On Bonds Payable will be debited and credited, respectively, for the portion of the balances in those accounts pertaining to the bonds redeemed. If the entire bond issue is redeemed, the entire balances in these accounts are eliminated.

Important: Make sure all appropriate subheads apply to your entry (see page v for instructions)

8000.1	**Bonds Payable**
8000.1.3	**Redemption or Other Reduction of Bonds Payable**
8000.1.3.4	**Extinguishment of Debt**
8000.1.3.4.2	**Early Extinguishment of Debt**
8000.1.3.4.2.3	**Bonds Originally Issued at a Discount**

**Gain On Redemption Of Bonds Payable is credited if the value of the cash and securities contributed to the trust are less than the carrying value (the debit to Bonds Payable less the credit to Discount On Bonds Payable) of the bonds redeemed. If the carrying value is less than the value of the cash and securities contributed, Loss On Redemption Of Bonds Payable is debited for the difference instead of this gain account. On rare occasions, the value of the cash and securities contributed may equal the carrying value of the bonds and there is no gain or loss recorded. If there are unamortized bond issuance costs, *see GEN8000.1.3.4.4.*

8000.1.3.4.4   **Unamortized Bond Issuance Cost at Reacquisition**

Bond Issuance Costs are amortized to expense on a straight-line basis over the life of the bonds. At defeasance, the amortization of bond issuance costs must be brought up to date. The remaining unamortized balance must then be written off, resulting in either a reduction in the gain on redemption or an increase in the loss on redemption.

Amortization Of Bond Issuance Costs	xxxx	
Unamortized Bond Issue Costs		xxxx
To record amortization of bond issuance costs to the date		
of redemption		
*Gain On Redemption Of Bonds Payable	xxxx	
Unamortized Bond Issue Costs		xxxx
To write off the remaining balance in Unamortized Bond		
Issue Costs		

*If Gain On Redemption Of Bonds Payable was originally credited at reacquisition, it is reduced as shown in this entry. If Loss On Redemption Of Bonds Payable was originally debited at reacquisition, it is increased (debited) instead of the gain account. If the amount of unamortized bond issue costs to write off exceeds the amount of gain originally recorded at redemption, the gain account is debited with an amount sufficient to reduce its balance to zero, and the loss account is debited with an amount sufficient to balance this entry. Any gain or loss should be reported as an extraordinary item.

8000.1.3.5   **Conversion of Bonds Payable into Stock**

Important: Make sure all appropriate subheads apply to your entry (see page v for instructions)

8000.1   **Bonds Payable**
8000.1.3   **Redemption or Other Reduction of Bonds Payable**
8000.1.3.5   **Conversion of Bonds Payable into Stock**

8000.1.3.5.1   **Market Value Approach to Conversion**

Under this method, the stock is recorded at its market value on the date of conversion (date of issuance of stock).

8000.1.3.5.1.1   **Bonds Originally Issued at Par**

Bonds Payable	xxxx	
*Loss On Conversion Of Bonds Payable	xxxx	
*Common (Preferred) Stock		xxxx
***Paid-In Capital In Excess Of Par (Stated) Value Of Common (Preferred) Stock		xxxx

To record loss on conversion of bonds payable

*The loss is calculated as the excess of the market value of stock given up over the carrying value of the bonds converted. If the carrying value of the bonds converted is in excess of the market value of the stock given up, Gain On Conversion Of Bonds Payable would be credited instead of this debit. If there are unamortized bond issuance costs, *see GEN8000.1.3.5.1.4.*

**Common (or Preferred) Stock is credited for the par (or stated) value of the stock issued.

***Paid-In Capital In Excess Of Par (or Stated) Value Of Common (or Preferred) Stock is credited for the excess of the market value of the stock issued over its par (or stated) value. This account is sometimes called Additional Paid-In Capital.

8000.1.3.5.1.2   **Bonds Originally Issued at a Premium**

*Premium On Bonds Payable	xxxx	
Bond Interest Expense		xxxx

To amortize premium up to the date of redemption

*Amortization of Premium on Bonds Payable must be brought up to date. Thus, amortization must be recorded for the period since the last time it was amortized. See note in *GEN8000.1.2.1.2* concerning how the premium is amortized.

Important: Make sure all appropriate subheads apply to your entry (see page v for instructions)

8000.1	**Bonds Payable**
8000.1.3	**Redemption or Other Reduction of Bonds Payable**
8000.1.3.5	**Conversion of Bonds Payable into Stock**
8000.1.3.5.1	**Market Value Approach to Conversion**
8000.1.3.5.1.2	**Bonds Originally Issued at a Premium**

---

*Bonds Payable	xxxx	
**Loss On Conversion Of Bonds Payable	xxxx	
*Premium On Bonds Payable	xxxx	
***Common (Preferred) Stock		xxxx
****Paid-In Capital In Excess Of Par (Stated) Value Of		
Common (Preferred) Stock		xxxx

To record loss on conversion of bonds payable

*Bonds Payable and Premium On Bonds Payable will be debited for the portion of the balances in those accounts pertaining to the bonds converted. If the entire bond issue is converted, the entire balances in these accounts are eliminated.

**The loss is calculated as the excess of the market value of stock given up over the carrying value (the sum of the debits to Bonds Payable and Premium On Bonds Payable) of the bonds converted. If the carrying value of the bonds converted is in excess of the market value of the stock given up, Gain On Conversion Of Bonds Payable would be credited instead of this debit. If there is unamortized bond issuance costs, see *GEN8000.1.3.5.1.4.*

***Common (or Preferred) Stock is credited for the par (or stated) value of the stock issued.

****Paid-In Capital In Excess Of Par (or Stated) Value Of Common (or Preferred) Stock is credited for the excess of the market value of the stock issued over its par (or stated) value. This account is sometimes called Additional Paid-In Capital.

8000.1.3.5.1.3   **Bonds Originally Issued at a Discount**

Bond Interest Expense	xxxx	
*Discount On Bonds Payable		xxxx

To amortize discount up to the date of redemption

*Amortization of Discount On Bonds Payable must be brought up to date. Thus, amortization must be recorded for the period since the last time it was amortized. See note in *GEN8000.1.2.1.3* concerning how the discount is amortized.

Important: Make sure all appropriate subheads apply to your entry (see page v for instructions)

8000.1	**Bonds Payable**
8000.1.3	**Redemption or Other Reduction of Bonds Payable**
8000.1.3.5	**Conversion of Bonds Payable into Stock**
8000.1.3.5.1	**Market Value Approach to Conversion**
8000.1.3.5.1.3	**Bonds Originally Issued at a Discount**

---

*Bonds Payable	xxxx	
**Loss On Conversion Of Bonds Payable	xxxx	
*Discount On Bonds Payable		xxxx
***Common (Preferred) Stock		xxxx
****Paid-In Capital In Excess Of Par (Stated) Value Of Common (Preferred) Stock		xxxx

To record loss on conversion of bonds payable

*Bonds Payable will be debited and Discount On Bonds Payable will be credited for the portion of the balances in those accounts pertaining to the bonds converted. If theentire bond issue is converted, the entire balances in these accounts are eliminated.

**The loss is calculated as the excess of the market value of stock given up over the carrying value (the debit to Bonds Payable less the credit to Discount On Bonds Payable) of the bonds converted. If the carrying value of the bonds converted is in excess of the market value of the stock given up, Gain On Conversion Of Bonds Payable would be credited instead of this debit. If there are unamortized bond issuance costs, *see GEN8000.1.3.5.1.4.*

***Common (or Preferred) Stock is credited for the par (or stated) value of the stock issued.

****Paid-In Capital In Excess Of Par (or Stated) Value Of Common (or Preferred) Stock is credited for the excess of the market value of the stock issued over its par (or stated) value. This account is sometimes called Additional Paid-In Capital.

8000.1.3.5.1.4   **Unamortized Bond Issuance Cost at Conversion**

Bond issuance costs are amortized to expense on a straight-line basis over the life of the bonds. At conversion, the amortization of bond issuance costs must be brought up to date. The remaining unamortized balance must then be written off, resulting in either a reduction in the gain on conversion or an increase in the loss on conversion.

Amortization Of Bond Issuance Costs	xxxx	
Unamortized Bond Issue Costs		xxxx

To record amortization of bond issuance costs to the date of redemption

---

Important: Make sure all appropriate subheads apply to your entry (see page v for instructions)

8000.1	**Bonds Payable**
8000.1.3	**Redemption or Other Reduction of Bonds Payable**
8000.1.3.5	**Conversion of Bonds Payable into Stock**
8000.1.3.5.1	**Market Value Approach to Conversion**
8000.1.3.5.1.4	**Unamortized Bond Issuance Cost at Conversion**

---

*Loss On Conversion Of Bonds Payable	xxxx	
Unamortized Bond Issue Costs		xxxx

To write off the remaining balance in Unamortized Bond Issue Costs

*If Loss On Conversion Of Bonds Payable was originally debited at conversion, it is increased as shown in this entry. If Gain On Conversion Of Bonds Payable was originally credited at conversion, it is debited (reduced) instead of the loss account. If the amount of unamortized bond issue costs to write off exceeds the amount of gain originally recorded at reacquisition, the gain account is debited with an amount sufficient to reduce its balance to zero, and the loss account is debited with an amount sufficient to balance this entry.

8000.1.3.5.2   **Book (Carrying) Value Approach to Conversion**

Under this method, the stock is recorded at the book (carrying) value of the bonds on the date of conversion (date of issuance of stock), and no loss or gain is recorded.

8000.1.3.5.2.1   **Bonds Originally Issued at Par**

Bonds Payable	xxxx	
*Common (Preferred) Stock		xxxx
**Paid-In Capital In Excess Of Par (Stated) Value Of Common (Preferred) Stock		xxxx

To record conversion of bonds payable at book value

*Common (or Preferred) Stock is credited for the par (or stated) value of the stock issued.

**Paid-In Capital In Excess Of Par (or Stated) Value Of Common (or Preferred) Stock is credited for the excess of the book value of the stock issued over its par (or stated) value. This account is sometimes called Additional Paid-In Capital.

8000.1.3.5.2.2   **Bonds Originally Issued at a Premium**

*Premium On Bonds Payable	xxxx	
Bond Interest Expense		xxxx

To amortize premium up to the date of redemption

Important: Make sure all appropriate subheads apply to your entry (see page v for instructions)

8000.1   **Bonds Payable**
8000.1.3   **Redemption or Other Reduction of Bonds Payable**
8000.1.3.5   **Conversion of Bonds Payable into Stock**
8000.1.3.5.2   **Book (Carrying) Value Approach to Conversion**
8000.1.3.5.2.2   **Bonds Originally Issued at a Premium**

---

*Amortization of Premium On Bonds Payable must be brought up to date. Thus, amortization must be recorded for the period since the last time it was amortized. See note in *GEN8000.1.2.1.2* concerning how the premium is amortized.

*Bonds Payable	xxxx	
*Premium On Bonds Payable	xxxx	
**Common (Preferred) Stock		xxxx
***Paid-In Capital In Excess Of Par (Stated) Value Of		
Common (Preferred) Stock		xxxx

To record conversion of bonds payable at book value

*Bonds Payable and Premium On Bonds Payable will be debited for the portion of the balances in those accounts pertaining to the bonds converted. If the entire bond issue is converted, the entire balances in these accounts are eliminated.

**Common (or Preferred) Stock is credited for the par (or stated) value of the stock issued.

***Paid-In Capital In Excess Of Par (or Stated) Value Of Common (or Preferred) Stock is credited for the excess of the book (carrying) value of the bonds converted over the par (or stated) value of the stock issued. This account is also called Additional Paid-In Capital.

8000.1.3.5.2.3   **Bonds Originally Issued at a Discount**

Bond Interest Expense	xxxx	
*Discount On Bonds Payable		xxxx

To amortize discount up to the date of redemption

*Amortization of Discount on Bonds Payable must be brought up to date. Thus, amortization must be recorded for the period since the last time it was amortized. See note in *GEN8000.1.2.1.3* concerning how the discount is amortized.

*Bonds Payable	xxxx	
*Discount On Bonds Payable		xxxx
**Common (Preferred) Stock		xxxx
***Paid-In Capital In Excess Of Par (Stated) Value Of		
Common (Preferred) Stock		xxxx

To record conversion of bonds payable at book value

Important: Make sure all appropriate subheads apply to your entry (see page v for instructions)

8000.1 **Bonds Payable**
8000.1.3   **Redemption or Other Reduction of Bonds Payable**
8000.1.3.5   **Conversion of Bonds Payable into Stock**
8000.1.3.5.2   **Book (Carrying) Value Approach to Conversion**
8000.1.3.5.2.3   **Bonds Originally Issued at a Discount**

---

*Bonds Payable will be debited and Discount On Bonds Payable will be credited for the portion of the balances in those accounts pertaining to the bonds converted. If the entire bond issue is converted, the entire balances in these accounts are eliminated.

**Common (or Preferred) Stock is credited for the par (or stated) value of the stock issued.

***Paid-In Capital In Excess Of Par (or Stated) Value Of Common (or Preferred) Stock is credited for the excess of the book (carrying) value of the bonds converted over the par (or stated) value of the stock issued. This account is also called Additional Paid-In Capital.

8000.1.3.5.3   **Induced Conversion**

Induced conversion occurs if additional cash or other consideration is offered to bond holders to induce conversion.

*Bond Conversion Expense	xxxx	
Cash ([Various Accounts])		xxxx
To record expense of induced conversion of bonds payable		

*The value of the additional cash or other consideration given to induce conversion is recorded in Bond Conversion Expense rather than as a loss (or reduction of a gain) on conversion. For other entries to record the conversion, *see GEN8000.1.3.5.1* (market value method) or *GEN8000.1.3.5.2* (book value method).

8000.2   **Long-Term Notes Payable**

8000.2.1   **Issuance of Long-Term Notes Payable**

8000.2.1.1   **Noninterest-Bearing Notes and Notes Bearing Interest at a Rate Different from the Market Rate of Interest**

Cash ([Various Assets])	xxxx	
*Discount On Notes Payable	xxxx	
**Notes Payable		xxxx
To record issuance of note payable		

Important: Make sure all appropriate subheads apply to your entry (see page v for instructions)

8000.2   **Long-Term Notes Payable**
8000.2.1   **Issuance of Long-Term Notes Payable**
8000.2.1.1   **Noninterest-Bearing Notes and Notes Bearing Interest at a Rate Different from the Market Rate of Interest**

---

*Discount On Notes Payable will be debited for the excess of the face value of the note payable over the amount of cash and/or fair market value of other assets received. Such an excess will occur if the market rate of interest exceeds the stated rate of the note. If the market rate of interest is less than the stated rate of the note, the cash and/or fair market value of other assets received will exceed the face value of the note, and Premium On Notes Payable will be credited for this excess. The discount or premium account is then amortized to interest expense over the life of the note.

**Notes Payable is credited for the face value of the note.

8000.2.1.2   **Notes Payable Exchanged for Cash Plus a Privilege or Right**

Cash	xxxx	
*Discount On Notes Payable	xxxx	
**Notes Payable		xxxx
*Unearned Revenue		xxxx
To record issuance of note payable		

*Discount On Notes Payable is debited and Unearned Revenue is credited for an equal amount that is the excess of the amount of cash received over the present value of the note payable issued. Thus, both the discount account and Unearned Revenue are initially debited and credited, respectively, for the value of the privilege or right given. The discount account is then amortized to interest expense over the life of the note. Unearned Revenue is recognized as revenue as the privilege or right is consumed or expires.

**Notes Payable is credited for the face value of the note.

8000.2.1.3   **Notes Payable Issued in a Noncash Transaction**

*Machinery ([Various Assets])	xxxx	
**Discount On Notes Payable	xxxx	
***Notes Payable		xxxx
To record issuance of note payable		

*The asset acquired is debited for its fair market value.

**The Discount On Notes Payable is debited for the excess of the face value of the note payable over the fair market value of the asset acquired. If the face value of the

Important: Make sure all appropriate subheads apply to your entry (see page v for instructions)

8000.2	**Long-Term Notes Payable**
8000.2.1	**Issuance of Long-Term Notes Payable**
8000.2.1.3	**Notes Payable Issued in a Noncash Transaction**

---

note payable is less than the fair market value of the asset acquired, Premium On Notes Payable is credited instead of this debit. The discount or premium account is then amortized to interest expense over the life of the note.

***Notes Payable is credited for the face value of the note.

8000.2.1.4   **Issuance of Mortgage Note Payable**

Cash	xxxx	
Mortgage Payable		xxxx
To record issuance of mortgage note payable		

8000.2.1.5   **Imputed Interest**

If the fair market value of the noncash assets received cannot be determined and if there is no ready market for the note payable, the present value of the note must be estimated by discounting the cash flows using an assumed market rate of interest. If the assumed market interest rate differs from the stated rate of interest on the note payable, this process is referred to as interest imputation.

*Machinery ([Various Assets])	xxxx	
**Discount On Notes Payable	xxxx	
***Notes Payable		xxxx
To record issuance of note payable		

*The asset acquired is debited for the present value of the note payable as determined by interest imputation.

**Discount On Notes Payable is debited for the excess of the face value of the note payable over its present value as determined by interest imputation. If the present value exceeds the face value, Premium On Notes Payable would be credited instead of this debit. Any discount or premium must be amortized to interest expense over the life of the note.

***Notes Payable is credited for the face value of the note.

Important: Make sure all appropriate subheads apply to your entry (see page v for instructions)

8000.2   **Long-Term Notes Payable**

8000.2.2   **Interest Rate Swaps**

No journal entries are required, but disclosures are required.

8000.2.3   **Take-or-Pay Contracts**

In a take-or-pay contract, a purchaser of goods signs a contract with a supplier and receives an option to take delivery of goods in return for an obligation to pay specified amounts periodically regardless of whether or not delivery of the goods is taken.

8000.2.3.1   **Issuance of Note Payable and Signing of Contract**

Goods Receivable	xxxx	
Notes Payable		xxxx
To record signing of take-or-pay contract		

8000.2.3.2   **Payment of Take-or-Pay Note Payable**

Notes Payable	xxxx	
Cash		xxxx
To record payment of take-or-pay note payable		

8000.2.3.3   **Receipt of Take-or-Pay Goods**

Inventory (Purchases, Supplies)	xxxx	
Goods Receivable		xxxx
To record receipt of take-or-pay goods		

8000.2.4   **Through-Put Contracts**

In a through-put contract, a purchaser of services signs a contract with a supplier and receives an option to take delivery of services in return for an obligation to pay specified amounts periodically regardless of whether or not delivery of the service is taken.

Important: Make sure all appropriate subheads apply to your entry (see page v for instructions)

8000.2   **Long-Term Notes Payable**
8000.2.4   **Through-Put Contracts**

8000.2.4.1   **Issuance of Through-Put Note Payable and Signing of Contract**

Services Receivable	xxxx	
Notes Payable		xxxx

To record signing of through-put contract

8000.2.4.2   **Payment of Through-Put Note Payable**

Notes Payable	xxxx	
Cash		xxxx

To record payment of through-put note payable

8000.2.4.3   **Receipt of Through-Put Services**

Transportation Expense ([Various Services Expense])	xxxx	
Services Receivable		xxxx

To record receipt of through-put services

8000.3   **Troubled Debt Restructuring**

In a troubled debt restructuring, debt is either settled at an amount less than its carrying (book) value, or it is continued with a modification of terms (interest rate, principal, etc).

8000.3.1   **Settlement of Debt at Less than Carrying (Book) Value**

8000.3.1.1   **Settlement by Transfer of Assets**

*Notes Payable	xxxx	
**Interest Payable	xxxx	
***Loss On Disposal Of Assets	xxxx	
****Gain On Debt Restructure		xxxx
*****[Various Assets]		xxxx

To record debt restructure

*Notes Payable is debited for the amount of any principle reduction.

Important: Make sure all appropriate subheads apply to your entry (see page v for instructions)

8000.3   **Troubled Debt Restructuring**
8000.3.1   **Settlement of Debt at Less than Carrying (Book) Value**
8000.3.1.1   **Settlement by Transfer of Assets**

**Interest Payable is debited for the amount of any interest forgiven.

***Loss On Disposal Of Assets is debited for the excess of the book (carrying) value of the assets given up over their fair market value. If the fair market value of the assets given up exceeds their book value, Gain On Disposal Of Assets is credited instead of this debit.

****Gain On Debt Restructure is credited for the total of the principle and interest forgiven. Any such gain is reported as an extraordinary item.

*****Various asset accounts may be credited. If there is accumulated depreciation related to these accounts, various accumulated depreciation accounts are debited as well.

8000.3.1.2   **Settlement by Transfer of Equity**

*Notes Payable	xxxx	
**Interest Payable	xxxx	
***Common (Preferred) Stock		xxxx
***Paid-In Capital In Excess Of Par (Stated) Value Of Common (Preferred) Stock		xxxx
****Gain On Debt Restructure		xxxx
To record debt restructure		

*Notes Payable is debited for the amount of any principal reduction.

**Interest Payable is debited for the amount of any interest forgiven.

***Common (Preferred) stock is credited for the par or stated value of the stock given. Paid-In Capital In Excess Of Par (or Stated) Value is credited for the excess of the fair market value of the stock given over its par or stated value.

****Gain On Debt Restructure is credited for the total of the principle and interest forgiven. Any gain is reported as an extraordinary item.

8000.3.2   **Continuation of Debt with Modification of Terms**

LONG-TERM LIABILITIES

GEN8000.3.2.1   GEN8000.3.2.2.1

Important: Make sure all appropriate subheads apply to your entry (see page v for instructions)

8000.3   **Troubled Debt Restructuring**
8000.3.2   **Continuation of Debt with Modification of Terms**

8000.3.2.1   **Present (Undiscounted) Value of Total Future Cash Payments Is More than Book Value of Debt**

In this situation, the carrying (book) value of the debt is not reduced. Interest is recognized as part of future payments.

8000.3.2.1.1   **Restructure**

    *Interest Payable   xxxx
      *Notes Payable   xxxx
    To record debt restructure*

*The accrued interest payable balance is transferred to Notes Payable.

8000.3.2.1.2   **Future Payments**

    Interest Expense   xxxx
    Notes Payable   xxxx
      Cash   xxxx
    To record payment on notes payable

8000.3.2.2   **Present (Undiscounted) Value of Total Future Cash Payments Is Less than Book Value of Debt**

8000.3.2.2.1   **Restructure**

    *Interest Payable   xxxx
    **Notes Payable   xxxx
      ***Gain On Debt Restructure   xxxx
    To record debt restructure*

*Accrued interest is removed from the books.

**Notes Payable is debited for the amount of principal reduction.

***Gain On Debt Restructure is credited to balance the entry.

Important: Make sure all appropriate subheads apply to your entry (see page v for instructions)

8000.3   **Troubled Debt Restructuring**
8000.3.2   **Continuation of Debt with Modification of Terms**
8000.3.2.2   **Present (Undiscounted) Value of Total Future Cash Payments Is Less than Book Value of Debt**

8000.3.2.2.2   **Future Payments**

*Notes Payable	xxxx	
Cash		xxxx

To record payment on notes payable

*Each payment reduces Notes Payable and no interest is recognized.

TABLE OF CONTENTS

9000.1	**Issuance of Stock**

9000.1.1	**Common (Preferred) Stock with Par Value**

9000.1.1.1	**Common (Preferred) Stock with Par Value Issued for Cash at a Price Equal to Par Value**

Cash	xxxx	
Common Stock		xxxx

To record issuance of stock

9000.1.1.2	**Common (Preferred) Stock with Par Value Issued for Cash at a Price Greater than Par Value**

Cash	xxxx	
*Common (Preferred) Stock		xxxx
**Additional Paid-In Capital - Common Preferred		
Stock		xxxx

To record issuance of stock

*Common (Preferred) Stock is credited for the par value of the shares issued.

**Common alternative account titles include:
- Contributed Capital In Excess Of Par - Common (Preferred) Stock
- Paid-In Capital In Excess Of Par - Common (Preferred) Stock
- Premium On Common (Preferred) Stock.

This account is credited for the excess of the issuance price over the par value of the shares issued.

9000.1.1.3	**Common (Preferred) Stock with Par Value Issued for Cash at a Price Less than Par Value**

Cash	xxxx	
*Additional Paid-In Capital - Common (Preferred) Stock	xxxx	
**Common (Preferred) Stock		xxxx

To record issuance of stock

Important: Make sure all appropriate subheads apply to your entry (see page v for instructions)

9000.1	**Issuance of Stock**
9000.1.1	**Common (Preferred) Stock with Par Value**
9000.1.1.3	**Common (Preferred) Stock with Par Value Issued for Cash at a Price Less than Par Value**

---

*Common alternative account titles include:
- Contributed Capital In Excess Of Par - Common (Preferred) Stock
- Paid-In Capital In Excess Of Par - Common (Preferred) Stock
- Premium On Common (Preferred) Stock.

This account is debited for the excess of the par value of the shares issued overthe issuance price. Stock is not usually issued at less than par if an entry like thiswould produce a debit balance in the account, because the buyer of the stock may be liable for such a difference. If a debit balance does result, a Discount On Common (Preferred) Stock account may be used for the debit balance. Some states may not allow stock to be issued at less than par value.

**Common (Preferred) Stock is credited for the par value of the shares issued.

9000.1.2   **Common (Preferred) Stock with Stated Value**

9000.1.2.1   **Common (Preferred) Stock with Stated Value Issued for Cash at Stated Value**

Cash	xxxx	
Common (Preferred) Stock		xxxx
To record issuance of stock		

9000.1.2.2   **Common (Preferred) Stock with Stated Value Issued for Cash at a Price Greater than Stated Value**

Cash	xxxx	
*Common (Preferred) Stock		xxxx
**Additional Paid-In Capital - Common (Preferred) Stock		xxxx
To record issuance of stock		

*Common (Preferred) Stock is credited for the stated value of the shares issued.

**Common alternative account titles include:
- Contributed Capital In Excess Of Stated Value - Common (Preferred) Stock
- Paid-In Capital In Excess Of Stated Value - Common (Preferred) Stock.

Important: Make sure all appropriate subheads apply to your entry (see page v for instructions)

9000.1   **Issuance of Stock**
9000.1.2   **Common (Preferred) Stock with Stated Value**
9000.1.2.2   **Common (Preferred) Stock with Stated Value Issued for Cash at a Price Greater than Stated Value**

This account is credited for the excess of the issuance price over the stated value of the shares issued.

9000.1.2.3   **Common (Preferred) Stock with Stated Value Issued for Cash at a Price Less than Stated Value**

Cash	xxxx
*Additional Paid-In Capital - Common (Preferred) Stock	xxxx
**Common (Preferred) Stock	xxxx

To record issuance of stock

*Common alternative account titles include:
- Contributed Capital In Excess Of Stated Value - Common (Preferred) Stock
- Paid-In Capital In Excess Of Stated Value - Common (Preferred) Stock.

This account is debited for the excess of the stated value of the shares issued over the issuance price. Stock is not usually issued for less than stated value if an entry such as this would produce a debit balance in this account.

**Common (Preferred) Stock is credited for the stated value of the shares issued.

9000.1.3   **Common (Preferred) Stock with No Par (Stated) Value**

Cash	xxxx
Common (Preferred) Stock	xxxx

To record issuance of stock

9000.1.4   **Stock Subscriptions**

When stock is issued on a subscription basis, an initial down payment may be received, and the balance of the issuance price is then received in one or more installments over a previously agreed-to period. The stock certificates are not issued until the entire subscription price has been received.

9000.1.4.1   **Initial Subscription**

Important: Make sure all appropriate subheads apply to your entry (see page v for instructions)

9000.1   **Issuance of Stock**
9000.1.4   **Stock Subscriptions**
9000.1.4.1   **Initial Subscription**

9000.1.4.1.1   **Common (Preferred) Stock with Par (Stated) Value**

> *Common (Preferred) Stock Subscriptions Receivable   xxxx
> **Common (Preferred) Stock Subscribed   xxxx
> ***Additional Paid-In Capital - Common (Preferred)
> Stock   xxxx
> *To record stock subscriptions*

*Common (Preferred) Stock Subscriptions Receivable is debited for the total subscription price of the shares. This account is normally shown in the balance sheet as a deduction from the total of stockholders' equity (as normally required by the Securities and Exchange Commission).

**Common (Preferred) Stock Subscribed is credited for the par or stated value of the shares. This account is shown in the balance sheet as part of stockholders' equity.

***Common alternative account titles include:
> - Contributed Capital In Excess Of Par (Stated) Value - Common (Preferred) Stock
> - Paid-In Capital In Excess Of Par (Stated) Value - Common (Preferred) Stock.

This account is credited for the excess of the subscription price over the par (stated) value of the shares.

9000.1.4.1.2   **Common (Preferred) Stock with No Par (Stated) Value**

> *Common (Preferred) Stock Subscriptions Receivable   xxxx
> **Common (Preferred) Stock Subscribed   xxxx
> *To record stock subscriptions*

**Common (Preferred) Stock Subscriptions Receivable is debited for the total subscription price of the shares. This account is usually shown in the balance sheet as a deduction from the total of stockholders' equity (as normally required by the Securities and Exchange Commission).

**Common (Preferred) Stock Subscribed is credited for the total subscription price of the shares. This account is shown on the balance sheet as part of stockholders' equity.

Important: Make sure all appropriate subheads apply to your entry (see page v for instructions)

9000.1   **Issuance of Stock**
9000.1.4   **Stock Subscriptions**

9000.1.4.2   **Receipt of Installment Payment (Down Payment) on a Stock Subscription**

Cash	xxxx	
Common (Preferred) Stock Subscriptions Receivable		xxxx

To record receipt of a stock subscription installment payment

9000.1.4.3   **Issuance of Stock After Last Installment Payment Is Received**

Common (Preferred) Stock Subscribed	xxxx	
Common (Preferred) Stock		xxxx

To record issuance of stock

9000.1.4.4   **Stock Subscription Defaults**

The method of accounting for stock subscription defaults is determined by the laws of the state in which the firm is incorporated.

9000.1.4.4.1   **All Cash Paid by Subscriber Is Returned to Subscriber**

*Common (Preferred) Stock Subscribed	xxxx	
**Additional Paid-In Capital - Common (Preferred) Stock	xxxx	
***Common (Preferred) Stock Subscriptions Receivable		xxxx
****Cash		xxxx

To record default of a stock subscription and return of cash paid by subscriber

*Common (Preferred) Stock Subscribed is debited sufficiently to remove the credit in the account relating to the defaulted subscription.

**Common alternative account titles include:
- Contributed Capital In Excess Of Par (Stated) Value - Common (Preferred) Stock
- Paid-In Capital In Excess Of Par (Stated) Value - Common (Preferred) Stock.

Important: Make sure all appropriate subheads apply to your entry (see page v for instructions)

9000.1	**Issuance of Stock**
9000.1.4	**Stock Subscriptions**
9000.1.4.4	**Stock Subscription Defaults**
9000.1.4.4.1	**All Cash Paid by Subscriber Is Returned to Subscriber**

This account is debited only if the subscribed-to shares have a par (stated) value. In this case, the account will be debitd for any excess of the original subscription price over the par (stated) value of the subscribed-to shares (i.e., the amount credited to this account when the original subscription was recorded). If the subscribed-to shares do not have a par (stated) value, the account is not involved in this entry.

***Common (Preferred) Stock Subscriptions Receivable is credited sufficiently to remove the uncollected balance of the original subscription price.

****Cash is credited in an amount equal to the cash returned to the defaulting subscriber.

9000.1.4.4.2   ## A Pro-Rated Amount of Stock Is Issued to Subscriber

*Common (Preferred) Stock Subscribed	xxxx	
**Additional Paid-In Capital - Common (Preferred) Stock	xxxx	
***Common (Preferred) Stock Subscriptions Receivable		xxxx
****Common (Preferred) Stock		xxxx

To record default of a stock subscription and issuance of a pro-rated amount of stock

*Common (Preferred) Stock Subscribed is debited sufficiently to remove the credit in the account relating to the shares that are the subject of the defaulted subscription.

**Common alternative account titles include:
- Contributed Capital In Excess Of Par (Stated) Value - Common (Pre-ferred) Stock
- Paid-In Capital In Excess Of Par (Stated) Value - Common (Preferred) Stock.

This account is debited only if the subscribed-to shares have a par or stated value. In this case, the account will be debited for any excess of the original subscription price over the par or stated value of the subscribed-to shares that are not now to be issued (i.e., the amount that had been credited to this account for the shares not now to be issued when the original subscription was recorded). If the subscribed-to shares do not have either a par or stated value, this account is not involved in this entry.

***Common (Preferred) Stock Subscriptions Receivable is credited sufficiently to remove the uncollected balance of the original subscription price.

Important: Make sure all appropriate subheads apply to your entry (see page v for instructions)

9000.1	**Issuance of Stock**
9000.1.4	**Stock Subscriptions**
9000.1.4.4	**Stock Subscription Defaults**
9000.1.4.4.2	**A Pro-Rated Amount of Stock Is Issued to Subscriber**

****Common (Preferred) Stock is credited to balance the entry. If the stock has a par or stated value, this credit will equal the par or stated value of the shares now issued.

9000.1.4.4.3   **No Refund Is Made or Stock Issued: the Company Keeps All Payments Previously Made by Defaulting Subscriber**

*Common (Preferred) Stock Subscribed	xxxx	
**Additional Paid-In Capital - Common (Preferred) Stock	xxxx	
***Common (Preferred) Stock Subscriptions Receivable		xxxx
****Paid-In Capital From Defaulted Stock Subscriptions - Common (Preferred) Stock		xxxx

To record a defaulted stock subscription

*Common (Preferred) Stock Subscribed is debited sufficiently to remove the credit in the account relating to the shares that are the subject of the defaulted subscription.

**Common alternative account titles include:
- Contributed Capital In Excess Of Par (Stated) Value - Common (Preferred) Stock
- Paid-In Capital In Excess Of Par (Stated) Value - Common (Preferred) Stock.

This account is debited only if the subscribed-to shares have a par or stated value. In this case, the account will be debited for any excess of the original subscription price over the par or stated value of the subscribed-to shares (i.e., the amount credited to this account when the original subscription was recorded). If the subscribed-to shares do not have either a par or stated value, the account is not involved in this entry.

***Common (Preferred) Stock Subscriptions Receivable is credited sufficiently to remove the uncollected balance of the original subscription price.

****Paid-In Capital From Defaulted Stock Subscriptions - Common (Preferred) Stock is credited to balance the entry. If the stock has a par or stated value, Additional Paid-In Capital - Common (Preferred) Stock may be credited instead of this account. If the stock does not have either a par or stated value, Paid-In Capital From Defaulted Stock Subscriptions - Common (Preferred) Stock may be credited as shown.

Important: Make sure all appropriate subheads apply to your entry (see page v for instructions)

9000.1   **Issuance of Stock**
9000.1.4   **Stock Subscriptions**
9000.1.4.4   **Stock Subscription Defaults**

9000.1.4.4.4   **Excess of Cash from Subsequent Resale Over Original Subscription Price Must Be Returned to Defaulting Subscriber**

In this case, there is usually no entry made until the subsequent resale. However, until the resale occurs, the related stock subscription receivable is deducted from the stock section.

9000.1.4.4.4.1   **Subsequent Resale Is at a Price Equal to or Greater than Original Subscription Price**

*Cash	xxxx	
**Common (Preferred) Stock Subscribed	xxxx	
***Common (Preferred) Stock		xxxx
****Common (Preferred) Stock Subscriptions Receivable		xxxx
To record sale of stock previously subscribed to and defaulted upon		

*Cash is debited for the amount of cash received.

**Common (Preferred) Stock Subscribed is debited sufficiently to remove the credit in the account relating to the shares which are the subject of the defaulted subscription.

***Common (Preferred) Stock is credited for the same amount as the debit to Common Stock Subscribed.

****Common (Preferred) Stock Subscriptions Receivable is credited for the same amount as the debit to Cash.

*Common (Preferred) Stock Subscriptions Receivable	xxxx	
*Cash		xxxx
To record a refund paid to defaulting subscriber		

*Common (Preferred) Stock Subscriptions Receivable is debited and Cash is credited for any excess of the cash received at resale of the stock (as recorded in the previous entry) over the amount of the stock subscription receivable that had not been collected from the defaulted subscriber. This entry will be necessary only if the resale of the stock was made at a price greater than the original subscription price. If the resale was made at a price equal to the original subscription price, no entry is necessary. If the

Important: Make sure all appropriate subheads apply to your entry (see page v for instructions)

9000.1	**Issuance of Stock**
9000.1.4	**Stock Subscriptions**
9000.1.4.4	**Stock Subscription Defaults**
9000.1.4.4.4	**Excess of Cash from Subsequent Resale Over Original Subscription Price Must Be Returned to Defaulting Subscriber**
9000.1.4.4.4.1	**Subsequent Resale Is at a Price Equal to or Greater than Original Subscription Price**

---

resale was made at a price less than the original subscription price, *see GEN9000.1.4.4.4.2.*

9000.1.4.4.4.2   **Subsequent Resale Is at a Price Less than Original Subscription Price**

*Cash	xxxx	
**Common (Preferred) Stock Subscribed	xxxx	
***Common (Preferred) Stock		xxxx
****Common (Preferred) Stock Subscriptions Receivable		xxxx

To record sale of stock previously subscribed to and defaulted upon

*Cash is debited for the amount of cash received.

**Common (Preferred) Stock Subscribed is debited sufficiently to remove the credit in the account relating to the shares that are the subject of the defaulted subscription.

***Common (Preferred) Stock is credited for the same amount as the debit to Common Stock Subscribed.

****Common (Preferred) Stock Subscriptions Receivable is credited for the same amount as the debit to Cash.

*Additional Paid-In Capital - Common (Preferred) Stock	xxxx	
**Common (Preferred) Stock Subscriptions Receivable		xxxx

To record removal of remaining stock subscription receivable

*Common alternative account titles include:
- Contributed Capital In Excess Of Par (Stated) Value - Common (Preferred) Stock
- Paid-In Capital In Excess Of Par (Stated) Value - Common (Preferred) Stock.

This account is debited to balance the entry if the stock has a par or stated value. If the stock does not have a par or stated value, the debit is made to Common (Preferred) Stock.

**Common (Preferred) Stock Subscriptions Receivable is credited for the excess of the amount of the uncollected receivable when the default occurred over the amount

Important: Make sure all appropriate subheads apply to your entry (see page v for instructions)

9000.1	**Issuance of Stock**
9000.1.4	**Stock Subscriptions**
9000.1.4.4	**Stock Subscription Defaults**
9000.1.4.4.4	**Excess of Cash from Subsequent Resale Over Original Subscription Price Must Be Returned to Defaulting Subscriber**
9000.1.4.4.4.2	**Subsequent Resale Is at a Price Less than Original Subscription Price**

---

of cash received upon resale of the stock. That is, the total of the credits to this account in this and the previous entry should equal the amount of subscription receivable that was never collected from the defaulting subscriber.

9000.1.5   **Lump Sum Issuances**

A lump sum issuance occurs if two or more classes of securities are issued for one price.

9000.1.5.1   **Common and Preferred Stock Are Issued for Cash**

The total cash received must be divided between the common and preferred stock.

If the fair market value of both securities can be determined, the cash is divided proportionately. For example, assume the fair market value of the common shares issued is $80,000 and the fair market value of the preferred shares issued is $40,000 for a total fair market value of $120,000 ($80,000 + $40,000). If the cash (price) received is $99,000, $66,000 ($99,000 X 80/120) is allotted to Common Stock and $33,000 ($99,000 X 40/120) is allotted to Preferred Stock.

If the fair market value of only one of the securities can be determined, it is recorded at its fair market value and any remainder is assigned to the other security. For example, assume the fair market value of the common stock can be determined to be $50,000. If the cash (price) received for both the common and preferred is $80,000, $50,000 is allotted to the common stock and $30,000 ($80,000 - $50,000) is assigned to the preferred stock.

If the fair market value of neither of the securities can be determined, the cash (price) received for both the common and preferred is usually allotted arbitrarily by the board of directors.

Cash	xxxx
*Common Stock	xxxx
*Preferred Stock	xxxx
**Additional Paid-In Capital - Common Stock	xxxx
**Additional Paid-In Capital - Preferred Stock	xxxx
To record issuance of preferred and common stock	

Important: Make sure all appropriate subheads apply to your entry (see page v for instructions)

9000.1   **Issuance of Stock**
9000.1.5   **Lump Sum Issuances**
9000.1.5.1   **Common and Preferred Stock Are Issued for Cash**

---

*Common Stock and Preferred Stock are credited for the par or stated value of the shares issued, or if the stock does not have a par or stated value, they are credited for amounts determined as explained above.

**Common alternative account titles include:
- Contributed Capital In Excess Of Par (Stated) Value - Common (Preferred) Stock
- Paid-In Capital In Excess Of Par (Stated) Value - Common (Preferred) Stock.

These accounts are credited only if the respective stocks have a par or stated value. Otherwise, the accounts are not used in this entry. If the stocks have par or stated values, these accounts are credited for the excess of the amounts allotted to the stocks over their par or stated value.

9000.1.5.2   **Stock and Bonds Payable Are Issued for a Lump Sum of Cash**

The total cash received must be divided between the stock and the bonds payable.

If the fair market value of both securities can be determined, the cash is divided proportionately. For example, assume the fair market value of the shares issued is $80,000 and the fair market value of the bonds payable is $40,000, for a total fair market value of $120,000 ($80,000 + $40,000). If the cash (price) received is $99,000, $66,000 ($99,000 X 80/120) is allotted to the stock and $33,000 ($99,000 X 40/120) is allotted to the bonds payable.

If the fair market value of only one of the securities can be determined, it is recorded at its fair market value and any remainder is assigned to the other security. For example, assume the fair market value of the bonds payable can be determined to be $50,000. If the cash (price) received for both the stock and the bonds payable is $80,000, $50,000 is assigned to the bonds payable and $30,000 ($80,000 - $50,000) is assigned to the stock.

*Cash	xxxx
**Common (Preferred) Stock	xxxx
***Additional Paid-In Capital - Common (Preferred) Stock	xxxx
****Bonds Payable	xxxx
*****Premium On Bonds Payable	xxxx

To record the issuance of bonds payable and stock

Important: Make sure all appropriate subheads apply to your entry (see page v for instructions)

9000.1	**Issuance of Stock**
9000.1.5	**Lump Sum Issuances**
9000.1.5.2	**Stock and Bonds Payable Are Issued for a Lump Sum of Cash**

---

*Cash is debited for the amount of cash received.

**Common (Preferred) Stock is credited for the par or stated value of the shares issued, or if the stock does not have a par or stated value, it is credited for the amount allotted to the stock as explained above.

***Common alternative account titles include:
- Contributed Capital In Excess Of Par (Stated) Value - Common (Pre-ferred) Stock
- Paid-In Capital In Excess Of Par (Stated) Value - Common (Preferred) Stock.

This account is used only if the stock has either a par or stated value. In that case, the account is credited for the excess of the amount assigned to the stock over the par or stated value of the shares issued.

****Bonds Payable is credited for the par value of the bonds issued.

*****Premium On Bonds Payable is credited for any excess of the amount appor-tioned to the bonds over the par value of the bonds issued. If the par value of the bonds issued exceeds the amount allotted to the bonds, Discount On Bonds Payable is debited for the excess instead of crediting this account.

9000.1.6   **Noncash Issuances of Stock**

9000.1.6.1   **Issuance of Stock for Noncash Assets, for Reduction of Liabilities, or for Expenses**

*[Various Assets] ([Various Liabilities, Various Expenses])	xxxx	
**Common (Preferred) Stock		xxxx
***Additional Paid-In Capital - Common (Preferred) Stock		xxxx
To record issuance of stock		

*Assets received or expenses incurred should be debited for the fair market value of the stock issued or the fair market value of the asset or expense, whichever is more clearly determined. If a liability is reduced, it is debited for its carrying (book) value.

Important: Make sure all appropriate subheads apply to your entry (see page v for instructions)

9000.1   **Issuance of Stock**
9000.1.6   **Noncash Issuances of Stock**
9000.1.6.1   **Issuance of Stock for Noncash Assets, for Reduction of Liabilities, or for Expenses**

**Common (Preferred) Stock is credited for the par or stated value of the shares issued. If the stock does not have a par or stated value, this account is credited to balance the entry.

***Common alternative account titles include:
- Contributed Capital In Excess Of Par (Stated) Value - Common (Preferred) Stock
- Paid-In Capital In Excess Of Par (Stated) Value - Common (Preferred) Stock.

This account is not used unless the stock issued has either a par or stated value. If the stock has a par or stated value, this account is credited to balance the entry.

9000.1.6.2   **Issuance of Stock for Noncash Assets or Expenses with the Assumption of a Liability**

*[Various Assets] ([Various Expenses])	xxxx
**[Various Liabilities]	xxxx
***Common (Preferred) Stock	xxxx
****Additional Paid-In Capital - Common (Preferred) Stock	xxxx

To record issuance of stock

*The assets acquired (or expenses incurred) should be recorded at (a) the fair market value of the stock given plus the value of the liabilities assumed, or (b) the fair market value of the assets acquired (or expenses incurred), whichever is more clearly determined.

**The liabilities assumed are credited for their respective amounts.

***Common (Preferred) Stock is credited for the par or stated value of the shares issued. If the stock does not have a par or stated value, this account is credited to balance the entry.

****Common alternative account titles include:
- Contributed Capital In Excess Of Par (Stated) Value - Common (Preferred) Stock
- Paid-In Capital In Excess Of Par (Stated) Value - Common (Preferred) Stock.

This account is not used unless the stock issued has either a par or stated value. If the stock has a par or stated value, this account is credited to balance the entry.

Important: Make sure all appropriate subheads apply to your entry (see page v for instructions)

9000.2   **Assessments on Stock**

The laws of some states allow or require under certain conditions that holders of common stock be assessed amounts in addition to what was originally paid in when the stock was issued. However, this rarely occurs.

9000.2.1   **Stock Was Originally Issued at a Discount Below Par**

> Cash   xxxx
>   *Discount On Common Stock   xxxx
> *To record an assessment on stock*

*If stock was originally issued at a discount below par, this discount account (or another account) will have been debited in the entry to record the issuance (*see GEN9000.1.1.3*). If an assessment is later made, the discount account (or other account debited) is credited as shown here. If a discount account was used when the stock was issued (*see GEN9000.1.1.3*), and if the amount of the assessment exceeds the amount of the debit balance in the discount account, the discount account is credited sufficiently to eliminate its debit balance and the excess assessment is credited to Additional Paid-In Capital - Common (Preferred) Stock.

9000.2.2   **Stock Was Originally Issued At Par or Above Par**

> Cash   xxxx
>   *Additional Paid-In Capital - Common (Preferred)
>   Stock   xxxx
> *To record an assessment on stock*

*Common alternative account titles include:
    - Contributed Capital In Excess Of Par Value - Common (Preferred) Stock
    - Paid-In Capital In Excess Of Par Value - Common (Preferred) Stock.
This account is not used unless the stock issued has either a par or stated value. If the stock has a par or stated value, this account is credited to balance the entry.

Important: Make sure all appropriate subheads apply to your entry (see page v for instructions)

9000.3   **Stock Issuance Costs**

Stock issuance costs include:
- Printing costs
- Registration and filing costs
- Legal and accounting fees
- Underwriting costs.

9000.3.1   **Stock Issuance Costs Treated as a Reduction of Proceeds from Issuance**

When stock issuance costs are incurred, they are debited to Stock Issuance Costs as shown below in the first entry. Subsequently, when the stock is issued, Stock Issuance Costs is credited as shown in the second entry.

Stock Issuance Costs	xxxx	
Cash ([Various Liabilities], [Various Expenses])		xxxx
To record stock issuance costs		
*Cash ([Various Accounts])	xxxx	
**Common (Preferred) Stock		xxxx
***Additional Paid-In Capital - Common (Preferred)		
Stock		xxxx
****Stock Issuance Costs		xxxx
To record the proceeds of stock issuance net of issuance costs		

*Cash ([Various Accounts]) is debited for the fair value of the assets received for the stock issued.

**Common (Preferred) Stock is credited for the par (stated) value of the shares issued. If the stock does not have a par (stated) value, it is credited to balance the entry.

***Common alternative account titles include:
- Contributed Capital In Excess Of Par (Stated) Value - Common (Preferred) Stock
- Paid-In Capital In Excess Of Par (Stated) Value - Common (Preferred) Stock.

This account is credited only if the stock has a par or stated value. Otherwise, the account is not used in this entry. If the stock has a par or stated value, this account is credited to balance the entry.

Important: Make sure all appropriate subheads apply to your entry (see page v for instructions)

9000.3   **Stock Issuance Costs**
9000.3.1   **Stock Issuance Costs Treated as a Reduction of Proceeds from Issuance**

****Stock Issuance Costs is credited for the amount of costs previously debited to this account when they were incurred. After this entry is made, the balance in this account should be zero.

9000.3.2   ## Stock Issuance Costs Treated as Organization Costs

*Organization Costs	xxxx	
Cash ([Various Liabilities], [Various Expenses])		xxxx

To record stock issuance costs

*Organization Costs is subsequently amortized over a period not to exceed 40 years. *See GEN6000.1.8.2.*

9000.4   ## Contingency Issuances of Stock

A contingency issuance of stock most often occurs as a result of a business combination agreement which may require that additional stock be issued if certain earnings goals or other conditions are met. Usually no formal journal entry is made to record contingency shares. Only a memorandum entry is made.

9000.5   ## Conversion of Preferred Stock

9000.5.1   ## Par (Stated) Value of Common Stock Does Not Equal Book Value of Preferred Stock

*Preferred Stock	xxxx	
*Premium On Preferred Stock	xxxx	
**Common Stock		xxxx
***Additional Paid-In Capital - Common (Preferred)		
Stock		xxxx

To record conversion of preferred stock to common stock

*Preferred Stock and Premium On Preferred Stock are debited sufficiently to remove any credit balances in these accounts that pertain to the shares of preferred stock converted. Common alternative account titles for Premium On Preferred Stock include:

Important: Make sure all appropriate subheads apply to your entry (see page v for instructions)

9000.5   **Conversion of Preferred Stock**
9000.5.1   **Par (Stated) Value of Common Stock Does Not Equal Book Value of Preferred Stock**

   - Contributed Capital In Excess Of Par (Stated) Value - Preferred Stock
   - Paid-In Capital In Excess Of Par (Stated) Value - Preferred Stock
   - Additional Paid-In Capital - Preferred Stock.

**Common Stock is credited for the par or stated value of the common shares issued in the conversion. If the common stock does not have a par or stated value, this account is credited to balance the entry.

***Common alternative account titles include:
   - Contributed Capital In Excess Of Par (Stated) Value - Common Stock
   - Paid-In Capital In Excess Of Par (Stated) Value - Common Stock
   - Additional Paid-In Capital - Common Stock.
This account is not used if the common stock does not have a par or stated value. If the common stock has a par or stated value, this account is credited to balance the entry.

9000.5.2   **Par (Stated) Value of Common Stock Exceeds Book Value of Preferred Stock**

*Preferred Stock	xxxx	
*Additional Paid-In Capital - Preferred Stock	xxxx	
**Retained Earnings		xxxx
***Common Stock		xxxx
****Additional Paid-In Capital - Common Stock		xxxx

To record conversion of preferred stock to common stock

*Preferred Stock and Additional Paid-In Capital - Preferred Stock are debited sufficiently to remove any credit balances in these accounts that pertain to the shares of preferred stock converted. Common alternative account titles for Additional Paid-In Capital - Preferred Stock include:
   - Contributed Capital In Excess Of Par (Stated) Value - Preferred
   - Paid-In Capital In Excess Of Par (Stated) Value - Preferred Stock
   - Premium on Preferred Stock.

**Retained Earnings is debited for the excess of par (stated) value of the common stock over the book value of the preferred stock.

***Common Stock is credited for the par (stated) value of the common shares issued in the conversion. If the common stock does not have a par (stated) value, this account is credited to balance the entry.

Important: Make sure all appropriate subheads apply to your entry (see page v for instructions)

9000.5   **Conversion of Preferred Stock**
9000.5.2   **Par (Stated) Value of Common Stock Exceeds Book Value of Preferred Stock**

****Common alternative account titles include:
- Contributed Capital In Excess Of Par (Stated) Value - Common Stock
- Paid-In Capital In Excess Of Par (Stated) Value - Common Stock
- Premium On Common Stock.

This account is not used if the common stock does not have a par or stated value. If the common stock has a par or stated value, this account is credited to balance the entry.

9000.6   **Stock Warrants**

Stock warrants enable the holder to purchase stock at a specific price during a specific period. Warrants may be issued to current shareholders proportionately to their holdings when a firm decides to issue additional shares. they may be sold by the firm, or they may be issued together with debt securities such as bonds to make the securities more attractive.

9000.6.1   **Issuance of Stock Warrants**

No entry is made to record the issuance of stock warrants unless detachable warrants are issued in conjunction with the issuance of debt securities such as bonds, or unless stock warrants are sold by the issuing firm. The sale of stock warrants by the issuing firm is recorded with the following entry:

Cash   xxxx
     *Additional Paid-In Capital - Common (Preferred)
        Stock Warrants   xxxx
     To record issuance of stock warrants

*Common alternative account titles include:
- Paid-In Capital - Common (Preferred) Stock Warrants
- Contributed Capital In Excess Of Par (Stated) Value - Common (Preferred) Stock Warrants.

Important: Make sure all appropriate subheads apply to your entry (see page v for instructions)

9000.6   Stock Warrants

9000.6.2   **Exercise of Stock Warrants**

*Cash	xxxx	
**Additional Paid-In Capital - Common (Preferred) Stock Warrants	xxxx	
***Common (Preferred) Stock		xxxx
****Additional Paid-In Capital - Common (Preferred) Stock		xxxx

To record exercise of stock warrants

*Cash is debited for the amount of cash received.

**Common alternative account titles include:
- Contributed Capital In Excess Of Par (Stated) Value - Common (Preferred) Stock Warrants
- Paid-In Capital In Excess Of Par (Stated) Value - Common (Preferred) Stock Warrants.

This account is debited sufficiently to remove any credit balance pertaining to the warrants being exercised that is in the account.

***Common (Preferred) Stock is credited for the par or stated value of the shares issued if the stock has a par or stated value. If the stock does not have a par or stated value, this account is credited to balance the entry.

****Common alternative account titles include:
- Contributed Capital In Excess Of Par (Stated) Value - Common (Preferred) Stock
- Paid-In Capital In Excess Of Par (Stated) Value - Common (Preferred) Stock.

This account is credited only if the stock has a par or stated value. Otherwise, this account is not used in this entry. If the stock has a par or stated value, this account is credited to balance the entry.

9000.6.3   **Expiration of Stock Warrants**

If stock warrants that were recorded when issued are not exercised within the exercise period allowed, they expire and the balance in the Additional Paid-In Capital - Common (Preferred) Stock Warrants account pertaining to the expired warrants must be removed from the books with the following entry:

Important: Make sure all appropriate subheads apply to your entry (see page v for instructions)

9000.6   **Stock Warrants**
9000.6.3   **Expiration of Stock Warrants**

---

*Additional Paid-In Capital - Common (Preferred) Stock Warrants	xxxx
Additional Paid-In Capital - Expired Common (Preferred) Stock Warrants	xxxx
To record expiration of stock warrants	

*Additional Paid-In Capital - Common (Preferred) Stock Warrants is debited sufficiently to remove the balance in this account pertaining to the expired warrants.

9000.7   **Stock Compensation Plans**

9000.7.1   **Stock Option Plans**

9000.7.1.1   **Noncompensatory Plans**

In a noncompensatory stock option plan, the primary purpose is to provide a means to issue stock to increase the capital of the firm or to ensure wide ownership by employees rather than to compensate employees. To be a noncompensatory plan, the plan must:
- be available to all full-time employees with minimum employment qualifications;
- offer employees stock equally or as a uniform percentage of salary or wages;
- set a reasonable time period for exercise of the option;
- offer no special discount from the prevailing market price beyond that which would be available under direct purchase agreements with stockholders or under other usual discounted offering situations.

Usually only a memorandum entry is made when stock options are issued under a noncompensatory plan. When stock is issued, it is recorded in the usual manner.

9000.7.1.2   **Compensatory Plans**

If any of the four qualifying conditions for a noncompensatory plan given in *GEN9000.7.1.1* are not met, the plan is a compensatory plan.

Important: Make sure all appropriate subheads apply to your entry (see page v for instructions)

9000.7	**Stock Compensation Plans**
9000.7.1	**Stock Option Plans**
9000.7.1.2	**Compensatory Plans**

The primary purpose of a compensatory plan is to provide compensation to employees to whom options are granted. Options may be grainted at a discount from market price at the time of the grant. Either the Intrinsic Value Based method (*GEN9000.7.1.2.1*) or the Fair Value Based Method (*GEN9000.7.1.2.2*) may be used to record the plan. (The FASB *encourages the use of the Fair Value Based Method.*)

9000.7.1.2.1   **Intrinsic Value Based Method**

Under the Intrinsic Value Based Method, the excess of the fair market value of the stock for which the option is granted over the exercise price on the grant date is deferred compensation expense. The FASB permits but does not favor this method. If this method is used, FASB Statement No. 123 requires disclosure of the pro forma net income for each year for which an income statement is presented, and pro forma earnings per share if earnings pcr share is presented, as if the Fair Value Based Method had been used. *see GEN9000.7.1.2.2.*

9000.7.1.2.1.1   **If Stock Option Is Recorded When Option Is Granted**

Under the Intrinsic Value Based Method, recording a stock option at the time the option is granted is *optional*.

With a *fixed-type stock option* (both the number of shares employees can purchase and the exercise price are known at the grant date, deferred compensation expense may be *calculated* when the option is granted. With *flexible or performance-type stock option* (either the number of shares employees can purchase or the exercise price are not known at the grant date), deferred compensation expense may be estimated when it is granted. In either case, the following entry may be made:

        *Deferred Compensation Expense   xxxx
           **Additional Paid-In Capital - Common (Preferred)
              Stock Options   xxxx
        To record the issuance of compensatory stock options

*Deferred Compensation Expense is debited for any excess market value of the stock, subject to the optionn over the exercise price on the date of grant. It is deducted from stockholders' equity in the balance sheet and amortized over the period in which employees are expected to perform to be entitled to the options (service period) *see below.*

Important: Make sure all appropriate subheads apply to your entry (see page v for instructions)

9000.7   **Stock Compensation Plans**
9000.7.1   **Stock Option Plans**
9000.7.1.2   **Compensatory Plans**
9000.7.1.2.1   **Intrinsic Value Based Method**
9000.7.1.2.1.1   **If Stock Option Is Recorded When Option Is Granted**

**Common alternative account titles include Contributed Capital In Excess Of Par (Stated) Value - Common (Preferred) Stock Options, and Paid-In Capital In Excess Of Par (Stated) Value - Common (Preferred) Stock Options.

If either the number of shares employees can purchase or the exercise price is not known at the grant date (flexible or performance-type stock option), the estimate of deferred compensation expense is adjusted annually as additional information becomes available or the underlying factors for the stock option change. If the above entry is made, Deferred Compensation Expense is then amortized to Compensation Expense over the period in which employees are expected to perform to be entitled to the options (service period) with the following entry:

Compensation Expense	xxxx	
*Deferred Compensation Expense		xxxx
To record compensation expense		

9000.7.1.2.1.2   **If Stock Option Is Not Recorded When Option Is Granted**

If the stock option (deferred compensation expense) is not recorded when granted, annual compensation expense is recognized over the period in which employees are expected to perform to be entitled to the options (service period) with the following entry:

Compensation Expense	xxxx	
Additional Paid-In Capital - Stock Options		xxxx
To record compensation expense		

9000.7.1.2.2   **Fair Value Based Method**

Under the Fair Value Based Method (favored by the FASB), deferred compensation expense is measured at the grant date based on the fair value of the option granted. A quoted market price is used for the fair value if available. Otherwise, fair value is estimated using an option-pricing model that takes into account the option exercise price and expected life, the current underlying stock price and its expected volatility, expected dividends, and the risk-free interest rate for the expected option term.

For example, assume XYZ Company grants executives options to purchase 1,000 shares of its common stock at $150 per share, the market price of the stock. If the

Important: Make sure all appropriate subheads apply to your entry (see page v for instructions)

9000.7	**Stock Compensation Plans**
9000.7.1	**Stock Option Plans**
9000.7.1.2	**Compensatory Plans**
9000.7.1.2.2	**Fair Value Based Method**

---

actual fair value of the stock option or an estimate using an option-pricing model is $15 per share, deferred compensation expense is $15,000 (1,000 shares X $15). Deferred compensation expense is recognized with the following entry:

Deferred Compensation Expense	xxxx	
Additional Paid-In Capital - Stock Options		xxxx
To record issuance of stock options		

Compensation expense is then recognized annually over the period in which employees are expected to perform to be entitled to the options (service period) as follows:

Compensation Expense	xxxx	
*Deferred Compensation Expense		xxxx
To record compensation expense		

Recognition of deferred income taxes may be required. *See GEN12000.2.*

9000.7.1.2.3

Exercise of Compensatory Stock Options

*Cash	xxxx	
**Additional Paid-In Capital - Common (Preferred) Stock Options	xxxx	
***Common Stock		xxxx
****Additional Paid-In Capital - Common (Preferred) Stock		xxxx
To record the exercise of compensatory stock options		

*Cash is debited for the amount of cash received.

**This account is debited to remove any credit balance pertaining to the options exercised. Common alternative account titles include:
- Contributed Capital In Excess Of Par (Stated) Value - Common (Preferred) Stock Options
- Paid-In Capital In Excess Of Par (Stated) Value - Common (Preferred) Stock Options.

***Common Stock is credited for the par or stated value, if any, or to balance the entry.

Important: Make sure all appropriate subheads apply to your entry (see page v for instructions)

9000.7   **Stock Compensation Plans**
9000.7.1   **Stock Option Plans**
9000.7.1.2   **Compensatory Plans**
9000.7.1.2.3   **Exercise of Compensatory Stock Options**

****This account is used only if the stock has a par or stated value and is then credited to balance the entry. Common alternative account titles include:
- Contributed Capital In Excess Of Par (Stated) Value - Common (Preferred) Stock
- Paid-In Capital In Excess Of Par (Stated) Value - Common (Preferred) Stock.

9000.7.1.2.4   **Expiration of Compensatory Stock Options (Compensatory Stock Options Not Exercised)**

9000.7.1.2.4.1   **Employee Fulfilled Obligations Under Stock Option**

*Additional Paid-In Capital - Common (Preferred) Stock Options	xxxx	
**Additional Paid-In Capital - Expired Common (Preferred) Stock Options		xxxx

To record expiration of stock options

*The debit is to remove any related credit balance. Common alternative account titles are:
- Contributed Capital In Excess Of Par (Stated) Value - Common (Preferred) Stock Options
- Paid-In Capital In Excess Of Par (Stated) Value - Common (Preferred) Stock Options.

**Common alternative account titles include:
- Contributed Capital In Excess Of Par (Stated) Value - Expired Common (Preferred) Stock Options
- Paid-In Capital In Excess Of Par (Stated) Value - Expired Common (Preferred) Stock Options.

9000.7.1.2.4.2   **Employee Did Not Fulfill Obligations Under Stock Option**

*Additional Paid-In Capital - Common (Preferred) Stock Options	xxxx	
Compensation Expense		xxxx

To record expiration of stock options

Important: Make sure all appropriate subheads apply to your entry (see page v for instructions)

9000.7   **Stock Compensation Plans**
9000.7.1   **Stock Option Plans**
9000.7.1.2   **Compensatory Plans**
9000.7.1.2.4   **Expiration of Compensatory Stock Options (Options Not Exercised)**
9000.7.1.2.4.2   **Employee Did Not Fulfill Obligations Under Stock Option**

---

*This account is debited to remove any credit balance pertaining to expired options.

9000.7.2   **Stock Appreciation Rights (SARs)**

A SAR is a right to receive cash or stock equal to market value appreciation of stock.

9000.7.2.1   **Issuance of Stock Appreciation Rights**

Only a memorandum entry is made. No formal journal entry is made.

9000.7.2.2   **Valuation of Liability for Stock Appreciation Rights At End of Each Year**

*Compensation Expense	xxxx	
*Liability For Stock Appreciation Rights		xxxx
To adjust liability for stock appreciation rights		

*This entry is for an increase in value. Debits and credits are reversed for a decrease.

9000.7.2.3   **Exercise of Stock Appreciation Rights**

Liability For Stock Appreciation Rights	xxxx	
*Cash		xxxx
**Common Stock		xxxx
***Additional Paid-In Capital - Stock Appreciation Rights		xxxx
To record exercise of stock appreciation rights		

*Cash is credited for the amount of cash paid to, if any, to satisfy the liability.

**Common Stock is credited for the par or stated value of the shares issued. Otherwise, this account is credited to balance the entry.

***Common alternative account titles include:
- Contributed Capital In Excess Of Par (Stated) Value - Stock Appreciation Rights
- Paid-In Capital In Excess Of Par (Stated) Value - Stock Appreciation Rights.

If the stock has a par or stated value, this account is credited to balance the entry.

Important: Make sure all appropriate subheads apply to your entry (see page v for instructions)

9000.8	**Treasury Stock**

Treasury stock is stock that has been issued and reacquired by the firm that issued it.

9000.8.1	**Cost Method of Accounting for Treasury Stock**

Under the cost method, Treasury Stock is debited for the cost of acquisition.

9000.8.1.1	**Acquisition of Treasury Stock - Cost Method**

    *Treasury Stock - Common (Preferred) Stock   xxxx
        Cash   xxxx
      To record the purchase of treasury stock

*Treasury Stock - Common (Preferred) Stock is debited for its acquisition   cost.

9000.8.1.2	**Reissuance of Treasury Stock - Cost Method**

9000.8.1.2.1	**Reissuance of Treasury Stock at a Price Equal to Its Acquisition Price**

    Cash   xxxx
        Treasury Stock - Common (Preferred) Stock   xxxx
      To record the reissuance of treasury stock

9000.8.1.2.2	**Reissuance of Treasury Stock at a Price Greater than Its Acquisition Price**

    Cash   xxxx
        *Treasury Stock - Common (Preferred) Stock   xxxx
        **Additional Paid-In Capital - Common (Preferred)
           Treasury Stock   xxxx
      To record the reissuance of treasury stock

*Treasury Stock - Common (Preferred) Stock is credited for its acquisition cost.

Important: Make sure all appropriate subheads apply to your entry (see page v for instructions)

9000.8   **Treasury Stock**
9000.8.1   **Cost Method of Accounting for Treasury Stock**
9000.8.1.2   **Reissuance of Treasury Stock - Cost Method**
9000.8.1.2.2   **Reissuance of Treasury Stock at a Price Greater than Acquisition Price**

**This account is credited for the excess of the reissuance price over the acquisition cost of the shares reissued. Common alternative account titles include:
- Contributed Capital In Excess Of Par (Stated) Value - Common (Pre-ferred) Treasury Stock
- Paid-In Capital In Excess Of Par (Stated) Value - Common (Preferred) Treasury Stock.

9000.8.1.2.3   **Reissuance of Treasury Stock at a Price Less than Acquisition Price**

Cash	xxxx	
*Additional Paid-In Capital - Common (Preferred) Treasury Stock	xxxx	
**Retained Earnings	xxxx	
***Treasury Stock - Common (Preferred) Stock		xxxx

To record reissuance of treasury stock

*Common alternative account titles include:
- Contributed Capital In Excess Of Par (Stated) Value - Common (Pre-ferred) Treasury Stock
- Paid-In Capital In Excess Of Par (Stated) Value - Common (Preferred) Treasury Stock.

This account is debited only if it has a credit balance. It is debited for the lesser of the amount of this credit or the excess of the acquisition cost of the treasury shares being reissued over the reissuance price. This account cannot be left with a debit balance after this entry.

**If necessary, Retained Earnings is debited to balance this entry. This is not necessary if the entire excess of the acquisition cost of the reissued treasury shares over the reissuance price can be debited to Additional Paid-In Capital - Common (Preferred) Treasury Stock. But, since this account cannot be left with a debit balance, Retained Earnings may be debited to absorb the extra debit to balance the entry.

***Treasury Stock - Common (Preferred) Stock is credited for its acquisition   cost.

9000.8.1.2.4   **Retirement of Treasury Stock**

Treasury stock may be retired if there are no plans to ever reissue the stock.

Important: Make sure all appropriate subheads apply to your entry (see page v for instructions)

9000.8   **Treasury Stock**
9000.8.1   **Cost Method of Accounting for Treasury Stock**
9000.8.1.2   **Reissuance of Treasury Stock - Cost Method**
9000.8.1.2.4   **Retirement of Treasury Stock**

---

*Common (Preferred) Stock	xxxx
**Additional Paid-In Capital - Common (Preferred) Stock	xxxx
***Retained Earnings	xxxx
****Additional Paid-In Capital - Retirement Of Common (Preferred) Treasury Stock	xxxx
*****Treasury Stock - Common (Preferred) Stock	xxxx

To record retirement of treasury stock

*Common (Preferred) Stock is debited for its par or stated value. If there is no par or stated value, it is debited for the average price paid for the stock; i.e., the balance in the account divided by the number of shares issued and multiplied by the number of shares being retired.

**Common alternative account titles include:
- Contributed Capital In Excess Of Par (Stated) Value - Common (Preferred) Stock
- Paid-In Capital In Excess Of Par (Stated) Value - Common (Preferred) Stock.

If the stock has a par or stated value, this account is debited sufficiently to remove any credit made to it when the shares now being retired were originally issued. This is usually calculated as an average amount by dividing the credit balance in this account by the number of shares of stock issued and multiplying by the number of shares being retired.

***Retained Earnings will be debited in this entry only if the acquisition cost of the treasury stock now being retired (the credit to Treasury Stock - Common (Preferred) Stock in this entry) exceeds the amount for which the stock was originally issued (the sum of the debits to Common (Preferred) Stock and Additional Paid-In Capital - Common (Preferred) Stock). In this case, Retained Earnings will be debited for the excess to balance the entry. (An alternative is to debit Retained Earnings only after all additional paid-in capital accounts are exhausted.)

****Common alternative account titles include:
- Contributed Capital In Excess Of Par (Stated) Value - Retirement Of Common (Preferred) Treasury Stock
- Paid-In Capital In Excess Of Par (Stated) Value - Retirement Of Common (Preferred) Treasury Stock.

This account is credited in this entry only if the acquisition cost of the treasury stock now being retired, i.e., the credit to Treasury Stock - Common (Preferred) Stock in this entry, is less than the amount for which the stock was originally issued, i.e., the

Important: Make sure all appropriate subheads apply to your entry (see page v for instructions)

9000.8   **Treasury Stock**
9000.8.1   **Cost Method of Accounting for Treasury Stock**
9000.8.1.2   **Reissuance of Treasury Stock - Cost Method**
9000.8.1.2.4   **Retirement of Treasury Stock**

---

sum of the debits to Common (Preferred) Stock and Additional Paid-In Capital - Common (Preferred) Stock. In this case, Additional Paid-In Capital - Retirement Of Common (Preferred) Treasury Stock will be credited for this difference to balance the entry.

*****Treasury Stock - Common (Preferred) Stock is credited for its acquisition cost.

9000.8.2   **Par Value Method of Accounting for Treasury Stock**

Under the par value method, when treasury stock is acquired, the transaction is treated as a retirement of the shares. Treasury Stock is debited for the par or stated value of the shares acquired. If the acquisition price exceeds the amount originally paid for the shares, the difference is debited to Retained Earnings. If the acquisition price is less than the amount originally paid for the shares, the difference is credited to Additional Paid-In Capital - Treasury Stock.

9000.8.2.1   **Acquisition of Treasury Stock at a Price Less than or Equal to Original Issuance Price**

*Treasury Stock - Common (Preferred) Stock	xxxx	
**Additional Paid-In Capital - Common (Preferred) Stock	xxxx	
***Additional Paid-In Capital - Common (Preferred) Treasury Stock		xxxx
****Cash		xxxx

To record the purchase of treasury stock

*Treasury Stock - Common (Preferred) Stock is debited for the par or stated value of the shares reacquired.

**Common alternative account titles include:
- Contributed Capital In Excess Of Par (Stated) Value - Common (Preferred) Stock
- Paid-In Capital In Excess Of Par (Stated) Value - Common (Preferred) Stock.

This account is debited sufficiently to remove any credit made to it when the shares now being retired were originally issued. This is usually calculated as an average amount by dividing the credit balance in this account by the number of shares of stock issued and multiplying by the number of shares being retired.

Important: Make sure all appropriate subheads apply to your entry (see page v for instructions)

9000.8　　　　　**Treasury Stock**
9000.8.2　　　　　　**Par Value Method of Accounting for Treasury Stock**
9000.8.2.1　　　　　　　**Acquisition of Treasury Stock at a Price Less than or Equal to Original Issuance Price**

***Common alternative account titles include:
- Contributed Capital In Excess Of Par (Stated) Value - Common (Preferred) Treasury Stock
- Paid-In Capital In Excess Of Par (Stated) Value - Common (Preferred) Treasury Stock.

This account is credited to balance the entry.

****Cash is credited for the amount of cash paid for the shares reacquired.

9000.8.2.2　　　　**Acquisition of Treasury Stock at a Price Greater than Original Issuance Price**

*Treasury Stock - Common (Preferred) Stock	xxxx	
**Additional Paid-In Capital - Common (Preferred) Stock	xxxx	
***Retained Earnings	xxxx	
****Cash		xxxx

To record the purchase of treasury stock

*Treasury Stock - Common (Preferred) Stock is debited for the par or stated value of the shares reacquired.

**Common alternative account titles include:
- Contributed Capital In Excess Of Par (Stated) Value - Common (Preferred) Stock
- Paid-In Capital In Excess Of Par (Stated) Value - Common (Preferred) Stock.

This account is debited sufficiently to remove any credit made to it when the shares now being retired were originally issued. This is usually calculated as an average amount by dividing the credit balance in this account by the number of shares of stock issued and multiplying by the number of shares being retired.

***Retained Earnings is debited to balance the entry.

****Cash is credited for the amount of cash paid for the shares reacquired.

Important: Make sure all appropriate subheads apply to your entry (see page v for instructions)

9000.8   **Treasury Stock**
9000.8.2   **Par Value Method of Accounting for Treasury Stock**

9000.8.2.3   **Reissuance of Treasury Stock**

Under the par value method, the reissuance of treasury stock is recorded in the same way as the original issuance of stock was recorded except that Treasury Stock - Common (Preferred) Stock is credited instead of Common (Preferred) Stock.

Cash	xxxx	
*Treasury Stock - Common (Preferred) Stock		xxxx
**Additional Paid-In Capital - Common (Preferred)		
Stock		xxxx

To record the reissuance of treasury stock

*Treasury Stock - Common (Preferred) Stock is credited for the par or stated value of the treasury stock reissued.

**Common alternative account titles include:
- Contributed Capital In Excess Of Par (Stated) Value - Common (Preferred) Stock
- Paid-In Capital In Excess Of Par (Stated) Value - Common (Preferred) Stock.

This account is credited for the excess of the reissuance price over the par or stated value of the shares reissued; i.e., it is credited to balance the entry.

9000.8.2.4   **Retirement of Treasury Stock**

*Common Stock	xxxx	
*Treasury Stock		xxxx

To record the retirement of treasury stock

*These accounts are debited and credited for the par or stated value of the shares retired.

9000.9   **Donated Capital**

Capital is sometimes donated (given) to a firm by stockholders or others such as a municipal or state government that hopes to attract industry to locate in its area.

Important: Make sure all appropriate subheads apply to your entry (see page v for instructions)

9000.9   **Donated Capital**

---

*[Various Assets]	xxxx
**Donated Capital	xxxx
To record donation of capital	

*The various assets acquired are debited for their fair market value.

**Donated Capital is credited to balance the entry.

9000.10   **Retained Earnings**

9000.10.1   **Appropriation of Retained Earnings**

Retained Earnings	xxxx
Retained Earnings Appropriated For Plant Expansion [Various Reasons]	xxxx
To record appropriation of retained earnings	

9000.10.2   **Reduction or Elimination of Appropriated Retained Earnings**

The only acceptable means of reduction or elimination of an appropriated retained earnings account is to return the amount to Retained Earnings.

Retained Earnings Appropriated For Plant Expansion [Various Reasons]	xxxx
Retained Earnings	xxxx
To reduce appropriated retained earnings	

9000.11   **Quasi-Reorganization**

A quasi-reorganization is a procedure allowed under the laws of some states whereby a firm may eliminate an accumulated deficit and revalue its assets. From an accounting point of view, this results in a "fresh start" for operations.

Important: Make sure all appropriate subheads apply to your entry (see page v for instructions)

9000.11   **Quasi-Reorganization**

9000.11.1   **Revaluation of Assets**

*[Various Assets]	xxxx	
*[Various Liabilities]	xxxx	
**Retained Earnings	xxxx	
*[Various Assets]		xxxx

To record revaluation of assets

*Assets and liabilities are revalued to fair market value by writing them up or down.

**Retained Earnings is debited to balance the entry. Because there should be no net write-up of net assets in this entry, a credit to Retained Earnings is not allowed.

9000.11.2   **Reduction of Par or Stated Value of Stock**

Common Stock, [Old Par Value]	xxxx	
Common Stock, [New Par Value]		xxxx
*Additional Paid-In Capital - Common Stock		xxxx

To record reduction of par (stated) value

*Common alternative account titles include:
- Contributed Capital In Excess Of Par (Stated) Value - Common Stock
- Paid-In Capital In Excess Of Par (Stated) Value - Common Stock.

9000.11.3   **Elimination of Deficit**

If eliminating the deficit in Retained Earnings requires a debit to Additional Paid-In Capital - Common Stock larger than its existing credit balance, the credit balance must first be increased by reducing the par or stated value of the stock with the following entry.

*Additional Paid-In Capital - Common Stock	xxxx	
**Retained Earnings		xxxx

To eliminate the deficit in Retained Earnings

*Common alternative account titles include:
- Contributed Capital In Excess Of Par (Stated) Value - Common Stock
- Paid-In Capital In Excess Of Par (Stated) Value - Common Stock.
This account is debited for the amount of credit to Retained Earnings but cannot have

Important: Make sure all appropriate subheads apply to your entry (see page v for instructions)

9000.11   **Quasi-Reorganization**
9000.11.3   **Elimination of Deficit**

---

a debit balance after this entry. Thus, if eliminating the deficit in Retained Earnings requires a debit to Additional Paid-In Capital - Common Stock larger than its existing credit balance, the credit balance must first be increased by reducing the par or stated value of the stock as shown in *GEN9000.11.2*.

**This credit to Retained Earnings should be sufficient to eliminate the existing debit balance (the deficit) and no larger. Retained Earnings may not be left with a credit balance after this entry.

9000.12   **Dividends**

9000.12.1   **Cash Dividends**

Cash dividends are dividends paid in cash.

9000.12.1.1   **Declaration of Cash Dividends**

Retained Earnings	xxxx	
Dividends Payable		xxxx
To record declaration of a cash dividend		

9000.12.1.2   **Payment of Cash Dividends**

Dividends Payable	xxxx	
Cash		xxxx
To record payment of cash dividends		

9000.12.2   **Property Dividends**

Property dividends are dividends paid by distribution of assets other than cash.

Important: Make sure all appropriate subheads apply to your entry (see page v for instructions)

9000.12   **Dividends**
9000.12.2   **Property Dividends**

9000.12.2.1   ### Declaration of Property Dividends

When a property dividend is declared, two entries must be made. The first entry is to revalue the asset to be distributed so that its account balance reflects current fair market value. The second entry is to record the declaration of the dividend.

*[Various Assets]	xxxx	
Gain On Revaluation Of [Various Assets]		xxxx
To record revaluation of asset to be distributed as a property dividend		

*The asset account is debited sufficiently to increase its balance to its fair market value. It is possible, but not at all likely, that the book value of the asset is greater than its fair market value. Should this be the case, Loss On Revaluation Of [Various Assets] is debited and the asset account is credited.

*Retained Earnings	xxxx	
*Property Dividends Payable		xxxx
To record declaration of property dividends		

*The debit and credit in this entry are equal to the fair market value of the asset to be distributed.

9000.12.2.2   ### Payment of Property Dividends

Property Dividends Payable	xxxx	
[Various Assets]		xxxx
To record declaration of property dividends		

9000.12.3   ### Scrip Dividends

A scrip dividend is paid by issuing debt securities to stockholders. Usually this involves the issuance of notes payable.

Important: Make sure all appropriate subheads apply to your entry (see page v for instructions)

9000.12   **Dividends**
9000.12.3   **Scrip Dividends**

9000.12.3.1   ## Declaration of Scrip Dividends

Retained Earnings	xxxx
Notes Payable To Stockholders (Dividend Notes	
Payable)	xxxx

To record declaration of scrip dividends

9000.12.3.2   ## Payment of Scrip Dividends

Notes Payable To Stockholders (Dividend Notes Payable)	xxxx
*Interest Expense	xxxx
Cash	xxxx

To record payment of scrip dividends and interest

*Interest expense is incurred and paid for the period the notes payable are outstanding; i.e., from the date the scrip dividend is declared until the date it is paid.

9000.12.4   ## Stock Dividends

A stock dividend is a dividend paid by distributing additional shares of stock to stockholders. If the number of additional shares to be issued as a stock dividend is less than 20-25% (according to the SEC) of the number of shares outstanding before the stock dividend, the stock dividend is called a "small" or "ordinary" stock dividend. If the number of additional shares to be issued is greater than 20-25% of the number of shares outstanding before the stock dividend, the stock dividend is called a "large" stock dividend. Large stock dividends are accounted for differently than small (ordinary) stock dividends. In either case, the total par or stated value of the shares outstanding will be increased (unlike a stock split).

9000.12.4.1   ## Small (Ordinary) Stock Dividends

If the number of additional shares to be issued as a stock dividend is less than 20-25% (according to the SEC) of the number of shares outstanding before the stock dividend, the stock dividend is called a "small" or "ordinary" stock dividend.

Important: Make sure all appropriate subheads apply to your entry (see page v for instructions)

9000.12   **Dividends**
9000.12.4   **Stock Dividends**
9000.12.4.1   **Small (Ordinary) Stock Dividends**

9000.12.4.1.1   **Declaration of Small (Ordinary) Stock Dividends**

*Retained Earnings	xxxx
**Common (Preferred) Stock Dividend Distributable	xxxx
***Additional Paid-In Capital - Common (Preferred)	
Stock Dividends	xxxx

To record declaration of stock dividends

*Retained Earnings is debited for the fair market value of the additional shares to be distributed as of the date the dividend is declared. If the fair market value cannot be determined, the par or stated value is used, but fair market value must be used if possible.

**Common (Preferred) Stock Dividend Distributable is credited for the par or stated value of the shares to be distributed. If the stock does not have a par or stated value, this account is credited to balance the entry.

***Common alternative account titles include:
- Contributed Capital In Excess Of Par (Stated) Value - Common (Preferred) Stock Dividends
- Paid-In Capital In Excess Of Par (Stated) Value - Common (Preferred) Stock Dividends.

This account is used in this entry only if the stock has a par or stated value, in which case the account is credited as needed to balance the entry.

9000.12.4.1.2   **Payment (Distribution) of Small (Ordinary) Stock Dividends**

Common (Preferred) Stock Dividend Distributable	xxxx
Common (Preferred) Stock	xxxx

To record payment (distribution) of stock dividend

9000.12.4.2   **Large Stock Dividends**

If the number of additional shares to be issued is greater than 20-25% (according to the SEC) of the number of shares outstanding before the stock dividend, the stock dividend is called a "large" stock dividend and is accounted for as if it were a stock split. *See GEN9000.13.*

Important: Make sure all appropriate subheads apply to your entry (see page v for instructions)

9000.12	**Dividends**
9000.12.4	**Stock Dividends**
9000.12.4.2	**Large Stock Dividends**

9000.12.4.2.1   Declaration of Large Stock Dividends

      *Retained Earnings   xxxx

           *Common (Preferred) Stock Dividend Distributable   xxxx

      To record declaration of a large stock dividend

*Retained Earnings is debited and Common (Preferred) Stock Dividend Distributable is credited for the par or stated value of the new shares to be distributed.

9000.12.4.2.2   Payment (Distribution) of Large Stock Dividends

      Common (Preferred) Stock Dividend Distributable   xxxx

           Common (Preferred) Stock   xxxx

      To record payment (distribution) of stock dividend

9000.12.5   Liquidating Dividends

See GEN5000.6.6.

9000.13   Stock Splits

A normal stock split occurs if additional shares of stock are distributed to stockholders so that the number of shares of stock outstanding is increased with no increase in the total par or stated value of the outstanding shares. Thus, the par or stated value per share is reduced proportionately to the increase in shares outstanding; e.g., in a 2 for 1 stock split, the number of shares outstanding is doubled, and the par or stated value per share is halved.

A reverse stock split occurs if the number of shares outstanding are decreased with no increase in the total par or stated value of the outstanding shares. Thus, the par or stated value per share is increased proportionately to the decrease in shares outstanding; e.g., in a 1 for 2 reverse stock split, the number of shares outstanding is halved, and the par or stated value per share is doubled.

No formal entry is necessary to record either a normal or a reverse stock split. A memorandum entry is made in the stock account to indicate the new par or stated value and the revised number of shares outstanding. A so-called stock split that results

Important: Make sure all appropriate subheads apply to your entry (see page v for instructions)

9000.13   **Stock Splits**

---

in a change in the aggregate par value of the stock but not in the per share par value is really a stock dividend and should be accounted for as shown in *GEN9000.13.*

9000.14   **Convertible Bonds (Debt)**

See GEN8000.1.3.5.

TABLE OF CONTENTS

10000.1.2.2.2.1	Increase in Fair Value
10000.1.2.2.2.2	Decrease in Fair Value
10000.1.2.2.3	Transfers Between Investment Categories
10000.1.2.2.3.1	Transfer from Short-Term Trading Category
10000.1.2.2.3.1.1	To Short-Term Available-for-Sale Category
10000.1.2.2.3.1.2	To Long-Term Available-for-Sale Category
10000.1.2.2.3.2	Transfer from Short-Term Available-for-Sale Category to Short-Term Trading Category
10000.1.2.2.3.2.1	Net Unrealized Holding Gain Accumulated on Securities Since Acquisition
10000.1.2.2.3.2.2	Net Unrealized Holding Loss Accumulated on Securities Since Acquisition
10000.1.2.2.3.3	Transfer from Short-Term Available-for-Sale Category to Long-Term Available-for-Sale Category
10000.1.2.3	Sale of Short-Term Marketable Equity Securities
10000.1.2.3.1	Sale of Short-Term Marketable Equity Securities Classified as Trading Securities
10000.1.2.3.2	Sale of Short-Term Marketable Equity Securities Classified as Available-for-Sale Securities
10000.1.2.3.2.1	Net Holding Gain Accumulated on Securities Since Acquisition
10000.1.2.3.2.2	Net Holding Loss Accumulated on Securities Since Acquisition
10000.1.2.4	Receipt of Cash Dividend
10000.1.2.5	Receipt of Stock Dividend or Stock Split
10000.2	**Long-Term Investments**
10000.2.1	Long-Term Debt Investments
10000.2.1.1	Purchase of Bonds
10000.2.1.1.1	Purchase at Par (Face, Stated, or Nominal) Value
10000.2.1.1.1.1	Purchase on Interest Payment Date
10000.2.1.1.1.2	Purchase Between Interest Payment Dates
10000.2.1.1.2	Purchase at a Premium
10000.2.1.1.2.1	Premium Not Separately Recorded
10000.2.1.1.2.2	Premium Separately Recorded
10000.2.1.1.3	Purchase at a Discount
10000.2.1.1.3.1	Discount Not Separately Recorded
10000.2.1.1.3.2	Discount Separately Recorded
10000.2.1.2	Accounting After Acquisition
10000.2.1.2.1	Held-to-Maturity Securities
10000.2.1.2.2	Available-for-Sale Securities
10000.2.1.2.2.1	Increase in Fair Value
10000.2.1.2.2.2	Decrease in Fair Value
10000.2.1.2.3	Transfers Between Investment Categories
10000.2.1.2.3.1	Transfer From Long-Term Available-for-Sale Category to Short-Term Trading Category
10000.2.1.2.3.1.1	Net Unrealized Holding Gain Accumulated on Securities Since Acquisition
10000.2.1.2.3.1.2	Net Unrealized Holding Loss Accumulated on Securities Since Acquisition
10000.2.1.2.3.2	Transfer from Long-Term Available-for-Sale Category to Short-Term Available-for-Sale Category

10000.2.2.1.1.2.2	Decrease in Fair Value
10000.2.2.1.1.3	Transfers Between Investment Categories
10000.2.2.1.1.3.1	Transfer from Long-Term Available-for-Sale Category to Short-Term Trading Category
10000.2.2.1.1.3.1.1	Net Unrealized Holding Gain Accumulated Since Acquisition
10000.2.2.1.1.3.1.2	Net Unrealized Holding Loss Accumulated Since Acquisition
10000.2.2.1.1.3.2	Transfer from Long-Term Available-for-Sale Category to Short-Term Available-for-Sale Category
10000.2.2.1.1.4	Sale of Long-Term Marketable Equity Securities
10000.2.2.1.1.4.1	Net Holding Gain Accumulated Since Acquisition
10000.2.2.1.1.4.2	Net Holding Loss Accumulated Since Acquisition
10000.2.2.1.1.5	Receipt of Cash Dividend
10000.2.2.1.1.6	Receipt of Stock Dividend or Stock Split
10000.2.2.1.2	Long-Term Investment in Nonmarketable Equity Securities
10000.2.2.1.2.1	Acquisition of Long-Term Nonmarketable Equity Securities
10000.2.2.1.2.2	Reclassification of Nonmarketable Equity Securities from Long-Term to Short-Term or from Short-Term to Long-Term
10000.2.2.1.2.3	Sale of Long-Term Nonmarketable Equity Securities
10000.2.2.1.2.4	Receipt of Cash Dividend
10000.2.2.1.2.5	Receipt of Stock Dividend or Stock Split
10000.2.2.2	Holdings of More than 20% of Voting Shares
10000.2.2.2.1	Acquisition of Stock
10000.2.2.2.2	Recognition of Portion of Net Income or Net Loss of Investee
10000.2.2.2.3	Receipt of Cash Dividend
10000.2.2.2.4	Sale of Investment in Stock

10000.3	**Investment in Stock Rights**
10000.3.1	Acquisition of Stock Rights
10000.3.1.1	Receipt of Stock Rights as a Current Stockholder
10000.3.1.2	Purchase of Stock Rights in the Market
10000.3.2	Sale of Stock Rights
10000.3.3	Exercise of Stock Rights (Use of Stock Rights to Purchase Additional Stock)
10000.3.4	Expiration of Stock Rights

10000.4	**Cash Surrender Value of Life Insurance**
10000.4.1	Payment of Premium and Recognition of Increase in Cash Surrender Value
10000.4.2	Payment of Premium and Recognition of Decrease in Cash Surrender Value
10000.4.3	Collection of Death Benefits

10000.5	**Special Long-Term Purpose Funds**
10000.5.1	Establishment of Fund
10000.5.2	Investment of Fund Cash
10000.5.3	Revenue Earned on Fund Investments
10000.5.4	Amortization of Premium or Discount on Bonds Held as Fund Investments
10000.5.4.1	Amortization of Premium on Bonds Held as Fund Investments
10000.5.4.2	Amortization of Discount on Bonds Held as Fund Investments

10000.1   **Short-Term (Temporary) Investments**

Short-Term (temporary) investments include:
- -Certificates of deposit (CDs)
- -Treasury bills
- -Commercial paper
- -Bonds
- -Stock
- -Stock warrants
- -Stock rights
- -Put and call options
- -Mutual funds

that are intended to be converted to cash within the longer of one year or the operating cycle.

10000.1.1   **Short-Term Debt Securities**

Short-term debt securities include certificates of deposit, treasury bills, commercial paper, bonds, and mutual funds investing in debt that otherwise fit the definition of temporary investments given in *GEN10000.1*. Equity (stock) securities are not included.

Short-term debt securities include three categories of investments:

1. Trading securities are debt securities intended to be sold in the near term. *See GEN10000.1.1.2.1.*

2. Held-to-maturity securities are debt securities intended to be held to maturity. These securities are considered short-term investments only if they fit the definition given in *GEN10000.1*; e.g., if they mature within the longer of one year or the operating cycle. *See GEN10000.2.1.2.1* for long-term investments classified as held-to-maturity.

3. Available-for-sale securities are debt securities not classified as either trading securities or held-to-maturity securities. Available-for-sale securities are considered short-term investments only if they fit the definition given in *GEN10000.1*. *See GEN10000.1.1.2.3* for long-term investments classified as available-for-sale.

Important: Make sure all appropriate subheads apply to your entry (see page v for instructions)

10000.1   **Short-Term (Temporary) Investments**
10000.1.1   **Short-Term Debt Securities**

Illustrations for investments in short-term debt securities in this section assume that any premium or discount on acquisition of the security is not amortized because of a lack of materiality. If premiums and discounts are material, they should be amortized as outlined in *GEN10000.2.1.1.2* and *GEN10000.2.1.1.3* for investments in long-term debt securities.

10000.1.1.1   **Acquisition of Short-Term Debt Securities**

10000.1.1.1.1   **Acquisition on Interest Payment Date**

*Short-Term Debt Securities - [Various Category]	xxxx	
Cash		xxxx
To record acquisition of short-term debt securities		

*Short-Term Debt Securities is debited for the cost of the securities which includes the basic purchase price plus any broker fees or other costs of acquisition paid by the purchaser. Trading, held-to-maturity, or available-for-sale categories may be indicated as shown in this entry. *See GEN10000.1.1.*

10000.1.1.1.2   **Acquisition Between Interest Payment Dates**

Many debt securities such as bonds pay interest periodically, e.g., every six months. If the securities are purchased between interest payment dates, interest calculated from the last interest payment date is added to the purchase price of the security. The purchaser will then collect a full period's interest on the next interest payment date, which will include reimbursement for the amount that was advanced to the seller.

*Short-Term Debt Securities - [Various Category]	xxxx	
**Interest Receivable	xxxx	
Cash		xxxx
To record acquisition of short-term debt securities between		
interest payment dates		

*Short-Term Debt Securities is debited for the cost of the securities, which includes the basic purchase price plus any broker fees or other costs of acquisition. Trading, held-to-maturity, or available-for-sale categories may be indicated as shown in this entry. *See GEN10000.1.1.*

Important: Make sure all appropriate subheads apply to your entry (see page v for instructions)

10000.1	**Short-Term (Temporary) Investments**
10000.1.1	**Short-Term Debt Securities**
10000.1.1.1	**Acquisition of Short-Term Debt Securities**
10000.1.1.1.2	**Acquisition Between Interest Payment Dates**

**Interest Receivable is debited for the amount of interest accrued since the last interest payment date. This amount is advanced to the seller along with the purchase price. Some companies prefer to debit Interest Revenue (Interest Income) for this amount so that when interest for the entire period is received, it can all be credited to Interest Revenue, resulting in a correct balance in the account. Either procedure produces the same result; i.e., the balance in Interest Revenue will ultimately be only the interest earned since the date of acquisition.

10000.1.1.2   **Application of Fair Value (Mark to Market) Principle After Acquisition**

At the end of the fiscal year, short-term debt securities classified either as trading securities or as available-for-sale securities are individually marked to market; i.e., adjusted to fair value. Both increases in fair value (unrealized holding gains) and decreases in fair value (unrealized holding losses) are recognized. Fair value is determined the same way for debt securities as for marketable equity securities if quoted market prices are available. (*See GEN10000.1.2.2* to determine fair value of marketable equity securities.) If quoted market prices are not available for debt securities, fair value is estimated using pricing techniques such as discounted cash flow analysis.

10000.1.1.2.1   **Trading Securities**

Trading securities are securities intended to be sold in the near term.

10000.1.1.2.1.1   **Increase in Fair Value**

*Short-Term Debt Securities - Trading	xxxx
**Unrealized Holding Gain On Short-Term Debt Trading Securities	xxxx
To record increase in fair value of short-term debt securities classified as trading securities	

*Short-Term Debt Securities - Trading is debited to adjust the carrying value of individual securities to their fair value at the end of the fiscal year.

Important: Make sure all appropriate subheads apply to your entry (see page v for instructions)

10000.1	**Short-Term (Temporary) Investments**
10000.1.1	**Short-Term Debt Securities**
10000.1.1.2	**Application of Fair Value (Mark to Market) Principle After Acquisition**
10000.1.1.2.1	**Trading Securities**
10000.1.1.2.1.1	**Increase in Fair Value**

**Unrealized Holding Gain On Short-Term Debt Trading Securities is credited for the increase in the fair value of the securities since the fair value was last updated (e.g., the date of acquisition, the end of the prior fiscal year, or the date of transfer between investment categories). This account is included on the income statement.

10000.1.1.2.1.2   **Decrease in Fair Value**

*Unrealized Holding Loss On Short-Term Debt Trading Securities	xxxx	
**Short-Term Debt Securities - Trading		xxxx

To record decrease in fair value of short-term debt securities classified as trading securities

*Unrealized Holding Loss On Short-Term Debt Trading Securities is debited for the decrease in the fair value of the securities since the fair value was last updated (e.g., the date of acquisition, the end of the prior fiscal year, or the date of transfer between investment categories). This account is included on the income statement.

**Short-Term Debt Securities - Trading is credited to adjust the carrying value of *individual securities* to their fair value at the end of the fiscal year.

10000.1.1.2.2   **Held-to-Maturity Securities**

Held-to-maturity securities are debt securities intended to be held to maturity. They are short-term investments only if they fit the definition given in *GEN10000.1*, e.g., if they mature within the longer of one year or the operating cycle. Held-to-maturity securities are accounted for at amortized cost. *See GEN10000.2.1.2.1.*

10000.1.1.2.3   **Available-for-Sale Securities**

Available-for-sale securities are securities other than trading securities or held-to-maturity securities. *See GEN10000.1.1.*

INVESTMENTS

Important: Make sure all appropriate subheads apply to your entry (see page v for instructions)

10000.1   **Short-Term (Temporary) Investments**
10000.1.1   **Short-Term Debt Securities**
10000.1.1.2   **Application of Fair Value (Mark to Market) Principle After Acquisition**
10000.1.1.2.3   **Available-for-Sale Securities**

10000.1.1.2.3.1   **Increase in Fair Value**

    *Short-Term Debt Securities - Available-For-Sale   xxxx
      **Net Unrealized Holding Gains And Losses On
          Short-Term Debt Available-For-Sale Securities   xxxx
    To record increase in fair value of short-term debt
    securities classified as available-for-sale securities

*Short-Term Debt Securities - Available For Sale is debited to adjust the carrying value of *individual securities* to fair value at the end of the fiscal year.

**Net Unrealized Holding Gains And Losses On Short-Term Debt Available-For-Sale Securities is credited for the increase in the fair value of the securities since the fair value of the securities was last updated (e.g., the date of acquisition, the end of the prior fiscal year, or the date of transfer between investment categories). This account nets all unrealized holding gains and losses on available-for-sale securities and is included as a separate component of Stockholders' Equity on the balance sheet.

10000.1.1.2.3.2   **Decrease in Fair Value**

    *Net Unrealized Holding Gains And Losses On Short-Term
        Debt Available-For-Sale Securities   xxxx
      **Short-Term Debt Securities - Available For Sale   xxxx
    To record decrease in fair value of short-term debt
    securities classified as available-for-sale

*Net Unrealized Holding Gains And Losses On Short-Term Debt Available-For-Sale Securities is debited for the decrease in the fair value of individual securities since the fair value of the securities was last updated (e.g., the date of acquisition, the end of the prior fiscal year, or the date of transfer between investment categories). This account nets all unrealized holding gains and losses on available-for-sale securities and is included as a separate component of Stockholders' Equity on the balance sheet.

**Short-Term Debt Securities - Available-For-Sale is credited to adjust the carrying value of *individual securities* to fair value at the end of the fiscal year.

Important: Make sure all appropriate subheads apply to your entry (see page v for instructions)

10000.1	**Short-Term (Temporary) Investments**
10000.1.1	**Short-Term Debt Securities**
10000.1.1.2	**Application of Fair Value (Mark to Market) Principle After Acquisition**

10000.1.1.2.4 **Transfers Between Investment Categories**

10000.1.1.2.4.1 **Transfer from Short-Term Trading Category**

10000.1.1.2.4.1.1 **To Short-Term Available-for-Sale Category**

> *Short-Term Debt Securities - Available-For-Sale   xxxx
>   **Short-Term Debt Securities - Trading   xxxx
>   ***Unrealized Holding Gains On Short-Term Debt
>   Trading Securities   xxxx
> *To record transfer of short-term debt securities from*
> *trading category to available-for-sale category*

*Short-Term Debt Securities - Available-For-Sale is debited for the fair value of the securities at the date of transfer.

**Short-Term Debt Securities - Trading is credited for the carrying value of the securities transferred. This is their fair value at the date of last adjustment.

***Unrealized Holding Gains On Short-Term Debt Trading Securities is credited for the increase in fair value of the transferred securities since the end of the prior fiscal year. If the fair value of the securities transferred has decreased, Unrealized Holding Loss On Short-Term Debt Trading Securities is debited instead. This account is included in the income statement. Subsequent changes in fair value of the securities transferred are recorded in Net Unrealized Holding Gains And Losses On Short-Term Debt Available-For-Sale Securities. This account is included as a separate component of Stockholders' Equity on the balance sheet. *See GEN10000.1.1.2.3.*

10000.1.1.2.4.1.2 **To Long-Term Available-for-Sale Category**

> *Long-Term Debt Securities - Available-For-Sale   xxxx
>   **Short-Term Debt Securities - Trading   xxxx
>   ***Unrealized Holding Gains On Short-Term Debt
>   Trading Securities   xxxx
> *To record transfer of short-term debt securities from*
> *trading category to long-term available-for-sale category*

Important: Make sure all appropriate subheads apply to your entry (see page v for instructions)

10000.1   **Short-Term (Temporary) Investments**
10000.1.1   **Short-Term Debt Securities**
10000.1.1.2   **Application of Fair Value (Mark to Market) Principle After Acquisition**
10000.1.1.2.4   **Transfers Between Investment Categories**
10000.1.1.2.4.1   **Transfer from Short-Term Trading Category**
10000.1.1.2.4.1.2   **To Long-Term Available-for-Sale Category**

---

*Long-Term Debt Securities - Available-For-Sale is debited for the fair value of the transferred securities at the date of transfer.

**Short-Term Debt Securities - Trading is credited for the carrying value of the securities transferred; i.e., their fair value at date of last adjustment.

***Unrealized Holding Gains On Short-Term Debt Trading Securities is credited for the increase in the fair value of the transferred securities since the end of the prior fiscal year. If the fair value of the securities transferred has decreased, Unrealized Holding Loss On Short-Term Debt Trading Securities is debited instead. This account is included in the income statement. Subsequent changes in fair value are recorded in Net Unrealized Holding Gains And Losses On Short-Term Debt Available-For-Sale Securities. This account is included as a separate component of Stockholders' Equity on the balance sheet. *See GEN10000.1.1.2.3.*

10000.1.1.2.4.1.3   **To Held-to-Maturity Category**

*Long-Term Debt Securities - Held-To-Maturity	xxxx	
**Short-Term Debt Securities - Trading		xxxx
***Unrealized Holding Gains On Short-Term Debt Trading Securities		xxxx

To record transfer of short-term debt securities from trading category to held-to-maturity category

*Long-Term Debt Securities - Held-To-Maturity is debited for the fair value of the transferred securities at the date of transfer. The securities are subsequently accounted for using the amortized cost method. The difference between the fair value of the debt securities at the date of transfer and their maturity value is a discount or premium that will be amortized as an adjustment to interest income over the remaining life of the securities. *See GEN10000.2.1.1.2* and *GEN10000.2.1.1.3* for premium and discount amortization for long-term debt securities.

**Short-Term Debt Securities - Trading is credited for the carrying value of the securities; i.e., their fair value at the date of last adjustment.

***Unrealized Holding Gains On Short-Term Debt Trading Securities is credited for the increase in the fair value of the transferred securities since the end of the prior fiscal year. If the fair value of the transferred securities has decreased, Unrealized Holding Loss On Short-Term Debt Trading Securities is debited instead. This account

Important: Make sure all appropriate subheads apply to your entry (see page v for instructions)

10000.1	**Short-Term (Temporary) Investments**
10000.1.1	**Short-Term Debt Securities**
10000.1.1.2	**Application of Fair Value (Mark to Market) Principle After Acquisition**
10000.1.1.2.4	**Transfers Between Investment Categories**
10000.1.1.2.4.1	**Transfer from Short-Term Trading Category**
10000.1.1.2.4.1.3	**To Held-to-Maturity Category**

---

is included on the income statement. Subsequent changes in fair value are no longer accounted for because the held-to-maturity securities are accounted for at amortized cost. *See GEN10000.2.1.2.1*

10000.1.1.2.4.2   Transfer from Short-Term Available-for-Sale Category

10000.1.1.2.4.2.1   To Short-Term Trading Category

10000.1.1.2.4.2.1.1   Net Unrealized Holding Gain Accumulated on Securities Since Acquisition

*Net Unrealized Holding Gains And Losses On Short-Term Debt Available-For-Sale Securities	xxxx	
**Short-Term Debt Securities - Trading	xxxx	
***Short-Term Debt Securities - Available-For-Sale		xxxx
****Unrealized Holding Gain On Short-Term Debt Trading Securities		xxxx

To record transfer of short-term debt securities from available-for-sale category to trading category

*Net Unrealized Holding Gains And Losses On Short-Term Debt Available-For-Sale Securities is debited to reverse (and realize) the net unrealized holding gain that has been recorded to reflect the increase in the fair value of the transferred securities since acquisition. This account has been previously reported as a separate component of Stockholders' Equity on the balance sheet. *See GEN10000.1.1.2.3* for accounting for available-for-sale debt securities at fair value.

**Short-Term Debt Securities - Trading is debited for the fair value of the securities at the date of transfer.

***Short-Term Debt Securities - Available-For-Sale is credited for the carrying value of the securities transferred. This is their fair value at the date of last adjustment.

INVESTMENTS

Important: Make sure all appropriate subheads apply to your entry (see page v for instructions)

10000.1	**Short-Term (Temporary) Investments**
10000.1.1	**Short-Term Debt Securities**
10000.1.1.2	**Application of Fair Value (Mark to Market) Principle After Acquisition**
10000.1.1.2.4	**Transfers Between Investment Categories**
10000.1.1.2.4.2	**Transfer from Short-Term Available-for-Sale Category**
10000.1.1.2.4.2.1	**To Short-Term Trading Category**
10000.1.1.2.4.2.1.1	**Net Unrealized Holding Gain Accumulated on Securities Since Acquisition**

****Unrealized Holding Gain On Short-Term Debt Trading Securities is credited to balance the entry and to record the unrealized holding gain that has accumulated on the transferred securities since the date of acquisition. This account is included on the income statement for the period in which the securities are transferred.

10000.1.1.2.4.2.1.2 **Net Unrealized Holding Loss Accumulated on Securities Since Acquisition**

*Unrealized Holding Loss On Short-Term Debt Trading Securities	xxxx	
**Short-Term Debt Securities - Trading	xxxx	
***Short-Term Debt Securities - Available-For-Sale		xxxx
****Net Unrealized Holding Gains And Losses On Short Term Debt Available-For-Sale Securities		xxxx

To record transfer of short-term debt securities from available-for-sale category to trading category

*Unrealized Holding Loss On Short-Term Debt Trading Securities is debited to balance the entry and to record the unrealized holding loss that has accumulated on the transferred securities since the date of acquisition. This account is included on the income statement for the period in which the securities are transferred.

**Short-Term Debt Securities - Trading is debited for the fair value of the securities at the date of transfer.

***Short-Term Debt Securities - Available-For-Sale is credited for the carrying value of the securities transferred; i.e., their fair value at the date of last adjustment.

****Net Unrealized Holding Gains And Losses On Short-Term Debt Available-For-Sale Securities is credited to reverse (and realize) the net unrealized holding loss that has been recorded to reflect the decrease in fair value of the securities transferred since acquisition. This account has been reported as a separate component of Stockholders' Equity on the balance sheet. *See GEN10000.1.1.2.3* on accounting for available-for-sale debt securities at fair value.

Important: Make sure all appropriate subheads apply to your entry (see page v for instructions)

10000.1	**Short-Term (Temporary) Investments**
10000.1.1	**Short-Term Debt Securities**
10000.1.1.2	**Application of Fair Value (Mark to Market) Principle After Acquisition**
10000.1.1.2.4	**Transfers Between Investment Categories**
10000.1.1.2.4.2	**Transfer from Short-Term Available-for-Sale Category**

10000.1.1.2.4.2.2   **To Long-Term Available-for-Sale Category**

*Long-Term Debt Securities - Available-For-Sale	xxxx	
*Short-Term Debt Securities - Available-For-Sale		xxxx
To record transfer of available-for-sale debt securities		
from short-term to long-term		

*The balance in Short-Term Debt Securities - Available-For-Sale for the securities transferred (generally their fair value at the end of the prior fiscal year) is transferred to Long-Term Debt Securities - Available-For-Sale.

10000.1.1.2.4.2.3   **To Held-to-Maturity Category**

*Long-Term Debt Securities - Held-To-Maturity	xxxx	
**Short-Term Debt Securities - Available-For-Sale		xxxx
***Net Unrealized Holding Gains And Losses On		
Short-Term Debt Available-For-Sale Securities		xxxx
To record transfer of short-term debt securities from		
available-for-sale category to held-to-maturity category		

*Long-Term Debt Securities - Held-To- Maturity is debited for the fair value of the securities at the date of transfer. The securities are subsequently accounted for using the amortized cost method. The difference between the fair value of the securities at the date of transfer and their maturity value is a discount or premium that will be amortized as an adjustment to interest income over the remaining life of the security. *See GEN10000.2.1.1.2* and *GEN10000.2.1.1.3* for premium and discount amortization on long-term debt securities.

**Short-Term Debt Securities - Available For Sale is credited for the carrying value of the securities transferred; i.e., their fair value at the date of last adjustment.

***Net Unrealized Holding Gains And Losses On Short-Term Debt Available-For-Sale Securities is credited for the increase in the fair value of the securities transferred since the carrying value was last adjusted. If the fair value of the securities decreased, this account is debited to balance the entry. (Subsequent increases or decreases in fair value are no longer accounted for because the held-to-maturity securities are accounted for at amortized cost.) This account is reported as a separate component of Stockholders' Equity on the balance sheet and is amortized over the

Important: Make sure all appropriate subheads apply to your entry (see page v for instructions)

10000.1	**Short-Term (Temporary) Investments**
10000.1.1	**Short-Term Debt Securities**
10000.1.1.2	**Application of Fair Value (Mark to Market) Principle After Acquisition**
10000.1.1.2.4	**Transfers Between Investment Categories**
10000.1.1.2.4.2	**Transfer from Short-Term Available-for-Sale Category**
10000.1.1.2.4.2.3	**To Held-to-Maturity Category**

---

remaining life of the securities similar to the amortization of other premiums and discounts. *See GEN10000.2.1.1.2* and *GEN10000.2.1.1.3* for premium and discount amortization.

10000.1.1.3   Sale of Short-Term Debt Securities

10000.1.1.3.1   Accrual of Interest to Date of Sale

Interest must be accrued from the last interest payment date or from the last time interest was accrued until the date of sale.

Interest Receivable	xxxx	
Interest Revenue		xxxx
To record accrual of interest to the date of sale		

10000.1.1.3.2   Sale of Short-Term Debt Securities Classified as Trading Securities

*Cash	xxxx	
**Interest Receivable		xxxx
***Short-Term Debt Securities - Trading		xxxx
****Realized Gain On Sale Of Short-Term Debt Securities		xxxx
To record sale of securities		

*Cash is debited for the sum of the sales price of the security plus the amount of accrued interest (*see GEN10000.1.2.4.1*) that the purchaser advances to the seller.

**Interest Receivable is credited for any interest accrued on the securities sold. This amount is advanced by the purchaser and included in the cash received. *See GEN10000.1.1.3.1* for the entry for accrued interest.

***Short-Term Debt Securities is credited for the carrying value of the securities sold; i.e., the fair value of the securities when the fair value of the securities was last updated (e.g., the date of acquisition, the end of the prior fiscal year, or the date of transfer between investment categories).

Important: Make sure all appropriate subheads apply to your entry (see page v for instructions)

10000.1   **Short-Term (Temporary) Investments**
10000.1.1   **Short-Term Debt Securities**
10000.1.1.3   **Sale of Short-Term Debt Securities**
10000.1.1.3.2   **Sale of Short-Term Debt Securities Classified as Trading Securities**

****Realized Gain On Sale Of Short-Term Debt Securities is credited to balance the entry. If a debit is needed to balance the entry, Realized Loss On Sale Of Short-Term Debt Securities is debited instead. This account is included on the Income Statement.

10000.1.1.3.3   **Sale of Short-Term Debt Securities Classified as Available-for-Sale Securities**

10000.1.1.3.3.1   **Net Unrealized Holding Gain Accumulated on Securities Since Acquisition**

*Cash	xxxx
**Net Unrealized Holding Gains And Losses On Short-Term Debt Available-For-Sale Securities	xxxx
***Interest Receivable	xxxx
****Short-Term Debt Securities - Available-For-Sale	xxxx
*****Realized Gain On Sale Of Short-Term Debt Securities	xxxx

To record sale of short-term debt securities classified as available-for-sale with accumulated net holding gain

*Cash is debited for the sum of the sales price plus the amount of accrued interest (*see GEN10000.1.2.4.1*) that the purchaser advances to the seller.

**Net Unrealized Holding Gains And Losses On Short-Term Debt Available-For-Sale Securities is debited to reverse (and realize) the net unrealized holding gain that has been recorded to reflect the increase in fair value of the securities sold since the date of acquisition. This account has been previously reported as a separate component of Stockholders' Equity on the balance sheet. *See GEN10000.1.1.2.3* for accounting for available-for-sale securities at fair value.

***Interest Receivable is credited for any interest accrued on the securities sold. This amount is advanced by the purchaser and included in the cash received. *See GEN10000.1.2.4.1* for the entry for accrued interest.

****Short-Term Debt Securities - Available For Sale is credited for the carrying value of the securities sold. This is the fair value of the securities at the date of last adjustment.

Important: Make sure all appropriate subheads apply to your entry (see page v for instructions)

10000.1	**Short-Term (Temporary) Investments**
10000.1.1	**Short-Term Debt Securities**
10000.1.1.3	**Sale of Short-Term Debt Securities**
10000.1.1.3.3	**Sale of Short-Term Debt Securities Classified as Available-for-Sale Securities**
10000.1.1.3.3.1	**Net Unrealized Holding Gain Accumulated on Securities Since Acquisition**

*****Realized Gain On Sale Of Short-Term Debt Securities is credited to balance the entry. If a debit is needed to balance the entry, Realized Loss On Sale Of Short-Term Debt Securities is debited instead. This account is included on the income statement.

10000.1.1.3.3.2   **Net Unrealized Holding Loss Accumulated on Securities Since Acquisition**

*Cash	xxxx
**Interest Receivable	xxxx
***Net Unrealized Holding Gains And Losses On Short-Term Debt Available-For-Sale Securities	xxxx
****Short-Term Debt Securities - Available-For-Sale	xxxx
*****Realized Gain On Sale Of Short-Term Debt Securities	xxxx

To record sale of short-term debt securities classified as available-for-sale with accumulated net holding loss

*Cash is debited for the sum of the sales price plus the amount of accrued interest (*see GEN10000.1.2.4.1*) that the purchaser advances to the seller.

**Interest Receivable is credited for any interest accrued on the securities sold. This amount is advanced by the purchaser and included in the cash received. *See GEN10000.1.2.4.1* for the entry for accrued interest.

***Net Unrealized Holding Gains And Losses On Short-Term Debt Available-For-Sale Securities is credited to reverse (and realize) the net unrealized holding loss that has been recorded to reflect the increase in fair value of the securities sold since the date of acquisition. This account has been previously reported as a separate component of Stockholders' Equity on the balance sheet. *See GEN10000.1.1.2.3* for accounting for available-for-sale securities at fair value.

****Short-Term Debt Securities - Available-For-Sale is credited for the carrying value of the securities sold; i.e., the fair value of the securities at the date of last adjustment.

*****Realized Gain On Sale Of Short-Term Debt Securities is credited to balance the entry. If a debit is needed to balance the entry, Realized Loss On Sale Of Short-Term Debt Securities is debited instead.

Important: Make sure all appropriate subheads apply to your entry (see page v for instructions)

10000.1   **Short-Term (Temporary) Investments**
10000.1.1   **Short-Term Debt Securities**

10000.1.1.4   ## Receipt of Interest

The following entry is for the receipt of regular interest payments. If interest is received from a purchaser upon sale of the securities, see GEN10000.1.1.3.

Cash	xxxx	
*Interest Receivable		xxxx
Interest Revenue		xxxx
To record receipt of interest revenue		

*Any interest receivable on the books as a result of interest accruals since the last interest payment date, including that resulting from advancement of interest to the seller at acquisition (as shown in *GEN10000.1.1.1.2*), must be written off when interest is received as shown here.

10000.1.2   ## Short-Term Marketable Equity Securities

Short-term marketable equity securities include stock, stock warrants, stock rights, put and call options, and mutual funds investing in stock that otherwise fit the definition of temporary investments given in *GEN10000.1*. Debt instruments are not included.

Short-term marketable equity securities include two categories of investments:

1. Trading securities are marketable equity securities that are intended to be sold in the near term.
2. Available-for-sale securities are investments in marketable equity securities that:
   - are not trading securities,
   - represent less than 20% of the outstanding voting shares of the company whose stock is owned, and
   - fit the definition of temporary investments given in *GEN10000.1*.

10000.1.2.1   ## Acquisition of Short-Term Marketable Equity Securities

*Short-Term Marketable Equity Securities - Trading		
(Available-For-Sale)	xxxx	
Cash		xxxx
To record acquisition of short-term marketable equity securities		

Important: Make sure all appropriate subheads apply to your entry (see page v for instructions)

10000.1   **Short-Term (Temporary) Investments**
10000.1.2   **Short-Term Marketable Equity Securities**
10000.1.2.1   **Acquisition of Short-Term Marketable Equity Securities**

---

*Short-Term Marketable Equity Securities - Trading (Available-For-Sale) is debited for the cost of the securities acquired. This cost includes the basic purchase price plus any broker fees or other costs necessary to acquire the securities.

10000.1.2.2   **Application of Fair Value (Mark to Market) Principle After Acquisition**

At the end of the fiscal year, short-term marketable equity securities are *individually* marked to market; i.e., adjusted to fair value. Both increases in fair value (unrealized holding gains) and decreases in fair value (unrealized holding losses) are recognized. For equity securities, fair value is determined using quoted market prices. For example, current sales prices on a national stock exchange, bid-and-ask prices in an over-the-counter market, or published share prices for mutual funds may be used for quoted market prices.

10000.1.2.2.1   **Trading Securities**

Trading securities are marketable equity securities that are intended to be sold in the near term.

10000.1.2.2.1.1   **Increase in Fair Value**

*Short-Term Marketable Equity Securities - Trading	xxxx
**Unrealized Holding Gain On Short-Term Marketable Equity Trading Securities	xxxx

To record increase in fair value of short-term equity securities classified as trading securities

*Short-Term Marketable Equity Securities - Trading is debited to adjust the carrying value of individual securities to their fair values at the end of the fiscal year.

**Unrealized Holding Gain On Short-Term Marketable Equity Trading Securities is credited for the increase in the fair value of individual securities since the fair value was last updated (e.g., the date of acquisition, the end of the prior fiscal year, or the date of transfer between investment categories). This account is included on the income statement.

Important: Make sure all appropriate subheads apply to your entry (see page v for instructions)

10000.1   **Short-Term (Temporary) Investments**
10000.1.2   **Short-Term Marketable Equity Securities**
10000.1.2.2   **Application of Fair Value (Mark to Market) Principle After Acquisition**
10000.1.2.2.1   **Trading Securities**

10000.1.2.2.1.2   **Decrease in Fair Value**

         *Unrealized Holding Loss On Short-Term Marketable
            Equity Trading Securities   xxxx
            **Short-Term Marketable Equity Securities - Trading   xxxx
         To record a decrease in the fair value of short-term
         marketable equity securities classified as trading securities

*Unrealized Holding Loss On Short-Term Marketable Equity Trading Securities is debited for the decrease in the fair value of *individual securities* since the fair value was last updated (e.g., the date of acquisition, the end of the prior fiscal year, or the date of transfer between investment categories). This account is included on the income statement.

**Short-Term Marketable Equity Securities - Trading is credited to adjust the carrying value of individual securities to their fair values at the end of the fiscal year.

10000.1.2.2.2   **Available-for-Sale Securities**

Available-for-sale securities are investments in marketable equity securities that:
     - are not trading securities,
     - represent less than 20% of the outstanding voting shares of the company
        whose stock is owned, and
     - fit the definition of temporary investments given in *GEN10000.1*.

10000.1.2.2.2.1   **Increase in Fair Value**

         *Short-Term Marketable Equity Securities - Available-For-
            Sale   xxxx
            **Net Unrealized Holding Gains And Losses On
              Short-Term Marketable Equity Available-For-
              Sale Securities   xxxx
         To record increase in fair value of short-term marketable
         equity securities classified as available-for-sale securities

*Short-Term Marketable Equity Securities - Available-For-Sale is debited to adjust the carrying value of individual securities to their fair value at the end of the fiscal year.

Important: Make sure all appropriate subheads apply to your entry (see page v for instructions)

10000.1   **Short-Term (Temporary) Investments**
10000.1.2   **Short-Term Marketable Equity Securities**
10000.1.2.2   **Application of Fair Value (Mark to Market) Principle After Acquisition**
10000.1.2.2.2   **Available-for-Sale Securities**
10000.1.2.2.2.1   **Increase in Fair Value**

**Net Unrealized Holding Gains And Losses On Short-Term Marketable Equity Available-For-Sale Securities is credited for the increase in fair value of *individual securities* since the fair value was last updated (e.g., the date of acquisition, the end of the prior fiscal year, or the date of transfer between investment categories). This account is included as a separate component of Stockholders' Equity on the balance sheet.

10000.1.2.2.2.2   **Decrease in Fair Value**

*Net Unrealized Holding Gains And Losses On Short-Term Marketable Equity Available-For-Sale Securities	xxxx
**Short-Term Marketable Equity Securities - Available-For-Sale	xxxx

To record a decrease in fair value of short-term marketable equity securities classified as available-for-sale securities

*Net Unrealized Holding Gains And Losses On Short-Term Marketable Equity Available-For-Sale Securities is debited for the decrease in fair value of individual securities since the fair value was last updated (e.g., the date of acquisition, the end of the prior fiscal year, or the date of transfer between investment categories). This account is included as a separate component of Stockholders' Equity on the balance sheet.

**Short-Term Marketable Equity Securities - Available-For-Sale is credited to adjust the carrying value of individual securities to their fair value at the end of the fiscal year.

10000.1.2.2.3   **Transfers Between Investment Categories**

10000.1.2.2.3.1   **Transfer from Short-Term Trading Category**

Important: Make sure all appropriate subheads apply to your entry (see page v for instructions)

10000.1	**Short-Term (Temporary) Investments**
10000.1.2	**Short-Term Marketable Equity Securities**
10000.1.2.2	**Application of Fair Value (Mark to Market) Principle After Acquisition**
10000.1.2.2.3	**Transfers Between Investment Categories**
10000.1.2.2.3.1	**Transfers from Short-Term Trading Company**

10000.1.2.2.3.1.1   **To Short-Term Available-for-Sale Category**

*Short-Term Marketable Equity Securities - Available-For-Sale	xxxx
**Short-Term Marketable Equity Securities - Trading	xxxx
***Unrealized Holding Gains On Short-Term Marketable Equity Trading Securities	xxxx

To record transfer of short-term marketable equity securities from trading category to short-term available-for-sale category

*Short-Term Marketable Equity Securities - Available-For-Sale is debited for the fair value of the securities at the date of transfer.

**Short-Term Marketable Equity Securities - Trading is credited for the carrying value of the securities transferred. This is their fair value at the date of last adjustment.

**Unrealized Holding Gains On Short-Term Marketable Equity Trading Securities is credited for the increase in the fair value of the transferred securities since the end of the prior fiscal year. If the fair value of the transferred securities has decreased, Unrealized Holding Loss On Short-]Term Marketable Equity Trading Securities is debited instead. Subsequent changes in the fair value of the securities transferred are recorded in Net Unrealized Holding Gains And Losses On Short-Term Marketable Equity Available-For-Sale Securities. This account is included as a separate component of Stockholders' Equity on the balance sheet. *See GEN10000.1.2.2.2* on accounting for available-for-sale securities.

10000.1.2.2.3.1.2   **To Long-Term Available-for-Sale Category**

*Long-Term Marketable Equity Securities - Available-For-Sale	xxxx
**Short-Term Marketable Equity Securities - Available-For-Sale	xxxx
***Unrealized Holding Gains On Short-Term Marketable Equity Available-For-Sale Securities	xxxx

To record transfer of short-term marketable equity securities from trading category to long-term available-for-sale category

GEN10000.1.2.2.3.1.2   GEN10000.1.2.2.3.2.1

Important: Make sure all appropriate subheads apply to your entry (see page v for instructions)

10000.1	**Short-Term (Temporary) Investments**
10000.1.2	**Short-Term Marketable Equity Securities**
10000.1.2.2	**Application of Fair Value (Mark to Market) Principle After Acquisition**
10000.1.2.2.3	**Transfers Between Investment Categories**
10000.1.2.2.3.1	**Transfer from Short-Term Trading Category**
10000.1.2.2.3.1.2	**To Long-Term Available-for-Sale Category**

---

*Long-Term Marketable Equity Securities - Available-For-Sale is debited for the fair value of the transferred securities at the date of transfer.

**Short-Term Marketable Equity Securities - Available-For-Sale is credited for the carrying value of the securities transferred; i.e., their fair value at the date of last adjustment.

***Unrealized Holding Gains On Short-Term Marketable Equity Available-For-Sale Securities is credited for the increase in the fair value of the securities transferred since last adjustment. If the fair value of the securities transferred has decreased instead, Unrealized Holding Loss On Short-Term Marketable Equity Available-For-Sale Securities is debited instead. These accounts are included on the income statement. Subsequent changes in fair value are recorded in Net Unrealized Holding Gains And Losses On Long-Term Available-For-Sale securities, which is included as a separate component of Stockholders' Equity on the balance sheet. *See GEN10000.2.1.2.2.*

10000.1.2.2.3.2	**Transfer from Short-Term Available-for-Sale Category to Short-Term Trading Category**

10000.1.2.2.3.2.1	**Net Unrealized Holding Gain Accumulated on Securities Since Acquisition**

*Net Unrealized Holding Gains And Losses On Short-Term
    Marketable Equity Available-For-Sale Securities xxxx
**Short-Term Marketable Equity Securities - Trading   xxxx
    ***Short-Term Marketable Equity Securities -
      Available-For-Sale   xxxx
    ****Unrealized Holding Gains On Short-Term
      Marketable Equity Available-For-Sale Securities   xxxx
*To record transfer of short-term marketable equity
securities from available-for-sale category to trading
category*

*Net Unrealized Holding Gains And Losses On Short-Term Marketable Equity Available-For-Sale Securities is debited to reverse (and realize) the net unrealized holding gain that has been recorded to reflect the increase in the fair value of the securities since the date of acquisition. This account has been previously reported as a

Important: Make sure all appropriate subheads apply to your entry (see page v for instructions)

10000.1	**Short-Term (Temporary) Investments**
10000.1.2	**Short-Term Marketable Equity Securities**
10000.1.2.2	**Application of Fair Value (Mark to Market) Principle After Acquisition**
10000.1.2.2.3	**Transfers Between Investment Categories**
10000.1.2.2.3.2	**Transfer from Short-Term Available-for-Sale Category to Short-Term Trading Category**
10000.1.2.2.3.2.1	**Net Unrealized Holding Gain Accumulated on Securities Since Acquisition**

separate component of Stockholders' Equity on the balance sheet. *See GEN10000.1.2.2.2* on accounting for available-for-sale securities.

**Short-Term Marketable Equity Securities - Trading is debited for the fair value of the securities at the date of transfer.

***Short-Term Marketable Equity Securities - Available-For-Sale is credited for the carrying value of the securities transferred; i.e., their fair value at the date of last adjustment.

***Unrealized Holding Gains On Short-Term Marketable Equity Available-For-Sale Securities is credited to balance the entry and to record the unrealized holding gain that has accumulated on the transferred securities since the date of acquisition. This account is included on the income statement for the period in which the securities are transferred.

10000.1.2.2.3.2.2   ## Net Unrealized Holding Loss Accumulated on Securities Since Acquisition

*Unrealized Holding Loss On Short-Term Marketable Equity Available-For-Sale Securities	xxxx
**Short-Term Marketable Equity Securities - Trading	xxxx
***Short-Term Marketable Equity Securities - Available-For-Sale	xxxx
****Net Unrealized Holding Gains And Losses On Short-Term Marketable Equity Available-For-Sale Securities	xxxx

To record transfer of short-term equity securities from available-for-sale category to trading category

*Unrealized Holding Loss On Short-Term Marketable Equity Available-For-Sale Securities is debited to balance the entry and to record the unrealized holding loss that has accumulated on the transferred securities since the date of acquisition. This account is included on the income statement for the period in which the securities are transferred.

**Short-Term Marketable Equity Securities - Trading is debited for the fair value of the securities at the date of transfer.

Important: Make sure all appropriate subheads apply to your entry (see page v for instructions)

10000.1	**Short-Term (Temporary) Investments**
10000.1.2	**Short-Term Marketable Equity Securities**
10000.1.2.2	**Application of Fair Value (Mark to Market) Principle After Acquisition**
10000.1.2.2.3	**Transfers Between Investment Categories**
10000.1.2.2.3.2	**Transfer from Short-Term Available-for-Sale Category to Short-Term Trading Category**
10000.1.2.2.3.2.2	**Net Unrealized Holding Loss Accumulated on Securities Since Acquisition**

***Short-Term Marketable Equity Securities - Available-For-Sale is credited for the carrying value of the securities transferred. This is their fair value at the date of last adjustment.

****Net Unrealized Holding Gains And Losses On Short-Term Marketable Equity Available-For-Sale Securities is credited to reverse (and realize) the net unrealized holding loss that has been recorded to reflect the decrease in the fair value of the transferred securities since acquisition. This account has been previously reported as a separate component of Stockholders' Equity on the balance sheet. *See GEN10000.1.2.2.2* on accounting for available-for-sale securities.

10000.1.2.2.3.3   **Transfer from Short-Term Available-for-Sale Category to Long-Term Available-for-Sale Category**

*Long-Term Marketable Equity Securities - Available-For-Sale	xxxx	
*Short-Term Marketable Equity Securities - Available-For-Sale		xxxx

To record transfer of marketable equity securities categorized as available-for-sale securities from short-term classification to long-term classification

*The balance in Short-Term Marketable Equity Securities - Available-For-Sale for the transferred securities is transferred to Long-Term Marketable Equity Securities - Available-For-Sale.

10000.1.2.3   **Sale of Short-Term Marketable Equity Securities**

10000.1.2.3.1   **Sale of Short-Term Marketable Equity Securities Classified as Trading Securities**

*Cash	xxxx	
**Short-Term Marketable Equity Securities - Trading		xxxx
***Realized Gain On Sale Of Short-Term Marketable Equity Securities		xxxx

To record gain on sale of short-term marketable equity securities classified as trading securities

Important: Make sure all appropriate subheads apply to your entry (see page v for instructions)

10000.1	**Short-Term (Temporary) Investments**
10000.1.2	**Short-Term Marketable Equity Securities**
10000.1.2.3	**Sale of Short-Term Marketable Equity Securities**
10000.1.2.3.1	**Sale of Short-Term Marketable Equity Securities Classified as Trading Securities**

---

*Cash is debited for the sales price of the securities sold.

**Short-Term Marketable Equity Securities - Trading is credited for the carrying value of the securities sold; i.e., the fair value of the securities when the fair value was last updated (e.g., the date of acquisition, the end of the prior fiscal year, or the date of transfer between investment categories).

***Realized Gain On Sale Of Short-Term Marketable Equity Securities is credited for the excess of the cash received over the carrying value of the securities sold. If the carrying value of the securities sold is greater than the cash received, Realized Loss On Sale Of Short-Term Marketable Equity Securities is debited instead.

10000.1.2.3.2 **Sale of Short-Term Marketable Equity Securities Classified as Available-for-Sale Securities**

10000.1.2.3.2.1 **Net Holding Gain Accumulated on Securities Since Acquisition**

*Cash	xxxx	
**Net Unrealized Holding Gains And Losses On Short-Term Marketable Equity Available-For-Sale Securities	xxxx	
***Short-Term Marketable Equity Securities - Available-For-Sale		xxxx
****Realized Gain On Sale Of Short-Term Marketable Equity Securities		xxxx

To record sale of short-term marketable equity securities classified as available-for-sale

*Cash is debited for the sales price of the security sold.

**Net Unrealized Holding Gains And Losses On Short-Term Marketable Equity Available-For-Sale Securities is debited to reverse (and realize) the net unrealized holding gain that has been recorded to reflect the increase in the fair value of the securities sold since the date of acquisition. This account has been previously reported as a separate component of Stockholders' Equity on the balance sheet. *See GEN10000.1.2.2.2* on accounting for available-for-sale securities.

Important: Make sure all appropriate subheads apply to your entry (see page v for instructions)

10000.1	**Short-Term (Temporary) Investments**
10000.1.2	**Short-Term Marketable Equity Securities**
10000.1.2.3	**Sale of Short-Term Marketable Equity Securities**
10000.1.2.3.2	**Sale of Short-Term Marketable Equity Securities Classified as Available-for-Sale Securities**
10000.1.2.3.2.1	**Net Holding Gain Accumulated on Securities Since Acquisition**

***Short-Term Marketable Equity Securities - Available-For-Sale is credited for the carrying value of the securities sold; i.e., the fair value of the securities when the fair value was last updated (e.g., the date of acquisition, the end of the prior fiscal year, or the date of transfer between investment categories).

****Realized Gain On Sale Of Short-Term Marketable Equity Securities is credited to balance the entry. If the cash received is less than the carrying value of the securities sold minus the net holding gain that is reversed, Realized Loss On Sale Of Short-Term Marketable Equity Securities is debited instead.

10000.1.2.3.2.2   **Net Holding Loss Accumulated on Securities Since Acquisition**

*Cash	xxxx
**Net Unrealized Holding Gains And Losses On Short-Term Marketable Equity Available-For-Sale Securities	xxxx
***Short-Term Marketable Equity Securities - Available-For-Sale	xxxx
****Realized Gain On Sale Of Short-Term Marketable Equity Securities	xxxx

To record sale of short-term marketable equity securities classified as available-for-sale

*Cash is debited for the sales price of the security sold.

**Net Unrealized Holding Gains And Losses On Short-Term Marketable Equity Available For Sale Securities is credited to reverse (and realize) the net unrealized holding loss that has been recorded to reflect the decrease in the fair value of the securities sold since the date of acquisition. This account has previously been reported as a separate component of Stockholders' Equity on the balance sheet. *See GEN10000.1.2.2.2* on accounting for available-for-sale securities.

***Short-Term Marketable Equity Securities - Available-For-Sale is credited for the carrying value of the securities sold; i.e., the fair value of the securities when the fair value was last updated (e.g., the date of acquisition, the end of the prior fiscal year, or the date of transfer between investment categories).

INVESTMENTS

Important: Make sure all appropriate subheads apply to your entry (see page v for instructions)

10000.1   **Short-Term (Temporary) Investments**
10000.1.2   **Short-Term Marketable Equity Securities**
10000.1.2.3   **Sale of Short-Term Marketable Equity Securities**
10000.1.2.3.2   **Sale of Short-Term Marketable Equity Securities Classified as Available-for-Sale Securities**
10000.1.2.3.2.2   **Net Holding Loss Accumulated on Securities Since Acquisition**

****Realized Gain On Sale Of Short-Term Marketable Equity Securities is credited to balance the entry. If the cash received is less than the carrying value of the securities sold plus the net holding loss which is reversed, Realized Loss On Sale Of Short-Term Marketable Equity Securities is debited instead.

10000.1.2.4   Receipt of Cash Dividend

Cash		xxxx
Dividend Income		xxxx
To record receipt of cash dividend		

10000.1.2.5   Receipt of Stock Dividend or Stock Split

A stock dividend is a dividend received in the form of additional shares of stock. A stock split occurs when the number of shares of stock outstanding is increased and the par (stated) value of the shares is decreased so that the total par (stated) value of the stock outstanding remains unchanged. In either case, from an investor's point of view all that has happened is that more shares are owned for the same total investment cost. Therefore, no journal entry is necessary.

10000.2   Long-Term Investments

Long-term investments include investments in debt and equity securities that a firm does not intend to convert to cash within the longer of one year or the operating cycle.

10000.2.1   Long-Term Debt Investments

Long-term debt investments include investments in long-term bonds, notes, and other debt securities. These securities are of two types:

1. Held-to-maturity securities are securities that a firm has the intent and ability to hold to maturity.
2. Available-for-sale securities are securities not classified as either trading (*see GEN10000.1* for definitions of types of short-term investments) or held-to-maturity investments. Available-for-sale debt securities are considered long-term investments if the firm does not intend to convert them to cash within the longer of one year or the operating cycle.

Important: Make sure all appropriate subheads apply to your entry (see page v for instructions)

10000.2   **Long-Term Investments**
10000.2.1   **Long-Term Debt Investments**

The illustrations that follow use investments in bonds as examples. However, the entries also apply to investments in other long-term debt securities.

10000.2.1.1   **Purchase of Bonds**

10000.2.1.1.1   **Purchase at Par (Face, Stated, or Nominal) Value**

Bonds are purchased at par (face, stated, or nominal) value when the current market rate of interest at issuance is equal to the interest rate (face, stated, coupon, or nominal rate) printed on the bond.

10000.2.1.1.1.1   **Purchase on Interest Payment Date**

> *Investment In Bonds - Available-For-Sale (Held-To-
> Maturity)   xxxx
> Cash   xxxx
> *To record investment in bonds*

*Investment In Bonds - Available-For-Sale (Held-To-Maturity) is debited for the cost of the bonds, which includes the purchase price plus brokerage fees and other costs of acquisition paid by the purchaser.

10000.2.1.1.1.2   **Purchase Between Interest Payment Dates**

Bonds normally pay half of the annual interest every six months. One of the interest payment dates is the maturity date of the bond; e.g., a bond that matures April 1, 2010 will pay interest on April 1 and October 1 each year. If bonds are purchased between interest payment dates, interest calculated from the last interest payment date (even though no interest may have been paid then) is added to the price of the bond. For example, if when the bonds are purchased there are only two months until the next interest payment date, four (6 - 2) months of interest will be advanced by the purchaser to the seller. Two months later, the purchaser will receive six months of interest, which will include two months of interest earned plus a reimbursement for the four months of interest advanced to the seller.

INVESTMENTS

Important: Make sure all appropriate subheads apply to your entry (see page v for instructions)

10000.2	**Long-Term Investments**
10000.2.1	**Long-Term Debt Investments**
10000.2.1.1	**Purchase of Bonds**
10000.2.1.1.1	**Purchase at Par (Face, Stated, or Nominal) Value**
10000.2.1.1.1.2	**Purchase Between Interest Payment Dates**

---

*Investment In Bonds	xxxx	
**Interest Receivable	xxxx	
***Cash		xxxx
To record investment in bonds		

*Investment In Bonds is debited for the purchase price of the bonds (excluding any accrued interest advanced to the seller but including broker fees and other costs of acquisition.

**Interest Receivable is debited for the amount of interest accrued since the last interest payment date. This amount is advanced to the seller along with the purchase price of the bonds. Alternative account titles include:
- Bond Interest Receivable
- Interest Revenue
- Bond Interest Revenue.

***Cash will be credited for the total of the cash paid. This includes the purchase price of the bonds as defined above plus interest accrued from the last interest payment date to the date of purchase.

10000.2.1.1.2   **Purchase at a Premium**

If the price of a bond exceeds its par (face or maturity) value, the excess is called a *premium*. This occurs if the interest rate paid on the bond exceeds the market rate.

10000.2.1.1.2.1   **Premium Not Separately Recorded**

Usually premiums on bonds purchased as an investment are not separately accounted for as they are with bonds payable. However, they may be accounted for separately (*see GEN10000.2.1.1.2.2*). Accounting for available-for-sale long-term debt securities after acquisition (*see GEN10000.2.1.2.2*) is facilitated if premiums are not separately recorded.

*Investments In Bonds - Available-For-Sale (Held-To-Maturity)	xxxx	
**Interest Receivable	xxxx	
***Cash		xxxx
To record bond investment		

Important: Make sure all appropriate subheads apply to your entry (see page v for instructions)

10000.2	**Long-Term Investments**
10000.2.1	**Long-Term Debt Investments**
10000.2.1.1	**Purchase of Bonds**
10000.2.1.1.2	**Purchase at a Premium**
10000.2.1.1.2.1	**Premium Not Separately Recorded**

---

*Investment In Bonds - Available-For-Sale (or Held-To-Maturity) is debited for the cost of the bonds including broker fees and other costs of acquisition.

**Interest Receivable is debited for the amount of interest accrued on the bonds purchased since the last interest payment date. This amount is advanced to the seller and recovered at the next interest payment date. If the purchase is made on an interest payment date, this account does not need to be debited.

***Cash is credited for the total amount paid, which includes the cost of the bond as defined above plus any accrued interest that is advanced to the seller.

10000.2.1.1.2.2

Premium Separately Recorded

Usually premiums on bonds purchased as an investment are not separately accounted for as they are with bonds payable. However, it is permissible to account for them separately as shown here. *See GEN10000.2.1.1.2.1* for entries when premiums are not accounted for separately.

*Investments In Bonds - Available-For-Sale (Held-To-Maturity)	xxxx	
**Premium On Investments In Bonds	xxxx	
***Interest Receivable	xxxx	
****Cash		xxxx
To record bond investment		

*Investment In Bonds - Available-For-Sale (Held-To-Maturity) is debited for the par (face or maturity) value of the bonds.

**Premium On Investments In Bonds is debited for the excess of the purchase price (excluding any accrued interest but including broker fees and other costs of acquisition) over the par (face or maturity) value of the bonds. The premium account is then amortized to interest revenue over the remaining life of the bond (time to maturity) as shown in *GEN10000.2.1.2.2*.

***Interest Receivable is debited for the amount of interest accrued on the bonds purchased since the last interest payment date. This amount is advanced to the seller and recovered at the next interest payment date. If the purchase is made on an interest payment date, this account does not need to be debited.

Important: Make sure all appropriate subheads apply to your entry (see page v for instructions)

10000.2	**Long-Term Investments**
10000.2.1	**Long-Term Debt Investments**
10000.2.1.1	**Purchase of Bonds**
10000.2.1.1.2	**Purchase at a Premium**
10000.2.1.1.2.2	**Premium Separately Recorded**

****Cash is credited for the total amount paid, which includes the cost of the bond as defined above plus any accrued interest which is advanced to the seller.

10000.2.1.1.3   **Purchase at a Discount**

If the par (face or maturity) value of a bond exceeds its price, the excess is called a discount. This will occur if the interest rate paid on the bond is less than the market rate.

10000.2.1.1.3.1   **Discount Not Separately Recorded**

Usually discounts are not separately accounted for as they are with bonds payable. However, it is permissible to account for them separately as shown in *GEN10000.2.1.1.3.2*. Accounting for available-for-sale long-term debt securities after acquisition (*see GEN10000.2.1.2.2*) is facilitated if discounts are not separately recorded.

*Investments In Bonds - Available-For-Sale (Held-To-Maturity)	XXXX	
**Interest Receivable	XXXX	
***Cash		XXXX
To record bond investment		

*Investment In Bonds - Available-For-Sale (Held-To-Maturity) is debited for the cost of the bonds including broker fees and other costs of acquisition. Discounts are not usually separately accounted for as they are with bonds payable.

**Interest Receivable is debited for the amount of interest accrued on the bonds purchased since the last interest payment date. This amount is advanced to the seller and recovered at the next interest payment date. If the purchase is made on an interest payment date, this account does not need to be debited.

***Cash is credited for the total amount paid, which includes the cost of the bond as defined above plus any accrued interest which is advanced to the seller.

Important: Make sure all appropriate subheads apply to your entry (see page v for instructions)

10000.2	**Long-Term Investments**
10000.2.1	**Long-Term Debt Investments**
10000.2.1.1	**Purchase of Bonds**
10000.2.1.1.3	**Purchase at a Discount**

10000.2.1.1.3.2   **Discount Separately Recorded**

Usually discounts are not separately accounted for as they are with bonds payable. However, it is permissible to account for them separately as shown here. *See GEN10000.2.1.1.3.1* for entries when discounts are not accounted for separately.

*Investments In Bonds - Available-For-Sale (Held-To-Maturity)	xxxx	
**Interest Receivable	xxxx	
***Discount On Investment In Bonds		xxxx
****Cash		xxxx
To record bond investment		

*Investment In Bonds - Available-For-Sale (Held-To-Maturity) is debited for the par (face or maturity) value of the bonds.

**Interest Receivable is debited for the amount of interest accrued on the bonds purchased since the last interest payment date. This amount is advanced to the seller and recovered at the next interest payment date. If the purchase is made on an interest payment date, this account does not need to be debited.

***Discount On Investments In Bonds is credited for the excess of the par (face or maturity) value of the bonds over the purchase price (excluding any accrued interest but including broker fees and other costs of acquisition). The discount account is then amortized to interest revenue over the life of the bond (time to maturity) as shown in *GEN10000.2.1.2.3*.

****Cash is credited for the total amount paid, which includes the price of the bond, any accrued interest that is advanced to the seller, and broker fees and other costs of acquisition.

10000.2.1.2   **Accounting After Acquisition**

10000.2.1.2.1   **Held-to-Maturity Securities**

Held-to-maturity securities are debt securities intended to be held to maturity. They are accounted for at amortized cost. Amortized cost at a given date is the acquisition

Important: Make sure all appropriate subheads apply to your entry (see page v for instructions)

10000.2   **Long-Term Investments**
10000.2.1   **Long-Term Debt Investments**
10000.2.1.2   **Accounting After Acquisition**
10000.2.1.2.1   **Held-to-Maturity Securities**

price adjusted for amortization of discount or premium to that date. For example, if $100,000 of five-year bonds that pay 10% annual interest (5% semi-annually) were purchased at a discount to yield 12% annually (6% semi-annually), the amortized cost at the end of each semi-annual period is shown in the following schedule:

Amortization Schedule

Date	Interest Received @5% (1)	Interest Income @6 (2)	Amortized Discount (3)	Cost (Carrying Value) (4)
1/1/03				$92,639.00 (5)
7/1/03	$5,000.00	$5,558.34	$558.34	93,197.34
12/31/03	5,000.00	5,591.84	591.84	93,789.18
7/1/04	5,000.00	5,627.35	627.35	94,416.53
12/31/04	5,000.00	5,664.99	664.99	95,081.52
7/1/05	5,000.00	5,704.89	704.89	95,786.41
12/31/05	5,000.00	5,747.18	747.18	96,533.60
7/1/06	5,000.00	5,792.02	792.02	97,325.62
12/31/06	5,000.00	5,839.54	839.54	98,165.15
7/1/07	5,000.00	5,889.91	889.91	99,055.06
12/31/07	5,000.00	5,943.30	944.94	100,000.00
	$50,000.00	$57,359.37	$7,359.37	

(1) Cash interest received semi-annually.
(2) Semi-annual interest earned (Column 4 at end of previous period X 6% semi-annual yield).
(3) Discount amortized each period (Column 2 - Column 1).
(4) Amortized cost (carrying value) at the end of the period (Column 4 at end of previous period + discount amortized in current period).
(5) Acquisition cost.

10000.2.1.2.2   **Available-for-Sale Securities**

At the end of the fiscal year, long-term investments in bonds classified as available-for-sale securities are *individually* marked to market; i.e., adjusted to fair value. Both increases in fair value (unrealized holding gains) and decreases in fair value (unrealized holding losses) are recognized.

Important: Make sure all appropriate subheads apply to your entry (see page v for instructions)

10000.2	**Long-Term Investments**
10000.2.1	**Long-Term Debt Investments**
10000.2.1.2	**Accounting After Acquisition**
10000.2.1.2.2	**Available-for-Sale Securities**

The total increase or decrease in fair value since acquisition is determined by comparing the current fair value of the securities with the current amortized cost of the securities. The increase or decrease in fair value for the current period is equal to the total increase or decrease in fair value since acquisition less the increase or decrease in fair value recorded in previous fiscal periods. For the example given in *GEN10000.2.1.2.1*, the increase in the fair value is recognized as follows:

		Amortized Cost	Fair Value
1/1/03	(Acquisition Date)	$99,639	$92,639
12/31/03	(Fiscal Year End)	93,789	95,000
12/31/04	(Fiscal Year End)	95,082	97,000

The increase in fair value that is recorded as of 12/31/03 is $1,211 ($95,000 fair value less $93,789 amortized cost). The increase in fair value that is recorded at 12/31/04 is $707 ($97,000 fair value less $95,082 amortized cost less $1,211 increase in fair value recorded as of 12/31/03). The amortization of discount or premium continues based on the original acquisition cost and maturity value of the bonds. *See GEN10000.2.1.3* and *GEN10000.2.1.4*.

10000.2.1.2.2.1   **Increase in Fair Value**

*Investment In Bonds - Available-For-Sale	xxxx
**Net Unrealized Holding Gains And Losses On Investment In Available-For-Sale Bonds	xxxx

To record increase in fair value of investment in bonds classified as available-for-sale securities

*Investment In Bonds - Available-For-Sale is debited to adjust the carrying value of individual securities to their fair values at the end of the fiscal year.

**Net Unrealized Holding Gains And Losses On Investment In Available-For-Sale Bonds is credited to record the increase in the fair value of the *individual securities* since the fair value was last updated (e.g., the date of acquisition, the end of the prior fiscal year, or the date of transfer between investment categories). *See GEN10000.2.1.2.2* for an explanation of the computation. This account is included as a separate component of Stockholders' Equity on the balance sheet.

Important: Make sure all appropriate subheads apply to your entry (see page v for instructions)

10000.2   **Long-Term Investments**
10000.2.1   **Long-Term Debt Investments**
10000.2.1.2   **Accounting After Acquisition**
10000.2.1.2.2   **Available-for-Sale Securities**

10000.2.1.2.2.2   **Decrease in Fair Value**

> *Net Unrealized Holding Gains And Losses On Investment
>   In Available-For-Sale Bonds   xxxx
>   **Investment In Bonds - Available-For-Sale   xxxx
> *To record decrease in fair value of investment in bonds*
> *classified as available-for-sale securities*

*Net Unrealized Holding Gains And Losses On Investment In Available-For-Sale Bonds is debited to record the decrease in the fair value of the individual securities since the fair value was last updated (e.g., the date of acquisition, the end of the prior fiscal year, or the date of transfer between investment categories). *See GEN10000.2.1.2.2* for an explanation of the computation. This account is included as a separate component of Stockholders' Equity on the balance sheet.

**Investment In Bonds - Available-For-Sale is credited to adjust the carrying values of individual securities to their fair values at the end of the fiscal year.

10000.2.1.2.3   **Transfers Between Investment Categories**

10000.2.1.2.3.1   **Transfer from Long-Term Available-for-Sale Category to Short-Term Trading Category**

Available-for-sale securities are other than trading or held-to-maturity securities.

Trading securities are securities intended to be sold in the near term.

10000.2.1.2.3.1.1   **Net Unrealized Holding Gain Accumulated on Securities Since Acquisition**

> *Net Unrealized Holding Gains And Losses On Investment
>   In Available-For-Sale Bonds   xxxx
>   **Short-Term Debt Securities - Trading   xxxx
>   ***Investment in Bonds - Available-For-Sale   xxxx
>   ****Unrealized Holding Gain On Long-Term Debt
>   Available-For-Sale Securities   xxxx
> *To record transfer of investment in long-term bonds from*
> *available-for-sale category to trading category*

Important: Make sure all appropriate subheads apply to your entry (see page v for instructions)

10000.2	**Long-Term Investments**
10000.2.1	**Long-Term Debt Investments**
10000.2.1.2	**Accounting After Acquisition**
10000.2.1.2.3	**Transfers Between Investment Categories**
10000.2.1.2.3.1	**Transfer from Long-Term Available-for-Sale Category to Short-Term Trading Category**
10000.2.1.2.3.1.1	**Net Unrealized Holding Gain Accumulated on Securities Since Acquisition**

---

*Net Unrealized Holding Gains And Losses On Investment In Available-For-Sale Bonds is debited to reverse (and realize) the net unrealized holding gain that has been recorded to reflect the increase in the fair value of the transferred securities since acquisition. This account has been previously reported as a separate component of Stockholders' Equity on the balance sheet.

**Short-Term Debt Securities - Trading is debited for the fair value of the securities at the date of transfer.

***Investment in Bonds - Available-For-Sale is credited for the carrying value of the securities transferred; i.e., their fair value at the end of the prior fiscal year or their fair value at the end of the prior fiscal year updated for any subsequent premium or discount amortization.

****Unrealized Holding Gain On Long-Term Debt Available-For-Sale Securities is credited to balance the entry and record the unrealized holding gain that has accumulated on the transferred securities since the date of acquisition. This account is included on the income statement for the period in which the securities are transferred.

10000.2.1.2.3.1.2   **Net Unrealized Holding Loss Accumulated on Securities Since Acquisition**

*Unrealized Holding Loss On Long-Term Debt Available-For-Sale Securities	xxxx	
**Short-Term Debt Securities - Trading	xxxx	
***Investment in Bonds - Available-For-Sale		xxxx
****Net Unrealized Holding Gains And Losses On Investment In Available-For-Sale Bonds		xxxx

To record transfer of investment in long-term bonds from available-for-sale category to trading category

*Unrealized Holding Loss On Long-Term Debt Available-For-Sale Securities is debited to balance the entry and record the unrealized holding loss that has accumulated on the transferred securities since the date of acquisition. This account is included on the income statement for the period in which the securities are transferred.

**Short-Term Debt Securities - Trading is debited for the fair value of the securities transferred at the date of transfer.

GEN10000.2.1.2.3.1.2   GEN10000.2.1.2.3.3

Important: Make sure all appropriate subheads apply to your entry (see page v for instructions)

10000.2	**Long-Term Investments**
10000.2.1	**Long-Term Debt Investments**
10000.2.1.2	**Accounting After Acquisition**
10000.2.1.2.3	**Transfers Between Investment Categories**
10000.2.1.2.3.1	**Transfer from Long-Term Available-for-Sale Category to Short-Term Trading Category**
10000.2.1.2.3.1.2	**Net Unrealized Holding Loss Accumulated on Securities Since Acquisition**

***Investment in Bonds - Available-For-Sale is credited for the carrying value of the securities transferred; i.e., their fair value at the end of the prior fiscal year or their fair value at the end of the prior fiscal year updated for any subsequent premium or discount amortization.

****Net Unrealized Holding Gains And Losses On Investment In Available-For-Sale Bonds is credited to reverse (and realize) the net unrealized holding loss that has been recorded to reflect the decrease in the fair value of the securities since the date of acquisition. This account has been previously reported as a separate component of Stockholders' Equity on the balance sheet.

10000.2.1.2.3.2   **Transfer from Long-Term Available-for-Sale Category to Short-Term Available-for-Sale Category**

*Short-Term Debt Securities - Available-For-Sale	xxxx	
*Investment In Bonds - Available-For-Sale		xxxx

To record transfer of long-term bond investment from long-term available-for-sale category to short-term available-for-sale category

*The balance in Investment In Bonds - Available-For-Sale for the bonds transferred (generally their fair value at the end of the prior fiscal year or their fair value at the end of the prior fiscal year updated for any subsequent premium or discount amortization) is transferred to Short-Term Debt Securities - Available-For-Sale.

10000.2.1.2.3.3   **Transfer from Long-Term Available-for-Sale Category to Held-to-Maturity Category**

*Investment In Bonds - Held-To-Maturity	xxxx	
**Investment In Bonds - Available-For-Sale		xxxx
***Net Unrealized Holding Gains And Losses On Investment In Available-For-Sale Bonds		xxxx

To record transfer of bond investment from long-term available-for-sale category to held-to-maturity category

*Investment In Bonds - Held-To-Maturity is debited for the fair value of the securities at the date of transfer. The securities are subsequently accounted for using the amortized cost method. The difference between the fair value of the securities at the

Important: Make sure all appropriate subheads apply to your entry (see page v for instructions)

10000.2   **Long-Term Investments**
10000.2.1   **Long-Term Debt Investments**
10000.2.1.2   **Accounting After Acquisition**
10000.2.1.2.3   **Transfers Between Investment Categories**
10000.2.1.2.3.3   **Transfer from Long-Term Available-for-Sale Category to Held-to-Maturity Category**

---

date of transfer and their maturity value is a discount or premium that will be amortized as an adjustment to interest income over the remaining life of the securities. *See GEN10000.2.1.2.1* for premium and discount amortization on long-term debt securities.

**Investment In Bonds - Available-For-Sale is credited for the carrying value of the securities transferred; i.e., their fair value at date of last adjustment.

**Net Unrealized Holding Gains And Losses On Investment In Available-For-Sale Bonds is credited for any increase in fair value to balance the entry. If a debit is needed to balance the entry because of a decrease in fair value, this account is debited instead. Subsequent increases or decreases in the fair value are not accounted for because the held-to-maturity securities are accounted for at amortized cost. The unrealized holding gain or loss at the date of transfer will continue to be reported as a separate component of Stockholders' Equity on the balance sheet and is amortized over the remaining life of the securities similar to the amortization of premiums and discounts. *See GEN10000.2.1.2.1* for premium and discount amortization of long-term debt securities.

10000.2.1.2.3.4   **Transfer from Held-to-Maturity Category to Long-Term Available-for-Sale Category**

      *Investment In Bonds - Available-For-Sale   xxxx
           **Investment In Bonds - Held-To-Maturity   xxxx
         ***Net Unrealized Holding Gains And Losses On
             Investment In Available-For-Sale Bonds   xxxx
      To record transfer of bond investment from held-to-maturity category to long-term available-for-sale category

*Investment In Bonds - Available-For-Sale is debited to increase the carrying value of the transferred securities to fair value at the date of transfer. If it is necessary to decrease the carrying value to fair value, this account is credited.

**Investment In Bonds - Held-To-Maturity is credited for the carrying value of the securities transferred.

***Net Unrealized Holding Gains And Losses On Investment In Available-For-Sale Bonds is credited to record the unrealized holding gain on the securities transferred. If

Important: Make sure all appropriate subheads apply to your entry (see page v for instructions)

10000.2	**Long-Term Investments**
10000.2.1	**Long-Term Debt Investments**
10000.2.1.2	**Accounting After Acquisition**
10000.2.1.2.3	**Transfers Between Investment Categories**
10000.2.1.2.3.4	**Transfer from Held-to-Maturity Category to Long-Term Available-for-Sale Category**

---

there is an unrealized holding loss, the same account is debited. This account is included as a separate component of Stockholders' Equity on the balance sheet. The securities transferred are subsequently accounted for at fair value. *See GEN10000.2.1.2.2* for the fair value method of accounting for long-term debt securities.

10000.2.1.2.3.5   **Transfer from Held-to-Maturity Category to Short-Term Available-for-Sale Category**

*Short-Term Debt Securities - Available-For-Sale	xxxx
**Investment In Bonds - Held-To-Maturity	xxxx
***Net Unrealized Holding Gains And Losses On Short-Term Available-For-Sale Securities	xxxx

To record transfer of bond investment from held-to-maturity category to short-term available-for-sale category

*Short-Term Debt Securities - Available-For-Sale is debited for the fair value of the securities at the date of transfer.

**Investment In Bonds - Held-To-Maturity is credited for the carrying value (amortized cost) of the transferred securities.

***Net Unrealized Holding Gains And Losses On Short-Term Available-For-Sale Securities is credited to record the unrealized holding gain on the securities transferred. If there is an unrealized holding loss, the same account is debited. This account is included as a separate component of Stockholders' Equity on the balance sheet. The securities transferred are subsequently accounted for at fair value. *See GEN10000.1.1.2.3* for the fair value method of accounting for short-term debt available-for-sale securities.

10000.2.1.3   **Receipt of Interest**

Important: Make sure all appropriate subheads apply to your entry (see page v for instructions)

10000.2   **Long-Term Investments**
10000.2.1   **Long-Term Debt Investments**
10000.2.1.3   **Receipt of Interest**

10000.2.1.3.1   **Bonds Originally Purchased at Par (Face or Maturity) Value**

Cash	xxxx	
*Interest Receivable		xxxx
Interest Revenue		xxxx

To record receipt of interest

*Interest Receivable is credited for any bond interest receivable previously recorded because of year-end interest revenue accruals or because Interest Receivable was debited for accrued interest paid at the time of purchase. *See GEN10000.2.1.1.1.2.*

10000.2.1.3.2   **Bonds Originally Purchased at a Premium**

10000.2.1.3.2.1   **Premium Amortized at Interest Payment Dates and at Year End**

10000.2.1.3.2.1.1   **Premium Not Separately Recorded**

Cash	xxxx	
*Investment In Bonds		xxxx
**Interest Receivable		xxxx
Interest Revenue		xxxx

To record receipt of interest and amortization of premium

*Investment In Bonds is credited for the amount of the premium amortized. The premium on bond investment (the excess of the amount debited to the investment account at the date of purchase over the par value of the bonds) is amortized over the life of the bonds (time from purchase to maturity). This may be done on interest payment dates and at year end (as assumed here) or only at year end. If the premium is amortized at interest payment dates, the credit to Interest Revenue is reduced by the amount of premium amortization credited to the investment account. If amortization is continued until the maturity date of the bonds, the balance in the investment account will equal the maturity value of the bonds. The premium should be amortized using the effective interest method, but the straight-line method may be used if the amounts are not materially different.

**Interest Receivable is credited for any bond interest receivable previously recorded because of year-end interest revenue accruals or because Interest Receivable was debited for accrued interest paid at the time of purchase. *See GEN10000.2.1.1.1.2.*

Important: Make sure all appropriate subheads apply to your entry (see page v for instructions)

10000.2	**Long-Term Investments**
10000.2.1	**Long-Term Debt Investments**
10000.2.1.3	**Receipt of Interest**
10000.2.1.3.2	**Bonds Originally Purchased at a Premium**
10000.2.1.3.2.1	**Premium Amortized at Interest Payment Dates and at Year End**

10000.2.1.3.2.1.2   **Premium Separately Recorded**

Cash	xxxx	
*Premium On Investment In Bonds		xxxx
**Interest Receivable		xxxx
Interest Revenue		xxxx

To record receipt of interest and amortization of premium

*Premium On Investment In Bonds is amortized over the life of the bonds (time from purchase to maturity). This may be done on interest payment dates and at year end (as assumed here) or only at year end. If the premium is amortized at interest payment dates, the credit to Interest Revenue is reduced by the amount of premium amortization. If amortization is continued until the maturity date of the bonds, the balance in the premium account willbe zero. The premium should be amortized using the effective interest method, but the straight-line method may be used if the amounts are not materially different.

**Interest Receivable is credited for any bond interest receivable previously recorded because of year-end interest revenue accruals or because Interest Receivable was debited for accrued interest paid at the time of purchase. *See GEN10000.2.1.1.1.2.*

10000.2.1.3.2.2   **Premium Not Amortized at Interest Payment Dates**

Cash	xxxx	
*Interest Receivable		xxxx
**Interest Revenue		xxxx

To record receipt of interest

*Interest Receivable is credited for any bond interest receivable previously recorded because of year-end interest revenue accruals or because Interest Receivable was debited for accrued interest paid at the time of purchase. *See GEN10000.2.1.1.1.2.*

**Interest Revenue is credited for whatever amount is necessary to balance the entry. Interest Revenue is adjusted at the end of the year for the amortization of the premium.

10000.2.1.3.3   **Bonds Originally Purchased at a Discount**

Important: Make sure all appropriate subheads apply to your entry (see page v for instructions)

10000.2   **Long-Term Investments**
10000.2.1   **Long-Term Debt Investments**
10000.2.1.3   **Receipt of Interest**
10000.2.1.3.3   **Bonds Originally Purchased at a Discount**

10000.2.1.3.3.1   **Discount Amortized at Interest Payment Dates and at Year End**

10000.2.1.3.3.1.1   **Discount Not Separately Recorded**

Cash	xxxx	
*Investments In Bonds	xxxx	
**Interest Receivable		xxxx
Interest Revenue		xxxx

To record receipt of interest and amortization of premium

*Investment In Bonds is debited for the amount of the discount amortized. The discount on bond investment (the excess of the par value of the bonds over the amount debited to the investment account at the date of purchase) is amortized over the life of the bonds (time from purchase to maturity). This may be done on interest payment dates and at year end (as assumed here) or only at year end. If the discount is amortized at interest payment dates, the credit to Interest Revenue is increased by the amount of discount amortization debited to the investment account. If such amortization is continued until the maturity date of the bonds, the balance in the investment account will equal the maturity value of the bonds. The discount should be amortized using the effective interest method, but the straight-line method may be used if the amounts are not materially different.

**Interest Receivable is credited for any bond interest receivable previously recorded because of year-end interest revenue accruals or because Interest Receivable was debited for accrued interest paid at the time of purchase. *See GEN10000.2.1.1.1.2.*

10000.2.1.3.3.1.2   **Discount Separately Recorded**

Cash	xxxx	
*Discount On Investment In Bonds	xxxx	
**Interest Receivable		xxxx
Interest Revenue		xxxx

To record receipt of interest and amortization of premium

*Discount On Investment In Bonds is amortized over the life of the bonds (time from purchase to maturity). This may be done on interest payment dates and at year end (as assumed here) or only at year end. If the discount is amortized at interest payment dates, the credit to Interest Revenue is increased by the amount of discount

Important: Make sure all appropriate subheads apply to your entry (see page v for instructions)

10000.2	**Long-Term Investments**
10000.2.1	**Long-Term Debt Investments**
10000.2.1.3	**Receipt of Interest**
10000.2.1.3.3	**Bonds Originally Purchased at a Discount**
10000.2.1.3.3.1	**Discount Amortized at Interest Payment Dates and at Year End**
10000.2.1.3.3.1.2	**Discount Separately Recorded**

---

amortization. The discount should be amortized using the effective interest method, but the straight-line method may be used if the amounts are not materially different.

**Interest Receivable is credited for any bond interest receivable previously recorded because of year-end interest revenue accruals or because Interest Receivable was debited for accrued interest paid at the time of purchase. *See GEN10000.2.1.1.1.2.*

10000.2.1.3.3.2   Discount Not Amortized at Interest Payment Dates

Cash	xxxx	
*Interest Receivable		xxxx
**Interest Revenue		xxxx
To record receipt of interest		

*Interest Receivable is credited for any bond interest receivable previously recorded because of year-end interest revenue accruals or because Interest Receivable was debited for accrued interest paid at the time of purchase. *See GEN10000.2.1.1.1.2.*

**Interest Revenue is credited for whatever is necessary to balance the entry. Interest Revenue is adjusted at the end of the year for the amortization of the discount.

10000.2.1.4   Accrual of Interest

10000.2.1.4.1   Bonds Originally Purchased at Par (Face or Maturity) Value

Interest Receivable	xxxx	
Interest Revenue		xxxx
To record receipt of interest		

10000.2.1.4.2   Bonds Originally Purchased at a Premium

Important: Make sure all appropriate subheads apply to your entry (see page v for instructions)

10000.2	**Long-Term Investments**
10000.2.1	**Long-Term Debt Investments**
10000.2.1.4	**Accrual of Interest**
10000.2.1.4.2	**Bonds Originally Purchased at a Premium**

10000.2.1.4.2.1 **Premium Not Separately Recorded**

Interest Receivable	xxxx	
*Investments In Bonds		xxxx
Interest Revenue		xxxx

To record accrual of interest and amortization of premium

*Investment In Bonds is credited for the amount of the premium amortized. The premium on bond investment (the excess of the amount debited to the investment account at the date of purchase over the par value of the bonds) is amortized over the life of the bonds (time from purchase to maturity). This may be done on interest payment dates and at year end or only at year end. The credit to Interest Revenue is reduced by the amount of premium amortization credited to the investment account. If amortization is continued until the maturity date of the bonds, the balance in the investment account will equal the maturity value of the bonds. The premium should be amortized using the effective interest method, but the straight-line method may be used if the amounts are not materially different.

10000.2.1.4.2.2 **Premium Separately Recorded**

Interest Receivable	xxxx	
*Premium On Investment In Bonds		xxxx
Interest Revenue		xxxx

To record accrual of interest and amortization of premium

*Premium On Investment In Bonds is amortized over the life of the bonds (time from purchase to maturity). The credit to Interest Revenue is reduced by the amount of premium amortization. The premium is usually amortized using the straight-line method, but occasionally the effective interest method is used.

10000.2.1.4.3 **Bonds Originally Purchased at a Discount**

10000.2.1.4.3.1 **Discount Not Separately Recorded**

Interest Receivable	xxxx	
*Investments In Bonds	xxxx	
Interest Revenue		xxxx

To record accrual of interest and amortization of discount

Important: Make sure all appropriate subheads apply to your entry (see page v for instructions)

10000.2	**Long-Term Investments**
10000.2.1	**Long-Term Debt Investments**
10000.2.1.4	**Accrual of Interest**
10000.2.1.4.3	**Bonds Originaly Purchased at a Discount**
10000.2.1.4.3.1	**Discount Not Separately Recorded**

---

*Investment In Bonds is credited for the amount of the discount amortized. The discount on bond investment (the excess of the par value of the bonds over the amount debited to the investment account at the date of purchase) is amortized over the life of the bonds (time from purchase to maturity). The credit to Interest Revenue is increased by the amount of discount amortization debited to the investment account. If amortization is continued until the maturity date of the bonds, the balance in the investment account will equal the maturity value of the bonds. The discount should be amortized using the effective interest method, but the straight-line method may be used if the amounts are not materially different.

10000.2.1.4.3.2   **Discount Separately Recorded**

Interest Receivable	xxxx	
*Discount On Investment In Bonds	xxxx	
Interest Revenue		xxxx

To record receipt of interest and amortization of discount

*Discount On Investment In Bonds is amortized over the life of the bonds (time from purchase to maturity). The credit to Interest Revenue is increased by the amount of discount amortization. The discount should be amortized using the effective interest method, but the straight-line method may be used if the amounts are not materially different.

10000.2.1.5   **Sale of Bond Investments**

10000.2.1.5.1   **Sale at Maturity (for Bond Investments Classified as Held-to-Maturity)**

10000.2.1.5.1.1   **Bonds Originally Purchased at Par (Face or Maturity) Value**

*Cash	xxxx	
**Investment In Bonds		xxxx
***Interest Receivable		xxxx
****Interest Revenue		xxxx

To record sale of bonds at maturity

*Cash is debited for the amount of cash received; i.e., the sum of the maturity value of the bonds plus interest since the last interest payment date.

Important: Make sure all appropriate subheads apply to your entry (see page v for instructions)

10000.2	**Long-Term Investments**
10000.2.1	**Long-Term Debt Investments**
10000.2.1.5	**Sale of Bond Investments**
10000.2.1.5.1	**Sale at Maturity (for Bond Investments Classified as Held-to-Maturity)**
10000.2.1.5.1.1	**Bonds Originally Purchased at Par (Face or Maturity) Value**

**Investment In Bonds is credited for the carrying value (maturity value) of the bonds.

***Interest Receivable is credited for any bond interest receivable previously recorded because of year-end interest revenue accruals or because Interest Receivable was debited for accrued interest paid at the time of purchase. *See GEN10000.2.1.1.1.2.*

****Interest Revenue is credited for whatever amount is necessary to balance the entry.

10000.2.1.5.1.2   **Bonds Originally Purchased at a Premium**

10000.2.1.5.1.2.1   **Premium Not Separately Recorded**

*Cash	XXXX	
**Investment In Bonds		XXXX
***Interest Receivable		XXXX
****Interest Revenue		XXXX

To record disposal of bonds at maturity

*Cash is debited for the amount of cash received; i.e., the sum of the maturity value of the bonds plus interest since the last interest payment date.

**Investment In Bonds is credited for the carrying value of the bonds. This amount is the maturity value plus any unamortized premium pertaining to the bonds maturing.

***Interest Receivable is credited for any bond interest receivable previously recorded because of year-end interest revenue accruals or because Interest Receivable was debited for accrued interest paid at the time of purchase. *See GEN10000.2.1.1.1.2.*

****Interest Revenue is credited for whatever amount is necessary to balance the entry.

Important: Make sure all appropriate subheads apply to your entry (see page v for instructions)

10000.2	**Long-Term Investments**
10000.2.1	**Long-Term Debt Investments**
10000.2.1.5	**Sale of Bond Investments**
10000.2.1.5.1	**Sale at Maturity (for Bond Investments Classified as Held-to-Maturity)**
10000.2.1.5.1.2	**Bonds Originally Purchased at a Premium**

10000.2.1.5.1.2.2 **Premium Separately Recorded**

*Cash	xxxx
**Investment In Bonds	xxxx
***Premium On Investment In Bonds	xxxx
****Interest Receivable	xxxx
*****Interest Revenue	xxxx

To record disposal of bonds at maturity

*Cash is debited for the amount of cash received; i.e., the sum of the maturity value of the bonds plus interest since the last interest payment date.

**Investment In Bonds is credited for the carrying (maturity) value of the bonds.

***Premium On Investment In Bonds is credited for an amount equal to the unamortized premium pertaining to the bonds maturing.

****Interest Receivable is credited for any bond interest receivable previously recorded because of year-end interest revenue accruals or because Interest Receivable was debited for accrued interest paid at the time of purchase. *See GEN10000.2.1.1.1.2.*

*****Interest Revenue is credited for whatever amount is necessary to balance the entry.

10000.2.1.5.1.3 **Bonds Originally Purchased at a Discount**

10000.2.1.5.1.3.1 **Discount Not Separately Recorded**

*Cash	xxxx
**Investment In Bonds	xxxx
***Interest Receivable	xxxx
****Interest Revenue	xxxx

To record disposal of bonds at maturity

*Cash is debited for the amount of cash received; i.e., the sum of the maturity value of the bonds plus interest since the last interest payment date.

**Investment In Bonds is credited for the carrying value of the bonds. This amount is the maturity value less any unamortized discount pertaining to the bonds maturing.

GEN10000.2.1.5.1.3.1

Important: Make sure all appropriate subheads apply to your entry (see page v for instructions)

10000.2	**Long-Term Investments**
10000.2.1	**Long-Term Debt Investments**
10000.2.1.5	**Sale of Bond Investments**
10000.2.1.5.1	**Sale at Maturity (for Bond Investments Classified as Held-to-Maturity)**
10000.2.1.5.1.3	**Bonds Originally Purchased at a Discount**
10000.2.1.5.1.3.1	**Discount Not Separately Recorded**

***Interest Receivable is credited for any bond interest receivable previously recorded because of year-end interest revenue accruals or because Interest Receivable was debited for accrued interest paid at the time of purchase. *See GEN10000.2.1.1.1.2.*

****Interest Revenue is credited for whatever amount is necessary to balance the entry.

10000.2.1.5.1.3.2   **Discount Separately Recorded**

*Cash	XXXX	
**Discount On Investment In Bonds	XXXX	
***Investment In Bonds		XXXX
****Interest Receivable		XXXX
*****Interest Revenue		XXXX
To record disposal of bonds at maturity		

*Cash is debited for the amount of cash received; i.e., the sum of the maturity value of the bonds plus interest since the last interest payment date.

**Discount On Investment In Bonds is debited for an amount equal to the unamortized discount of the bonds maturing.

***Investment In Bonds is credited for the carrying (maturity) value of the bonds.

****Interest Receivable is credited for any bond interest receivable previously recorded because of year-end interest revenue accruals or because Interest Receivable was debited for accrued interest paid at the time of purchase. *See GEN10000.2.1.1.1.2.*

*****Interest Revenue is credited for whatever amount is necessary to balance the entry.

10000.2.1.5.2   **Sale Before Maturity (for Bond Investments Classified as Available-for-Sale)**

Important: Make sure all appropriate subheads apply to your entry (see page v for instructions)

10000.2	**Long-Term Investments**
10000.2.1	**Long-Term Debt Investments**
10000.2.1.5	**Sale of Bond Investments**
10000.2.1.5.2	**Sale Before Maturity (for Bond Investments Classified as Available-for-Sale)**

10000.2.1.5.2.1   **Bonds Originally Purchased at Par (Face or Maturity) Value**

        *Interest Receivable   xxxx
             Interest Revenue   xxxx
        To record accrued interest

*Interest Receivable is debited for the amount of interest accrued since the last interest payment date or since the last time it was accrued, whichever is the most recent date.

        *Cash   xxxx
             **Investment In Bonds   xxxx
             ***Interest Receivable   xxxx
             ****Gain On Sale Of Bond Investment   xxxx
        To record sale of bond investment

*Cash is debited for the amount of cash received; i.e., the sum of the sales price of the bonds plus interest accrued since the last interest payment date.

**Investment In Bonds is credited for the carrying value (fair value at last adjustment) of the bonds. *See GEN10000.2.1.2.2* for the fair value method of accounting for investments in long-term debt securities.

***Interest Receivable is credited for any bond interest receivable previously recorded because of interest accruals or because Interest Receivable was debited for accrued interest paid at the time of purchase. *See GEN10000.2.1.1.1.2.*

****Gain On Sale Of Bond Investment is credited for whatever amount is necessary to balance the entry. If a debit amount is necessary to balance the entry, Loss On Sale Of Bond Investment is debited instead.

        *Net Unrealized Holding Gains And Losses   xxxx
             **Realized Gain On Sale Of Bond Investment   xxxx
        To record realization of previously unrealized holding gain recorded since acquisition of investment

*Net Unrealized Holding Gains And Losses is debited to eliminate the unrealized holding gain that has been recorded to reflect the increase in fair value of the securities since date of acquisition. *See GEN10000.2.1.2.2.1* for the fair value method of accounting for investment in long-term debt securities. If an unrealized holding loss has been recorded to reflect a decrease in fair value since acquisition, this account is credited.

Important: Make sure all appropriate subheads apply to your entry (see page v for instructions)

10000.2	**Long-Term Investments**
10000.2.1	**Long-Term Debt Investments**
10000.2.1.5	**Sale of Bond Investments**
10000.2.1.5.2	**Sale Before Maturity (for Bond Investments Classified as Available-for-Sale)**
10000.2.1.5.2.1	**Bonds Originally Purchased at Par (Face or Maturity) Value**

**Realized Gain On Sale Of Bond Investment is credited to realize the previously unrealized holding gain recorded since the date of acquisition. If a previously unrealized holding loss is realized, Realized Loss On Sale Of Bond Investment is debited instead.

10000.2.1.5.2.2   Bonds Originally Purchased at a Premium

10000.2.1.5.2.2.1   Premium Not Separately Recorded

*Interest Receivable	xxxx	
**Investment In Bonds		xxxx
***Interest Revenue		xxxx

To record accrued interest and amortization of premium

*Interest must be accrued since the last interest payment date or since the last time it was accrued, whichever is the most recent date.

**Investment In Bonds must be credited to amortize the premium from the date of the last amortization to the date of disposal.

***Interest Revenue is credited for whatever amount is necessary to balance the entry.

*Cash	xxxx	
**Investment In Bonds		xxxx
***Interest Receivable		xxxx
****Gain On Sale Of Bond Investment		xxxx

To record sale of bond investment

*The amount of cash received will be the sum of the sales price of the bonds plus interest since the last interest payment date.

**Investment In Bonds is credited for the carrying value (the fair value at last adjustment minus the amortization of premium for the current period) of the bonds (*see GEN10000.2.1.5.2.2.1*). See *GEN10000.2.1.2.2* for the fair value method of accounting for investment in long-term debt securities.

***Interest Receivable is credited for any bond interest receivable previously recorded because of interest accruals or because Interest Receivable was debited for accrued interest paid at the time of purchase. *See GEN10000.2.1.1.1.2.*

INVESTMENTS

Important: Make sure all appropriate subheads apply to your entry (see page v for instructions)

10000.2	**Long-Term Investments**
10000.2.1	**Long-Term Debt Investments**
10000.2.1.5	**Sale of Bond Investments**
10000.2.1.5.2	**Sale Before Maturity (for Bond Investments Classified as Available-for-Sale)**
10000.2.1.5.2.2	**Bonds Originally Purchased at a Premium**
10000.2.1.5.2.2.1	**Premium Not Separately Recorded**

****Gain On Sale Of Bond Investment is credited for whatever amount is necessary to balance the entry. If a debit amount is necessary to balance the entry, Loss On Sale Of Bond Investment is debited instead.

*Net Unrealized Holding Gains And Losses	xxxx	
**Realized Gain On Sale Of Bond Investment		xxxx

To record realization of previously unrealized holding gain recorded since acquisition of investment

*Net Unrealized Holding Gains And Losses is debited to eliminate the unrealized holding gain that has been recorded to reflect the increase in fair value of the securities since the date of acquisition. *See GEN10000.2.1.2.2* for the fair value method of accounting for investment in long-term debt securities. If an unrealized holding loss has been recorded to reflect a decrease in fair value since acquisition, this account is credited instead.

**Realized Gain On Sale Of Bond Investment is credited to realize the previously unrealized holding gain recorded since the date of acquisition. If a previously unrealized holding loss is realized, Realized Loss On Sale Of Bond Investment is debited instead.

10000.2.1.5.2.2.2   Premium Separately Recorded

*Interest Receivable	xxxx	
**Premium On Investment In Bonds		xxxx
***Interest Revenue		xxxx

To record accrued interest and amortization of premium

*Interest Receivable is debited for the amount of interest accrued since the last interest payment date or since the last time it was accrued, whichever is the most recent date.

**Premium On Investment In Bonds must be credited to amortize the premium from the date of the last amortization to the date of disposal.

INVESTMENTS

Important: Make sure all appropriate subheads apply to your entry (see page v for instructions)

10000.2	**Long-Term Investments**
10000.2.1	**Long-Term Debt Investments**
10000.2.1.5	**Sale of Bond Investments**
10000.2.1.5.2	**Sale Before Maturity (for Bond Investments Classified as Available-for-Sale)**
10000.2.1.5.2.2	**Bonds Originally Purchased at a Premium**
10000.2.1.5.2.2.2	**Premium Separately Recorded**

***Interest Revenue is credited for whatever amount is necessary to balance the entry.

*Cash	xxxx	
**Investment In Bonds		xxxx
***Premium On Investment In Bonds		xxxx
****Interest Receivable		xxxx
*****Gain On Sale Of Bond Investment		xxxx

To record sale of bond investment

*Cash is debited for the amount of cash received; i.e., the sum of the sales price of the bonds plus interest since the last interest payment date.

**Investment In Bonds is credited for the carrying value (the fair value at last adjustment) of the bonds. *See GEN10000.2.1.2.2* for the fair value method of accounting for investment in long-term debt securities.

***Premium On Investment In Bonds is credited for an amount equal to the unamortized premium of the bonds maturing.

****Interest Receivable is credited for any bond interest receivable previously recorded because of year-end interest revenue accruals or because Interest Receivable was debited for accrued interest paid at the time of purchase. *See GEN10000.2.1.1.1.2.*

*****Gain On Sale Of Bond Investment is credited for whatever amount is necessary to balance the entry. If a debit amount is necessary to balance the entry, Loss On Sale Of Bond Investment is debited instead.

*Net Unrealized Holding Gains And Losses	xxxx	
**Realized Gain On Sale Of Bond Investment		xxxx

To record realization of previously unrealized holding gain
recorded since acquisition of investment

*Net Unrealized Holding Gains And Losses is debited to eliminate the unrealized holding gain that has been recorded to reflect the increase in fair value of the securities since date of acquisition. *See GEN10000.2.1.2.2* for the fair value method of accounting for investment in long-term debt securities. If an unrealized holding loss has been recorded to reflect a decrease in fair value since acquisition, this account is credited.

Important: Make sure all appropriate subheads apply to your entry (see page v for instructions)

10000.2	**Long-Term Investments**
10000.2.1	**Long-Term Debt Investments**
10000.2.1.5	**Sale of Bond Investments**
10000.2.1.5.2	**Sale Before Maturity (for Bond Investments Classified as Available-for-Sale)**
10000.2.1.5.2.2	**Bonds Originally Purchased at a Premium**
10000.2.1.5.2.2.2	**Premium Separately Recorded**

**Realized Gain On Sale Of Bond Investment is credited to realize the previously unrealized holding gain recorded since the date of acquisition. If a previously unrealized holding loss is realized, Realized Loss On Sale Of Bond Investment is debited instead.

10000.2.1.5.2.3   **Bonds Originally Purchased at a Discount**

10000.2.1.5.2.3.1   **Discount Not Separately Recorded**

*Interest Receivable	xxxx	
**Investment In Bonds	xxxx	
***Interest Revenue		xxxx

To record accrued interest and amortization of discount

*Interest must be accrued since the last interest payment date or since the last time it was accrued, whichever is the most recent date.

**Investment In Bonds must be debited to amortize the discount from the date of the last amortization to the date of disposal.

***Interest Revenue is credited for whatever amount is necessary to balance the entry.

*Cash	xxxx	
**Investment In Bonds		xxxx
***Interest Receivable		xxxx
****Gain On Sale Of Bond Investment		xxxx

To record sale of bond investment

*Cash is debited for the amount of cash received; i.e., the sum of the sales price of the bonds plus interest since the last interest payment date.

**Investment In Bonds is credited for the carrying value (the fair value at last adjustment to fair value plus the amortization of discount for the current period) of the bonds (*see GEN10000.2.1.5.2.3.1*). See *GEN10000.2.1.2.2* for the fair value method of accounting for investment in long-term debt securities.

***Interest Receivable is credited for any bond interest receivable previously recorded because of interest accruals or because Interest Receivable was debited for accrued interest paid at the time of purchase. See *GEN10000.2.1.1.1.2.*

Important: Make sure all appropriate subheads apply to your entry (see page v for instructions)

10000.2	**Long-Term Investments**
10000.2.1	**Long-Term Debt Investments**
10000.2.1.5	**Sale of Bond Investments**
10000.2.1.5.2	**Sale Before Maturity (for Bond Investments Classified as Available-for-Sale)**
10000.2.1.5.2.3	**Bonds Originally Purchased at a Discount**
10000.2.1.5.2.3.1	**Discount Not Separately Recorded**

****Gain On Sale Of Bond Investment is credited for whatever amount is necessary to balance the entry. If a debit amount is necessary to balance the entry, Loss On Sale Of Bond Investment is debited instead.

*Net Unrealized Holding Gains And Losses	xxxx	
**Realized Gain On Sale Of Bond Investment		xxxx

To record realization of previously unrealized holding gain recorded since acquisition of investment

*Net Unrealized Holding Gains And Losses is debited to eliminate the unrealized holding gain that has been recorded to reflect the increase in fair value of the securities since the date of acquisition. *See GEN10000.2.1.2.2* for the fair value method of accounting for investment in long-term debt securities. If an unrealized holding loss has been recorded to reflect a decrease in fair value since acquisition, this account is credited instead.

**Realized Gain On Sale Of Bond Investment is credited to realize the previously unrealized holding gain recorded since the date of acquisition. If a previously unrealized holding loss is realized, Realized Loss On Sale Of Bond Investment is debited instead.

10000.2.1.5.2.3.2   **Discount Separately Recorded**

*Interest Receivable	xxxx	
**Discount On Investment In Bonds	xxxx	
***Interest Revenue		xxxx

To record accrual of interest and amortization of discount

*Interest Receivable is debited for the amount of interest accrued since the last interest payment date or since the last time it was accrued, whichever is the most recent date.

**Discount On Investment In Bonds must be debited to amortize the discount from the date of the last amortization to the date of disposal.

***Interest Revenue is credited for whatever amount is necessary to balance the entry.

Important: Make sure all appropriate subheads apply to your entry (see page v for instructions)

10000.2	**Long-Term Investments**
10000.2.1	**Long-Term Debt Investments**
10000.2.1.5	**Sale of Bond Investments**
10000.2.1.5.2	**Sale Before Maturity (for Bond Investments Classified as Available-for-Sale)**
10000.2.1.5.2.3	**Bonds Originally Purchased at a Discount**
10000.2.1.5.2.3.2	**Discount Separately Recorded**

---

*Cash	xxxx
**Discount On Investment In Bonds	xxxx
***Investment In Bonds	xxxx
****Interest Receivable	xxxx
*****Gain On Sale Of Bond Investment	

To record sale of bond investment

*Cash is debited for the amount of cash received; i.e., the sum of the sales price of the bonds plus interest since the last interest payment date.

**Discount On Investment In Bonds is debited for an amount equal to the unamortized discount of the bonds maturing.

***Investment In Bonds is credited for the carrying value (the fair value at last adjustment to fair value) of the bonds. *See GEN10000.2.1.2.2* for the fair value method of accounting for investment in long-term debt securities.

****Interest Receivable is credited for any bond interest receivable previously recorded because of year-end interest revenue accruals or because Interest Receivable was debited for accrued interest paid at the time of purchase. *See GEN10000.2.1.1.1.2.*

*****Gain On Sale Of Bond Investment is credited for whatever amount is necessary to balance the entry. If a debit amount is necessary to balance the entry, Loss On Sale Of Bond Investment is debited instead.

*Net Unrealized Holding Gains And Losses	xxxx
**Realized Gain On Sale Of Bond Investment	xxxx

To record realization of previously unrealized holding gain recorded since acquisition of investment

*Net Unrealized Holding Gains And Losses is debited to eliminate the unrealized holding gain that has been recorded to reflect the increase in the fair value of the securities since the date of acquisition. *See GEN10000.2.1.2.2* for the fair value method of accounting for investment in long-term debt securities. If an unrealized holding loss has been recorded to reflect a decrease in fair value since acquisition, this account is credited instead.

**Realized Gain On Sale Of Bond Investment is credited to realize the previously unrealized holding gain recorded since the date of acquisition. If a previously unrealized holding loss is realized, Realized Loss On Sale Of Bond Investment is debited instead.

Important: Make sure all appropriate subheads apply to your entry (see page v for instructions)

10000.2 **Long-Term Investments**

10000.2.2 **Long-Term Equity Investments**

Long-term equity investments include investments in the types of securities listed in *GEN10000.1.1.* Investments in equity securities are considered long-term investments if the company does not intend to convert them to cash within the longer of one year or the operating cycle.

10000.2.2.1 **Holdings of Less than 20% of Voting Shares**

If less than 20% of the outstanding voting shares of a company are owned, it is assumed there is no significant influence over the operations of the investee. In this circumstance, the fair value method is used for long-term investments in marketable equity securities (stocks readily marketable) and the cost method is used for long-term investments in nonmarketable equity securities (stocks not readily marketable). If significant influence can be shown with ownership of less than 20% of the out-standing voting shares, the equity method procedures given in *GEN10000.2.2.2* apply.

10000.2.2.1.1 **Investment in Marketable Equity Securities**

The fair value method must be used when accounting for investments in marketable equity securities representing less than 20% of the outstanding voting shares of the company whose stock is owned unless significant influence can be shown (*see GEN10000.2.2.1*). Long-term investments in marketable equity securities of this type are available-for-sale securities.

10000.2.2.1.1.1 **Acquisition of Long-Term Marketable Equity Securities**

*Long-Term Marketable Equity Securities - Available-For-
    Sale   xxxx
    Cash   xxxx
*To record acquisition of long-term marketable equity
securities*

*Long-Term Marketable Equity Securities - Available-For-Sale is debited for the cost of the securities which includes the purchase price plus broker fees and other costs of acquisition.

Important: Make sure all appropriate subheads apply to your entry (see page v for instructions)

10000.2	**Long-Term Investments**
10000.2.2	**Long-Term Equity Investments**
10000.2.2.1	**Holdings of Less than 20% of Voting Shares**
10000.2.2.1.1	**Investment in Marketable Equity Securities**

10000.2.2.1.1.2 **Application of Fair Value (Mark to Market) Principle**

At the end of the fiscal year, long-term marketable equity securities representing ownership of less than 20% of the outstanding voting shares of the company whose stock is owned are individually adjusted to fair value (i.e., marked to market). Both increases in fair value (unrealized holding gains) and decreases in fair value (unrealized holding losses) are recognized. *See GEN10000.1.2* for the application of the fair value (mark to market) principle to investments in short-term marketable equity securities and for a definition of fair value for equity investments.

10000.2.2.1.1.2.1 **Increase in Fair Value**

> *Long-Term Marketable Equity Securities - Available-For-Sale xxxx
> **Net Unrealized Holding Gains And Losses On Long-Term Marketable Equity Available-For-Sale Securities xxxx
> *To record an increase in fair value of long-term marketable equity securities*

*Long-Term Marketable Equity Securities - Available-For-Sale is debited to adjust the carrying value of individual securities to their fair value at the end of the fiscal year.

**Net Unrealized Holding Gains And Losses On Long-Term Marketable Equity Available-For-Sale Securities is credited for the increase in the fair value of the individual securities since the fair value was last updated (e.g., since the date of acquisition, the end of the prior fiscal year, or the date of transfer between investment categories). The unrealized holding gain is combined with other unrealized holding gains and losses on available-for-sale securities and is included as a separate component of Stockholders' Equity on the balance sheet.

10000.2.2.1.1.2.2 **Decrease in Fair Value**

> *Net Unrealized Holding Gains And Losses On Long-Term Marketable Equity Available-For-Sale Securities xxxx
> **Long-Term Marketable Equity Securities - Available-For-Sale xxxx
> *To record decrease in fair value of long-term marketable equity securities*

Important: Make sure all appropriate subheads apply to your entry (see page v for instructions)

10000.2	**Long-Term Investments**
10000.2.2	**Long-Term Equity Investments**
10000.2.2.1	**Holdings of Less than 20% of Voting Shares**
10000.2.2.1.1	**Investment in Marketable Equity Securities**
10000.2.2.1.1.2	**Application of Fair Value (Mark to Market) Principle**
10000.2.2.1.1.2.2	**Decrease in Fair Value**

---

*Net Unrealized Holding Gains And Losses On Long-Term Marketable Equity Available-For-Sale Securities is debited for the decrease in the fair value of individual securities since the fair value was last updated (e.g., since the date of acquisition, the end of the prior fiscal year, or the date of transfer between investment categories). The unrealized holding loss is combined with other unrealized holding gains and losses on available-for-sale securities and is included as a separate component of Stockholders' Equity on the balance sheet.

**Long-Term Marketable Equity Securities - Available-For-Sale is credited to adjust the carrying value of individual securities to their fair value at the end of the fiscal year.

10000.2.2.1.1.3   **Transfers Between Investment Categories**

10000.2.2.1.1.3.1   **Transfer from Long-Term Available-for-Sale Category to Short-Term Trading Category**

Trading securities are securities intended to be sold in the near term.

10000.2.2.1.1.3.1.1   **Net Unrealized Holding Gain Accumulated Since Acquisition**

*Net Unrealized Holding Gains And Losses On Short-Term Marketable Equity Available-For-Sale Securities	xxxx	
**Short-Term Marketable Equity Securities - Trading	xxxx	
***Long-Term Marketable Equity Securities - Available-For-Sale		xxxx
****Unrealized Holding Gain On Long-Term Marketable Equity Available-For-Sale Securities		xxxx

To record transfer from available-for-sale category to trading category

*Net Unrealized Holding Gains And Losses On Short-Term Marketable Equity Available-For-Sale Securities is debited to reverse (and realize) the net unrealized holding gain that has been recorded to reflect the increase in the fair value of the transferred securities since the date of acquisition. This account has been previously reported as a separate component of Stockholders' Equity on the balance sheet. *See GEN10000.2.2.1.1.2* for accounting for the fair value of long-term marketable equity securities.

GEN10000.2.2.1.1.3.1.1   GEN10000.2.2.1.1.3.1.2

Important: Make sure all appropriate subheads apply to your entry (see page v for instructions)

10000.2	**Long-Term Investments**
10000.2.2	**Long-Term Equity Investments**
10000.2.2.1	**Holdings of Less than 20% of Voting Shares**
10000.2.2.1.1	**Investment in Marketable Equity Securities**
10000.2.2.1.1.3	**Transfers Between Investment Categories**
10000.2.2.1.1.3.1	**Transfer from Long-Term Available-for-Sale Category to Short-Term Trading Category**
10000.2.2.1.1.3.1.1	**Net Unrealized Holding Gain Accumulated Since Acquisition**

**Short-Term Marketable Equity Securities - Trading is debited for the fair value of the securities at the date of transfer.

***Long-Term Marketable Equity Securities - Available-For-Sale is credited for the carrying value of the securities transferred; i.e., their fair value at the end of the prior fiscal year.

****Unrealized Holding Gain On Long-Term Marketable Equity Available-For-Sale Securities is credited to balance the entry and to record the unrealized holding gain that has accumulated on the transferred securities since the date of acquisition. This account is included on the income statement in the period in which the securities are transferred.

10000.2.2.1.1.3.1.2   **Net Unrealized Holding Loss Accumulated Since Acquisition**

*Unrealized Holding Loss On Long-Term Marketable Equity Available-For-Sale Securities	xxxx
**Short-Term Marketable Equity Securities - Trading	xxxx
***Long-Term Marketable Equity Securities - Available-For-Sale	xxxx
****Net Unrealized Holding Gains And Losses On Short-Term Marketable Equity Available-For-Sale Securities	xxxx

To record transfer from available-for-sale category to trading category

*Unrealized Holding Loss On Long-Term Marketable Equity Available-For-Sale Securities is debited to balance the entry and to record the unrealized holding loss that has accumulated on the transferred securities since the date of acquisition. This account is included on the income statement in the period in which the securities are transferred.

**Short-Term Marketable Equity Securities - Trading is debited for the fair value of the securities at the date of transfer.

***Long-Term Marketable Equity Securities - Available-For-Sale is credited for the carrying value of the securities transferred; i.e., their fair value at the end of the prior fiscal year.

INVESTMENTS

Important: Make sure all appropriate subheads apply to your entry (see page v for instructions)

10000.2	**Long-Term Investments**
10000.2.2	**Long-Term Equity Investments**
10000.2.2.1	**Holdings of Less than 20% of Voting Shares**
10000.2.2.1.1	**Investment in Marketable Equity Securities**
10000.2.2.1.1.3	**Transfers Between Investment Categories**
10000.2.2.1.1.3.1	**Transfer from Long-Term Available-for-Sale Category to Short-Term Trading Category**
10000.2.2.1.1.3.1.2	**Net Unrealized Holding Loss Accumulated Since Acquisition**

****Net Unrealized Holding Gains And Losses is credited to reverse (and realize) the net unrealized holding loss that has been recorded to reflect the decrease in the fair value of the transferred securities since the date of acquisition. This account has been reported as a separate component of Stockholders' Equity on the balance sheet. *See GEN10000.2.2.1.1.2* for accounting for the fair value of long-term marketable equity securities.

10000.2.2.1.1.3.2   **Transfer from Long-Term Available-for-Sale Category to Short-Term Available-for-Sale Category**

*Short-Term Marketable Equity Securities - Available-For-Sale	xxxx	
*Long-Term Marketable Equity Securities - Available-For-Sale		xxxx
To record transfer of investment in marketable equity securities from long-term available-for-sale category to short-term available-for-sale category		

*The balance in Long-Term Marketable Equity Securities - Available-For-Sale for the securities transferred (generally the fair value at the end of the prior fiscal year) is transferred to Short-Term Marketable Equity Securities - Available-For-Sale. *See GEN10000.1.2* for accounting for short-term available-for-sale securities.

10000.2.2.1.1.4   **Sale of Long-Term Marketable Equity Securities**

10000.2.2.1.1.4.1   **Net Holding Gain Accumulated Since Acquisition**

*Cash	xxxx	
**Net Unrealized Holding Gains And Losses On Long-Term Marketable Equity Available-For-Sale Securities	xxxx	
***Long-Term Marketable Equity Securities - Available-For-Sale		xxxx
****Realized Gain On Sale Of Long-Term Marketable Equity Securities		xxxx
To record sale of long-term marketable equity securities classified as available-for-sale with accumulated net holding gain		

GEN10000.2.2.1.1.4.1

GEN10000.2.2.1.1.4.2

Important: Make sure all appropriate subheads apply to your entry (see page v for instructions)

10000.2	**Long-Term Investments**
10000.2.2	**Long-Term Equity Investments**
10000.2.2.1	**Holdings of Less than 20% of Voting Shares**
10000.2.2.1.1	**Investment in Marketable Equity Securities**
10000.2.2.1.1.4	**Sale of Long-Term Marketable Equity Securities**
10000.2.2.1.1.4.1	**Net Holding Gain Accumulated Since Acquisition**

---

*Cash is debited for the sales price of the securities sold.

**Net Unrealized Holding Gains And Losses On Long-Term Marketable Equity Available-For-Sale Securities is debited to reverse (and realize) the net unrealized holding gain that has been recorded to reflect the increase in the fair value of the securities since the date of acquisition. This account has previously been reported as a separate component of Stockholders' Equity in the balance sheet. *See GEN10000.2.2.1* for accounting for the fair value of long-term marketable equity securities classified as available-for-sale.

***Long-Term Marketable Equity Securities - Available-For-Sale is credited for the carrying value of the securities sold; i.e., the fair value of the securities when the fair value was last updated (e.g., the date of acquisition, the end of the prior fiscal year, or the date of transfer between investment categories).

****Realized Gain On Sale Of Long-Term Marketable Equity Securities is credited to balance the entry. If a debit is necessary to balance the entry, Realized Loss On Sale Of Long-Term Marketable Equity Securities is debited instead. This account is included on the income statement.

10000.2.2.1.1.4.2   **Net Holding Loss Accumulated Since Acquisition**

*Cash	xxxx
**Net Unrealized Holding Gains And Losses On Long-Term Marketable Equity Available-For-Sale Securities	xxxx
***Long-Term Marketable Equity Securities - Available-For-Sale	xxxx
****Realized Gain On Sale Of Long-Term Marketable Equity Securities	xxxx

To record sale of long-term marketable equity securities classified as available-for-sale with accumulated net holding loss

*Cash is debited for the sales price of the securities sold.

**Net Unrealized Holding Gains And Losses On Long-Term Marketable Equity Available-For-Sale Securities is credited to reverse (and realize) the net unrealized holding loss that has been recorded to reflect the decrease in the fair value of the securities since the date of acquisition. This account has previously been reported as a

Important: Make sure all appropriate subheads apply to your entry (see page v for instructions)

10000.2	**Long-Term Investments**
10000.2.2	**Long-Term Equity Investments**
10000.2.2.1	**Holdings of Less than 20% of Voting Shares**
10000.2.2.1.1	**Investment in Marketable Equity Securities**
10000.2.2.1.1.4	**Sale of Long-Term Marketable Equity Securities**
10000.2.2.1.1.4.2	**Net Holding Loss Accumulated Since Acquisition**

---

separate component of Stockholders' Equity on the balance sheet. *See GEN10000.2.2.1* for accounting for the fair value of long-term marketable equity securities classified as available-for-sale.

***Long-Term Marketable Equity Securities - Available-For-Sale is credited for the carrying value of the securities sold; i.e., the fair value of the securities when the fair value was last updated (e.g., the date of acquisition, the end of the prior fiscal year, or the date of transfer between investment categories).

****Realized Gain On Sale Of Long-Term Marketable Equity Securities is credited to balance the entry. If a debit is necessary to balance the entry, Realized Loss On Sale Of Long-Term Marketable Equity Securities is debited instead.

10000.2.2.1.1.5   **Receipt of Cash Dividend**

Cash	xxxx	
Dividend Income		xxxx
To record receipt of cash dividend		

10000.2.2.1.1.6   **Receipt of Stock Dividend or Stock Split**

A stock dividend is a dividend received in the form of additional shares of stock with the same par (stated) value. A stock split occurs when the number of shares of stock outstanding is increased and the par (stated) value of the shares is decreased, so that the total par (stated) value of the stock outstanding remains unchanged. In either case, from an investor's point of view all that has happened is that more shares are owned for the same total investment cost. Therefore, no journal entry is necessary.

10000.2.2.1.2   **Long-Term Investment in Nonmarketable Equity Securities**

Long-term investments in nonmarketable equity securities are accounted for using the cost method. The lower-of-cost-or-market method is not applied to long-term nonmarketable equity securities.

INVESTMENTS

Important: Make sure all appropriate subheads apply to your entry (see page v for instructions)

10000.2	**Long-Term Investments**
10000.2.2	**Long-Term Equity Investments**
10000.2.2.1	**Holdings of Less than 20% of Voting Shares**
10000.2.2.1.2	**Long-Term Investment in Nonmarketable Equity Securities**

10000.2.2.1.2.1 **Acquisition of Long-Term Nonmarketable Equity Securities**

*Long-Term Nonmarketable Equity Securities	xxxx	
Cash		xxxx

To record acquisition of long-term nonmarketable equity securities

*Long-Term Nonmarketable Equity Securities is debited for the cost of the securities acquired, which includes the purchase price plus broker fees and other costs of acquisition.

10000.2.2.1.2.2 **Reclassification of Nonmarketable Equity Securities from Long-Term to Short-Term or from Short-Term to Long-Term**

*Short-Term Nonmarketable Equity Securities	xxxx	
*Long-Term Nonmarketable Equity Securities		xxxx

To record reclassification of long-term nonmarketable equity securities to short-term

*This entry shows the reclassification of long-term nonmarketable equity securities to short-term. If the reclassification were from short-term to long-term, the entry would be reversed. In any case, the accounts are debited or credited for the cost of the securities reclassified.

10000.2.2.1.2.3 **Sale of Long-Term Nonmarketable Equity Securities**

Cash	xxxx	
*Long-Term Nonmarketable Equity Securities		xxxx
**Realized Gain On Sale Of Long-Term Nonmarketable Equity Securities		xxxx

To record gain on sale of long-term nonmarketable equity securities

*Long-Term Nonmarketable Equity Securities is credited for the cost of the securities sold. Cost is defined as the debit balance in this account attributable to the securities sold.

INVESTMENTS

Important: Make sure all appropriate subheads apply to your entry (see page v for instructions)

10000.2   **Long-Term Investments**
10000.2.2   **Long-Term Equity Investments**
10000.2.2.1   **Holdings of Less than 20% of Voting Shares**
10000.2.2.1.2   **Long-Term Investment in Nonmarketable Equity Securities**
10000.2.2.1.2.3   **Sale of Long-Term Nonmarketable Equity Securities**

**Realized Gain On Sale Of Long-Term Nonmarketable Equity Securities is credited for the excess of the cash received over the cost of the securities sold. If the cost of securities sold exceeds the amount of cash received, Realized Loss On Sale Of Long-Term Nonmarketable Equity Securities is debited for the excess instead.

10000.2.2.1.2.4   **Receipt of Cash Dividend**

Cash	xxxx	
Dividend Income		xxxx
To record receipt of cash dividend		

10000.2.2.1.2.5   **Receipt of Stock Dividend or Stock Split**

A stock dividend is a dividend received in the form of additional shares of stock with the same par (stated) value. A stock split occurs when the number of shares of stock outstanding is increased and the par (stated) value of the shares is decreased, so that the total par or stated value of the stock outstanding remains unchanged. In either case, from an investor's point of view all that has happened is that more shares are owned for the same total investment cost. Therefore, no journal entry is necessary.

10000.2.2.2   **Holdings of More than 20% of Voting Shares**

If more than 20% of the outstanding voting shares of a company are owned, the equity method of accounting is used to recognize significant influence over the operations of the investee. If 50% or more of the voting shares are owned consolidated statements are usually prepared, but the equity method is still used to account for the investment on the parent company's books. If significant influence does not exist with more than 20% ownership, the equity method cannot be used; the procedures shown in *GEN10000.2.2.1* apply.

10000.2.2.2.1   **Acquisition of Stock**

Investment In Stock	xxxx	
Cash		xxxx
To record acquisition of stock		

Important: Make sure all appropriate subheads apply to your entry (see page v for instructions)

10000.2	**Long-Term Investments**
10000.2.2	**Long-Term Equity Investments**
10000.2.2.2	**Holdings of More than 20% of Voting Shares**

10000.2.2.2.2 **Recognition of Portion of Net Income or Net Loss of Investee**

*Investment In Stock	xxxx	
**Loss From Investment - Extraordinary	xxxx	
***Revenue From Investment - Ordinary		xxxx

To record portion of net income of investee

*Investment In Stock is debited (credited) for the proportionate share of the net income (loss) of the investee attributable to the shares of stock owned; e.g., if 22% of the outstanding voting shares are owned, 22% of the net income of the investee would be recognized.

**Loss From Investment - Extraordinary is debited for the investor's proportionate share of any extraordinary loss of the investee. If the investee has an extraordinary gain, Gain From Investment - Extraordinary is credited for the investor's proportionate share. Any extraordinary losses and gains must be recognized separately from the rest of the net income or net loss.

***Revenue From Investment - Ordinary is credited for whatever amount is necessary to balance the entry. If a debit is necessary to balance the entry, Loss From Investment - Ordinary is debited instead.

10000.2.2.2.3 **Receipt of Cash Dividend**

Cash	xxxx	
*Investment In Stock		xxxx

To record receipt of cash dividend from investment in stock

*The investment account is credited instead of a revenue account because the dividend represents a distribution of the revenue already recognized, as shown in *GEN10000.2.2.2.2.*

10000.2.2.2.4 **Sale of Investment in Stock**

*Cash	xxxx	
**Investment In Stock		xxxx
***Gain On Sale Of Investment		xxxx

To record sale of investment in stock

Important: Make sure all appropriate subheads apply to your entry (see page v for instructions)

10000.2	**Long-Term Investments**
10000.2.2	**Long-Term Equity Investments**
10000.2.2.2	**Holdings of More than 20% of Voting Shares**
10000.2.2.2.4	**Sale of Investment in Stock**

---

*Cash is debited for the amount of cash received.

**Investment In Stock is credited for the balance in that account pertaining to the shares of stock sold.

***Gain On Sale Of Investment is credited for whatever is necessary to balance the entry. If a debit is necessary to balance the entry, Loss On Sale Of Investment is debited instead of this credit.

10000.3   **Investment in Stock Rights**

Stock rights are certificates issued by a corporation that intends to offer for sale additional shares of a stock issue already outstanding. These stock rights are issued to present stockholders of the stock issue in proportion to the shares they currently own, and permit the shareholders to purchase a sufficient quantity of the new shares to be issued to maintain their proportionate ownership of the increased number of total outstanding shares. Once issued, stock rights may be traded separately from the stock itself until they are used to purchase the additional shares from the company (i.e., they are exercised), or until they expire due to passage of time.

10000.3.1   **Acquisition of Stock Rights**

10000.3.1.1   **Receipt of Stock Rights as a Current Stockholder**

*Investment In Stock Rights	xxxx	
Investment in Stock		xxxx
To record receipt of stock rights		

*Investment In Stock Rights is debited for a proportionate share of the cost of the original shares of stock owned. The cost of the original shares is apportioned between those shares of stock and the stock rights received, on the basis of the relative market value of the stock and the stock rights after the stock rights begin to be traded in the market.

For Example: Assume a company owned 10,000 shares at a cost of $110,000 and received 10,000 stock rights. If when the rights begin to be traded on the market they have a market value of $3 per right and the stock trades at $12 per share, the cost of the rights is determined as follows:

INVESTMENTS

Important: Make sure all appropriate subheads apply to your entry (see page v for instructions)

10000.3   **Investment in Stock Rights**
10000.3.1   **Acquisition of Stock Rights**
10000.3.1.1   **Receipt of Stock Rights as a Current Stockholder**

Market value of rights: $3 X 10,000 ∇ $ 30,000
Market value of stock: $12 X 10,000 ∇ 120,000
Total market value: $150,000

Cost of rights: $110,000 X 30 / 150 X $22,000

Therefore, the entry on the previous page would be made for $22,000.

10000.3.1.2   **Purchase of Stock Rights in the Market**

Investment In Stock Rights	xxxx	
Cash		xxxx
To record purchase of stock rights		

10000.3.2   **Sale of Stock Rights**

Cash	xxxx	
*Investment In Stock Rights		xxxx
**Gain On Sale Of Investments		xxxx
To record sale of stock rights		

*Investment In Stock Rights is credited for the cost (carrying value) of the stock rights sold.

**Gain On Sale Of Investments is credited for the excess of the cash received over the cost of the stock rights sold. If the cost of the stock rights sold exceeds the amount of cash received, Loss On Sale Of Investments would be debited for this excess instead.

10000.3.3   **Exercise of Stock Rights (Use of Stock Rights to Purchase Additional Stock)**

*Investment In Stock	xxxx	
Investment In Stock Rights		xxxx
Cash		xxxx
To record exercise of stock rights		

Important: Make sure all appropriate subheads apply to your entry (see page v for instructions)

10000.3	**Investment in Stock Rights**
10000.3.3	**Exercise of Stock Rights (Use of Stock Rights to Purchase Additional Stock)**

---

*Investment In Stock is debited for the sum of the cost of the stock rights exercised and the cash paid.

10000.3.4   Expiration of Stock Rights

*Loss On Expiration Of Stock Rights	xxxx	
*Investment In Stock Rights		xxxx
To record expiration of stock rights		

*Loss On Expiration Of Stock Rights is debited and Investment In Stock Rights is credited for the cost of the stock rights that have expired.

10000.4   Cash Surrender Value of Life Insurance

If a company takes out life insurance on its officers and lists itself as the beneficiary, any cash surrender value of the policy is an asset to the company.

In the early years of a whole-life (constant premium) policy, the cash surrender value will increase because the actual cost of the insurance is less than the premium paid. As the individual insured grows older, the actual cost of the insurance increases until it begins to exceed the premium paid. At this point, the cash surrender value begins to decline.

10000.4.1   Payment of Premium and Recognition of Increase in Cash Surrender Value

Insurance Expense (Prepaid Insurance)	xxxx	
*Cash Surrender Value Of Life Insurance	xxxx	
Cash		xxxx
To record payment of premium on life insurance		

*Cash Surrender Value Of Life Insurance is debited for the excess of the premium paid over the actual cost of the insurance. This figure will be supplied by the insurance company.

Important: Make sure all appropriate subheads apply to your entry (see page v for instructions)

10000.4   **Cash Surrender Value of Life Insurance**

10000.4.2   **Payment of Premium and Recognition of Decrease in Cash Surrender Value**

Insurance Expense (Prepaid Insurance)	xxxx	
*Cash Surrender Value Of Life Insurance		xxxx
Cash		xxxx

To record payment of premium on life insurance

*Cash Surrender Value Of Life Insurance is credited for the excess of the actual cost of the insurance over the premium paid. This figure will be supplied by the insurance company.

10000.4.3   **Collection of Death Benefits**

Cash	xxxx	
*Cash Surrender Value Of Life Insurance		xxxx
**Insurance Expense (Prepaid Insurance)		xxxx
***Gain From Life Insurance		xxxx

To record collection of life insurance benefit

*Cash Surrender Value Of Life Insurance is credited sufficiently to remove any balance in the account attributed to the policy collected.

**Insurance Expense (Prepaid Insurance) is credited to remove any balance in the account pertaining to life insurance coverage for periods after the death of the insured.

***Gain From Life Insurance is credited for whatever amount is necessary to balance the entry.

10000.5   **Special Long-Term Purpose Funds**

Special long-term purpose funds are cash and securities set aside for special long-term purposes such as:
- Plant expansion
- Special projects
- Retirement of long-term debt (sinking fund)
- Retirement of stock (probably preferred stock)
- General contingencies.

Important: Make sure all appropriate subheads apply to your entry (see page v for instructions)

10000.5   **Special Long-Term Purpose Funds**

10000.5.1   **Establishment of Fund**

*Bond Sinking ([Various]) Fund Cash	xxxx	
Cash		xxxx
To record establishment of fund		

*Bond Sinking Fund ([Various]) Cash is set up to establish the fund. This is a special cash account.

10000.5.2   **Investment of Fund Cash**

*Bond Sinking ([Various]) Fund Investments	xxxx	
Bond Sinking ([Various]) Fund Cash		xxxx
To record purchase of securities for the fund		

*Bond Sinking ([Various]) Fund Investments is set up to keep track of investments separately from the cash in the fund. This is a special investments account.

10000.5.3   **Revenue Earned on Fund Investments**

Bond Sinking ([Various]) Fund Cash	xxxx	
Bond Sinking ([Various]) Fund Revenue		xxxx
To record revenue earned on fund investments		

10000.5.4   **Amortization of Premium or Discount on Bonds Held as Fund Investments**

10000.5.4.1   **Amortization of Premium on Bonds Held as Fund Investments**

See GEN10000.2.1.2.2 for a general discussion of the amortization of premium on long-term investments in bonds.

Bond Sinking ([Various]) Fund Revenue	xxxx	
Bond Sinking ([Various]) Fund Investments		xxxx
To record amortization of premium on bonds held as fund		
investments		

Important: Make sure all appropriate subheads apply to your entry (see page v for instructions)

10000.5	**Special Long-Term Purpose Funds**
10000.5.4	**Amortization of Premium or Discount on Bonds Held as Fund Investments**

10000.5.4.2 **Amortization of Discount on Bonds Held as Fund Investments**

See GEN10000.2.1.2.3 for a general discussion of the amortization of discount on long-term investments in bonds.

Bond Sinking ([Various]) Fund Investments	xxxx	
Bond Sinking ([Various]) Fund Revenue		xxxx
To record amortization of discount on bonds held as fund investments		

10000.5.5 **Accrual of Interest on Fund Investments**

Interest Receivable on Bond Sinking ([Various]) Fund Investments	xxxx	
Bond Sinking ([Various]) Fund Revenue		xxxx
To record accrual of interest on fund investments		

10000.5.6 **Sale of Fund Investments**

Bond Sinking ([Various]) Fund Cash	xxxx	
*Bond Sinking ([Various]) Fund Investments		xxxx
**Gain On Sale Of Bond Sinking ([Various]) Fund Investments		xxxx
To record sale of fund investments		

*Bond Sinking ([Various]) Fund Investments is credited for the carrying value of the investments sold.

**Gain On Sale Of Bond Sinking ([Various]) Fund Investments is credited for the excess of the cash received over the carrying value of the investments sold. If the carrying value of the investments sold exceeds the amount of cash received, Loss On Sale Of Bond Sinking ([Various]) Fund Investments is debited for this excess instead. If this entry is to record the sale of bonds in which the fund has invested, any unamortized premium or discount on the bonds sold must be amortized to the date of sale as shown in *GEN10000.5.4* before this entry is made.

Important: Make sure all appropriate subheads apply to your entry (see page v for instructions)

10000.5   **Special Long-Term Purpose Funds**

10000.5.7   **Use of Fund for Its Intended Purpose**

Bonds Payable (Various Accounts Consistent With The Use Of The Fund)	xxxx	
Bond Sinking ([Various]) Fund Cash		xxxx

To record use of fund

10000.5.8   **Derivative Instruments**

Derivative financial instruments, or simply derivatives, are designed to manage the risks due to changes in market prices. Examples of derivatives include financial forwards or financial futures, options, and interest rate swaps. These financial instruments derive their values from values of other assets such as stocks, bonds, or commodities. Or, their values may be related to a market-determined index such as Standard and Poor's 500 stock composite index. The accounting provisions for derivatives depend on the intention for which the derivatives were designed. Accounting provisions for speculation, hedging fair value, and cash flow hedge are covered here.

10000.5.8.1   **Derivatives for Speculative Purposes**

Examples of derivatives for speculative purposes are call options and put options. These give the holder the right, but not the obligation, to buy shares at a pre-determined price, often called the strike price or the exercise price. In a call option, the buyer speculates that the price of the underlying stock increase in the future. In a put option, the buyer speculates that the price will decrease in the future. This call option (derivative) derives its value from the changes in the value of the underlying stock or other commodities. Thus, the option value is affected by two factors:
- Changes in the intrinsic value of the underlying stock
- The time value of the option.

10000.5.8.1.1   **Purchase of Call Option or Put Option**

Call Option (Put Option)	xxxx	
Cash		xxxx

To record purchase of call option (put option)

Important: Make sure all appropriate subheads apply to your entry (see page v for instructions)

10000.5   **Special Long-Term Purpose Funds**
10000.5.8   **Derivative Instruments**
10000.5.8.1   **Derivatives for Speculative Purposes**

10000.5.8.1.2   ### Increase or Decrease in the Intrinsic Value of an Option

If the fair market value of the underlying stock increases in a call option or decreases in a put option, there is an unrealized gain (an increase in the intrinsic value of the option) that is recognized as follows:

Call Option (Put Option)	xxxx	
*Unrealized Holding Gain or Loss		xxxx

To record increase (decrease) in the intrinsic value of call (put) option

*This account will be debited in the case of an call option if there is a decrease in the market value of the underlying stock. In the case of a put option, if there is an increase in the market value of the underlying stock, this account will also be debited. This unrealized holding gain or loss is recognized in the income statement.

10000.5.8.1.3   ### Increase or Decrease in the Time Value of an Option

The time value of an option reflects the possibility that the expectation that the price of the underlying stock will increase above the strike price (in a call option), or decrease below the strike price (in a put option) during the option term. A market appraisal determines the change in the time value of an option and an unrealized holding gain or loss is recognized accordingly as follows:

*Unrealized Holding Gain or Loss	xxxx	
Call Option (Put Option)		xxxx

To record decrease in time value of option

*This account will be debited, if there is an decrease in the time value of the option, or credited if there is an increase.

10000.5.8.2   ### Interest Rate Swaps (Fair Value Hedges)

A derivative designed to offset the exposure to changes in the fair value of an asset or a liability is called a fair value hedge. An example of a fair value hedge is an interest rate swap. Assume company A issues bonds at 6% to third parties. Companies A and B engage in an interest rate swap where B will pay interest at 6% to A on the borrowed money and A, in return, will pay interest to B on the borrowed money at a variable rate.

Important: Make sure all appropriate subheads apply to your entry (see page v for instructions)

10000.5   **Special Long-Term Purpose Funds**
10000.5.8   **Derivative Instruments**
10000.5.8.2   **Interest Rate Swaps (Fair Value Hedges)**

10000.5.8.2.1   **Settlement Payments on an Interest Rate Swap**

If the variable rate in an interest rate swap declines, Company A (see example in *GEN10000.5.8.2*) that issued the debt will receive an amount from Company which is the difference between the fixed rate and the variable rate times the amount of the debt. The receipt recorded by Company A as follows:

Cash	xxxx	
Interest Expense		xxxx

To record receipt of settlement amount in interest rate swap

Company B will record this payment to Company A as additional interest expense.

If the variable rate in an interest rate swap increases, Company A will pay an amount to Company B which is the difference between the fixed rate and the variable rate times the amount of the debt. The payment is recorded as follows:

Interest Expense	xxxx	
Cash		xxxx

To record payment of settlement amount in interest rate swap

Company B will record the amount received from Company A as a reduction in interest expense.

10000.5.8.2.2   **Changes in the Value of a Swap Contract**

If the variable rate in the interest rate swap contract declines, the value of the interest rate swap contract from the point of view of Company A (see example in *GEN10000.5.8.2*) increases. The increase is recorded as follows:

Swap Contract	xxxx	
*Unrealized Holding Gain or Loss		xxxx

To record increase value of interest rate swap contract

*This account is debited to recognize a loss if the variable rate increases. This unrealized gain or loss is recognized in the income statement.

Important: Make sure all appropriate subheads apply to your entry (see page v for instructions)

10000.5	**Special Long-Term Purpose Funds**
10000.5.8	**Derivative Instruments**
10000.5.8.2	**Interest Rate Swaps (Fair Value Hedges)**

10000.5.8.2.3   **Changes in the Fair Market Value of the Liability (Debt) Due to Change in the Variable Interest Rate in the Interest Rate Swap**

If the variable rate in the interest rate swap declines, the fair value of the liability (debt) increases and a loss must be recognized by Company A (see example in *GEN10000.5.8.2*) as follows:

*Unrealized Holding Gain or Loss	xxxx	
Bonds Payable [Various Debt]		xxxx

To record increase in the fair market value of debt due to change in the variable rate of interest rate swap

*This account is credited and an unrealized holding gain is recognized if the variable rate increases. On the income statement, this unrealized loss will offset the unrealized gain recognized from the increase in the value of the swap contract (*see* GEN10000.5.8.2.2*).

10000.5.8.3   **Accounting for a Cash Flow Hedge**

A derivative designed to offset the exposure to the variability in future cash flows is called a cash flow hedge. An example of cash flow hedge is a futures contract.

Assume, for example, a company plans to buy a commodity in the future. To hedge against the risk of rising prices for this commodity, which would require more cash to purchase it, the company enters into a futures contract. A futures contract gives the holder the right and the obligation to purchase an asset at a pre-established price for the duration of the term of the contract. The underlying value of this derivative is the price of the commodity.

10000.5.8.3.1   **Changes in the Value of a Futures Contract**

There is no entry to record when the futures contract is signed. But, as the price of the underlying asset changes, an unrealized gain or loss is recognized as follows:

Futures Contract	xxxx	
*Unrealized Holding Gain or Loss		xxxx

To record increase in value of futures contract

INVESTMENTS

Important: Make sure all appropriate subheads apply to your entry (see page v for instructions)

10000.5	**Special Long-Term Purpose Funds**
10000.5.8	**Derivative Instruments**
19999.5.8.3	**Accounting for a Cash Flow Hedge**
10000.5.8.3.1	**Changes in the Value of a Futures Contract**

*This account will be debited and a loss is recognized, if the price of the underlying asset declines. Any unrealized holding gain or loss arising from a futures contract is recorded in equity, as part of other comprehensive income.

10000.5.8.3.2   **Recording the Purchase of the Underlying Asset**

Inventory	xxxx	
Cash		xxxx
To record purchase of the asset		

10000.5.8.3.3   **Recording Settlement of a Futures Contract**

After the commodity is purchased at the current price, the futures contract is settled for the difference between the pre-established price and the current actual price as follows:

*Cash	xxxx	
Futures Contract		xxxx
To record final settlement of futures contract		

*Company A would have paid cash, if the actual price for the commodity had declined below its pre-established price.

10000.5.8.3.4   **Closing the Unrealized Holding Gain or Loss Account**

After the inventory is sold, any remaining balance in the Unrealized Holding Gain Or Loss account is closed to Cost of Goods Sold as follows:

Unrealized Holding Gain or Loss	xxxx	
*Cost of Goods Sold		xxxx
To record final settlement of futures contract		

*This account would be debited if there was an unrealized holding loss. The effect of the futures contract is recognized in the income statement as a result of this entry.

TABLE OF CONTENTS

| 11000.1 | **General Revenue Recognition Guidelines** |

According to the Financial Accounting Standards Board (FASB), revenues are "inflows . . . of assets . . . or settlements of . . . liabilities (or a combination of both) from delivering or producing goods, rendering services, or other activities that constitute the entity's ongoing major or central operations." (FASB Concepts Statement No. 6, par. 78) Revenue should be recognized (recorded) when it is realized or realizable and earned. In general, revenues are realized or realizable when goods or services are exchanged for cash or receivables. Revenues are earned when the earnings process is complete or virtually complete (i.e., the activities that entitle the seller to cash or receivables have been substantially accomplished).

| 11000.1.1 | **Revenue Earned upon Sale of Inventory** |

| 11000.1.1.1 | **Sale of Inventory for Cash and/or Receivables** |

Revenue is generally recorded at the time goods are shipped.

*Cash	xxxx	
**Accounts (Notes) Receivable	xxxx	
Sales		xxxx
To record sales		

*This account will not be involved if cash is not received.

**This account will not be involved if only cash is received.

| 11000.1.1.2 | **Sale of Inventory for Other than Cash and/or Receivables** |

Revenue is generally recorded at the time goods are shipped.

[Various Assets]	xxxx	
Sales		xxxx
To record sales		

Important: Make sure all appropriate subheads apply to your entry (see page v for instructions)

11000.1   **General Revenue Recognition Guidelines**
11000.1.1   **Revenue Earned upon Sale of Inventory**

11000.1.1.3   **Sales Accompanied by a Buyback Agreement**

A buyback agreement is a product financing arrangement. If a sale of inventory is accompanied by a buyback agreement that specifies a set buyback price sufficient to cover the cost of inventory plus related holding costs of the other party, no sale is recorded. A liability recognizing the obligation to repurchase the goods must be recorded and the inventory "sold" must be transferred to another account.

Cash (Accounts Receivable, Notes Receivable)	xxxx	
Obligations Under Inventory Buyback Agreements		xxxx
To record obligation to repurchase goods		
Inventory Financed Under Buyback Agreement	xxxx	
Inventory		xxxx
To record inventory financed under buyback agreement		

11000.1.1.4   **Sales Accompanied by Right of Return**

If customers have the right to return their purchases, the FASB prohibits the recognition of revenue at the time of sale unless all of the following conditions are met (FASB Statement No. 48, par. 6):

a. The seller's price is substantially fixed or determinable at the date of sale;

b. The buyer has paid the seller or is obligated to pay and the obligation is not contingent upon the buyer's resale of the goods;

c. The buyer's obligation to pay is not changed if the goods are stolen or destroyed;

d. The buyer acquiring the goods for resale has economic substance apart from that provided by the seller;

e. The seller does not have significant obligations for future performance to directly assist the buyer in reselling the goods; and

f. The amount of future returns can be reasonably estimated.

Cash (Accounts Receivable, Notes Receivable)	xxxx	
*Sales		xxxx
To record sales		

Important: Make sure all appropriate subheads apply to your entry (see page v for instructions)

11000.1	**General Revenue Recognition Guidelines**
11000.1.1	**Revenue Earned upon Sale of Inventory**
11000.1.1.4	**Sales Accompanied by Right of Return**

---

*The sale is recorded when the right to return expires or when the above six conditions are met, whichever occurs first. Estimated sales returns should be accounted for using the allowance method discussed at GEN3000.1.4.2.

11000.1.2   **Revenue Earned for Services Rendered**

Revenue is generally recorded once services have been rendered and billing rights exist.

Cash (Accounts Receivable, Notes Receivable)	xxxx	
[Various Assets]	xxxx	
[Various Liabilities]		xxxx
*Service Revenue Earned		xxxx
To record service revenue		

*Other common account titles include:
- Commissions Earned
- Fees Earned.

11000.1.3   **Gains (Losses) on Disposition of Assets Other than Inventory**

Gains (losses) resulting from the sale or exchange of assets other than inventory (e.g., investments and property, plant, and equipment) are not revenues (expenses) because they do not arise from the ongoing, major and central operations of the firm but from peripheral or incidental activities. *See GEN5000.3* for a discussion of the disposition of such assets.

11000.1.4   **Revenue Earned as a Result of Passage of Time**

Some revenues such as Rental Income and Interest Income are earned over time. These revenues should be accrued at the end of each accounting period to the extent they have not previously been recorded. *See GEN1000.2.3.2* for a discussion of end-of-period adjusting entries.

11000.2   ### Installment Sales Method

Installment sales are sales for which payment is required in periodic installments over a specified period of time. Although the installment sales method can be used to account for installment sales, the use of this method to account for most installment sales is rarely justified. The use of the installment sales method is justified only when there is sufficient uncertainty to require postponement of revenue recognition. Uncertainty may exist if there is no reasonable basis for estimating the degree of collectibility of the related installment receivables. Under the installment sales method, revenue is recognized as cash is collected rather than at the time the installment sales are made. If the installment sales method is not used, an installment sale is accounted for like any other sale.

11000.2.1   ### Installment Sales

*Installment Accounts Receivable - Year X	xxxx
**Installment Sales	xxxx
To record installment sales	

*Rather than debiting Accounts Receivable as is usual with a sale, when the installment sales method is used, a separate Installment Accounts Receivable account is used for *each year in which installment sales are made*. Thus, Installment Accounts Receivable - Year X is used only to record receivables from installment sales made in year X. If the installment sales contract specifies that interest is to be charged to the buyer on the unpaid balance of the receivable, this debit to Installment Account Receivable should *exclude* any such interest. Thus, if the periodic payment stipulated in the contract includes interest, this debit will be less than the total of all the payments by the amount of interest included.

**Installment Sales is credited instead of Sales. Sales would be credited only for a sale that was not an installment sale, or for an installment sale for which the installment sales method was not used. Any interest chargeable to the buyer on the unpaid balance of the related receivable should be *excluded* from this entry. Thus, if the periodic payment stipulated in the contract includes interest, this credit will be less than the total of all the payments by the amount of interest included.

REVENUE RECOGNITION

Important: Make sure all appropriate subheads apply to your entry (see page v for instructions)

11000.2 **Installment Sales Method**

11000.2.2 **Collection of Installment Accounts Receivable**

11000.2.2.1 **Installment Payments Do Not Include Interest**

Cash	XXXX	
Installment Accounts Receivable - Year W		XXXX
Installment Accounts Receivable - Year X		XXXX

To record collection of installment receivables

11000.2.2.2 **Installment Payments Include Interest**

Cash	XXXX	
*Interest Revenue		XXXX
**Installment Accounts Receivable - Year W		XXXX
**Installment Accounts Receivable - Year X		XXXX

To record collection of installment receivables

*Interest Revenue is credited for the amount computed by multiplying the balance of unpaid installment receivables by the interest rate specified in the installment sales contract.

**Installment Accounts Receivable for each year is credited for the difference between the total payments collected from installment receivables of that year and the amount credited to Interest Revenue relating to unpaid installment receivables of that year.

11000.2.3 **Cost of Installment Sales**

*Cost Of Installment Sales	XXXX	
**Inventory (Finished Goods)		XXXX

To record cost of installment sales

*Cost Of Installment Sales is debited instead of Cost Of Sales (Cost Of Goods Sold) because the cost of installment sales must be kept separate from the cost of other sales.

**Purchases is credited if the periodic inventory system is used.

Important: Make sure all appropriate subheads apply to your entry (see page v for instructions)

11000.2   **Installment Sales Method**

11000.2.4   ## Deferral of Gross Profit on Installment Sales

During each period in which installment sales are made for which the installment sales method is used, the following entry must be made to close Installment Sales and Cost Of Installment Sales and to defer the gross profit on those installment sales.

Installment Sales	xxxx	
Cost Of Installment Sales		xxxx
*Deferred Gross Profit On Installment Sales - Year X		xxxx
To close installment sales and cost of installment sales		

*The amount of gross profit to be deferred in Year X is Year X's total installment sales revenue less the cost of Year X's installment sales. A separate Deferred Gross Profit On Installment Sales account must be used for installment sales of each year. Thus, to the extent that installment receivables are not fully collected in the same year the installment sales are made, there will be more than one Deferred Gross Profit On Installment Sales account on the books at any one time.

11000.2.5   ## Recognition of Gross Profit on Installment Sales Realized

Gross profit on installment sales is realized as collections of installment receivables are made. The amount realized is a percentage of the collections made on Install-ment Accounts Receivable during the period. This percentage is the gross profit percentage. For example, if installment sales of $100,000 are made in Year X and the related Cost Of Installment Sales is $60,000, Gross Profit On Installment Sales made in Year X is $40,000 ($100,000 - $60,000), and the gross profit percentage is 40% ($40,000 / $100,000). If $80,000 of installment receivables are collected in Year X from installment sales made that year, $32,000 of gross profit is realized (40% X $80,000). Different gross profit percentages may apply to installment sales made in different years.

*Deferred Gross Profit - Year W	xxxx	
*Deferred Gross Profit - Year X	xxxx	
Realized Gross Profit On Installment Sales		xxxx
To recognize gross profit realized on installment sales		

*Collections during the current year may be from installment sales made in the current year or in previous years. Because different gross profit percentages may

Important: Make sure all appropriate subheads apply to your entry (see page v for instructions)

| 11000.2 | **Installment Sales Method** |
| 11000.2.5 | **Recognition of Gross Profit on Installment Sales Realized** |

---

apply to sales made in different years, separate Deferred Gross Profit accounts must be maintained for each year (*see GEN11000.2.4*). Therefore, separate calculations of the type discussed in the preceding paragraph must be made to determine the amount of gross profit realized on collections of installment receivables from sales made in different years.

11000.2.6

Closing Realized Gross Profit on Installment Sales at the End of the Accounting Period

Realized Gross Profit On Installment Sales	xxxx	
*Income Summary		xxxx
To close Realized Gross Profit On Installment Sales		

*Common alternative account titles include:
- Expense And Revenue Summary
- Profit Or Loss Summary.

11000.2.7

Defaults and Repossessions Related to Installment Sales

When merchandise sold on the installment basis and accounted for using the installment sales method is repossessed due to the purchaser's failure to make payments, the amount of deferred gross profit related to the repossessed merchandise must be removed from the books.

*Repossessed Merchandise	xxxx	
**Deferred Gross Profit On Installment Sales - Year X	xxxx	
***Loss (Gain) On Repossession	xxxx	
****Installment Accounts Receivable - Year X		xxxx
To record repossession of goods sold on consignment		

*Repossessed Merchandise should be debited for the fair market value of the goods repossessed. The normal inventory account should not be used here.

**Deferred Gross Profit On Installment Sales should be debited for the amount of the deferred gross profit in the account that is applicable to the repossessed merchandise. This amount is found by multiplying the gross profit rate originally earned on the sale by the remaining uncollected receivable balance pertaining to the repossessed merchandise.

Important: Make sure all appropriate subheads apply to your entry (see page v for instructions)

11000.2   **Installment Sales Method**
11000.2.7   **Defaults and Repossessions Related to Installment Sales**

***Loss On Repossession is debited (or Gain On Repossession is credited) to balance the entry.

****Installment Accounts Receivable - Year X is credited for the amount of the receivable remaining that pertains to the repossessed merchandise. This will be equal to the original selling price less all payments received to date.

11000.3   ### Cost Recovery Method

Under the cost recovery method, no profit is recognized until collections exceed the cost of goods sold.

The cost recovery method may be used to account for sales that require periodic payments by the buyer and for which the collectibility of the receivable cannot be reasonably estimated. The cost recovery method is a much more conservative method than the installment sales method. It is usually applied to installment sales only when there is an extreme risk of collectibility of the receivable. The cost recovery method may be applied to noninstallment sales that may require more than one payment and for which a provision for uncollectible accounts cannot be reasonably estimated.

11000.3.1   ### Receivable Is Noninterest Bearing

11000.3.1.1   ### Sales

Accounts Receivable (Installment Accounts Receivable)	xxxx	
Sales		xxxx
To record sales		

11000.3.1.2   ### Collection of Accounts Receivable

Cash	xxxx	
Accounts Receivable (Installment Accounts Receivable)		xxxx
To record collection of receivables		

Important: Make sure all appropriate subheads apply to your entry (see page v for instructions)

11000.3	**Cost Recovery Method**
11000.3.1	**Receivable Is Noninterest Bearing**

11000.3.1.3   **Cost of Sales**

Cost Of Sales (Cost Of Goods Sold)	xxxx	
*Inventory (Finished Goods)		xxxx
To record cost of sales		

*Purchases may be credited if the periodic inventory system is used.

11000.3.1.4   **Deferral of Gross Profit on Sales**

During each period in which sales are made for which the cost recovery method is used, the following entry must be made to close Sales and Cost Of Sales and to defer the gross profit on those sales.

*Sales	xxxx	
**Cost Of Sales (Cost Of Goods Sold)		xxxx
***Deferred Gross Profit		xxxx
To defer gross profit on sales		

*Sales is debited for the amount of sales for which the cost recovery method was used.

**Cost Of Sales (Cost Of Goods Sold) is credited for the cost of the sales for which the cost recovery method was used.

***Deferred Gross Profit is credited to balance the entry.

11000.3.1.5   **Recognition of Gross Profit Realized**

Gross profit is realized when the cumulative amount collected exceeds the cost of the sale.

*Deferred Gross Profit	xxxx	
*Realized Gross Profit		xxxx
To record realized gross profit		

*This entry is made for an amount equal to the excess of cash collected over the cost of goods sold. For example, if an item that cost $600 was sold for $1,000, there

Important: Make sure all appropriate subheads apply to your entry (see page v for instructions)

11000.3   **Cost Recovery Method**
11000.3.1   **Receivable Is Noninterest Bearing**
11000.3.1.5   **Recognition of Gross Profit Realized**

---

would be deferred gross profit of $400 ($1,000 - $600). This entry would not be made until $600 (the amount of cost of goods sold) in cash was collected. Subsequently, this entry would be made to realize gross profit (in addition to the entry to reduce the receivable presented in *GEN11000.3.2.2*) as the remaining $400 was collected.

11000.3.1.6   **Closing Realized Gross Profit at the End of the Accounting Period**

Realized Gross Profit	xxxx	
*Income Summary		xxxx
To close realized gross profit		

*Common alternative account titles include Expense And Revenue Summary and Profit Or Loss Summary.

11000.3.2   **Receivable Is Interest Bearing**

11000.3.2.1   **Sales**

Accounts Receivable (Installment Accounts Receivable)	xxxx	
Sales		xxxx
To record sales		

11000.3.2.2   **Collection of Accounts Receivable**

Cash	xxxx	
*Deferred Interest Revenue		xxxx
Accounts Receivable (Installment Accounts Receivable)		xxxx
To record collection of receivables		

*The amount of interest collected is deferred until the entire cost of goods sold has been recovered. Once the entire cost of goods sold has been recovered, this credit will be made to Interest Revenue instead of Deferred Interest Revenue, and the interest previously recorded as deferred will be realized (*see GEN11000.3.2.6*). The interest amount is found with the usual interest formula: Outstanding Principal

Important: Make sure all appropriate subheads apply to your entry (see page v for instructions)

11000.3   **Cost Recovery Method**
11000.3.2   **Receivable Is Interest Bearing**
11000.3.2.2   **Collection of Accounts Receivable**

Amount X Interest Rate X Time, where the interest rate and time period are stated on an annual basis.

11000.3.2.3   **Cost of Sales**

> Cost Of Sales (Cost Of Goods Sold)   xxxx
>   *Inventory (Finished Goods)   xxxx
> *To record cost of sales*

*Purchases may be credited if the periodic inventory system is used.

11000.3.2.4   **Deferral of Gross Profit on Sales**

During each period in which sales are made for which the cost recovery method is used, the following entry must be made to close Sales and Cost Of Sales and to defer the gross profit on those sales.

> *Sales   xxxx
>   **Cost Of Sales (Cost Of Goods Sold)   xxxx
>   ***Deferred Gross Profit   xxxx
> *To defer gross profit on sales*

*Sales is debited for the amount of sales for which the cost recovery method was used.

**Cost Of Sales (Cost Of Goods Sold) is credited for the cost of the sales for which the cost recovery method was used.

***Deferred Gross Profit is credited to balance the entry.

11000.3.2.5   **Recognition of Gross Profit Realized**

> *Deferred Gross Profit   xxxx
>   *Realized Gross Profit   xxxx
> *To record realized gross profit*

Important: Make sure all appropriate subheads apply to your entry (see page v for instructions)

11000.3	**Cost Recovery Method**
11000.3.2	**Receivable Is Interest Bearing**
11000.3.2.5	**Recognition of Gross Profit Realized**

*This entry is made for an amount equal to the excess of cash collected over the cost of goods sold. For example, if an item that cost $600 was sold for $1,000, there would be deferred gross profit of $400 ($1,000 - $600). This entry would not be made until $600 (the amount of cost of goods sold) in cash was collected. Subsequently, this entry would be made to realize gross profit (in addition to the entry to reduce the receivable presented in *GEN11000.3.2.2*) as the remaining $400 was collected.

11000.3.2.6

Recognition of Interest Revenue Realized

Until cash equal to the total cost of goods sold is received, any interest revenue collected is deferred as noted in *GEN11000.3.2.2*. When the total cash received equals the cost of goods sold, any interest revenue that has been deferred must be recognized with the following entry:

Deferred Interest Revenue	xxxx	
Interest Revenue		xxxx
To record interest revenue realized		

11000.3.2.7

Closing Realized Gross Profit and Interest Revenue at the End of the Accounting Period

Realized Gross Profit	xxxx	
Interest Revenue	xxxx	
*Income Summary		xxxx
To close realized gross profit		

*Common alternative account titles include:
- Expense And Revenue Summary
- Profit Or Loss Summary.

11000.4

Consignment Sales

A consignment is an arrangement whereby a company (the consignor) ships goods to another company (the consignee) that attempts to sell the goods on behalf of the consignor. The consignor retains title to the goods until they are sold by the consignee.

Important: Make sure all appropriate subheads apply to your entry (see page v for instructions)

11000.4   **Consignment Sales**

11000.4.1   **Accounting by the Consignor**

11000.4.1.1   **Shipment of Consigned Goods**

*Inventory On Consignment	xxxx	
Inventory (Finished Goods)		xxxx
**Cash (Freight-Out)		xxxx

To record shipment of consigned goods

*Inventory On Consignment is debited for the cost of the inventory shipped on consignment plus any freight costs incurred by the consignor to ship the goods to the consignee.

**Cash (or Freight-Out) is credited for any freight costs incurred by the consignor to ship the goods to the consignee.

11000.4.1.2   **Notification by Consignee of Consignment Sales and Expenses and Receipt of Amounts Due**

Cash	xxxx	
Commission Expense	xxxx	
*[Various Expenses]	xxxx	
Consignment Sales Revenue		xxxx

To record consignment sales and commissions

Cost Of Consignment Sales	xxxx	
Inventory On Consignment		xxxx

To record cost of consignment goods sold

*If reimbursable expenses are incurred by the consignee (e.g., for advertising or promotion), appropriate expense accounts are debited if the cash received from the consignee has been reduced accordingly.

GEN11000.4.2   GEN11000.4.2.4

Important: Make sure all appropriate subheads apply to your entry (see page v for instructions)

11000.4   **Consignment Sales**

11000.4.2   ## Accounting by the Consignee

11000.4.2.1   ## Receipt of Goods on Consignment from the Consignor

No entries are required on the books of the consignee upon the receipt of consigned goods.

11000.4.2.2   ## Reimbursable Expenses Incurred in Selling Consigned Goods

*Receivable From Consignor	xxxx	
Cash (Accounts Payable, [Various Expenses])		xxxx
To record reimbursable expenses		

*Alternatively, Payable To Consignor may be debited to reduce its balance.

11000.4.2.3   ## Sale of Goods Held on Consignment

Cash (Accounts Receivable)	xxxx	
Payable To Consignor		xxxx
To record sales		

11000.4.2.4   ## Notification to Consignor of Consignment Sales and Expenses and Remittance of Amounts Due

Payable To Consignor	xxxx	
*Receivable From Consignor		xxxx
Commission Revenue		xxxx
Cash		xxxx
To record consignment sales commissions and remittance to consignor		

*Receivable From Consignor is credited sufficiently to eliminate any debit balance in the account that may have been generated by entries of the kind discussed in *GEN11000.4.2.2.*

Important: Make sure all appropriate subheads apply to your entry (see page v for instructions)

11000.5   **Long-Term Construction Contracts**

11000.5.1   **Percentage-of-Completion Method**

The percentage-of-completion method of revenue recognition is used for long-term construction contracts meeting the following conditions:
- the construction contract specifies legally enforceable rights involving goods or services to be provided and received by the parties to the con-tract, the consideration, and the terms of settlement;
- parties to the contract can be expected to satisfy their obligations under the contract; and
- reasonable estimates can be made of the seller's progress toward completion, revenues, and costs.

Under the percentage-of-completion method, revenues and gross profit are recognized each period based on the percentage of the work that has been completed to date.

11000.5.1.1   **Construction Costs**

*Construction In Process	xxxx	
**[Various Accounts]		xxxx
To record construction costs		

*All construction costs are accumulated in Construction In Process, which is an inventory-type account. (Gross profit will also be accumulated in this account; see *GEN11000.5.1.3.*)

**Credits may be made to Cash, Accounts Payable, and various expense or liability accounts.

11000.5.1.2   **Billings (Progress Billings)**

Accounts Receivable	xxxx	
*Billings On Construction In Process		xxxx
To record progress billings		

Important: Make sure all appropriate subheads apply to your entry (see page v for instructions)

11000.5	**Long-Term Construction Contracts**
11000.5.1	**Percentage-of-Completion Method**
11000.5.1.2	**Billings (Progress Billings)**

---

*Billings On Construction In Process is a contra inventory account, i.e., it is subtracted from Construction In Process on the Balance Sheet.

11000.5.1.3

Receipt of Progress Payments (Collections)

Cash	xxxx	
Accounts Receivable		xxxx
To record receipt of progress payments		

11000.5.1.4

Recognition of Revenue and Gross Profit

*Construction In Process	xxxx	
**Construction Expenses	xxxx	
***Revenue From Long-Term Construction Contract		xxxx
To record revenue and gross profit		

*Construction In Process is debited for the portion of the estimated total gross profit that is applicable to the work done during the period. The gross profit to be recognized in the current period is found as follows:

If:

CGP = Gross profit to be recognized in current period

$\%$ = Percentage of total work completed (total costs incurred to date / estimated total costs at completion)

TGP = Estimated total gross profit from the contract

PGP = Gross profit recognized in prior periods

Then:

$$CGP = (\% \times TGP) - PGP$$

The estimated total gross profit expected from the contract should be recomputed each period because it is possible that unexpected events (e.g., increase in costs) may affect the gross profit. Likewise, when computing the percentage of total work completed, the estimate of total contract costs should be revised as appropriate.

**Construction Expenses is debited to balance the entry. This account is similar to Cost Of Goods Sold.

***The amount of revenue to be recognized during the current period is found as follows:

REVENUE RECOGNITION

Important: Make sure all appropriate subheads apply to your entry (see page v for instructions)

11000.5	**Long-Term Construction Contracts**
11000.5.1	**Percentage-of-Completion Method**
11000.5.1.4	**Recognition of Revenue and Gross Profit**

If:

CR = Revenue to be recognized in current period

% = Percentage of total work completed (total costs incurred to date / estimated total costs at completion)

TR = Estimated total revenue from the contract

PR = Revenue recognized in prior periods

Then:

$$CR = (\% \ X \ TR) - PR$$

11000.5.1.5 **Current Period Loss on a Profitable Contract**

If total costs significantly increase (but not to the point of making the contract unprofitable in the sense that there will be no gross profit), it is possible that too much gross profit may have been recognized in previous periods. In this case, an adjustment to remove some of the previously recognized gross profit must be made by recognizing a loss in the current period.

*Construction Expenses	xxxx	
**Construction In Process		xxxx
***Revenue From Long-Term Construction Contract		xxxx
To recognize loss on a profitable long-term contract		

*Construction Expenses is debited for the amount of expense incurred during the period.

**Construction In Process is credited to balance the entry.

***Revenue From Long-Term Construction Contract is credited for the amount of revenue to be recognized in the current period. This amount is calculated as noted in *GEN11000.5.1.4*.

11000.5.1.6 **Current Period Loss on an Unprofitable Contract**

If total costs increase to the point of making the contract unprofitable (i.e., there will be a loss on the entire contract), the entire expected loss should be recognized in the current period.

Important: Make sure all appropriate subheads apply to your entry (see page v for instructions)

11000.5   **Long-Term Construction Contracts**
11000.5.1   **Percentage-of-Completion Method**
11000.5.1.6   **Current Period Loss on an Unprofitable Contract**

---

    *Construction Expenses   xxxx
      **Construction In Process   xxxx
      ***Revenue From Long-Term Construction Contract   xxxx
    To recognize loss on long-term contract

*Construction Expenses is debited to balance the entry.

**Construction In Process is credited for the amount of loss to be recognized. This is the excess of the total expected contract costs over the contract sales price plus all gross profit that has been recognized in previous periods.

***Revenue From Long-Term Construction Contract is credited for the amount of revenue to be recognized in the current period. This amount is calculated as noted in *GEN11000.5.1.4.*

11000.5.1.7

Final Settlement of the Contract

After all construction costs and gross profit (or loss) have been recorded and the work is 100% complete, the debit balance in Construction In Process should equal the credit balance in Billings On Construction In Process. These two accounts are then closed out against each other with the following entry:

    Billings On Construction In Process   xxxx
      Construction In Process   xxxx
    To record final settlement of contract

11000.5.2

Completed Contract Method

The percentage-of-completion method must be used to account for long-term construction contracts if the conditions noted in *GEN11000.5.1* are met. If any of these conditions are not met, the completed contract method must be used.

11000.5.2.1

Construction Costs

    *Construction In Process   xxxx
      **[Various Accounts]   xxxx
    To record construction costs

Important: Make sure all appropriate subheads apply to your entry (see page v for instructions)

11000.5	**Long-Term Construction Contracts**
11000.5.2	**Completed Contract Method**
11000.5.2.1	**Construction Costs**

---

*All construction costs are accumulated in Construction In Process, which is an inventory-type account.

**Credits may be made to Cash, Accounts Payable, and various expense or liability accounts.

11000.5.2.2   **Billings (Progress Billings)**

Accounts Receivable	xxxx	
*Billings On Construction In Process		xxxx
To record progress billings		

*Billings On Construction In Process is a contra inventory account; i.e., it is subtracted from Construction In Process on the Balance Sheet.

11000.5.2.3   **Receipt of Progress Payments (Collections)**

Cash	xxxx	
Accounts Receivable		xxxx
To record receipt of progress payments		

11000.5.2.4   **Recognition of Revenue and Closing of Accounts**

No revenue is recognized under the completed contract method until the contract is completed. At that time, the following entries are made:

*Billings On Construction In Process	xxxx	
*Revenue From Long-Term Construction Contract		xxxx
To close billings account and recognize revenue		

*The debit and credit in this entry are for the total revenue from the contract.

**Costs Of Construction	xxxx	
**Construction In Process		xxxx
To close Construction In Process		

**The debit and credit in this entry are for the total cost of construction.

Important: Make sure all appropriate subheads apply to your entry (see page v for instructions)

11000.5   **Long-Term Construction Contracts**
11000.5.2   **Completed Contract Method**

11000.5.2.5   ## Current Period Loss on an Unprofitable Contract

If total costs increase to the point of making the contract unprofitable (i.e., there will be a loss on the entire contract), the entire expected loss should be recognized in the current period.

> *Loss On Long-Term Contract   xxxx
>   Construction In Process   xxxx
> *To recognize loss on unprofitable long-term contract*

*The amount of loss to be recognized is the excess of the total expected contract costs over the contract sales price (contract revenue).

11000.6   ## Short-Term Construction Contracts

The completed contract method should be used to account for short-term construction contracts.

11000.6.1   ## Construction Costs

> *Construction In Process   xxxx
>   **[Various Accounts]   xxxx
> *To record construction costs*

*All construction costs are accumulated in Construction In Process.

**Credits may be made to Cash, Accounts Payable, and various expense or liability accounts.

11000.6.2   ## Billings (Progress Billings)

> Accounts Receivable   xxxx
>   *Billings On Construction In Process   xxxx
> *To record progress billings*

Important: Make sure all appropriate subheads apply to your entry (see page v for instructions)

11000.6   **Short-Term Construction Contracts**
11000.6.2   **Billings (Progress Billings)**

---

*Billings On Construction In Process is a contra inventory account; i.e., it is subtracted from Construction In Process on the Balance Sheet.

11000.6.3   ## Receipt of Progress Payments (Collections)

Cash	xxxx	
Accounts Receivable		xxxx

To record receipt of progress payments

11000.6.4   ## Recognition of Revenue and Closing of Accounts

No revenue is recognized under the completed contract method until the contract is completed and the goods are transferred to the buyer. At that time, the following entries are made:

Billings On Construction In Process	xxxx	
Revenue From Short-Term Construction Contract		xxxx

To close billings account and recognize revenue

Costs Of Construction	xxxx	
Construction In Process		xxxx

To close Construction In Process

11000.6.5   ## Current Period Loss on an Unprofitable Contract

If total costs increase to the point of making the contract unprofitable (i.e., there will be a loss), the entire expected loss should be recognized in the current period.

*Loss On Short-Term Contract	xxxx	
Construction In Process		xxxx

To recognize loss on unprofitable short-term contract

*The amount of loss to be recognized is the excess of the total expected contract costs over the contract sales price.

Important: Make sure all appropriate subheads apply to your entry (see page v for instructions)

11000.7

Revenue from Production of Certain Precious Metals and Agricultural Products

For products (e.g., certain precious metals) where:
- the product's selling price is reasonably assured,
- the units are interchangeable, and
- no significant costs are involved in distributing the product,

production rather than sale is considered to be the most critical event in the earnings process, and revenue may be recognized when production of the product is completed.

Other products (e.g., agricultural products) increase in value as they grow. For products that possess immediate marketability at quoted prices that cannot be influenced by the producer, accounting principles allow revenue to be recognized at the completion of production.

*Inventory	xxxx	
*Revenue Earned On Completed Production		xxxx
To recognize revenue		

*The debit and credit in this entry are for the net realizable value (selling price less costs of delivery, etc.) of the product. Costs of production are recorded as usual.

11000.8

Revenue Related to Sales for Which There Is No Reasonable Basis for Estimating Collectibility

The cost recovery method is used to record sales in which there is no reasonable basis for estimating the collectibility of the receivable. Under this method, no profit is recognized until the seller has collected an amount sufficient to cover the cost of the goods sold. The cost recovery method is usually preferred over the installment sales method when the degree of uncertainty is extremely high. *See GEN11000.3.*

11000.9

Franchise-Related Revenues

A franchise is the right to use property or to provide a product or service under a specific tradename.

Important: Make sure all appropriate subheads apply to your entry (see page v for instructions)

11000.9   **Franchise-Related Revenues**

11000.9.1   **Initial Franchise Fees**

The franchise agreement often allows the franchisee to pay a portion of the initial franchise fee in cash and to finance the remainder. In general, revenue is recorded only when the franchisor makes substantial performance of the services to be provided under the franchise agreement and collection of the fees is reasonably assured. In cases where collection of the amount financed is extremely uncertain, revenue may be recognized under the installment method described in *GEN11000.2* or the cost recovery method described in *GEN11000.3*.

11000.9.1.1   **Down Payment (or Entire Franchise Fee) Initially Received**

11000.9.1.1.1   **Initial Nonrefundable Franchise Fee Amounts Received**

The following entry concerns only cash initially received. If a receivable is involved in whole or in part (as with a down payment), *see GEN11000.9.1.2*.

Cash	xxxx	
*Revenue From Franchise Fees		xxxx
**Unearned Franchise Fees		xxxx
To record receipt of franchise fee		

*If nonrefundable initial franchise fee amounts received represent payment for services already provided to the franchisee, or no future services are required, they are recorded as revenue.

**Nonrefundable initial franchise fee amounts received for which future services must be performed by the franchisor are recorded as unearned revenue until the services have been performed and the fee has been earned.

11000.9.1.1.2   **Initial Refundable Franchise Fee Amounts Received**

The following entry concerns only cash initially received. If a receivable is involved in whole or in part (as with a down payment), *see GEN11000.9.1.2*.

Important: Make sure all appropriate subheads apply to your entry (see page v for instructions)

11000.9	**Franchise-Related Revenues**
11000.9.1	**Initial Franchise Fees**
11000.9.1.1	**Down Payment (or Entire Franchise Fee) Initially Received**
11000.9.1.1.2	**Initial Refundable Franchise Fee Amounts Received**

Cash	xxxx	
*Unearned Franchise Fees		xxxx
To record receipt of franchise fee		

*No revenue should be recognized when franchise fee amounts received are refundable or substantial services are yet to be performed. Such amounts are recorded as unearned revenue until the amounts become nonrefundable and the services have been performed.

11000.9.1.2   ### Franchise Fee Financed by Franchisor

The following entry concerns receipt of only a note receivable. If cash is also received, *see GEN11000.9.1.1.*

*Notes Receivable	xxxx	
**Discount On Notes Receivable		xxxx
***Unearned Franchise Fees		xxxx
To record initial franchise fee		

*Notes Receivable should be debited for the principal (face) amount of the note.

**The note should be discounted to its present value using the interest rate specified in the loan agreement. The present value is found by multiplying the annual payment amount by the appropriate present value of an annuity interest factor. The difference between the face amount and the present value amount (i.e., the discount) is credited to Discount On Notes Receivable. This discount is then recognized as interest revenue over the life of the note as discussed in *GEN3000.2.1.1.2.2*. If no rate or an unrealistically low rate is specified in the loan agreement, a realistic interest rate must be imputed as discussed in *GEN8000.2.1.5*.

***The difference between the face amount of the note and the discount amount (i.e., the present value of the note receivable) should be credited to Unearned Franchise Fees if substantial services remain to be performed by the franchisor or the fee is refundable. If the franchisor has no remaining obligation to refund any down payment received or to perform any future services, Revenue From Franchise Fees should be credited instead of this unearned revenue account.

Important: Make sure all appropriate subheads apply to your entry (see page v for instructions)

11000.9   **Franchise-Related Revenues**

11000.9.2   **Franchisor Retains an Option to Purchase the Franchise**

The franchise agreement may provide the franchisor with an option to purchase the franchise if certain conditions are met.

11000.9.2.1   **Recording Unearned Franchise Fees**

If it is probable that the franchisor will reacquire the franchise, no revenue should be recognized by the franchisor when initial franchise fees are received. Instead, Unearned Franchise Fees should be recorded as follows:

Cash	xxxx	
Unearned Franchise Fees		xxxx
To record receipt of franchise fees		

11000.9.2.2   **Option to Purchase Is Exercised**

Unearned Franchise Fees	xxxx	
Investment In Franchise		xxxx
To reduce the investment in franchise by the amount of		
unearned franchise fees that will not be earned		

11000.9.2.3   **Option to Purchase Is Not Exercised and Services Are Performed**

Unearned Franchise Fees	xxxx	
Revenue From Franchise Fees		xxxx
To record franchise fee revenue		

11000.9.3   **Continuing Franchise Fees**

Cash (Franchise Fees Receivable)	xxxx	
*Revenue From Franchise Fees		xxxx
To record continuing franchise fees		

*If a portion of the fees are designated for a specific purpose (e.g., local advertising), then this designated amount should be credited to Unearned Franchise Fees instead

---

Important: Make sure all appropriate subheads apply to your entry (see page v for instructions)

11000.9   **Franchise-Related Revenues**
11000.9.3   **Continuing Franchise Fees**

---

of Revenue From Franchise Fees. It would subsequently be recorded as earned when the services are performed.

11000.9.4   **Franchisee Given Right to Make Bargain Purchases of Supplies or Equipment after Initial Franchise Fee Is Paid**

11000.9.4.1   **Receipt of Initial Franchise Fee**

Cash	xxxx	
Revenue From Franchise Fees		xxxx
*Unearned Sales Revenue		xxxx
To record receipt of franchise fee		

*If equipment and/or supplies are to be sold to the franchisee at a bargain purchase price, a portion of the initial franchise fee should be deferred as Unearned Sales Revenue until the sale occurs. The amount deferred should be sufficient to allow the franchisor to recognize a reasonable profit on the sale.

11000.9.4.2   **Sale of Supplies or Equipment under a Bargain Purchase Agreement**

Cash (Accounts Receivable)	xxxx	
*Unearned Sales Revenue	xxxx	
**Sales		xxxx
To record sale of inventory to franchisee at bargain purchase amount		

*Unearned Sales Revenue is debited to balance the entry but not in excess of its credit balance.

**Sales is credited for the normal sales price (not the bargain price).

TABLE OF CONTENTS

INCOME TAXES

12000.1   **Estimated Income Tax**

Corporations are required to make estimated tax payments to the Internal Revenue
Service (IRS) and to many states each quarter.

12000.1.1   **Recording Estimated Income Tax**

Prepaid Income Tax	xxxx	
Income Tax Payable		xxxx
To record estimated income tax		

12000.1.2   **Payment of Estimated Income Tax**

*Income Tax Payable	xxxx	
Cash		xxxx
To record payment of estimated income tax		

*Income Tax Payable is debited if the entry at *GEN12000.1.1* was made. Otherwise,
Prepaid Income Tax is debited.

12000.1.3   **Recognition of Income Tax Expense**

The entry shown below transfers the balance in Prepaid Income Tax to Income Tax
Expense. This may be done periodically during the year as one of the usual adjusting
entries or as part of a larger entry that would also record deferred tax assets and
liabilities (*see GEN12000.2*).

Income Tax Expense	xxxx	
Prepaid Income Tax		xxxx
To recognize income tax expense		

12000.2   **Deferred Income Taxes Related to Temporary Differences**

Taxable income and accounting income may differ for two reasons:
- Permanent differences: A permanent difference occurs if an expense for
  accounting purposes is *never allowed* as a deduction for tax purposes

Important: Make sure all appropriate subheads apply to your entry (see page v for instructions)

12000.2   **Deferred Income Taxes Related to Temporary Differences**

(e.g., fines and penalties) or a revenue is recognized for accounting purposes that is *never taxable* (e.g., interest earned on state and local obligations).

- *Temporary differences:* A temporary difference occurs if an expense or revenue recognized in one period for accounting purposes is recognized in a different period for tax purposes (e.g., use of a different depreciation method for tax purposes than for accounting purposes). Certain other events, e.g., business combinations, may also create temporary differences.

Because permanent differences affect only the calculation of the tax liability for the period in which they occur, there are no deferred tax consequences associated with such differences. Deferred tax amounts are associated only with temporary differences.

12000.2.1   **Recognizing Deferred Tax Liabilities**

Cumulative effects of temporary differences resulting from expensing items faster for tax purposes than for accounting (book) purposes, or from recognizing revenue more slowly for tax purposes than for accounting purposes, will cause accounting (book) income to exceed taxable income in early years and taxable income to exceed accounting income in later years. If there is at least one temporary timing difference at year-end, the cumulative effect of which is to produce future taxable income in excess of accounting (book) income, then a deferred tax liability must be reported on the balance sheet at the end of the current year.

*Income Tax Expense	xxxx	
**Income Tax Payable		xxxx
***Deferred Tax Liability		xxxx
To record income tax		

*Income Tax Expense is debited sufficiently to balance the entry. In this entry, Income Tax Expense includes both the current and the deferred income tax expense. Alternatively, the components of the expense may be recorded separately by debiting both Income Tax Expense - Current and Income Tax Expense - Deferred.

**Income Tax Payable is credited for the amount of the tax liability as calculated on the tax return.

Important: Make sure all appropriate subheads apply to your entry (see page v for instructions)

12000.2   **Deferred Income Taxes Related to Temporary Differences**
12000.2.1   **Recognizing Deferred Tax Liabilities**

***Deferred Tax Liability is credited (or debited) *sufficiently to increase (or decrease) the balance in the account to properly reflect the total amount of the liability.* The total amount of the liability is recalculated at the end of the current period.

The amount of the Deferred Tax Liability at the end of the current period is found by multiplying the total cumulative temporary differences pertaining to all assets and liabilities at the end of the current period that will cause taxable income in future periods to be greater than accounting (book) income by the applicable tax rate (i.e., the firm's expected average tax rate).

The cumulative temporary difference for each asset or liability is computed as follows:

Current Book Value of Asset (or Liability)	xxxx
Less: Current Tax Basis	xxxx
Total Difference	xxxx
Less: Permanent Difference (if Any)	xxxx
Cumulative Temporary Difference	xxxx

All calculations that result in cumulative temporary differences *which will result in greater taxable income than accounting income in future years* are then totaled to arrive at the total cumulative temporary difference for the deferred tax liability calculation. This amount is then multiplied by the expected average tax rate to determine the desired balance in Deferred Tax Liability.

The expected average tax rate is the enacted tax rate that the entity expects to be applied to taxable income in the periods in which the deferred tax liability is expected to be settled.

The amount of the increase (credit) or decrease (debit) in Deferred Tax Liability recorded in the above entry is then calculated as follows:

Desired Balance in Deferred Tax Liability	xxxx
Less: Current Balance in Deferred Tax Liability	xxxx
Amount of Increase (Credit) or Decrease (Debit)	xxxx

Important: Make sure all appropriate subheads apply to your entry (see page v for instructions)

12000.2   **Deferred Income Taxes Related to Temporary Differences**

12000.2.2   ## Recognizing Deferred Tax Assets

Cumulative effects of temporary differences resulting from expensing items more slowly for tax purposes than for accounting (book) purposes, or from recognizing revenue faster for tax purposes than for accounting purposes will cause taxable income to exceed accounting income in early years and accounting income to exceed taxable income in later years. If cumulative temporary differences at the end of the current year will cause accounting (book) income to exceed taxable income in future years, then a deferred tax asset must be reported on the balance sheet at the end of the current year.

*Income Tax Expense	xxxx	
**Deferred Tax Asset	xxxx	
***Income Tax Payable		xxxx
To record income tax		

*Income Tax Expense is debited sufficiently to balance the entry. In this entry, Income Tax Expense includes both the current and the deferred income tax expense. Alternatively, the components of the expense may be recorded separately by debiting Income Tax Expense - Current and debiting or crediting Income Tax Expense - Deferred.

**Deferred Tax Asset is debited (or credited) *sufficiently to increase (or decrease) the balance in the account to properly reflect the total amount of the asset*. The total amount of the asset is recalculated at the end of the current period.

The amount of the Deferred Tax Asset at the end of the current period is found by multiplying the total cumulative temporary differences pertaining to all assets and liabilities at the end of the current period that will cause taxable income in future periods to be less than accounting (book) income by the applicable tax rate (i.e., the firm's expected average tax rate).

***Income Tax Payable is credited for the amount of the tax liability as calculated on the tax return.

The cumulative temporary difference for each asset or liability is computed as follows:

Important: Make sure all appropriate subheads apply to your entry (see page v for instructions)

12000.2   **Deferred Income Taxes Related to Temporary Differences**
12000.2.2   **Recognizing Deferred Tax Assets**

Current Book Value of Asset (or Liability)	xxxx
Less: Current Tax Basis	xxxx
Total Difference	xxxx
Less: Permanent Difference (if Any)	xxxx
Cumulative Temporary Difference	xxxx

All calculations that result in cumulative temporary differences *which will result in less taxable income than accounting income in future years* are then totaled to arrive at the total cumulative temporary difference for the deferred tax asset calculation. This amount is then multiplied by the expected average tax rate to determine the desired balance in Deferred Tax Asset.

The expected average tax rate is the enacted tax rate that the entity expects to be applied to taxable income in the periods in which the deferred tax asset is expected to be realized.

The amount of the increase (debit) or decrease (credit) in Deferred Tax Asset recorded in the above entry is then calculated as follows:

Desired Balance in Deferred Tax Asset	xxxx
Less: Current Balance in Deferred Tax Asset	xxxx
Amount of Increase (Debit) or Decrease (Credit)	xxxx

12000.2.3   **Deferred Tax Asset Valuation Account**

If, based on all available evidence, there is more than a 50% likelihood that some portion (or all) of a deferred tax asset will not be realized, then the deferred tax asset should be reduced to its expected realizable value using a valuation account.

Income Tax Expense	xxxx
*Allowance To Reduce Deferred Tax Asset To	
Expected Realizable Value	xxxx
To record reduction in deferred tax asset expected realizable value	

*Allowance To Reduce Deferred Tax Asset To Expected Realizable Value is adjusted at the end of each period so that its balance represents the amount of the

Important: Make sure all appropriate subheads apply to your entry (see page v for instructions)

12000.2   **Deferred Income Taxes Related to Temporary Differences**
12000.2.3   **Deferred Tax Asset Valuation Account**

Deferred Tax Asset not expected to be realized. If the balance in the allowance account needs to be reduced, Allowance To Reduce Deferred Tax Asset To Expected Realizable Value is debited and Income Tax Expense is credited. The allowance account is subtracted from Deferred Tax Asset on the balance sheet and cannot have a debit balance.

12000.2.4   Changes in Federal Income Tax Rates

When tax rate changes occur, the effect on deferred income tax accounts should be recognized in the period the rate change is enacted into law.

12000.2.4.1   Adjusting Deferred Tax Liability

12000.2.4.1.1   Reflecting a Decrease in Tax Rates

Lower future income tax rates reduce currently recognized deferred tax liabilities because future taxes will be lower.

*Deferred Tax Liability	xxxx	
Income Tax Expense		xxxx
To adjust Deferred Tax Liability		

*To determine the debit to Deferred Tax Liability, the new amount of the liability must first be determined by using the new tax rates for the periods affected. That is, the cumulative temporary differences pertaining to all assets and liabilities at the end of the current period that will cause taxable income in future periods to be greater than accounting (book) income (i.e., that will cause future taxable amounts) must be analyzed according to the years in which the future taxable amounts will occur. The total future taxable amounts for each year are then multiplied by the tax rate applicable to that year to determine that year's portion of the total deferred tax liability. The total deferred tax liability is then found by adding the individual yearly amounts.

The debit to Deferred Tax Liability is determined by subtracting the new amount of the liability just determined from the current account balance.

Important: Make sure all appropriate subheads apply to your entry (see page v for instructions)

12000.2   **Deferred Income Taxes Related to Temporary Differences**
12000.2.4   **Changes in Federal Income Tax Rates**
12000.2.4.1   **Adjusting Deferred Tax Liability**

12000.2.4.1.2   **Reflecting an Increase in Tax Rates**

Higher future income tax rates increase currently recognized deferred tax liabilities because future taxes will be higher.

Income Tax Expense	xxxx	
*Deferred Tax Liability		xxxx
To adjust Deferred Tax Liability		

*To determine the credit to Deferred Tax Liability, the new amount of the liability must first be determined by using the new tax rates for the periods affected. That is, the cumulative temporary differences pertaining to all assets and liabilities at the end of the current period that will cause taxable income in future periods to be greater than accounting (book) income (i.e., that will cause future taxable amounts) must be analyzed according to the years in which the future taxable amounts will occur. The total future taxable amounts for each year are then multiplied by the tax rate applicable to that year to determine that year's portion of the total deferred tax liability. The total deferred tax liability is then found by adding the individual yearly amounts.

The credit to Deferred Tax Liability is determined by subtracting the current De-ferred Tax Liability balance from the new amount of the liability just determined.

12000.2.4.2   **Adjusting Deferred Tax Asset**

12000.2.4.2.1   **Reflecting a Decrease in Tax Rates**

Lower future income tax rates decrease currently recognized deferred tax assets because future taxes will be lower.

Income Tax Expense	xxxx	
*Deferred Tax Asset		xxxx
To adjust Deferred Tax Asset		

*To determine the credit to Deferred Tax Asset, the new amount of the asset must first be determined by using the new tax rates for the periods affected. That is, the cumulative temporary differences pertaining to all assets and liabilities at the end of the current period that will cause taxable income in future periods to be less than

Important: Make sure all appropriate subheads apply to your entry (see page v for instructions)

12000.2	**Deferred Income Taxes Related to Temporary Differences**
12000.2.4	**Changes in Federal Income Tax Rates**
12000.2.4.2	**Adjusting Deferred Tax Asset**
12000.2.4.2.1	**Reflecting a Decrease in Tax Rates**

accounting (book) income (i.e., that will cause future deductible amounts) must be analyzed according to the years in which the future deductible amounts will occur. The total future deductible amounts for each year are then multiplied by the tax rate applicable to that year to determine that year's portion of the total deferred tax asset. The total deferred tax asset is then found by adding the individual yearly amounts.

The credit to Deferred Tax Asset is determined by subtracting the new amount of the asset just determined from the current Deferred Tax Asset balance.

12000.2.4.2.2   **Reflecting an Increase in Tax Rates**

Higher future income tax rates increase currently recognized deferred tax assets because future taxes will be higher.

> *Deferred Tax Asset   xxxx
>   Income Tax Expense   xxxx
>   *To adjust Deferred Tax Asset*

*To determine the debit to Deferred Tax Asset, the new amount of the asset must first be determined by using the new tax rates for the periods affected. That is, the cumulative temporary differences pertaining to all assets and liabilities at the end of the current period that will cause taxable income in future periods to be less than accounting (book) income (i.e., that will cause future deductible amounts) must be analyzed according to the years in which the future deductible amounts will occur. The total future deductible amounts for each year are then multiplied by the tax rate applicable to that year to determine that year's portion of the total deferred tax asset. The total deferred tax asset is then found by adding the individual yearly amounts.

The debit to Deferred Tax Asset is determined by subtracting the current Deferred Tax Asset balance from the new amount of the asset just determined.

12000.2.5   **Computing Deferred Tax Assets and Liabilities Subject to Multiple Tax Rates**

The average expected enacted tax rate should be applied to taxable income in the periods in which the deferred tax liability is to be settled or the deferred tax asset is to be realized.

Important: Make sure all appropriate subheads apply to your entry (see page v for instructions)

12000.2   **Deferred Income Taxes Related to Temporary Differences**

12000.2.5   **Computing Deferred Tax Assets and Liabilities Subject to Multiple Tax Rates**

If taxable income is expected in the year(s) that temporary differences are expected to be realized, then the tax rate in effect during those years should be used to compute the current period deferred tax liability or asset. If, on the other hand, the entity expects a taxable loss during the year(s) that temporary differences are expected to be realized, then the entity must determine whether it will carry its net operating loss (NOL) back or forward. If the NOL is expected to be carried back, then the tax rate in effect during the 3 earlier years should be used. If the NOL is expected to be carried forward, then the tax rate expected to be in effect in the future periods should be used.

12000.3   **Net Operating Losses (NOL)**

A net operating loss occurs when tax-deductible expenses are greater than taxable revenues (i.e., there is negative taxable income and no tax liability for the current period). Net operating losses may be carried back to previous tax years and/or forward to future tax years to offset taxable income in those periods.

12000.3.1   **Net Operating Loss Carrybacks**

Net operating losses may be carried back 2 years and forward 20 years to offset taxable income in those periods. (The taxpayer may elect not to carry back and to only carry forward.) An amended tax return must be filed for each year to which an NOL is carried back in order to claim refunds for taxes paid in those years. The NOL carried back must be applied to the earliest year first (e.g., if the current period is 2004, then the NOL must be used to reduce the taxable income of 2002 first). If any NOL remains, it is then applied to the next earliest year (e.g., the NOL would next be used to reduce the taxable income of 2003). Finally, if any NOL remains, it may be carried forward for up to 20 years.

*Income Tax Refund Receivable	xxxx	
Benefit Due To Loss Carryback		xxxx
To record the tax effect of an NOL carryback		

*The amount of the income tax refund receivable equals the amount of prior years' taxes refundable due to the NOL carryback.

Important: Make sure all appropriate subheads apply to your entry (see page v for instructions)

12000.3 Net Operating Losses (NOL)

12000.3.2 ### Net Operating Loss Carryforwards

If the net operating loss (NOL) is not fully absorbed by carrying it back 2 years, the remaining NOL may be carried forward for up to 20 years. A taxpayer may choose not to carry the NOL back if it is not advantageous to do so. In that case, the entire NOL may be carried forward.

12000.3.2.1 ### A Valuation Account Is Not Used

If, based on all available evidence, there is at least a 50% likelihood that all of the deferred tax asset created by an NOL carryforward will be realized, then no valuation account is required.

12000.3.2.1.1 ### To Record Loss Carryforward Without a Valuation Account

*Deferred Tax Asset		xxxx
Benefit Due To Loss Carryforward (Income Tax Expense)		xxxx
To record NOL carryforward		

*The amount of the future tax savings (the Deferred Tax Asset) is found by multiplying the remaining NOL amount by the enacted tax rate(s) assumed to be in effect in the future periods in which the benefit will be received.

12000.3.2.1.2 ### To Record Reduction of Income Tax Payable Caused by an NOL Carryforward from a Previous Year Without a Valuation Account

Income Tax Expense		xxxx
*Deferred Tax Asset		xxxx
**Income Tax Payable		xxxx
To record income taxes		

*Deferred Tax Asset is credited (reduced) for the amount of taxes saved as a result of the carryforward (i.e., the carryforward amount allowable this year X the average tax rate).

Important: Make sure all appropriate subheads apply to your entry (see page v for instructions)

12000.3   **Net Operating Losses (NOL)**
12000.3.2   **Net Operating Loss Carryforwards**
12000.3.2.1   **A Valuation Account Is Not Used**
12000.3.2.1.2   **To Record Reduction of Income Tax Payable Caused by an NOL Carryforward from a Previous Year Without a Valuation Account**

**The credit to Income Tax Payable is found as follows. First, the current period taxable income without regard to the NOL carryforward is reduced by the amount of the carryforward. If the carryforward exceeds the year's taxable income, the excess amount may be carried forward to following years (up to 20 years). Second, the tax on any remaining taxable income is found by multiplying the remaining taxable income by the average tax rate. This should be the amount of tax liability as calculated on the tax return.

12000.3.2.2   **A Valuation Account Is Used**

If, based on all available evidence, there is more than a 50% likelihood that some portion (or all) of the deferred tax asset created by an NOL carryforward will not be realized, then the deferred tax asset should be reduced to its expected realizable value using a valuation account.

12000.3.2.2.1   **To Record Loss Carryforward with a Valuation Account**

*Deferred Tax Asset	xxxx
Benefit Due To Loss Carryforward (Income Tax Expense)	xxxx
To record the tax effect of an NOL carryforward	

*The amount of the future tax savings (the Deferred Tax Asset) is found by multiplying the remaining NOL amount by the enacted tax rate(s) assumed to be in effect in the future periods in which the benefit will be received.

Benefit Due To Loss Carryforward (Income Tax Expense)	xxxx
**Allowance To Reduce Deferred Tax Asset To Expected Realizable Value	xxxx
To record reduction in deferred tax asset to expected realizable value	

**The allowance account is credited for the amount not expected to be realized. The balance of this account must be reconsidered at the end of each year and revalued if necessary. The account is debited or credited as appropriate to ensure that the balance in the account represents the amount not expected to be realized as of the end of the period in question. In periods where the balance needs to be reduced, the allowance account is debited and Benefit Due To Loss Carryforward (Income Tax

Important: Make sure all appropriate subheads apply to your entry (see page v for instructions)

12000.3   **Net Operating Losses (NOL)**
12000.3.2   **Net Operating Loss Carryforwards**
12000.3.2.1   **A Valuation Account Is Not Used**
12000.3.2.2.1   **To Record Loss Carryforward with a Valuation Account**

Expense) is credited. This account is deducted from Deferred Tax Asset in the Balance Sheet.

12000.3.2.2.2   **To Record Reduction of Income Tax Payable Caused by an NOL Carryforward from a Previous Year with a Valuation Account**

Income Tax Expense	xxxx	
*Deferred Tax Asset		xxxx
**Income Tax Payable		xxxx

To record the effect of an NOL carryforward on current period tax liability

*Deferred Tax Asset is credited (reduced) by the amount of taxes saved as a result of the carryforward (i.e., the carryforward amount allowable in the current year X the average tax rate).

**The credit to Income Tax Payable is found as follows. First, the current period taxable income without regard to the NOL carryforward is reduced by the amount of the carryforward. If the carryforward exceeds the year's taxable income, the excess amount may be carried forward to the following years (up to 20 years). Second, the tax on any remaining taxable income is found by multiplying the remaining taxable income by the average tax rate. This should be the amount of tax liability as calculated on the tax return.

Allowance To Reduce Deferred Tax Asset To Expected Realizable Value	xxxx	
*Benefit Due To Loss Carryforward		xxxx

To eliminate the allowance and recognize loss carryforward

*The credit to Benefit Due To Loss Carryforward is found by multiplying the loss carryforward amount by the average tax rate.

12000.4   **Collection of Income Tax Receivable**

Cash	xxxx	
Income Tax Receivable		xxxx
Interest Income		xxxx

To record collection of income tax receivable and interest

Important: Make sure all appropriate subheads apply to your entry (see page v for instructions)

12000.5   **Assessment of Additional Income Tax**

Income Tax Expense	xxxx	
*Interest Expense	xxxx	
*Penalties Expense	xxxx	
Income Tax Payable (Cash)		xxxx

To record additional income tax assessment

*Interest and penalty expense are recorded in separate accounts because interest is deductible for tax purposes and penalties are not. If the amount of penalties is not material the debit to Penalties Expense may be made instead to Miscellaneous Expense.

TABLE OF CONTENTS

GEN13000   PENSIONS AND POSTRETIREMENT BENEFITS

13000.1   **Pension Plans**

A pension plan is an agreement between an employer and its employees under which the employer promises to provide benefits to its retired employees for services they rendered while employed. A pension plan under which employees as well as employers make contributions is called a contributory plan. If only the employer makes contributions, the plan is a noncontributory plan.

13000.1.1   **Defined Contribution Pension Plan**

In a defined contribution plan, the amount of the contribution is defined but not the benefits to be received by employees at retirement. The employer's contribution to the plan is determined by a specified formula, and any benefits paid to employees in the future are limited to those that can be provided by the contributions to the plan and the returns earned on the plan's investments.

The only entry made by a firm with a defined contribution pension plan is to record its periodic contribution and expense.

13000.1.1.1   **Contribution Is Equal to Current Pension Expense**

*Pension Expense	xxxx	
Cash		xxxx
To record pension expense		

*In a defined contribution plan, the annual pension expense is the amount that the entity is required to contribute to the plan as determined by the formula specified in the plan.

13000.1.1.2   **Contribution Is Greater than Current Pension Expense**

*Pension Expense	xxxx	
**Prepaid Pension Expense (Pension Liability)	xxxx	
Cash		xxxx
To record pension expense		

Important: Make sure all appropriate subheads apply to your entry (see page v for instructions)

13000.1   **Pension Plans**
13000.1.1   **Defined Contribution Pension Plan**
13000.1.1.2   **Contribution Is Greater than Current Pension Expense**

---

*In a defined contribution plan, the annual pension expense is the amount that the entity is required to contribute to the plan as determined by the formula specified in the plan.

**Prepaid Pension Expense is debited for the excess payment unless there is a balance in Pension Liability, in which case Pension Liability is debited.

13000.1.1.3   **Contribution Is Less than Current Pension Expense**

According to the Employee Retirement Income Security Act of 1974 (ERISA), annual funding of pension plans is no longer at the employer's discretion. Under ERISA, employers must fund their pension plans in accordance with an actuarial funding method that over time will be sufficient to pay for all pension obligations.

*Pension Expense		xxxx
**Pension Liability (Prepaid Pension Expense)		xxxx
Cash		xxxx

To record pension expense

*In a defined contribution plan, the annual pension expense is the amount that the entity is required to contribute to the plan as determined by the formula specified in the plan.

**Pension Liability is credited for the excess expense unless there is a balance in Prepaid Pension Expense, in which case Prepaid Pension Expense is credited.

13000.1.2   **Defined Benefit Pension Plan**

In a defined benefit plan, the benefits to be received by retirees (rather than the contributions to be made) are specified. Benefits are determined by a specified formula that typically takes into consideration factors such as length of employment and salary level. One measure of the employer's obligation for deferred compensation to its employees is the Projected Benefit Obligation (PBO). The PBO is based on all years of service performed by both vested and nonvested employees using their expected future salaries. The estimated future benefits must be discounted to the present using an actuarial present value approach.

Important: Make sure all appropriate subheads apply to your entry (see page v for instructions)

13000.1   **Pension Plans**
13000.1.2   **Defined Benefit Pension Plan**

13000.1.2.1   **Recording Current Period Pension Expense in a Defined Benefit Plan**

In a defined benefit plan, the pension expense recognized each period is not necessarily equal to the cash contributed to the plan. The computation of current pension expense is affected by the following items:

(1) *Service Cost* - This is the actuarial present value of benefits that must be paid in the future for services provided by employees during the current period. Future pay levels must be used if required by the pension benefit formula.

(2) *Interest Cost* - Interest must be accrued on the pension obligation because the obligation is calculated on a discounted basis. The interest included in the current period pension expense is based on the "projected benefit obligation" (defined in *GEN13000.1.2*) outstanding during the period.

(3) *Actual Return On Plan Assets* - This is the actual increase or decrease in the plan's assets resulting from interest, dividends, and changes in market value. The actual return is adjusted for employer contributions and the benefits paid during the period.

(4) *Amortization Of Unrecognized Prior Service Cost* - If the plan gives employees retroactive credit for services performed prior to the date the plan is adopted or amended, the resulting increase in the projected benefit obligation is called "prior service cost" (PSC). This cost must be amortized over the remaining service life of the covered active employees.

(5) *Gain Or Loss* - These gains and losses are associated with changes in market value of plan assets and changes in the actuarial assumptions that affect the amount of the projected benefit obligation. If the gain or loss exceeds 10% of the larger of the beginning balance of the projected benefit obligation or the market-related value of the plan assets, the excess should be amortized over the average remaining service period of active employees expected to receive benefits under the plan. This is referred to as the "corridor approach" of amortizing pension gains or losses. See explanation (*h*) below for a detailed example of the corridor approach.

Pension Plan Worksheet

Item	Annual Pension Expense (1)	Cash (2)	Prepaid/ Accrued Pension Cost (3)	Additional Liability (4)	Pension Intangible (5)	Contra Equity (6)	Plan Assets (7)	Projected Benefit Obligation (8)	Unrecognized Prior Service Cost (9)	Unrecognized Net Gain or Loss (10)
			Journal Entries					*Disclosure Amounts*		
(a) Beginning Balances			xxxxDr./Cr.				xxxx Dr.	xxxx Cr.	xxxx Dr.	xxxx Dr./Cr.
(b) Prior Service Cost (PSC)								xxxx Cr.	xxxx Dr.	
Beginning balances restated [total of line (a) + line (b)]										
(c) Current Service Cost	xxxx Dr.							xxxx Cr.		
(d) Interest on Obligation	xxxx Dr.							xxxx Cr.		
(e) Actual Return on Plan Assets	xxxx Cr.						xxxx Dr.			
(f) Amortization of Unrecognized PSC	xxxx Dr.								xxxx Cr.	
(g) Unexpected Loss/Gain on Plan Assets	xxxx Dr./Cr.									xxxx Dr./Cr.
(h) Amortization of Unrecognized Net Loss/Gain	xxxx Dr./Cr.									xxxx Dr./Cr.
(i) Annual Contribution		xxxx Cr.					xxxx Dr.			
(j) Benefits Paid to Retirees							xxxx Cr.	xxxx Dr.		
(k) Increase/Decrease in Obligation								xxxx Dr./Cr.		xxxx Dr./Cr.
Pension expense journal entry:										
(l) Minimum Liability Adjustment				xxxx Cr.	xxxx Dr.	xxxx Dr.				
End of year balances	xxxx	xxxx	xxxx	xxxx	xxxx	xxxx	xxxx	xxxx	xxxx	xxxx

Each entry (item) included in the worksheet is described on pages 393 through 396:

Important: Make sure all appropriate subheads apply to your entry (see page v for instructions)

13000.1	**Pension Plans**
13000.1.2	**Defined Benefit Pension Plan**
13000.1.2.1	**Recording Current Period Pension Expense in a Defined Benefit Plan**

---

(6) When Statement of Financial Accounting Standards No. 87 went into effect in 1987, the manner in which pension-related assets and liabilities were measured significantly changed. Any "transition loss or gain" that may have been incurred because of the change in measurement is either added to the gain or loss on plant assets or separately amortized over the average remaining service period of employees expected to receive benefits under the plan. However, the amortization should not be less than 15 years.

Accounting for defined benefit plans is complex because the Financial Accounting Standards Board chose not to formally recognize in the books several items that affect the determination of current period pension expense. However, even though not recorded in the books, these items must still be disclosed in the notes to the financial statements. Therefore, many firms have developed memorandum entries or worksheets for use in computing the amount of pension expense to be recognized in the current period and for keeping track of the nonrecognized items for disclosure purposes. The worksheet format recommended by Paul D.W. Miller (*Journal of Accountancy,* February 1987, pp. 86-94) is used to develop the required journal entries illustrated below.

In the worksheet on the previous page, the columns are numbered. Columns 1-6 are items that are formally recognized in the books (i.e., journal entries are made for the amounts in these columns). Columns 7-10 are used to calculate amounts needed for disclosure in financial statements.

(a) Beginning balance.
(b) This entry recognizes the increase in the pension obligation that occurs when employees are granted credit for services rendered prior to the date of plan adoption or amendment. Prior Service Cost (PSC) must be amortized over the years that the employees who were granted credit are expected to provide services to the firm.
(c) This entry recognizes the actuarial present value of benefits earned by employees during the current period.
(d) This entry accrues interest on the pension obligation. The amount of interest is found by multiplying the beginning of the period balance of the projected benefit obligation by the plan settlement rate (the interest rate which reflects the rates at which pension benefits could be effectively settled).

Important: Make sure all appropriate subheads apply to your entry (see page v for instructions)

13000.1	**Pension Plans**
13000.1.2	**Defined Benefit Pension Plan**
13000.1.2.1	**Recording Current Period Pension Expense in a Defined Benefit Plan**

(e) This entry recognizes the actual return earned on plan assets during the period. The amount is found as follows:

Plan Assets, End of Year Fair Value	xxxx
Less: Plan Assets, Beginning of Year Fair Value	(xxxx)
Increase (Decrease) in Plan Assets Fair Value	xxxx
Plus: Benefits Paid During the Year	xxxx
Less: Annual Contribution to the Plan	(xxxx)
Actual Return on Plan Assets	xxxx

The above worksheet entry assumes a positive actual return (i.e., pension expense is decreased). If the actual return is negative (i.e., pension expense is increased), the entry is reversed, and Pension Expense is debited on the worksheet and Plan Assets is credited.

(f) This entry recognizes the amortization of unrecognized prior service cost. The amortization amount may be based on the straight-line method or the years-of-service method. Under the years-of-service method, the amount is found by multiplying the service years consumed during the year by the cost per service year. The service years consumed during the year is equal to the number of employees who were granted credit for prior service and are working in the current year. The cost per service year is found by dividing the amount of prior service cost by the total number of service years to be worked by all of the participating employees. The total number of service years is found by summing the total years each covered employee is expected to work prior to retirement. Because the service years consumed during the year decrease over time as employees who were granted credit for prior service begin to retire, the amortization amount decreases each year.

(g) Unexpected gains or losses may result from the actual return on plan assets being more or less than the expected return (beginning of year plan assets times the expected rate of return).

(h) Gains or losses resulting from unexpected fluctuations in pension expense or pension assets are not recognized immediately. To prevent these unrecognized gains or losses from becoming too large, the balance in Unrecognized Net Gain Or Loss must be amortized when it exceeds 10% of the larger of the beginning balances of the projected benefit obligation (defined in *GEN13000.1.2*) or the market-related value of the plan assets. Because both gains and losses are recognized in the same account, the 10% criterion represents a corridor (e.g., if the larger of the two balances is

Important: Make sure all appropriate subheads apply to your entry (see page v for instructions)

13000.1	**Pension Plans**
13000.1.2	**Defined Benefit Pension Plan**
13000.1.2.1	**Recording Current Period Pension Expense in a Defined Benefit Plan**

$1,000,000, then the lower limit is -$100,000 and the upper limit is $100,000). If the beginning balance in Unrecognized Net Gain Or Loss exceeds the corridor, the excess (i.e., the amount outside the corridor) must be amortized over the remaining service life of all employees. The amortization amount is found by dividing the excess amount by the average remaining service life of all employees. The amortization of excess gains or losses is included in current period pension expense only if the unrecognized gain or loss exceeded the corridor as of the beginning of the year.

(i) This entry recognizes the firm's annual contribution to the plan.

(j) This entry recognizes the benefits paid to retirees during the period.

(k) This entry recognizes an increase or decrease in the projected benefit obligation because of changes in the actuarial assumptions of the plan (e.g., estimates relating to the mortality rate, turnover rate, retirement rate, and salary levels) or differences between experience and expectation regarding the obligation. The amount of the entry is the amount needed to adjust Projected Benefit Obligation at the end of the year (after all other entries affecting the account have been entered into the worksheet) to the actuary's estimate of the end of year projected benefit obligation.

(l) If, in any period, the Accumulated Benefit Obligation (ABO) exceeds the fair value of the plan assets, a minimum pension liability must be recognized. The ABO is the pension obligation calculated for all years (vested and nonvested) of employee service using *current* salary levels. The minimum pension liability is equal to the amount by which the accumulated (not projected) benefit obligation at the end of the year exceeds the fair value (not the market-related asset value) of the pension plan assets. If there is already a credit balance in Prepaid/Accrued Pension Cost (Column 3), then the additional liability amount is found by subtracting the balance in Prepaid/Accrued Pension Cost from the minimum pension liability amount. If there is a debit balance in Prepaid/Accrued Pension Cost, the balance in the account is added to the minimum pension liability amount. The amount of the required worksheet entry is the amount necessary to adjust the beginning balance of the additional liability to this calculated amount. If the amount of additional liability is less than or equal to the balance in Unrecognized Prior Service Cost plus any unrecognized transition loss, the full amount of the additional liability is assumed to represent goodwill and is therefore debited to

Important: Make sure all appropriate subheads apply to your entry (see page v for instructions)

13000.1   **Pension Plans**
13000.1.2   **Defined Benefit Pension Plan**
13000.1.2.1   **Recording Current Period Pension Expense in a Defined Benefit Plan**

Intangible Asset - Deferred Pension Cost. If the additional liability exceeds the balance in Unrecognized Prior Service Cost plus any unrecognized transition loss, the excess amount is debited to Excess of Additional Pension Liability Over Unrecognized Prior Service Cost, which is a contra stockholders' equity account. The entry recorded in the above worksheet assumes that the additional liability exceeds the balance in Unrecognized Prior Service Cost. On the other hand, if the fair value of the plan exceeds the accumulated pension obligation, no asset may be recognized.

Once the worksheet has been completed, formal journal entries can be developed. First, compute sums for worksheet Columns 1 and 2. Next, using the first three columns of the worksheet, develop the necessary journal entry for the current period pension expense as illustrated in the example provided below. Then, recompute the ending balances in Columns 3 and 7 to 10. The balance in Prepaid/Accrued Pension Cost (Column 3) should equal the net balance of the disclosure amounts (Columns 7-10). Next, do the additional liability adjustment. Finally, make a formal journal entry for the current period pension expense and for the additional liability adjustment. See *GEN13000.1.2.3* for a comprehensive illustration of the worksheet and the resulting entries.

Pension Expense	xxxx	
Cash		xxxx
*Prepaid/Accrued Pension Cost		xxxx
To record current period pension expense		

*When the year's Pension Expense exceeds the cash contribution, Prepaid/Accrued Pension Cost is credited for the difference and a credit balance represents a liability. If the cash contribution exceeds the current period pension expense, Prepaid/Accrued Pension Cost is debited for the difference and a debit balance represents an asset.

13000.1.2.2   **Recognition of the Minimum Pension Liability**

Important: Make sure all appropriate subheads apply to your entry (see page v for instructions)

13000.1   **Pension Plans**
13000.1.2   **Defined Benefit Pension Plan**
13000.1.2.2   **Recognition of the Minimum Pension Liability**

13000.1.2.2.1   **Additional Liability Is Less than Unrecognized Prior Service Cost**

> *Intangible Asset - Deferred Pension Cost   xxxx
>   *Additional Pension Liability   xxxx
> *To record additional pension liability*

*Because the minimum liability must be computed each year, in some years the accounts in this entry will be increased (as in this entry), while in other years the balances in the accounts may need to be decreased.

13000.1.2.2.2   **Additional Liability Is Greater than Unrecognized Prior Service Cost**

> Intangible Asset - Deferred Pension Cost   xxxx
> *Excess Of Additional Pension Liability Over
>   Unrecognized Prior Service Cost   xxxx
>   Additional Pension Liability   xxxx
> *To record additional pension liability*

*This debit is needed only when the additional pension liability amount exceeds the amount of the balance of Unrecognized Prior Service Cost plus any unrecognized transition loss. Because the minimum liability must be computed each year, in some years the accounts in this entry will be increased, while in other years the balances in the accounts may be decreased.

13000.1.2.3   **Example Illustrating Use of the Pension Worksheet**

Assume the partial pension worksheet provided on the following page is to be used to develop the required journal entries. All numbers are assumed (not calculated) for the purpose of this illustration.

Pension Plan Worksheet

Item	Journal Entries						Disclosure Amounts			
	Annual Pension Expense (1)	Cash (2)	Prepaid/ Accrued Pension Cost (3)	Additional Liability (4)	Pension Intangible (5)	Contra Equity (6)	Plan Assets (7)	Projected Benefit Obligation (8)	Unrecognized Prior Service Cost (9)	Unrecognized Net Gain or Loss (10)
(a) Beginning Balances										
(b) Prior Service Cost (PSC)										
Beginning balances restated [total of line (a) + line (b)]										
(c) Current Service Cost										
(d) Interest on Obligation										
(e) Actual Return on Plan Assets										
(f) Amortization of Unrecognized PSC										
(g) Unexpected Loss/Gain on Plan Assets										
(h) Amortization of Unrecognized Net Loss/Gain			FOR PURPOSES OF ILLUSTRATION — NOT ALL FIGURES ARE SHOWN							
(i) Annual Contribution										
(j) Benefits Paid to Retirees										
(k) Increase/Decrease in Obligation										
Pension expense journal entry:	9,999 Dr.	6,666 Cr.	3,333 Cr.							
(l) Minimum Liability Adjustment			5,555 Cr.	5,555 Cr.	4,500 Dr.	1,055 Dr.				
End of year balances			7,777 Cr.	5,555 Cr.	4,500 Dr.	1,055 Dr.	12,000 Dr.	27,777 Dr.	4,500 Dr.	3,500 Dr.

400

Important: Make sure all appropriate subheads apply to your entry (see page v for instructions)

13000.1   **Pension Plans**
13000.1.2   **Defined Benefit Pension Plan**
13000.1.2.3   **Example Illustrating Use of the Pension Worksheet**

Pension Expense	9,999	
Cash		6,666
*Prepaid/Accrued Pension Cost		3,333

To record pension expense

*Prepaid/Accrued Pension Cost is credited because pension expense exceeded the cash contribution.

**Intangible Asset - Deferred Pension Cost	4,500	
***Excess Of Additional Pension Liability Over		
Unrecognized Prior Service Cost	1,055	
Additional Pension Liability		5,555

To record additional pension liability

**The amount cannot be more than the balance of Unrecognized Prior Service Cost (Column 9, $4,500).

***In this plan, the additional pension liability end of year balance exceeds the end of year balance in Unrecognized Prior Service Cost. Therefore, a portion of the additional liability is recognized as an asset (similar to goodwill), and the remainder is charged against stockholders' equity ($5,555 - $4,500 = $1,055).

13000.2   **Postretirement Benefits Other than Pensions**

Postretirement benefits other than pensions include health care and other welfare benefits provided to retirees and their spouses, dependents, and beneficiaries. As in the case of pensions, firms must measure their postretirement benefit obligation and accrue an appropriate amount of cost during the years that employees provide services.

13000.2.1   **Recording Current Period Postretirement Expense**

The amount of current period postretirement expense is affected by the following items:

Important: Make sure all appropriate subheads apply to your entry (see page v for instructions)

13000.2　　　　　　　**Postretirement Benefits Other than Pensions**
13000.2.1　　　　　　　**Recording Current Period Postretirement Expense**

---

(1) *Service Cost* - This is the portion of the Expected Postretirement Benefit Obligation (EPBO) applicable to the service provided by employees during the current period. The EPBO is the actuarial present value of all postretirement benefits that must be paid in the future.

(2) *Interest Cost* - Interest must be recognized on the Accumulated Postretirement Benefit Obligation (APBO). The APBO is the actuarial present value of future benefits attributed to employees' services performed up to the current date.

(3) *Actual Return On Plan Assets* - This is the actual increase or decrease in the plan's assets resulting from interest, dividends, and changes in market value.

(4) *Amortization Of Unrecognized Prior Service Cost* - If the plan gives employees retroactive credit for services performed prior to the date the plan is adopted or amended, the Expected Postretirement Benefit Obligation is increased. The cost of these retroactive benefits must be amortized.

(5) *Gain Or Loss* - These gains and losses are changes in the APBO resulting from changes in actuarial assumptions and differences between actual and expected returns on plan assets.

(6) *Amortization Of Transition Obligation* - A transition amount is computed at the beginning of the year of adoption of FAS 106 (the accounting standard prescribing the treatment of postretirement benefits). The transition amount is the difference between the APBO and the fair value of the plan assets. The fair value of the plan assets is adjusted for any accrued obligation (added to the fair value) or prepaid costs (subtracted from the fair value).

As with pensions, the accounting for postretirement benefits is complex because the FASB chose not to formally recognize in the books several items that affect the determination of current period postretirement expense. In addition, even though not recorded in the books, these items still have to be disclosed in the notes to the financial statements. Therefore, many firms use the same worksheet approach described in *GEN13000.1.2.3*. The worksheet format recommended by Paul D.W. Miller (*Journal of Accountancy*, February 1987, pp. 86-94) is used to develop the required journal entries illustrated below.

In the worksheet on the following page, Columns 1-3 are items that are formally recognized in the books. Columns 4-8 are amounts needed for disclosure in financial statements.

Postretirement Benefits Worksheet

Item	Journal Entries					Disclosure Amounts		
	Annual Postretirement Expense (1)	Cash (2)	Prepaid/Accrued Postretirement Cost (3)	Accumulated Postretirement Benefit Obligations (4)	Plan Assets (5)	Unrecognized Transition Amount (6)	Unrecognized Prior Service Cost (7)	Unrecognized Net Gain or Loss (8)
(a) Beginning Balances			xxxx Dr./Cr.	xxxx Cr.	xxxx Dr.	xxxx Dr.	xxxx Dr.	xxxx Dr.
(b) Prior Service Cost (PSC)				xxxx Cr.			xxxx Dr.	
Beginning balances restated [total of line (a) + line (b)]								
(c) Current Service Cost	xxxx Dr.			xxxx Cr.				
(d) Interest on Obligation	xxxx Dr.			xxxx Cr.				
(e) Actual Return on Plan Assets	xxxx Cr.				xxxx Dr.			
(f) Amortization of Unrecognized PSC	xxxx Dr.						xxxx Cr.	
(g) Unexpected Loss/Gain on Plan Assets	xxxx Dr./Cr.							xxxx Dr./Cr.
(h) Amortization of Transition Amount	xxxx Dr./Cr.					xxxx Cr		
(i) Annual Contribution		xxxx Cr.			xxxx Dr.			
(j) Benefits Paid to Retirees				xxxx Dr.	xxxx Cr.			
(k) Increase/Decrease in Obligation				xxxx Dr./Cr.				xxxx Dr./Cr.
Postretirement benefits expense journal entry								
End of year balances	xxxx	xxxx	xxxx	xxxx Cr.	xxxx Dr.	xxxx	xxxx Dr.	xxxx

Each entry (item) included in the worksheet is described on pages 402 through 403.

Important: Make sure all appropriate subheads apply to your entry (see page v for instructions)

13000.2   **Postretirement Benefits Other than Pensions**
13000.2.1   **Recording Current Period Postretirement Expense**

(a) This entry establishes the unrecognized transition amount and the related Accumulated Postretirement Benefit Obligation (APBO).

(b) This entry recognizes the increase in the APBO that occurs when employees are granted retroactive credit for services rendered prior to the date the credit is granted (either the date of plan adoption or plan amendment). Prior Service Cost is amortized over the period beginning on the date that the credit is effective to the date that the employees are fully eligible to receive benefits.

(c) This entry recognizes the actuarial present value of benefits earned by employees during the current period.

(d) This entry accrues interest on the APBO. The amount of interest is found by multiplying the beginning of the year APBO (adjusted for benefit payments expected to be made during the year) by the beginning of the year discount rate (i.e., a rate comparable to that earned on currently available high-quality, fixed-income investments).

(e) This entry recognizes the actual return earned on plan assets during the period and is found as follows:

Plan Assets, End of Year Fair Value	xxxx
Less: Plan Assets, Beginning of Year Fair Value	(xxxx)
Increase (Decrease) in Plan Assets Fair Value	xxxx
Plus: Benefits Paid During the Year	xxxx
Less: Annual Contribution to the Plan	(xxxx)
Actual Return on Plan Assets	xxxx

The above worksheet entry assumes a positive actual return (i.e., postretirement expense is decreased). If the actual return is negative (i.e., postretirement expense is increased), the entry is reversed, and Postretirement Expense is debited on the worksheet and Plan Assets is credited.

(f) This entry recognizes the amortization of unrecognized prior service cost. Prior service cost is generally amortized over the remaining service periods of covered employees (i.e., until they are fully eligible for the benefits).

Important: Make sure all appropriate subheads apply to your entry (see page v for instructions)

13000.2   **Postretirement Benefits Other than Pensions**
13000.2.1   **Recording Current Period Postretirement Expense**

(g) Unexpected gains or losses from differences in actual and expected returns on plan assets and from changes in the APBO due to actuarial assumptions may be recognized entirely in the current period or may be deferred or amortized based on a corridor approach similar to that used for pensions. (*See GEN13000.1.2.1.*) Unrecognized Net Gain Or Loss must be amortized when the beginning balance exceeds 10% of the larger of the beginning balances of the APBO or the market-related value of the plan assets. If the corridor is exceeded, then the minimum amount that must be amortized is the excess (i.e., the amount outside the corridor) divided by the average remaining service life to expected retirement of all active employees. This entry illustrates the amortization of a loss.

(h) This entry illustrates the amortization of the unrecognized transition amount. Employers may choose to immediately recognize the transition amount or to defer the amount and amortize it over the remaining service period to expected retirement of the employees who are employed at the time of transition and who are expected to receive benefits. Amortization must be computed on a straight-line basis. If the remaining service period is less than 20 years, a 20-year period may be used. In any case, the transition amount may not be amortized more slowly than it is actually paid off.

(i) This entry recognizes the firm's annual contribution to the plan.

(j) This entry recognizes the benefits paid to retirees under the plan during the period.

(k) This entry recognizes an increase in the APBO resulting from changes in the actuarial assumptions of the plan. If changes in the assumptions resulted in an unexpected decrease in the obligation balance, the APBO would be debited on the worksheet and Unrecognized Net Gain Or Loss would be credited.

Once the worksheet has been completed, the formal journal entry can be developed. First, compute sums for worksheet Columns 1 and 2. Next, using Columns 1-3 of the worksheet, develop the necessary journal entry for the current period postretirement expense as illustrated in the example provided below. Then, compute the ending balances in Columns 3-8. The balance in Prepaid/Accrued Postretirement Cost (Column 3) should equal the net balance in the disclosure entries (Columns 4-8). Finally, make a formal journal entry for the current period postretirement expense. See the example given in *GEN13000.2.2* provided below.

Important: Make sure all appropriate subheads apply to your entry (see page v for instructions)

13000.2   **Postretirement Benefits Other than Pensions**
13000.2.1   **Recording Current Period Postretirement Expense**

Postretirement Expense	xxxx	
Cash		xxxx
*Prepaid/Accrued Pension Cost		xxxx

To record postretirement plan expense

*When the year's Postretirement Expense exceeds the cash contribution, Prepaid/Accrued Postretirement Cost is credited for the difference and a credit balance represents a liability. If the cash contribution exceeds the current period postretirement expense, then this account is debited for the difference and a debit balance represents an asset.

13000.2.2   **Example Illustrating Use of the Postretirement Benefits Worksheet**

Assume the partial postretirement benefits worksheet provided on the following page is to be used to develop the required journal entry. All numbers are assumed (not calculated) for the purpose of this illustration.

Postretirement Expense	6,666	
Cash		4,444
*Prepaid/Accrued Postretirement Benefits Cost		2,222

To record postretirement benefits cost

*Prepaid/Accrued Postretirement Benefits Cost is credited because postretirement expense exceeded the cash contribution.

Postretirement Benefits Worksheet

Item	Annual Postretirement Expense (1)	Cash (2)	Journal Entries — Prepaid/Accrued Postretirement Cost (3)	Accumulated Postretirement Benefit Obligations (4)	Plan Assets (5)	Disclosure Amounts — Unrecognized Transition Amount (6)	Unrecognized Prior Service Cost (7)	Unrecognized Net Gain or Loss (8)
(a) Beginning Balances								
(b) Prior Service Cost (PSC)								
Beginning balances restated [total of line (a) + line (b)]								
(c) Current Service Cost								
(d) Interest on Obligation								
(e) Actual Return on Plan Assets								
(f) Amortization of Unrecognized PSC								
(g) Unexpected Loss/Gain on Plan Assets								
(h) Amortization of Transition Amount								
(i) Annual Contribution								
(j) Benefits Paid to Retirees								
(k) Increase/Decrease in Obligation								
Postretirement Benefits Expense								
journal entry	6,666 Dr.	4,444 Cr.	2,222 Cr.					
End of year balances			9,999 Cr.	43,999 Cr.	6,000 Dr.	19,000 Dr.	5,000 Dr.	4,000 Dr.

FOR PURPOSES OF ILLUSTRATION — NOT ALL FIGURES ARE SHOWN

TABLE OF CONTENTS

GEN14000   LEASES

14000.1

Lease Provisions

A lease is a contract under which an owner (lessor) grants the right to use property to a renter (lessee) for one or more rental payments. Lease provisions (e.g., duration, amount of lease payment, liability for taxes, insurance, maintenance, lessee restrictions, rights upon termination or default) vary widely from contract to contract. A lease that transfers substantially all of the benefits and risks of ownership to the lessee should be capitalized. Leases that do not transfer substantially all of the benefits and risks of ownership to the lessee are operating leases.

14000.2

Operating Leases

A lease agreement that fails to transfer substantially all of the benefits and risks of ownership is an operating lease. All leases that are not capital leases are operating leases.

14000.2.1

Accounting by Lessee - Operating Leases

14000.2.1.1

Recording by Lessee of Rent Expense for Operating Lease

Rent Expense	xxxx	
*Cash (Prepaid Rent, Rent Payable)		xxxx
To record rent expense		

*The account credited depends on whether or not other entries have preceded this one. If payment is being made, the credit is to Cash. Otherwise, the credit is to a previously established asset (Prepaid Rent) or liability (Rent Payable).

Important: Make sure all appropriate subheads apply to your entry (see page v for instructions)

14000.2   **Operating Leases**

14000.2.2   ## Accounting by Lessor - Operating Leases

14000.2.2.1   ### Recording by Lessor of Rental Income (Rental Revenue) for Operating Lease

*Cash (Rent Receivable, Unearned Rental Income)	xxxx	
Rental Income (Rental Revenue)		xxxx
To record rent earned		

*The account debited depends on whether cash is received at the time this entry is made and whether other entries have preceded this one. If cash is received at the time of this entry, the debit is to Cash. If cash has not yet been received, the debit is to Rent Receivable. If cash was previously received and at that time Unearned Rental Income was credited, Unearned Rental Income is now debited.

14000.2.2.2   ### Recording by Lessor of Ownership Costs of Property Leased to Others

*Property Tax Expense	xxxx	
*Insurance Expense	xxxx	
*Maintenance Expense	xxxx	
*[Various Expenses]	xxxx	
Cash		xxxx
*[Various Liabilities]		xxxx
To record ownership costs of property leased to others		

*Various other expenses and liabilities may be debited or credited. Individual expenses will probably be recorded in individual entries rather than all in one entry as illustrated here.

14000.2.2.3   ### Recording Depreciation Expense on Property Leased to Others

*Depreciation Expense - Leased [Various Property]	xxxx	
Accumulated Depreciation - Leased [Various Property]		xxxx
To record depreciation of leased property		

*Depreciation is computed and recorded in the same way as it is for similar non-leased assets.

Important: Make sure all appropriate subheads apply to your entry (see page v for instructions)

14000.2   **Operating Leases**
14000.2.2   **Accounting by Lessor - Operating Leases**

14000.2.2.4   **Impairment of Value of Property Leased to Others Under Operating Leases**

If the value of property leased to others under an operating lease has been impaired, an impairment loss is recognized.

*Loss Due To Impairment Of Leased Property	xxxx	
Accumulated Depreciation - [Leased Property]		xxxx

To record loss due to impairment of leased property

*The loss recognized is the excess of the asset's carrying value over its fair market value, if known, or its discounted net future cash flow. *See GEN5000.5.1.*

14000.2.2.5   **Recording Initial Direct Costs of Operating Lease - Lessor**

Initial direct costs are the expenditures or expenses associated with originating a lease contract. They may include legal fees, appraisal costs, costs of credit investigations, commissions, processing costs, and costs of negotiating and closing the lease agreement.

Deferred Initial Direct Leasing Costs	xxxx	
Cash ([Various Liabilities])		xxxx

To record initial direct costs of an operating lease

*Rental Income (Rental Revenue)	xxxx	
*Deferred Initial Direct Leasing Costs		xxxx

To record amortization of initial direct leasing costs

*Initial direct leasing costs are allocated over the term of the lease in proportion to the rental income recognized. An alternative to debiting Rental Income (Rental Revenue) is to debit Amortization Of Initial Direct Leasing Costs.

14000.3   **Capital Leases**

Capital leases transfer substantially all of the benefits and risks of ownership to the lessee. If a lease is a capital lease, the lessee recognizes an asset and related liability, and the lessor records the lease as a sale.

Important: Make sure all appropriate subheads apply to your entry (see page v for instructions)

14000.3 **Capital Leases**

14000.3.1

Accounting by Lessee - Capital Leases

A noncancellable lease meeting *one or more* of the following criteria at inception must be classified and accounted for as a capital lease (FASB Statement 13, par. 7):

   a. the lease agreement transfers ownership of the property to the lessee at the end of the lease term;

   b. the lease agreement contains a bargain purchase option;

   c. the lease term is equal to 75% or more of the estimated economic life of the leased property; or

   d. the present value at the beginning of the lease term of the minimum lease payments (excluding executory costs included in the payments) equals or exceeds 90% of the fair value of the leased property.

However, criteria *c* and *d* do not apply when the lease inception occurs during the last 25% of the asset's economic life or for leases of land.

14000.3.1.1

Recording a Capital Lease by Lessee at Date of Inception

The lessee capitalizes a leased asset at *the lower of* the present value of the (discounted) minimum lease payments (excluding executory costs included in the payments; i.e., ownership costs such as maintenance, insurance, taxes) or the asset's fair market value. Minimum lease payments include the following items (FASB Statement 13, par. 5j):

   a. minimum rental payments - the minimum periodic payment the lessee is obligated to make;

   b. guaranteed residual value - the amount the lessor is guaranteed to realize (either from the lessee or from sale of the leased property to another party) at the end of the lease term exclusive of amounts owed due to excessive wear and tear, damage, etc., to the leased asset. Any unguaranteed residual value is not included in the minimum lease payments;

   c. penalty for failure to renew or extend the lease - the amount payable to the lessor when the lessee fails to renew or extend a lease as required by the lease agreement;

   d. bargain purchase option - the price at which the lessee may purchase the leased asset after the date the option becomes exercisable or at the end of the lease term. To be a bargain purchase option, the option price must, at the time the lease is signed, be sufficiently below the expected fair value of the leased asset at the end of the lease term so that the lessee's exercise of the purchase option is reasonably assured.

Important: Make sure all appropriate subheads apply to your entry (see page v for instructions)

14000.3	**Capital Leases**
14000.3.1	**Accounting by Lessee - Capital Leases**
14000.3.1.1	**Recording a Capital Lease by Lessee at Date of Inception**

The minimum lease payments are found by multiplying the periodic lease payment (less executory costs) by the number of payments required. (For lessor's computation of the annual lease payment see *GEN14000.3.2.1.2* and *GEN14000.3.2.2.3*).

The present value of the minimum lease payments is determined by using the lower of (a) the lessee's incremental borrowing rate or (b) the implicit rate earned by the lessor (assuming the lessor's rate is known or can be determined). The lessee's incremental borrowing rate is the rate that the lessee would have to pay to borrow the funds to purchase the asset rather than lease it. The lessor's implicit rate is that rate equating the present value of the minimum lease payments and any unguaranteed residual value with the fair market value of the leased asset at the lease inception.

The amount to be capitalized and the amount of the lease liability depend on whether there is a guaranteed residual value.

The lease liability may be found as follows:

Amount of Periodic Lease Payment	xxxx
Less: Executory Costs Included in the Lease Payment	xxxx
Equals: Lease Payment Exclusive of Executory Costs	xxxx
Multiplied by: Present Value Interest Factor (from the Appropriate Annuity Due Table)	X factor
Equals: Present Value of Rental Payments	xxxx
Plus: Present Value of Any Guaranteed Residual Value *(see points 1 and 2 below)*	xxxx
Equals: Present Value of Minimum Lease Payments *(see point 3 below)*	xxxx

Three points need to be noted:

1. Only *graranteed* residual value increase the amount capitalized by the lessee.

2. If a capital lease has a bargain purchase option, the purchase option is accounted for like a guaranteed residual value. That is, the present value of the option price is added to the present value of the minimum lease payments.

3. A leased asset is not capitalized at more than its fair value at the date of inception.

Leased [Various Property] Under Capital Leases	xxxx	
Liability Under Capital Leases		xxxx
To record capital lease		

Important: Make sure all appropriate subheads apply to your entry (see page v for instructions)

14000.3	**Capital Leases**
14000.3.1	**Accounting by Lessee - Capital Leases**

14000.3.1.2   **Recording Lease Payments by Lessee Under a Capital Lease**

14000.3.1.2.1   **Recording the Initial Lease Payment at Lease Inception by Lessee Under a Capital Lease**

Most lease contracts require the lessee to make the first lease payment at the inception of the lease. This situation is referred to as an annuity due-type lease arrangement.

*[Various Expenses ([Various Prepaid Expenses])]	xxxx
Liability Under Capital Leases	xxxx
**Cash	xxxx

To record first lease payment under a capital lease

*If the lease payment includes amounts stipulated by the lease agreement to be applied to executory costs (e.g., property taxes, insurance, maintenance), such amounts are credited to the appropriate expense accounts (e.g., Property Tax Expense, Insurance Expense, Maintenance Expense) or prepaid expense accounts (e.g., Prepaid Property Tax, Prepaid Insurance, Prepaid Maintenance) when received.

**The amount of the lease payment is computed by the lessor and is stipulated in the lease. *See GEN14000.3.1.2.2* for further discussion.

14000.3.1.2.2   **Recording Lease Payments (Subsequent to Initial Payment at Lease Inception) by Lessee Under a Capital Lease**

*[Various Expenses ([Various Prepaid Expenses])]	xxxx
Liability Under Capital Leases	xxxx
**Interest Expense	xxxx
Cash	xxxx

To record lease payment under a capital lease

*If the lease payment includes amounts stipulated by the lease agreement to be applied to executory costs (e.g., property taxes, insurance, maintenance), such amounts are credited to the appropriate expense accounts (e.g., Property Tax Expense, Insurance Expense, Maintenance Expense) or prepaid expense accounts (e.g.,Prepaid Property Tax, Prepaid Insurance, Prepaid Maintenance) when received.

LEASES

Important: Make sure all appropriate subheads apply to your entry (see page v for instructions)

14000.3	**Capital Leases**
14000.3.1	**Accounting by Lessee - Capital Leases**
14000.3.1.2	**Recording Lease Payments by Lessee Under a Capital Lease**
14000.3.1.2.2	**Recording Lease Payments (Subsequent to Initial Payment at Lease Inception) by Lessee Under a Capital Lease**

**The effective interest method (shown below) must be used to allocate each lease payment between principal and interest. The interest rate should be the same as that used in *GEN14000.3.1.1*. The existence of any guaranteed residual value will also affect the amount of interest expense that is recognized by the lessee. The following schedules may be used to compute the interest expense on the unpaid lease liability:

Unguaranteed Residual Value:
(Steps to complete the schedules are given below.)

Date	Periodic Lease Payments (1)	Executory Costs (2)	Interest on Unpaid Liability (3)	Reduction of Liability (4)	Lease Liability Balance (5)
Beg. Bal.					xxxx
mm/dd/yy	xxxx	xxxx	xxxx	xxxx	xxxx
mm/dd/yy	xxxx	xxxx	xxxx	xxxx	xxxx
(Other dates, etc.)					
mm/dd/yy	xxxx	xxxx	xxxx	xxxx	-0-

Guaranteed Residual Value (GRV):
(Steps to complete the schedules are given below.

Date	Periodic Lease Payments and GRV (1)	Executory Costs (2)	Interest on Unpaid Liability (3)	Reduction of Liability (4)	Lease Liability Balance (5)
Beg. Bal.					xxxx
mm/dd/yy	xxxx	xxxx	xxxx	xxxx	xxxx
mm/dd/yy	xxxx	xxxx	xxxx	xxxx	xxxx
(Other dates, etc.)					
GRV	xxxx	-0-	xxxx	xxxx	-0-

LEASES

Important: Make sure all appropriate subheads apply to your entry (see page v for instructions)

14000.3   **Capital Leases**
14000.3.1   **Accounting by Lessee - Capital Leases**
14000.3.1.2   **Recording Lease Payments by Lessee Under a Capital Lease**
14000.3.1.2.2   **Recording Lease Payments (Subsequent to Initial Payment at Lease Inception) by Lessee Under a Capital Lease**

Steps to complete these schedules are as follows:

1. Enter the beginning balance of the lease liability (the amount capitalized by the lessee) in Column 5. The amount will be different in each sched-ule depending on whether a residual value is guaranteed.
2. Enter the periodic lease payment amounts in Column 1.
3. Enter any executory costs included in the lease payments in Column 2.
4. Enter the appropriate amount of interest on the unpaid lease liability in Column 3. The interest amount is found by multiplying the preceding period's ending balance of the lease liability (Column 5, last period) by the same interest rate used to compute the present value of the minimum lease payments.
5. Enter the amount of each lease payment that goes toward liability reduction in Column 4. The amount is found by subtracting the amounts in Columns 2 and 3 for the period from the amount in Column 1 for the period.
6. Enter the amount of the remaining lease liability in Column 5. This amount is found by subtracting the amount of the lease liability reduction for a period (Column 4) from the previous lease liability balance (i.e., from the balance in Column 5 for the previous period).
7. If any part of the residual value is guaranteed, enter the guaranteed amount as an additional payment in Column 1 as of the end of the lease term. Interest is computed on the payment as described above.

The amount of interest to be recognized each period may be found by referring to Column 3 of the schedule. If the accounting period does not fall on a lease payment date, then interest expense should be accrued for the period since interest expense was last recognized.

14000.3.1.3   ### Recording Periodic Depreciation Expense on the Leased Asset

> *Depreciation Expense - Capital Leases   xxxx
>   Accumulated Depreciation - Capital Leases   xxxx
>   *To record depreciation expense*

*The leased asset should be depreciated in the same manner as other similar assets owned by the lessee. The leased asset should be depreciated over its economic life if

Important: Make sure all appropriate subheads apply to your entry (see page v for instructions)

14000.3	**Capital Leases**	
14000.3.1	**Accounting by Lessee - Capital Leases**	
14000.3.1.3	**Recording Periodic Depreciation Expense on the Leased Asset**	

---

the lease agreement transfers ownership to the lessee or includes a bargain purchase option. Otherwise, it should be depreciated over the term of the lease.

14000.3.1.4

Recording Executory Costs Not Included in Lease Payment (Paid Separately by Lessee)

*Property Tax Expense	XXXX	
*Insurance Expense	XXXX	
*Maintenance Expense	XXXX	
*[Various Expenses]	XXXX	
Cash ([Various Prepaid Expenses])		XXXX
*[Various Liabilities]		XXXX

To record executory costs on a capital lease

*Various other expenses and liabilities may be debited or credited. Individual expenses will probably be recorded in individual entries rather than all in one entry as illustrated here.

14000.3.1.5

Recording Disposition or Acquisition of Leased Asset

At the end of the lease term, the lessee may return the leased asset to or may pur-chase it from the lessor. Purchase of the leased asset is likely if the lease includes a bargain purchase option.

A lessee may occasionally purchase a leased asset prior to the end of the lease. In that case, the carrying value of the lease liability should be adjusted by any differ-ence between the purchase price and the balance of the lease liability.

14000.3.1.5.1

Return of Leased Asset to Lessor at End of Lease - Lease Includes a Guaranteed Residual Value

*Accumulated Depreciation - Capital Leases	XXXX	
*Interest Expense	XXXX	
*Liability Under Capital Leases	XXXX	
*Leased Asset Under Capital Leases		XXXX

To record return of leased asset at the end of the lease term

Important: Make sure all appropriate subheads apply to your entry (see page v for instructions)

14000.3 **Capital Leases**
14000.3.1 **Accounting by Lessee - Capital Leases**
14000.3.1.5 **Recording Disposition or Acquisition of Leased Asset**
14000.3.1.5.1 **Return of Leased Asset to Lessor at End of Lease - Lease Includes a Guaranteed Residual Value**

**Loss On Capital Leases	xxxx
**Cash	xxxx

To record loss from guarantee of residual value

*Accumulated Depreciation and Leased Asset Under Capital Leases will not have equal credit and debit balances when there is a guaranteed residual value. The difference between the balances in the two accounts is the asset's book value, which then represents the guaranteed residual value. In the interest amortization schedule shown in *GEN14000.3.1.2.2*, the return of the leased asset with a guaranteed residual value is treated as a final lease payment and is allocated to Interest Expense and Liability Under Capital Leases. See the lease payment amortization schedule given in *GEN14000.3.1.2.2* to determine the amounts to be debited to Interest Expense and Liability Under Capital Leases.

 **If the fair value of the leased asset returned is less than the guaranteed residual value, the lessee may have to pay the difference. If so, a loss account must be debited and Cash credited. If the asset's fair value exceeds the guaranteed residual value, the lease may provide for a refund to be paid the lessee by the lessor. If this occurs, Cash would be debited and Gain On Capital Leases would be credited.

14000.3.1.5.2 **Return of Leased Asset to Lessor at End of Lease - Nonguaranteed Residual Value**

Assuming the leased asset has been fully depreciated and the lease liability fully paid, all that remains is to remove the asset and accumulated depreciation from the books. (Costs of removal and return of the leased asset should be charged to expense as incurred.)

Accumulated Depreciation - Capital Leases	xxxx
Leased Asset Under Capital Leases	xxxx

To record return of leased asset at the end of the lease term

14000.3.1.5.3 **Recording by Lessee of Purchase of Leased Asset from Lessor at End of Lease**

An entry is needed to transfer the balance from the leased asset account to the appropriate long-term asset account and transfer the balance from the accumulated depreciation on capital leases to accumulated depreciation on the owned asset as follows:

LEASES

Important: Make sure all appropriate subheads apply to your entry (see page v for instructions)

14000.3	**Capital Leases**
14000.3.1	**Accounting by Lessee - Capital Leases**
14000.3.1.5	**Recording Disposition or Acquisition of Leased Asset**
14000.3.1.5.3	**Recording by Lessee of Purchase of Leased Asset from Lessor at End of Lease**

*Machinery ([Various Assets])	xxxx	
Accumulated Depreciation - Capital Leases	xxxx	
Leased Asset Under Capital Leases		xxxx
Accumulated Depreciation - Machinery ([Various Assets])		xxxx
Cash		xxxx

To record purchase of leased asset at end of the lease term

*The appropriate asset account (e.g., Land, Vehicles, Equipment) should be debited for the sum of the credit balance in Leased Asset Under Capital Leases and the credit to Cash.

14000.3.2   **Accounting by Lessor - Capital Leases**

If, at the inception of the lease, the lease agreement meets one or more of the first four of the following criteria and both of the criteria in 5 and 6, then the lease must be capitalized and classified by the lessor as either a direct financing or a sales-type capital lease (FASB Statement No. 13, par. 7):

1. The lease agreement transfers ownership of the property to the lessee by the end of the lease term.

2. The lease agreement contains a bargain purchase option.

3. The lease term is equal to 75% or more of the estimated economic life of the leased property (not applicable to an asset leased during the last 25% of its economic life).

4. The present value of the minimum lease payments (excluding executory costs) equals or exceeds 90% of the fair value of the leased property.

5. Collectibility of the lease payments is reasonably predictable.

6. There are no significant uncertainties surrounding the amount of unreimbursable costs yet to be incurred by the lessor under the lease contract.

14000.3.2.1   **Direct Financing Capital Leases**

Direct Financing leases do not include any manufacturer's or dealer's profit. That is, the leased asset's fair value and cost to the lessor are substantially equal.

Important: Make sure all appropriate subheads apply to your entry (see page v for instructions)

14000.3   **Capital Leases**
14000.3.2   **Accounting by Lessor - Capital Leases**
14000.3.2.1   **Direct Financing Capital Leases**

14000.3.2.1.1   **Recording a Direct Financing Lease at Inception - Lessor**

*Lease Payments Receivable	xxxx	
**Equipment ([Various Assets])		xxxx
***Unearned Interest Revenue - Leases		xxxx

To record a direct financing capital lease by the lessor

*Lease Payments Receivable is debited for the lease investment, which is the sum of the minimum lease payments and any unguaranteed residual value at the end of the lease term. Because the amount of the minimum lease payments includes any guaranteed residual value (see the discussion in *GEN14000.3.1.1*), the inclusion of any unguaranteed residual value in the lease payment receivable results in the full residual value amount (whether or not guaranteed) being included in the lease payments. If the lessor pays any executory costs (e.g., maintenance, insurance, property taxes), the rental payment (a component of the minimum lease payments amount) should be reduced by the amount of executory costs paid. Finally, any initial direct costs incurred in originating the lease contract (e.g., legal fees, appraisal costs, credit investigations, commissions, processing costs, and negotiation and closing costs) should be added to the net investment amount.

**The leased asset is removed from the books.

***The credit to Unearned Interest Revenue (a liability) is found by subtracting the fair value of the leased asset from the Lease Payments Receivable debit. Unearned Interest Revenue is amortized over the lease term using the effective interest method *(see GEN14000.3.2.1.3)*. On the balance sheet, Lease Payments Receivable will be reported net of the unearned interest revenue.

14000.3.2.1.2   **Recording Initial Lease Payment Under a Direct Financing Capital Lease at Lease Inception by Lessor**

Most lease contracts require the lessee to make the first lease payment at the inception of the lease. This situation is referred to as an annuity-due-type lease arrangement.

Important: Make sure all appropriate subheads apply to your entry (see page v for instructions)

14000.3	**Capital Leases**
14000.3.2	**Accounting by Lessor - Capital Leases**
14000.3.2.1	**Direct Financing Capital Leases**
14000.3.2.1.2	**Recording Initial Lease Payment Under a Direct Financing Capital Lease at Lease Inception by Lessor**

---

*Cash	xxxx	
**[Various Expenses] ([Various Prepaid Expenses])		xxxx
***Lease Payments Receivable		xxxx

To record receipt of first lease payment under a direct financing lease

*The amount of the lease payment is found as follows:

Amount to Be Recovered by the Lessor	xxxx
Divided by: Present Value Interest Factor (from the Appropriate Annuity Due Table)	/ factor
Equals: Lease Payment Required	<u>xxxx</u>

The amount to be recovered by the lessor is the fair market value of the leased asset reduced by the present value of any residual value accruing to the lessor. The present value of the residual value is found as follows:

Residual Value of Leased Asset	xxxx
Multiplied by: Present Value Interest Factor (from the Appropriate Present Value of $1 Table)	X factor
Equals: Present Value of Leased Asset Residual Value	<u>xxxx</u>

If the lease contract requires the lessee to pay executory costs, the lease payment is increased by the amount specified.

**If the lease payment includes amounts stipulated by the lease agreement to be applied to executory costs (e.g., property taxes, insurance, maintenance), such amounts are credited to the appropriate expense accounts (e.g., Property Tax Expense, Insurance Expense, Maintenance Expense) or prepaid expense accounts (e.g., Prepaid Property Tax, Prepaid Insurance, Prepaid Maintenance) when received.

***Lease Payments Receivable is reduced by the difference between the total lease payment amount and the executory costs included in the lease payment.

LEASES

Important: Make sure all appropriate subheads apply to your entry (see page v for instructions)

14000.3   **Capital Leases**
14000.3.2   **Accounting by Lessor - Capital Leases**
14000.3.2.1   **Direct Financing Capital Leases**

14000.3.2.1.3   **Recording Receipt of Lease Payments (Subsequent to Receipt of Initial Payment at Lease Inception) by Lessor Under a Direct Financing Capital Lease**

Cash	xxxx
Lease Payments Receivable	xxxx
[Various Expenses]	xxxx

To record receipt of lease payment under a direct financing lease

Unearned Interest Revenue - Leases	xxxx
*Interest Revenue - Leases	xxxx

To record interest revenue

*The effective interest method must be used to allocate each lease payment between principal and interest. The schedule provided below may be used to compute the interest revenue on the net lease investment. A single schedule works for both a guaranteed and an unguaranteed residual value because the amount of the lessor's net investment is the same in either case.

Date	Periodic Lease Payment and Residual Value (1)	Executory Costs (2)	Interest on Net Investment (3)	Net Investment Recovery (4)	Net Investment Balance (5)
Balance					xxxx
mm/dd/yy	xxxx	xxxx	xxxx	xxxx	xxxx
mm/dd/yy	xxxx	xxxx	xxxx	xxxx	xxxx
(Other dates, etc.)					
Residual Value	xxxx	-0-	xxxx	xxxx	-0-

Steps to complete this schedule are as follows:

> 1. Enter the beginning net lease investment in Column 5. The amount is the same regardless of whether or not the residual value is guaranteed.

Important: Make sure all appropriate subheads apply to your entry (see page v for instructions)

14000.3   **Capital Leases**
14000.3.2   **Accounting by Lessor - Capital Leases**
14000.3.2.1   **Direct Financing Capital Leases**
14000.3.2.1.3   **Recording Receipt of Lease Payments (Subsequent to Receipt of Initial Payment at Lease Inception) by Lessor Under a Direct Financing Capital Lease**

---

2. Enter the periodic lease payment amounts in Column 1.

3. Enter any executory costs included in the lease payment in Column 2.

4. Enter the appropriate amount of interest earned on the net lease investment in Column 3. The interest amount is found by multiplying the preceding balance of the net lease investment (Column 5, last period) by the same interest rate used to compute the present value of the minimum lease payments.

5. Enter the amount of each lease payment that goes toward investment recovery in Column 4. The amount is found by subtracting the amounts in Columns 2 and 3 for the period from the amount in Column 1 for the period.

6. Enter the amount of the remaining net lease investment in Column 5. This amount is found by subtracting the lease recovery amount for a period (Column 4) from the previous net lease investment balance (i.e., from the balance in Column 5 for the previous period).

7. Enter the residual value (whether or not guaranteed) as an additional payment in Column 1 at the end of the lease term. Interest is computed on the payment in the same way as described above.

The amount of interest revenue to be recognized each period may be found by referring to Column 3 of the schedule. If the accounting period does not fall on a date that a lease payment is received, then interest revenue must be accrued for the period since interest revenue was last recognized.

14000.3.2.1.4   **Recording Disposition or Reacquisition (Return) of Leased Asset**

At the end of the lease term the lessee may return the leased asset or may purchase it from the lessor. In either case, no balances will remain in the Lease Payments Receivable (after recording the receipt of the cash or return of the asset) and Unearned Interest Revenue accounts.

14000.3.2.1.5   **Recording Reacquisition (Return) of Leased Asset at End of Lease Term**

Important: Make sure all appropriate subheads apply to your entry (see page v for instructions)

14000.3	**Capital Leases**
14000.3.2	**Accounting by Lessor - Capital Leases**
14000.3.2.1	**Direct Financing Capital Leases**
14000.3.2.1.5	**Recording Reacquisition (Return) of Leased Asset at End of Lease Term**

14000.3.2.1.5.1

Recording Reacquisition (Return) of Leased Asset at End of Lease Term - Residual Value Originally Included in Lease Payments Receivable

*Equipment ([Various Assets])	xxxx
**Accumulated Depreciation - Equipment [(Various Assets])	xxxx
***Lease Payments Receivable	xxxx

To record return of leased asset at the end of the lease term

*Equipment (or other asset) is debited for the original cost of the asset leased.

**Accumulated Depreciation is credited for the difference between the original cost of the asset leased and the amount of residual value (guaranteed and unguaranteed) that was originally included in the total lease payments receivable.

***Lease Payments Receivable is credited sufficiently to remove any debit balance pertaining to the lease. This amount should equal the amount of residual value (guaranteed and unguaranteed) that was originally included in the total lease payments receivable.

14000.3.2.1.5.2

Recording Reacquisition (Return) of Leased Asset at End of Lease Term - No Residual Value Originally Included in Lease Payments Receivable

*Salvaged Rental Equipment ([Various Salvaged Rental Assets])	xxxx
*Gain On Salvaged Rental Equipment (Gain On Salvaged Rental [Various Assets])	xxxx

To record return of leased asset at the end of the lease term

*This entry is made for the amount of the fair value (if any) of the salvaged equipment. If the rental asset that is returned has no fair value, no entry is made.

14000.3.2.1.6

Recording Sale of Leased Asset to Lessee at End of Lease Term

LEASES

Important: Make sure all appropriate subheads apply to your entry (see page v for instructions)

14000.3	**Capital Leases**
14000.3.2	**Accounting by Lessor - Capital Leases**
14000.3.2.1	**Direct Financing Capital Leases**
14000.3.2.1.6	**Recording Sale of Leased Asset to Lessee at End of Lease Term**

14000.3.2.1.6.1 **Recording Sale of Leased Asset to Lessee at End of Lease Term - No Residual Value Originally Included in Lease Payments Receivable**

Cash	xxxx	
Gain On Sale Of Leased Asset		xxxx

To record sale of leased asset to lessee at end of the lease term

14000.3.2.1.6.2 **Recording Sale of Leased Asset to Lessee at End of Lease Term - Residual Value Originally Included in Lease Payments Receivable**

Cash	xxxx	
Lease Payments Receivable		xxxx
Gain On Sale Of Leased Asset		xxxx

To record sale of leased asset to lessee at end of the lease term

14000.3.2.2 **Sales-Type Capital Leases**

A sales-type lease includes a manufacturer's or dealer's profit. The amount of this profit is equal to the difference between (a) the present (discounted) value of the minimum lease payments and (b) the cost of the leased asset less the present value of any unguaranteed residual value.

14000.3.2.2.1 **Recording a Sales-Type Lease at Inception - Lessor**

*Cost Of Goods Sold	xxxx	
**Lease Payments Receivable	xxxx	
***Sales		xxxx
****Unearned Interest Revenue		xxxx
*****Inventory		xxxx

To record a sales-type capital lease by the lessor

*The debit to Cost Of Goods Sold is for the cost of goods sold less the present value of any unguaranteed residual value. This debit assumes the perpetual inventory method is used. If the periodic inventory method is used, Cost Of Goods Sold will

---

Important: Make sure all appropriate subheads apply to your entry (see page v for instructions)

14000.3	**Capital Leases**
14000.3.2	**Accounting by Lessor - Capital Leases**
14000.3.2.2	**Sales-Type Capital Leases**
14000.3.2.2.1	**Recording a Sales-Type Lease at Inception - Lessor**

---

not appear in this entry. *See GEN4000.1.1* and *GEN4000.1.2* for a discussion of periodic and perpetual inventory methods, respectively.

**The amount debited to Lease Payments Receivable is the sum of the minimum lease payments and any unguaranteed residual value at the end of the lease term.

Because the amount of the minimum lease payments includes any guaranteed residual value, the inclusion of any unguaranteed residual value in the lease payment receivable results in the full residual value amount (whether or not guaranteed) being included in the lease payments receivable. If the lessee pays any executory costs, the rental payment (a component of the minimum lease payments amount) should be reduced by the amount of executory costs included.

***Sales Revenue is credited for the sales price, which is equal to the present value of the annual rental payments plus the present value of any guaranteed residual value.

****The amount of Unearned Interest Revenue (a liability) is determined by subtracting the fair value of the leased asset from the Lease Payments Receivable amount. The unearned interest is amortized over the lease term using the effective interest method *(see GEN14000.3.2.2.4)*.

*****This credit assumes the perpetual inventory method is used. If the periodic inventory method is used, Inventory will not appear in this entry. *See GEN4000.1.1* and *GEN4000.1.2* for a discussion of periodic and perpetual inventory methods, respectively.

14000.3.2.2.2   **Recording Initial Direct Costs Associated with a Sales-Type Lease**

Initial direct costs are the costs associated with originating a lease contract. Initial direct costs include items such as legal fees, appraisal costs, credit investigations, commissions, processing costs, and negotiating and closing costs. For sales-type leases, these are expensed during the year of sale.

[Various Expenses]		xxxx
Cash		xxxx

To record initial direct costs associated with a sales-type lease

---

Important: Make sure all appropriate subheads apply to your entry (see page v for instructions)

14000.3   **Capital Leases**
14000.3.2   **Accounting by Lessor - Capital Leases**
14000.3.2.2   **Sales-Type Capital Leases**

14000.3.2.2.3   **Recording the Initial Lease Payment Under a Sales-Type Capital Lease at Lease Inception by a Lessor**

Most lease contracts require the lessee to make the first lease payment at the inception of the lease. This situation is referred to as an annuity-due-type lease arrangement.

*Cash	xxxx	
**[Various Expenses] ([Various Prepaid Expenses])		xxxx
***Lease Payments Receivable		xxxx
To record receipt of initial lease payment under a sales-type capital lease		

*The amount of the lease payment is determined as follows:

Amount to Be Recovered by the Lessor	xxxx
Divided by: Present Value Interest Factor (from the Appropriate Annuity Due Table)	/ factor
Equals: Lease Payment Required	<u>xxxx</u>

The amount to be recovered by the lessor is the fair market value of the leased asset reduced by the present value of any residual value accruing to the lessor. The present value of the residual value may be found as follows:

Residual Value of Leased Asset	xxxx
Multiplied by: Present Value Interest Factor (from the Appropriate Present Value of $1 Table)	X factor
Equals: Present Value Of Leased Asset Residual Value	<u>xxxx</u>

If the lease contract requires the lessee to pay executory costs, the lease payment is increased by the amount specified.

Important: Make sure all appropriate subheads apply to your entry (see page v for instructions)

14000.3	**Capital Leases**
14000.3.2	**Accounting by Lessor - Capital Leases**
14000.3.2.2	**Sales-Type Capital Leases**
14000.3.2.2.3	**Recording the Initial Lease Payment Under a Sales-Type Capital Lease at Lease Inception by a Lessor**

**If the lease payment includes amounts stipulated by the lease agreement to be applied to executory costs (e.g., property taxes, insurance, maintenance), such amounts are credited to the appropriate expense accounts (e.g., Property Tax Expense, Insurance Expense, Maintenance Expense) or prepaid expense accounts (e.g., Prepaid Property Tax, Prepaid Insurance, Prepaid Maintenance) when received.

***Lease Payments Receivable is reduced by the difference between the total lease payment amount and the executory costs included in the lease payment; i.e., it is credited to balance the entry.

14000.3.2.2.4   **Recording Receipt of Lease Payments (Subsequent to Receipt of Initial Payment at Lease Inception) by a Lessor Under a Sales-Type Capital Lease**

Cash	xxxx	
Lease Payments Receivable		xxxx
*[Various Expenses] ([Various Prepaid Expenses])		xxxx

To record receipt of a lease payment under a sales-type lease

*If the lease payment includes amounts stipulated by the lease agreement to be applied to executory costs (e.g., property taxes, insurance, maintenance), such amounts are credited to the appropriate expense accounts (e.g., Property Tax Expense, Insurance Expense, Maintenance Expense) or prepaid expense accounts (e.g., Prepaid Property Tax, Prepaid Insurance, Prepaid Maintenance) when received.

Unearned Interest Revenue	xxxx	
*Interest Revenue		xxxx

To record interest revenue

*The effective interest method must be used to allocate each lease payment between principal and interest. The schedule provided below may be used to compute the interest revenue on the net lease investment. A single schedule for the lessor works for both a guaranteed and an unguaranteed residual value because the amount of the lessor's net investment is the same in both cases.

LEASES

Important: Make sure all appropriate subheads apply to your entry (see page v for instructions)

14000.3	**Capital Leases**
14000.3.2	**Accounting by Lessor - Capital Leases**
14000.3.2.2	**Sales-Type Capital Leases**
14000.3.2.2.4	**Recording Receipt of Lease Payments (Subsequent to Receipt of Initial Payment at Lease Inception) by a Lessor Under a Sales-Type Capital Lease**

Date	Periodic Lease Payments and Residual Value (1)	Executory Costs (2)	Interest on Net Investment (3)	Net Investment Recovery (4)	Net Investment Balance (5)
Balance					xxxx
mm/dd/yy	xxxx	xxxx	xxxx	xxxx	xxxx
mm/dd/yy	xxxx	xxxx	xxxx	xxxx	xxxx
(Other dates, etc.)					
Residual Value	xxxx	-0-	xxxx	xxxx	-0-

Steps to complete this schedule are as follows:

1. Enter the beginning net lease investment in Column 5. The amount is the same regardless of whether or not the residual value is guaranteed.

2. Enter the periodic lease payment amounts in Column 1.

3. Enter any executory costs included in the lease payment in Column 2.

4. Enter the appropriate amount of interest earned on the net lease investment in Column 3. The interest amount is determined by multiplying the preceding balance of the net lease investment (Column 5, last period) by the same interest rate used to compute the present value of the minimum lease payments.

5. Enter the amount of each lease payment that goes toward investment recovery in Column 4. The amount is determined by subtracting the amounts in Columns 2 and 3 for the period from the amount in Column 1 for the period.

6. Enter the amount of the remaining net lease investment in Column 5. This amount is determined by subtracting the lease recovery amount for a period (Column 4) from the previous net lease investment balance (i.e., from the balance in Column 5 for the previous period).

7. Enter the residual value (whether or not guaranteed) as an additional payment in Column 1 as of the end of the lease term when the asset or cash is received. Interest is computed on the payment as described above.

Important: Make sure all appropriate subheads apply to your entry (see page v for instructions)

14000.3	**Capital Leases**
14000.3.2	**Accounting by Lessor - Capital Leases**
14000.3.2.2	**Sales-Type Capital Leases**
14000.3.2.2.4	**Recording Receipt of Lease Payments (Subsequent to Receipt of Initial Payment at Lease Inception) by a Lessor Under a Sales-Type Capital Lease**

The amount of interest revenue to be recognized each period may be determined by referring to Column 3 of the schedule. If the accounting period does not fall on a date that a lease payment is received, interest revenue must be accrued for the period since interest revenue was last recognized.

14000.3.2.2.5   **Recording Receipt of Residual Value by Lessor at End of Lease**

*Inventory	xxxx	
**Cash	xxxx	
Lease Payments Receivable		xxxx

To record receipt of residual value on a sales-type lease at the end of the lease term

*Inventory is debited for only the fair value of the leased asset whether or not the residual value is guaranteed.

**If the residual value is guaranteed, the lessee generally is required to pay an amount equal to any excess of the guaranteed residual amount and the asset's fair value at the end of the lease. If the residual value is unguaranteed, then Loss On Capital Lease is debited for the amount by which the expected but unguaranteed residual value exceeds the asset's fair value. It is possible no cash is received, in which case Cash is not involved in this entry.

14000.4   **Sale-Leaseback Contracts**

In a sale-leaseback transaction, an owner sells an asset with the provision that the purchaser lease the asset back to the owner. If the seller-lessee does not give up the right to use the asset, no gain or loss is recognized on the sale-leaseback transaction.

14000.4.1   **Accounting by the Seller-Lessee for Sale-Leaseback Transactions**

The seller-lessee applies the same four criteria described in *GEN14000.3.1* in classifying the lease as a capital or operating lease.

If the lease is a capital lease, any profit or loss on the sale is amortized over the asset's economic life (if Criterion 1 or 2 is met) or over the term of the lease in proportion to the amortization of the leased assets.

Important: Make sure all appropriate subheads apply to your entry (see page v for instructions)

14000.4   **Sale-Leaseback Contracts**
14000.4.1   **Accounting by the Seller-Lessee for Sale-Leaseback Transactions**

If the lease is an operating lease, any profit or loss on the sale is amortized in proportion to the rental payments over the period the asset is used by the lessee.

However, gains and losses are recognized in two instances for either capital or operating leases:

1. If the transaction is classified as a minor leaseback (i.e., the present value of the rental payments is 10% or less of the asset's fair value), the full amount of the profit or loss is recognized immediately.
2. Second, if the fair value of the leased asset is less than its book value, a loss is recognized immediately up to the extent of the difference between the two amounts.

The following journal entries assume the lease is classified as a capital lease *(see GEN4000.3.1)*:

14000.4.1.1   **Recording Sale and Leaseback of Asset by the Seller-Lessee**

Cash	xxxx	
*Accumulated Depreciation - Equipment ([Various Assets])	xxxx	
*Equipment ([Various Assets])		xxxx
**Unearned Profit On Sale-Leaseback Transaction		xxxx
To record sale and leaseback of asset		

*Equipment (or other asset) is credited and Accumulated Depreciation is debited sufficiently to remove the carrying value of the asset sold.

**The unearned profit is found by subtracting the carrying value of the asset sold from the selling price.

*Leased Equipment ([Various Assets]) Under Capital Leases	xxxx	
*Liability Under Capital Leases		xxxx
To record leaseback agreement		

*The amount for this entry is found as described in *GEN14000.3.1.1*.

Important: Make sure all appropriate subheads apply to your entry (see page v for instructions)

14000.4   **Sale-Leaseback Contracts**
14000.4.1   **Accounting by the Seller-Lessee for Sale-Leaseback Transactions**

14000.4.1.2   **Recording the Initial Lease Payment Under a Sale and Leaseback Contract at Lease Inception by a Seller-Lessee**

> Liability Under Capital Leases   xxxx
>   *Cash   xxxx
> *To record initial lease payment*

*The amount of the periodic lease payment is contained in the lease agreement. It may be computed as described in *GEN14000.3.2.2.3.*

14000.4.1.3   **Recording Periodic Depreciation Expense on the Leased Asset**

> *Depreciation Expense - Capital Leases   xxxx
>   Accumulated Depreciation - Capital Leases   xxxx
> *To record depreciation expense*

*The leased asset should be depreciated in the same manner as other similar assets owned by the lessee.

14000.4.1.4   **Recording Executory Costs Not Included in the Lease Payment (Paid Separately by the Lessee)**

> *Property Tax Expense   xxxx
> *Insurance Expense   xxxx
> *Maintenance Expense   xxxx
> *[Various Expenses]   xxxx
>   Cash ([Various Prepaid Expenses])   xxxx
>   *[Various Liabilities]   xxxx
> *To record executory costs on a capital lease*

*Various other expenses and liabilities may be debited or credited. Individual expenses will probably be recorded in individual entries rather than all in one entry as illustrated here.

Important: Make sure all appropriate subheads apply to your entry (see page v for instructions)

14000.4   **Sale-Leaseback Contracts**
14000.4.1   **Accounting by the Seller-Lessee for Sale-Leaseback Transactions**

14000.4.1.5   **Recording Annual Interest Expense on Lease Liability by Lessee**

*Interest Expense	xxxx	
Interest Payable		xxxx
To record interest expense on lease liability		

*The amount of interest expense to be recognized is determined on an effective interest basis using an amortization schedule as described in *GEN14000.3.2.1.3.*

14000.4.1.6   **Recording Amortization of Profit or Loss on Sale-Leaseback Transactions**

*Unearned Profit On Sale-Leaseback Transaction	xxxx	
Depreciation Expense		xxxx
To record amortization of profit on a sale-leaseback transaction		

*Profit or loss on the sale in a sale-leaseback transaction is amortized over the asset's economic life (if ownership is expected to transfer as a result of the lease terms) or over the term of the lease (if ownership is not expected to transfer), in proportion to the amortization of the leased assets. For example, if the straight-line depreciation method is used to depreciate the leased asset, then the gross profit amount would also be amortized on a straight-line basis. The amount to be recog-nized during the current period can be found by dividing the total amount of gross profit by the appropriate number of years (i.e., either the years of expected economic life or years in the lease term).

14000.4.2   **Accounting by the Purchaser-Lessor for Sale-Leaseback Transactions**

The purchaser-lessor applies the same criteria described in GEN14000.3.2 in classi-fying the lease as a capital or operating lease. If the lease qualifies as a capital lease, a purchase of the asset is recorded as shown below. Subsequently, the transaction is accounted for as a direct financing lease as discussed in *GEN14000.3.2.1.*

Important: Make sure all appropriate subheads apply to your entry (see page v for instructions)

14000.4   **Sale-Leaseback Contracts**
14000.4.2   **Accounting by the Purchaser-Lessor for Sale-Leaseback Transactions**

14000.4.2.1   **Recording Purchase and Lease of Asset**

*Equipment ([Various Assets])	xxxx	
Cash		xxxx
To record purchase of asset from lessee		

*The asset account is debited for the purchase price (fair value) of the purchased asset.

*Lease Payments Receivable	xxxx	
Equipment ([Various Assets])		xxxx
**Unearned Interest Revenue		xxxx
To record lease of asset in a sale-leaseback transaction		

*The amount debited to Lease Payments Receivable is found in the same manner as described for a direct financing lease in *GEN14000.3.2.1.1.*

**The amount credited to Unearned Interest Revenue is found by subtracting the credit to Equipment ([Various Assets]) from the amount of the lease payments receivable.

14000.4.2.2   **Recording Receipt of Initial Lease Payment at Lease Inception**

Cash	xxxx	
Lease Payments Receivable		xxxx
To record receipt of initial lease payment		

14000.4.2.3   **Recording Interest Revenue**

*Unearned Interest Revenue	xxxx	
*Interest Revenue		xxxx
To record interest revenue		

*The amount of interest revenue to be recognized is found using the effective interest method described in *GEN14000.3.2.1.3.*

TABLE OF CONTENTS

| 15000.1 | **Change in Accounting Principle** |

A change in accounting principle occurs when an entity switches from one generally accepted accounting principle to another generally accepted accounting principle. A change in accounting principle does not occur as a result of switching from an unaccepted accounting principle to one that is accepted (which is a correction of an error; *see GEN15000.3*). Nor does a change in accounting principle occur as a result of applying a new principle to newly occurring events or to items that were previously immaterial but that have now become material.

There are three types of accounting changes differentiated by accounting method:

1. Those accounted for retroactively (*see GEN15000.1.1*),
2. A change to the Last-In-First-Out (LIFO) inventory method (*see GEN15000.1.2*), and
3. Those accounted for by reporting the cumulative effect of the change (*see GEN15000.1.3*).

| 15000.1.1 | **Changes in Accounting Principle that Must Be Accounted for Retroactively** |

There are five situations in which change in accounting principles must be accounted for on a retroactive basis; i.e., previous years' financial statements must be revised:

1. A change *from* (not to) the LIFO inventory flow assumption to some other flow assumption (*see GEN15000.1.1.1*);
2. A change in the method of accounting for long-term construction contracts; e.g., to or from the percentage of completion method (*see GEN15000.1.1.2*);
3. A change to or from the full-cost method of accounting in extractive industries (*see GEN15000.1.1.3*);
4. First-time issuance of financial statements by a closely held firm attempting to issue additional stock, register securities, or enter into a business combination; and

Important: Make sure all appropriate subheads apply to your entry (see page v for instructions)

15000.1   **Changes in Accounting Principle**
15000.1.1   **Changes in Accounting Principle that Must Be Accounted for**
Retroactively

---

5. If retroactive treatment is required by an official pronouncement of an authoritative professional standard-setting organization.

A retroactive change is accounted for as follows:

1. The change's cumulative effect on the financial statements of prior years is computed;
2. The financial statements of prior years are restated to what they would have reflected had the new method been used in those years;
3. The portion of the cumulative effect that applies to years prior to those included in the current statements is recorded as an adjustment to Retained Earnings as of the beginning of the earliest year presented.

The journal entry needed to record a retroactive change may be developed from a schedule similar to the one provided below. All numbers are assumed, including an income tax rate of 40%.

Change Made In Year 20X3
Comparative Statements For Years 20X1-20X3 Presented

Year(s)	Pretax Income Under Principle One	Pretax Income Under Principle Two	Increase (Decrease) In Income	Income Tax Effect (40%)	Effect on Income Net of Tax
(a) Prior to 20X1	$ 6,000	$ 7,000	$1,000	$ 400	$ 600
(b) 20X1	2,300	3,900	1,600	640	960
20X2	2,700	4,100	1,400	560	840
(c) Total Effect	$11,000	$15,000	$4,000	$1,600	$2,400

where:

(a) = The effect on income for all years prior to the first year presented in the current set of financial statements (e.g., if comparative statements are presented for years 20X1-20X3, this would be the effect on income for all years prior to 20X1).

Important: Make sure all appropriate subheads apply to your entry (see page v for instructions)

15000.1   **Changes in Accounting Principle**
15000.1.1   **Changes in Accounting Principle that Must Be Accounted for Retroactively**

(b) = The effect on income of the prior years that are included in the current set of financial statements (e.g., if comparative statements are presented for years 20X1-20X3, this would be the effect on income for 20X1 and 20X2). The effect on income of each of the prior years would be calculated and shown separately in this schedule.

(c) = The total effect on income of all prior years as of the beginning of the current year (i.e., the total effect on income as of the beginning of 20X3, the year in which the change is made).

15000.1.1.1   ### Change *from* Last-In-First-Out (LIFO) Inventory Flow Method

A change from the LIFO inventory flow method results in higher reported earnings than other methods (assuming increasing prices over time). The journal entry needed to record the change may be developed from a schedule similar to that illustrated in *GEN15000.1.1* above. In this instance, Principle One is the LIFO inventory flow method and Principle Two (the new principle) is another inventory flow method (i.e., FIFO or Weighted Average).

*Inventory	xxxx	
**Income Tax Payable		xxxx
***Retained Earnings		xxxx

To record a change from the LIFO inventory flow method

*Inventory is debited for the total effect on prior years' earnings due to the change in inventory method. For example, this would be $4,000 using the example in the schedule given in *GEN15000.1.1*.

**Income Tax Payable is credited for the total income tax effect of the change. For example, this would be $1,600 using the example in the schedule given in *GEN15000.1.1*.

***Retained Earnings is credited for the effect on prior years net income net of tax. For example, this would be $2,400 using the example in the schedule given in *GEN15000.1.1*.

Important: Make sure all appropriate subheads apply to your entry (see page v for instructions)

15000.1   **Changes in Accounting Principle**
15000.1.1   **Changes in Accounting Principle that Must Be Accounted for Retroactively**

15000.1.1.2   **Change in Method of Accounting for Long-Term Construction Contracts**

15000.1.1.2.1   **Change from Completed Contract Method to Percentage-of-Completion Method**

The journal entry needed to record the change from the completed contract method to the percentage-of-completion method (or vice versa) may be developed from a schedule similar to that illustrated in *GEN15000.1.1*. In that illustration, Principle One is the completed contract method, while Principle Two is the percentage-of-completion method.

*Construction In Process	xxxx	
**Income Tax Payable		xxxx
***Retained Earnings		xxxx

To record a change to the percentage-of-completion method

*Construction In Process is debited for the total effect on prior years' income resulting from this accounting change. For example, this would be $4,000 using the example given in the schedule in *GEN15000.1.1*.

**Income Tax Payable is credited for the total income tax effect of the change. For example, this would be $1,600 using the example in the schedule given in *GEN15000.1.1*. IRS regulations may allow certain sized companies to use a different method to account for long-term construction contracts for financial accounting purposes than for tax purposes. If different methods are used, deferred income taxes must be adjusted instead of Income Taxes Payable. *See GEN12000.2* for a discussion of deferred income taxes.

***Retained Earnings is credited for the effect on prior years' income net of tax. For example, this would be $2,400 using the example in the schedule given in *GEN15000.1.1*.

15000.1.1.2.2   **Change to Completed Contract Method from Percentage-of-Completion Method**

The journal entry needed to record the change to the completed contract method from the percentage-of-completion method (or vice versa) may be developed from a

Important: Make sure all appropriate subheads apply to your entry (see page v for instructions)

15000.1	**Changes in Accounting Principle**
15000.1.1	**Changes in Accounting Principle that Must Be Accounted for Retroactively**
15000.1.1.2	**Change in Method of Accounting for Long-Term Construction Contracts**
15000.1.1.2.2	**Change to Completed Contract Method from Percentage-of-Completion Method**

---

schedule similar to that illustrated in *GEN15000.1.1*. In that illustration, Principle One is the completed contract method, while Principle Two is the percentage-of-completion method.

*Retained Earnings	xxxx
**Income Taxes Receivable	xxxx
***Construction In Process	xxxx

To record a change to the completed contract method

*Retained Earnings is debited for the effect on prior years' income net of tax. For example, this would be $2,400 using the example in the schedule given in *GEN15000.1.1*.

**Income Tax Receivable is debited for the total income tax effect of the change. For example, this would be $1,600 using the example in the schedule given in *GEN15000.1.1*. IRS regulations may allow certain sized companies to use a different method to account for long-term construction contracts for financial accounting purposes than for tax purposes. If different methods are used, deferred income taxes must be adjusted instead of Income Taxes Receivable. *See GEN12000.2* for a discussion of deferred income taxes.

***Construction In Process is credited for the total effect on prior years' income resulting from this accounting change. For example, this would be $4,000 using the example given in the schedule in *GEN15000.1.1*.

15000.1.1.3   **Change to or from Full Cost Method of Accounting in Extractive Industries**

15000.1.1.3.1   **Change from Successful Efforts Method to Full Cost Method**

A change to the full cost method results in higher reported earnings. The journal entry needed to record the change may be developed from a schedule similar to that illustrated in *GEN15000.1.1*. In this instance, Principle One refers to the successful efforts method, while Principle Two refers to the full cost method.

ACCOUNTING CHANGES AND ERROR CORRECTIONS

Important: Make sure all appropriate subheads apply to your entry (see page v for instructions)

15000.1   **Changes in Accounting Principle**
15000.1.1   **Changes in Accounting Principle that Must Be Accounted for Retroactively**
15000.1.1.3   **Change to or from Full Cost Method of Accounting in Extractive Industries**
15000.1.1.3.1   **Change from Successful Efforts Method to Full Cost Method**

---

*Oil Deposits ([Various Natural Resources])   xxxx
　　**Income Tax Payable   xxxx
　　***Retained Earnings   xxxx
　　To record change to the full cost method

*Oil Deposits ([Various Natural Resources]) is debited for the total effect on prior years' income resulting from this accounting change. For example, this would be $4,000 using the example given in the schedule at *GEN15000.1.1.*

**Income Tax Payable is credited for the total income tax effect of the change. For example, this would be $1,600 using the example in the schedule given in *GEN15000.1.1.* IRS regulations may allow certain sized companies to use a different method to account for extraction of natural resources for financial accounting purposes than for tax purposes. If different methods are used, deferred income taxes must be adjusted instead of Income Taxes Payable. *See GEN12000.2* for a discussion of deferred income taxes.

***Retained Earnings is credited for the effect on prior years' income net of tax. For example, this would be $2,400 using the example in the schedule given in *GEN15000.1.1.*

15000.1.1.3.2   Change to Successful Efforts Method from Full Cost Method

A change from the full cost method results in lower reported earnings. The journal entry needed to record the change may be developed from a schedule similar to that illustrated in *GEN15000.1.1.* In this instance, Principle One is the successful efforts method, while Principle Two is the full cost method.

*Retained Earnings   xxxx
　**Income Tax Receivable   xxxx
　　***Oil Deposits ([Various Natural Resources])   xxxx
　　To record change to the successful efforts method

*Retained Earnings is debited for the effect on prior years' income net of tax. For example, this would be $2,400 using the example in the schedule given in *GEN15000.1.1.*

**Income Tax Receivable is debited for the total income tax effect of the change. For example, this would be $1,600 using the example in the schedule given in

Important: Make sure all appropriate subheads apply to your entry (see page v for instructions)

15000.1	**Changes in Accounting Principle**
15000.1.1	**Changes in Accounting Principle that Must Be Accounted for Retroactively**
15000.1.1.3	**Change to or from Full Cost Method of Accounting in Extractive Industries**
15000.1.1.3.2	**Change to Successful Efforts Method from Full Cost Method**

GEN15000.1.1. IRS regulations may allow certain sized companies to use a different method to account for extraction of natural resources for financial accounting purposes than for tax purposes. If different methods are used, deferred income taxes must be adjusted instead of Income Taxes Receivable. *See GEN12000.2* for a discussion of deferred income taxes.

***Oil Deposits ([Various Natural Resources]) is credited for the total effect on prior years' income resulting from this accounting change. For example, this would be $4,000 using the example given in the schedule in *GEN15000.1.1.*

15000.1.2

Change *to* LIFO Inventory Method

Neither a cumulative effect (*see GEN15000.1.3*) nor a retroactive adjustment (*see GEN15000.1.1*) is made when a firm changes to the LIFO inventory method because the effects on income for prior years cannot be reasonably determined. Thus, no journal entry is required unless the inventory has been written down below cost under the lower-of-cost-or-market (LCM) approach. If the inventory has been written down under LCM, the following entry is required to restore the inventory to cost:

*Inventory (Allowance To Reduce Inventory To Market)	xxxx	
**Adjustment To Record Inventory At Cost		xxxx
To adjust Inventory to cost		

*Inventory (Allowance To Reduce Inventory To Market) is debited to restore the balance of Inventory to cost (or to eliminate the allowance account). *See GEN4000.1.1.8* for discussion of the application of LCM to inventory.

**This account will appear in the income statement and will increase net income.

15000.1.3

Cumulative-Effect Type Changes in Accounting Principle

A change in accounting principle that does not require retroactive treatment (i.e., that does not involve any of the five situations described in *GEN15000.1.1*) and that does not involve a change to the LIFO inventory flow method is accounted for on a current ("catch-up" or cumulative-effect) basis. The cumulative effect of the change as of the beginning of the year is included in current period income. Financial

Important: Make sure all appropriate subheads apply to your entry (see page v for instructions)

15000.1	**Changes in Accounting Principle**
15000.1.3	**Cumulative-Effect Type Changes in Accounting Principle**

statements of prior years are not restated. However, the effects on income and earnings per share (EPS) for the current and prior years must be presented in pro forma form, i.e., as if the new principle had been applied in prior years as well as in the current year. The journal entry needed to record a cumulative-effect type change may be developed from a schedule similar to the following:

Year	Effect on Pretax Income Under Principle One	Effect on Pretax Income Under Principle Two	Before Tax Increase (Decrease) In Income	Income Tax Effect (40%)	Effect on Income Net of Tax
(a)	$16,000	$7,000	$9,000	$3,600	$5,400
(b)	14,000	7,000	7,000	2,800	4,200
(c)	12,000	7,000	5,000	2,000	3,000
(T)	$42,000	$21,000	$21,000	$8,400	$12,600

where:

(a), (b), and (c) = The effect on income for each year affected by the change up to the beginning of the current year.

(T) = The total effect on income as of the beginning of the current year (i.e., the total effect on income as of the beginning of the year in which the change is made).

For example, assume a firm that uses the sum-of-the-years'-digits method of depreciation for financial accounting purposes (and accelerated cost recovery system, or ACRS, depreciation for tax purposes) decides to switch to the straight-line method. The journal entry provided below would be required (assuming the amounts shown in the above schedule that are based on an asset costing $56,000, an 8-year life, and no salvage value) to record this change in accounting principle. Principle One is the sum-of-the-years'-digits method and Principle Two is the straight-line method.

*Accumulated Depreciation		xxxx
**Deferred Tax Asset		xxxx
***Cumulative Effect Of Change In Accounting Principle - Depreciation		xxxx

To record a change to the straight-line depreciation method

Important: Make sure all appropriate subheads apply to your entry (see page v for instructions)

15000.1   **Changes in Accounting Principle**
15000.1.3   **Cumulative-Effect Type Changes in Accounting Principle**

---

*Accumulated Depreciation is debited for the pre-tax effect of the change. For example, this would be $21,000 in the schedule shown above.

**Deferred Tax Asset is credited for the total income tax effect of the change. For example, this would be $8,400 using the example in the schedule given above. Because tax depreciation (ACRS) in previous years was less than financial depreciation, a deferred tax asset had been previously recorded. That account balance is now reduced by $8,400. If the same depreciation method was used for tax and financial accounting, no deferred tax asset was created, and this credit would be to Income Tax Payable.

A different cumulative-effect type of change in accounting principle may require Deferred Tax Asset and Deferred Tax Liability to be adjusted differently than illustrated in this example. *See GEN12000.2* for a discussion of deferred taxes.

***Cumulative Effect Of Change In Accounting Principle Depreciation is credited for the cumulative effect of the change, net of tax. This account will increase income in the income statement. For example, this increase is $12,600 using the example in the schedule given above.

15000.2   **Change in Accounting Estimate**

A change in accounting estimate occurs when a firm revises an estimate as a result of new information or experience. Common examples include changes in the percentages used to estimate the amount of bad debt expense or uncollectible accounts, revision of estimates of service lives or salvage values for plant assets, and revision of estimates of warranty costs. Changes in accounting estimates are accounted for prospectively. That is, changes in estimates require neither retroactive nor cumulative-effect (catch-up) treatment. Instead, the effects of such changes are accounted for in the period of change if only a single period is affected, or in the period of change and future periods if the change affects multiple periods.

15000.2.1   **Change in Estimate of Bad Debt Expense (Estimated Percentage Applied to Sales to Arrive at Bad Debt Expense)**

If a change is made in the percentage factor usually applied to sales to arrive at bad debt expense (uncollectible accounts expense), no special journal entry is made. All

Important: Make sure all appropriate subheads apply to your entry (see page v for instructions)

15000.2   **Changes in Accounting Estimate**
15000.2.1   **Change in Estimate of Bad Debt Expense (Estimated Percentage Applied to Sales to Arrive at Bad Debt Expense)**

that is necessary is to apply the new percentage the next time bad debt expense is recorded and make the normal journal entry given below. (*See GEN3000.1.3* for a discussion of bad debt expense.)

*Bad Debt Expense (Uncollectible Accounts Expense)	xxxx	
**Allowance For Bad Debts (Allowance For Uncollectible Accounts)		xxxx
To record bad debt expense		

*The debit to Bad Debt Expense (Uncollectible Accounts Expense) is determined by applying the new revised percentage to sales.

**Allowance For Bad Debts (Allowance For Uncollectible Accounts) is credited to balance the entry.

15000.2.2   ## Change in Estimate of Uncollectible Accounts (Estimated Percentages Applied to Accounts Receivable to Arrive at Desired Balance of the Allowance Account (Aging of Accounts))

If a change is made in the percentage factor usually applied to Accounts Receivable to arrive at the desired balance of Allowance For Bad Debts (Allowance For Uncollectible Accounts), no special journal entry is made. All that is necessary is to apply the new percentage the next time the desired balance in the Allowance account is calculated and make the normal journal entry as follows:

*Bad Debt Expense (Uncollectible Accounts Expense)	xxxx	
**Allowance For Bad Debts (Allowance For Uncollectible Accounts)		xxxx
To record bad debt expense		

*Bad Debt Expense (Uncollectible Accounts Expense) is debited to balance the entry.

**The credit to Allowance For Bad Debts (Allowance For Uncollectible Accounts) is determined by first applying the new percentage to Accounts Receivable to arrive at the desired credit balance in the allowance account and then adjusting the current balance in the allowance account to produce the desired balance. If the allowance account needs to be increased (as will usually be the case), Allowance For Bad

Important: Make sure all appropriate subheads apply to your entry (see page v for instructions)

15000.2   **Changes in Accounting Estimate**
15000.2.2   **Change in Estimate of Uncollectible Accounts (Estimated Percentages Applied to Accounts Receivable to Arrive at Desired Balance of the Allowance Account (Aging of Accounts))**

Debts is credited and Bad Debt Expense is debited as shown in this entry. If the allowance account needs to be decreased, Allowance For Bad Debts is debited and Bad Debt Expense is credited. *See GEN3000.1.3* for a discussion of bad debt expense.

15000.2.3   **Change in Estimate of Service Life and/or Salvage Value**

When a change is made in the estimate of service life or salvage value for a plant asset, the remaining undepreciated book value of the asset as of the beginning of the year in which the change is made is depreciated over the current and future years using the new salvage value and/or service life.

For example, assume equipment costing $10,000 has been depreciated on a straight-line basis using a 10-year life and no salvage value. At the beginning of Year 6 of the equipment's life, management now believes that the equipment will last 7 more years (for a total of 12 years) and will have a $1,500 salvage value. The undepreciated book value of the equipment at the beginning of Year 6 is $5,000 (calculated below). The entry to record Year 6 depreciation is as follows:

*Depreciation Expense	500	
Accumulated Depreciation - Equipment		500
To record current period depreciation		

*The debit to Depreciation Expense is found as follows:

Cost	$10,000
Less: Depreciation Taken Through Year 5	
(($10,000/10) X 5)	5,000
Undepreciated Book Value at Beginning of Year 6	5,000
Less: Newly Estimated Salvage Value	1,500
Amount to Depreciate	$3,500

New Annual Depreciation: $3,500/7 = $500

15000.2.4   **Change in Estimated Liability**

When a change in estimate of a liability occurs, the current balance in the estimated liability account is adjusted (increased or decreased) to equal the newly estimated amount.

Important: Make sure all appropriate subheads apply to your entry (see page v for instructions)

15000.2   Changes in Accounting Estimate
15000.2.4   Change in Estimated Liability

---

*Warranty Expense ([Various Expense])   xxxx
*Estimated Liability For Warranties
([Various Estimated Liability])   xxxx
To adjust estimated liability

*Warranty Expense ([Various Expense]) is debited and Estimated Liability For Warranties ([Various Estimated Liability]) is credited to increase the balance in the liability account to the newly estimated amount. If the balance in the liability account needs to be reduced, Estimated Liability For Warranties ([Various Estimated Liability]) is debited and Warranty Expense ([Various Expense]) is credited.

15000.3   Correction of Accounting Errors

Accounting errors result from math errors, application of improper accounting principles, oversight, and misuse of facts at the time financial statements were prepared. Some errors involve both income statement and balance sheet accounts. Such errors may or may not be counterbalancing. Errors discovered in the current year that relate to operations of prior years should be accounted for as prior period adjustments; i.e., adjustments to the beginning balance of Retained Earnings.

15000.3.1   Counterbalancing Errors

Counterbalancing errors are errors that will correct themselves over two periods. (But financial statements for each *individual* period will still show the effects of the error.) For example, such an error might result in an overstatement of income in one year and an equal understatement of income in the following year. Counterbalancing errors may involve the failure to properly accrue or defer expenses and revenues at year end or the understatement or overstatement of ending inventory balances.

15000.3.1.1   Failure to Accrue Expense at End of Last Year

The entry below is made if the error is found and corrected in the year following the year in which the error was made (before the books for the year following the year of the error are closed). If the error is not found until the second year following the year in which the error was made, no journal entry is necessary to correct the error because it corrects itself over two years (i.e., it is a counterbalancing error).

Important: Make sure all appropriate subheads apply to your entry (see page v for instructions)

15000.3	**Correction of Accounting Errors**	
15000.3.1	**Counterbalancing Errors**	
15000.3.1.1	**Failure to Accrue Expense at End of Last Year**	

However, the financial statements for the two individual years (the year of the error and the next year) will each show errors unless the following entry is made:

*Retained Earnings	xxxx	
**Income Tax Receivable	xxxx	
***[Various Expense]		xxxx

*To correct error resulting from failure to accrue expense
at the end of last year*

*Because expenses were understated last year, net income for last year was over-stated and Retained Earnings is overstated. Retained earnings therefore must be debited for the amount of the expense that was not accrued net of the tax effect.

**Income Tax Receivable is debited because, in effect, taxes have been prepaid as a result of reporting overstated earnings in the previous year. The amount of the debit is found by multiplying the amount of the error (the credit to expense) by the marginal tax rate.

***When the expense was first paid this year, the expense account was debited for the amount of the expense that should have been accrued last year. Thus, the expense account for the current year is overstated and must be reduced.

15000.3.1.2

Failure to Defer Expense at End of Last Year

The entry below is made if the error is found and corrected in the year following the year in which the error was made (before the books for the year following the year of the error are closed). If the error is not found until the second year following the year in which the error was made, no journal entry is necessary to correct the error (except in the unusual case in which there would still be prepaid amounts) because it corrects itself over two years (i.e., it is a counterbalancing error). However, the financial state-ments for the two individual years (the year of the error and the next year) will each show errors unless the following entry is made:

*[Various Expense]	xxxx	
**Income Tax Payable		xxxx
***Retained Earnings		xxxx

*To correct error resulting from failure to defer expense at
end of last year*

Important: Make sure all appropriate subheads apply to your entry (see page v for instructions)

15000.3   **Correction of Accounting Errors**
15000.3.1   **Counterbalancing Errors**
15000.3.1.2   **Failure to Defer Expense at End of Last Year**

---

*The relevant expense account is debited for the amount of expense that should have been deferred last year and is properly an expense of the current period.

**Income Tax Payable is credited because, in effect, taxes have been underpaid as a result of reporting understated earnings in the previous year. The amount of the credit is found by multiplying the amount of the error by the marginal tax rate.

***Because expenses were overstated last year, net income for last year was understated and Retained Earnings is understated. Retained earnings therefore must be credited for the amount of the expense that was not deferred net of tax effects.

15000.3.1.3   **Failure to Accrue Revenue at End of Last Year**

The entry below is made if the error is found and corrected in the year following the year in which the error was made (before the books for the year following the year of the error are closed). If the error is not found until the second year following the year in which the error was made, no journal entry is necessary to correct the error because it corrects itself over two years (i.e., it is a counterbalancing error). However, the financial statements for the two individual years (the year of the error and the next year) will each show errors unless the following entry is made:

*[Various Revenue]	xxxx	
**Income Tax Payable		xxxx
***Retained Earnings		xxxx

*To correct error resulting from failure to accrue revenue
at the end of last year*

*When the revenue was received this year, the revenue account was credited for the amount of the revenue that should have been accrued last year. Thus, the revenue account for the current year is overstated and must be reduced (debited).

**Income Tax Payable is credited because, in effect, taxes have been underpaid as a result of reporting understated earnings in the previous year. The amount of the credit is found by multiplying the amount of the error (the debit to revenue) by the marginal tax rate.

***Because revenue was understated last year, net income for last year was understated and Retained Earnings is understated. Retained earnings therefore must be credited for the amount of the revenue that was not accrued (net of tax effects).

Important: Make sure all appropriate subheads apply to your entry (see page v for instructions)

15000.3   **Correction of Accounting Errors**
15000.3.1   **Counterbalancing Errors**

15000.3.1.4   **Failure to Defer Revenue at End of Last Year**

The entry below is made if the error is found and corrected in the year following
the year in which the error was made (before the books for the year following the year
of the error are closed). If the error is not found until the second year following the
year in which the error was made, no journal entry is necessary to correct the error
(except in the unusual case in which there would still be unearned amounts) because it
corrects itself over two years (i.e., it is a counterbalancing error). However, the
financial statements for the two individual years (the year of the error and the next
year) will each show errors unless the following entry is made:

*Retained Earnings	xxxx	
**Income Tax Receivable	xxxx	
***[Various Revenue]		xxxx

*To correct error resulting from failure to accrue revenue
at the end of last year*

*Because revenue was overstated last year, net income for last year was overstated
and Retained Earnings is overstated. Retained Earnings therefore must be reduced
(debited) for the amount of the revenue that was not deferred net of tax effects.

**Income Tax Receivable is debited because, in effect, taxes have been overpaid as a
result of reporting overstated earnings in the previous year. The amount of the debit is
found by multiplying the amount of the error by the marginal tax rate.

***The relevant revenue account is credited for the amount of revenue that should
have been deferred last year and is properly a revenue of the current period.

15000.3.1.5   **Understatement of Prior Year Ending Inventory Balance**

The entry below is made if the error is found and corrected in the year following
the year in which the error was made (before the books for the year following the year
of the error are closed). If the error is not found until the second year following the
year in which the error was made, no journal entry is necessary to correct the error
because it corrects itself over two years (i.e., it is a counterbalancing error). However,
the financial statements for the two individual years (the year of the error and the next
year) will each show errors unless the following entry is made:

Important: Make sure all appropriate subheads apply to your entry (see page v for instructions)

15000.3   **Correction of Accounting Errors**
15000.3.1   **Counterbalancing Errors**
15000.3.1.5   **Understatement of Prior Year Ending Inventory Balance**

---

*Inventory	xxxx	
**Income Tax Payable		xxxx
***Retained Earnings		xxxx
To correct inventory error		

*Inventory is increased (debited) for the amount it was understated at the end of last year.

**Income Tax Payable is credited because, in effect, taxes have been underpaid as a result of reporting understated earnings in the previous year. The amount of the credit is found by multiplying the amount of the error by the marginal tax rate.

***Because ending inventory was understated last year, net income for last year was understated and Retained Earnings is understated. Retained Earnings therefore must be credited for the amount of the understatement net of tax effects.

15000.3.1.6   Overstatement of Prior Year Ending Inventory Balance

The entry below is made if the error is found and corrected in the year following the year in which the error was made (before the books for the year following the year of the error are closed). If the error is not found until the second year following the year in which the error was made, no journal entry is necessary to correct the error because it corrects itself over two years (i.e., it is a counterbalancing error). However, the financial statements for the two individual years (the year of the error and the next year) will each show errors unless the following entry is made:

*Income Tax Receivable	xxxx	
**Retained Earnings	xxxx	
***Inventory		xxxx
To correct inventory error		

*Income Tax Receivable is debited because, in effect, taxes have been overpaid as a result of reporting overstated earnings in the previous year. The amount of the debit is found by multiplying the amount of the error by the marginal tax rate.

**Because ending inventory was overstated last year, net income for last year was overstated and Retained Earnings is overstated. Retained Earnings therefore must be reduced (debited) for the amount of overstatement net of tax effects.

Important: Make sure all appropriate subheads apply to your entry (see page v for instructions)

15000.3	**Correction of Accounting Errors**
15000.3.1	**Counterbalancing Errors**
15000.3.1.6	**Overstatement of Prior Year Ending Inventory Balance**

***Inventory is credited for the amount it was overstated at the end of last year.

15000.3.2   **Noncounterbalancing Errors**

Noncounterbalancing errors are errors that are not self-correcting over two periods.

15000.3.2.1   **Failure to Record Prior Year Amortization or Depreciation**

15000.3.2.1.1   **Books Have Not Been Closed for Year of the Error**

*Amortization (Depreciation) Expense	xxxx	
*Patents ([Various Amortized Assets],		
Accumulated Depreciation)		xxxx
To correct amortization (depreciation) error		

*Amortization (Depreciation) Expense is debited and Patents ([Various Amortized Asset], Accumulated Depreciation) is credited for the amount of expense that should have been recorded but was not.

*Income Tax Payable	xxxx	
*Income Tax Expense		xxxx
To correct income tax accounts for error in understating		
amortization (depreciation)		

*This entry reduces the Income Tax Payable and Income Tax Expense balances for the prior year by an amount equal to the amount of the amortization (depreciation) error multiplied by the marginal tax rate. If different methods are used for financial accounting and tax, deferred taxes may have to be adjusted. *See GEN12000.2* for a discussion of deferred income taxes.

15000.3.2.1.2   **Books Have Been Closed for Year of the Error**

*Retained Earnings (Prior Period Adjustment)	xxxx	
*Patents ([Various Amortized Assets], Accumulated		
Depreciation)		xxxx
To correct amortization (depreciation) error		

Important: Make sure all appropriate subheads apply to your entry (see page v for instructions)

15000.3	**Correction of Accounting Errors**
15000.3.2	**Noncounterbalancing Errors**
15000.3.2.1	**Failure to Record Prior Year Amortization or Depreciation**
15000.3.2.1.2	**Books Have Been Closed for Year of the Error**

---

*Retained Earnings is credited for the amount of expense that should have been recorded but was not.

*Income Tax Payable	xxxx	
*Retained Earnings (Prior Period Adjustment)		xxxx
To correct income tax accounts for error in understating amortization (depreciation)		

*This entry reduces Income Tax Payable and increases Retained Earnings (Prior Period Adjustment) by an amount equal to the amount of the amortization (depreciation) error multiplied by the marginal tax rate. If no Income Tax Payable account exists, Income Tax Receivable is debited instead. If different methods are used for financial accounting and tax, deferred taxes may have to be adjusted. *See GEN12000.2* for a discussion of deferred income taxes.

15000.3.2.2   **Failure to Capitalize an Asset (Asset Is Erroneously Expensed)**

15000.3.2.2.1   **Books Have Not Been Closed for Year of the Error**

*Machinery ([Various Assets])	xxxx	
**Depreciation Expense	xxxx	
**Accumulated Depreciation		xxxx
*[Various Expense]		xxxx
To correct error of expensing a capital asset		

*Machinery ([Various Assets]) is debited for the cost of the asset acquired. This is the amount that was erroneously expensed. The offsetting credit should be to the expense account that was erroneously debited.

**Depreciation Expense is debited and Accumulated Depreciation is credited for the amount of depreciation for the year that should have been recorded but was not.

*Income Tax Expense	xxxx	
*Income Tax Payable		xxxx
To correct tax error caused by error of expensing a capital asset		

Important: Make sure all appropriate subheads apply to your entry (see page v for instructions)

15000.3	**Correction of Accounting Errors**
15000.3.2	**Noncounterbalancing Errors**
15000.3.2.2	**Failure to Capitalize an Asset (Asset is Erroneously Expensed)**
15000.3.2.2.1	**Books Have Not Been Closed for Year of the Error**

---

*This entry increases Income Tax Payable and Income Tax Expense by an amount equal to the amount of the amortization (depreciation) error multiplied by the marginal tax rate. If different methods are used for financial accounting and tax, deferred taxes may have to be adjusted. *See GEN12000.2* for a discussion of deferred income taxes.

15000.3.2.2.2   **Books Have Been Closed for Year of the Error**

*Machinery ([Various Assets])	xxxx	
**Accumulated Depreciation		xxxx
***Retained Earnings (Prior Period Adjustment)		xxxx
To correct error of expensing a capital asset		

*Machinery ([Various Assets]) is debited for the cost of the asset acquired. This is the amount that was erroneously expensed.

**Accumulated Depreciation is credited for the amount of depreciation that should have been recorded but was not.

***Retained Earnings (Prior Period Adjustment) is credited to balance the entry. It may be calculated as the excess of the overstatement of expense caused by erroneously expensing the asset, over the understatement of expense caused by failure to record depreciation (net of tax effects).

*Retained Earnings (Prior Period Adjustment)	xxxx	
*Income Tax Payable		xxxx
To correct tax error caused by error of expensing a capital asset		

*This entry increases Income Tax Payable and decreases Retained Earnings by an amount equal to the amount of the amortization (depreciation) error multiplied by the marginal tax rate. If different methods are used for financial accounting and tax, deferred taxes may have to be adjusted. *See GEN12000.2* for a discussion of deferred income taxes.

TABLE OF CONTENTS

| 16000.1 | **Job Order Cost Accounting** |

| 16000.1.1 | **Materials (Parts)** |

| 16000.1.1.1 | **Materials (Parts) Purchases** |

| Raw Materials (Parts) Inventory | xxxx | |
| Accounts Payable | | xxxx |

To record purchase of raw materials or parts

| 16000.1.1.2 | **Materials (Parts) Use (Requisition)** |

| 16000.1.1.2.1 | **Direct Materials Used** |

Direct materials are materials (parts) that can be directly traced to and physically become a part of the product produced.

| Work-In-Process (Jobs-In-Process) Inventory - [Various Jobs] | xxxx | |
| Raw Materials (Parts) Inventory | | xxxx |

To record use of direct materials

| 16000.1.1.2.2 | **Indirect Materials Used** |

Indirect materials are materials used in production that cannot be directly traced to and do not become part of the product produced.

| *Factory (Manufacturing) Overhead - Indirect Materials Expense | xxxx | |
| Raw Materials Inventory | | xxxx |

To record use of indirect materials

See GEN16000.1.3.1 for use of this account.

Important: Make sure all appropriate subheads apply to your entry (see page v for instructions)

16000.1   **Job Order Cost Accounting**

16000.1.2   **Labor**

16000.1.2.1   **Labor Expense Incurred**

In addition to the entries shown below, *see GEN7000.10* for a more complete discussion of payroll, payroll taxes, and other employee-related liabilities.

16000.1.2.1.1   **Inside Labor**

Inside labor is labor performed by employees of the company.

Factory Wages Expense	xxxx	
*Federal Income Tax Withheld		xxxx
*State Income Tax Withheld		xxxx
**F.I.C.A. Tax Withheld		xxxx
***[Other Withholdings Payable]		xxxx
****Factory Wages Payable		xxxx
To record payroll		

*Federal and state withholdings are found by referring to tax withholding tables provided by the federal and state governments.

**A common alternative account title is Social Security Tax Withheld.

***Other withholdings may include amounts for insurance premiums, savings plans, union dues, and uniform costs.

****Factory Wages Payable is credited for the amount of net salaries and wages; i.e., gross salaries and wages minus all the payroll deductions.

16000.1.2.1.2   **Outside Labor**

Outside labor is labor performed by employees of another company with which a contract to supply labor is held. These employees will be paid by the labor supplying company which will account for all withholdings and payroll taxes. All that is necessary is to record the labor expense and the liability to the labor supplying company.

Important: Make sure all appropriate subheads apply to your entry (see page v for instructions)

16000.1	**Job Order Cost Accounting**
16000.1.2	**Labor**
16000.1.2.1	**Labor Expense Incurred**
16000.1.2.1.2	**Outside Labor**

Factory Outside Labor Expense	xxxx	
Factory Outside Labor Payable		xxxx
To record outside labor expense		

16000.1.2.2   **Labor Application**

16000.1.2.2.1   **Direct Labor**

Direct labor is labor that can be directly traced to a particular job.

Work-In-Process (Jobs-In-Process) Inventory		
- [Various Jobs]	xxxx	
*Factory Wages Expense (Factory Outside		
Labor Expense)		xxxx
To record transfer of direct labor costs to work-in-process		

See GEN16000.1.2.1 for the initial entry to record factory wages expense or outside labor expense.

16000.1.2.2.2   **Indirect Labor**

Indirect labor is labor that cannot be directly traced to a particular job.

*Factory (Manufacturing) Overhead		
- Indirect Labor Expense	xxxx	
**Factory Wages Expense (Factory Outside		
Labor Expense)		xxxx
To record transfer of indirect labor costs to Factory		
(Manufacturing) Overhead		

See GEN16000.1.3.1 for use of this account.

**See GEN16000.1.2.1* for the initial entry to record factory wages expense or outside labor expense.

Important: Make sure all appropriate subheads apply to your entry (see page v for instructions)

16000.1   **Job Order Cost Accounting**

16000.1.3   **Factory (Manufacturing) Overhead**

16000.1.3.1   **Recording Factory (Manufacturing) Overhead Expense**

The following four entries are typical examples of recording factory (manufacturing) overhead:

Factory (Manufacturing) Overhead - Depreciation Expense	xxxx	
Accumulated Depreciation		xxxx
To record factory-related depreciation expense		

Factory (Manufacturing) Overhead - Utilities Expense	xxxx	
Accounts Payable (Utilities Payable)		xxxx
To record factory-related utility expense		

Factory (Manufacturing) Overhead - Insurance Expense	xxxx	
Accounts Payable (Prepaid Insurance)		xxxx
To record factory-related insurance expense		

Factory (Manufacturing) Overhead - Property Tax Expense	xxxx	
Property Taxes Payable (Prepaid Property Taxes)		xxxx
To record factory-related insurance expense		

Factory (Manufacturing) Overhead - Indirect Materials Expense	xxxx	
*Raw Materials Inventory		xxxx
To record use of indirect materials		

*See GEN16000.1.1 for use of this account.

Factory Overhead (Manufacturing Overhead) - Indirect Labor Expense	xxxx	
*Factory Wages Expense (Factory Outside Labor Expense)		xxxx
To record transfer of indirect labor costs to Factory Overhead		

Important: Make sure all appropriate subheads apply to your entry (see page v for instructions)

16000.1   **Job Order Cost Accounting**
16000.1.3   **Factory (Manufacturing) Overhead**
16000.1.3.1   **Recording Factory (Manufacturing) Overhead Expense**

See GEN16000.1.2.1 for the initial entry to record factory wages expense or outside labor expense.

16000.1.3.2   **Application of Overhead to Work-in-Process (Jobs-in-Process) Inventory**

> *Work-In-Process (Jobs-In-Process) Inventory
> - [Various Jobs]   xxxx
>   Factory (Manufacturing) Overhead   xxxx
> *To apply factory (manufacturing) overhead to jobs*

*The amount transferred out of Factory (Manufacturing) Overhead to an individual job is determined by multiplying a predetermined application (overhead or burden) rate times a prescribed base such as direct labor hours or machine hours used on the job. The predetermined application (overhead or burden) rate can be calculated by the following formula:

$$\frac{\text{Estimated Total Annual Factory Overhead}}{\text{Estimated Total Annual Direct Labor Hours}}$$
$$\text{(Or another base)}$$

This calculation will provide an amount per direct labor hour (or other base) that can be used to apply overhead costs to individual jobs. Because this application is based on estimates, some overhead costs may be left in Factory (Manufacturing) Overhead at the end of an accounting period. The following entries illustrate how to dispose of an ending balance in Factory (Manufacturing) Overhead.

16000.1.3.3   **Over-Applied or Under-Applied Factory (Manufacturing) Overhead**

Because the application of overhead to Work-In-Process (Jobs-In-Process) Inventory is accomplished by using a predetermined application rate based on estimates *(see GEN16000.1.3.2)*, there will usually be a debit (under-applied) balance or a credit (over-applied) balance in Factory (Manufacturing) Overhead. This section covers what to do with this balance.

COST ACCOUNTING

Important: Make sure all appropriate subheads apply to your entry (see page v for instructions)

16000.1   **Job Order Cost Accounting**
16000.1.3   **Factory (Manufacturing) Overhead**
16000.1.3.3   **Over-Applied or Under-Applied Factory (Manufacturing) Overhead Expense**

16000.1.3.3.1 **Over-Applied or Under-Applied Balance in the Factory (Manufacturing) Overhead Account Is Not Significant Compared with Total Factory (Manufacturing) Overhead During the Period**

16000.1.3.3.1.1 **Over-Applied Factory (Manufacturing) Overhead**

Factory (Manufacturing) Overhead	xxxx	
Cost Of Goods Sold		xxxx

To transfer the under-applied balance in Factory (Manufacturing) Overhead to Cost of Goods Sold

16000.1.3.3.1.2 **Under-Applied Factory (Manufacturing) Overhead**

Cost Of Goods Sold	xxxx	
Factory (Manufacturing) Overhead		xxxx

To transfer over-applied balance in Factory (Manufacturing) Overhead to Cost Of Goods Sold

16000.1.3.3.2 **Over-Applied or Under-Applied Balance in the Factory (Manufacturing) Overhead Account Is Significant Compared with Total Factory (Manufacturing) Overhead During the Period**

16000.1.3.3.2.1 **Over-Applied Factory (Manufacturing) Overhead**

*Factory (Manufacturing) Overhead	xxxx	
Cost Of Goods Sold		xxxx
Finished Goods Inventory - [Various Jobs]		xxxx
Work-In-Process (Jobs-In-Process) Inventory - [Various Jobs]		xxxx

To allocate the over-applied balance in Factory (Manufacturing) Overhead

*Factory (Manufacturing) Overhead is debited for the amount of the credit balance remaining (i.e., Factory (Manufacturing) Overhead is zeroed out). The amount of this debit is then allocated with credits to:

Important: Make sure all appropriate subheads apply to your entry (see page v for instructions)

16000.1	**Job Order Cost Accounting**
16000.1.3	**Factory (Manufacturing) Overhead**
16000.1.3.3	**Over-Applied or Under-Applied Factory (Manufacturing) Overhead Expense**
16000.1.3.3.2	**Over-Applied or Under-Applied Balance in the Factory (Manufacturing) Overhead Account Is Significant Compared with Total Factory (Manufacturing) Overhead During the Period**
16000.1.3.3.2.1	**Over-Applied Factory (Manufacturing) Overhead**

-Cost Of Goods Sold
-Finished Goods Inventory - [Various Jobs]
-Work-In-Process (Jobs-In-Process) Inventory

on the basis of the relative amounts of factory (manufacturing) overhead earlier applied to those accounts. *For example,* if the amounts of factory (manufacturing) overhead in Cost Of Goods Sold, Finished Goods Inventory, and Work-In-Process (Jobs-In-Process) Inventory are $80,000, $50,000, and $30,000, respectively (a total of $160,000), the amount of the debit to Factory (Manufacturing) Overhead is allocated by crediting Cost of Goods Sold for 8/16, Finished Goods Inventory for 5/16, and Work-In-Process (Jobs-In-Process) Inventory for 3/16 of the amount debited to Factory (Manufacturing) Overhead.

16000.1.3.3.2.2   **Under-Applied Factory (Manufacturing) Overhead**

Cost Of Goods Sold	XXXX	
Finished Goods Inventory - [Various Jobs]	XXXX	
Work-In-Process (Jobs-In-Process) Inventory		
- [Various Jobs]	XXXX	
*Factory (Manufacturing) Overhead		XXXX

To allocate the under-applied balance in the Factory (Manufacturing) Overhead

*Factory (Manufacturing) Overhead is credited for the amount of the debit balance remaining; i.e., Factory (Manufacturing) Overhead is zeroed out. The amount of this credit is then allocated with debits to:
-Cost Of Goods Sold
-Finished Goods Inventory - [Various Jobs]
-Work-In-Process (Jobs-In-Process) Inventory
on the basis of relative amounts of factory (manufacturing) overhead earlier applied to those accounts. *For example,* if the amounts of factory (manufacturing) overhead in Cost of Goods Sold, Finished Goods Inventory, and Work-in-Process (Jobs-In-Process) Inventory are $80,000, $50,000, and $30,000, respectively (a total of $160,000), the amount of the credit to Factory (Manufacturing) Overhead is allocated by debiting Cost of Goods Sold for 8/16, Finished Goods Inventory for 5/16, and Work-In-Process (Jobs-In-Process) Inventory for 3/16 of the amount credited to Factory (Manufacturing) Overhead.

Important: Make sure all appropriate subheads apply to your entry (see page v for instructions)

16000.1 **Job Order Cost Accounting**

16000.1.4 **Completion and Sale of Jobs**

16000.1.4.1 **Completion of Jobs**

Finished Goods Inventory - [Various Jobs]	xxxx
Work-In-Process (Jobs-In-Process) Inventory - [Various Jobs]	xxxx

To transfer costs of jobs from Work-In-Process (Jobs-in-Process) Inventory to Finished Goods Inventory

16000.1.4.2 **Sale of Jobs**

Cost Of Goods Sold	xxxx
Finished Goods Inventory - [Various Jobs]	xxxx

To transfer costs of jobs from Finished Goods Inventory to Cost of Goods Sold

Accounts Receivable (Cash)	xxxx
Sales Revenue	xxxx

To record sale

16000.2 **Process Costing**

16000.2.1 **Materials (Parts)**

16000.2.1.1 **Materials (Parts) Purchases**

Raw Materials (Parts) Inventory	xxxx
Accounts Payable	xxxx

To record purchase of raw materials or parts

Important: Make sure all appropriate subheads apply to your entry (see page v for instructions)

16000.2   **Process Costing**
16000.2.1   **Materials (Parts)**

16000.2.1.2   **Materials (Parts) Use (Requisition)**

16000.2.1.2.1   **Direct Materials (Parts) Used**

Direct materials are materials (parts) that can be directly traced to and physically become part of the product produced.

*Work-In-Process Inventory - [Various Departments]	xxxx	
Raw Materials (Parts) Inventory		xxxx
To record direct materials (parts) used in departments		

*If direct materials (parts) are added in subsequent departments, similar entries are made charging the Work-In-Process accounts for those departments.

16000.2.1.2.2   **Indirect Materials Used**

Indirect materials are materials used in production that cannot be directly traced to or do not become a part of the product produced. *See GEN16000.2.2* to record indirect materials used in a process cost system.

16000.2.2   **Conversion Costs (Labor and Overhead)**

16000.2.2.1   **Labor Expense Incurred**

In addition to the entries shown below, *see GEN7000.10* for a more complete discussion of payroll, payroll taxes, and other employee-related liabilities.

Important: Make sure all appropriate subheads apply to your entry (see page v for instructions)

16000.2	**Process Costing**
16000.2.2	**Conversion Costs (Labor and Overhead)**
16000.2.2.1	**Labor Expense Incurred**

16000.2.2.1.1   **Inside Labor**

Inside labor is labor performed by employees of the company.

Factory Wages Expense	xxxx	
*Federal Income Tax Withheld		xxxx
*State Income Tax Withheld		xxxx
**F.I.C.A. Tax Withheld		xxxx
***[Other Withholdings Payable]		xxxx
****Factory Wages Payable		xxxx
To record payroll		

*Federal and state withholdings are found by referring to tax withholding tables provided by the federal and state governments.

**A common alternative account title is Social Security Tax Withheld.

***Other withholdings may include amounts for insurance premiums, savings plans, union dues, and uniform costs.

****Factory Wages Payable is credited for the amount of net salaries and wages; i.e., gross salaries and wages minus all payroll deductions.

16000.2.2.1.2   **Outside Labor**

Outside labor is labor performed by employees of another company with which a contract to supply labor is held. These employees will be paid by the labor supplying company which will account for all withholdings and payroll taxes. All that is necessary is to record the labor expense and the liability to the labor supplying company.

Factory Outside Labor Expense	xxxx	
Factory Outside Labor Payable		xxxx
To record outside labor expense		

16000.2.2.2   **Recording Factory (Manufacturing) Overhead Expense**

The following six entries are typical examples of recording factory overhead:

Important: Make sure all appropriate subheads apply to your entry (see page v for instructions)

16000.2   **Process Costing**
16000.2.2   **Conversion Costs (Labor and Overhead)**
16000.2.2.2   **Recording Factory (Manufacturing) Overhead Expense**

Factory (Manufacturing) Overhead - Depreciation Expense   xxxx
    Accumulated Depreciation - [Various Assets]   xxxx
To record factory-related depreciation expense

Factory (Manufacturing) Overhead - Utilities Expense   xxxx
    Accounts (Utilities) Payable   xxxx
To record factory-related utility expense

Factory (Manufacturing) Overhead - Insurance Expense   xxxx
    Accounts Payable (Prepaid Insurance)   xxxx
To record factory-related insurance expense

Factory (Manufacturing) Overhead - Property Tax Expense   xxxx
    Property Taxes Payable (Prepaid Property Taxes)   xxxx
To record factory-related property tax expense

Factory (Manufacturing) Overhead - Indirect Materials
    Expense   xxxx
    *Raw Materials Inventory   xxxx
To record use of indirect materials

*See GEN16000.1.1 for use of this account.

Factory (Manufacturing) Overhead - Indirect Labor
    Expense   xxxx
    **Factory Wages Expense (Factory Outside Labor
        Expense)   xxxx
*To record transfer of indirect labor costs to Factory
(Manufacturing) Overhead*

**See GEN16000.1.2.1 for the initial entry to record factory wages expense or outside labor expense.

16000.2.2.3   **Allocation of Conversion Costs**

Important: Make sure all appropriate subheads apply to your entry (see page v for instructions)

16000.2	**Process Costing**	
16000.2.2	**Conversion Costs (Labor and Overhead)**	
16000.2.2.3	**Allocation of Conversion Costs**	

16000.2.2.3.1   **Simplified Allocation Approach**

In the simplified approach illustrated in the entry below, factory overhead is not applied using predetermined application (overhead or burden) rates, and direct labor is not recorded separately from indirect labor.

Work-In-Process Inventory - [Various Departments]	xxxx
*Raw Materials Inventory	xxxx
**Factory Wages Expense (Factory Outside	
Labor Expense)	xxxx
***[Various Accounts]	xxxx
To record conversion costs for departments	

*This account is credited for the amount of indirect materials used. *See GEN16000.2.1.2.2.*

**This account is credited for the amount of indirect labor. *See GEN16000.2.2.1* for the initial entry to record factory wages expense or outside labor expense.

***Examples of other accounts that may be credited include those for:
- -supplies
- -labor
- -depreciation
- -utilities
- -other overhead items.

Similar entries would be made charging each department's separate work-in-process inventory account for the conversion costs incurred in that department.

16000.2.2.3.2   **Expanded Allocation Approach**

In the expanded allocation approach, factory (manufacturing) overhead is applied using predetermined application (overhead or burden) rates, and direct labor is recorded separately from indirect labor. The predetermined application (overhead or burden) rate can be calculated by the following formula:

$$\frac{\text{Estimated Total Annual Factory Overhead}}{\text{Estimated Total Annual Direct Labor Hours}}$$
(Or another base)

Important: Make sure all appropriate subheads apply to your entry (see page v for instructions)

16000.2	**Process Costing**
16000.2.2	**Conversion Costs (Labor and Overhead)**
16000.2.2.3	**Allocation of Conversion Costs**
16000.2.2.3.2	**Expanded Allocation Approach**

This calculation provides an amount per direct labor hour (or other base) that can be used to apply overhead costs to individual jobs. Because this application is based on estimates, some overhead costs may be left in Factory (Manufacturing) Overhead at the end of an accounting period.

16000.2.2.3.2.1   **Direct Labor**

Direct labor is labor that can be directly traced to a particular product.

> *Work-In-Process Inventory - [Various Departments]   xxxx
> Factory Wages Expense (Factory Outside
>   Labor Expense)   xxxx
> *To record direct labor in [various departments]*

*Similar entries are made for subsequent departments to record direct labor incurred in those departments.

16000.2.2.3.2.2   **Factory (Manufacturing) Overhead**

16000.2.2.3.2.2.1   **Recording Actual Factory (Manufacturing) Overhead**

> *Factory (Manufacturing) Overhead Control   xxxx
>   **Raw Materials Inventory   xxxx
>   ***Factory Wages Expense (Factory Outside
>   Labor Expense)   xxxx
>   ****[Various Accounts]   xxxx
> *To record actual factory (manufacturing) overhead*

*This account is used to accumulate actual overhead costs.

**This account is credited for the amount of indirect materials used. *See GEN16000.2.1.2.2.*

***This account is credited for the amount of indirect labor used. *See GEN16000.2.2.1* for the initial entry to record factory wages expense or outside labor expense.

Important: Make sure all appropriate subheads apply to your entry (see page v for instructions)

16000.2	**Process Costing**
16000.2.2	**Conversion Costs (Labor and Overhead)**
16000.2.2.3	**Allocation of Conversion Costs**
16000.2.2.3.2	**Expanded Allocation Approach**
16000.2.2.3.2.2	**Factory (Manufacturing) Overhead**
16000.2.2.3.2.2.1	**Recording Actual Factory (Manufacturing) Overhead**

****Examples of other accounts that may be credited include:
- -supplies
- -depreciation
- -utilities
- -other overhead items.

Similar entries are made charging each department's separate work-in-process inventory account for the conversion costs incurred in that department.

16000.2.2.3.2.2.2 Recording Application of Factory (Manufacturing) Overhead to Departments

*Work-In-Process - [Various Departments]	xxxx	
**Applied Factory (Manufacturing) Overhead		xxxx
To record application of factory (manufacturing) overhead to departments		

*Similar entries are made for factory (manufacturing) overhead applied in subsequent departments.

**This account is used to accumulate amounts of overhead applied to production. Factory (Manufacturing) Overhead Control is not used for this purpose under this system. (*See GEN16000.2.2.3.2.2.1* for use of the Factory (Manufacturing) Overhead Control account.) The amount for this entry is determined by using a predetermined application (overhead or burden) rate. *See GEN16000.2.2.3.2* for an explanation of this rate.

16000.2.2.3.2.2.3 Over-Applied or Under-Applied Factory (Manufacturing) Overhead

Because the application of overhead to Work-In-Process Inventory is accomplished by using a predetermined application (overhead or burden) rate based on estimates (*see GEN16000.1.3.2*), the debit balance in Factory (Manufacturing) Overhead Control will not usually equal the credit balance in Applied Factory (Manufacturing) Overhead at the end of the period. If the credit balance in Applied Factory (Manufacturing) Overhead is less than the debit balance in Factory (Manufacturing) Overhead Control, the overhead is said to be under-applied. If the credit balance in Applied Factory (Manufacturing) Overhead is greater than the debit balance in Factory (Manufacturing) Overhead Control, the overhead is said to be over-applied. This section covers what to do with these differences.

Important: Make sure all appropriate subheads apply to your entry (see page v for instructions)

16000.2	**Process Costing**
16000.2.2	**Conversion Costs (Labor and Overhead)**
16000.2.2.3	**Allocation of Conversion Costs**
16000.2.2.3.2	**Expanded Allocation Approach**
16000.2.2.3.2.2	**Factory (Manufacturing) Overhead**
16000.2.2.3.2.2.3	**Over-Applied or Under-Applied Factory (Manufacturing) Overhead**

16000.2.2.3.2.2.3.1   **Over-Applied or Under-Applied Overhead Is Not Significant Compared with Total Actual Factory (Manufacturing) Overhead During the Period**

Over-Applied Factory (Manufacturing) Overhead:

*Applied Factory (Manufacturing) Overhead	xxxx	
**Factory (Manufacturing) Overhead Control		xxxx
Cost Of Goods Sold		xxxx

To close over-applied factory (manufacturing) overhead to Cost Of Goods Sold

Under-Applied Factory (Manufacturing) Overhead:

Cost Of Goods Sold	xxxx	
*Applied Factory (Manufacturing) Overhead	xxxx	
**Factory (Manufacturing) Overhead Control		xxxx

To close under-applied factory (manufacturing) overhead to Cost Of Goods Sold

*Applied Factory (Manufacturing) Overhead is debited for the amount of its credit balance. *See GEN16000.2.2.3.2.2.2* for use of this account.

**Factory (Manufacturing) Overhead Control is credited for the amount of its debit balance. *See GEN16000.2.2.3.2.2.1* for use of this account.

16000.2.2.3.2.2.3.2   **Over-Applied or Under-Applied Factory (Manufacturing) Overhead Is Significant Compared with Total Factory (Manufacturing) Overhead During the Period**

Over-Applied Factory (Manufacturing) Overhead:

*Applied Factory (Manufacturing) Overhead	xxxx	
**Factory (Manufacturing) Overhead Control		xxxx
***Cost Of Goods Sold		xxxx
***Finished Goods Inventory		xxxx
***Work-In-Process Inventory		xxxx

To close over-applied factory (manufacturing) overhead to Cost Of Goods Sold, Finished Goods Inventory, and Work-In-Process Inventory

Important: Make sure all appropriate subheads apply to your entry (see page v for instructions)

16000.2	**Process Costing**
16000.2.2	**Conversion Costs (Labor and Overhead)**
16000.2.2.3	**Allocation of Conversion Costs**
16000.2.2.3.2	**Expanded Allocation Approach**
16000.2.2.3.2.2	**Factory (Manufacturing) Overhead**
16000.2.2.3.2.2.3	**Over-Applied or Under-Applied Factory (Mfg.) Overhead**
16000.2.2.3.2.2.3.2	**Over-Applied or Under-Applied Factory (Mfg) Overhead is Significant Compared with Total Factory (Mfg) Overhead During the Period**

*Applied Factory (Manufacturing) Overhead is debited for the amount of its credit balance. *See GEN16000.2.2.3.2.2.2* for use of this account.

**Factory (Manufacturing) Overhead Control is credited for the amount of its debit balance. *See GEN16000.2.2.3.2.2.1* for use of this account.

***The amount of the over-applied factory (manufacturing) overhead is allocated with credits to:
> -Cost Of Goods Sold
> -Finished Goods Inventory
> -Work-In-Process Inventory

on the basis of relative amounts of factory (manufacturing) overhead earlier applied to those accounts. *For example,* if the amounts of factory (manufacturing) overhead in Cost of Goods Sold, Finished Goods Inventory, and Work-in-Process Inventory are, $80,000, $50,000, and $30,000, respectively (a total of $160,000), the amount of the over-applied factory (manufacturing) overhead is allocated by crediting Cost of Goods Sold for 8/16, Finished Goods Inventory for 5/16, and Work-In-Process Inventory for 3/16 of the over-applied amount.

Under-Applied Factory (Manufacturing) Overhead:

***Cost Of Goods Sold	xxxx	
***Finished Goods Inventory	xxxx	
***Work-In-Process Inventory	xxxx	
**Applied Factory (Manufacturing) Overhead	xxxx	
*Factory (Manufacturing) Overhead Control		xxxx
To close over-applied factory (manufacturing) overhead		

*Factory (Manufacturing) Overhead Control is credited for the amount of its debit balance. *See GEN16000.2.2.3.2.2.1* for use of this account.

**Applied Factory (Manufacturing) Overhead is debited for the amount of its credit balance.

***The amount of the under-applied factory (manufacturing) overhead is allocated with debits to:
> -Cost Of Goods Sold
> -Finished Goods Inventory
> -Work-In-Process Inventory

Important: Make sure all appropriate subheads apply to your entry (see page v for instructions)

16000.2	**Process Costing**
16000.2.2	**Conversion Costs (Labor and Overhead)**
16000.2.2.3	**Allocation of Conversion Costs**
16000.2.2.3.2	**Expanded Allocation Approach**
16000.2.2.3.2.2	**Factory (Manufacturing) Overhead**
16000.2.2.3.2.2.3	**Over-Applied or Under-Applied Factory (Mfg.) Overhead**
16000.2.2.3.2.2.3.2	**Over-Applied or Under-Applied Factory (Mfg) Overhead is Significant Compared with Total Factory (Mfg) Overhead During the Period**

on the basis of relative amounts of factory (manufacturing) overhead earlier applied to those accounts. *For example,* if the amounts of factory (manufacturing) overhead in Cost of Goods Sold, Finished Goods Inventory, and Work-in-Process Inventory are $80,000, $50,000, and $30,000, respectively (a total of $160,000), the amount of the under-applied factory (manufacturing) overhead is allocated by debiting Cost Of Goods Sold for 8/16, Finished Goods Inventory for 5/16, and Work-In-Process Inventory for 3/16 of the under-applied amount.

16000.2.3   Transfer of Units

16000.2.3.1   Transfer Between Departments

*Work-In-Process Inventory - [Department #2]	xxxx	
*Work-In-Process Inventory - [Department #1]		xxxx
To record completion of units in Department #1 and		
subsequent transfer to Department #2		

*As work is completed and transferred to the next department, an entry is made transferring the cost of the completed units, based on the production cost report, to the subsequent department.

16000.2.3.2   Transfer from Last Department to Finished Goods Inventory

Finished Goods Inventory	xxxx	
Work-In-Process Inventory - [Last Department]		xxxx
To record completion of units in the last department and		
subsequent transfer to Finished Goods Inventory		

16000.3   Standard Costing

16000.3.1   Materials (Parts)

Important: Make sure all appropriate subheads apply to your entry (see page v for instructions)

16000.3   **Standard Costing**
16000.3.1   **Materials (Parts)**

16000.3.1.1   **Materials (Parts) Purchases**

*Raw Materials (Parts) Inventory	xxxx	
Direct Material Price Variance		xxxx
Accounts Payable		xxxx
To record purchase of materials or parts		

*Raw Materials (Parts) Inventory is debited for the actual quantity purchased at the standard unit price. Accounts Payable is credited for the actual quantity at the actual unit price, and Direct Material Price Variance is credited (favorable) or debited (unfavorable) to balance the entry. The amount of this debit or credit will be equal to the actual quantity times the difference between the actual unit price and the standard unit price.

16000.3.1.2   **Materials (Parts) Use (Requisition)**

16000.3.1.2.1   **Direct Materials (Parts)**

Direct materials are materials (parts) that can be directly traced to and physically become a part of the product produced.

*Work-In-Process Inventory	xxxx	
Direct Materials Efficiency Variance	xxxx	
Raw Materials (Parts) Inventory		xxxx
To record direct materials used in production		

*Work-In-Process Inventory is debited for the standard quantity required for the job at the standard unit price. Raw Materials (Parts) Inventory is credited for the actual quantity issued at the standard unit price. Direct Materials Efficiency Variance is debited (unfavorable) or credited (favorable) for the difference to balance the entry. The amount of this debit or credit will be equal to the standard unit price times the actual quantity issued, less the standard quantity required for the job.

16000.3.2   **Labor**

Important: Make sure all appropriate subheads apply to your entry (see page v for instructions)

16000.3   **Standard Costing**
16000.3.2   **Labor**

16000.3.2.1   **Labor Expense Incurrence**

In addition to the entries shown below, *see GEN7000.10* for a more complete discussion of payroll, payroll taxes, and other employee-related liabilities.

16000.3.2.1.1   **Inside Labor**

Inside labor is labor performed by employees of the company.

Factory Wage Expense	xxxx	
*Federal Income Tax Withheld		xxxx
*State Income Tax Withheld		xxxx
**F.I.C.A. Tax Withheld		xxxx
***[Other Withholdings Payable]		xxxx
****Factory Wages Payable		xxxx
To record payroll		

*Federal and state withholdings are found by referring to tax withholding tables provided by the federal and state governments.

**A common alternative account title is Social Security Tax Withheld.

***Other withholdings may include amounts for insurance premiums, savings plans, union dues, and uniform costs.

****Factory Wages Payable is credited for the amount of net salaries and wages; i.e., gross salaries and wages minus all payroll deductions.

16000.3.2.1.2   **Outside Labor**

Outside labor is labor performed by employees of another company with which a contract to supply labor is held. These employees will be paid by the labor supplying company which will account for all withholdings and payroll taxes. All that is necessary is to record the labor expense and the liability to the labor supplying company.

Factory Outside Labor Expense	xxxx	
Factory Outside Labor Payable		xxxx
To record outside labor expense		

Important: Make sure all appropriate subheads apply to your entry (see page v for instructions)

16000.3   **Standard Costing**
16000.3.2   **Labor**

16000.3.2.2   **Direct Labor**

*Work-In-Process Inventory	xxxx	
***Direct Labor Efficiency Variance	xxxx	
****Direct Labor Price Variance		xxxx
**Factory Wages Expense (Factory Outside Labor Expense)		xxxx

To record direct labor

*Work-In-Process Inventory is debited for the standard hours allowed at the standard labor rate per hour.

**Factory Wages Expense (Factory Outside Labor Expense) is credited for the actual hours at the actual hourly rate. *See GEN16000.3.2.1* for initial entry to this account.

***Direct Labor Efficiency Variance is either debited (unfavorable) for the excess of the actual hours used over the standard hours required times the standard labor rate per hour, or credited (favorable) for the excess of the standard hours required over the actual hours used times the standard labor rate per hour.

****Direct Labor Price Variance is either credited (favorable) for the excess of the standard hourly rate over the actual hourly rate times the actual hours used, or debited (unfavorable) for the excess of the actual hourly rate over the standard hourly rate times the actual hours used.

16000.3.3   **Factory (Manufacturing) Overhead**

16000.3.3.1   **Recording Actual Factory (Manufacturing) Overhead**

*Factory (Manufacturing) Overhead Control	xxxx	
**Raw Materials Inventory		xxxx
Factory Wages Expense (Factory Outside Labor Expense)		xxxx
***[Various Accounts]		xxxx

To record actual overhead incurred

*This account is used to accumulate actual overhead costs.

Important: Make sure all appropriate subheads apply to your entry (see page v for instructions)

16000.3   **Standard Costing**
16000.3.3   **Factory (Manufacturing) Overhead**
16000.3.3.1   **Recording Actual Factory (Manufacturing) Overhead**

**Raw Materials Inventory is credited for the amount of indirect materials used.

***Examples of other accounts that may be credited include:
   -Supplies
   -Depreciation (Accumulated Depreciation)
   -[Various Expenses]
   -[Various Assets]
   -[Various Liabilities].

16000.3.3.2   **Applying Factory (Manufacturing) Overhead**

*Work-In-Process Inventory	xxxx	
**Applied Factory (Manufacturing) Overhead		xxxx

To record application of overhead to production

*Work-In-Process Inventory and Applied Factory (Manufacturing) Overhead are debited and credited, respectively, for the standard overhead rate times the standard hours (or other standard base) allowed for the job.

**This account is used to accumulate amounts of overhead applied to production. Factory (Manufacturing) Overhead Control is not used for this purpose under this system. *See GEN16000.2.2.3.2.2.1 for use of Factory (Manufacturing) Overhead Control.* The amount for this entry is determined by multiplying the standard overhead cost per unit times the equivalent whole units flowing through the Work-In-Process Inventory as calculated in a production report.

16000.3.4   **Closing Variance Accounts**

16000.3.4.1   **Net Amount of Variances Is Not Significant Compared with Total Manufacturing Costs for the Period**

Direct Material Price Variance	xxxx	
Direct Labor Price Variance	xxxx	
*Cost Of Goods Sold	xxxx	
Direct Material Efficiency Variance		xxxx
Direct Labor Efficiency Variance		xxxx

To close variance accounts to Cost of Goods Sold

Important: Make sure all appropriate subheads apply to your entry (see page v for instructions)

16000.3 **Standard Costing**
16000.3.4   **Closing Variance Accounts**
16000.3.4.1   **Net Amount of Variances Is Not Significant Compared with Total Manufacturing Costs for the Period**

---

*Direct material price and efficiency variances and direct labor price and efficiency variances are closed to Cost of Goods Sold (which is debited or credited as necessary to balance the journal entry) if their net balances are not significant compared with total manufacturing costs for the period. If their net balances are significant compared with total manufacturing costs for the period, *see GEN16000.3.4.2.*

16000.3.4.2   **Net Amount of Variances Is Significant Compared with the Total Manufacturing Costs for the Period**

Direct Material Price Variance	xxxx	
Direct Labor Price Variance	xxxx	
*Work-In-Process Inventory	xxxx	
*Finished Goods Inventory	xxxx	
*Cost Of Goods Sold	xxxx	
Direct Material Efficiency Variance		xxxx
Direct Labor Efficiency Variance		xxxx

To close variance accounts to Work-In-Process Inventory, Finished Goods Inventory, and Cost Of Goods Sold

*Direct material price and efficiency variances and direct labor price and efficiency variances are closed to:
    -Work-In-Process Inventory
    -Finished Goods Inventory
    -Cost Of Goods Sold
if the net balances of these variance accounts are significant compared with total manufacturing costs for the period. These accounts are debited or credited as necessary to balance the journal entry. (If their net balances are not significant compared with total manufacturing costs for the period, *see GEN16000.3.4.1.*) The total amount to be closed to Work-In-Process Inventory, Finished Goods Inventory, and Cost of Goods Sold is allocated among these accounts on the basis of the relative amounts of materials and labor costs contained in the balances of these accounts. *For example,* if the amounts of materials and labor costs contained in the balances of these accounts are $50,000, $70,000, and $80,000, respectively (a total of $200,000), 5/20 of the total amount to be closed is allocated to Work-In-Process Inventory, 7/20 to Finished Goods Inventory, and 8/20 to Cost Of Goods Sold.

Important: Make sure all appropriate subheads apply to your entry (see page v for instructions)

16000.3   **Standard Costing**

16000.3.5   **Under-Applied or Over-Applied Factory (Manufacturing) Overhead**

If the balance in Factory (Manufacturing) Overhead exceeds the balance in Applied Factory (Manufacturing) Overhead, overhead is said to be under-applied. If the balance in Applied Factory (Manufacturing) Overhead exceeds the balance in Factory (Manufacturing) Overhead, overhead is said to be over-applied.

16000.3.5.1   **Under-Applied or Over-Applied Factory (Manufacturing) Is Not Significant Compared with Total Factory (Manufacturing) Overhead for the Period**

*Applied Factory (Manufacturing) Overhead	xxxx	
Factory (Manufacturing) Overhead Control		xxxx
**Cost Of Goods Sold		xxxx

To close under-applied or over-applied overhead to Cost Of Goods Sold

*See GEN16000.3.3.2 for a discussion of how this account is used to apply overhead to production.

**Cost Of Goods Sold is debited (if overhead is under-applied) or credited (if overhead is over-applied) to balance the entry. Over-applied or under-applied factory (manufacturing) overhead is closed to Cost Of Goods Sold if the amount is not significant compared with the total overhead costs during the period. If the amount is significant compared with the total overhead costs during the period, *see* GEN16000.3.5.2.

16000.3.5.2   **Under-Applied or Over-Applied Factory (Manufacturing) Overhead Is Significant Compared with Total Factory (Manufacturing) Overhead During the Period**

*Applied Factory (Manufacturing) Overhead	xxxx	
Factory (Manufacturing) Overhead Control		xxxx
**Work-In-Process Inventory		xxxx
**Finished Goods Inventory		xxxx
**Cost Of Goods Sold		xxxx

To close under-applied or over-applied overhead to Cost Of Goods Sold

Important: Make sure all appropriate subheads apply to your entry (see page v for instructions)

16000.3	**Standard Costing**
16000.3.5	**Under-Applied or Over-Applied Factory (Manufacturing) Overhead**
16000.3.5.2	**Under-Applied or Over-Applied Factory (Manufacturing) Overhead is Significant Compared with Total Factory (Manufacturing) Overhead During the Period**

*See GEN16000.3.3.2 for a discussion of how this account is used to apply overhead to production.

**Work-In-Process Inventory, Finished Goods Inventory, and Cost Of Goods Sold are debited (in the case of under-applied overhead) or credited (in the case of over-applied overhead) to balance the entry. If the amount of under-applied or over-applied overhead is significant compared with the total overhead costs during the period, this amount is closed to:

-Work-In-Process Inventory
-Finished Goods Inventory
-Cost Of Goods Sold

on the basis of the relative amounts of overhead contained in the balances of those accounts. For example, if the amount of overhead contained in the balances of those accounts is $60,000, $30,000, and $70,000, respectively (a total of $160,000), 6/16 of the under-applied or over-applied overhead is allocated to Work-In-Process Inventory, 3/16 to Finished Goods Inventory, and 7/16 to Cost Of Goods Sold.

16000.3.6   **Completion of Product**

Finished Goods	xxxx	
Work-In-Process Inventory		xxxx
To record completion of product and transfer to Finished Goods Inventory		

16000.4   **Variable (Direct) Costing**

Variable (direct) costing is a cost reporting system under which only variable costs that include direct materials, direct labor, and variable factory (manufacturing) overhead are allocated to Work-In-Process Inventory, Finished Goods Inventory, and Cost Of Goods Sold. Fixed production costs are treated as period costs and expensed as incurred. Variable costing is useful for cost control and management decision-making purposes, but it is not permitted for the purposes of financial accounting. Thus, if variable costing is used as the primary costing system, Work-In-Process Inventory, Finished Goods Inventory, and Cost Of Goods Sold must be adjusted at the end of the period to include the fixed costs of manufacturing for financial accounting purposes.

Important: Make sure all appropriate subheads apply to your entry (see page v for instructions)

16000.4   **Variable (Direct) Costing**

16000.4.1   **Adjusting Accounts from Variable (Direct) Costing to Include Fixed Costs of Manufacturing**

Work-In-Process Inventory	xxxx	
Finished Goods Inventory	xxxx	
Cost Of Goods Sold	xxxx	
*[Various Accounts]		xxxx

To adjust inventory accounts and Cost of Goods Sold for a pro rata share of fixed factory overhead for financial accounting purposes

*Any accounts that include fixed factory (manufacturing) overhead costs that would normally be inventoried if variable costing were not used should be credited in this entry.

16000.5   **Spoilage, Scrap, and Reworked Product**

16000.5.1   **Spoilage**

Spoilage is the cost of unacceptable units of production that are discarded or sold for scrap value. Normal spoilage arises under efficient operations. Abnormal spoilage is not expected to arise under efficient operating conditions.

16000.5.1.1   **Normal Spoilage**

16000.5.1.1.1   **Normal Spoilage Recorded**

*Spoiled Production Inventory	xxxx	
**Factory (Manufacturing) Overhead - Normal Spoilage	xxxx	
***Work-In-Process Inventory - [Various Jobs]		xxxx

To record normal spoilage in a job cost system

*Spoiled production is recorded in Spoiled Production Inventory at estimated scrap value until sold.

COST ACCOUNTING

Important: Make sure all appropriate subheads apply to your entry (see page v for instructions)

16000.5	**Spoilage, Scrap, and Reworked Product**
16000.5.1	**Spoilage**
16000.5.1.1	**Normal Spoilage**
16000.5.1.1.1	**Normal Spoilage Recorded**

**Factory (Manufacturing) Overhead is charged with the net cost of spoilage (gross cost of the spoiled production less estimated cost of disposal). This net cost is spread over all production as factory (manufacturing) overhead is allocated through use of the predetermined overhead rate. (*See GEN16000.2.2.3.2.*)

***The inclusion of a job designation here indicates that this entry is for a job-order costing system. In a process cost system, normal spoilage flows through the system as a normal cost of operations, and a separate entry to record normal spoilage is not required.

16000.5.1.1.2   **Normal Spoilage Sold**

Accounts Receivable (Cash)	xxxx	
Spoiled Production Inventory		xxxx
*Gain On Sale Of Spoiled Production		xxxx
To record sale of spoiled production		

*A gain is recorded if the sales price is greater than the estimated scrap value at which it was carried in Spoiled Production Inventory. If the sales price is less than the estimated scrap value at which it was carried, Loss On Sale Of Spoiled Production is recorded. If the sales price is exactly equal to the estimated scrap value at which it was carried, no gain or loss is recorded.

16000.5.1.2   **Abnormal Spoilage**

Loss From Abnormal Spoilage	xxxx	
Work-In-Process Inventory		xxxx
To record the costs of abnormal spoilage for the period in		
a process costing system or a job order cost system		

16000.5.2   **Scrap**

Scrap may be defined as a product that has minimal or no sales value compared with the sales value of the main or joint products. Scrap is not usually inventoried.

Important: Make sure all appropriate subheads apply to your entry (see page v for instructions)

16000.5	**Spoilage, Scrap, and Reworked Product**
16000.5.2	**Scrap**

16000.5.2.1

Sale of Scrap if Amount Received Is Recorded as Scrap Revenue

Accounts Receivable (Cash)	xxxx	
Sales of Scrap (Scrap Revenue)		xxxx
To record sale of scrap		

16000.5.2.2

Sale of Scrap if Amount Received Is Used to Offset Cost of All Production

Accounts Receivable (Cash)	xxxx	
Factory (Manufacturing) Overhead		xxxx
To record sale of scrap		

16000.5.2.3

Sale of Scrap if Amount Received Is Used to Offset the Cost of a Particular Job in a Job Cost System

Accounts Receivable (Cash)	xxxx	
Work-In-Process Inventory - [Various Jobs]		xxxx
To record sale of scrap		

16000.5.3

Reworked Units

*Factory (Manufacturing) Overhead - Reworked Units	xxxx	
Raw Materials (Parts) Inventory		xxxx
**Factory Wages Expense (Factory Outside Labor Expense)		xxxx
***Applied Factory (Manufacturing) Overhead		xxxx
To record the cost of reworking defective units		

*Under this method, the cost of reworking units will be spread over all units produced using a predetermined overhead rate. *See GEN16000.2.2.3.2* for the calculation and use of overhead rates.

**See GEN16000.3.2.1* for the initial use of this account.

***See GEN16000.3.3.2* for a discussion of how this account is used to apply overhead to production.

Important: Make sure all appropriate subheads apply to your entry (see page v for instructions)

16000.6

Operations (Hybrid) Costing

*Operations (hybrid) costing is a costing system used for production runs of homogeneous products. Each production order flows through a sequence of departments or processes. Every unit of product is treated the same within each department or process it goes through. Product costs are compiled for each individual production run. Direct materials, which may differ by production order, are specifically identified with the appropriate order as they are in a job order costing system (*see GEN16000.1.1.2.1*). Conversion costs (all other manufacturing costs) are compiled for each department or process and applied to all units passing through the department or process using a basis of volume such as the number of units in the production order. Thus, conversion costs are accounted for in a manner similar to that used in a process costing system.

16000.6.1

Materials (Parts) Use (Requisition)

Work-In-Process Inventory - [Various Departments (Processes)]	xxxx	
Raw Materials (Parts) Inventory		xxxx
To record the use of direct materials in a specific department or process		

16000.6.2

Recording Actual Conversion Costs

Conversion costs are all manufacturing costs other than direct materials; i.e., all indirect materials, labor, and overhead.

Conversion Costs	xxxx	
*[Various Accounts]		xxxx
To record actual conversion costs		

*Credits will be made to Raw Materials Inventory (for indirect materials), Factory Wages Expense (Factory Outside Labor Expense) (for indirect and direct labor), and any account that would normally be credited as actual factory (manufacturing) overhead is recorded.

Important: Make sure all appropriate subheads apply to your entry (see page v for instructions)

16000.6   **Operations (Hybrid) Costing**

16000.6.3   **Application of Conversion Costs to Production**

             *Work-In-Process Inventory - [Various Departments
                 (Process)]   xxxx
                *Applied Conversion Costs   xxxx
             To record application of conversion costs to production

*The amount debited to Work-In-Process Inventory and credited to Applied Conversion Costs is determined by using a predetermined application (overhead or burden) rate. *See GEN16000.2.2.3.2* for a discussion of predetermined application (overhead or burden) rates.

16000.6.4   **Transfer of Production Between Departments (Processes)**

            Work-In-Process Inventory - [Department (Process) #2]   xxxx
                Work-In-Process Inventory - [Department (Process)
                   #1]   xxxx
            To record transfer of production from Department
            (Process) #1 to Department (Process) #2

16000.6.5   **Transfer of Production Out of Last Department (Process) to Finished Goods Inventory**

            Finished Goods Inventory   xxxx
                Work-In-Process Inventory - [Last Department
                   (Process)]   xxxx
            To record completion of production and transfer of
            production to Finished Goods Inventory

16000.7   **Backflush (Post-Deduct or Delayed) Costing**

Backflush (post-deduct or delayed) costing is a modified form of standard cost accounting that was developed to reduce the clerical effort and cost of traditional standard cost accounting systems. The traditional standard cost system tracks costs from material requisitions and time tickets through direct materials and direct labor to work in process then to finished goods. This can be an expensive process. The term "backflush" arose because inventory costing can be delayed until as late as the

---

Important: Make sure all appropriate subheads apply to your entry (see page v for instructions)

16000.7 **Backflush (Post-Deduct or Delayed) Costing**

time of sale, when costs are then "backflushed" through the system, and inventories are costed. This system is often used with a just-in-time (JIT) production system in which amounts of direct materials and work in process are constant or small.

16000.7.1 **Purchase of Raw Materials (Parts)**

*Raw Materials (Parts) And Work-In-Process Inventory	xxxx	
**Raw Materials Price Variance	xxxx	
Accounts Payable		xxxx

To record the purchase of raw materials or parts

*The combined raw materials (parts) and work-in-process inventory account is debited for the actual quantity of materials acquired times the standard unit cost of materials (parts) acquired.

**Raw Materials Price Variance is debited for the excess of actual unit cost over standard unit cost of materials acquired times the actual quantity of materials acquired. If the standard unit cost of materials acquired is in excess of the actual unit cost, this excess times the actual quantity of materials acquired is credited to this account.

16000.7.2 **Recording Actual Conversion Costs**

Conversion costs are all manufacturing costs other than direct materials; i.e., all indirect materials, labor, and overhead.

Conversion Costs	xxxx	
*[Various Accounts]		xxxx

To record actual conversion costs

*Credits will be made to Raw Materials (Parts) Inventory (for indirect materials), Factory Wages Expense (Factory Outside Labor Expense) (for indirect and direct labor), and any account that would normally be credited as actual factory (manufacturing) overhead is recorded.

Important: Make sure all appropriate subheads apply to your entry (see page v for instructions)

16000.7   **Backflush (Post-Deduct or Delayed) Costing**

16000.7.3   **Recording Finished Goods**

Finished Goods Inventory	xxxx	
Raw Materials (Parts) And Work-In-Process		
Inventory		xxxx
*Applied Conversion Costs		xxxx

To transfer the standard costs of goods completed to Finished Goods Inventory

*The amount credited to Applied Conversion Costs is determined by using a predetermined application (overhead or burden) rate. *See GEN16000.2.2.3.2* for a discussion of predetermined application (overhead or burden) rates.

16000.7.4   **Recording Cost of Goods Sold**

Cost Of Goods Sold	xxxx	
Finished Goods Inventory		xxxx

To record cost of goods sold

16000.7.5   **Recording Raw Materials Efficiency Variance**

*Raw Materials Efficiency Variance	xxxx	
Raw Materials (Parts) And Work-In-Process		
Inventory		xxxx

To record materials efficiency variance

*Raw Materials Efficiency Variance is debited (unfavorable) and Raw Materials (Parts) And Work-In-Process Inventory is credited for any excess of actual direct materials cost in Raw Materials (Parts) And Work-In-Process Inventory over the standard unit price of materials (parts) times the standard quantity of materials (parts) needed (standard cost) for the current work-in-process given its current stage of completion. If the standard cost is in excess of the actual direct materials cost in Raw Materials (Parts) And Work-In-Process Inventory, Raw Materials Efficiency Variance would be credited (favorable) and Raw Materials (Parts) And Work-In-Process Inventory would be debited.

Important: Make sure all appropriate subheads apply to your entry (see page v for instructions)

16000.7   **Backflush (Post-Deduct or Delayed) Costing**

16000.7.6   **Recording Under-Applied or Over-Applied Conversion Costs**

If the credit balance in Applied Conversion Costs is in excess of the debit balance in Conversion Costs, conversion costs are said to be under-applied. If the debit balance in Conversion Costs is in excess of the credit balance in Applied Conversion Costs, conversion costs are said to be over-applied.

16000.7.6.1   **Recording Under-Applied Conversion Costs**

Applied Conversion Costs	xxxx	
*Cost Of Goods Sold	xxxx	
Conversion Costs		xxxx
To record under-applied conversion costs		

*Under-applied conversion costs are usually closed to Cost Of Goods Sold, regardless of how significant or insignificant the amount is.

16000.7.6.2   **Recording Over-Applied Conversion Costs**

Applied Conversion Costs	xxxx	
*Cost Of Goods Sold		xxxx
Conversion Costs		xxxx
To record over-applied conversion costs		

*Over-applied conversion costs are usually closed to Cost Of Goods Sold, regardless of how significant or insignificant the amount is.

TABLE OF CONTENTS

GEN17000   BUSINESS COMBINATIONS

17000.1   **A Single Legal Entity (Corporation) Survives Combination**

17000.1.1   **Merger-Type Combination (One Combining Legal Entity Is the Survivor, and the Other Combining Legal Entity Is Dissolved)**

17000.1.1.1   **Purchase Method of Accounting**

*[Various Assets]	xxxx	
**Goodwill	xxxx	
***[Various Liabilities]		xxxx
****Cash		xxxx
*****[Various Debt And Equity]		xxxx

To record business combination

*The various assets acquired, including identifiable and separable intangible assets are debited for their fair market value at the date of combination, unless the expected future use indicates a lower value to the acquirer.

**Goodwill is debited in a business combination accounted for by the purchase method when the purchase price exceeds the total of the fair market values assigned to the various separately identifiable net assets acquired. Goodwill and other intangible assets that have indefinite useful lives will not be amortized but rather will be tested at least annually for impairment. *See GEN6000.1.1.3.*

***The various liabilities assumed are credited for their fair market value at the date of combination.

****The credit to Cash may (in addition to amounts paid as part of the purchase price) include amounts paid for legal and accounting fees (but not costs of registering and issuing debt or equity securities) directly related to the business combination.

*****Accounts for the various debt (bonds payable, long-term notes payable, mortgages payable, etc.) and equity (preferred stock, common stock, rights, warrants, etc.) given in the combination are credited for their fair market value at the date of combination.

Important: Make sure all appropriate subheads apply to your entry (see page v for instructions)

17000.1   A Single Legal Entity (Corporation) Survives Combination

---

17000.1.2   Consolidation-Type Combination (a New Legal Entity Is Formed, and Both Old Legal Entities Are Dissolved)

17000.1.2.1   Purchase Method of Accounting

*[Various Assets]	xxxx	
**Goodwill	xxxx	
***[Various Liabilities]		xxxx
****Cash		xxxx
*****[Various Debt And Equity]		xxxx

To record business combination

*The various assets acquired are debited for their fair market value at the date of combination.

**Goodwill is debited in a business combination accounted for by the purchase method when the purchase price exceeds the total of the fair market values assigned to the various separately identifiable net assets acquired. Goodwill and other intangible assets that have indefinite useful lives will not be amortized but rather will be tested at least annually for impairment.. *See GEN6000.1.1.3.*

***The various liabilities assumed are credited for their fair market value at the date of combination.

****The credit to Cash may (in addition to amounts paid as part of the purchase price) include amounts paid for legal and accounting fees (but not costs of registering and issuing debt or equity securities) directly related to the business combination.

*****Accounts for the various debt (bonds payable, long-term notes payable, mortgages payable, etc.) and equity (preferred stock, common stock, rights, warrants, etc.) and equity (preferred stock, common stock, rights, warrants, etc.) given in the combination are credited for their fair market value at the date of combination.

17000.2   Both Legal Entities (Corporations) Survive Combination in a Parent/Subsidiary Relationship

---

Important: Make sure all appropriate subheads apply to your entry (see page v for instructions)

17000.2   **Both Legal Entities (Corporations) Survive Combination in a Parent/Subsidiary Relationship**

17000.2.1   **Parent Corporation Acquires 100% of Subsidiary Corporation's Stock Shares**

17000.2.1.1   **Purchase Method of Accounting**

Investment In Subsidiary	xxxx	
*Cash		xxxx
**[Various Debt And Equity Accounts]		xxxx
To record business combination		

*The credit to Cash may (in addition to amounts paid as part of the purchase price) include amounts paid for legal and accounting fees (but not costs of registering and issuing debt or equity securities) directly related to the business combination.

**Accounts for the various debt (bonds payable, long-term notes payable, mortgages payable, etc.) and equity (preferred stock, common stock, rights, warrants, etc.) accounts given in the combination are credited for their fair market value at the date of combination.

17000.2.1.2   **Post-Combination Entries**

See the section on "Long-Term Equity Investments" (*GEN10000.2.2*).

17000.2.2   **Parent Corporation Acquires a Majority (but less than 100%) of Subsidiary Corporation's Stock Shares**

17000.2.2.1   **Purchase Method of Accounting**

Investment in Subsidiary	xxxx	
*Cash		xxxx
** [Various Debt And Equity Accounts]		xxxx
To record business combination		

*The credit to Cash may (in addition to amounts paid as part of the purchase price) include amounts paid for legal and accounting fees (but not costs of registering and issuing debt or equity securities) directly related to the business combination.

Important: Make sure all appropriate subheads apply to your entry (see page v for instructions)

17000.2   **Both Legal Entities (Corporations) Survive Combination in a Parent/Subsidiary Relationship**

17000.2.2   **Parent Corporation Acquires a Majority (but Less than 100%) of Subsidiary Corporation's Stock Shares**

17000.2.2.1   **Purchase Method of Accounting**

**Accounts for the various debt (bonds payable, long-term notes payable, mortgages payable, etc.) and equity (preferred stock, common stock, rights, warrants, etc.) accounts given in the combination are credited for their fair market value at the date of combination.

17000.2.2.2   **Post-Combination Entries**

See the section on "Long-Term Equity Investment" (*GEN10000.2.2*).

17000.3   **A New Subsidiary Legal Entity (a New Corporation) Is Chartered by the Parent, Which then Holds the Subsidiary Corporation's Stock**

17000.3.1   **Chartering New Entity (Corporation)**

Investment in Subsidiary	xxxx	
Cash ([Various Assets])		xxxx
[Various Debt And Equity Accounts]		xxxx
To record charter of new subsidiary		

17000.3.2   **Post-Chartering Entries**

See the section on "Long-Term Equity Investment" (*GEN10000.2.2*).

17000.4   **Pushdown Accounting**

Pushdown accounting is the direct adjustment of assets and liabilities on a subsidiary corporation's books to reflect their fair market values at the date of acquisition by a parent.

*[Various Assets]	xxxx	
**Goodwill	xxxx	
***[Various Liabilities]		xxxx
****Additional Paid-In Capital - Revaluation		xxxx
To revalue assets and liabilities to fair market value		

Important: Make sure all appropriate subheads apply to your entry (see page v for instructions)

17000.4   **Pushdown Accounting**

---

*Various asset accounts are debited (or credited) sufficiently to adjust their balances to fair market value.

**Goodwill is debited for any excess of the purchase price of the acquired corporation over the sum of the fair market values of its separately identified assets and liabilities (i.e., over the sum of the book values of the assets and liabilities plus the adjustments made with this entry).

***The various liability accounts are credited (or debited) sufficiently to adjust their balances to fair market values.

****Additional Paid-In Capital - Revaluation is credited sufficiently to balance the entry.

TABLE OF CONTENTS

18000.1   **Entries on Home Office Books (Separate Accounting Records Created and Maintained at Branch Office)**

18000.1.1   **Transfer of Assets to Branch**

18000.1.1.1   **Transfer of Cash to Branch**

Investment In Branch (Branch Office)	xxxx	
Cash		xxxx
To record transfer of cash to branch office		

18000.1.1.2   **Transfer of Inventory to Branch**

18000.1.1.2.1   **Periodic Inventory System Used**

Investment In Branch (Branch Office)	xxxx	
Shipments To Branch		xxxx
To record transfer of inventory to branch office		

18000.1.1.2.2   **Perpetual Inventory System Used**

Investment In Branch (Branch Office)	xxxx	
Inventory		xxxx
To record transfer of inventory to branch office		

18000.1.1.3   **Transfer of Various Assets to Branch**

Investment In Branch (Branch Office)	xxxx	
[Various Assets]		xxxx
To record transfer of assets to branch office		

Important: Make sure all appropriate subheads apply to your entry (see page v for instructions)

18000.1   **Entries on Home Office Books (Separate Accounting Records Created and Maintained at Branch Office)**

18000.1.2   **Obtaín Fixed Assets for Branch Office (Record-Keeping for Fixed Assets Remains on Home Office Books)**

[Various Fixed Assets] - Branch	xxxx	
Cash		xxxx

To record acquisition of fixed assets to be used for branch office

18000.1.3   **Recognize Results of Operations by Branch Office**

*Investment In Branch (Branch Office)	xxxx	
*Branch Income (Loss)		xxxx

To record results of operations by branch office

*If the branch office incurs a loss, Branch Loss is debited and Investment In Branch is credited instead of this entry. At the end of the accounting period, Branch Income or Branch Loss is closed to Income Summary in the usual manner together with the other revenue and expense accounts of the home office.

18000.1.4   **Transfer of Assets to Home Office from Branch Office**

18000.1.4.1   **Transfer of Cash from Branch Office**

Cash	xxxx	
Investment In Branch (Branch Office)		xxxx

To record transfer of cash from branch office

18000.1.4.2   **Transfer of Other Assets from Branch Office**

[Various Assets]	xxxx	
Investment In Branch (Branch Office)		xxxx

To record transfer of assets from branch office

Important: Make sure all appropriate subheads apply to your entry (see page v for instructions)

18000.1   **Entries on Home Office Books (Separate Accounting Records Created and Maintained at Branch Office)**

18000.1.5   **Discontinuation of Branch Operations (Close All Branch Office Accounts and Transfer All Assets to Home Office**

[Various Assets]	xxxx	
[Various Liabilities]		xxxx
Investment In Branch (Branch Office)		xxxx

To record transfer of remaining assets to home office and close all accounts on branch office books

18000.2   **Entries on Branch Office Books (Separate Accounting Records Created and Maintained at Branch Office)**

18000.2.1   **Transfer of Assets from Home Office**

18000.2.1.1   **Transfer of Cash from Home Office**

Cash	xxxx	
Home Office		xxxx

To record cash transferred from home office

18000.2.1.2   **Transfer of Inventory from Home Office**

18000.2.1.2.1   **Periodic Inventory System Used**

Shipments From Home Office	xxxx	
Home Office		xxxx

To record inventory transferred from home office

18000.2.1.2.2   **Perpetual Inventory System Used**

Inventory	xxxx	
Home Office		xxxx

To record inventory transferred from home office

Important: Make sure all appropriate subheads apply to your entry (see page v for instructions)

18000.2   **Entries on Branch Office Books (Separate Accounting Records Created and Maintained at Branch Office**

18000.2.1   **Transfer of Assets from Home Office**

18000.2.1.3   **Transfer of Other Assets from Home Office**

[Various Assets]	xxxx	
Home Office		xxxx
To record assets transferred from home office		

18000.2.1.4   **Recording Results of Operations at Branch Office**

*Income Summary	xxxx	
Home Office		xxxx
To close Income Summary to home office		

*The branch office records revenue and expense transactions as they occur and closes these accounts to Income Summary. This entry transfers a resulting credit balance in Income Summary (indicating a net profit) to Home Office. If it is necessary to transfer a debit balance in Income Summary (indicating a net loss) to Home Office, this entry would debit Home Office and credit Income Summary.

18000.2.2   **Transfer Assets to Home Office from Branch Office**

18000.2.2.1   **Transfer of Cash to Home Office**

Home Office	xxxx	
Cash		xxxx
To record transfer of cash to home office		

18000.2.2.2   **Transfer of Other Assets to Home Office**

Home Office	xxxx	
[Various Assets]		xxxx
To record transfer of assets to home office		

Important: Make sure all appropriate subheads apply to your entry (see page v for instructions)

18000.2   **Entries on Branch Office Books (Separate Accounting Records Created and Maintained at Branch Office**

18000.2.3   ### Discontinuation of Branch Operations (Close All Branch Office Accounts and Transfer All Assets to Home Office)

Home Office	XXXX	
[Various Liabilities]	XXXX	
[Various Assets]		XXXX

To record transfer of remaining assets to home office and close all accounts on branch office books

18000.3   ### Sales Agency (All Accounting Records Maintained at Home Office)

18000.3.1   ### Acquisition or Dedication of Assets to Be Used at Sales Agency

*[Various Assets] - Sales Agency	XXXX	
**Cash [Various Assets And Liabilities]		XXXX

To recognize acquisition or dedication of assets to be used at sales agency

*The various assets acquired or dedicated are debited.

**Cash and liabilities given to acquire the assets are credited. If already owned assets are dedicated to the sales agency, those asset accounts are credited.

18000.3.2   ### Transfer of Sample Inventory to Sales Agency Location

Sample Inventory - Sales Agency	XXXX	
Inventory		XXXX

To record transfer of sample inventory to sales agency

18000.3.3   ### Creation of Petty Cash Fund for Sales Agency

Petty Cash - Sales Agency	XXXX	
Cash		XXXX

To record establishment of petty cash fund at sales agency

Important: Make sure all appropriate subheads apply to your entry (see page v for instructions)

18000.3   **Sales Agency (All Accounting Records Maintained at Home Office)**

18000.3.4   ## Recording Sales Agency Operating Transactions

18000.3.4.1   ### Recording Sales Originating at Sales Agency

Accounts Receivable	xxxx
Sales - Sales Agency	xxxx

To record sales transactions originating at sales agency

18000.3.4.2   ### Recording Cost of Sales for Sales Agency Sales

Cost of sales is recorded at sale only when the perpetual inventory system is used.

Cost of Sales - Sales Agency	xxxx
Inventory	xxxx

To record cost of sales originating at sales agency

18000.3.4.3   ### Replenishing Petty Cash of Sales Agency

[Various Operating Expenses] - Sales Agency	xxxx
Cash	xxxx

To record replenishment of petty cash at sales agency

18000.3.4.4   ### Recording Operating Expenses of Sales Agency

*[Various Operating Expenses] - Sales Agency	xxxx
[Various Accounts]	xxxx

To record operating expenses incurred at sales agency

*These operating expenses are closed to Income Summary (Expense And Revenue Summary) as are all other usual expenses.

TABLE OF CONTENTS

19000.1   **Sales Transactions (Exports) Denominated in Foreign Currency (Foreign Currency Is Required Medium of Payment per Sales Contract)**

19000.1.1   **Cash Sale with Foreign Currency Received**

*Foreign Currency	xxxx	
*Sales		xxxx

To record sale to foreign customer and receipt of foreign currency in payment

*This entry is recorded at the U.S. dollar equivalent of the foreign currency, net of costs to convert to U.S. dollars, using the spot exchange rate at the time of sale.

19000.1.1.1   **Immediate Conversion of Foreign Currency to U.S. Dollars**

There is no exchange gain or loss if conversion is made immediately at the time of sale.

Cash	xxxx	
Foreign Currency		xxxx

To record exchange of foreign currency for U.S. dollars

19000.1.1.2   **Delayed Conversion of Foreign Currency to U.S. Dollars**

Exchange rate fluctuations will likely result in exchange gain or loss if conversion is delayed past the time of sale. If there is only a slight delay and an immaterial exchange gain or loss, companies often net the gain or loss in the sales price.

Cash	xxxx	
*Exchange Loss	xxxx	
Foreign Currency		xxxx

To record exchange of foreign currency for U.S. dollars

Important: Make sure all appropriate subheads apply to your entry (see page v for instructions)

19000.1   **Sales Transactions (Exports) Denominated in Foreign Currency (Foreign Currency Is Required Medium of Payment per Sales Contract)**

19000.1.1   **Cash Sale with Foreign Currency Received**

19000.1.1.2   **Delayed Conversion of Foreign Currency to U.S. Dollars**

---

*Exchange Loss is debited for the excess of the carrying (book) value of the foreign currency exchanged over the U.S. dollars (cash) received. If U.S. dollars (cash) received exceed the carrying (book) value of the foreign currency exchanged, Exchange Gain is credited instead.

19000.1.2   **Credit Sale**

In addition to the journal entry explanations given in *GEN19000.1.2.1* through *GEN19000.1.2.3*, see the example given in *GEN19000.1.2.4*.

19000.1.2.1   **Recording the Sale**

*Accounts Receivable	xxxx	
*Sales		xxxx
To record sale on account		

*This entry is recorded at the U.S. dollar equivalent of the foreign currency value of the sale using the spot exchange rate at the time of sale. For an example, *see GEN19000.1.2.4*.

19000.1.2.2   **End-of-Period Adjustment of Accounts Receivable Value**

*Accounts Receivable	xxxx	
*Exchange Gain		xxxx
To adjust Accounts Receivable to the current U.S. dollar equivalent of foreign currency receivable		

*Accounts Receivable is debited and Exchange Gain is credited for the amount of any increase in the U.S. dollar equivalent of the foreign currency value of the accounts receivable determined by applying the current exchange rate. If the U.S. dollar equivalent of the foreign currency value of the accounts receivable has decreased, Exchange Loss is debited and Accounts Receivable is credited. For an example, *see GEN19000.1.2.4*.

Important: Make sure all appropriate subheads apply to your entry (see page v for instructions)

19000.1 **Sales Transactions (Exports) Denominated in Foreign Currency (Foreign Currency Is Required Medium of Payment per Sales Contract)**

19000.1.2 **Credit Sale**

19000.1.2.3 ### Collection of Accounts Receivable

*Foreign Currency	xxxx	
**Exchange Loss	xxxx	
Accounts Receivable		xxxx

To record collection of accounts receivable denominated in foreign currency

*Foreign Currency is debited for the U.S. dollar equivalent of the foreign currency collected using the spot exchange rate at the time of settlement. For an example, *see* GEN19000.1.2.4.

**Exchange Loss is debited to balance the entry. If a credit is needed to balance the entry, Exchange Gain is credited instead.

Cash	xxxx	
Foreign Currency		xxxx

To record conversion of foreign currency to U.S. dollars

19000.1.2.4 ### Example of Credit Sale Denominated in Foreign Currency

Assume that on December 1, 20X1, a U.S. company sells merchandise to a British company. The sale is denominated in British pounds (£) at £100,000. Payment for the merchandise is to be received by the U.S. company in British pounds on January 30, 20X2. Assuming the following spot exchange rates, the journal entries to be made by the U.S. company on the relevant dates are:

December 1, 20X1	$1.50/£
December 31, 20X1	$1.52/£
January 30, 20X2	$1.48/£

At Date of Sale (12/1/X1):

Accounts Receivable	150,000	
Sales		150,000

To record sale on account

(£100,000 X $1.50 = $150,000)

Important: Make sure all appropriate subheads apply to your entry (see page v for instructions)

19000.1   **Sales Transactions (Exports) Denominated in Foreign Currency (Foreign Currency Is Required Medium of Payment per Sales Contract)**

19000.1.2   **Credit Sale**

19000.1.2.4   **Example of Credit Sale Denominated in Foreign Currency**

At End-of-Period Reporting Date (12/31/X1):

*Accounts Receivable	2,000	
*Exchange Gain		2,000

To adjust Accounts Receivable to its current U.S. dollar equivalent value

*Due to exchange rate movements, the U.S. dollar value of the accounts receivable has risen to $152,000. The $2,000 increase in the dollar value of the accounts receivable is debited to Accounts Receivable and credited to Exchange Gain.

At Collection of Accounts Receivable Date (1/30/X2):

*Foreign Currency	148,000	
**Exchange Loss	4,000	
Accounts Receivable		152,000

To record collection of accounts receivable denominated in foreign currency

*Due to exchange rate movements, the £100,000 received by the U.S. company on settlement date is worth $148,000.

**The difference between the carrying (book) value of the accounts receivable ($152,000) and the U.S. dollar value of the foreign currency received ($148,000) is debited to Exchange Loss.

Cash	148,000	
Foreign Currency		148,000

To record conversion of foreign currency to U.S. dollars

19000.2   **Purchases (Imports) Denominated in Foreign Currency (Foreign Currency Is Required Medium of Payment per Purchase Contract)**

19000.2.1   **Cash Purchase with Foreign Currency Paid**

Foreign Currency	xxxx	
Cash		xxxx

To record exchange of U.S. dollars for foreign currency

Important: Make sure all appropriate subheads apply to your entry (see page v for instructions)

19000.2   **Purchases (Imports) Denominated in Foreign Currency (Foreign Currency Is Required Medium of Payment per Purchase Contract)**

19000.2.1   **Cash Purchase with Foreign Currency Paid**

Inventory (Purchases)	xxxx	
Foreign Currency		xxxx

To record purchase from a foreign supplier and payment in foreign currency

19000.2.2   **Credit Purchase**

19000.2.2.1   **Recording the Purchase**

*Inventory (Purchases)	xxxx	
*Accounts Payable		xxxx

To record purchase on account

*Inventory (Purchases) is debited and Accounts Payable is credited for an amount equal to the U.S. dollar equivalent of the foreign currency value of the purchase determined by using the spot exchange rate at the time of purchase.

19000.2.2.2   **End-of-Period Adjustment of Accounts Payable Value**

*Accounts Payable	xxxx	
Exchange Gain		xxxx

To adjust Accounts Payable to the current U.S. dollar equivalent of foreign currency payable

*Accounts Payable is debited and Exchange Gain is credited for the amount of any decrease in the U.S. dollar equivalent of the foreign currency value of the accounts payable determined by applying the current exchange rate. If the U.S. dollar equivalent of the foreign currency value of the accounts payable has increased, Exchange Loss is debited and Accounts Payable is credited for the amount of the increase instead.

19000.2.2.3   **Payment of Accounts Payable**

Foreign Currency	xxxx	
Cash		xxxx

To record conversion of U.S. dollars to foreign currency

Important: Make sure all appropriate subheads apply to your entry (see page v for instructions)

19000.2   **Purchases (Imports) Denominated in Foreign Currency (Foreign Currency Is Required Medium of Payment per Purchase Contract)**

19000.2.2   **Credit Purchase**

19000.2.2.3   **Payment of Accounts Payable**

Accounts Payable	xxxx	
*Exchange Loss	xxxx	
**Foreign Currency		xxxx

To record payment of accounts payable denominated in foreign currency

*Exchange Loss is debited to balance the entry. If a credit is needed, Exchange Gain is credited instead.

**Foreign Currency is debited for the U.S. dollar equivalent of the foreign currency collected using the spot exchange rate at the date of settlement.

19000.3   **Lending, Including Acquisition of Debt Securities Denominated in Foreign Currency (Foreign Currency Is Medium Required to Repay Loan)**

19000.3.1   **At Loan Origination Date**

Notes Receivable ([Various Receivables])	xxxx	
Cash		xxxx

To record loan

19000.3.2   **End-of-Period Adjustment of Receivable**

*Notes Receivable ([Various Receivables])	xxxx	
*Exchange Gain		xxxx

To adjust a receivable to the current U.S. dollar equivalent of foreign currency receivable

*Notes Receivable (or other receivable) is debited and Exchange Gain is credited for the amount of any increase in the U.S. dollar equivalent of the foreign currency value of the receivable determined by applying the current exchange rate. If the U.S. dollar equivalent of the foreign currency value of the receivable has decreased, Exchange Loss is debited and the receivable is credited for the amount of the decrease instead.

Important: Make sure all appropriate subheads apply to your entry (see page v for instructions)

19000.3	**Lending, Including Acquisition of Debt Securities Denominated in Foreign Currency (Foreign Currency Is Medium Required to Repay Loan)**
19000.3.2	**End-of-Period Adjustment of Receivable**

Interest Receivable	xxxx	
Interest Earned		xxxx

To accrue interest earned at end of period

19000.3.3	**Settlement of Receivable**

*Foreign Currency	xxxx	
**Exchange Loss	xxxx	
Notes Receivable ([Various Receivables])		xxxx
Interest Receivable		xxxx
Interest Earned		xxxx

To record collection of receivable

*Foreign Currency is debited for the U.S. dollar equivalent of the foreign currency collected using the spot exchange rate at the date of settlement.

**Exchange Loss is debited for the excess of the total credits to notes receivable (or other receivable), Interest Receivable, and Interest Earned over the debit to Foreign Currency. If the debit to Foreign Currency exceeds the credits to Notes Receivable (or other receivable), Interest Receivable, and Interest Earned, Exchange Gain is credited instead.

Cash	xxxx	
*Foreign Currency		xxxx

To record conversion of foreign currency to U.S. dollars

*Foreign Currency is credited for the U.S. dollar equivalent of the foreign currency converted using the spot exchange rate at the date of conversion.

19000.4	**Borrowing (Loan Payable Denominated in Foreign Currency)**

In addition to the journal entry explanations given in *GEN19000.4.1* through *GEN19000.4.3*, see the example in *GEN19000.4.4.*

Important: Make sure all appropriate subheads apply to your entry (see page v for instructions)

19000.4   **Borrowing (Loan Payable Denominated in Foreign Currency)**

19000.4.1   **At Loan Origination Date**

Cash (Foreign Currency)	xxxx	
Notes Payable [Various Payables]		xxxx

To record loan from lender

For an example, *see GEN19000.4.4.*

19000.4.2   **End-of-Period Adjustment of Payable**

*Notes Payable [Various Payables]	xxxx	
*Exchange Gain		xxxx

To adjust a payable to the current U.S. dollar equivalent of foreign currency payable

*Notes Payable [Various Payables] is debited and Exchange Gain is credited for the amount of any decrease in the U.S. dollar equivalent of the foreign currency value of the payable determined by applying the current exchange rate. If the U.S. dollar equivalent of the foreign currency value of the payable has increased, Exchange Loss is debited and the payable is credited for the amount of the increase instead.

Interest Expense	xxxx	
Interest Payable		xxxx

To accrue interest expense at end of period

For an example, *see GEN19000.4.4.*

19000.4.3   **Settlement of Payable**

Foreign Currency	xxxx	
Cash		xxxx

To record acquisition of foreign currency

Important: Make sure all appropriate subheads apply to your entry (see page v for instructions)

19000.4   **Borrowing (Loan Payable Denominated in Foreign Currency)**
19000.4.3   **Settlement of Payable**

Notes Payable [Various Payables]	xxxx	
Interest Payable	xxxx	
Interest Expense	xxxx	
*Exchange Loss	xxxx	
**Foreign Currency		xxxx
To record payment of liability		

*Exchange Loss is debited for the excess of the credit to Foreign Currency over the debits to Notes Payable (or other payable), Interest Payable, and Interest Expense. If the debits to Notes Payable (or other payable), Interest Payable, and Interest Expense exceed the credit to Foreign Currency, Exchange Gain is credited instead.

**Foreign Currency is credited for the U.S. dollar equivalent of the foreign currency paid using the spot exchange rate at the date of settlement.

For an example, *see GEN19000.4.4.*

19000.4.4   **Example of Borrowing Denominated in Foreign Currency**

Assume that on October 1, 20X1, a U.S. company borrowed 1,000,000 French francs (FF) on a six-month, 10% interest-bearing note payable. The principal and interest on the note is payable at maturity date (March 31, 20X2) in French francs. Assuming the following spot exchange rates, the journal entries to be made by the U.S. company on the relevant dates are:

October 1, 20X1	$.1750/FF
December 31, 20X1	$.1700/FF
March 31, 20X2	$.1720/FF

At Loan Origination Date (10/1/X1):

Foreign Currency	175,000	
Notes Payable		175,000
To record loan from lender		
(FF1,000,000 X $.1750 = $175,000)		

Important: Make sure all appropriate subheads apply to your entry (see page v for instructions)

19000.4	**Borrowing (Loan Payable Denominated in Foreign Currency)**
19000.4.4	**Example of Borrowing Denominated in Foreign Currency**

At End-of-Period Reporting Date (12/31/X1):

*Notes Payable	5,000	
*Exchange Gain		5,000
To adjust Notes Payable to its current U.S. dollar equivalent value		

*Due to exchange rate movements, the U.S. dollar value of the notes payable has decreased to $170,000. The $5,000 decrease in the dollar value of the notes payable is debited to Notes Payable and credited to Exchange Gain.

Interest Expense	4,250	
Interest Payable		4,250
To accrue interest at the end of the period		

(FF1,000,000 X .10 X 3/12 X $.1700 = $4,250)

At Settlement Date (3/31/X2):

*Foreign Currency	180,600	
*Cash		180,600
To record acquisition of foreign currency to pay off the principal and interest accrued on the notes payable		

*Due to exchange rate movements, the U.S. dollar equivalent value of the principal and interest that is to be paid on the note by the U.S. company is $180,600 on settlement date. (Principal: FF1,000,000 X .1720 = $172,000; Interest: FF1,000,000 X .10 X 6/12 X .1720 = $8,600; $172,000 + $8,600 = $180,600.)

Notes Payable	170,000	
Interest Payable	4,250	
*Interest Expense	4,300	
**Exchange Loss	2,050	
Foreign Currency		180,600
To record payment of liability		

*(FF1,000,000 X .10 X 3/12 X .1720 = $4,300)

Important: Make sure all appropriate subheads apply to your entry (see page v for instructions)

| **19000.4** | **Borrowing (Loan Payable Denominated in Foreign Currency)** |
| **19000.4.4** | **Example of Borrowing Denominated in Foreign Currency** |

**Exchange loss is debited for the excess of the dollar value of the foreign currency paid over the carrying (book) values of the notes payable, interest payable, and the interest expense recorded for the period.

19000.5   **Forward Exchange Contracts**

Forward exchange contracts are contracts with a currency broker to either buy or sell foreign currency in the future at a specified price (the forward rate).

19000.5.1   **Hedge of Accounts Receivable (Forward Contract to Sell Foreign Currency)**

In addition to the journal entry explanations given in *GEN19000.5.1.1* through *GEN19000.5.1.4*, see the example in *GEN19000.5.1.5*.

19000.5.1.1   **At Contract Origination Date**

*U.S. Dollars Receivable - [Exchange Dealer]	xxxx	
**Discount On Forward Exchange Contract	xxxx	
***Foreign Currency Payable - [Exchange Dealer]		xxxx
To record forward exchange contract		

*U.S. Dollars Receivable is debited for the U.S dollar equivalent of the amount of foreign currency to be sold determined by applying the exchange rate specified in the forward exchange contract.

**Discount On Forward Exchange Contract is debited to balance the entry. If a credit (rather than a debit) is needed to balance the entry, Premium On Forward Exchange Contract is debited.

***Foreign Currency Payable is credited for the U.S. dollar equivalent of the amount of foreign currency payable in the future determined by applying the spot exchange rate at the contract origination date.

For an example, *see GEN19000.5.1.5.*

Important: Make sure all appropriate subheads apply to your entry (see page v for instructions)

19000.5	**Forward Exchange Contracts**
19000.5.1	**Hedge of Accounts Receivable (Forward Contract to Sell Foreign Currency)**

19000.5.1.2   **End-of-Period Adjustment of Foreign Currency Payable**

*Foreign Currency Payable - [Exchange Dealer]	xxxx	
*Exchange Gain		xxxx
To adjust Foreign Currency Payable to the current U.S.		
dollar equivalent		

*Foreign Currency Payable is debited and Exchange Gain is credited for the amount of any decrease in the U.S. dollar equivalent of the foreign currency payable determined by applying the current exchange rate. If the U.S. dollar equivalent of the foreign currency payable has increased, Exchange Loss is debited and the payable is credited for the amount of the increase instead.

For an example, *see GEN19000.5.1.5.*

19000.5.1.3   **End-of-Period Amortization of Premium or Discount**

A premium or discount on a forward exchange contract is amortized over the life of the contract using the straight-line method.

*Amortization Expense - Discount On Forward Exchange		
Contract	xxxx	
*Discount On Forward Exchange Contract		xxxx
To amortize Discount on Forward Exchange Contract		

*This entry is for the amortization of a discount. To amortize a premium, Premium On Forward Exchange Contract is debited and Revenue From Forward Exchange Contract is credited.

For an example, *see GEN19000.5.1.5.*

19000.5.1.4   **Settlement of Forward Exchange Contract**

Foreign Currency Payable - Exchange Dealer	xxxx	
*Exchange Loss	xxxx	
**Foreign Currency		xxxx
To record settlement of foreign currency payable		

Important: Make sure all appropriate subheads apply to your entry (see page v for instructions)

19000.5	**Forward Exchange Contracts**
19000.5.1	**Hedge of Accounts Receivable (Forward Contract to Sell Foreign Currency)**
19000.5.1.4	**Settlement of Forward Exchange Contract**

---

*Exchange Loss is debited to balance the entry. If a credit is needed, Exchange Gain is credited.

**Foreign Currency is credited for the U.S. dollar equivalent of the foreign currency given determined by using the spot exchange rate at the date of settlement.

Cash	xxxx	
U.S. Dollars Receivable - [Exchange Dealer]		xxxx
To record collection of amount due from exchange dealer		
*Amortization Expense - Discount On Forward Exchange Contract	xxxx	
*Discount On Forward Exchange Contract		xxxx
To amortize balance of Discount On Forward Exchange Contract		

*This entry is for the amortization of a discount. To amortize a premium, Premium On Forward Exchange Contract is debited and Revenue From Forward Exchange Contract is credited.

For an example, *see GEN19000.5.1.5.*

19000.5.1.5

Example of Forward Exchange Contract - Hedge of Accounts Receivable

Assume that, to hedge an exposed accounts receivable position denominated in British pounds, a U.S. company enters into a forward contract with an exchange dealer on November 1, 20X1. The forward contract specifies that on March 1, 20X2, the U.S. company will deliver £100,000 to the exchange dealer in exchange for U.S. dollars at a forward rate of $1.48/£. Assuming the following spot exchange rates, the journal entries to be made by the U.S. company on the relevant dates are:

November 1, 20X1	$1.52/£
December 31, 20X1	$1.50/£
March 1, 20X2	$1.54/£

FOREIGN CURRENCY TRANSACTIONS

Important: Make sure all appropriate subheads apply to your entry (see page v for instructions)

19000.5	**Forward Exchange Contracts**
19000.5.1	**Hedge of Accounts Receivable (Forward Contract to Sell Foreign Currency)**
19000.5.1.5	**Example of Forward Exchange Contract - Hedge of Accounts Receivable**

At Contract Origination Date (11/1/X1):

*U.S. Dollars Receivable - [Exchange Dealer]	148,000	
**Discount on Forward Exchange Contract	4,000	
***Foreign Currency Payable - [Exchange Dealer]		152,000
To record forward exchange contract		

*The U.S. dollar receivable is debited for the contracted dollars (£100,000 X $1.48) that will be paid by the exchange dealer to the U.S. company for the £100,000 on March 1, 20X2.

**The excess of the value of the foreign currency payable over the value of the U.S. dollars receivable is debited to Discount On Forward Exchange Contract.

***The foreign currency payable is credited for the current dollar equivalent value (£100,000 X $1.52) of the £100,000 to be delivered by the company to the exchange dealer on March 1, 20X2.

At End-of-Period Reporting Date (12/31/X1):

*Foreign Currency Payable - [Exchange Dealer]	2,000	
*Exchange Gain		2,000
To adjust Foreign Currency Payable to its current U.S.		
dollar equivalent value		

*Due to exchange rate movements, the dollar value of the foreign currency payable has decreased to $150,000. The $2,000 decrease in the dollar value of the foreign currency payable is debited to Foreign Currency Payable and credited to Exchange Gain.

*Amortization Expense	2,000	
*Discount On Forward Exchange Contract		2,000
To amortize Discount On Forward Exchange Contract		
($4,000 X 2/4 = $2,000)		

Important: Make sure all appropriate subheads apply to your entry (see page v for instructions)

19000.5   **Forward Exchange Contracts**
19000.5.1   **Hedge of Accounts Receivable (Forward Contract to Sell Foreign Currency)**
19000.5.1.5   **Example of Forward Exchange Contract - Hedge of Accounts Receivable**

At Settlement Date (3/1/X2):

*Foreign Currency Payable - [Exchange Dealer]	150,000	
*Exchange Loss	4,000	
*Foreign Currency		154,000

To record settlement of foreign currency payable

*Due to exchange rate movements, the £100,000 paid by the U.S. company on settlement date is worth $154,000. The difference between the carrying (book) value of the foreign currency payable ($150,000) and the dollar value of the foreign currency paid ($154,000) is debited to Exchange Loss.

Cash	148,000	
U.S. Dollars Receivable - [Exchange Dealer]		148,000

To record receipt of cash (U.S. dollars) from exchange dealer

Amortization Expense	2,000	
Discount On Forward Exchange Contract		2,000

To amortize balance of Discount On Forward Exchange Contract

19000.5.2   **Hedge of Accounts Payable (Forward Contract to Buy Foreign Currency)**

19000.5.2.1   **At Contract Origination Date**

*Foreign Currency Receivable - [Exchange Dealer]	xxxx	
**Premium On Forward Exchange Contract	xxxx	
***U.S. Dollars Payable - [Exchange Dealer]		xxxx

To record forward exchange contract

*Foreign Currency Receivable is debited for the U.S. dollar equivalent of the foreign currency to be received determined by using the spot exchange rate at the contract origination date.

Important: Make sure all appropriate subheads apply to your entry (see page v for instructions)

19000.5   **Forward Exchange Contracts**
19000.5.2   **Hedge of Accounts Payable (Forward Contract to Buy Foreign Currency)**
19000.5.2.1   **At Contract Origination Date**

**Premium On Forward Exchange Contract is debited to balance the entry. If a credit is needed to balance the entry, it is made to Discount On Forward Exchange Contract. Any premium or discount is amortized over the life of the forward exchange contract using the straight-line method.

***U.S. Dollars Payable is credited for the U.S. dollar equivalent of the foreign currency to be received determined by applying the exchange rate specified in the forward exchange contract.

19000.5.2.2   **End-of-Period Adjustment of Foreign Currency Receivable**

> *Foreign Currency Receivable - [Exchange Dealer]   xxxx
>   *Exchange Gain   xxxx
> *To adjust Foreign Currency Receivable to the current U.S.*
> *dollar equivalent*

*Foreign Currency Receivable is debited and Exchange Gain is credited for the amount of any increase in the U.S. dollar equivalent of the foreign currency receivable determined by applying the current exchange rate. If the U.S. dollar equivalent of the foreign currency receivable has decreased, Exchange Loss is debited and the receivable is credited for the amount of the increase instead.

19000.5.2.3   **End-of-Period Amortization of Premium or Discount**

A premium or discount on a forward exchange contract is amortized over the life of the contract using the straight-line method.

> *Amortization Expense - Premium On Forward Exchange
>   Contract   xxxx
>   *Premium On Forward Exchange Contract   xxxx
> *To amortize Premium On Forward Exchange Contract*

*This entry is for the amortization of a premium. To amortize a discount, Discount On Forward Exchange Contract is debited and Revenue From Forward Exchange Contract is credited.

Important: Make sure all appropriate subheads apply to your entry (see page v for instructions)

19000.5   **Forward Exchange Contracts**
19000.5.2   **Hedge of Accounts Payable (Forward Contract to Buy Foreign Currency)**

19000.5.2.4   **Settlement of Forward Exchange Contract**

U.S. Dollars Payable - [Exchange Dealer]	xxxx	
Cash		xxxx

To record payment of amount due to exchange broker

*Foreign Currency	xxxx	
**Exchange Loss	xxxx	
Foreign Currency Receivable - [Exchange Dealer]		xxxx

To record receipt of foreign currency from exchange dealer

*Foreign Currency is debited for the U.S. dollar equivalent of the foreign currency received determined by using the spot exchange rate at the date of settlement.

**Exchange Loss is debited to balance the entry. If a credit is needed, Exchange Gain is credited.

*Amortization Expense - Premium On Forward Exchange Contract	xxxx	
*Premium On Forward Exchange Contract		xxxx

To amortize balance of Premium On Forward Exchange Contract

*This entry is for the amortization of a premium. To amortize a discount, Discount On Forward Exchange Contract is debited and Revenue From Forward Exchange Contract is credited.

19000.5.3   **Hedge of Foreign Currency Commitment (Sales) with Future Receivable (Forward Contract to Sell Foreign Currency)**

19000.5.3.1   **Discount or Premium on Forward Exchange Contract Is Deferred**

A discount or premium on a forward exchange contract that is made to hedge a foreign currency commitment with a future receivable may be either deferred and closed to Sales at settlement of the contract or amortized over the life of the contract. *See GEN19000.5.3.2 for entries when the discount or premium is amortized.*

Important: Make sure all appropriate subheads apply to your entry (see page v for instructions)

19000.5	**Forward Exchange Contracts**
19000.5.3	**Hedge of Foreign Currency Commitment (Sales) with Future Receivable (Forward Contract to Sell Foreign Currency)**
19000.5.3.1	**Discount or Premium on Forward Exchange Contract Is Deferred**

19000.5.3.1.1   ## At Contract Origination Date

*U.S. Dollars Receivable - [Exchange Dealer]	xxxx	
**Deferred Discount On Forward Exchange Contract	xxxx	
***Foreign Currency Payable - [Exchange Dealer]		xxxx
To record forward exchange contract		

*U.S. Dollars Receivable is debited for the U.S. dollar equivalent of the foreign currency to be paid determined by using the exchange rate specified in the forward exchange contract.

**Deferred Discount On Forward Exchange Contract is debited to balance the entry. If a credit is needed to balance the entry, it is made to Deferred Premium On Forward Exchange Contract. Any deferred premium or discount is closed to Sales when the forward exchange contract is settled.

***Foreign Currency Payable is credited for the U.S. dollar equivalent of the foreign currency to be paid determined by using the spot exchange rate at the contract origination date.

19000.5.3.1.2   ## End-of-Period Adjustment of Foreign Currency Payable

*Foreign Currency Payable - [Exchange Dealer]	xxxx	
**Deferred Exchange Gain		xxxx
To adjust Foreign Currency Payable to its current U.S. dollar equivalent		

*Foreign Currency Payable is debited and Deferred Exchange Gain is credited for the amount of any decrease in the U.S. dollar equivalent of the foreign currency payable determined by applying the current exchange rate. If the U.S. dollar equivalent of the foreign currency payable has increased, Deferred Exchange Loss would be debited and the payable would be credited for the amount of the increase.

**Deferred Exchange Gain is credited (or Deferred Exchange Loss is debited). The gain or loss is deferred because an unrecorded commitment is being hedged. The deferred gain or loss is subsequently closed to Sales at settlement of the forward exchange contract.

Important: Make sure all appropriate subheads apply to your entry (see page v for instructions)

19000.5   **Forward Exchange Contracts**
19000.5.3   **Hedge of Foreign Currency Commitment (Sales) with Future Receivable (Forward Contract to Sell Foreign Currency)**
19000.5.3.1   **Discount or Premium on Forward Exchange Contract Is Deferred**

19000.5.3.1.3   **Settlement of Forward Exchange Contract**

Foreign Currency	xxxx	
Sales		xxxx
To record sales		

Foreign Currency Payable - [Exchange Dealer]	xxxx	
*Deferred Exchange Loss	xxxx	
**Foreign Currency		xxxx
To record payment of foreign currency to exchange dealer		

*Deferred Exchange Loss is debited to balance the entry. If a credit is needed to balance the entry, Deferred Exchange Gain is debited. The deferred gain or loss is closed to Sales in the next entry.

**Foreign Currency is credited for the U.S. dollar equivalent of the foreign currency paid determined by using the spot exchange rate at the date of settlement.

Sales	xxxx	
*Deferred Exchange Gain	xxxx	
*Deferred Exchange Loss		xxxx
**Deferred Discount On Forward Exchange Contract		xxxx
To close deferred loss and discount		

*Deferred Exchange Loss is credited to eliminate any debit balance pertaining to this contract. If there is a Deferred Exchange Gain, it is debited to eliminate any credit balance pertaining to the contract.

**Deferred Discount On Forward Exchange Contract is credited to eliminate any debit balance pertaining to this contract. Alternatively, if there is a Deferred Premium On Forward Exchange Contract, it is debited to eliminate any credit balance pertaining to the contract.

Cash	xxxx	
U.S. Dollars Receivable - [Exchange Dealer]		xxxx
To record cash received from exchange dealer		

Important: Make sure all appropriate subheads apply to your entry (see page v for instructions)

19000.5   **Forward Exchange Contracts**
19000.5.3   **Hedge of Foreign Currency Commitment (Sales) with Future Receivable (Forward Contract to Sell Foreign Currency)**

19000.5.3.2   **Discount or Premium on Forward Exchange Contract Is Not Deferred**

A discount or premium on a forward exchange contract that is made to hedge a foreign currency commitment with a future receivable may be either deferred and closed to Sales at settlement of the contract or amortized over the life of the contract. *See GEN19000.5.3.1 for entries when the discount or premium is deferred.*

19000.5.3.2.1   **At Contract Origination Date**

*U.S. Dollars Receivable - [Exchange Dealer]	xxxx	
**Discount On Forward Exchange Contract	xxxx	
***Foreign Currency Payable - [Exchange Dealer]		xxxx
To record forward exchange contract		

*U.S. Dollars Receivable is debited for the U.S. dollar equivalent of the foreign currency to be paid determined by using the exchange rate specified in the forward exchange contract.

**Discount On Forward Exchange Contract is debited to balance the entry. If a credit is needed to balance the entry it is made to Premium On Forward Exchange Contract. Any premium or discount is amortized over the life of the forward exchange contract using the straight-line method.

***Foreign Currency Payable is credited for the U.S. dollar equivalent of the foreign currency to be paid determined by using the spot exchange rate at the contract origination date.

19000.5.3.2.2   **End-of-Period Adjustment of Foreign Currency Payable**

*Foreign Currency Payable - [Exchange Dealer]	xxxx	
**Deferred Exchange Gain		xxxx
To adjust Foreign Currency Payable to its current U.S. dollar equivalent		

Important: Make sure all appropriate subheads apply to your entry (see page v for instructions)

19000.5	**Forward Exchange Contracts**
19000.5.3	**Hedge of Foreign Currency Commitment (Sales) with Future Receivable (Forward Contract to Sell Foreign Currency)**
19000.5.3.2	**Discount or Premium on Forward Exchange Contract Is Not Deferred**
19000.5.3.2.2	**End-of-Period Adjustment of Foreign Currency Payable**

---

*Foreign Currency Payable is debited and Deferred Exchange Gain is credited for the amount of any decrease in the U.S. dollar equivalent of the foreign currency payable determined by applying the current exchange rate. If the U.S. dollar equivalent of the foreign currency payable has increased, Deferred Exchange Loss is debited and the payable is credited instead.

**Deferred Exchange Gain is credited (or Deferred Exchange Loss is debited). The gain or loss is deferred because an unrecorded commitment is being hedged. This deferred gain or loss is subsequently recognized at settlement of the forward exchange contract.

19000.5.3.2.3   **End-of-Period Amortization of Premium or Discount**

A premium or discount on a foreign exchange contract is amortized over the life of the contract using the straight-line method.

*Amortization Expense - Discount On Forward Exchange Contract	xxxx	
*Discount On Forward Exchange Contract		xxxx
To amortize Discount On Forward Exchange Contract		

*This entry is for the amortization of a discount. To amortize a premium, Premium On Forward Exchange Contract is debited and Revenue From Foreign Exchange Contract is credited.

19000.5.3.2.4   **Settlement of Forward Exchange Contract**

Foreign Currency	xxxx	
Sales		xxxx
To record sales		

Foreign Currency Payable - [Exchange Dealer]	xxxx	
*Deferred Exchange Loss	xxxx	
**Foreign Currency		xxxx
To record payment of foreign currency to exchange dealer		

Important: Make sure all appropriate subheads apply to your entry (see page v for instructions)

19000.5   **Forward Exchange Contracts**
19000.5.3   **Hedge of Foreign Currency Commitment (Sales) with Future Receivable (Forward Contract to Sell Foreign Currency)**
19000.5.3.2   **Discount or Premium on Forward Exchange Contract Is Not Deferred**
19000.5.3.2.4   **Settlement of Forward Exchange Contract**

---

*Deferred Exchange Loss is debited to balance the entry. If a credit is needed to balance the entry, Deferred Exchange Gain is credited. The deferred gain or loss is closed to Sales in the next entry.

**Foreign Currency is credited for the U.S. dollar equivalent of the foreign currency paid determined by using the spot exchange rate at the date of settlement.

Sales	xxxx	
*Deferred Exchange Gain	xxxx	
*Deferred Exchange Loss		xxxx
**Discount On Forward Exchange Contract		xxxx
To close deferred loss and discount		

*Deferred Exchange Loss is credited to eliminate any debit balance pertaining to this contract. If there is a Deferred Exchange Gain, it is debited to eliminate any credit balance pertaining to this contract.

**Discount On Forward Exchange Contract is credited to eliminate any debit balance pertaining to this contract. Alternatively, if there is a Premium On Forward Exchange Contract, it is debited to eliminate any credit balance pertaining to this contract.

Cash	xxxx	
U.S. Dollars Receivable - [Exchange Dealer]		xxxx
To record cash received from exchange dealer		

19000.5.4   **Hedge of Foreign Currency Commitment (Purchase) with Future Payable (Forward Contract to Buy Foreign Currency)**

19000.5.4.1   **Discount or Premium on Forward Contract Is Deferred**

A discount or premium on a forward exchange contract that is made to hedge a foreign currency commitment with a future payable may be either deferred and closed to Inventory (Purchases) at settlement of the contract or amortized over the life of the contract. *See GEN19000.5.4.2* for entries when the discount or premium is amortized.

FOREIGN CURRENCY TRANSACTIONS

Important: Make sure all appropriate subheads apply to your entry (see page v for instructions)

19000.5   **Forward Exchange Contracts**
19000.5.4   **Hedge of Foreign Currency Commitment (Purchase) with Future Payable (Forward Contract to Buy Foreign Currency)**
19000.5.4.1   **Discount or Premium on Forward Contract Is Deferred**

In addition to the journal entry explanations given in *GEN19000.5.4.1.1* through *GEN19000.5.4.1.3*, see the example in *GEN19000.5.4.1.4*.

19000.5.4.1.1   **At Contract Origination Date**

*Foreign Currency Receivable - [Exchange Dealer]	xxxx
**Deferred Premium On Forward Exchange Contract	xxxx
***U.S. Dollars Payable - [Exchange Dealer]	xxxx

To record forward exchange contract

*Foreign Currency Receivable is debited for the U.S. dollar equivalent of the foreign currency to be received determined by using the spot exchange rate at the contract origination date.

**Deferred Premium On Forward Exchange Contract is debited to balance the entry. If a credit is needed to balance the entry, it is made to Deferred Discount On Forward Exchange Contract. Any deferred discount or premium is closed to Inventory (Purchases) at settlement of the contract.

***U.S. Dollars Payable is credited for the U.S. dollar equivalent of the foreign currency to be received determined by using the exchange rate specified in the forward exchange contract.

For an example, *see GEN19000.5.4.1.4*.

19000.5.4.1.2   **End-of-Period Adjustment of Foreign Currency Receivable**

*Foreign Currency Receivable - [Exchange Dealer]	xxxx
**Deferred Exchange Gain	xxxx

To adjust Foreign Currency Receivable to its current U.S. dollar equivalent

*Foreign Currency Receivable is debited and Deferred Exchange Gain is credited for the amount of any increase in the U.S. dollar equivalent of the foreign currency receivable determined by applying the current exchange rate. If the U.S. dollar equivalent of the foreign currency receivable has decreased, Deferred Exchange Loss is debited and the receivable is credited for the amount of the decrease.

FOREIGN CURRENCY TRANSACTIONS

Important: Make sure all appropriate subheads apply to your entry (see page v for instructions)

19000.5	**Forward Exchange Contracts**
19000.5.4	**Hedge of Foreign Currency Commitment (Purchase) with Future Payable (Forward Contract to Buy Foreign Currency)**
19000.5.4.1	**Discount or Premium on Forward Contract Is Deferred**
19000.5.4.1.2	**End-of-Period Adjustment of Foreign Currency Receivable**

**Deferred Exchange Gain is credited (or Deferred Exchange Loss is debited). The gain or loss is deferred because an unrecorded commitment is being hedged. The deferred gain or loss is subsequently recognized at settlement of the forward exchange contract.

For an example, *see GEN19000.5.4.1.4.*

19000.5.4.1.3   **Settlement of Forward Exchange Contract**

U.S. Dollars Payable - [Exchange Dealer]	xxxx	
Cash		xxxx
To record payment of obligation to exchange dealer		

*Foreign Currency	xxxx	
**Deferred Exchange Loss	xxxx	
Foreign Currency Receivable - [Exchange Dealer]		xxxx
To record receipt of foreign currency from exchange dealer		

*Foreign Currency is debited for the U.S. dollar equivalent of the foreign currency received determined by using the spot exchange rate at the date of settlement.

**Deferred Exchange Loss is debited to balance the entry. If a credit is needed to balance the entry, Deferred Exchange Gain is credited. The deferred gain or loss is closed to Inventory (Purchases) in a subsequent entry.

Inventory (Purchases)	xxxx	
Foreign Currency		xxxx
To record purchases		

Inventory (Purchases)	xxxx	
*Deferred Exchange Gain	xxxx	
*Deferred Exchange Loss		xxxx
**Deferred Premium On Forward Exchange Contract		xxxx
To close deferred exchange gain and deferred premium to		
Inventory (Purchases)		

*Deferred Exchange Gain is debited sufficiently to remove any credit balance pertaining to the contract. If there is a Deferred Exchange Loss, it is credited to eliminate any debit balance pertaining to the contract.

Important: Make sure all appropriate subheads apply to your entry (see page v for instructions)

19000.5	**Forward Exchange Contracts**
19000.5.4	**Hedge of Foreign Currency Commitment (Purchase) with Future Payable (Forward Contract to Buy Foreign Currency)**
19000.5.4.1	**Discount or Premium on Forward Contract Is Deferred**
19000.5.4.1.3	**Settlement of Forward Exchange Contract**

**Deferred Premium On Forward Exchange Contract is credited to eliminate any debit balance pertaining to the contract. Alternatively, if there is a Deferred Discount On Forward Exchange Contract, it is debited to eliminate any credit balance pertaining to the contract.

For an example, *see GEN19000.5.4.1.4.*

19000.5.4.1.4   **Example of Hedge of Foreign Currency Commitment (Purchase) with Future Payable - Discount or Premium on Forward Contract Is Deferred**

Assume that, to hedge a purchase commitment denominated in French francs (FF), a U.S. company enters into a forward contract with an exchange dealer on December 1, 20X1. The forward contract specifies that on February 1, 20X2, the U.S. company will receive FF1,000,000 from the exchange dealer in exchange for U.S. dollars at a forward rate of $.1695/FF. Assuming the following spot exchange rates, the journal entries to be made by the U.S. company on the relevant dates are:

December 1, 20X1	$.1680/FF
December 31, 20X1	$.1700/FF
February 1, 20X2	$.1690/FF

At Contract Origination Date (12/1/X1):

*Foreign Currency Receivable - [Exchange Dealer]	168,000	
**Deferred Premium On Forward Exchange Contract	1,500	
***U.S. Dollars Payable - [Exchange Dealer]		169,500
To record forward exchange contract		

*The foreign currency receivable is debited for the current dollar equivalent value (FF1,000,000 X $.1680) of the FF1,000,000 to be received by the company from the exchange dealer on February 1, 20X2.

**The excess of the value of the U.S. dollar payable over the value of the foreign currency receivable is debited to Deferred Premium On Forward Exchange Contract.

***The U.S. dollar payable is credited for the contracted dollars (FF1,000,000 X $.1695) that will be paid by the U.S. company to the exchange dealer for FF1,000,000 on February 1, 20X2.

FOREIGN CURRENCY TRANSACTIONS

Important: Make sure all appropriate subheads apply to your entry (see page v for instructions)

19000.5	**Forward Exchange Contracts**
19000.5.4	**Hedge of Foreign Currency Commitment (Purchase) with Future Payable (Forward Contract to Buy Foreign Currency)**
19000.5.4.1	**Discount or Premium on Forward Contract Is Deferred**
19000.5.4.1.4	**Example of Hedge of Foreign Currency Commitment (Purchase) with Future Payable - Discount or Premium on Forward Contract Is Deferred**

At End-of-Period Reporting Date (12/31/X1):

*Foreign Currency Receivable - [Exchange Dealer]	2,000	
*Deferred Exchange Gain		2,000
To adjust Foreign Currency Receivable to its current U.S. dollar equivalent value		

*Due to exchange rate movements, the dollar value of the foreign currency receivable has increased to $170,000. The $2,000 increase in the dollar value of the foreign currency receivable is debited to Foreign Currency Receivable and credited to Exchange Gain.

At Settlement Date (2/1/X2):

U.S. Dollars Payable - [Exchange Dealer]	169,500	
Cash		169,500
To record payment of cash (U.S. dollars) to exchange dealer		

*Foreign Currency	169,000	
*Deferred Exchange Loss	1,000	
*Foreign Currency Receivable - [Exchange Dealer]		170,000
To record receipt of foreign currency from exchange dealer		

*Due to exchange rate movements, the FF1,000,000 received by the U.S. company on settlement date is worth $169,000. The difference between the carrying (book) value of the foreign currency receivable (FF170,000) and the dollar value of the foreign currency received ($169,000) is debited to Deferred Exchange Loss.

Inventory (Purchases)	169,000	
Foreign Currency		169,000
To record purchases		

Inventory (Purchases)	500	
Deferred Exchange Gain	2,000	
Deferred Exchange Loss		1,000
Deferred Premium On Forward Exchange Contract		1,500
To close Deferred Exchange Gain, Deferred Exchange Loss, and the deferred premium to Inventory (Purchases)		

Important: Make sure all appropriate subheads apply to your entry (see page v for instructions)

19000.5   **Forward Exchange Contracts**
19000.5.4   **Hedge of Foreign Currency Commitment (Purchase) with Future Payable**
              (Forward Contract to Buy Foreign Currency)

19000.5.4.2   **Discount or Premium on Forward Contract Is Not Deferred**

A discount or premium on a forward exchange contract that is made to hedge a foreign currency commitment with a future payable may be either deferred and closed to Inventory (Purchases) at settlement of the contract or amortized over the life of the contract. *See GEN19000.5.4.1 for entries when the discount or premium is deferred.*

19000.5.4.2.1   **At Contract Origination Date**

    *Foreign Currency Receivable - [Exchange Dealer]   xxxx
    **Premium On Forward Exchange Contract   xxxx
        ***U.S. Dollars Payable - [Exchange Dealer]   xxxx
    To record forward exchange contract

*Foreign Currency Receivable is debited for the U.S. dollar equivalent of the foreign currency to be received determined by using the spot exchange rate at the contract origination date.

**Premium On Forward Exchange Contract is debited to balance the entry. If a credit is needed to balance the entry, it is made to Discount On Forward Exchange Contract. Any premium or discount is amortized over the life of the forward exchange contract using the straight-line method.

***U.S. Dollars Payable is credited for the U.S. dollar equivalent of the foreign currency to be received determined by using the exchange rate specified in the forward exchange contract.

19000.5.4.2.2   **End-of-Period Adjustment of Foreign Currency Receivable**

    *Foreign Currency Receivable - [Exchange Dealer]   xxxx
        **Deferred Exchange Gain   xxxx
    To adjust Foreign Currency Receivable to its current U.S.
    dollar equivalent

Important: Make sure all appropriate subheads apply to your entry (see page v for instructions)

19000.5	**Forward Exchange Contracts**
19000.5.4	**Hedge of Foreign Currency Commitment (Purchase) with Future Payable (Forward Contract to Buy Foreign Currency)**
19000.5.4.2	**Discount or Premium on Forward Contract Is Not Deferred**
19000.5.4.2.2	**End-of-Period Adjustment of Foreign Currency Receivable**

---

*Foreign Currency Receivable is debited and Deferred Exchange Gain is credited for the amount of any increase in the U.S. dollar equivalent of the foreign currency receivable determined by applying the current exchange rate. If the U.S. dollar equivalent of the foreign currency receivable has decreased, Deferred Exchange Loss is debited and the receivable is credited for the amount of the decrease.

**Deferred Exchange Gain is credited (or Deferred Exchange Loss is debited). The gain or loss is deferred because an unrecorded commitment is being hedged. This deferred gain or loss is subsequently recognized at settlement of the forward exchange contract.

19000.5.4.2.3   **End-Of-Period Amortization of Premium or Discount**

A premium or discount on a foreign exchange contract is amortized over the life of the contract using the straight-line method.

*Amortization Expense - Forward Exchange Contract	xxxx	
Premium On Forward Exchange Contract		xxxx
To amortize Premium On Forward Exchange Contract		

*This entry is for the amortization of a premium. To amortize a discount, Discount On Forward Exchange Contract is debited and Revenue From Foreign Exchange Contract is credited.

19000.5.4.2.4   **Settlement of Forward Exchange Contract**

U.S. Dollars Payable - [Exchange Dealer]	xxxx	
Cash		xxxx
To record payment of obligation to exchange dealer		

*Foreign Currency	xxxx	
**Deferred Exchange Loss	xxxx	
Foreign Currency Receivable - [Exchange Dealer]		xxxx
To record receipt of foreign currency from exchange dealer		

*Foreign Currency is debited for the U.S. dollar equivalent of the foreign currency received determined by using the spot exchange rate at the date of settlement.

Important: Make sure all appropriate subheads apply to your entry (see page v for instructions)

19000.5   **Forward Exchange Contracts**
19000.5.4   **Hedge of Foreign Currency Commitment (Purchase) with Future Payable (Forward Contract to Buy Foreign Currency)**
19000.5.4.2   **Discount or Premium on Forward Contract Is Not Deferred**
19000.5.4.2.4   **Settlement of Forward Exchange Contract**

**Deferred Exchange Loss is debited to balance the entry. If a credit is needed to balance the entry, Deferred Exchange Gain is credited. The deferred gain or loss is closed to Inventory (Purchases) in a subsequent entry.

Inventory (Purchases)	xxxx	
Foreign Currency		xxxx
To record purchases		

Inventory (Purchases)	xxxx	
*Deferred Exchange Gain	xxxx	
*Deferred Exchange Loss		xxxx
**Premium On Forward Exchange Contract		xxxx
To close deferred exchange gain and deferred premium to		
Inventory (Purchases)		

*Deferred Exchange Gain and Deferred Exchange Loss are debited and credited, respectively, to eliminate any balances in those accounts pertaining to the contract.

**Premium On Forward Exchange Contract is credited sufficiently to remove any debit balance pertaining to the contract. Alternatively, if there is a Discount On Forward Exchange Contract account, it is debited sufficiently to remove any credit balance pertaining to the contract.

19000.5.5   **Speculation (Forward Contract to Sell Foreign Currency)**

In addition to the journal entry explanations given in *GEN19000.5.5.1* through *GEN19000.5.5.3*, see the example given in *GEN19000.5.5.4*.

19000.5.5.1   **At Contract Origination Date**

This transaction is recorded at the forward rate specified in the contract.

U.S. Dollars Receivable - [Exchange Dealer]	xxxx	
Foreign Currency Payable - [Exchange Dealer]		xxxx
To record forward exchange contract		

For an example, *see GEN19000.5.5.4.*

Important: Make sure all appropriate subheads apply to your entry (see page v for instructions)

19000.5   **Forward Exchange Contracts**
19000.5.5   **Speculation (Forward Contract to Sell Foreign Currency)**

19000.5.5.2   **End-of-Period Adjustment of Foreign Currency Payable**

> *Foreign Currency Payable - [Exchange Dealer]   xxxx
>   *Exchange Gain   xxxx
>   *To adjust Foreign Currency Payable to its current U.S.*
>   *dollar equivalent*

*Foreign Currency Payable is debited and Exchange Gain is credited for the amount of any decrease in the U.S. dollar equivalent of the foreign currency payable determined by applying the current forward rate applicable to the remaining maturity of the forward contract. If the U.S. dollar equivalent of the foreign currency payable has increased, Exchange Loss is debited and the Foreign Currency Payable is credited for the amount of the increase.

For an example, *see GEN19000.5.5.4.*

19000.5.5.3   **Settlement of Forward Exchange Contract**

> Foreign Currency   xxxx
>   Cash   xxxx
>   *To record acquisition of foreign currency*

> Foreign Currency Payable - [Exchange Dealer]   xxxx
> *Exchange Loss   xxxx
>   **Foreign Currency   xxxx
>   *To record payment of foreign currency to exchange dealer*

*Exchange Loss is debited to balance the entry. If a credit is necessary to balance the entry, it is made to Exchange Gain.

**Foreign Currency is credited for the U.S. dollar equivalent of the foreign currency paid determined by applying the exchange rate current at the settlement date.

> Cash   xxxx
>   U.S. Dollars Receivable - [Exchange Dealer]   xxxx
>   *To record receipt of U.S. dollars from exchange dealer*

For an example, *see GEN19000.5.5.4.*

Important: Make sure all appropriate subheads apply to your entry (see page v for instructions)

19000.5	**Forward Exchange Contracts**
19000.5.5	**Speculation (Forward Contract to Sell Foreign Currency)**

19000.5.5.4   ### Example of Speculation (Forward Contract to Sell Foreign Currency)

Assume that on December 1, 20X1, a U.S. company enters into a forward contract with an exchange dealer. The forward contract specifies that on February 1, 20X2, the U.S. company will deliver £100,000 to the exchange dealer in exchange for U.S. dollars at a forward rate of $1.55/£. Assuming the following exchange rates, the journal entries to be made by the U.S. company on the relevant dates are as shown below:

	Spot Rate	Forward Rate
December 1, 20X1	$1.48/£	$1.55/£ (60 day)
December 31, 20X1	$1.50/£	$1.54/£ (30 day)
February 1, 20X2	$1.56/£	

At Contract Origination Date (12/1/X1):

U.S. Dollars Receivable - [Exchange Dealer]	155,000	
Foreign Currency Payable - [Exchange Dealer]		155,000

To record forward exchange contract
(£100,000 X $1.55 = 155,000)

At End-of-Period Reporting Date (12/31/X1):

*Foreign Currency Payable - [Exchange Dealer]	1,000	
*Exchange Gain		1,000

*To adjust Foreign Currency Payable to its expected U.S.
dollar equivalent value at maturity*

*Due to exchange rate movements, the expected dollar value of the foreign currency payable has decreased to $154,000. The $1,000 decrease in the expected dollar value of the foreign currency payable is debited to Foreign Currency Payable and credited to Exchange Gain.

At Settlement Date (2/1/X2):

Foreign Currency	156,000	
Cash		156,000

To record acquisition of foreign currency

Important: Make sure all appropriate subheads apply to your entry (see page v for instructions)

19000.5	**Forward Exchange Contracts**	
19000.5.5	**Speculation (Forward Contract to Sell Foreign Currency)**	
19000.5.5.4	**Example of Speculation (Forward Contract to Sell Foreign Currency)**	

---

*Foreign Currency Payable - [Exchange Dealer]	154,000	
*Exchange Loss	2,000	
*Foreign Currency		156,000
To record payment of foreign currency to exchange dealer		

*Due to exchange rate movements, the £100,000 paid by the U.S. company on settlement date is worth $156,000. The difference between the carrying (book) value of the foreign currency payable ($154,000) and the dollar value of the foreign currency paid ($156,000) is debited to Exchange Loss.

Cash	155,000	
U.S. Dollars Receivable - [Exchange Dealer]		155,000
To record receipt of U.S. dollars from exchange dealer		

19000.5.6   Speculation (Forward Contract to Buy Foreign Currency)

19000.5.6.1   At Contract Origination Date

Foreign Currency Receivable - [Exchange Dealer]	xxxx	
U.S. Dollars Payable - Exchange Dealer		xxxx
To record forward exchange contract		

19000.5.6.2   End-of-Period Adjustment of Foreign Currency Receivable

*Foreign Currency Receivable - [Exchange Dealer]	xxxx	
Exchange Gain		xxxx
To adjust Foreign Currency Receivable to its current U.S. dollar equivalent		

*Foreign Currency Receivable is debited and Exchange Gain is credited for the amount of any increase in the U.S. dollar equivalent of the foreign currency receivable, determined by applying the current forward rate applicable to the remaining maturity of the forward contract. If the U.S. dollar equivalent of the foreign currency receivable has decreased, Exchange Loss is debited and the receivable is credited for the amount of the decrease.

Important: Make sure all appropriate subheads apply to your entry (see page v for instructions)

19000.5   **Forward Exchange Contracts**
19000.5.6   **Speculation (Forward Contract to Buy Foreign Currency)**

19000.5.6.3   **Settlement of Forward Exchange Contract**

Dollars Payable - [Exchange Dealer]	xxxx	
Cash		xxxx

To record payment of U.S. dollar obligation to exchange dealer

*Foreign Currency	xxxx	
**Exchange Loss	xxxx	
Foreign Currency Receivable - [Exchange Dealer]		xxxx

To record receipt of foreign currency from exchange dealer

*Foreign Currency is debited for the U.S. dollar equivalent of the foreign currency received determined by applying the exchange rate current at the settlement date.

**Exchange Loss is debited to balance the entry. If a credit is necessary to balance the entry, Exchange Gain is credited.

Cash	xxxx	
Foreign Currency		xxxx

To record conversion of foreign currency to U.S. dollars

TABLE OF CONTENTS

GEN20000   REORGANIZATION AND LIQUIDATION

20000.1	**Reorganization**

20000.1.1	**Reorganization by Contractual Agreement Between Debtor and Creditors**

20000.1.1.1	**Accounting by Debtor**

20000.1.1.1.1	**Restructure of Debt**

20000.1.1.1.1.1	**Future Payments Equal or Exceed Book Value of Debt Including Interest**

No journal entries are necessary by the debtor. A new effective interest rate is computed based on the renegotiated future payments. This new rate is used to record future interest payments.

20000.1.1.1.1.2	**Future Payments Are Less than Book Value of Debt Including Interest**

[Various Liabilities]	xxxx	
Accrued Interest Payable	xxxx	
Gain On Debt Restructure		xxxx

To record reduction of liabilities and to recognize gain due to debt restructure

20000.1.1.1.2	**Assignment of Assets to Satisfy Creditors**

*[Various Assets]	xxxx	
*Gain On Revaluation Of Assets		xxxx

To revalue assets to fair market value prior to assigning assets to creditors

Important: Make sure all appropriate subheads apply to your entry (see page v for instructions)

20000.1   **Reorganization**
20000.1.1   **Reorganization by Contractual Agreement Between Debtor and Creditors**
20000.1.1.1   **Accounting by Debtor**
20000.1.1.1.2   **Assignment of Assets to Satisfy Creditors**

---

*Various asset accounts are debited sufficiently to adjust their balances upward to reflect fair market values and a corresponding gain is recognized. If assets must be written down to reflect fair market values, the asset accounts are credited, and Loss On Revaluation Of Assets is debited.

[Various Liabilities]	xxxx	
Accrued Interest Payable	xxxx	
[Various Assets]		xxxx
Gain On Assignment Of Assets To Creditors		xxxx

To record assignment of assets to creditors

20000.1.1.1.3   Exchange of Debt for Equity

*[Various Liabilities]	xxxx	
*Accrued Interest Payable	xxxx	
**Common (Preferred) Stock		xxxx
**Additional Paid-In Capital - Common (Preferred) Stock		xxxx
***Gain On Reorganization		xxxx

To recognize exchange of debt for equity

*The various liability accounts and Accrued Interest Payable pertaining to the particular liabilities involved in the exchange are debited to eliminate their balances.

**The appropriate stock account is credited for the par (stated) value of the stock issued. If the stock has no par (stated) value, the stock account is credited for the fair market value of the stock issued if it can be reasonably determined. Otherwise, the stock account is credited for an amount equal to the sum of the debits to the various liability accounts and to Accrued Interest Payable.

***Gain On Reorganization is credited for the excess of (a) the sum of the debits to the various liability accounts and to Accrued Interest Payable over (b) the sum of the credits to Common (Preferred) Stock and Additional Paid-In Capital. If the sum of the credits to Common (Preferred) Stock and Additional Paid-In Capital exceeds the sum of the debits to the various liability accounts and to Accrued Interest Payable, the excess is debited to Loss On Reorganization instead of this credit.

Important: Make sure all appropriate subheads apply to your entry (see page v for instructions)

20000.1	**Reorganization**
20000.1.1	**Reorganization by Contractual Agreement Between Debtor and Creditors**
20000.1.1.1	**Accounting by Debtor**

20000.1.1.1.4 **Administrative and Professional Service Costs of Reorganization**

Reorganization Expense	xxxx	
Cash		xxxx

To record administrative and professional service costs of the debt restructure or reorganization

20000.1.1.2 **Accounting by Creditor**

20000.1.1.2.1 **Restructure of Debt**

*Loss On Concessions To Debtors	xxxx	
[Various Receivables]		xxxx
Accrued Interest Receivable		xxxx

To record reduction of receivable and to recognize loss due to concessions to debtor

*Loss On Concessions To Debtors is debited for the difference between the present value of all expected future cash receipts (discounted at the effective interest rate when the receivables originated) and the carrying (book) value of the debt.

The above entry is consistent with Statement of Financial Accounting Standard No. 114.

20000.1.1.2.2 **Receipt of Assets Assigned to Satisfy Receivable**

*[Various Assets]	xxxx	
**Loss On Concessions To Debtors	xxxx	
***[Various Receivables]		xxxx
***Accrued Interest Receivable		xxxx

To record receipt of assets assigned to satisfy receivable and recognize loss

Important: Make sure all appropriate subheads apply to your entry (see page v for instructions)

20000.1	**Reorganization**
20000.1.1	**Reorganization by Contractual Agreement Between Debtor and Creditors**
20000.1.1.2	**Accounting by Creditor**
20000.1.1.2.2	**Receipt of Assets Assigned to Satisfy Receivable**

---

*Various asset accounts are debited for the fair market value of the assets received.

**Loss On Concessions To Debtors is debited for the excess of the credits made to eliminate the receivables and accrued interest over the fair market value of the assets received. If the fair market value of the assets received exceeds the credits made to eliminate the receivables and accrued interest, the excess is credited to Gain On Concessions To Debtors instead of this debit.

***These accounts are credited to eliminate their balances.

20000.1.1.2.3   **Exchange of Receivables for Stock of Debtor**

*Investment In [Various] Stock	xxxx	
**Loss On Concessions To Debtors	xxxx	
***[Various Receivables]		xxxx
***Accrued Interest Receivable		xxxx

To record exchange of receivables for stock of debtor and to recognize loss

*Investment In [Various] Stock is debited for the fair market value of the stock received. If the fair market value of the stock is not reasonably determined, this investment account is debited for an amount equal to the carrying (book) value of the receivables (including accrued interest) exchanged.

**Loss On Concessions To Debtors is debited for any excess of the credits made to eliminate the carrying (book) value of the receivables (including accrued interest) exchanged over the fair market value of the stock received. If the fair market value of the stock received exceeds the credits made to eliminate the carrying (book) value of the receivables (including accrued interest) exchanged, this excess is credited to Gain On Concessions To Debtors instead of this debit.

***Credits are made to various receivable accounts (including Accrued Interest Receivable) to eliminate their carrying (book) value.

20000.1.2   **Reorganization Under Chapter 11 of the Reform (Bankruptcy) Act**

Important: Make sure all appropriate subheads apply to your entry (see page v for instructions)

20000.1	**Reorganization**
20000.1.2	**Reorganization Under Chapter 11 of the Reform (Bankruptcy) Act**

20000.1.2.1 **Accounting by Debtor**

20000.1.2.1.1 **Debt Restructured (Renegotiated); Future Payments Equal or Exceed Book Value of Debt Including Accrued Interest**

No journal entries are necessary by the debtor. A new effective interest rate is computed based on the renegotiated future payments. This new rate is used to record future interest payments.

20000.1.2.1.2 **Debt and Equity Restructured (Renegotiated); Future Payments Less than Book Value of Debt Including Accrued Interest**

20000.1.2.1.2.1 **Conditions for Fresh Start Accounting Are Met**

The following two conditions must be met before fresh start accounting may be used:

- The total value of the assets immediately before the reorganization is confirmed is less than the total value of the post-petition liabilities; and
- Holders of existing voting shares receive less than 50 percent of the voting shares of the post-reorganization entity.

[Various Old Liabilities]	xxxx	
Accrued Interest Payable [New]	xxxx	
[Various New Liabilities]		xxxx
*Common Stock [New]		xxxx
*Additional Paid-In Capital		xxxx
Gain On Debt Restructure		xxxx

To record restructure of liabilities and equity

*The amount for total contributed capital of the new entity is determined in the reorganization negotiations between the interested parties. This amount is then allocated between Common Stock and Additional Paid-In Capital. Common Stock is credited for the par (stated) value of the shares in the new entity received by the creditors. Additional Paid-In Capital is credited for a pro-rated amount based on the shares received by the creditors.

Important: Make sure all appropriate subheads apply to your entry (see page v for instructions)

Common Stock [Old]	xxxx	
Preferred Stock [Old]	xxxx	
*Common Stock [New]		xxxx
*Additional Paid-In Capital		xxxx

To record exchange of old stock for new stock in the emerging entity

*The old Common Stock and old Preferred Stock accounts are closed to the new Common Stock and Additional Paid-In Capital accounts. Common Stock (new) is credited for the par (stated) value of the shares in the new entity received by the old equity holders.

20000.1.2.1.2.2   **Adopting Fresh Start Accounting for the Emerging Entity**

*[Various Assets]	xxxx	
**Additional Paid-In Capital	xxxx	
***Gain On Debt Restructure	xxxx	
****Reorganization Value In Excess Of Amounts Allocable To Identifiable Assets	xxxx	
*[Various Assets]		xxxx
***Retained Earnings (Deficit)		xxxx

To revalue assets to fair market value and to eliminate the deficit

*Assets are written up or down to their fair market value.

**Additional Paid-In Capital is adjusted to the predetermined amount.

***Gain On Debt Restructure and Retained Earnings (Deficit) are adjusted to have a zero balance.

****Reorganization value is a value assigned to the entity as part of the reorganization plan. If the fair market value of all identifiable assets exceeds the reorganization value, the difference is debited to Reorganization Value In Excess Of Amounts Allocable To Identifiable Assets.

Important: Make sure all appropriate subheads apply to your entry (see page v for instructions)

20000.1	**Reorganization**
20000.1.2	**Reorganization Under Chapter 11 of the Reform (Bankruptcy) Act**
20000.1.2.1	**Accounting by Debtor**
20000.1.2.1.2	**Debt and Equity Restructured (Renegotiated); Future Payments Less than Book Value of Debt Including Accrued Interest**

20000.1.2.1.2.3   ## Conditions for Fresh Start Accounting Are Not Met

If either of the following two conditions are not met, fresh start accounting may *not* be used:

- The total value of the assets immediately before confirmation of the reorganization is less than the total value of the post-petition liabilities; and
- Holders of existing voting shares receive less than 50 percent of the voting shares of the post-reorganization entity.

20000.1.2.1.2.3.1   ## Restructure of Debt

[Various Liabilities]	xxxx	
Accrued Interest Payable	xxxx	
Gain On Debt Restructure		xxxx

To record reduction of liabilities and to recognize gain due to debt restructure

20000.1.2.1.2.3.2   ## Assignment of Assets to Satisfy Creditors

*[Various Assets]	xxxx	
*Gain On Revaluation Of Assets		xxxx

To revalue assets to fair market value prior to assigning assets to creditors

*Various asset accounts are debited sufficiently to adjust their balances upward to reflect fair market values, and a corresponding gain is recognized. If assets must be written down to reflect fair market values, the asset accounts would be credited, and Loss On Revaluation Of Assets would be debited.

[Various Liabilities]	xxxx	
Accrued Interest Payable	xxxx	
[Various Assets]		xxxx
Gain On Assignment Of Assets To Creditors		xxxx

To record assignment of assets to creditors

Important: Make sure all appropriate subheads apply to your entry (see page v for instructions)

20000.1	**Reorganization**
20000.1.2	**Reorganization Under Chapter 11 of the Reform (Bankruptcy) Act**
20000.1.2.1	**Accounting by Debtor**
20000.1.2.1.2	**Debt and Equity Restructured (Renegotiated); Future Payments Less than Book Value of Debt Including Accrued Interest**
20000.1.2.1.2.3	**Conditions for Fresh Start Accounting Are Not Met**

20000.1.2.1.2.3.3 **Exchange of Debt for Equity**

*[Various Liabilities]	xxxx	
*Accrued Interest Payable	xxxx	
**Common (Preferred) Stock		xxxx
**Additional Paid-In Capital - Common (Preferred) Stock		xxxx
***Gain On Reorganization		xxxx

To recognize exchange of debt for equity

*The various liability accounts and Accrued Interest Payable pertaining to the particular liabilities involved in the exchange are debited to eliminate their balances.

**The appropriate stock account is credited for the par (stated) value of the stock issued. If the stock has no par (stated) value, the stock account is credited for the fair market value of the stock issued if it can be reasonably determined. Otherwise, the stock account is credited for an amount equal to the sum of the debits to the various liability accounts and to Accrued Interest Payable.

***Gain On Reorganization is credited for the excess of (a) the sum of the debits to the various liability accounts and to Accrued Interest Payable over (b) the sum of the credits to Common (Preferred) Stock and Additional Paid-In Capital. If the sum of the credits to Common (Preferred) Stock and Additional Paid-In Capital exceeds the sum of the debits to the various liability accounts and to Accrued Interest Payable, the excess is debited to Loss On Reorganization instead of this credit.

20000.1.2.1.2.3.4 **Administrative and Professional Service Costs of Reorganization**

Reorganization Expense	xxxx	
Cash		xxxx

To record administrative and professional service costs of the debt restructure or reorganization

---

20000.1.2.2 **Accounting by Creditor**

Important: Make sure all appropriate subheads apply to your entry (see page v for instructions)

20000.1   **Reorganization**
20000.1.2   **Reorganization Under Chapter 11 of the Reform (Bankruptcy) Act**
20000.1.2.2   **Accounting by Creditor**

20000.1.2.2.1

Debt Restructured (Renegotiated); Present Value of Future Receivables Is Less than Current Book Value of Receivables Including Accrued Interest

*Loss On Concessions To Debtors	xxxx
[Various Receivables]	xxxx
Accrued Interest Receivable	xxxx

To record reduction of receivable and to recognize loss due to concessions to debtor

*Loss On Concessions To Debtors is debited for the difference between the present value of all expected future cash receipts (discounted at the effective interest rate when the receivables originated) and the carrying (book) value of the debt.

The above entry is consistent with Statement of Financial Accounting Standard No. 114.

20000.1.2.2.2

Receipt of Assets Assigned to Satisfy Receivables

*[Various Assets]	xxxx
**Loss On Concessions To Debtors	xxxx
***[Various Receivables]	xxxx
***Accrued Interest Receivable	xxxx

To record receipt of assets assigned to satisfy receivables and to recognize loss

*Various asset accounts are debited for the fair market value of the assets received.

**Loss On Concessions To Debtors is debited for the excess of the credits made to eliminate the receivables and accrued interest satisfied over the fair market value of the assets received. If the fair market value of the assets received exceeds the credits made to eliminate the receivables and accrued interest satisfied, the excess is credited to Gain On Concessions To Debtors instead of this debit.

Important: Make sure all appropriate subheads apply to your entry (see page v for instructions)

20000.1   **Reorganization**
20000.1.2   **Reorganization Under Chapter 11 of the Reform (Bankruptcy) Act**
20000.1.2.2   **Accounting by Creditor**
20000.1.2.2.2   **Receipt of Assets Assigned to Satisfy Receivables**

***Credits are made to various receivable accounts (including Accrued Interest Receivable) to eliminate their book value.

20000.1.2.2.3   **Exchange of Receivables for Stock of Debtor**

*Investment In [Various] Stock	xxxx	
**Loss On Concessions To Debtors	xxxx	
***[Various Receivables]		xxxx
***Accrued Interest Receivable		xxxx

To record exchange of receivables for stock of debtor and to recognize loss

*Investment In [Various] Stock is debited for the fair market value of the stock received. If the fair market value of the stock is not reasonably determined, this investment account is debited for an amount equal to the carrying (book) value of the receivables (including accrued interest) exchanged.

**Loss On Concessions To Debtors is debited for any excess of the credits made to eliminate the carrying (book) value of the receivables (including accrued interest) exchanged over the fair market value of the stock received. If the fair market value of the stock received exceeds the credits made to eliminate the carrying (book) value of the receivables (including accrued interest) exchanged, this excess is credited to Gain On Concessions To Debtors instead of this debit.

***Credits are made to various receivable accounts (including Accrued Interest Receivable) to eliminate their book value.

20000.2   **Receivership Under Chapter 7 of the Reform (Bankruptcy) Act**

Receivership occurs when the courts appoint a trustee (receiver) to administer the assets and liabilities of a bankrupt firm.

20000.2.1   **Accounting by Debtor**

Important: Make sure all appropriate subheads apply to your entry (see page v for instructions)

20000.2   **Receivership Under Chapter 7 of the Reform (Bankruptcy) Act**
20000.2.1   **Accounting by Debtor**

20000.2.1.1   **Trustee Continues to Use Existing Books of Debtor**

20000.2.1.1.1   **Business Operations During Liquidation Period**

If business operations continue during the liquidation period, they are accounted for as usual; i.e., they are recorded the same way they would be for a firm that was not in bankruptcy or receivership.

20000.2.1.1.2   **Conversion of Noncash Assets to Cash**

Cash	xxxx	
*Accumulated Depreciation - [Various Assets]	xxxx	
**Liquidation Clearing Account	xxxx	
*[Various Assets]		xxxx
To record sale of noncash assets		

*The carrying (book) value of the various assets sold is written off.

**Liquidation Clearing Account is debited for the excess of the carrying (book) value of the assets sold over the amount of Cash received. If the carrying (book) value of the assets sold is less than the amount of Cash received, this account is credited for the difference.

200000.2.1.1.3   **Recording Administrative and Professional Service Costs**

Liquidation Clearing Account	xxxx	
Cash		xxxx
To record administrative and professional service costs of bankruptcy liquidation		

20000.2.1.1.4   **Payment to Creditors and Settlement of Liabilities**

*[Various Liabilities]	xxxx	
**Liquidation Clearing Account		xxxx
Cash		xxxx
To record payment to creditors		

Important: Make sure all appropriate subheads apply to your entry (see page v for instructions)

20000.2   **Receivership Under Chapter 7 of the Reform (Bankruptcy) Act**
20000.2.1   **Accounting by Debtor**
20000.2.1.1   **Trustee Continues to Use Existing Books of Debtor**
20000.2.1.1.4   **Payment to Creditors and Settlement of Liabilities**

---

*The carrying (book) value of the various liabilities settled is eliminated from the accounts.

**Liquidation Clearing Account is credited for any excess of the carrying (book) value of the various liabilities settled over the amount of cash paid to the creditors.

20000.2.1.1.5   **Closing the Books**

Common (Preferred) Stock	xxxx	
Additional Paid-In Capital - [Various]	xxxx	
Retained Earnings		xxxx
Liquidation Clearing Account		xxxx

To close out all remaining accounts

20000.2.1.2   **Trustee Opens New Books to Account for Liquidation Activities**

20000.2.1.2.1   **Transfer of Assets to Trustee's Records**

Accumulated Depreciation - [Various Assets]	xxxx	
[Various], Trustee	xxxx	
[Various Assets]		xxxx

To record transfer of assets to trustee's records

20000.2.1.2.2   **Receipt of Cash from Trustee**

*Cash	xxxx	
**Liquidation Clearing Account	xxxx	
***[Various], Trustee		xxxx

To record receipt of cash from trustee

*Cash is debited for the amount of cash received from the trustee as proceeds from the sale of assets.

**Liquidation Clearing Account is debited for the excess of the carrying (book) value of the assets sold by the trustee (previously debited to the trustee account (*see* GEN20000.2.1.2.1*) over the amount of cash received from the trustee.

Important: Make sure all appropriate subheads apply to your entry (see page v for instructions)

20000.2   Receivership Under Chapter 7 of the Reform (Bankruptcy) Act
20000.2.1   Accounting by Debtor
20000.2.1.2   Trustee Opens New Books to Account for Liquidation Activities
20000.2.1.2.2   Receipt of Cash from Trustee

***The trustee account is credited for the carrying (book) value of the assets sold (previously debited to the trustee account (*see GEN20000.2.1.2.1*).

20000.2.1.2.3   **Payment to Creditors and Settlement of Liabilities**

*[Various Liabilities]	xxxx	
**Liquidation Clearing Account		xxxx
Cash		xxxx

To record payment to creditors

*The carrying (book) value of the various liabilities settled is eliminated from the accounts.

**Liquidation Clearing Account is credited for any excess of the carrying (book) value of the various liabilities settled over the amount of cash paid to the creditors.

20000.2.1.2.4   **Closing the Books**

Common (Preferred) Stock	xxxx	
Additional Paid-In Capital - [Various]	xxxx	
Retained Earnings		xxxx
Liquidation Clearing Account		xxxx

To close out all remaining accounts

20000.2.2   **Accounting by Creditor**

The only entry necessary is to record the final settlement of the receivable with the debtor.

Cash	xxxx	
*Loss From Bankrupt Debtor	xxxx	
**[Various Receivables]		xxxx
**Accrued Interest Receivable		xxxx

To record receipt of cash from bankrupt debtor and to recognize loss

Important: Make sure all appropriate subheads apply to your entry (see page v for instructions)

20000.2   **Receivership Under Chapter 7 of the Reform (Bankruptcy) Act**
20000.2.2   **Accounting by Creditor**

---

*Loss From Bankrupt Debtor (Allowance For Uncollectible Accounts if appropriate) is debited for the excess of the carrying (book) value of the receivables (including Accrued Interest Receivable) settled over the amount of cash received.

**The carrying (book) value of the various receivables (including any Accrued Interest Receivable) is eliminated.

20000.2.3   ## Accounting by Trustee (New Books Are Established)

20000.2.3.1   ## Setting Up New Books When Assets Are Transferred from Debtor

*[Various Assets]	xxxx	
*Accumulated Depreciation - [Various Assets]		xxxx
**[Various Company] - In Receivership		xxxx
To record receipt of trusteeship of assets		

*The assets received are recorded at their carrying (book) value on the books of the bankrupt firm.

**[Various Company] - In Receivership is credited for the net carrying (book) value of the assets received from the bankrupt firm.

20000.2.3.2   ## Operations During Liquidation Period

If business operations continue during the liquidation period, they are recorded as if the firm were not in bankruptcy or receivership. All nominal accounts are closed to Income Summary, which is then closed to [Various Company] - In Receivership.

20000.2.3.3   ## Conversion of Assets to Cash

Cash	xxxx	
*[Various Company] - In Receivership	xxxx	
**Accumulated Depreciation - [Various Assets]	xxxx	
**[Various Assets]		xxxx
To record sale of assets		

Important: Make sure all appropriate subheads apply to your entry (see page v for instructions)

20000.2   **Receivership Under Chapter 7 of the Reform (Bankruptcy) Act**
20000.2.3   **Accounting by Trustee (New Books Are Established)**
20000.2.3.3   **Conversion of Assets to Cash**

---

*[Various Company] - In Receivership is debited for the excess of the carrying (book) value of the assets sold over the cash received. If the cash received exceeds the carrying (book) value of the assets sold, this account would be credited for the difference instead of debited.

**The carrying (book) value of the assets sold is eliminated from the accounts.

20000.2.3.4   **Administrative and Professional Service Costs**

        *[Various Company] - In Receivership   xxxx
           Cash   xxxx
        To record administrative and professional service costs of the debt restructure or reorganization

*Instead of debiting [Various Company] - In Receivership directly, an expense account may be debited. The expense account would be closed to Income Summary, which would be closed to [Various Company] - In Receivership.

20000.2.3.5   **Return of Cash to Debtor (or Direct Payment to Creditors)**

        [Various Company] - In Receivership   xxxx
           Cash   xxxx
        To record transfer of cash to debtor (or direct payment to creditors)

TABLE OF CONTENTS

21000.1	**Organization (Creation) of a Partnership**

21000.1.1   **Individual Partner's Contribution Is Equal to His/Her Initial Capital Balance**

*[Various Assets]	xxxx	
[Partner A], Capital		xxxx

To record initial contribution of Partner A to the partnership

*Each asset contributed is debited for an amount equal to its fair market value at the time of contribution.

21000.1.2   **Individual Partner's Contribution Is Less than His/Her Initial Capital Balance**

21000.1.2.1   **Goodwill Method**

*[Various Assets]	xxxx	
**Goodwill	xxxx	
[Partner A], Capital		xxxx

To record initial contribution of Partner A to the partnership

*Each asset contributed is debited for its fair market value at the time of contribution.

**Goodwill is debited for the amount indicated in the partnership agreement; i.e, the difference between the amount of capital indicated by the partnership agreement and the fair market value of the assets contributed.

21000.1.2.2   **Bonus Method - Old Partner Provides Bonus to New Partner**

*[Various Assets]	xxxx	
**[Partner B], Capital	xxxx	
***[Partner A], Capital		xxxx

To record initial contribution of Partner A to the partnership

Important: Make sure all appropriate subheads apply to your entry (see page v for instructions)

21000.1	**Organization (Creation) of a Partnership**
21000.1.2	**Individual Partner's Contribution is Less than His/Her Initial Capital Balance**
21000.1.2.2	**Bonus Method - Old Partner Provides Bonus to New Partner**

---

*Each asset contributed by the new partner is debited for an amount equal to its fair market value at time of contribution.

**The old partner's capital account is debited for the amount of bonus given by the old partner to the new partner as indicated in the partnership agreement. The total bonus is indicated by the difference between the amount of capital indicated in the partnership agreement and the fair value of the assets contributed.

21000.2	**Operations**

21000.2.1	**Normal Operating Activities**

There are no unusual entries necessary to record normal operating activities of a partnership.

21000.2.2	**Drawings**

Drawings is a term used to refer to normal withdrawals of a partner's share of earnings as provided for in the partnership agreement.

[Partner A], Drawings	xxxx	
Cash		xxxx
To record Partner A's normal drawings		

21000.2.3	**Close Income Summary (Expense And Revenue Summary)**

21000.2.3.1	**Net Profit Occurs**

*Income Summary	xxxx	
**[Partner A], Capital		xxxx
**[Partner B], Capital		xxxx
**[Partner C], Capital		xxxx
To close Income Summary		

Important: Make sure all appropriate subheads apply to your entry (see page v for instructions)

21000.2	**Operations**
21000.2.3	**Close Income Summary (Expense And Revenue Summary)**
21000.2.3.1	**Net Profit Occurs**

---

*Common alternative account titles are Expense And Revenue Summary and Profit And Loss Summary.

**Each partner's capital account is credited for that partner's share of profit as provided for in the partnership agreement. Partners' shares of income will not necessarily be equal.

21000.2.3.2	**Net Loss Occurs**		
	*[Partner A], Capital	xxxx	
	*[Partner B], Capital	xxxx	
	*[Partner C], Capital	xxxx	
	**Income Summary		xxxx
	To close Income Summary		

*Each partner's capital account is debited for that partner's share of loss as provided for in the partnership agreement. Partners' shares of loss will not necessarily be equal.

**Common alternative account titles are Expense And Revenue Summary and Profit And Loss Summary.

21000.3	**One Partner's Capital Investment Changed**

21000.3.1	**Additional Assets Are Invested**		
	*[Various Assets]	xxxx	
	[Partner A], Capital		xxxx
	To record additional assets invested by Partner A		

*Each asset contributed is debited for an amount equal to its fair value at time of contribution.

Important: Make sure all appropriate subheads apply to your entry (see page v for instructions)

21000.3   **One Partner's Capital Investment Changed**

21000.3.2   **Unscheduled Withdrawal of Assets**

An unscheduled withdrawal of assets is a withdrawal that is not a drawing under the terms of the partnership agreement. Thus, a Drawings account is not used to record such a withdrawal.

*[Various Assets]	xxxx	
*Gain On Revaluation Of Assets		xxxx
To record revaluation of assets		

*The assets to be withdrawn are written up to fair market value and Gain On Revaluation Of Assets is credited. If the assets must be written down to fair market value, they are credited and Loss On Revaluation Of Assets is debited.

[Partner A], Capital	xxxx	
[Various Assets]		xxxx
To record the unscheduled withdrawal of assets by Partner A		

21000.4   **Admission of New Partner**

The admission of a new partner results in a change in the partnership entity; i.e., the result is considered to be a new and different partnership from the old partnership. Even though this is the case, the old accounting records are usually carried over to the new partnership.

21000.4.1   **New Partner Contributes Assets to Partnership**

21000.4.1.1   **Assets Contributed by New Partner Have a Fair Market Value Equal to New Partner's Capital Balance**

*[Various Assets]	xxxx	
[Partner N], Capital		xxxx
To record the admission of Partner N to the partnership		

*Each asset contributed is debited for an amount equal to its fair market value at the time of contribution.

Important: Make sure all appropriate subheads apply to your entry (see page v for instructions)

21000.4   **Admission of New Partner**
21000.4.1   **New Partner Contributes Assets to Partnership**

21000.4.1.2   **Assets Contributed by New Partner Have a Fair Market Value Greater than New Partner's Implied Capital Balance (New Partner Pays a Premium for Admission)**

21000.4.1.2.1   **Goodwill Method**

*[Various Assets]	xxxx	
[Partner N], Capital		xxxx

To record the admission of Partner N to the partnership

*Each asset contributed is debited for an amount equal to its fair market value at the time of contribution.

*Goodwill	xxxx	
**[Partner O], Capital		xxxx
**[Partner P], Capital		xxxx

To record goodwill implied by admission of new partner

*Goodwill is debited for the amount of goodwill implied by the terms under which the new partner was admitted. *For example,* if the new partner contributed assets with a fair market value of $150,000 for a one-third interest in the partnership, a 100% interest must be worth $450,000 ($150,000 / 1/3). This suggests that the value of the remaining two-thirds interest held by the old partners is $300,000. If the capital balances of the two old partners at the time totaled only $240,000, goodwill of $60,000 ($300,000 - $240,000) is implied.

**The capital accounts of each of the old partners will be credited for each partner's share of the goodwill recorded. Goodwill is allocated among the old partners according to their current profit and loss ratios as indicated in the old partnership agreement.

21000.4.1.2.2   **Bonus Method - New Partner Provides Bonus to Old Partners**

*[Various Assets]	xxxx	
**[Partner N], Capital		xxxx
***[Partner O], Capital		xxxx
***[Partner P], Capital		xxxx

To record admission of Partner N

Important: Make sure all appropriate subheads apply to your entry (see page v for instructions)

21000.4	**Admission of New Parnter**
21000.4.1	**New Partner Contributes Assets to Partnership**
21000.4.1.2	**Assets Contributed by New Partner Have a Fair Market Value Greater than New Partner's Implied Capital Balance (New Partner Pays a Premium for Admission)**
21000.4.1.2.2	**Bonus Method - New Partner Provides Bonus to Old Partners**

*Each asset contributed is debited for an amount equal to its fair value at time of contribution.

**The new partner's capital account ([Partner N], Capital) is credited for the amount agreed to by the new and old partners under the terms of admission of the new partner.

***The old partners' capital accounts are credited for the excess of the fair market value of the assets contributed by the new partner over the credit made to the new partner's capital account ([Partner A], Capital). The old partners will share this difference according to their profit and loss ratio as indicated in the old partnership agreement.

21000.4.1.3

Assets Contributed by New Partner Have Market Value Less than New Partner's Implied Capital Balance (New Partner Admitted by Old Partners at a Discount)

The likely cause of this situation is the purchase of intangibles by the new partner.

21000.4.1.3.1

Goodwill Method

*[Various Assets]	xxxx
**Goodwill	xxxx
***[Partner N], Capital	xxxx
To record the admission of Partner N	

*Each asset contributed is debited for an amount equal to its fair market value at the time of contribution.

**Goodwill is debited for the excess of the credit to the new partner's capital account ([Partner N], Capital) over the fair market value of the assets contributed.

***The new partner's capital account ([Partner N], Capital) is credited for the amount agreed to by the old and new partners.

Important: Make sure all appropriate subheads apply to your entry (see page v for instructions)

21000.4	**Admission of New Parnter**
21000.4.1	**New Partner Contributes Assets to Partnership**
21000.4.1.3	**Assets Contributed by New Partner Have Market Value Less than New Partner's Implied Capital Balance (New Partner Admitted by Old Partners at a Discount)**

21000.4.1.3.2   **Bonus Method - Old Partners Provide Bonus to New Partner**

*[Various Assets]	xxxx
**[Partner O], Capital	xxxx
**[Partner P], Capital	xxxx
***[Partner N], Capital	xxxx
To record admission of Partner N	

*Each asset contributed is debited for an amount equal to its fair market value at the time of contribution.

**The old partners' capital accounts are debited for the excess of the credit to the new partner's capital account ([Partner N], Capital) over the fair market value of the assets contributed. The old partners' share the total reduction in old partner capital according to their profit and loss ratio as indicated in the old partnership agreement.

***The new partner's capital account ([Partner N], Capital) is credited for the amount agreed to by the old and new partners.

21000.4.2   **New Partner Makes External Payment to Old Partners; No New Assets Are Invested in Partnership**

21000.4.2.1   **External Payment by New Partner Is Equal to New Partner's Capital Balance**

*[Partner O], Capital	xxxx
*[Partner P], Capital	xxxx
**[Partner N], Capital	xxxx
To record admission of Partner N	

*The old partners' capital accounts are debited sufficiently to reduce their balances to reflect their agreed-to new percentage ownership in the new partnership. *For example,* assume the book value of the partnership assets (and therefore the sum of the old partners' capital balances before admission of the new partner) is $300,000; i.e., $150,000 each. Also assume the new partner purchased a one-third interest equally from the old partners, so that after admission of the new partner each partner was to have a one-third interest. Each of the old partners' accounts would be debited for $50,000 to reduce its balance to $100,000 ($300,000 / 3).

Important: Make sure all appropriate subheads apply to your entry (see page v for instructions)

21000.4   **Admission of New Parnter**

21000.4.2   **New Partner Makes External Payment to Old Partners; No New Assets Are Invested in Partnership**

21000.4.2.1   **External Payment by New Partner Is Equal to New Partner's Capital Balance**

**The new partner's capital account ([Partner N], Capital) is credited sufficiently to represent his/her purchased share of the total equity of the partnership.

21000.4.2.2

External Payment Made by New Partner Is Greater than New Partner's Implied Capital Balance Based on Old Partners' Capital Balances Before Admission (New Partner Pays Premium for Admission)

21000.4.2.2.1

Goodwill Method

*Goodwill	xxxx	
**[Partner O], Capital		xxxx
**[Partner P], Capital		xxxx

To record goodwill implied by admission of new partner

*Goodwill is debited for the amount of goodwill implied by the terms under which the new partner was admitted. *For example,* assume the new partner paid the two old partners $150,000 for a one-third interest in the partnership. A 100% interest must be worth $450,000 ($150,000 / 1/3). This suggests that the value of the remaining two-thirds interest held by the old partners is $300,000. If the capital balances of the two old partners at the time totaled only $240,000, goodwill of $60,000 ($300,000 - $240,000) is implied.

**The capital accounts of each of the old partners will be credited for each partner's share of the goodwill recorded. Goodwill is allocated among the old partners according to their current profit and loss ratios as indicated in the old partnership agreement.

*[Partner O], Capital	xxxx	
*[Partner P], Capital	xxxx	
**[Partner N], Capital		xxxx

To record admission of Partner N

*The old partners' capital accounts are debited sufficiently to reduce their balances to reflect their agreed-to new percentage ownership in the new partnership. For example, assume the book value of the partnership assets (and therefore the sum of the partners' capital balances after recording goodwill) is $450,000. If the new partner purchased a one-third interest equally from the old partners so that after admission of the new partner each partner was to have a one-third interest, each of the old partners'

Important: Make sure all appropriate subheads apply to your entry (see page v for instructions)

21000.4	**Admission of New Parnter**
21000.4.2	**New Partner Makes External Payment to Old Partners; No New Assets Are Invested in Partnership**
21000.4.2.2	**External Payment Made by New Partner Is Greater than New Partner's Implied Capital Balance Based on Old Partners' Capital Balances Before Admission (New Partner Pays Premium for Admission)**
21000.4.2.2.1	**Goodwill Method**

---

accounts would be debited for $75,000 to reduce its balance by one-half of the $150,000 credit to the new partner's capital account.

**The new partner's capital account ([Partner N], Capital) is credited sufficiently to represent his/her purchased share of the total equity of the partnership.

21000.4.2.2.2   **Bonus Method - New Partner Provides Bonus to Old Partners**

*[Partner O], Capital	xxxx	
*[Partner P], Capital	xxxx	
**[Partner N], Capital		xxxx
To record admission of Partner N		

*The old partners' capital accounts are debited sufficiently to reduce their balances to reflect their agreed-to new percentage ownership in the new partnership.

**The credit to the new partner's capital account will be for an amount that is less than the external payment made to the old partners.

21000.4.2.3   **External Payment Made by New Partner Is Less than New Partner's Implied Capital Balance Based on Old Partners' Capital Balances Before Admission (New Partner Admitted at a Discount)**

21000.4.2.3.1   **Goodwill Method**

*Goodwill	xxxx	
*[Partner O], Capital	xxxx	
*[Partner P], Capital	xxxx	
*[Partner N], Capital		xxxx
To record admission of Partner N		

*All debits and credits in this entry are made according to negotiations among the old and new partners. The goodwill recorded is that brought to the partnership by the new partner. The credit to the new partner's capital account ([Partner N], Capital) will be for more than the external payment.

Important: Make sure all appropriate subheads apply to your entry (see page v for instructions)

21000.4   **Admission of New Parnter**
21000.4.2   **New Partner Makes External Payment to Old Partners; No New Assets Are Invested in Partnership**
21000.4.2.3   **External Payment Made by New Partner Is Less than New Partner's Implied Capital Balance Based on Old Partners' Capital Balances Before Admission (New Partner Admitted at a Discount)**

21000.4.2.3.2   **Bonus Method - Old Partners Provide Bonus to New Partner**

*[Partner O], Capital	xxxx	
*[Partner P], Capital	xxxx	
*[Partner N], Capital		xxxx
To record admission of Partner N		

*All debits and credits in this entry are made according to negotiations among the old and new partners. The credit to the new partner's capital account ([Partner N], Capital) will be for more than the external payment.

21000.5   **Changing Ownership - Old Partner Withdraws from the Partnership (Voluntarily or for Reasons of Retirement, Death, etc.)**

The withdrawal of a partner from a partnership regardless of the reason results in a change in the partnership entity; i.e, the old partnership is technically dissolved and a new partnership takes its place. Usually the accounting records of the old partnership are continued in the name of the new partnership.

21000.5.1   **Partnership Assets Distributed to Withdrawing Partner**

21000.5.1.1   **Assets Distributed Have Book Value Equal to Old Partner's Capital Balance**

[Partner W], Capital	xxxx	
*[Various Assets]		xxxx
To record withdrawal of Partner W from the partnership		

*Asset accounts are credited for the book value of the assets distributed.

21000.5.1.2   **Assets Distributed to Old Partner Have Book Value Greater than Old Partner's Capital Balance (Old Partner Given Premium at Withdrawal)**

Important: Make sure all appropriate subheads apply to your entry (see page v for instructions)

21000.5	**Changing Ownership - Old Partner Withdraws from the Partnership (Voluntarily or for Reasons of Retirement, Death, etc.)**
21000.5.1	**Partnership Assets Distributed to Withdrawing Partner**
21000.5.1.2	**Assets Distributed to Old Partner Have Book Value Greater than Old Partner's Capital Balance (Old Partner Given Premium at Withdrawal)**

21000.5.1.2.1   **Goodwill Method**

*Goodwill	xxxx	
[Partner W], Capital		xxxx
[Partner O], Capital		xxxx
[Partner P], Capital		xxxx

To record goodwill implicit in the partnership

*Goodwill is debited for the amount of goodwill implicit in the partnership as determined by negotiations when the partner withdraws. *For example,* assume the partners agree to pay the withdrawing partner $20,000 more than the balance in his/her capital account, which represents a one-third partnership interest. The amount of partnership goodwill implicit in the agreement is $60,000 ($20,000/ 1/3). The partners' capital accounts will be credited to allocate the goodwill on the basis of their profit sharing ratios as contained in the partnership agreement.

[Partner W], Capital	xxxx	
*[Various Assets]		xxxx

To record withdrawal of Partner W from the partnership

*Asset accounts are credited for their book value.

21000.5.1.2.2   **Bonus Method - Remaining Partners Provide Bonus to Withdrawing Partner**

*[Partner O], Capital	xxxx	
*[Partner P], Capital	xxxx	
**[Partner W], Capital	xxxx	
***[Various Assets]		xxxx

To record the withdrawal of Partner W from the partnership

*The surviving partners' capital balances are debited for the excess of the book value of the assets given to the withdrawing partner over the balance in the withdrawing partner's capital account ([Partner W], Capital).

**The withdrawing partner's capital account ([Partner W], Capital) is debited sufficiently to eliminate its credit balance.

Important: Make sure all appropriate subheads apply to your entry (see page v for instructions)

21000.5   **Changing Ownership - Old Partner Withdraws from the Partnership (Voluntarily or for Reasons of Retirement, Death, etc.)**

21000.5.1   **Partnership Assets Distributed to Withdrawing Partner**

21000.5.1.2   **Assets Distributed to Old Partner Have Book Value Greater than Old Partner's Capital Balance (Old Partner Given Premium at Withdrawal**

21000.5.1.2.2   **Bonus Method - Remaining Partners Provide Bonus to Withdrawing Partner**

***Asset accounts are credited for their book value.

21000.5.1.3   **Assets Distributed to Old Partner Have a Book Value Less than Old Partner's Capital Balance (Old Partner Withdraws at a Discount)**

21000.5.1.3.1   **Overvalued Assets**

*[Partner W], Capital	xxxx	
*[Partner O], Capital	xxxx	
*[Partner P], Capital	xxxx	
**[Various Assets]		xxxx

To write down overvalued assets

*The partners' capital accounts are debited for the amount the assets are written down.

**The assets are written down by the amount resulting from negotiations when the partner withdraws.

[Partner W], Capital	xxxx	
*[Various Assets]		xxxx

To record withdrawal of Partner W from the partnership

*Because the assets were written down in the preceding entry, the book value of the assets given to Partner W equals Partner W's capital balance.

21000.5.1.3.2   **Bonus Method - Withdrawing Partner Provides a Bonus to Remaining Partners**

*[Partner W], Capital	xxxx	
**[Various Assets]		xxxx
***[Partner O], Capital		xxxx
***[Partner P], Capital		xxxx

To record withdrawal of Partner W from the partnership

PARTNERSHIPS

Important: Make sure all appropriate subheads apply to your entry (see page v for instructions)

21000.5   **Changing Ownership - Old Partner Withdraws from the Partnership (Voluntarily or for Reasons of Retirement, Death, etc.)**

21000.5.1   **Partnership Assets Distributed to Withdrawing Partner**

21000.5.1.3   **Assets Distributed to Old Partner Have a Book Value Less than Old Partner's Capital Balance (Old Partner Withdraws at a Discount)**

21000.5.1.3.2   **Bonus Method - Withdrawing Partner Provides a Bonus to Remaining Partners**

---

*The withdrawing partner's capital account ([Partner W], Capital) is debited sufficiently to eliminate its credit balance.

**The assets are written down by the amount resulting from negotiations when the partner withdraws.

***The surviving partners' capital accounts are credited for the excess of the debit to the withdrawing partner's capital account over the amount of the write down of the assets. The surviving partners will share the total credit according to their profit sharing ratio as contained in the partnership agreement.

21000.5.2   **Remaining Partners Make External Payment to Withdrawing Partner; No Partnership Assets Distributed**

21000.5.2.1   **External Payment by Remaining Partners Is Equal to Old Partner's Capital Balance**

[Partner W], Capital	xxxx	
[Partner O], Capital		xxxx
[Partner P], Capital		xxxx

To record the withdrawal of Partner W

21000.5.2.2   **External Payment Made by Remaining Partners Is Greater than Withdrawing Partner's Capital Balance (Remaining Partners Pay Premium to Withdrawing Partner)**

21000.5.2.2.1   **Goodwill Method**

*Goodwill	xxxx	
[Partner O], Capital		xxxx
[Partner P], Capital		xxxx
[Partner W], Capital		xxxx

To record Goodwill implicit in the partnership

*Goodwill is debited for the amount of goodwill implicit in the partnership as determined by negotiations when the partner withdraws. For example, assume the

Important: Make sure all appropriate subheads apply to your entry (see page v for instructions)

21000.5   **Changing Ownership - Old Partner Withdraws from the Partnership (Voluntarily or for Reasons of Retirement, Death, etc.)**

21000.5.2   **Remaining Partners Make External Payment to Withdrawing Partner; No Partnership Assets Distributed**

21000.5.2.2   **External Payment Made by Remaining Partners Is Greater than Withdrawing Partner's Capital Balance (Remaining Partners Pay Premium to Withdrawing Partner)**

21000.5.2.2.1   **Goodwill Method**

---

partners agree to externally pay the withdrawing partner $20,000 more than the balance in his/her capital account, which represents a one-third partnership interest. The amount of partnership goodwill implicit in the agreement is $60,000 ($20,000/ 1/3). The partners' capital accounts will be credited to allocate the goodwill on the basis of their profit sharing ratios as contained in the partnership agreement.

*[Partner W], Capital	xxxx	
**[Partner O], Capital		xxxx
**[Partner P], Capital		xxxx

To record the withdrawal of Partner W from the partnership and transfer of capital to remaining partners

*[Partner W], Capital is debited to eliminate its balance.

**Credits to the remaining partners' capital accounts will be based on their profit and loss sharing ratios as contained in the partnership agreement, unless a different agreement has been reached by the remaining partners.

21000.5.2.2.2   **Bonus Method - Remaining Partners Provide Bonus to Withdrawing Partner**

[Partner W], Capital	xxxx	
*[Partner O], Capital		xxxx
*[Partner P], Capital		xxxx

To record withdrawal of Partner W from the partnership and transfer of capital to remaining partners

*Credits to the remaining partners' capital accounts will be based on their profit and loss sharing ratios as contained in the partnership agreement unless a different agreement has been reached by the remaining partners.

21000.5.2.3   **External Payment Made by Remaining Partners Is Less than Withdrawing Partner's Capital Balance (Partner Withdraws at a Discount)**

Important: Make sure all appropriate subheads apply to your entry (see page v for instructions)

21000.5   **Changing Ownership - Old Partner Withdraws from the Partnership (Voluntarily or for Reasons of Retirement, Death, etc.)**

21000.5.2   **Remaining Partners Make External Payment to Withdrawing Partner; No Partnership Assets Distributed**

21000.5.2.3   **External Payment Made by Remaining Partners Is Less than Withdrawing Partner's Capital Balance (Partner Withdraws at a Discount)**

21000.5.2.3.1   **Overvalued Assets**

[Partner W], Capital	XXXX	
[Partner O], Capital	XXXX	
[Partner P], Capital	XXXX	
*[Various Assets]		XXXX
To write down overvalued assets		

*Assets are written down for the amount of the overvaluation implicit in the partnership as determined by negotiations when the partner withdraws. *For example,* assume the partners agree to externally pay the withdrawing partner $20,000 less than the balance in his/her capital account, which represents a one-third partnership interest. The amount of overvaluation of assets implicit in the agreement is $60,000 ($20,000/ 1/3). The partners' capital accounts will be debited to allocate the write down on the basis of their profit sharing ratios as contained in the partnership agreement.

*[Partner W], Capital	XXXX	
**[Partner O], Capital		XXXX
**[Partner P], Capital		XXXX
To record the withdrawal of Partner W from the partnership		

*[Partner W], Capital is debited to eliminate its balance.

**Credits to the remaining partners' capital accounts will be based on their profit and loss sharing ratios as contained in the partnership agreement unless a different agreement has been reached by the remaining partners.

21000.5.2.3.2   **Bonus Method - Withdrawing Partner Provides Bonus to Remaining Partners**

*[Partner W], Capital	XXXX	
**[Partner O], Capital		XXXX
**[Partner P], Capital		XXXX
To record withdrawal of Partner W from the partnership and transfer of capital to remaining partners		

Important: Make sure all appropriate subheads apply to your entry (see page v for instructions)

21000.5	**Changing Ownership - Old Partner Withdraws from the Partnership (Voluntarily or for Reasons of Retirement, Death, etc.)**
21000.5.2	**Remaining Partners Make External Payment to Withdrawing Partner; No Partnership Assets Distributed**
21000.5.2.3	**External Payment Made by Remaining Partners Is Less than Withdrawing Partner's Capital Balance (Partner Withdraws at a Discount)**
21000.5.2.3.2	**Bonus Method - Withdrawing Partner Provides Bonus to Remaining Partner**

---

*[Partner W], Capital is debited to eliminate its balance.

**Credits to the remaining partners' capital accounts will be based on their profit and loss sharing ratios as contained in the partnership agreement, unless a different agreement has been reached by the remaining partners.

21000.6

Changing Ownership - Old Partner Transfers Interest in Partnership to New Partner

The withdrawal of a partner from a partnership regardless of the reason results in a change in the partnership entity; i.e, the old partnership is technically dissolved and a new partnership takes its place. Usually the accounting records of the old partnership are continued in the name of the new partnership. Replacement of a withdrawing partner by a new partner normally does not affect partnership assets.

*[Partner W], Capital	xxxx	
*[Partner N], Capital		xxxx
To record replacement of old partner with new partner		

*The balance of the old partner's capital account is transferred to the new partner.

21000.7

Partnership Liquidation

If a partnership is liquidated, all operations of the partnership are discontinued, and all partnership assets are distributed to creditors and partners.

21000.7.1

Sale of All Partnership Assets for Cash

Cash	xxxx	
*Gain On Liquidation		xxxx
**[Various Assets]		xxxx
To record sale of partnership assets for cash		

*Gain On Liquidation is credited to balance the entry. Alternatively, if a debit is needed to balance the entry, Loss On Liquidation is debited.

**Asset accounts are credited for their book value.

Important: Make sure all appropriate subheads apply to your entry (see page v for instructions)

21000.7　　　　**Partnership Liquidation**

21000.7.2

Additional Contributions by Partners

Additional contributions by solvent partners may be necessary to offset one or more negative (debit) partner capital balances or to satisfy partnership liabilities if partnership assets are otherwise inadequate.

Cash	xxxx	
[Partner A], Capital		xxxx
To recognize additional contribution by solvent partner		

21000.7.3

Payment of Partnership Liabilities

Payment of creditors takes priority over distribution of assets to partners.

*[Various Liabilities]	xxxx	
Cash		xxxx
To record payment of liabilities		

*Liability accounts are debited to eliminate their balances.

21000.7.4

Absorption of Negative (Debit) Partner Capital Balance by Solvent Partners

If one or more partners have a negative (debit) capital balance that is not removed by additional contributions, it must be absorbed by the solvent partners.

*[Partner A], Capital	xxxx	
*[Partner B], Capital	xxxx	
[Partner I], Capital		xxxx
To record absorption of negative capital balance of		
Partner I by solvent partners		

*The solvent partners will absorb the negative capital balance of the insolvent partner based on their profit and loss sharing ratios as contained in the partnership agreement.

Important: Make sure all appropriate subheads apply to your entry (see page v for instructions)

21000.7　　　　　　**Partnership Liquidation**

21000.7.5　　　　　**Distribution of Remaining Assets to Partners**

*[Partner A], Capital	xxxx	
*[Partner B], Capital	xxxx	
Cash		xxxx
To record final liquidation of partnership		

*Partners will receive cash in amounts equal to their capital balances. Only partners with credit capital balances will receive cash. Any debit capital balances should have been eliminated as indicated in *GEN21000.7.4.*

TABLE OF CONTENTS

22000.1   **Estates**

The personal representative of an estate is the fiduciary accountable to the beneficiaries, the court, and to the taxing authorities. The personal representative may also
be called an executor or executrix, if named by the decedent's will, or an
administrator, if named by the court for a decedent dying intestate.

The personal representative is responsible for taking inventory of all the assets in the
estate, for safeguarding the assets during the life of the estate, for distributing the
assets to the beneficiaries, for the filing of the necessary forms and payment of estate
and inheritance taxes to the proper taxing authorities, and for accounting to the courts
for the disposition of the assets.

Throughout the accounting for an estate, the personal representative must distinguish between assets that are part of the principle of the estate and assets that come
into the estate as income. The determination of principal and income items is not
always clear. If the decedent specified how to treat certain items in the will, that
direction controls; in the absence of testamentary direction, however, state laws
govern this determination. A number of states have adopted the Revised Uniform
Principal and Income Act in whole or in part. Treatment of the items in this section
follows this act. Accounting income as determined by the trust document or state law
may differ from estate taxable income and income determined under generally
accepted accounting procedures.

Unless otherwise directed, estates use the cash basis of accounting during the
administration of the estate with two exceptions:

1. Items of income earned by the decedent prior to death are accrued by the
   estate and become part of the estate principal.
2. Items of income earned by the estate but not received at the time the estate
   is closed must also be accrued to complete the closing process.

22000.1.1   **Recording the Initial Inventory of Estate Assets**

The personal representative must file an inventory of assets with the probate court.
The principal of the estate includes all assets owned (except certain items that pass
directly to the beneficiaries without inclusion in the probate estate; e.g., insurance
proceeds payable to a beneficiary other than the estate, items in which the decedent

Important: Make sure all appropriate subheads apply to your entry (see page v for instructions)

22000.1	**Estates**
22000.1.1	**Recording the Initial Inventory of Estate Assets**

---

was a joint tenant, and in some states, real property and certain personal property items). The principal also includes all items of income accrued at the date of the decedent's death. Assets are recorded at their fair market (appraisal) value at the date of the decedent's death. Assets encumbered by debt are also recorded at their fair value; i.e., liabilities do not reduce the value of the asset. Because the initial recording of inventory is *not* a determination of the net worth of the estate, liabilities of the decedent or liens against property do not have to be included in the initial inventory. Debts owed by the decedent at the date of death and debts incurred by the estate are not recorded in the accounts until they are paid from estate principal or income. However, the personal representative should keep a separate listing of all liabilities of the decedent and may, if desired, record the liens against estate property as liabilities in the initial inventory. This latter practice conforms the initial inventory more closely to the estate net worth.

It is normally unnecessary to identify each item, except cash, as an item of principal. Generally, estate income is received in the form of cash only and will not be invested in other forms of assets unless the estate cannot be settled within a reasonable period. If, however, the estate receives income in other than cash or invests the cash income in other assets, the personal representative may designate each item in the initial inventory as a principal item to ensure the segregation of principal and income items; for example: Stock of MNO Company - Principal.

Cash - Principal	xxxx	
Certificate Of Deposit	xxxx	
*Interest Receivable	xxxx	
*Rent Receivable	xxxx	
*Dividends Receivable	xxxx	
Stock Of [Various]	xxxx	
Real Estate - [Various]	xxxx	
**Life Insurance Receivable	xxxx	
Household Furnishings	xxxx	
Personal Residence	xxxx	
Clothing	xxxx	
Jewelry	xxxx	
Automobile	xxxx	
[Various Assets]	xxxx	
***Mortgage Payable		xxxx
***[Various Liabilities]		xxxx
Estate Principal		xxxx

To record initial inventory of estate assets

Important: Make sure all appropriate subheads apply to your entry (see page v for instructions)

22000.1   **Estates**
22000.1.1   **Recording the Initial Inventory of Estate Assets**

---

*Interest and rents accrued to the date of death and dividends declared but not yet received are recorded as part of the estate principal. In some states, however, the date of record for dividends declared must precede the date of death to be considered principal.

**Life insurance payable to the estate as beneficiary is included in the inventory of assets.

***All liabilities that must be satisfied using estate property are recorded.

22000.1.2   **Recording the Collection of Receivables**

Cash - Principal	xxxx	
Interest Receivable		xxxx
Rent Receivable		xxxx
Dividends Receivable		xxxx
Life Insurance Receivable		xxxx
[Various Receivables]		xxxx

To record collection of receivables

22000.1.3   **Recording Assets Discovered Subsequent to Filing the Initial Asset Inventory**

Often other assets are discovered after the initial inventory is filed with the probate court. Although these assets are ultimately treated as part of estate principal, for probate purposes they are separately designated as Assets Subsequently Discovered to indicate that they were not part of the initial inventory.

[Various Assets]	xxxx	
Assets Subsequently Discovered		xxxx

To record assets subsequently discovered

22000.1.4   **Recording Income Earned on Principal Assets**

Certain principal assets in an estate, such as rental properties, stocks, and bonds, will earn income. Only the income accrued to the date of the decedent's death constitutes

Important: Make sure all appropriate subheads apply to your entry (see page v for instructions)

22000.1   **Estates**
22000.1.4   **Recording Income Earned on Principal Assets**

---

estate principal; income earned on these assets from the date of death forward is income to the estate.

*Cash - Income	xxxx	
Rental Income		xxxx
Interest Income		xxxx
Dividend Income		xxxx
[Various Income]		xxxx

To record income earned on estate principal assets

*Most income items will be received in the form of cash. If, however, property is received as income, it is recorded with a designation as an income item (like Cash shown in the entry above) to maintain separation of income and principal items.

22000.1.5   Investing Cash in Income-Producing Assets

*Investment In [Various Income-Producing Assets]		
- Principal	xxxx	
**Investment In [Various Income-Producing Assets]		
- Income	xxxx	
*Cash - Principal		xxxx
**Cash - Income		xxxx

To record investment in income-producing assets

*Investments of cash from principal should be designated "principal."

**Investments of cash from income should be designated "income."

22000.1.6   Recording Expenses Paid by Estate

22000.1.6.1   Payment of Expense Incurred Prior to Death of Decedent

Unless otherwise directed, debts existing at the time the estate is created are paid out of the principal assets in the estate.

Important: Make sure all appropriate subheads apply to your entry (see page v for instructions)

22000.1   **Estates**
22000.1.6   **Recording Expenses Paid by Estate**
22000.1.6.1   **Payment of Expense Incurred Prior to Death of Decedent**

Debts Of Decedent Paid	xxxx	
Cash - Principal		xxxx

To record payment of debts incurred by the decedent prior to death

22000.1.6.2   Payment of Expense Incurred by Estate

The majority of the expenses of an estate will be paid out of estate principal unless otherwise directed in the decedent's will. Expenses related to income items, however, are paid out of income. The most common of these expenses are income taxes on income earned by estate assets, expenses directly related to estate income (for example, expenses related to rental property while in the estate), and a portion of administrative expenses related to managing the income of the estate.

Estates are of relatively short duration and often do not have complex income-producing assets requiring depreciation, depletion, and amortization of intangibles or bond discounts and premiums. If required, the treatment of depreciation, depletion, and amortization as expenses from principal or from income follows directives in the will or state law. *See GEN22000.2* covering Trusts, which includes the treatment of these items as recommended in the Revised Uniform Principal and Income Act. (This act applies to estates as well as to trusts.)

22000.1.6.2.1   Payment of Expense from Estate Principal

Funeral Expense - Principal	xxxx	
Administrative Expense - Principal	xxxx	
Estate Tax Expense - Principal	xxxx	
[Various Expenses] - Principal	xxxx	
Cash - Principal		xxxx

To record payment of expenses chargeable to principal

Important: Make sure all appropriate subheads apply to your entry (see page v for instructions)

22000.1   **Estates**
22000.1.6   **Recording Expenses Paid by Estate**
22000.1.6.2   **Payment of Expense Incurred by Estate**

22000.1.6.2.2   ### Payment of Expense from Estate Income

Income Tax Expense - Income	xxxx	
Administrative Expense - Income	xxxx	
[Various Expenses] - Income	xxxx	
Cash - Income		xxxx

To record payment of expenses

If the income of the estate is insufficient to pay the expenses related to income, then they must be paid partly (or wholly) from principal:

Administrative Expense - Income	xxxx	
Administrative Expense - Principal	xxxx	
[Various Expenses] - Income	xxxx	
[Various Expenses] - Principal	xxxx	
Cash - Income		xxxx
Cash - Principal		xxxx

To record payment of expenses

22000.1.7   ### Sale of Principal Assets

Unless otherwise directed, gains and losses on the sale of principal assets are treated as increases and decreases in the estate principal.

22000.1.7.1   ### Sale of Principal Assets at a Gain

Cash - Principal	xxxx	
[Various Assets]		xxxx
*Gain On Principal Assets Sold		xxxx

To record gain on sale of principal assets

*Gain On Principal Assets Sold is credited for the excess of the proceeds over the carrying value of the asset sold.

Important: Make sure all appropriate subheads apply to your entry (see page v for instructions)

22000.1   **Estates**
22000.1.7   **Sale of Principal Assets**

22000.1.7.2   **Sale of Principal Assets at a Loss**

Cash - Principal	xxxx	
*Loss On Principal Assets Sold	xxxx	
[Various Assets]		xxxx
To record sale of principal assets		

*Loss On Principal Assets Sold is debited for the excess of the carrying value of the asset sold over the proceeds received.

22000.1.8   **Distributions to Beneficiaries**

Legacies refer to gifts of personal property; devises are gifts of real property. Distributions to beneficiaries may be in the form of a:
- specific legacy or devise - a specified noncash item;
- demonstrative legacy - a cash gift from a specific source;
- general legacy - a cash property gift from an unspecified source; and
- residual legacy or devise - a gift of the personal or real property remaining in the estate after all other legacies and devises have been satisfied.

22000.1.8.1   **Distribution of Estate Principal Assets**

Legacy Distributed - [Beneficiary A]	xxxx	
Devise Distributed - [Beneficiary B]	xxxx	
Household Furnishings		xxxx
Clothing		xxxx
Jewelry		xxxx
Automobile		xxxx
[Various Assets]		xxxx
To record distribution of estate principal assets		

Important: Make sure all appropriate subheads apply to your entry (see page v for instructions)

22000.1   **Estates**
22000.1.8   **Distributions to Beneficiaries**

22000.1.8.2   **Distribution of Estate Income Assets**

Legacy Distributed - [Beneficiary C]	xxxx	
Legacy Distributed - [Beneficiary D]	xxxx	
[Various Assets] - Income		xxxx
Cash - Income		xxxx

To record distribution of estate income assets

22000.1.8.3   **Satisfaction of a Specific Legacy or Devise with Alternative Estate Property**

If a beneficiary receives alternative property in place of a specific legacy or devise of personal or real property, the estate recognizes a gain or loss if the value of the property distributed differs from the value of the specific legacy. (The personal representative can be held liable if the alternative distribution impairs the value of legacies to other beneficiaries.)

Legacy Distributed - [Beneficiary E]	xxxx	
Cash - Principal		xxxx
Gain On Satisfaction Of Legacy With Alternative Property		xxxx

To record distribution of cash in place of a specific legacy

22000.1.9   **Transfer of Assets to a Testamentary Trust**

Often a decedent's will directs certain assets to be placed in trust (a testamentary trust) for the benefit of a beneficiary. This is frequently done when the beneficiary is a minor, disabled, or has special needs. An entry similar to the following is made to transfer principal assets to the trustee:

Important: Make sure all appropriate subheads apply to your entry (see page v for instructions)

22000.1   **Estates**
22000.1.9   **Transfer of Assets to a Testamentary Trust**

Assets Transferred To [Various Trustee] - Principal	xxxx	
Assets Transferred To [Various Trustee] - Income	xxxx	
Personal Residence		xxxx
Certificate Of Deposit		xxxx
[Various Assets]		xxxx
Cash - Principal		xxxx
Cash - Income		xxxx

To record transfer of assets to the testamentary trust

22000.1.10   **Closing the Estate**

The personal representative of the estate has the responsibility to close the books of the estate and report to the court. After the personal representative closes the books, a Charge and Discharge Statement is prepared that summarizes all the transactions and events that affected the estate during its life. If the estate is complex, the Charge and Discharge Statement will also include supporting schedules that provide details for each of the accounts.

22000.1.10.1   **Closing Income Accounts**

The entries to close the estate's income accounts are as follows:

Rental Income	xxxx	
Interest Income	xxxx	
Dividend Income	xxxx	
[Various Income]	xxxx	
Income Tax Expense - Income		xxxx
Administrative Expense - Income		xxxx
Assets Transferred To [Various Trustee] - Income		xxxx
Legacy Distributed - [Beneficiary C]		xxxx
Legacy Distributed - [Beneficiary D]		xxxx

To close income accounts

Important: Make sure all appropriate subheads apply to your entry (see page v for instructions)

22000.1   **Estates**
22000.1.10   **Closing the Estate**

22000.1.10.2   ## Closing Principal Accounts

Estate Principal	xxxx	
Assets Subsequently Discovered	xxxx	
Gain On Principal Assets Sold	xxxx	
Gain On Satisfaction Of Legacy With Alternative Property	xxxx	
Loss On Principal Assets Sold		xxxx
Administrative Expense - Principal		xxxx
Funeral Expense - Principal		xxxx
Debts Of The Decedent Paid		xxxx
Devise Distributed - [Beneficiary B]		xxxx
Legacy Distributed - [Beneficiary A]		xxxx
Legacy Distributed - [Beneficiary B]		xxxx
Legacy Distributed - [Beneficiary E]		xxxx
Assets Transferred To [Various Trustee] - Principal		xxxx

To close principal accounts

22000.2   ## Trusts

A trust is a separate entity created by a grantor (or a settler) and administered by a fiduciary (trustee) for the benefit of one or more beneficiaries. The grantor transfers cash and/or other assets to the trust. If the trust is set up by a living grantor, it is an inter vivos trust. If a trust is established by the will of a decedent, it is a testamentary trust.

The grantor has the right to select the trustee and to name the beneficiaries of the trust. The grantor can also specify the parameters within which the trustee must operate, whether income beneficiaries are to receive all or only part of the income during the trust year, whether the trustee may invade the principal (corpus) for the benefit of the beneficiaries, the bases of accounting for trust income and principal, and the disposition of the assets remaining when the trust is closed. The person receiving the assets when the trust is closed is called the remainderman.

The trust document may specify exactly how items are to be treated for accounting purposes. Regardless of state law or generally accepted accounting principles, the accounting treatment follows the dictates of the grantor. In the absence of any direction, the relevant state law will control the treatment of various items as either income or principal. Many states have adopted the Revised Uniform Principal and

Important: Make sure all appropriate subheads apply to your entry (see page v for instructions)

22000.2   **Trusts**

Income Act in whole or in part. The following presentation is based on the most common practices prescribed therein.

The trustee has several responsibilities. The first responsibility is to safeguard the assets. A trustee can be held personally liable for failure to manage the assets appropriately.

Another trustee responsibility is to maintain separation between trust income and trust principal because it is common to have different income and principal beneficiaries. The trustee must accurately determine trust income and allocation of expenses so that beneficiaries receive accurate amounts of income and principal as directed by the grantor.

Unlike an estate, a trust does not require a formal accounting to a court. However, a trustee is required to file fiduciary income tax returns for a trust on a timely basis. (The determination of taxable income is separate and distinct from the determination of accounting income.)

Trusts normally use the cash method of accounting, with two exceptions:
- Income accrued at the date that the trust is established is considered part of the principal unless the trust document directs otherwise.
- When the trust is about to close and the principal is distributed, income must be accrued to the date of distribution.

22000.2.1   **Opening the Trust - Transfer of Assets to the Trust**

Cash - Principal	xxxx	
Dividend Receivable	xxxx	
*[Various Assets]	xxxx	
Trust Principal		xxxx
To record receipt of trust assets		

*If trust income is expected to be received in other than cash, the trustee should identify the principal assets in some manner; for example: XYZ Stock - Principal.

Important: Make sure all appropriate subheads apply to your entry (see page v for instructions)

22000.2   **Trusts**

22000.2.2   **Investment of Cash in Income-Producing Assets**

A primary responsibility of a trustee is to invest wisely in income-producing assets in a manner consistent with the grantor's purpose for the trust.

Investment In [Various Income-Producing Assets]	xxxx	
Cash - Principal		xxxx

To record investment of principal cash in [various assets]

22000.2.3   **Receipt of Trust Income Items**

22000.2.3.1   **Trust Receipts Credited to Income**

22000.2.3.1.1   **Income on Principal Assets**

The following items are considered income of a trust:
- rents
- royalties
- interest
- cash and property dividends
- net income from a business.

Gains and losses on principal assets and stock dividends are considered items of principal rather than of income.

Cash	xxxx	
Rental Income		xxxx
Royalty Income		xxxx
Dividend Income		xxxx
Interest Income		xxxx

To record receipt of income

22000.2.3.1.2   **Amortization of Bond Premium**

Amortization of bond discount and premium is inconsistent and depends on the origin of the bonds. If the bonds are in the trust at its inception, neither discount nor

Important: Make sure all appropriate subheads apply to your entry (see page v for instructions)

22000.2	**Trusts**
22000.2.3	**Receipt of Trust Income Items**
22000.2.3.1	**Income on Principal Assets**
22000.2.3.1.2	**Amortization of Bond Premium**

---

premium is amortized. If the bonds are acquired by a trust after the trust is established, a premium is amortized and credited to principal, but a discount is not amortized.

Cash - Income	xxxx	
Interest Income		xxxx
Investment In [Various] Bonds		xxxx

To record receipt of interest income and amortization of bond premium

Cash - Principal	xxxx	
Cash - Income		xxxx

To transfer cash from income to principal to restore principal for the amortization

22000.2.3.1.3   **Amortization of Bond Discount**

Bond discount is not amortized in a trust.

22000.2.3.2   **Trust Receipts Credited to Principal**

Cash - Principal	xxxx	
[Various Assets]		xxxx
Gain On Sale Of [Various Assets]		xxxx

To record gain on the sale of assets

22000.2.4   **Trust Expenses**

22000.2.4.1   **Expenses Charged to Income**

22000.2.4.1.1   **Ordinary Expenses**

Ordinary expenses related to the production of income such as the taxes, repairs, maintenance, and insurance on rental properties, business expenses, and taxes on income are charged to income.

Important: Make sure all appropriate subheads apply to your entry (see page v for instructions)

22000.2   **Trusts**
22000.2.4   **Trust Expenses**
22000.2.4.1   **Expenses Charged to Income**
22000.2.4.1.1   **Ordinary Expenses**

Repairs Expense	xxxx	
Insurance Expense	xxxx	
[Various Expenses]	xxxx	
Cash - Income		xxxx

To record income-related expenses

22000.2.4.1.2   **Administrative Expenses**

Expenses of a trustee in administering the trust are generally apportioned between trust income and principal. The Revised Uniform Principal and Income Act provides that 50% of the trustee's regular compensation is to be charged to income and the rest to principal. This or an alternate allocation must also be used to apportion expenses that are the result of management of income and principal such as accounting and legal fees.

Trustee's Fee - Income	xxxx	
Legal Fees - Income	xxxx	
[Various] - Income	xxxx	
Cash - Income		xxxx

To record administrative expense

22000.2.4.1.3   **Depreciation and Depletion Expense**

The treatment of depreciation and depletion may vary. If the grantor of the trust intended to maintain the principal of the trust intact, income is charged with these expenses. The Revised Uniform Principal and Income Act provides that income will be charged with depreciation of real and personal property and that 27.5% of gross receipts for royalties on interests in mineral deposits is to be added to principal as a depletion allowance. However, it is not uncommon for state laws to depart from this section of the act and consider depreciation as a charge against principal (*see GEN22000.2.4.2.4*). *See GEN5000.4* and *GEN5000.6.4* for general discussions of depreciation and depletion accounting, respectively.

22000.2.4.1.3.1   **Depreciation**

Depreciation Expense - Income	xxxx	
Accumulated Depreciation - [Various Assets]		xxxx

To record depreciation

Important: Make sure all appropriate subheads apply to your entry (see page v for instructions)

22000.2   **Trusts**
22000.2.4   **Trust Expenses**
22000.2.4.1   **Expenses Charged to Income**
22000.2.4.1.3   **Depreciation and Depletion Expenses**
22000.2.4.1.3.1   **Depreciation**

Cash - Principal	xxxx	
Cash - Income		xxxx

To transfer income assets to principal to offset depreciation

22000.2.4.1.3.2   **Depletion**

Depletion Expense - Income	xxxx	
[Various Assets]		xxxx

To record depletion

Cash - Principal	xxxx	
Cash - Income		xxxx

To transfer income to principal to cover depletion

22000.2.4.2   **Expenses Charged to Principal**

The most common expenses charged to principal are for capital improvements, extraordinary repairs, debt repayments, losses on the sale of principal assets, and taxes paid on gains on the sale of principal assets.

22000.2.4.2.1   **Capital Expenditures**

[Various Assets]	xxxx	
Cash - Principal		xxxx

To record a capital expenditure

22000.2.4.2.2   **Debt Repayment**

Note Payable	xxxx	
Cash - Principal		xxxx

To record payment of a note

Important: Make sure all appropriate subheads apply to your entry (see page v for instructions)

22000.2	**Trusts**
22000.2.4	**Trust Expenses**
22000.2.4.2	**Expenses Charged to Principal**

22000.2.4.2.3 Other Expenses

Extraordinary Repairs Expense - Principal	xxxx	
Income Tax Expense - Principal	xxxx	
Administrative Expense - Principal	xxxx	
Legal Fees - Principal	xxxx	
Cash - Principal		xxxx

To record tax on sale of a principal asset and
administrative and legal fees chargeable to principal

22000.2.4.2.4 Depreciation and Depletion Expense

If the trust document or state law charges principal with the depreciation and depletion expense, the following entries are made:

22000.2.4.2.4.1 Depreciation

See GEN5000.4 for a general discussion of depreciation accounting.

Depreciation Expense - Principal	xxxx	
Accumulated Depreciation - [Various Assets]		xxxx

To record depreciation expense

22000.2.4.2.4.2 Depletion

See GEN5000.6.4 for a general discussion of depletion accounting.

Depletion Expense - Principal	xxxx	
[Various Assets]		xxxx

To record depletion expense

22000.2.5 Distributions to Beneficiaries

Many trusts limit the distributions during the accounting period to the net income from the trust. However, the grantor may direct that distributions of principal be

Important: Make sure all appropriate subheads apply to your entry (see page v for instructions)

22000.2	**Trusts**
22000.2.5	**Distributions to Beneficiaries**

---

made under a number of circumstances; for example, when income is less than a stated amount, for the payment of unusual medical expenses, or for college expenses.

22000.2.5.1   Distribution from Income

Trust Income Distributed - [Beneficiary A]	xxxx	
Trust Income Distributed - [Beneficiary B]	xxxx	
Cash - Income		xxxx

To record distribution of income to beneficiaries

22000.2.5.2   Distribution from Principal

Trust Principal Distributed - [Beneficiary B]	xxxx	
Cash - Principal		xxxx
[Various Assets]		xxxx

To record distribution of principal to beneficiaries

22000.2.6   Periodic Closing of Trust Books

22000.2.6.1   Closing Nominal Accounts - Income Items

Rental Income	xxxx	
Royalty Income	xxxx	
Dividend Income	xxxx	
Interest Income	xxxx	
Repairs Expense		xxxx
Insurance Expense		xxxx
Trustee's Fee - Income		xxxx
Legal Fees - Income		xxxx
Depreciation Expense		xxxx
Depletion Expense		xxxx
Trust Income Distributed - [Beneficiary A]		xxxx
Trust Income Distributed - [Beneficiary B]		xxxx

To close nominal accounts related to income

Important: Make sure all appropriate subheads apply to your entry (see page v for instructions)

22000.2	**Trusts**
22000.2.6	**Periodic Closing of Trust Books**
22000.2.6.1	**Closing Nominal Accounts - Income Items**

Many trusts require the distribution of all net accounting income to the beneficiaries annually. However, if all income is not distributed, the excess income is closed to Trust Income Retained or to Trust Principal, depending on the direction of the grantor.

22000.2.6.2 ## Closing Nominal Accounts - Principal Items

Gain On Sale Of [Various Assets]	xxxx	
Trust Principal	xxxx	
Income Tax Expense - Principal		xxxx
Administrative Expense - Principal		xxxx
Legal Fees - Principal		xxxx
Trust Principal Distributed - [Beneficiary B]		xxxx
Extraordinary Repairs Expense - Principal		xxxx
[Various Expenses] - Principal		xxxx

To close nominal accounts related to principal to trust principal

22000.2.7 ## Closing the Trust

When the trust terminates, the trustee must accrue income to the date of termination and distribute the income and principal items according to the directions of the grantor of the trust.

22000.2.7.1 ## Accruing Income

Interest Receivable	xxxx	
Interest Income		xxxx

To accrue interest income

Important: Make sure all appropriate subheads apply to your entry (see page v for instructions)

22000.2   **Trusts**
22000.2.7   **Closing the Trust**

22000.2.7.2   **Distributions to Beneficiaries**

Trust Income Distributed - [Beneficiary A]	xxxx	
Trust Income Distributed - [Beneficiary B]	xxxx	
Trust Principal Distributed - [Beneficiary D]	xxxx	
Interest Receivable		xxxx
Cash - Income		xxxx
Cash - Principal		xxxx
Investment In [Various] Bonds		xxxx
[Various Assets]		xxxx

*To record final distributions to income beneficiaries and
the residual of the trust to the remainderman*

22000.2.7.3   **Closing Remaining Trust Accounts**

Interest Income	xxxx	
Trust Principal	xxxx	
Trust Income Distributed - [Beneficiary A]		xxxx
Trust Income Distributed - [Beneficiary B]		xxxx
Trust Principal Distributed - [Beneficiary D]		xxxx

To close remaining trust accounts

ACCOUNT TITLE INDEX

The references for each of the following accounts are to sections illustrating typical usage. Many of these accounts appear throughout this book in other sections in addition to those referenced here. The following symbols are used in brackets after each account title to indicate the nature of the account:

A= Asset

AA = Adjunct Asset

AC = Adjunct Capital

AL = Adjunct Liability

C = Capital or Equity

CC = Contra Capital or Contra Equity

CE = Contra Expense

CL = Contra Liability

CR = Contra Revenue

G = Gain

L = Liability

O = Loss

R = Revenue

Allowance For Collection Expense [CA]:
GEN3000.1.5.2

Allowance For Depreciation [CA]: see
Accumulated Depreciation

Allowance For Doubtful Accounts [CA]:
GEN3000.1.3.1; GEN3000.1.3.2

Allowance For Finance Charges [CA]:
GEN3000.1.2.1.2.2

Allowance For Repairs And Maintenance
[CA]: GEN5000.2.1.2

Allowance For Sales Discounts [CA]:
GEN3000.1.2.1.2.2

Allowance For Sales Returns And
Allowances [CA]: GEN3000.1.4.2

Allowance For Uncollectible Accounts [CA]:
GEN3000.1.3.1; GEN3000.1.3.2;
GEN15000.2

Allowance For Unearned Discounts [CA]:
GEN3000.1.2.1.2.2

Allowance To Reduce Deferred Tax Asset To
Expected Realizable Value [CA]:
GEN12000.2.3; GEN12000.3.2.2

Allowance To Reduce Inventory To LIFO
[CA]: GEN4000.3.1.2

Allowance To Reduce Inventory To Market
[CA]: GEN4000.1.1.8; GEN4000.1.2.8;
GEN4000.3.1.1

Amortization Expense - Purchased Computer
Software [E]: GEN6000.1.6.2

Amortization Expense - Copyrights [E]:
GEN6000.1.3.3

Amortization Expense - Discount On Forward
Exchange Contract [E]: GEN19000.5.1;
GEN19000.5.3.2.3

Amortization Expense - Franchises [E]:
GEN6000.1.5.2

Amortization Expense - Leasehold
Improvements [E]: GEN6000.1.7.2

Amortization Expense - Licenses [E]:
GEN6000.1.5.2

Amortization Expense - Organization Costs
[E]: GEN6000.1.8.2

Amortization Expense - Premium On Forward
Exchange Contract [E]: GEN19000.5.2;
GEN19000.5.3.2.3

Amortization Expense - Relocation Costs [E]:
GEN5000.2.6.1.1

Amortization Expense - Software
Development Costs [E]:
GEN6000.1.9.1.3

Amortization Expense - Trademarks [E]:
GEN6000.1.4.3

Amortization Expense - Trade Names [E]:
GEN6000.1.4.3

Amortization Of Bond Issuance Costs [E]:
GEN8000.1.1.4.3; GEN8000.1.3

Amortization Of Excess Of Fair Market Value
Over Cost Of Net Assets Acquired [R]:
GEN6000.1.1.2.2

Applied Conversion Costs [CE]:
GEN16000.6.3; GEN16000.7

Applied Factory Overhead [CE]:
GEN16000.2.2.3.2.2; GEN16000.3.3.2;
GEN16000.3.5; GEN16000.5.3

Assets Subsequently Discovered [C]:
GEN22000.1.3; GEN22000.1.10.2

Assets Transferred To [Various Trustee] -
Income [E]: GEN22000.1.9;
GEN22000.1.10.1

Assets Transferred To [Various Trustee] -
Principal [E]: GEN22000.1.9;
GEN22000.1.10.1

Automobile [A]: GEN22000.1.1

Autos And Trucks [A]: GEN5000.1.1.3

B

Bad Debt Expense [E]: GEN3000.1.3.1;
GEN3000.1.3.2; GEN3000.1.3.3;
GEN15000.2

Banking Expense [E]: GEN2000.1.4.3

Bank Service Charges [E]: GEN2000.1.4.3

Benefit Due To Loss Carryforward [R]:
GEN12000.3.2

Billings On Construction In Process [CA]:
GEN11000.5; GEN11000.6

Bond Conversion Expense [E]:
GEN8000.1.3.5.3

Bond Interest Expense [E]: GEN8000.1.2.1

Bond Interest Payable [L]: GEN8000.1

Bond Sinking Fund Cash [A]: GEN10000.5

Bond Sinking Fund Investments [A]:
GEN10000.5

Bond Sinking Fund Revenue [R]:
GEN10000.5

Bonds Payable [L]: GEN8000.1;
GEN9000.1.5.2

Branch Office [A]: see *Investment In Branch*

Branch Income [R]: GEN18000.1.3

Branch Loss [E]: GEN18000.1.3

Buildings [A]: GEN5000.1.1.2

C

Call Option/Put Option [A]:
GEN10000.5.8.1.1

Capital [C]: GEN1000.2.2.2.1.1

Cash [A]: GEN2000

Cash Discounts Forfeited [E]:
GEN3000.1.2.2.3.1

Cash - Income [A]: GEN22000.1.4;
GEN22000.2.3.1.2
Cash Over And Short [G or O]:
GEN2000.2.1.3
Cash - Principal [A]: GEN22000.1.2;
GEN22000.2.1
Cash Surrender Value Of Life Insurance [A]:
GEN10000.4
Certificate Of Deposit [A]: GEN22000.1.1
Clothing [A]: GEN22000.1.1
Collection Expense [E]: GEN3000.1.5
Commission Expense [E]: GEN4000.6.2.2;
GEN11000.4.1.2
Commission Revenue [R]: GEN11000.4.2.4
Common Stock [C]: GEN9000.1
Common Stock Dividend Distributable [C]:
GEN9000.12.4
Common Stock Subscribed [C]:
GEN9000.1.4
Common Stock Subscriptions Receivable [A]:
GEN9000.1.4
Compensation Expense [E]:
GEN9000.7.1.2.1; GEN9000.7.2.2
Computer Software [A]: GEN6000.1.6.1
Construction Expenses [E]: GEN11000.5.1.4;
GEN11000.5.1.6
Construction In Process [A]: GEN11000.5.1;
GEN11000.5.2; GEN11000.6;
GEN15000.1.1.2
Contribution Expense [E]: GEN5000.3.5
Conversion Costs [E]: GEN16000.6.2;
GEN16000.7
Copyrights [A]: GEN6000.1.3.1
Cost Of Consignment Sales [E]:
GEN4000.6.2.2; GEN11000.4.1.2
Cost Of Goods Sold [E]: GEN4000.1.1.7.1.2;
GEN4000.1.2.5; GEN4000.2.3.2.2;
GEN14000.3.2.2; GEN16000
Cost Of Installment Sales [E]: GEN11000.2.3
Cost Of Sales [E]: see *Cost Of Goods Sold*
Costs Of Construction [A]: GEN11000.5.2.4
Cumulative Effect Of Change In Accounting
Principle [G or O]: GEN4000.3;
GEN15000.1.3
Customer Deposits Payable [L]: GEN7000.4

D
Dealer Deposits Payable [L]: GEN7000.4
Debts of Decedent Paid [A]: GEN22000.1.6
Deferred Compensation Expense [A]:
GEN9000.7.1.2
Deferred Discount On Forward Exchange
Contract [CA or CL]: GEN19000.5.3.1

Deferred Exchange Gain [G]: GEN19000.5.3;
GEN19000.5.4
Deferred Exchange Loss [O]: GEN19000.5.3;
GEN19000.5.4
Deferred Gross Profit [L]: GEN11000.3.1;
GEN11000.3.2
Deferred Gross Profit On Installment Sales
[L]: GEN11000.2.4
Deferred Initial Direct Leasing Costs [A]:
GEN14000.2.2.4
Deferred Interest Revenue [L]:
GEN11000.3.2
Deferred Pension Cost [A]: see *Intangible
Asset - Deferred Pension Cost*
Deferred Premium On Forward Exchange
Contract [CA or CL]: GEN19000.5.4.1
Deferred Tax Asset [A]: GEN12000.2.2;
GEN12000.2.4.2; GEN12000.3.2;
GEN15000
Deferred Tax Liability [L]: GEN12000.2.1;
GEN12000.2.4.1; GEN15000
Delivery Equipment [A]: GEN5000.1.1.3
Depletion Expense [E]: GEN5000.6.4
Deposits On Utilities [A]: GEN2000.1.1.4
Deposits Payable [L]: GEN7000.4
Depreciation Expense [E]: GEN5000.4;
GEN14000.2.2.3; GEN14000.3.1.3;
GEN14000.4.1.3; GEN15000.2.3
Devise Distributed [E]: GEN22000.1.2.1;
GEN22000.1.10.2
Direct Labor [E]: GEN4000.2.2.2.1
Direct Labor Efficiency Variance [G or O]:
GEN16000.3.2; GEN16000.3.4
Direct Labor Price Variance [G or O]:
GEN16000.3.2; GEN16000.3.4
Direct Materials Efficiency Variance [G or O]:
GEN16000.3.1; GEN16000.3.4
Direct Materials Price Variance [G or O]:
GEN16000.3.1; GEN16000.3.4
Discount On Bonds Payable [CL]:
GEN8000.1.1.3; GEN8000.1.3
Discount On Common Stock [CC]:
GEN9000.2.1
Discount On Forward Exchange Contract [CA
or CL]: GEN19000.5.1; GEN19000.5.3;
GEN19000.5.4
Discount On Investment In Bonds [CA]:
GEN10000.2.1.1.3.2;
GEN10000.2.1.3.3.1.2
Discount On Notes Payable [CL]:
GEN7000.2; GEN8000.2
Discount On Notes Receivable
[CA]:GEN3000.2.1

Gain On Redemption Of Bonds Payable [G]: GEN8000.1.3.4

Gain On Reorganization [G]: GEN20000.1.1.1.3; GEN20000.1.2.1.4

Gain On Repossession [G]: GEN11000.2.7

Gain On Restructuring Of Debt [G]: GEN8000.3.2.2.1

Gain On Revaluation Of Assets [G]: GEN9000.12.2.1; GEN20000.1.1.1.2; GEN20000.1.2.1.3

Gain On Sale Of Bond Investment [G]: GEN10000.2.1.5.2.1

Gain On Sale Of Bond Sinking Fund Investments [G]: GEN10000.5.6

Gain On Sale Of Leased Asset [G]: GEN14000.3.2.1.6

Gain On Sale Of Plant Asset [G]: GEN5000.3.1; GEN5000.3.2

Gain On Sale Of Spoiled Production [G]: GEN16000.5.1.1.2

Gain On Salvaged Rental Equipment [G]: GEN14000.3.2.1.5

Gain On Satisfaction Of Legacy With Alternative Property [G]: GEN22000.1.8.3

Goods Receivable [A]: GEN8000.2.3

Goodwill [A]: GEN6000.1.1: GEN17000.2.2.2: GEN21000.1.2.1; GEN21000.4.1.2.1; GEN21000.4.1.3.1; GEN21000.4.2.2.1; GEN21000.4.2.3.1; GEN21000.5.1.2.1; GEN21000.5.2.2.1

Goodwill Amortization Expense [E]: GEN6000.1.1.2.1

H

Home Office [L]: GEN18000.2

Household Furnishings [A]: GEN22000.1.1

I

Income Summary [CC or AC]: GEN1000.2.3.5.1; GEN1000.2.3.5.2; GEN1000.2.3.5.3

Income Tax Expense [E]: GEN7000.8

Income Tax Payable [L]: GEN7000.8; GEN12000.1

Income Tax Refund Receivable [A]: GEN12000.3.1

In Receivership, XX Co. [C]: GEN20000.2.3

Installment Accounts Receivable [A]: GEN11000.2: GEN11000.3

Installment Sales [R]: GEN11000.2

Insurance Expense [E]: GEN1000.2.2.2.5.2; GEN14000.2.2.2; GEN14000.3.1.4

Intangible Asset - Deferred Pension Cost [A]: GEN13000.1.2

Interest Expense [E]: GEN1000.2.3.2.2.2; GEN7000.2

Interest Income [R]: see *Interest Revenue*

Interest Payable [L]: GEN1000.2.3.2.2.2; GEN7000.2

Interest Receivable [A]: GEN1000.2.3.2.2.1; GEN3000.2; GEN10000.1.1.1.2; GEN10000.1.1.3.1; GEN10000.2.1.1.1.2

Interest Revenue [R]: GEN1000.2.2.2.4.3; GEN3000.2; GEN10000.1.1.3.1

Interest Revenue - Leases [R]: GEN14000.3.2.1

Inventory [A]: GEN4000

Inventory Financed Under Buyback Agreement [A]: GEN11000.1.1.3

Inventory On Consignment [A]: GEN4000.6.2; GEN11000.4

Inventory Over And Short [G or O]: GEN4000.1.2.7.1

Investment In Bonds [A]: GEN1000.2.1

Investment In Bonds - Available-For-Sale [A]: GEN10000.2.1.1; GEN10000.2.1.2.2

Investment In Bonds - Held-To-Maturity [A]: GEN10000.2.1.1

Investment In Branch [A]: GEN18000

Investment In [Various Income-Producing Assets] [A]: GEN22000.2.2

Investment In [Various Income-Producing Assets] - Income [A]: GEN22000.1.5

Investment In [Various Income-Producing Assets] - Principal [A]: GEN22000.1.5

Investment In Stock [A]: GEN10000.2.2.2; GEN10000.3.1

Investment In Stock Rights [A]: GEN10000.3.1

Investment In Subsidiary [A]: GEN17000

J

Jewelry [A]: GEN22000.1.1

Jobs-In-Process Inventory [A]: GEN16000.1

L

Land [A]: GEN5000.1.1.1

Land Improvements [A]: GEN5000.1.1.1.5

Leased Asset Under Capital Leases [A]: GEN14000.3.1

Leased Equipment Under Capital Leases [A]: GEN14000.4.1.1

Leasehold Improvements [A]: GEN6000.1.7

Lease Payments Receivable [A]: GEN14000.3.2; GEN14000.4.2

Legacy Distributed [E]: GEN22000.1.8.1;
GEN22000.1.8.2; GEN22000.1.10.2

Legal Fees [E]: GEN22000.2.4.1.2

Liability For Postretirement Medical Benefits
[L]: GEN7000.10.4

Liability For Probable Expropriation Of Assets
[L]: GEN7000.9.2

Liability For Stock Appreciation Rights [L]:
GEN9000.7.2

Liability For Uninsured Accident [L]:
GEN7000.9.6

Liability On Notes Receivable Discounted [L]:
GEN3000.2.4.2.3

Liability On Sold Accounts Receivable [L]:
GEN3000.1.7.2.1

Liability On Transferred Accounts Receivable
[L]: GEN3000.1.7.2.1

Liability Under Capital Leases [L]:
GEN14000.3.1; GEN14000.4.1

Licenses [A]: GEN6000.1.5

Life Insurance Receivable [A]:
GEN22000.1.1; GEN22000.1.2

Liquidation Clearing Account [A or L]:
GEN20000.2.1.1; GEN20000.2.1.2

Long-Term Debt Securities - Available-For-
Sale [A]: GEN10000.1.1.2.4.1.2;
GEN10000.1.1.2.4.2.2

Long-Term Debt Securities - Held-To-Maturity
[A]: GEN10000.1.1.2.4.1.3;
GEN10000.1.1.2.4.2.3

Long-Term Marketable Equity Securities -
Available-For-Sale [A]:
GEN10000.1.2.2.3.1.2;
GEN10000.2.2.1.1

Long-Term Nonmarketable Equity Securities
[A]: GEN10000.2.2.1.2

Loss Due To Discounts Forfeited [O]:
GEN5000.1.1.3.3.1

Loss Due To Equipment Obsolescence [O]:
GEN5000.5.1

Loss Due To Impairment Of Copyright [O]:
GEN6000.1.3.3

Loss Due To Impairment Of Franchises and
Licenses [O]: GEN6000.1.5.2

Loss Due To Impairment Of Goodwill [O]:
GEN6000.1.1.2

Loss Due To Impairment of Patents [O]:
GEN6000.1.2.3

Loss Due To Impairment of Trademark or
Trade Name [O]: GEN6000.1.4.3

Loss Due To Probable Expropriation Of
Assets [O]: GEN7000.9.2.1

Loss Due To Write Down Of Inventory To
Market [O]: GEN4000.1.1.8;
GEN4000.1.2.8

Loss From Abnormal Spoilage [O]:
GEN16000.5.1.2

Loss From Bankrupt Debtor [O]:
GEN20000.2.2

Loss From Expropriation Of Assets [O]:
GEN7000.9.2.2

Loss From Investment - Extraordinary [O]:
GEN10000.2.2.2.2

Loss From Lawsuit [O]: GEN7000.9.1.2

Loss From Uninsured Accident [O]:
GEN7000.9.6

Loss On Capital Lease [O]:
GEN14000.3.1.5.1

Loss On Concessions To Debtors [O]:
GEN20000.1.1.2; GEN20000.1.2.2

Loss On Conversion Of Bonds Payable [O]:
GEN8000.1.3.5

Loss On Disposal Of Assets [O]:
GEN8000.3.1.1

Loss On Disposal Of Plant Asset [O]:
GEN5000.3.2; GEN5000.3.5

Loss On Expiration Of Stock Rights [O]:
GEN10000.3.4

Loss On Exploration [O]: GEN5000.6.1.2.4

Loss On Long-Term Contract [O]:
GEN11000.5.2.5

Loss On Principal Assets Sold [O]:
GEN22000.1.7.2

Loss On Purchase Commitment [O]:
GEN4000.5.1.2.2; GEN4000.5.2.3

Loss On Reorganization [O]:
GEN20000.1.1.1.3

Loss On Repossession [O]: GEN11000.2.7

Loss On Retirement Of Plant Assets [O]:
GEN5000.2.2

Loss On Sale Of Plant Asset [O]:
GEN5000.3.1.2.3; GEN5000.3.4

Loss On Sale Of Notes Receivable [O]:
GEN3000.2.4.1.1

Loss On Sale Of Receivables [O]:
GEN3000.1.7

Loss On Sale Of Spoiled Production [O]:
GEN16000.5.1.1.2

Loss On Short-Term Contract [O]:
GEN11000.6.5

Loss On Transfer Of Receivables [O]:
GEN3000.1.7

Loss On Unsuccessful Defense Of Copyright
[O]: GEN6000.1.3.2.2

Loss On Unsuccessful Defense Of
  Trademark [O]: GEN6000.1.4.2.2
Loss On Unsuccessful Defense Of Trade
  Name [O]: GEN6000.1.4.2.2

M

Machinery [A]: GEN5000.1.1.3
Machinery And Equipment [A]:
  GEN5000.1.1.3
Maintenance Expense [E]: GEN14000.2.2.2;
  GEN14000.3.1.4
Manufacturing Overhead [E]:
  GEN4000.2.1.2.5.2; GEN4000.2.2.2.1;
  GEN16000
Manufacturing Overhead Control [E]:
  GEN16000.2.2.3.2.2; GEN16000.3.3;
  GEN16000.3.5
Manufacturing Summary [E]:
  GEN4000.2.2.1.3; GEN4000.2.3.1.3
Mortgage Payable [L]: GEN5000.1.1.1.2;
  GEN8000.2.1.4; GEN22000.1.1

N

Net Unrealized Holding Gains And Losses
  On Investment In Available-For-Sale
  Bonds [C or CE]: GEN10000.2.1.2.2;
  GEN10000.2.1.2.3
Net Unrealized Holding Gains And Losses
  On Long-Term Marketable Equity
  Available-For-Sale Securities [C or CE]:
  GEN10000.2.2.1.1.2
Net Unrealized Holding Gains And Losses
  On Short-Term Debt Available-For-Sale
  Securities [C or CE]:
  GEN10000.1.1.2.3.1;
  GEN10000.1.1.2.3.2;
  GEN10000.1.1.2.4.2.1.1;
  GEN10000.1.1.3.3.1
Net Unrealized Holding Gains And Losses
  On Short-Term Marketable Equity
  Available-For-Sale Securities [C or CE]:
  GEN10000.1.2.2.2.1;
  GEN10000.1.2.2.3.2.2;
  GEN10000.1.2.3.2
Notes Payable [L]: GEN7000.2; GEN8000.2
Notes Payable To Stockholders [L]:
  GEN9000.12.3
Notes Receivable [A]: GEN3000.2
Notes Receivable - Past Due [A]:
  GEN3000.2.4.1.3

O

Obligations (Liability) Under Capital Leases
  [L]: GEN14000.3.1.5.1
Office Equipment [A]: GEN5000.1.1.3
Office Furnishings [A]: GEN5000.1.1.3
Oil Deposits [A]: GEN5000.6.1;
  GEN5000.6.2.2; GEN5000.6.3.2;
  GEN15000.1.1.3
Organization Costs [A]: GEN6000.1.8;
  GEN9000.3.2

P

[Partner X], Capital [C]: GEN21000
Parts Inventory [A]: GEN16000
Patents [A]: GEN6000.1.2.1;
  GEN15000.3.2.1
Payable To Consignor [L]: GEN11000.4.2.4
Payroll Tax Expense [E]: GEN7000.10.2.1
Penalties Expense [E]: GEN12000.5
Pension Expense [E]: GEN13000.1
Pension Liability [L]: GEN13000.1.1
Personal Residence [A]: GEN22000.1.1
Petty Cash [A]: GEN2000.2.1; GEN2000.2.2
Postretirement Expense [E]: GEN13000.2.1
Postretirement Medical Benefits Expense [E]:
  GEN7000.10.4
Preferred Stock [C]: GEN9000.1
Preferred Stock Dividend Distributable [C]:
  GEN9000.12.4
Preferred Stock Subscribed [C]:
  GEN9000.1.4
Preferred Stock Subscriptions Receivable [A]:
  GEN9000.1.4
Premium Expense [E]: GEN7000.9.5
Premium On Bonds Payable [AL]:
  GEN8000.1.1.2; GEN8000.1.3;
  GEN9000.1.5.2
Premium On Common Stock [C]: see
  *Additional Paid-In Capital - Common
  Stock*
Premium On Forward Exchange Contract
  [AA or AL]: GEN19000.5.1.4;
  GEN19000.5.4.2
Premium On Investments In Bonds [AA]:
  GEN10000.2.1.1.2.2;
  GEN10000.2.1.3.2.1.2
Premium On Preferred Stock [C]: see
  *Additional Paid-In Capital - Preferred
  Stock*
Prepaid Income Tax [A]: GEN12000.1
Prepaid Insurance [A]: GEN1000.2.2.2.5.2
Prepaid/Accrued Pension Cost [A or L]:
  GEN13000.1.2

Prepaid Pension Expense [A]:
GEN13000.1.1.2
Prepaid Property Tax [A]: GEN7000.7.2
Prepaid Rent [A]: GEN14000.2
Prior Period Adjustment [CC or AC]:
GEN4000.4.1.2; GEN15000.3.2.2.2
Property Dividends Payable [L]:
GEN9000.12.2
Property Tax Expense [E]: GEN7000.7;
GEN14000.2.2.2; GEN14000.3.1.4
Property Tax Payable [L]: GEN7000.7
Purchase Discounts [CA]: GEN4000.1.1
Purchase Discounts Lost [E]:
GEN4000.1.2.4.2.2
Purchase Returns And Allowances [CA]:
GEN4000.1.1
Purchases [A]: GEN4000.1.1

R

Raw Materials Inventory [A]: GEN4000.2.1;
GEN16000
Raw Materials And Work-In-Process
Inventory [A]: GEN16000.7
Raw Materials Efficiency Variance [G or O] :
GEN16000.7; also see *Materials Effi-
ciency Variance*
Raw Materials Price Variance [G or O]:
GEN16000.7; also see *Materials
Efficiency Variance*
Realized Gain (Loss) On Sale Of Bond
Investment [G (O)]: GEN10000.2.1.5.2
Realized Gain (Loss) On Sale Of Long-Term
Marketable Equity Securities [G (O)]:
GEN10000.2.2.1.1.4
Realized Gain (Loss) On Sale Of Long-Term
Nonmarketable Equity Securities [G (O)]:
GEN10000.2.2.1.2.3
Realized Gain (Loss) On Sale Of Short-Term
Debt Securities [G (O)]:
GEN10000.1.1.3.2; GEN10000.1.1.3.3.1
Realized Gain (Loss) On Sale Of Short-Term
Marketable Equity Securities [G (O)]:
GEN10000.1.2.3
Realized Gross Profit [R]: GEN11000.3.1;
GEN11000.3.2
Realized Gross Profit On Installment Sales
[R]: GEN11000.5; GEN11000.6
Receivable From Consignor [A]:
GEN11000.4.2
Relocation Costs [A]: GEN5000.2.6.1
Relocation Expense [E]: GEN5000.2.6.2
Rental Income [R]: GEN14000.2.2.4

Rent Expense [E]: GEN1000.2.3.5.2;
GEN14000.2
Rent Payable [L]: GEN14000.2
Rent Receivable [A]: GEN1000.2.3.2.2.1;
GEN14000.2.2
Rent Revenue [R]: GEN1000.2.2.2.4.4
Reorganization Expense [E]:
GEN20000.1.1.1.4; GEN20000.1.2.1.5
Reorganization Value In Excess Of Amounts
Allocable To Identifiable Assets [A]:
GEN20000.1.2.1.2.2
Repairs And Maintenance Expense [E]:
GEN5000.2.1
Repossessed Merchandise [A]:
GEN11000.2.7
Research And Development Expense [E]:
GEN6000.1.9.1.1; GEN6000.3
Retained Earnings [C]: GEN1000.2.3.5.3;
GEN1000.2.3.5.4; GEN4000.4.1.2;
GEN5000.6.6; GEN9000; GEN15000;
GEN17000
Retained Earnings Appropriated For Plant
Expansion [C]: GEN9000.10
Revenue Earned On Completed Production
[R]: GEN11000.7
Revenue From Franchise Fees [R]:
GEN11000.9.1
Revenue From Investment - Ordinary [R]:
GEN10000.2.2.2.2
Revenue From Long-Term Construction
Contract [R]: GEN11000.5.1;
GEN11000.5.2
Revenue From Short-Term Construction
Contract [R]: GEN11000.6.4

S

Salaries And Wages Expense [E]:
GEN7000.10
Sales [R]: GEN2000.1.2.9; GEN3000.1.2.1.1;
GEN14000.3.2.2
Sales Discounts [CR]: GEN3000.1.2.1.2.1;
GEN3000.1.2.1.2.2
Sales Discounts Forfeited [R]:
GEN3000.1.2.2.3.1
Sales Of Scrap [R]: GEN16000.5.2.1
Sales Returns And Allowances [CR]:
GEN3000.1.4
Sales Taxes Payable [L]: GEN7000.6
Salvaged Rental Equipment [A]:
GEN14000.3.2.1.5
Sample Inventory [A]: GEN18000.3.2
Scrap Revenue [R]: GEN16000.5.2.1
Service Revenue [R]: GEN1000.2.2.2.4.1

Services Receivable [A]: GEN8000.2.4

Shipments From Home Office [L]: GEN18000.2.1.2

Shipments To Branch [A]: GEN18000.1.1.2.1

Short-Term Debt Securities - Available-For-Sale [A]: GEN10000.1.1.2.3.1; GEN10000.1.1.2.3.2; GEN10000.1.1.2.4.1.1; GEN10000.1.1.2.4.2.1.1

Short-Term Debt Securities - Trading [A]: GEN1000.1.1.2.1.1; GEN10000.1.1.2.4.1; GEN10000.1.1.2.4.2.1.1; GEN10000.1.2.2.3.1

Short-Term Marketable Equity Securities - Available-For-Sale [A]: GEN10000.1.2.2.2.1; GEN10000.1.2.2.2

Short-Term Marketable Equity Securities - Trading [A]: GEN10000.1.2.1

Short-Term Nonmarketable Equity Securities [A]: GEN10000.2.2.1.2.2

Sick Pay Wages Payable [L]: GEN7000.10.5

Software Development Costs [A]: GEN6000.1.9.1

Software Development Expense [E]: GEN6000.1.9.2

Spoiled Production Inventory [A]: GEN16000.5.1.1

State Income Tax Withheld [L]: GEN7000.10.1

State Unemployment Tax Payable [L]: GEN7000.10.2

Stock Issuance Costs [CC]: GEN9000.3.1

Subscription Revenue [R]: GEN1000.2.3.2.1.3.1

Supplies [A]: GEN1000.2.2.2.5.2

Supplies Expense [E]: GEN1000.2.2.2.5.2

Swap Contract [A]: GEN10000.5.8.2.2

T

Telephone Poles [A]: GEN5000.4.1.6

Theft Loss [O]: GEN4000.2.1.2.6.2

Tools [A]: GEN5000.4.1.5

Trademarks [A]: GEN6000.1.4.1

Trade Names [A]: GEN6000.1.4.1

Transportation Expense [E]: GEN8000.2.4.3

Transportation-In [AA]: GEN4000.1.1.7.2

Treasury Bonds Payable [L]: GEN8000.1.3.3

Treasury Stock - Common [CC]: GEN9000.8

Treasury Stock - Preferred [CC]: GEN9000.8

Trucks [A]: GEN5000.2.2

Trustee's Fee [E]: GEN22000.2.4.1.2

Trust Income Distributed [E]: GEN22000.2.5.1; GEN22000.2.6.1; GEN22000.2.7.3

Trust Principal [C]: GEN22000.2.1; GEN22000.2.7.3

Trust Principal Distributed [E]: GEN20000.2.6.2; GEN22000.2.7.2; GEN22000.2.7.3

U

Unamortized Bond Issue Cost [A]: GEN8000.1.1.4; GEN8000.1.3

Uncollectible Accounts Expense [E]: GEN3000.1.3.1; GEN3000.1.3.2

Uncollectible Amounts Recovered [R]: GEN3000.1.3.3.2

Undeveloped Oil Rights [A]: GEN5000.6.1.2.2

Undeveloped Property [A]: GEN5000.6.1.2

Unearned Franchise Fees [L]: GEN11000.9.1

Unearned Interest Revenue - Leases [L]: GEN14000.3.2; GEN14000.4.2

Unearned Profit On Sale-Leaseback Transaction [L]: GEN14000.4.1

Unearned Rent [L]: GEN1000.2.3.2.1.3.1

Unearned Revenue [L]: GEN8000.2.1.2

Unearned Sales Revenue [L]: GEN11000.9.1.5

Unearned Subscription Revenue [L]: GEN1000.2.3.2.1.3.1

Unearned Warranty Revenue [L]: GEN7000.9.4

Unrealized Holding Gain On Long-Term Debt Available-For-Sale Securities [G]: GEN10000.2.1.2.3.1.1

Unrealized Holding Gain On Short-Term Debt Trading Securities [G]: GEN10000.1.1.2.4.1.1; GEN10000.1.1.2.4.1.2; GEN10000.1.1.2.4.1.3; GEN10000.1.1.2.4.2.1.1

Unrealized Holding Gain On Short-Term Marketable Equity Available-For-Sale Securities [G]: GEN10000.1.2.2.3.1.2

Unrealized Holding Gain On Short-Term Marketable Equity Trading Securities [G]: GEN10000.1.2.2.1.1; GEN10000.1.2.2.3.1.1

Unrealized Holding Loss On Long-Term Debt Available-For-Sale Securities [O]: GEN10000.2.1.2.3.1.2

Unrealized Holding Loss On Short-Term
Marketable Equity Available-For-Sale
Securities [O]: GEN10000.1.2.2.3.2.2
Unrealized Holding Loss On Short-Term
Marketable Equity Trading Securities [O]:
GEN10000.1.2.2.1.2
Unrealized Loss On Valuation Of Computer
Software Costs [O]: GEN6000.1.9.1.4
Utility Expense [E]: GEN1000.2.3.5.2
U.S. Dollars Payable [L]: GEN19000.5
U.S. Dollars Receivable [A]: GEN19000.5

V
Vacation Wages Payable [L]: GEN7000.10.5
Vehicles [A]: GEN5000.1.1.3
Vouchers Payable [L]: GEN2000.1.1.2; also
see *Accounts Payable*

W
Wages Expense [E]: GEN1000.2.1.2
Wages Payable [L]: GEN1000.2.1.2
Warranty Expense [E]: GEN7000.9.3;
GEN15000.2.4
Warranty Revenue [R]: GEN7000.9.4.2
Withdrawals [CC]: GEN1000.2.3.5.4; also
see *Drawings*
Work-In-Process Inventory [A]:
GEN4000.2.1.2.5.1; GEN4000.2.2;
GEN4000.2.3.2.1; GEN16000

TOPICAL INDEX

Abandonment

D

F

Factoring: *see Accounts Receivable - Sale of*

Factory equipment: *see Property, plant & equipment - Equipment*

Factory overhead: *see Manufacturing costs - Factory overhead* and *Cost accounting - Factory overhead*

Federal Unemployment Tax: GEN7000.10.2

FICA

    Employees' share: GEN7000.10.1.1

    Employer's share: GEN7000.10.2.1

FIFO

    Applied to inventory

        Change from FIFO

            Permanent change: GEN4000.3.1.1

            Temporary adjustment: GEN4000.3.1.2

        Change to FIFO: GEN4000.3.2

Finished Goods Inventory: GEN4000.2.3

        End of period adjustment: GEN4000.2.3.1.3

        Periodic inventory system: GEN4000.2.3.1

        Perpetual inventory system: GEN4000.2.3.2

        Sale of: GEN4000.2.3.1.2; GEN4000.2.3.2.2

        Transfer from work-in-process: GEN4000.2.3.1.1; GEN4000.2.3.2.1

        Transfer to cost of goods sold: GEN4000.2.3.1.2; GEN4000.2.3.2.2

Fire loss

    Inventory: GEN4000.1.2.7.2; GEN4000.2.1.2.6.2

    Plant assets: GEN5000.3.3.2

First-in-first-out method: *see FIFO*

Fixed assets: *see Property, plant & equipment*

Foreign currency transactions: GEN19000

    Borrowing abroad (payable denominated in foreign currency): GEN19000.4

        End-of-period adjustment: GEN19000.4.2

        Origination: 19000.4.1

        Settlement: GEN19000.4.3

    Exports: *see Foreign currency transactions - Sales*

    Forward exchange contracts: GEN19000.5

        Contract to buy foreign currency: GEN19000.5.2; GEN19000.5.4; see also *Foreign currency transactions - Forward exchange contracts - Hedge of account payable, Foreign currency transactions - Forward exchange contracts - Hedge of foreign currency commitment with future payable,* and *Foreign currency transactions -Forward exchange contracts - Speculation - Forward contract to buy*

        Contract to sell foreign currency: GEN19000.5.1; GEN19000.5.3; see also *Foreign currency transactions - Forward exchange contracts - Hedge of account receivable, Foreign currency transactions - Forward exchange contracts - Hedge of foreign currency commitment with future receivable, Foreign currency transactions - Forward exchange contracts - Speculation, Cash Flow Hedge - Forward contract to sell*

        Definition: GEN19000.5

        Hedge of account payable (forward contract to buy): GEN19000.5.2

            Amortization of premium or discount, end-of-period: GEN19000.5.2.3

            End-of-period adjustment of Foreign Currency Receivable: GEN19000.5.2.2

            Origination: GEN19000.5.2.1

            Settlement: GEN19000.5.2.4

        Hedge of account receivable (forward contract to sell): GEN19000.5.1

G

Insurance proceeds: GEN5000.3.3.3
Intangible assets: GEN6000
    Acquisition of: GEN6000.1
        Basket purchase: GEN6000.2
        Lump-sum purchase: GEN6000.2
    Amortization of: GEN6000.1
    Basket purchase: GEN6000.2
    Computer Software: GEN6000.1.6; see also *Computer Software*
    Computer Software Development Costs: GEN6000.1.9; see also *Computer Software Development Costs*
    Copyrights: GEN6000.1.3; see also *Copyrights*
    Definition: GEN6000.1
    Franchises: GEN6000.1.5; see also *Franchises*
    Goodwill: GEN6000.1.1; see also *Goodwill*
    Impairment of value, goodwill: GEN5000.1.1.3
    Leasehold improvements: GEN6000.1.7; see also *Leasehold Improvements*
    Licenses: GEN6000.1.5; see also *Franchises*
    Lump-sum purchase: GEN6000.2
    Organization costs: GEN6000.1.8; see also *Organization Costs*
    Patents: GEN6000.1.2; see also *Patents*
    R&D: GEN6000.3
    Research and development costs: GEN6000.3
    Software: GEN6000.1.6; see also *Computer Software*
    Software development costs: GEN6000.1.9; see also *Computer Software Development Costs*
    Trademarks: GEN6000.1.4; see also *Trademarks*
    Trade names: GEN6000.1.4; see also *Trademarks*
Interest Expense
    Bonds payable, on: GEN8000.1.2; see also *Bonds Payable - Interest On*
Interest rate swaps: GEN10000.5.8.2
    Changes in value: GEN10000.5.8.2.2; GEN10000.5.8.2.3
    Settlement payments: GEN10000.5.8.2.1
Interest received in advance: *see Unearned Revenues*
Inventory: GEN4000
    Casualty loss: GEN4000.1.2.7.2; GEN4000.2.1.2.6.2
    Changes in valuation method: GEN4000.3
        FIFO, change from
            Permanent change: GEN4000.3.1.1
            Temporary adjustment: GEN4000.3.1.2
        FIFO, change to: GEN4000.3.2
        LIFO, change from: GEN4000.3.2; GEN15000.1.1.1
        LIFO, change to
            Permanent change: GEN4000.3.1.1; GEN15000.1.2
            Temporary adjustment to LIFO: GEN4000.3.1.2
        Other than from or to LIFO: GEN4000.3.3
        Weighted average
            Change from: GEN4000.3.1
            Change to: GEN4000.3.2
    Consignment of: GEN4000.6; GEN11000.4
        Consignee, accounting by: GEN4000.6.1; GEN11000.4.2
            Receipt of goods: GEN11000.4.2.1
            Reimbursable expenses: GEN11000.4.2.2

Sale of: GEN10000.2.2.2.4
Mark-to-market principle: *see Investments - Fair value principle*
Short-term: GEN10000.1
   Debt securities: GEN10000.1.1
      Acquisition: GEN10000.1.1.1
      Available-for-sale securities: GEN10000.1.1.2.3
         Transferred to held-to-maturity category: GEN10000.1.1.2.4.2.3
         Transferred to long-term available-for-sale category: GEN10000.1.1.2.4.2.2
         Transferred to short-term trading category: GEN10000.1.1.2.4.2.1
      Fair value principle applied to: GEN10000.1.1.2
      Held-to-maturity securities: GEN10000.1.1.2.2
      Interest received: GEN10000.1.1.4
      Sale of: GEN10000.1.1.3
         Available-for-sale securities: GEN10000.1.1.3.3
         Trading securities: GEN10000.1.1.3.2
      Trading securities: GEN10000.1.1.2.1
         Transferred to held-to-maturity category: GEN10000.1.1.2.4.1.3
         Transferred to long-term available-for-sale category: GEN10000.1.1.2.4.1.2
         Transferred to short-term available-for-sale category: GEN10000.1.1.2.4.1.1
      Transfers between investment categories: GEN10000.1.1.2.4.1
   Marketable equity securities
      Acquisition: GEN10000.1.2.1
      Available-for-sale securities: GEN10000.1.2.2.2
         Transferred to long-term available-for-sale category: GEN10000.1.2.2.3.3
         Transferred to short-term trading category: GEN10000.1.2.2.3.2
      Dividends received
         Cash: GEN10000.1.2.4
         Stock: GEN10000.1.2.5
      Fair value principle applied to: GEN10000.1.2.2
      Sale of: GEN10000.1.2.3
         Available-for-sale securities: GEN10000.1.2.3.2
         Trading securities: GEN10000.1.2.3.1
      Stock split received: GEN10000.1.2.5
      Trading securities: GEN10000.1.2.2.1
         Transferred to long-term available-for-sale category: GEN10000.1.2.2.3.1.2
         Transferred to short-term available-for-sale category: GEN10000.1.2.2.3.1.1
  Stock rights: GEN10000.3
     Acquisition: GEN10000.3.1
       Purchase: GEN10000.3.1.2
       Receipt of as stockholder: GEN10000.3.1.1
     Exercise of: GEN10000.3.3
     Expiration of: GEN10000.3.4
     Sale of: GEN10000.3.2
  Temporary investments: *see Investments - Short-term*
  Trading securities: GEN10000.1.1.2.1; GEN10000.1.2.2.1
Involuntary conversion of assets: GEN5000.3.3

J

Job order cost accounting system: GEN16000.1; see also *Cost accounting - Job order system*

L

Labor: *see Cost accounting - Job order system - Labor, Cost accounting - Process cost system - Labor, and Cost accounting - Standard costing - Labor*

Land: *see Property, plant, & equipment - Land*

Leasehold improvements: GEN6000.1.7
    Acquisition: GEN6000.1.7.1
    Amortization: GEN6000.1.7.2
    Definition: GEN6000.1.7

Leases: GEN14000
    Impairment of value of property lease under: GEN14000.3.1.5.4
    Capital: GEN14000.3
        Lessee, accounting by: GEN14000.3.1
            Depreciation of leased asset: GEN14000.3.1.3
            Executory costs: GEN14000.3.1.4
            Impairment of value of property lease under: GEN14000.3.1.5.4
            Lease, recording: GEN14000.3.1.1
            Lease payments, recording: GEN14000.3.1.2
                Initial lease payments: GEN14000.3.1.2.1
                Subsequent lease payments: GEN14000.3.1.2.2
            Purchase of leased asset: GEN14000.3.1.5; GEN14000.3.1.5.3
            Return of leased asset to lessor: GEN14000.3.1.5
                Guaranteed residual value: GEN14000.3.1.5.1
                Nonguaranteed residual value: GEN14000.3.1.5.2
        Lessor, accounting by: GEN14000.3.2
            Direct financing leases: GEN14000.3.2.1
                Lease, recording: GEN14000.3.2.1.1
                Lease payments, recording
                    Initial lease payment: GEN14000.3.2.1.2
                    Subsequent lease payments: GEN14000.3.2.1.3
                Reacquisition of leased asset: GEN14000.3.2.1.4; GEN14000.3.2.1.5
                    No residual value included in lease payments receivable: GEN14000.3.2.1.5.2
                    Residual value included in lease payments receivable: GEN14000.3.2.1.5.1
                Sale of leased asset to lessee: GEN14000.3.2.1.4; GEN14000.3.2.1.6
            Sales-type leases: GEN14000.3.2.2
                Initial direct costs of lease: GEN14000.3.2.2.2
                Lease, recording: GEN14000.3.2.2.1
                Lease payments, recording
                    Initial lease payment: GEN14000.3.2.2.3
                    Subsequent lease payments: GEN14000.3.2.2.4
                Reacquisition of leased asset: GEN14000.3.2.2.5
    Definition: GEN14000.1
    Operating: GEN14000.2
        Impairment of value of property leased to others: GEN14000.2.2.4
        Lessee, accounting by: GEN14000.2.1
            Rent expense: GEN14000.2.1.1
        Lessor, accounting by: GEN14000.2.2
            Impairment of value of property leased to others: GEN14000.2.2.4
            Initial direct lease costs: GEN14000.2.2.4
            Rental income: GEN14000.2.2.1
            Rental property (property leased to others)

M

Purchase Returns And Allowances: GEN4000.1.1.3; GEN4000.1.2.3
  Sale of: GEN4000.1.1.5; GEN4000.1.2.5
  Theft loss: GEN4000.1.2.7.2: GEN4000.2.1.2.6.2
Merger: GEN17000.1.1; see also *Business combination - Merger*
Minimum pension liability: GEN13000.1.2.2; see also *Pensions - Defined benefit plans - Minimum pension liability*
Mortgage note payable: GEN8000.2.1.4

N

Natural resources: *see Property, Plant, & Equipment - Natural Resources*
Negative goodwill: GEN6000.1.1.1.2
  Amortization of: GEN6000.1.1.2
Net Operating Losses: GEN12000.3; see also Income taxes - Net operating losses
Notes Payable: GEN7000.2; GEN8000.2; see also Long-Term Notes Payable
  Currently maturing portion: GEN7000.2.2
  Definition: GEN7000.2
  Discount on: GEN7000.2.1.2
  Interest expense on: GEN7000.2.3
    Interest bearing note: GEN7000.2.3.1
    Non-interest bearing note: GEN7000.2.3.2
  Long-term: *see Long-Term Notes Payable*
  Payment of: GEN2000.1.1.10; GEN7000.2.4
    Interest bearing note: GEN7000.2.4.1
  Recording: GEN7000.2.1
    Interest-bearing: GEN7000.2.1.1
    Noninterest bearing: GEN7000.2.1.2
  Short-term: GEN7000.2
  Trade notes payable: GEN7000.2
Notes Receivable: GEN3000.2
  Accrual of interest on: GEN3000.2.1.2.1
    Discount on notes receivable *is* involved: GEN3000.2.1.1.2.2
    Discount on notes receivable *is not* involved: GEN3000.2.1.1.1.2
  Collection of: GEN3000.2.3
  Defaulted
    Discounted note: GEN3000.2.4.1.3
  Discount on
    Accrual of interest and: GEN3000.2.1.1.2.2
    Receipt of interest and: GEN3000.2.1.1.2
    When note is collected: GEN3000.2.3
    When note is received to replace Accounts Receivable: GEN3000.2.1.2
    When note is received for cash: GEN3000.2.1.1.2.1
    When note is received for sales: GEN3000.2.1.3
    When note is received for prepaid rights: GEN3000.2.1.4
    When note is received for property or goods: GEN3000.2.1.5
    When note is received for services: GEN3000.2.1.6
  Discounting of: GEN3000.2.4
    Default by maker: GEN3000.2.4.1.3
    Liability on discounted notes receivable: GEN3000.2.4.2.3
    Payment by maker at maturity: GEN3000.2.4.1.2
    Recorded as a borrowing with recourse: GEN3000.2.4.2

Recorded as a sale with recourse: GEN3000.2.4.1
Interest on
    Accrual of: GEN3000.2.1.1.1.2; GEN3000.2.1.1.2.2;
    Receipt of
        Discount on notes receivable *is* involved: GEN3000.2.1.1.2.3; GEN3000.2.1.1.2.4
        Discount on notes receivable *is not* involved: GEN3000.2.1.1.1.3; GEN3000.2.1.1.1.4
        Reversing entries made: GEN3000.2.1.1.2.4
        Reversing entries not made: GEN3000.2.1.1.2.3
Liability Notes Receivable Discounted: GEN3000.2.4.2.3
Noninterest-Bearing: GEN3000.2.1.1.2
Past-due: *see Defaulted*
Received: GEN3000.2.1.1
    For Accounts Receivable: GEN3000.2.1.2
    For cash: GEN3000.2.1.1
        Interest rate realistic: GEN3000.2.1.1.1
        Interest rate unrealistic: GEN3000.2.1.1.2
    For prepaid rights: GEN3000.2.1.4
    For property or goods: GEN3000.2.1.5
    For Sales: GEN3000.2.1.3
    For Services: GEN3000.2.1.6
    Unrealistic interest rate and: GEN3000.2.1.1.2
Notes Receivable Discounted: GEN3000.2.4.1.1

O

Office Equipment: *see Property, Plant & Equipment - Equipment*
Office Furnishings: *see Property, Plant & Equipment - Equipment*
Operating leases: GEN14000.2; see also *Leases - Operating*
Operating losses, net: GEN12000.3; see also *Income taxes - Net operating losses*
Operations costing: GEN16000.6; see also *Cost accounting - Operations costing*
Options, call or put: GEN10000.5.8.1.1
    Intrinsic value, increase or decrease in: GEN10000.5.8.1.2
    Time value, increase or decrease in: GEN10000.5.8.1.3
Organization costs: GEN6000.1.8
    Amortization: GEN6000.1.8.2
    Recording: GEN6000.1.8.1
    Stock issuance costs treated as: GEN9000.3.2
Overage or shortage in inventory: GEN4000.1.2.7; GEN4000.2.1.2.6.1
Overhead: *see Manufacturing costs - Factory overhead* and *Cost accounting - Factory overhead*

P

Paid-In Capital In Excess Of Par Or Stated Value: *see Additional Paid-In Capital*
Partnerships: GEN21000
    Admission of new partner: GEN21000.4
        Assets contributed to old partners: GEN21000.4.2
            Fair value equal to new partner's capital balance: GEN21000.4.2.1
            Fair value greater than new partner's capital balance: GEN21000.4.2.2
                Bonus method of accounting for: GEN21000.4.2.2.2
                Goodwill method of accounting for: GEN21000.4.2.2.1
            Fair value less than new partner's capital balance: GEN21000.4.2.3
                Bonus method of accounting for: GEN21000.4.2.3.2

Debt repayment: GEN22000.2.4.2.2
Definition: GEN22000.2
Distribution
    Beneficiaries, to: GEN22000.2.5; GEN22000.2.7.2
        Income, from: GEN22000.2.5.1
        Principal, from: GEN22000.2.5.2
Establishment of trust: GEN22000.2.1
Expenses incurred by trust: GEN22000.2.4
    Administrative expenses: GEN22000.2.4.1.2
    Depletion expense: GEN22000.2.4.1.3; GEN22000.2.4.2.4
    Depreciation expense: GEN22000.2.4.1.3; GEN22000.2.4.2.4
    Ordinary expenses: GEN22000.2.4.1
Income distribution: GEN22000.2.5.1
Income from principle assets: GEN22000.2.3.1.1; GEN22000.2.2.2
Principle assets
    Investment of: GEN22000.2.2
    Received: GEN22000.2.1
Receipts credited to principal: GEN22000.2.2.2

U

Uncollectible Accounts Receivable: GEN3000.1.3
    Change in estimate of: GEN15000.2.2; GEN15000.2.1
    Percentage of Receivables Approach: GEN3000.1.3.2
    Percentage of Sales Approach: GEN3000.1.3.1
    Recovery of: GEN3000.1.3.1.4; GEN3000.1.3.2.3
    Write-Off: GEN3000.1.3.1.3; GEN3000.1.3.2.2
Uncollectible Amounts Recovered: GEN3000.1.3.3.2; see also *Uncollectible Accounts Receivable -*
  Recovery of
Unearned revenues: GEN1000.2.3.2.1.3; GEN7000.5
    Realizing: GEN7000.5.2
    Recording: GEN7000.5.1
Uninsured losses: GEN7000.9.6

V

Vacation pay: GEN7000.5
Variable costing: GEN16000.4
Variances: *see Standard costing - Variances*
Vehicles: *see Property, Plant & Equipment - Equipment*
Vouchers Payable: *see Accounts Payable*

W

Wages And Salaries
    Accrued: GEN7000.10.3
    Payable: GEN7000.10.1
Warranties and Guarantees: *see Guarantees And Warranties*
Warrants, stock: GEN9000.6; see also *Stock - Warrants*
Warranty revenue: GEN7000.9.4
Weighted average inventory method
    Change from: GEN4000.3.1
    Change to: GEN4000.3.2